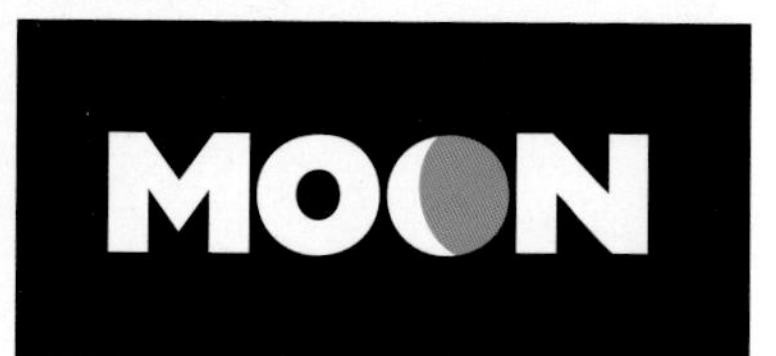

MOON HANDBOOKS

MINNESOTA

TIM BEWER WITH TRICIA CORNELL

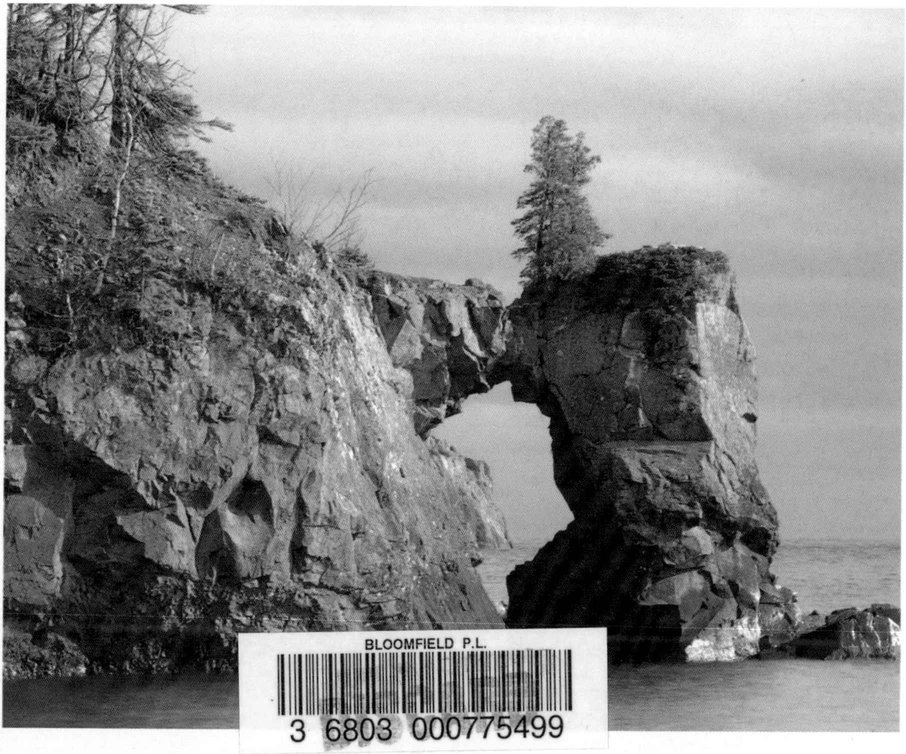

MINNESOTA
CANADA
MANITOBA
ONTARIO
MICHIGAN
NORTH DAKOTA
0 40 mi
0 40 km
Winnipeg
Morris
Falcon Lake
Melick
Dryden
Piney
Angle Inlet
Lake of the Woods
Eagle Lake
White Otter Lake
Rainy Lake
Marmion Lake
Lac des Mille Lacs
Atikokan
Kashabowie
Thunder Bay
Hallock
Lake Bronson State Park
Warroad
Roseau
Baudette
Franz Jevne State Park
Fort Frances
International Falls
Voyageurs National Park
Hayes Lake State Park
Argyle
Fourtown
Thief River Falls
Grand Falls
Bois Forte Reservation
Grand Forks
Red Lake Reservation
Red Lake
Redby
Northome
Effie
Cook
Ely
Superior National Forest
Grand Marais
Grand Portage
Crookston
Chippewa National Forest
Lake Winnibigoshish
McCarthy Beach State Park
Chisholm
Virginia
Temperance River State Park
Lake Superior
Red River of the North
Twin Valley
White Earth Reservation
Bemidji
Leech Lake Reservation
Hibbing
Illgen City
Grand Rapids
Gooseberry Falls State Park
Itasca State Park
Walker
Remer
Two Harbors
Fargo
Moorhead
Hill City
Red Cliff
Buffalo River State Park
Detroit Lakes
Park Rapids
Fond du Lac Reservation
Duluth
Ottawa National Forest
Aitkin
McGregor
Poplar
Ashland
Bad River Reservation
Ironwood
Wahpeton
Staples
Moose Lake State Park
Fergus Falls
Brainerd
Mille Lacs Lake
Crow Wing State Park
Chequamegon National

WISCONSIN
IOWA
SOUTH DAKOTA
NEBRASKA
ILLINOIS
ST. PAUL
Minneapolis
St. Cloud
Cambridge
North Branch
Taylors Falls
Milaca
Mora
Alexandria
Wheaton
Browns Valley
Morris
Ortonville
Milbank
Belgrade
Litchfield
Willmar
Watertown
Montevideo
Granite Falls
Canby
Lake Benton
Marshall
New Ulm
Mankato
Jordan
Northfield
Red Wing
Owatonna
Rochester
Winona
Sanborn
Pipestone
St. James
Windom
Luverne
Worthington
Fairmont
Albert Lea
Austin
Preston
Sioux Falls
Rock Rapids
Spencer
Algona
Clear Lake
Mason City
Decorah
Le Mars
Sioux City
South Sioux City
Ida Grove
Moorland
Carroll
Waterloo
Oelwein
Dubuque
Prairie du Chien
Readstown
La Crosse
Onalaska
Tomah
Black River Falls
Eau Claire
Chippewa Falls
Forest
Abbotsford
Wausau
Heafford Junction
Lake Maria State Park
Upper Sioux Agency State Park
Minneopa State Park
Blue Mounds State Park
Myre-Big Island State Park
John A. Latsch State Park
Chequamegon National Forest
Lac Courte Oreilles Reservation
Reservation
Winnebago Reservation
Minnesota River
Mississippi River
Missouri River
Wisconsin River
St. Croix
Petenwell Lake
© AVALON TRAVEL

Contents

STOP

Discover Minnesota

Diversity is not usually the first word that comes to mind when you think of Minnesota, but it should be. From skyscrapers to sod houses, from timeless steamboat towns on the Mississippi and St. Croix Rivers to Wobegonic farm country in the west, and from Minneapolis's world-class arts scene to a record-setting ball of twine, even seasoned travelers are likely to be impressed.

The one thing just about everyone does know about Minnesota is that this is some beautiful country. The boreal forests of the northeast fade into the tallgrass prairie of the southwest, and in between are the lakes – far more than the sloganned 10,000. I've been around the globe but have yet to find any place more beautiful than the Boundary Waters – thousands of lakes rimmed by ancient bedrock and littered with islands. Just next door, the rocky Lake Superior shore, lined with cliffs and waterfalls, is as lovely a coast as you'll ever see. In the south, towering bluffs reach high above the Mississippi River, largely unchanged since Mark Twain and Henry David Thoreau rode by in steamboats.

Other than mountain climbing, your options for getting out into this glorious wilderness are endless. With one million acres, but no roads, the Boundary Waters Canoe Area Wilderness just might be the best quiet-water paddling in the world. Bikers can bypass the traffic since Minnesota

is a leader in rail-to-trail conversions. Rock hounds can scale some of the best walls between Seneca and Boulder. And, of course, the fun doesn't stop when the snow falls: from snowboards to dogsleds, you can try it all.

While it's easy to joke about Minnesota's Scandinavian heritage – which does in fact live on in church-basement lutefisk dinners and the quiet exclamation, "Uff-da!" – that doesn't do justice to the state's real ethnic diversity. Native American communities in the north work hard to maintain their traditions, and Minnesota is home to the largest Somali population in the United States and the largest urban Hmong population in the world, as well as sizable and established Mexican, Russian, Tibetan, Asian, and East African communities.

Add in the state's high wages and low cost of living, and it's not surprising when Minnesota regularly tops nationwide rankings in quality of life. Don't be surprised if, after your visit, you just can't bring yourself to leave: Every year thousands of people arrive as visitors and return as residents.

Planning Your Trip

▸ WHERE TO GO

The bluff-lined Mississippi River, the waterfall-rich North Shore, the arts-loving Twin Cities, and the lake-filled Boundary Waters Canoe Area Wilderness all lie on the eastern side of Minnesota, but there are superb surprises in the west, and you can't really know Minnesota without taking a turn through the prairies.

Twin Cities

With four internationally known art museums, three Tony Award–winning theaters, and a full slate of festivals year-round, Minneapolis is one of the country's most cultured cities, while quiet St. Paul, where the primary attractions are its historic buildings, is one of its most stately. Together the pair makes an easily navigable and satisfying urban destination.

St. Croix Valley

Some people, in their rush to get "Up North," drive through this region and never know what they're missing: postcard-perfect towns like Marine-on-St. Croix and Stillwater, and gorgeous gorges in the state parks to the north. The St. Croix River is protected as a National Scenic Riverway and serves up some superb quiet-water paddling while other rivers have wild white water.

The Arrowhead

The northeast corner has more than its fair share of Minnesota's best and most beautiful, starting with the port city of Duluth. Minnesotans themselves named the stunning views along the North Shore of Lake Superior among 150 iconic state treasures. And, on

The Minnesota State Capitol in St. Paul was designed by local architect Cass Gilbert.

IF YOU HAVE...

- **THREE DAYS:** Visit Minneapolis and St. Paul.
- **FIVE DAYS:** Add Stillwater, Red Wing, and Winona.
- **ONE WEEK:** Add Duluth.
- **TWO WEEKS:** Add Two Harbors, Grand Marais, and Ely.

the other side of the region, Old World culture lives on in the mining towns of the Iron Range. Tucked in the middle are Voyageurs National Park and the Boundary Waters Canoe Area Wilderness, arguably the best canoeing destination in the world.

Central Lakes

Minnesota's lake country, much of it covered by the 1,042-square-mile Chippewa National Forest, is the most popular family vacation destination for Minnesotans. The waters are lined with resorts, and the towns are full of gift shops and amusement parks. The Mississippi River is born in Itasca State Park (one of many lovely state parks), and this region is also the epicenter of Minnesota's giant sculpture habit, so oversized animals and Paul Bunyans welcome you to many small towns.

Red River Valley

The farm fields of the Red River Valley stretch seemingly forever, broken only by scattered small towns and parks, including the wonderful Agassiz National Wildlife Refuge. Unheralded Moorhead is home to the Scandinavian-focused Historical and Cultural Society of Clay County, and nearby is Buffalo River State Park, with one of the largest and healthiest remaining prairies. The towns and parks along the Otter Trail Scenic Byway are Minnesota in microcosm.

Prairieland

While southwest Minnesota is mostly farm country—broken by the deep, tree-lined Minnesota River Valley—it has a surprisingly varied assortment of attractions, including the sacred—Pipestone National Monument and Jeffers Petroglyphs—and the weird—Belle Plaine's two-story outhouse. Fans trek to Walnut Grove, home of Laura Ingalls Wilder, and a few scattered patches of prairie remain, most notably at Blue Mounds State Park.

Bluff Country

In southeast Minnesota, steep bluffs rise as much as 500 feet over the Mississippi River, which widens to form the stunning Lake Pepin, a popular summer playground for water buffs. Glimpses of the river's shipping heyday live on in picturesque towns like Red Wing and Winona and farther inland, in Amish country, pleasant villages like Lanesboro and Harmony hearken back to a simpler time.

▸ WHEN TO GO

Minnesota's glorious summers, with long, lingering evenings and temperatures in the 80s, are the most popular with tourists, but visitors shouldn't write off winter, when locals make the most of the snow with outdoor activities and even festivals.

Spring comes in like a lion and races through like a cheetah, lasting as little as a couple of weeks—if you can even be sure just when it begins. Few visitors come at this time, but a profusion of wildflowers and the cheapest lodging of the year are bonuses for those who do. Fall—with mild, sunny, dry weather, beautiful foliage, and off-season discounts—is my pick for the best time to visit.

Locals make the most of winter with outdoor activities, like cross-country skiing in Voyageurs National Park.

▸ BEFORE YOU GO

Transportation

While smaller regional airports serve Duluth, St. Cloud, and other cities outstate, these connections are often expensive and inconvenient. Consider landing at Minneapolis-St. Paul International Airport and driving to your final destination.

You'll need your own wheels, anyhow, outside the Twin Cities. The state's only passenger rail line—the Empire Builder—passes through Red Wing, the Twin Cities, St. Cloud, and Moorhead, but runs only once a day in each direction. Bus connections exist, but don't always land you in the best part of town. A car will give you the flexibility to get off the highway and make worthwhile stops at regional and state parks.

What to Take

Minnesota is a decidedly casual place. Whatever duds you're comfortable in at home will be just fine here, even at a theater or nice restaurant (dance clubs, which usually have dress codes, are the exception).

The only way to enjoy a Minnesota winter is properly dressed: hat, scarf, gloves, overcoat or parka, and boots from at least November through March. Late spring and early fall are often rainy. If you're planning outdoor treks, you may be able to rent everything you need from an outfitter.

The mist rises off Lake Superior, a lake so large that it creates its own weather.

Explore Minnesota

▸ THE BEST OF MINNESOTA

Since Minnesota is a big state, this 11-day tour is necessarily limited despite all the driving involved, but combining history, culture, technology, nature, arts, and world-class kitsch, it highlights the variety that makes Minnesota such a wonderful place.

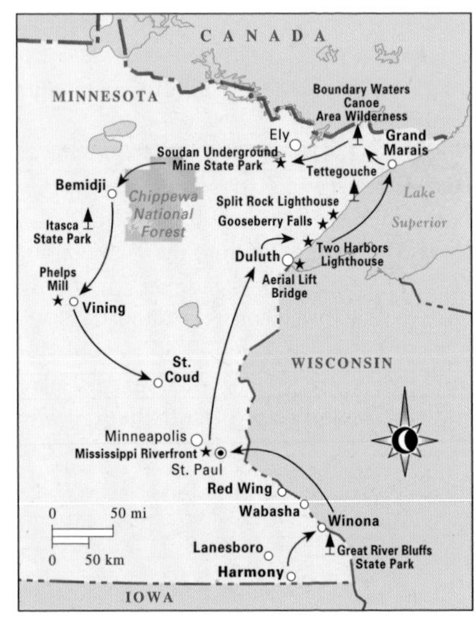

Day 1

Start your tour in Minnesota's southeastern corner in Harmony, the center of the state's largest Amish community. After stopping in lovely little Lanesboro, take the Historic Bluff Country Scenic Byway through the deep and narrow Root River Valley to the Mississippi River.

Day 2

Follow the Great River Road north alongside the Mississippi, shopping and

The Stone Arch Bridge curves gracefully across the Mississippi near downtown Minneapolis.

Recent years have brought new development to downtown St. Paul.

sightseeing in the historic river towns of Winona, Wabasha, and Red Wing. Along the way, stop at some of the bluff-top parks, such as Great River Bluffs State Park, for spectacular valley views.

Days 3-4

Spend a day each getting to know Minneapolis and St. Paul. In Minneapolis, stroll the Mississippi Riverfront and the Sculpture Garden and visit an art museum of your choice—they're all good. St. Paul's must-see is Summit Avenue. Afterward, visit Historic Fort Snelling, Mall of America, or Stillwater, depending on your tastes.

Day 5

Spend the day in Duluth watching ships slip under the Aerial Lift Bridge and visiting the many museums in and around Canal Park, including the Lake Superior Maritime Visitor Center and the Great Lakes Floating Maritime Museum. If you can get a reservation, spend the night in the Two Harbors Lighthouse.

Days 6-7

Highway 61, one of only 27 officially designated All-American Roads, hugs Lake Superior for just 150 miles, but two days is the minimum time needed to do the North Shore justice. Wild waterfalls and rugged coast run between the few small towns, and all eight state parks warrant a stop. The first three you meet are the most impressive: Gooseberry Falls is the most visited state park for good reason; Split Rock Lighthouse is a Minnesota icon; and Tettegouche has some of the most impressive shoreline on the whole lake. The featured waterfall at far less crowded Judge C. R. Magney seemingly disappears into the rock.

Other than the parks, enchanting little Grand Marais, both a fishing village and an artists' community, and the fur-trade reenactment at Grand Portage National Monument are must-sees in this area.

Day 8

Paddle the glorious Boundary Waters Canoe Area Wilderness, one of the world's most beautiful and wildlife-rich wildernesses.

Split Rock Lighthouse, on Lake Superior's North Shore, is a Minnesota icon.

Take several days rather than just one if you can spare them.

Day 9

Journey into the center of the earth at Soudan Underground Mine State Park, and look at one of the city-sized strip mines between Virginia and Hibbing. Head west through the Chippewa National Forest, a lovely drive, especially if you get off U.S. Highway 2, on your way to Bemidji for a look at the giant Paul Bunyan and Babe the Blue Ox statues.

Day 10

Spend most of the day exploring Itasca State Park, which not only surrounds the humble headwaters of the Mississippi River, but has thousands of acres of old-growth forest and many historic sites. When done, head south to Otter Tail County and spend the night in one of the distinctive B&Bs.

Day 11

Drive as much of the Otter Trail Scenic Byway as you can, making sure not to miss Phelps Mill and the statues in Vining. Then head back to the Twin Cities early enough to allow a walk in St. Cloud's Munsinger and Clemens Gardens.

Take a walk in St. Cloud's Munsinger and Clemens Gardens.

SMALL-TOWN FESTIVALS

Just about every city in Minnesota sets aside a day or a weekend each year to come together, set out a few carnival rides, and eat deep-fried treats. Some of these events have a certain insiders-only feel; others attract visitors from a few towns over or even around the state. Either way, these small-town festivals – usually some sort of "Days" – are a great way to experience Minnesota.

One of the biggest, thanks in part to its proximity to the Cities, is Northfield's **Defeat of Jesse James Days,** celebrating that town's claim to fame the weekend after Labor Day. Another Western icon is recognized in Lanesboro's **Buffalo Bill Days** the first weekend in August. Among the oldest community celebrations are two classics: Glenwood's **Waterama,** the last full weekend in July and the **Cokato Corn Carnival** in mid-August.

Several towns celebrate their ethnic heritage. You can get a little taste of Scandinavia at Moorhead's **Hjemkomst Festival,** one of the nation's largest celebrations of Nordic heritage, held the fourth weekend of June. Scandia and Nisswa both hold similar, but smaller fests. Finnish-Americans celebrate the **Finnish-American Summer Festival,** held the first Saturday in June in Embarrass, and the **Finn Creek Festival,** the last weekend of August in New York Mills. New Ulm goes all out for its **Bavarian Blast,** the third weekend in July, and Pelican Rapids has a little something for everyone at the **International Friendship Festival** in June, marking its status as one of the most diverse cities in the state.

While most festivals are held in June, July, and August, some communities like to celebrate the cold weather as well – and what better place to do that than in International Falls, which holds **Icebox Days** every January, complete with a polar bear dip. The **Ely Winter Festival,** which starts the first Thursday in February, attracts folks from all the way down in the Cities. Little Aitkin starts the season with a **Fish House Parade** on the day after Thanksgiving.

Other cities take an "any excuse for a good party approach": **Potato Days** in Barnesville, **Oxcart Days** in Crookston, **Buffalo Days** in Luverne, **Box Car Days** in Tracy, **Applefest** in La Crescent, and, of course, **Dylan Days** in Hibbing.

Defeat of Jesse James Days, in Northfield

The Science Museum of Minnesota sits on the riverfront in St. Paul.

▸ MINNESOTA WITH KIDS

Minnesota is a terrific place to travel with children. While you won't find the kind of big, flashy attractions that you might elsewhere, you will find that your children are welcomed and even catered to just about everywhere you go. (Folks looking for an escape from kids may want to take note of that, as well.) All but the very fanciest of restaurants have high chairs and children's menus on hand, and nearly every museum has something to offer even the youngest of visitors.

An outstate lakeside resort—of which there are hundreds, particularly in the Central Lakes—is a great place to park the family for the week, alternating time on the lake with forays to local attractions. While you're out there, away from the crowds and high ticket prices in the cities, take the kids to a small-town festival or a Northwoods League baseball game. You don't need themed rides and costumed mice to make memories.

Twin Cities

The metro area has a handful of indoor water parks attached to chain hotels. The Depot, in downtown Minneapolis, is the most conveniently situated. Another hotel that does double duty as an attraction is the Marriott

Lakeside family resorts and campgrounds are classic Minnesota summer experiences.

WACKY AND TACKY MINNESOTA

Best known to fans of the fantastical as the land of giant sculptures, Minnesota offers plenty of bizarre and humorous attractions.

You can make your own judgments about the exhibits at the Twin Cities' larger art museums and sculpture parks, but many of the smaller galleries are brave enough to skirt the edges of wacky, if not tacky. And searching the **Mall of America** for tackiness is shooting fish in a barrel.

South of town, in Wykoff, the incomparable **Ed's Museum** is all about one nobody and his stuff. You can't seriously search for wacky and tacky Minnesota without seeing Austin's **SPAM Museum,** Blue Earth's 47-foot-tall **Jolly Green Giant statue,** Belle Plaine's **two-story outhouse,** and Darwin's giant **twine ball.**

If that's not enough for you, you can learn about the silly legend of the **Kensington Runestone** in Alexandria, where the 28-foot-tall Viking **Big Ole** welcomes you to the "Birthplace of America." There's an abundance of **oversized statuary** farther north, in and around Fergus Falls, including the world's largest otter, prairie chicken, and pelican. Brainerd is positively overrun with **giant Paul Bunyan statues,** including one that talks. There are also some **giant walleye sculptures** around Lake Mille Lacs and a **fishing-bobber water tower** in Pequot Lakes.

Bemidji's **Paul Bunyan and Babe the Blue Ox statues** inspired the whole trend of oversized sculptures in Minnesota, and Akeley claims **Minnesota's tallest Paul Bunyan** (well, he would be if he stood up).

Minnesota loves its giant fiberglass sculptures. This walleye is in Garrison on Lake Mille Lacs.

The Great Lakes Aquarium is Duluth's top family attraction.

Residence Inn in Edina, which is connected to an indoor park and climbing structure.

Young kids should never be bored in the Twin Cities. The excellent Minnesota Zoo and Minnesota Children's Museum can each fill a kid-sized day. The Sculpture Garden at the Walker Art Center is a great place to run off energy. And the south Minneapolis neighborhood of Linden Hills, with toy shops, a children's bookstore, and trolley rides, is a relaxing place to spend an afternoon.

Older kids will get more out of the Science Museum of Minnesota, The Bakken (all about electricity), and the Minnesota History Center.

Kids here even get their own Tony Award–winning theater: Definitely get tickets to whatever's at the Children's Theatre while you're here. Or, during the summer, be sure to catch a St. Paul Saints baseball game.

And, of course, what's a trip to Minnesota without a visit to the amusement park in the Mall of America?

St. Croix Valley

On your way up toward the North Shore, the excellent North West Company Fur Post, populated with knowledgeable costumed reenactors, is a great place to learn about Minnesota's fur trade and the lives of the Ojibwe.

The Arrowhead

Duluth is another especially family-friendly destination. The Edgewater Resort and Waterpark, a short distance from Canal Park, offers plenty of entertainment right onsite. Canal Park itself is compact and easily traversed by little legs, and is adjacent to the city's top family attraction, the Great Lakes Aquarium. Best of all, two scenic train rides depart from Duluth, and what kid wouldn't enjoy that?

Much of Arrowhead's beauty lies in remote wilderness—daunting for some families. Gooseberry Falls State Park is accessible and well-suited to young feet. North of Grand Marais, Grand Portage National Monument is another excellent historical site with costumed interpreters.

Inland, in Ely, the International Wolf Center and North American Bear Center offer animal-loving kids a chance to learn about two fascinating denizens of the Northwoods.

Decades of school groups have made

a pilgrimage to Chisholm's Minnesota Discovery Center to learn about the mining heritage of the Iron Range. You can spend much of a day exploring the vast museum and grounds.

Central Lakes

The Central Lakes area is truly Minnesota's playground. This is where you'll find the state's biggest, poshest, and best-known family resorts. Alexandria is a good home base for families exploring the lakes. Older kids, in particular, will enjoy the Runestone Museum, based on a hoax some people just can't let go of.

For the right kind of kid, the Minnesota Military Museum in Camp Ripley, south of Brainerd, and the Mille Lacs Indian Museum, in the city of Mille Lacs, are absolute must-sees. The Headwaters Science Center in Bemidji does a great job spanning various ages and interests.

Little Grand Rapids is a surprisingly good family destination, with the varied and well-developed Forest History Center and an excellent Children's Discovery Museum.

Prairieland

This area of the state is the home of two beloved children's literature classics—the *Little House* books in Walnut Grove and the *Betsy-Tacy* books in Mankato. Fans of both series make pilgrimages to Minnesota and both towns—though Walnut Grove in particular—work hard to satisfy them.

The annual trip to the apple orchard and pumpkin field is sacrosanct for most Minnesota families. While there are great orchards all over, Emma Krumbee's in Belle Plaine does it up right, with a petting zoo, playgrounds, and more.

A popular, one-of-a-kind attraction for families is the Harkin Store outside of New Ulm, where costumed guides show off wares dating back to the late 1800s.

Thanks to its location deep in the southwest corner of the state, Blue Mounds State Park doesn't get the crowds you'll find elsewhere. It's also among the easiest state parks for families to enjoy, with gentle trails and a herd of bison.

Bluff Country

Watching hundreds of eagles soar over the Mississippi River at the National Eagle Center in Wabasha is an unforgettable experience for kids and adults. Combine it with a trip to LARK Toys in nearby Kellogg and your kids will think they've gone to heaven. And, if they've got a sense of humor, they'll get a kick out of Austin's SPAM Museum as well.

bison herd at Blue Mounds State Park

NATURE AND WILDLIFE TOUR

This tour doesn't encompass all of Minnesota's wonderful natural attractions—there are just too many—but in 10 days you will get an in-depth look at both the beauty and the diversity of the state.

Day 1

Head to Interstate State Park, a 45-mile ride outside the Twin Cities, for a look at some awesome geological formations carved by the water from melting glaciers during the last ice age. There are further examples in Banning State Park, which also has a wonderful wildflower display each spring. Gaze at the gorge in Jay Cooke State Park before stopping in Duluth for some late afternoon bird-watching on Park Point.

Day 2

Before leaving town, climb Hawk Ridge, where each fall tens of thousands of migrating raptors pass by. Head up the waterfall-rich North Shore, stopping at Gooseberry Falls State Park and Tettegouche State Park, including Palisade Head, to explore Lake Superior's rocky shoreline. Leave the lake behind and head north on Highway 1, where you stand a good chance of seeing a moose, through the Superior National Forest.

Days 3-5

Depending on your preference, take an extended camping trip by canoe into the Boundary Waters Canoe Area Wilderness (book in advance) or by motorboat through Voyageurs National Park, two of the most beautiful places on earth. If you are here in the winter, you can cross the frozen lakes by ski, snowshoe, dogsled, or snowmobile. After getting back to civilization, join the International Wolf Center in Ely for a howling trip into the forest, or travel to Orr to meet the bears at the Vince Shute Wildlife Sanctuary.

Day 6

Stop at Hill Annex Mine State Park for the morning fossil-hunting tour and then head into the Chippewa National Forest, home to a greater percentage of breeding bald eagles than anywhere else in the Lower 48, for a few hikes. Make sure you see the old-growth forest in the Lost Forty.

Day 7

Look for insectivorous plants along the Bog Walk at Lake Bemidji State Park, and spend the rest of the day pondering the minute Mississippi River and admiring all the other attractions at Itasca State Park.

Day 8

Tamarac National Wildlife Refuge lies on

GETTING INTO THE GREAT OUTDOORS

Minnesota is a great place to indulge your outdoor recreation habits, and many visitors are here for nothing but.

TWIN CITIES

Right in the Twin Cities, **Fort Snelling State Park,** at the junction of the Mississippi and Minnesota Rivers, and the **Louisville Swamp Unit of the Minnesota Valley National Wildlife Refuge** up the Minnesota, are surprisingly wild places with some worthy hiking and ski trails. **Lebanon Hills Regional Park** has one of the best mountain bike trails in Minnesota and a canoe portage trail linking seven lakes.

ST. CROIX VALLEY

The upper reaches of the **St. Croix National Scenic Riverway** offer a leisurely paddle through some pretty deep wilderness. And, if you want white water, the **Kettle River** in **Banning State Park** and the **St. Louis River** near Duluth deliver in a big way. Some of the Midwest's best rock climbers flock to **Interstate State Park.**

THE ARROWHEAD

The possibilities are nearly endless in the **Superior National Forest,** but the highlight is the **Boundary Waters Canoe Area Wilderness,** one of the world's best canoe destinations. The **Superior Hiking Trail,** one of the country's premier long-distance foot paths, climbs the hills above Lake Superior. The state's three best downhill ski areas, **Lutsen Mountains, Giants Ridge,** and **Spirit Mountain,** all rise near each other, and hundreds of kilometers of **world-class cross-country skiing** trails wind through the forests along the North Shore.

CENTRAL LAKES

Though most famous for harboring the headwaters of the Mississippi River (which can be canoed in the spring), **Itasca State Park** has some of the best hiking trails in the north, including a great section of the **North Country National Scenic Trail.** The clear water in **Cuyuna Country State Recreation Area**'s old mine pits attracts scuba divers.

PRAIRIELAND

With excellent rock climbing and hiking, **Blue Mounds State Park** is the adventure center of southwest Minnesota. There is plenty of good paddling on the Minnesota River, particularly between the Big Stone National Wildlife Refuge and Lac Qui Parle State Park.

BLUFF COUNTRY

The **Blufflands State Trail** and **Cannon Valley Trail,** two paved rail-to-trail bike routes, are great ways to enjoy the Driftless Area's unique beauty, as is paddling the **Root and Cannon Rivers,** which cut the deep valleys the trails follow. It's also a lot of fun to poke around the labyrinth backwaters of the **Mississippi River.** Extensively bolted **Barn Bluff** in **Red Wing** has some good rock climbing.

sunset at Boundary Waters Canoe Area Wilderness

headwaters of the Mississippi River in Itasca State Park

a convergence of Minnesota's three primary ecosystems—prairie, northern hardwood forest, and northern pine forest—and so it is one of the state's best wildlife-watching destinations, particularly for birds. Cross through the remarkably flat Red River Valley to Buffalo River State Park, which protects one of Minnesota's largest and healthiest prairies and is a premier place to see prairie chickens doing their spring mating dance. Turn south, continuing through endless farm fields until you hit the Minnesota River near the Big Stone National Wildlife Refuge. Bird-watchers will want to detour to Salt Lake to expand their life lists. You'll have to go pretty fast to squeeze this all into a day, but it can be done.

Day 9

The wildlife-watching is always wonderful at Lac Qui Parle State Park, but especially in fall when hundreds of thousands of geese gather. Bald eagles congregate over the winter. Leave the river to see some fantastic prairie scenery at Jeffers Petroglyphs and the Sod House on the Prairie, and then stop at Minneopa State Park to see southern Minnesota's largest waterfall and a field full of glacial erratics.

Day 10

Your last day twists through the deep, rugged valleys of Minnesota's Pseudo Driftless Area. Forestville and Mystery Cave State Park has some especially lovely scenery and also Minnesota's longest cave. Make a quick stop in Fountain, the "Sink Hole Capital of the U.S.A.," before reaching the spectacular 500-foot bluffs lining the Mississippi River. Climb the bluffs at John A. Latsch State Park for some wonderful views before heading home. (In the fall, watch the migrating tundra swans near Weaver, or, in the winter, do some eagle watching around Wabasha.)

▸ MINNESOTA'S CULTURAL MÉLANGE

Listen to *A Prairie Home Companion* long enough and you might think Minnesota's entire population comes from Scandinavia and Germany. These are the largest ethnic groups, but today's Minnesotans have come from all corners of the globe.

Twin Cities

St. Paul is the more Irish of the Twin Cities, but there are good pubs on both sides of the river. Northeast Minneapolis (Nordeast), once the destination of choice for Eastern European immigrants, is still graced by many Eastern Orthodox churches. Other than some street names (Nicollet and Hennepin), the most noteworthy remnant from the French-Canadians are the *tourtieres* (meat pies) sold at Our Lady of Lourdes Church in Minneapolis. Minneapolis's American Swedish Institute is a busy cultural center, and St. Paul's Penumbra Theatre Company is one of the nation's premier African American dramatic groups. The Shakopee Mdewakanton Sioux Reservation in Prior Lake, where the massive casino has made millionaires out of all tribal members, isn't your typical reservation, though they do host a powwow in August. The Twin Cities has the largest urban Hmong population in the world, and the Hmong New Year celebration in St. Paul is a mighty big event.

Our Lady of Lourdes Church in Minneapolis

St. Croix Valley

Little Scandia commemorates the state's first Swedish settlers with a pair of museums and a host of festivals. The Fond du Lac Cultural Center and Museum in Cloquet looks at Ojibwe history.

The Arrowhead

In the early 20th century the Iron Range was an impressive cultural melting pot. These days the diversity is mostly celebrated in edible form and foods like pasties and potica are available at many restaurants and bakeries. Minnesota Discovery Center in Chisholm looks at the Range's ethnic heritage as well as mining. Embarrass, settled by Finns who wanted to farm instead of mine, remains a deeply Finnish town at heart.

The Bois Forte Ojibwe Reservation near Orr is still a very traditional place, and the tribe runs the Bois Forte Heritage Center near Tower. There's more Native American history on display at Grand Portage National Monument on the Grand Portage Ojibwe Reservation. You can see ancient pictographs in the Boundary Waters Canoe Area Wilderness and Voyageurs National Park.

Central Lakes

The Mille Lacs Indian Museum on Lake Mille Lacs is a great place to learn about Ojibwe culture and purchase Native American crafts. The Red Lake Ojibwe Reservation, centered around the namesake lake, is one of the most traditional Native American communities in the country and just one of two reservations where all land is still owned collectively by the tribe. The Leech Lake Ojibwe Reservation sits within the Chippewa National Forest, and the band hosts three popular powwows in the city of Cass Lake. The Native American arts and crafts collection at the Pope County Historical Museum in Glenwood is so good the Smithsonian wanted to have it.

Red River Valley

The Historical and Cultural Society of Clay County in Moorhead contains a 76-foot Viking-style ship, the Hopperstad Stave Church, and other Norwegian displays. Half of the population of Thief River Falls claims at least some Norse ancestry, making this statistically the most Norwegian city in the nation. The Finn Creek Museum in New York Mills is a Finnish farm site with many original buildings. Nearby, little Pelican Rapids is one of the most ethnically diverse towns in the state.

Prairieland

The lovely city of Pipestone is brimming with Dakota culture and hosts many Native American events. The city is also home to the Pipestone National Monument, which, along with Jeffers Petroglyphs, is one of the most important Native American spiritual sites in the state. Several other Native American historic sites, including the interesting Lac Qui Parle Mission, lie along the Minnesota River, as do the Lower Sioux Reservation near Morton and the Upper Sioux Reservation near Granite Falls.

Sixty-six percent of New Ulm residents have German ancestry, making it the most German city in the nation, and the Teutonic heritage, from the Glockenspiel to schnitzel, is ever-present. Farther up the river, Milan has emerged as a Scandinavian arts center. Walnut Grove, one-time home of Laura Ingalls Wilder, author of the *Little House* books, and the Sod House on the Prairie are good places to learn about the lives of pioneers.

Bluff Country

Winona once produced more sauerkraut than any city west of Chicago, and the east end still has the largest concentration of Poles from the Kashubian region in the United States. Farther up the Mississippi is the Prairie Island Dakota Reservation, and Minnesota's largest Amish communities are centered on Harmony.

TWIN CITIES

With downtowns just eight miles apart, the Twin Cities moniker is certainly appropriate, but it is definitely a fraternal pairing. The English journalist Trevor Fishlock quipped that Minneapolis and St. Paul "are divided by the Mississippi River and united by the belief that the inhabitants of the other side of the river are inferior." This tale of two cities no longer has the acrimony of the past, when census counts were illegally padded in an effort to outrank the other, but these friendly rivals have not completely lost their competitive edge: The two still go head-to-head to attract new businesses, and locals' loyalties to one or the other run deep.

While people who have never been here naturally lump the two together, visitors will quickly see the differences. Energetic Minneapolis with soaring skyscrapers is the more modern and cosmopolitan of the two, while conservative St. Paul with its winding streets and downtown parks promotes its European charm. In a nutshell, Minneapolis is slick and St. Paul is sober—though ironically two of the most notable developments in recent years are the return of nightlife to downtown St. Paul and the historic restoration along Minneapolis's riverfront. Citizens tend to reflect their cities' demeanors. Some smug west bank natives consider St. Paul nothing more than Minneapolis's most enjoyable suburb, while St. Paulites sometimes judge their neighbors to be arrogant.

Despite all the differences, the many similarities best define the area. Twin Cities residents are full of hometown pride, prices are

HIGHLIGHTS

Mississippi Riverfront: The heart of historic Minneapolis encompasses St. Anthony Falls, the landmark Stone Arch Bridge, the river's final lock and dam, a host of historic buildings, and much more (page 36).

Walker Art Center and Minneapolis Sculpture Garden: Minneapolis has arts galore, and these two spots are world class. The Walker Art Center focuses on modern art, and the Minneapolis Sculpture Garden, home of the iconic *Spoonbridge and Cherry,* is one of the nation's largest urban sculpture gardens (page 38).

Historic Fort Snelling: What would become Minnesota more or less began in this imposing fortress perched high above the confluence of the Mississippi and Minnesota rivers. Today, dozens of costumed reenactors relive the days of 1827 (page 42).

Summit Avenue: F. Scott Fitzgerald, who once lived on this swank St. Paul street, called it "a mausoleum of American architectural monstrosities," and Frank Lloyd Wright declared it "the worst collection of architecture in the world." Even if you agree with them, odds are you'll be impressed by the longest stretch of Victorian homes in the nation. The massive James J. Hill House and the jam-packed Julian H. Sleeper House let you look inside that era (page 65).

Minnesota History Center: This large, engaging museum takes a broad look at the who, what, when, where, and why behind the making of the North Star State (page 67).

Science Museum of Minnesota: Not just for kids, this excellent and often hands-on museum, Minnesota's most visited, spans the course of science from the ancient world to what we can expect in the future. There is also an IMAX theater and 3-D cinema (page 68).

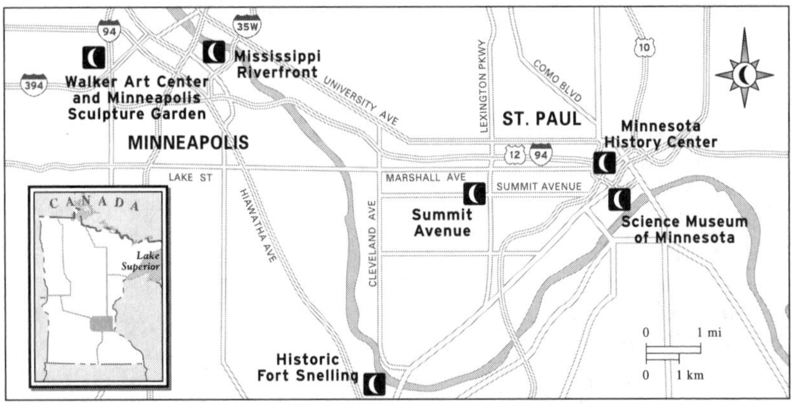

LOOK FOR TO FIND RECOMMENDED SIGHTS, ACTIVITIES, DINING, AND LODGING.

lower than in most similarly sized cities, and the quality of life here is second to none. Also, you don't have to head out of town to enjoy the outdoors—the riverside parks are stunningly beautiful, especially as fall color takes hold, and around 800 of the state's nearly 12,000 lakes wet the metro area.

While many locals find little reason to go "across the river," exploring either city without at least a quick visit to the other would be a mistake. The combination of the best of both makes for a wonderful trip indeed.

PLANNING YOUR TIME

You can't do the Twin Cities justice in a day, and you'll miss several highlights with only two, so let's lay out a busy three-day visit with a home base in Minneapolis. On your first morning, do some people and sculpture watching along **Nicollet Mall** (come back in the early evening if you are here between Thanksgiving and Christmas, when Holidazzle parades light up the winter darkness) before admiring more statuary at the **Minneapolis Sculpture Garden.** Pick an art museum—the **Walker Art Center** if your tastes lean toward the contemporary or the **Minneapolis Institute of Arts** for the classics—and then stroll along the **Mississippi Riverfront.** For dinner, pick a country and cuisine from the dozens of choices along **Eat Street** and then enjoy a night of theater at the **Guthrie Theater, Children's Theatre Company,** or one of the many respected smaller theaters.

On your second day, step back in time in St. Paul. Start out admiring the mansions lining **Summit Avenue** and tour the grandest of them all, the **James J. Hill House.** Also visit the **Cathedral of St. Paul** and take a quick trip through the **Minnesota History Center** before cruising the Mississippi River Mark Twain style with **Padelford Riverboat Company** in the summer months. At the heart of downtown is **Landmark Center,** a castle-like cultural center best admired from **Rice Park,** which will be filled with ice sculptures if you are here during the Winter Carnival. Take a gander at **St. Paul City Hall** and **Ramsey County Courthouse, Minnesota State Capitol,** and the homes fronting the **Irvine Park Historic District**'s village green before heading back to Minneapolis for some nightlife, perhaps polkaing at **Nye's Polonaise** or seeing who's on stage at **First Avenue, Dakota Jazz Club,** or **Cedar Cultural Center.**

Everything on day three can be reached by light rail. On your way to a morning at **Mall of America,** stop for a look at the waterfall and historic buildings in **Minnehaha Park.** In the afternoon, watch costumed reenactors fire cannons at **Historic Fort Snelling** (a 15-minute walk from the light rail station) and then take a hike through the Minnesota River Valley in **Fort Snelling State Park.**

MEDIA

In a sense, the Twin Cities maintain competing daily newspapers, though realistically the ***Star Tribune*** (www.startribune.com) is the Minneapolis and west metro paper, while the smaller ***Pioneer Press*** (www.pioneerpress.com) focuses on St. Paul and the east metro. For arts and entertainment information pick up ***City Pages*** (www.citypages.com), the alternative weekly paper, or the local edition of ***The Onion*** (www.theonion.com). ***Lavender*** (www.lavendermagazine.com) is a free biweekly covering the Twin Cities gay scene. ***Minnesota Monthly*** (www.minnesotamonthly.com) and ***Mpls.St.Paul*** (www.mspmag.com) are the two competing high-class lifestyle magazines sold at newsstands and bookstores. For kid-oriented tips and events, look for the free monthly ***Minnesota Parent*** (www.mnparent.com). Also free on racks, particularly in the U of M area, is the ***Minnesota Daily*** (www.mndaily.com), one of the largest student-run newspapers in the country.

Twin Cities radio offers everything every other big city does, from corporate pop music to lunatic political rants. **KNOW** (91.1) is the home of Minnesota Public Radio (www.mpr.org), which plays classical music at **KSJN** (99.5) and contemporary music at **KCMP** 89.3, known as the Current. **KFAI** (www.kfai.org, 90.3 and 106.7 FM) is a lefty volunteer-run

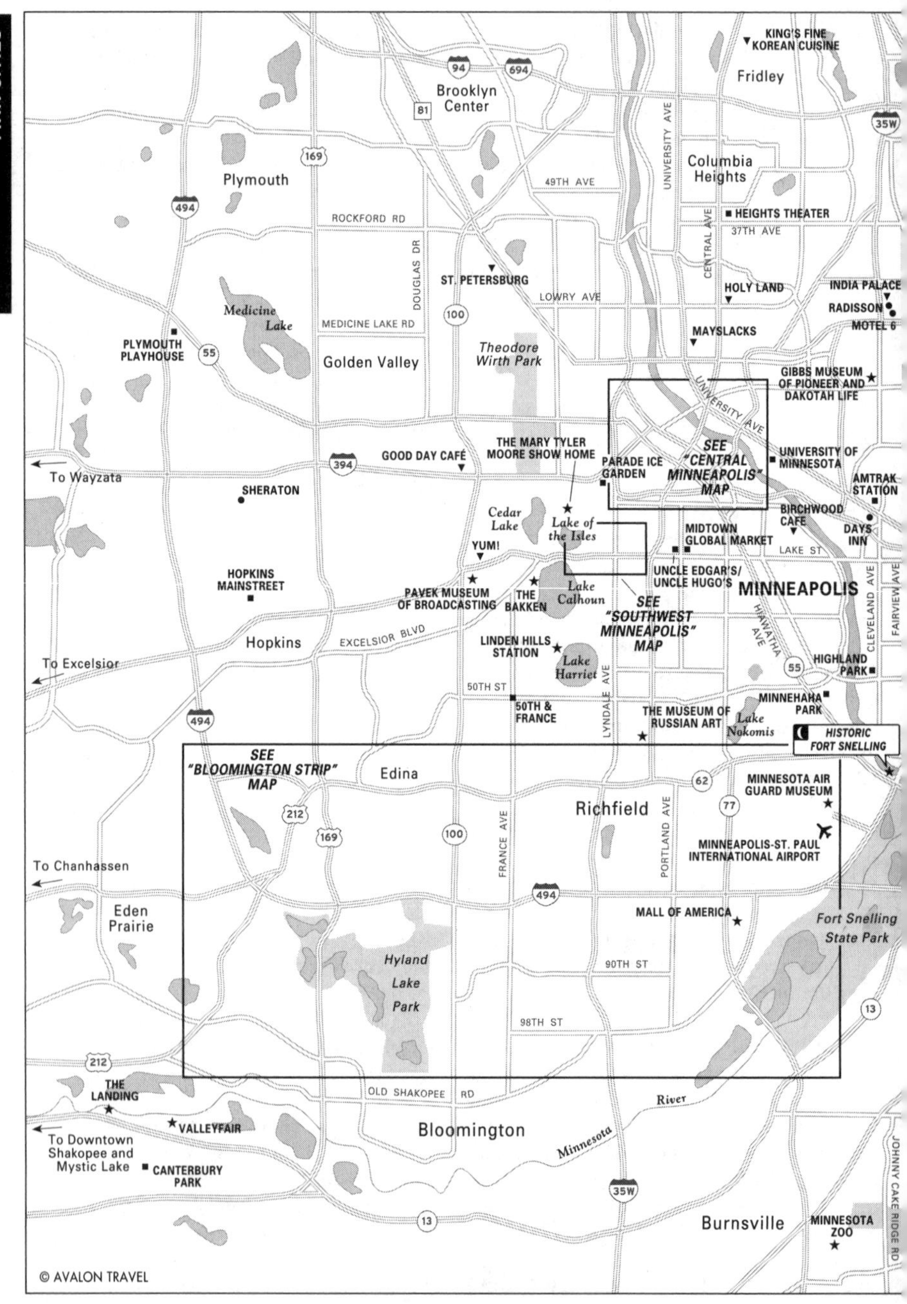

KING'S FINE KOREAN CUISINE
Fridley
Brooklyn Center
Plymouth
Columbia Heights
49TH AVE
UNIVERSITY AVE
HEIGHTS THEATER
37TH AVE
CENTRAL AVE
ROCKFORD RD
DOUGLAS DR
ST. PETERSBURG
LOWRY AVE
HOLY LAND
INDIA PALACE
RADISSON
MOTEL 6
Medicine Lake
MEDICINE LAKE RD
MAYSLACKS
PLYMOUTH PLAYHOUSE
Golden Valley
Theodore Wirth Park
GIBBS MUSEUM OF PIONEER AND DAKOTAH LIFE
UNIVERSITY AVE
SEE "CENTRAL MINNEAPOLIS" MAP
UNIVERSITY OF MINNESOTA
THE MARY TYLER MOORE SHOW HOME
GOOD DAY CAFÉ
PARADE ICE GARDEN
AMTRAK STATION
To Wayzata
SHERATON
BIRCHWOOD CAFE
Cedar Lake
Lake of the Isles
MIDTOWN GLOBAL MARKET
DAYS INN
YUM!
LAKE ST
HOPKINS MAINSTREET
PAVEK MUSEUM OF BROADCASTING
THE BAKKEN
Lake Calhoun
UNCLE EDGAR'S/ UNCLE HUGO'S
MINNEAPOLIS
SEE "SOUTHWEST MINNEAPOLIS" MAP
HIAWATHA AVE
CLEVELAND AVE
FAIRVIEW AVE
Hopkins
EXCELSIOR BLVD
LINDEN HILLS STATION
Lake Harriet
To Excelsior
HIGHLAND PARK
50TH ST
MINNEHAHA PARK
50TH & FRANCE
LYNDALE AVE
THE MUSEUM OF RUSSIAN ART
Lake Nokomis
HISTORIC FORT SNELLING
SEE "BLOOMINGTON STRIP" MAP
Edina
MINNESOTA AIR GUARD MUSEUM
Richfield
FRANCE AVE
PORTLAND AVE
MINNEAPOLIS-ST. PAUL INTERNATIONAL AIRPORT
To Chanhassen
Eden Prairie
MALL OF AMERICA
Fort Snelling State Park
Hyland Lake Park
90TH ST
98TH ST
THE LANDING
OLD SHAKOPEE RD
River
VALLEYFAIR
Bloomington
Minnesota
To Downtown Shakopee and Mystic Lake
CANTERBURY PARK
JOHNNY CAKE RIDGE RD
Burnsville
MINNESOTA ZOO

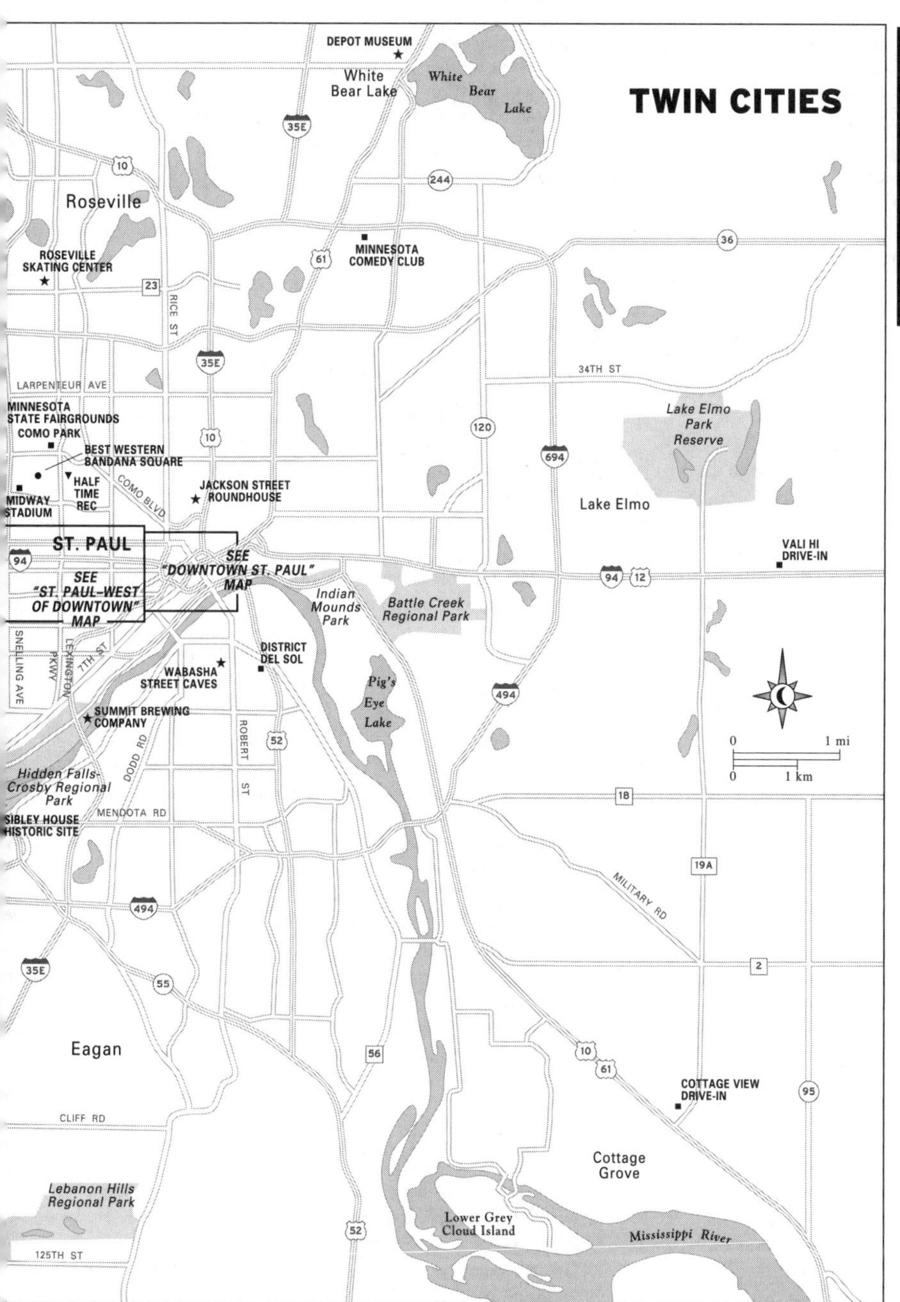

TWIN CITIES
DEPOT MUSEUM
White Bear Lake
White Bear Lake
Roseville
ROSEVILLE SKATING CENTER
MINNESOTA COMEDY CLUB
RICE ST
LARPENTEUR AVE
34TH ST
MINNESOTA STATE FAIRGROUNDS
COMO PARK
BEST WESTERN BANDANA SQUARE
HALF TIME REC
MIDWAY STADIUM
COMO BLVD
JACKSON STREET ROUNDHOUSE
Lake Elmo Park Reserve
Lake Elmo
ST. PAUL
SEE "ST. PAUL–WEST OF DOWNTOWN" MAP
SEE "DOWNTOWN ST. PAUL" MAP
VALI HI DRIVE-IN
Indian Mounds Park
Battle Creek Regional Park
SNELLING AVE
PKWY
LEXINGTON
7TH ST
DISTRICT DEL SOL
WABASHA STREET CAVES
SUMMIT BREWING COMPANY
Pig's Eye Lake
DODD RD
ROBERT ST
Hidden Falls-Crosby Regional Park
MENDOTA RD
SIBLEY HOUSE HISTORIC SITE
0 1 mi
0 1 km
MILITARY RD
Eagan
COTTAGE VIEW DRIVE-IN
CLIFF RD
Cottage Grove
Lebanon Hills Regional Park
Lower Grey Cloud Island
Mississippi River
125TH ST

public radio station with a global programming schedule, including Democracy Now. **KTLK** (www.ktlkfm.com, 100.3) fills the air with talk from the other end of the spectrum.

GETTING THERE AND AWAY

By Air

Minneapolis-St. Paul International Airport (612/726-5555, www.mspairport.com), immediately south of the two cities, is one of the Midwest's largest hubs. When arranging your flight, be sure to find out whether you will be using the Lindbergh or Humphrey terminal; both are on the Hiawatha light rail line.

By Train

Though located in St. Paul, the **Amtrak** station (730 Transfer Rd., 651/644-6012 or 800/872-7245, www.amtrak.com) is almost exactly between the two downtowns. The eastbound train heads out at 7:50 A.M., stopping in Red Wing and Winona, while the westbound, with stops in St. Cloud and Detroit Lakes, departs at 11:15 P.M. Be aware that weather frequently delays the eastbound train in the Rockies for hours.

In late 2009, the Twin Cities' first commuter rail line, **Northstar** (www.metrotransit.org/northstar) began carrying passengers from downtown Minneapolis to Big Lake, about 45 miles to the north, via Fridley, Coon Rapids, Anoka, and Elk River. Five departures in each direction serve morning commuters (between 6:30 and 8:45 A.M.), and five serve evening commuters (between 3:30 and 5:30 P.M.) for the 50-minute trip. The ride from Minneapolis to Big Lake costs about $8 and rides between other stations cost $3.25, with 25 percent discounts on the weekends.

By Bus

Minneapolis's downtown **bus station** (950 Hawthorne Ave., 612/371-3325) handles departures for Greyhound, Jefferson Lines, and other bus companies. **Megabus,** with service to Chicago, uses the 4th Street North Parking Garage along North 3rd Avenue. Many of these routes also stop at the U of M campus and St. Paul's little bus station (166 University Ave. W., St. Paul, 651/222-0507).

GETTING AROUND

By Bus and Train

Overall, **Metro Transit** (612/373-3333, www.metrotransit.org) is pretty good. The regular cash fare is $1.75 for local routes and $2.25 for express routes. Add $0.50 and $0.75 respectively during rush hour (6–9 A.M. and 3–6:30 P.M. weekdays). Seniors and youth (ages 6–12) ride for $0.75, except during rush hour, when they pay regular fares. Disabled riders (all buses are equipped with ramps) pay $0.75 at all times. Request a transfer when boarding, and your fare is valid for unlimited travel on any combination of buses and trains for 2.5 hours. A ride anywhere in Minneapolis's or St. Paul's Downtown Zone costs just $0.50. A **Day Pass,** good for 24 hours of unlimited travel from the time of first use, costs $6 and is valid throughout the entire metro area. They are sold at the two transit stores (719 Marquette Ave., Minneapolis, 7:30 A.M.–5:30 P.M. Mon.–Fri.; 101 E. 5th St., St. Paul, skyway level, 7:30 A.M.–4:45 P.M. Mon.–Fri.), ticket machines at rail stations, and from the driver. All tickets for light rail must be bought from the machines on the platform before boarding the train—it's a $180 fine if you are caught without one. Bikes can be rolled right onto light rail trains and placed in the racks on the front of every bus.

The **Hiawatha Line Light Rail** (612/373-3333, www.metrotransit.org) connects downtown Minneapolis to the airport and Mall of America. To reach the airport and mall from St. Paul, take bus #54.

By Taxi

Hailing a taxi isn't easy in either downtown—and downright impossible outside of downtown. Your best bet is to look for a taxi rank outside of a hotel or call one. Expect a flag fall of $2.50 and $2.35 per mile after that, plus a $3 airport surcharge. A ride between the airport and either downtown or between downtowns costs about $30. **Suburban Taxi** (612/522-2222 in Minneapolis, 651/522-2222 in St. Paul) covers the entire metro area and has 24-hour radio dispatch.

Organized Tours

Down In History Tours (651/292-1220, www.wabashastreetcaves.com) serves up a bevy of wacky two-hour Twin Cities tours focused on Irish history, tacky sights, ghosts and ghouls, and—most popular—St. Paul's gangster history. Led by costumed reenactors, they revisit the homes and hideouts of the most infamous crooks of the Roaring '20s. Most tours are summer only, though the St. Paul Gangster outing runs year-round. All tours depart from the **Wabasha Street Caves** (215 S. Wabasha St, $22.) near downtown St. Paul. They also lead short tours of the caves themselves, once a fashionable nightclub, for $5.

You can get a unique view of the Minneapolis Riverfront on a Segway scooter with **Magical History Tours** (125 Main St. SE, 952/888-9200, www.humanonastick.com, 10 A.M. and 3 P.M. daily Apr.–Nov., $80, includes admission to the Mill City Museum and discounts at nearby eateries). Knowledgeable and upbeat guides lead the three-hour guided tours (including training and a snack break). Reservations are recommended; arrive 30 minutes early.

Metro Connections (612/333-8687 or 800/747-8687, www.metroconnections.com, $32, children 12 and under $22) runs three-hour highlights tours that run in a loop, picking up at several downtown hotels and the Mall of America. Tours run daily in the summer and less often as it gets colder. The holiday lights tour in November and December is particularly popular.

Gray Line Tours (952/469-5020, www.grayline-mpls.com, Sat. in summer only, $35, children 14 and under $25) runs tours that start at the Mall of America. Make reservations in advance.

Minneapolis

The larger, more polished, and—as St. Paulites would say—pompous half of the Twin Cities is a world-class city. Capped by four internationally renowned art museums and a trio of Tony Award–winning theaters, few cities this small can boast of such superb and diverse cultural opportunities. The vibrant nightlife spans smart political humor to classic burlesque cabaret, while the always thriving music scene has birthed such legends as Prince, Morris Day and The Time, Hüsker Dü, The Replacements, Soul Asylum, Babes in Toyland, Dillinger Four, and Atmosphere. The city is as beautiful as it is energetic. The shimmering skyline belies the many historic structures preserved behind it, and, with the mighty Mississippi rushing through the heart of town and a dozen lakes dotting the rest of it, the appropriately named City of Water (*minne* is the Dakota word for water and *polis* is Greek for city) is not lacking in natural beauty either. When you get here, take your time. Minneapolis may be small, but it has so much to offer visitors that you'll need at least a couple of days to do it justice and several more to do it all.

History

Minneapolis was born at St. Anthony Falls. Settlers began to roll into the area immediately after an 1838 treaty with the Dakota opened up the river's east bank. Franklin Steele set out from Fort Snelling by moonlight and beat all other intended claimants to the falls, although, because he lacked financing, it would take 11 years before he could develop his town. When the money finally came through, he erected a dam, opened a sawmill, and plotted the town of St. Anthony. Minneapolis technically began on the opposite shore in 1849, when Colonel John H. Stevens received permission to operate a ferry and so built his home there. Though a few farmers soon joined him, this land, still a part of Fort Snelling's holdings, wasn't officially opened up for settlement until 1855.

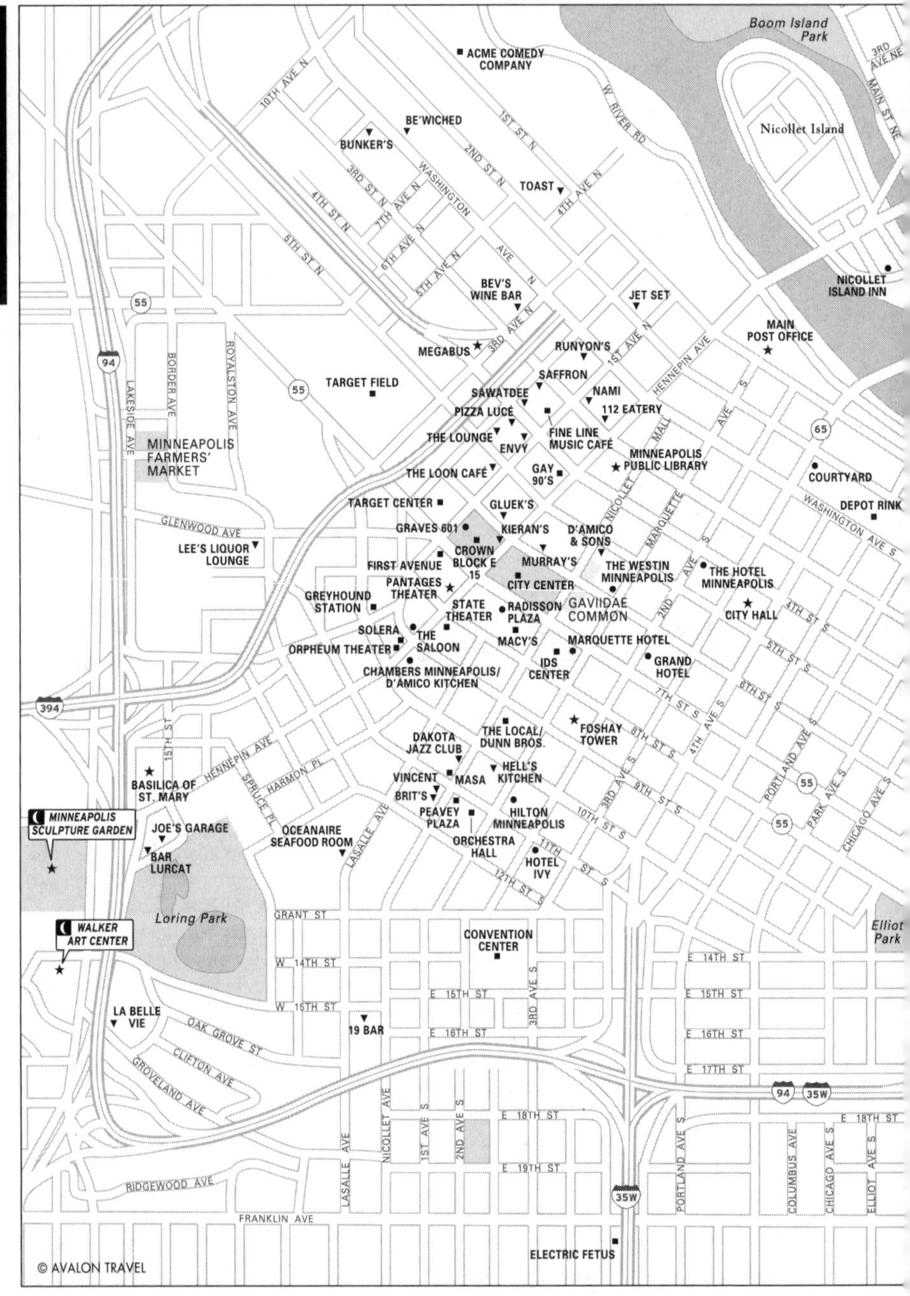

Boom Island Park
Nicollet Island
ACME COMEDY COMPANY
BE'WICHED
BUNKER'S
TOAST
NICOLLET ISLAND INN
BEV'S WINE BAR
JET SET
MAIN POST OFFICE
MEGABUS
RUNYON'S
SAFFRON
TARGET FIELD
SAWATDEE
NAMI
PIZZA LUCÉ
112 EATERY
THE LOUNGE
ENVY
FINE LINE MUSIC CAFÉ
MINNEAPOLIS PUBLIC LIBRARY
COURTYARD
MINNEAPOLIS FARMERS' MARKET
THE LOON CAFÉ
GAY 90'S
TARGET CENTER
GLUEK'S
DEPOT RINK
GRAVES 601
KIERAN'S
D'AMICO & SONS
LEE'S LIQUOR LOUNGE
CROWN BLOCK E 15
MURRAY'S
FIRST AVENUE
THE WESTIN MINNEAPOLIS
THE HOTEL MINNEAPOLIS
PANTAGES THEATER
CITY CENTER
GREYHOUND STATION
STATE THEATER
RADISSON PLAZA
GAVIIDAE COMMON
CITY HALL
SOLERA
THE SALOON
MACY'S
MARQUETTE HOTEL
ORPHEUM THEATER
IDS CENTER
GRAND HOTEL
CHAMBERS MINNEAPOLIS/ D'AMICO KITCHEN
THE LOCAL/ DUNN BROS.
FOSHAY TOWER
DAKOTA JAZZ CLUB
BASILICA OF ST. MARY
VINCENT
MASA
HELL'S KITCHEN
BRIT'S
MINNEAPOLIS SCULPTURE GARDEN
PEAVEY PLAZA
HILTON MINNEAPOLIS
JOE'S GARAGE
OCEANAIRE SEAFOOD ROOM
ORCHESTRA HALL
BAR LURCAT
HOTEL IVY
Loring Park
Elliot Park
WALKER ART CENTER
CONVENTION CENTER
LA BELLE VIE
19 BAR
ELECTRIC FETUS
10TH AVE N
1ST ST N
W RIVER RD
3RD AVE NE
MAIN ST NE
2ND ST N
WASHINGTON AVE N
3RD ST N
4TH ST N
7TH AVE N
4TH AVE N
6TH ST N
6TH AVE N
5TH AVE N
3RD AVE N
1ST AVE N
HENNEPIN AVE
BORDER AVE
ROYALSTON AVE
LAKESIDE AVE
GLENWOOD AVE
NICOLLET MALL
MARQUETTE AVE S
2ND AVE S
WASHINGTON AVE S
4TH ST S
5TH ST S
6TH ST S
7TH ST S
8TH ST S
9TH ST S
10TH ST S
11TH ST S
12TH ST S
3RD AVE S
4TH AVE S
PORTLAND AVE S
PARK AVE S
CHICAGO AVE S
15TH ST
HARMON PL
SPRUCE PL
LASALLE AVE
GRANT ST
W 14TH ST
W 15TH ST
E 14TH ST
E 15TH ST
E 16TH ST
E 17TH ST
E 18TH ST
E 19TH ST
OAK GROVE ST
CLIFTON AVE
GROVELAND AVE
RIDGEWOOD AVE
FRANKLIN AVE
NICOLLET AVE
1ST AVE S
2ND AVE S
COLUMBUS AVE
ELLIOT AVE S
94
394
35W
55
65
© AVALON TRAVEL

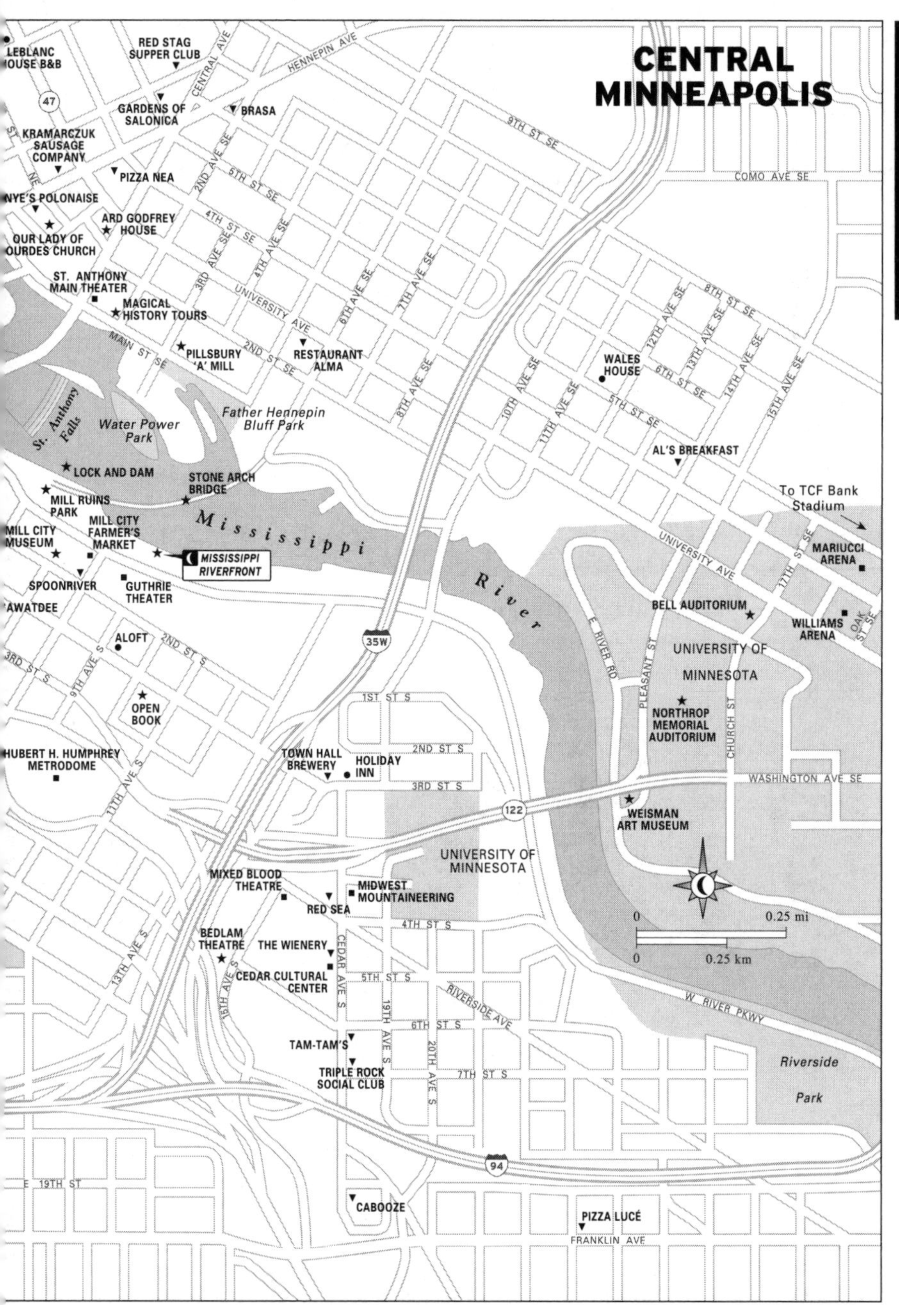
CENTRAL MINNEAPOLIS
RED STAG SUPPER CLUB
GARDENS OF SALONICA
BRASA
KRAMARCZUK SAUSAGE COMPANY
PIZZA NEA
NYE'S POLONAISE
ARD GODFREY HOUSE
OUR LADY OF LOURDES CHURCH
ST. ANTHONY MAIN THEATER
MAGICAL HISTORY TOURS
PILLSBURY 'A' MILL
RESTAURANT ALMA
WALES HOUSE
AL'S BREAKFAST
Father Hennepin Bluff Park
Water Power Park
St. Anthony Falls
LOCK AND DAM
STONE ARCH BRIDGE
MILL RUINS PARK
MILL CITY MUSEUM
MILL CITY FARMER'S MARKET
MISSISSIPPI RIVERFRONT
Mississippi River
SPOONRIVER
GUTHRIE THEATER
ALOFT
OPEN BOOK
HUBERT H. HUMPHREY METRODOME
To TCF Bank Stadium
MARIUCCI ARENA
BELL AUDITORIUM
WILLIAMS ARENA
UNIVERSITY OF MINNESOTA
NORTHROP MEMORIAL AUDITORIUM
WEISMAN ART MUSEUM
TOWN HALL BREWERY
HOLIDAY INN
UNIVERSITY OF MINNESOTA
MIXED BLOOD THEATRE
MIDWEST MOUNTAINEERING
RED SEA
BEDLAM THEATRE
THE WIENERY
CEDAR CULTURAL CENTER
TAM-TAM'S
TRIPLE ROCK SOCIAL CLUB
CABOOZE
PIZZA LUCÉ
Riverside Park
0 0.25 mi
0 0.25 km
HENNEPIN AVE
CENTRAL AVE
9TH ST SE
COMO AVE SE
5TH ST SE
4TH ST SE
UNIVERSITY AVE
MAIN ST SE
2ND ST SE
8TH ST SE
6TH ST SE
UNIVERSITY AVE
E RIVER RD
PLEASANT ST
CHURCH ST
WASHINGTON AVE SE
2ND ST S
3RD ST S
1ST ST S
4TH ST S
5TH ST S
6TH ST S
7TH ST S
CEDAR AVE S
19TH AVE S
20TH AVE S
RIVERSIDE AVE
W RIVER PKWY
E 19TH ST
FRANKLIN AVE
35W
122
94
47

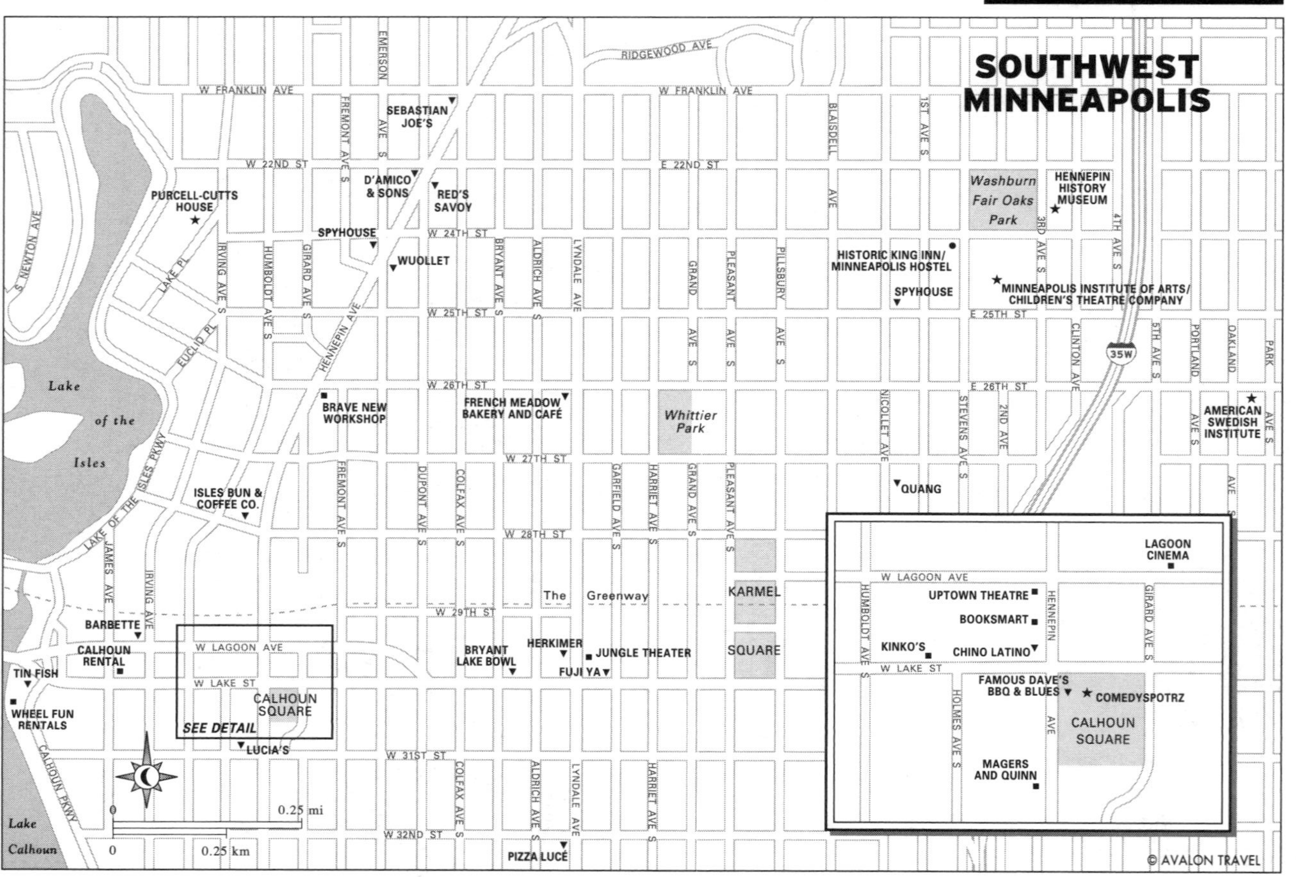
SOUTHWEST MINNEAPOLIS
Washburn Fair Oaks Park
HENNEPIN HISTORY MUSEUM
MINNEAPOLIS INSTITUTE OF ARTS/ CHILDREN'S THEATRE COMPANY
AMERICAN SWEDISH INSTITUTE
HISTORIC KING INN/ MINNEAPOLIS HOSTEL
SPYHOUSE
QUANG
Whittier Park
KARMEL SQUARE
The Greenway
JUNGLE THEATER
FUJI YA
HERKIMER
BRYANT LAKE BOWL
FRENCH MEADOW BAKERY AND CAFÉ
PIZZA LUCÉ
SEBASTIAN JOE'S
RED'S SAVOY
D'AMICO & SONS
WUOLLET
SPYHOUSE
BRAVE NEW WORKSHOP
ISLES BUN & COFFEE CO.
PURCELL-CUTTS HOUSE
CALHOUN SQUARE
LUCIA'S
SEE DETAIL
BARBETTE
CALHOUN RENTAL
TIN FISH
WHEEL FUN RENTALS
Lake of the Isles
Lake Calhoun
LAGOON CINEMA
UPTOWN THEATRE
BOOKSMART
KINKO'S
CHINO LATINO
FAMOUS DAVE'S BBQ & BLUES
COMEDYSPOTRZ
CALHOUN SQUARE
MAGERS AND QUINN
W FRANKLIN AVE
RIDGEWOOD AVE
EMERSON AVE S
FREMONT AVE S
W 22ND ST
E 22ND ST
BLAISDELL AVE
1ST AVE S
3RD AVE S
4TH AVE S
W 24TH ST
IRVING AVE S
HUMBOLDT AVE S
GIRARD AVE S
BRYANT AVE S
ALDRICH AVE S
LYNDALE AVE
GRAND AVE S
PLEASANT AVE S
PILLSBURY AVE S
W 25TH ST
E 25TH ST
CLINTON AVE
5TH AVE S
PORTLAND AVE S
OAKLAND AVE
PARK AVE S
35W
HENNEPIN AVE
W 26TH ST
E 26TH ST
NICOLLET AVE
STEVENS AVE S
2ND AVE
W 27TH ST
DUPONT AVE S
COLFAX AVE S
GARFIELD AVE S
HARRIET AVE S
W 28TH ST
W 29TH ST
LAKE PL
EUCLID PL
S NEWTON AVE
LAKE OF THE ISLES PKWY
JAMES AVE
IRVING AVE
W LAGOON AVE
W LAKE ST
HOLMES AVE S
HENNEPIN AVE
GIRARD AVE S
HUMBOLDT AVE S
W 31ST ST
W 32ND ST
CALHOUN PKWY
0
0.25 mi
0.25 km
© AVALON TRAVEL

Despite the delay, west bank supremacy was such a foregone conclusion that right after the Territorial Legislature created Hennepin County in 1852, the first commissioners chose that side for the county seat, even though no town existed.

Though Scandinavian and French Canadian immigrants came to both towns in large numbers, many educated New Englanders also settled here in order to strike it rich when the United States opened up the West. Hydropower made lumber the initial industry, and by 1852, four mills trimmed the pine brought down the Mississippi. The falls were also a major tourist attraction and many wealthy southerners—plus some East Coast luminaries like Henry David Thoreau—traveled up the Mississippi by steamboat to see them. The luxurious Winslow Hotel opened in St. Anthony in 1857 to house the visiting elite and helped the towns prosper. In 1860 St. Anthony had a population of 3,258, and 2,564 more lived in Minneapolis. The Civil War (1861–1865) ended the tourist trade and stunted the region's growth, though following General Lee's surrender settlers headed out into the prairies and money once again poured into the towns fronting St. Anthony Falls. When the state legislature officially incorporated Minneapolis in 1866, it combined the two small communities into one.

The same year that the Winslow turned down its first bed, industrialists dug a canal along the river's west bank, creating the West Side Milling District. As wheat replaced big bluestem on the western prairies, new flour mills continued to open, and by 1870, a dozen were grinding the golden grain, while 18 sawmills also operated in the area. Ten years later another dozen flour mills, utilizing the most modern methods available, were turning out not only more flour than anywhere else in the world, but the absolute best flour money could buy. These mills not only made Minneapolis a major city—the population swelled from 13,000 in 1870 to 165,000 by 1890—but ensured that it, rather than St. Paul, became the state's metropolis. Flour had eclipsed lumber in importance, though the latter continued to thrive, and, as the 19th century spun into the 20th, Minneapolis also enjoyed a short run as the nation's largest lumber center; however, the forests were soon felled, and most of the sawmills shut down by 1910.

A variety of factors, including cheap electricity, eliminated the need for waterpower to produce flour, so Mill City's 50-year run as the "Flour Milling Capital of the World" came to an end in 1930. The last commercial mill at the falls closed in 1965; however, companies that had been born on the river—Pillsbury, General Mills, and Cargill—evolved into diversified food manufacturers and remain headquartered here. Additionally, the Minneapolis Grain Exchange, established in 1881, remains one of the world's largest commodities markets—about one million bushels are traded daily.

Like most large middle-American cities, Minneapolis experienced suburban flight in the mid-20th century, but unlike most others, the downtown has always remained a vibrant shopping and social center. Significant civic investment began in the 1950s and, though it involved razing many gorgeous historic buildings, it also included the creation of the first all-weather pedestrian skyway and the nation's second downtown pedestrian mall. The skyline was forever changed in the 1970s with the construction of the 57-story IDS tower, and the upward growth has continued largely uninterrupted ever since. Downtown's evolution continues today with expanding options in the Warehouse District and the conversion of the western riverfront into a cultural destination.

Orientation

The heart of the city is **Nicollet Mall,** a 12-block pedestrian and transit corridor lined with restaurants and shops. **Hennepin Avenue,** one block to the west, is home to four top theaters and some decent dining options. The historic **Warehouse District,** the center of the city's entertainment scene, covers the northwest corner of downtown. The renovated buildings are now filled with swank restaurants and nightclubs, and this is where the beautiful people come to be seen, though there are destinations for all tastes here. Most of downtown is linked by an eight-mile elevated indoor skyway system that will keep you warm in the winter and dry when it rains. There is no shortage of parking ramps downtown, though street parking can be hard to come by.

Right across the river from downtown, where the city began, historic **St. Anthony Main** has many of the city's oldest buildings, and the great river and skyline views attract many for a meal and a stroll. **East Hennepin Avenue** behind Main Street has plenty of good restaurants, including Nye's Polonaise, a Minneapolis landmark. Collectively East Hennepin and all the other neighborhoods of northeast Minneapolis are known as **Nordeast.** This working-class region, known for the figurative church and bar on every corner, maintains strong Eastern European roots, though it now has a much wider international flair, especially along Central Avenue, and the many artists' studios have made it the center of the city's visual arts scene. East of the falls, on the edge of the University of Minnesota Campus, is **Dinkytown,** a fun four-block commercial district with student-focused shops, bars, and restaurants. Note that all addresses east of the river have a SE or NE suffix, with Hennepin Avenue forming the north–south divide.

The University of Minnesota (U of M) campus stretches across the river to the **West Bank,** now filled with as many East African immigrants as students. The eclectic mix of restaurants and live music venues makes it one of the most enjoyable nightspots in the city if you like your entertainment beyond the mainstream; don't worry, the southern end isn't nearly as rough and tumble as it appears at first glance.

Nicollet Avenue, between downtown and Lake Street, has been officially designated **Eat Street,** and dozens of restaurants representing cuisines from all corners of the globe line it. **Uptown,** often fancifully described as Minneapolis's answer to Greenwich Village, is the trendiest neighborhood in town. Officially Uptown is just a small area centered on Hennepin Avenue and Lake Street, but realistically the triangle formed by Lake Street and Hennepin and Lyndale Avenues is a continuous commercial district. After the Warehouse District, this is the city's best late-night destination.

The **Chain of Lakes**—Lake Calhoun, Lake Harriet, Lakes of the Isles, and Cedar Lake—runs up the city's southwest side. The crown jewels of Minneapolis, these park-encased gems are one of the things that make the city such a wonderful place to live, and, naturally, they are ringed by some of the city's fanciest homes. Paved bike and pedestrian trails hug their shores, and, since motorboats are prohibited, sailors, windsurfers, and paddlers have the waves to themselves.

SIGHTS

Mississippi Riverfront

The Father of Waters has only one natural waterfall, **St. Anthony Falls.** The 50-foot drop was known as Minirara (Curling Water) to the Dakota and Kakabikah (The Severed Rock) by the Ojibwe before Father Louis Hennepin honored his patron saint (Anthony of Padua) by bestowing it with the boring modern name. Hennepin was one of the first Europeans to see this spot when his Dakota captors led his exploration party past in 1680. Today a stroll through the old milling district is both a beautiful and educational experience.

The closest you can get to the falls is at **Water Power Park,** on Hennepin Island. A bridge leads from Main Street, past the Xcel Energy Plant. Standing on the viewing platform, you can feel sometimes feel the spray from one of the best natural sources of waterpower in the nation. One of the country's first hydroelectric plants was built here on Hennepin Island more than 120 years ago, and, to this day, Xcel Energy operates a plant on the island that powers downtown Minneapolis.

The 1.8-mile **St. Anthony Falls Heritage Trail** follows the riverfront past the falls, ruined mills, and other sights composing this National Historic District, and numerous historical markers recount the fascinating natural, engineering, and industrial history along the way. A good place to begin the tour is on the east bank, at Old St. Anthony, where many of

© TRICIA CORNELL

Joggers and bicyclists now enjoy the Stone Arch Bridge, which once carried trains into the heart of Minneapolis.

the renovated mid-19th-century buildings now house shops, restaurants, and watering holes—perfect for a bit of refreshment after you complete your loop.

Perched above Main Street is the small but tall **Our Lady of Lourdes Church,** the city's oldest church still in continuous use. Originally built in the Greek temple style by the First Universalist Society in 1854, the Catholic French-Canadian St. Anthony of Padua Parish purchased it 20 years later and added the bell tower and other features. To fund restoration projects, the parish office sells frozen *tourtieres* (meat pies).

Heading down Main Street you'll pass the **Pillsbury 'A' Mill,** a National Historic Landmark that was the world's largest when built in 1881; it could turn out 5,000 bushels a day. It ground its last wheat in 2003 and is scheduled to become condos. Across from the mill is **Father Hennepin Bluff Park.** You can either walk alongside it or follow the steps down to the trails, bridges, and overlooks at the river's edge.

Past the park the trail crosses the river over the one-of-a-kind **Stone Arch Bridge.** Beginning in 1881, 600 men worked around the clock for 22 months to finish this vital link in James J. Hill's railroad empire. Trains crossed the 23 granite and limestone arches for 101 years, but today bikers and pedestrians roll and stroll across the 2,100-foot span to take in the panoramic views it offers. The singular structure, built of 100,000 tons of stone, is now not only a Minneapolis icon, but a National Historic Civil Engineering Landmark.

The west end of the bridge passes the **Upper St. Anthony Falls Lock and Dam,** the last of the 29 locks along the Upper Mississippi River. The 49-foot lift accounts for 12 percent of the river's total rise between here and St. Louis. Free guided tours (www.nps.gov/miss, 877/552-1416, usually four or five times daily 10 A.M.–4 P.M. Mon., Thurs., and Fri., 10 A.M.–5 P.M. Sat.–Sun. May–Oct., times are posted daily) discuss the engineering history, including details about the complicated process of shoring up the waterfall with its concrete apron, and the area's unique geology.

The ancient-looking—if you ignore the steel beams and engine remnants—industrial ruins next to the lock are part of **Mill Ruins Park** (103 Portland Ave. S., 612/313-7793). Archeological excavations will continue on the walls, canals, and tailraces for many more years. Call about tours and opportunities to assist in the digs.

Rising within the ruins of the Washburn-Crosby 'A' Mill, also a National Historic Landmark, is the **Mill City Museum** (704 2nd St. S., 612/341-7555, www.millcitymuseum.org, 10 A.M.–5 P.M. Tues.–Sat., noon–5 P.M. Sun., $10 adults). The creatively constructed glass center has exhibits and performances about milling and associated topics such as railroads, agriculture, and waterpower. Guides lead riverfront walking tours (11 A.M. Sat., 1 P.M. Sun. June–Sept., $12). Perched above it all is an 8th-floor observation deck with superb views.

A block over, the longest cantilevered space in the country open to the public (178 feet) extends out from the **Guthrie Theater** (818 2nd St. S., 612/377-2224, 9 A.M.–1 A.M. daily) and offers another fantastic view. Ask at the ticket office about self-guided audio tours. Backstage tours (612/377-2224, 10 A.M. Fri.–Sun., $10 adults) last about 75 minutes.

Coming back across the Mississippi along the Hennepin Avenue Bridge, you will descend onto the 50-acre enigma that is **Nicollet Island,** home to the Nicollet Island Inn—a respected hotel and fancy restaurant—and a hidden neighborhood of 19th-century homes.

Walker Art Center and Minneapolis Sculpture Garden

The **Walker Art Center** (1750 Hennepin Ave., 612/375-7600, www.walkerart.org, 11 A.M.–5 P.M. Tues.–Wed. and Fri.–Sun., 11 A.M.–9 P.M. Thurs., $10 adults, free Thurs. after 5 P.M. and first Sat. of each month) began in 1879 when lumber baron Thomas Barlow Walker's art collection outgrew his house. He added a new wing to his mansion and opened the Midwest's first public art gallery. It has now grown into one of the world's most lauded modern art centers. Best known for its major exhibitions of cutting-edge 20th-century art, the Walker is a multifaceted center, and the performing arts do not take a backseat to visual arts—there are always music, dance, film, and similar events going on.

Across the street from the Walker is one of the largest urban sculpture gardens in the country. Best known for the iconic ***Spoonbridge and Cherry,*** the 11-acre landscaped grounds of the **Minneapolis Sculpture Garden** (6 A.M.–midnight daily; free tours 2 P.M. Sat.–Sun. May–Sept., free admission) contain over 40 mostly massive sculptures. The small **Cowles Conservatory** (10 A.M.–8 P.M. Tues.–Sat., 10 A.M.–5 P.M. Sun., free admission) has some horticultural displays, but most interesting is the palm room's 25-foot *Standing Glass Fish* by Frank Gehry, the design architect of the Weisman Art Museum. Unfortunately, picnics are not allowed at this great spot, but you can cross the Irene Hixon Whitney Bridge to **Loring Park** for an outdoor meal. (Read what must be one of the world's "longest" poems as you amble over.)

Other Art Museums

There is something for everyone at the Twin Cities' largest and most popular art museum. The encyclopedic collection of the **Minneapolis Institute of Arts** (2400 3rd Ave. S., 612/870-3131, www.artsmia.org, 10 A.M.–5 P.M. Tues.–Wed. and Fri.–Sat., 10 A.M.–9 P.M. Thurs., 11 A.M.–5 P.M. Sun., free admission) spans the globe and the ages with the oldest of the more than 100,000 objects dating back to 20,000 B.C. Highlights include paintings by masters such as Rembrandt, Monet, and Georgia O'Keeffe; a varied African collection; 17th- and 18th-century Chinese period rooms; and one of the world's premier assemblages of Prairie School objects.

For such a large building, the University of Minnesota's **Frederick R. Weisman Art Museum** (333 E. River Rd., 612/625-9494, www.weisman.umn.edu, 10 A.M.–5 P.M. Tues.–Wed. and Fri., 10 A.M.–8 P.M. Thurs., 11 A.M.–5 P.M. Sat.–Sun., free admission) displays very little art. Instead, the building itself is the highlight of the collection. Perched above the Mississippi River, the wonderful jumble of shapes was once described as an "exploding silver artichoke." Inside the naturally lit galleries, equal space is given to temporary exhibitions of contemporary art and highlights from the 17,000-piece permanent collection, which is especially rich in American art from the first half of the 20th century.

The Museum of Russian Art (5500 Stevens Ave. S., 612/821-9045, www.tmora.org, 10 A.M.–5 P.M. Mon.–Fri., 10 A.M.–4 P.M. Sat., 1–5 P.M. Sun., $5 adults) is the country's only museum dedicated to 20th-century Russian art. The museum, in a renovated Spanish Colonial church, is helping these largely unknown artists, who flourished despite strict state control, to finally get their deserved recognition outside the old USSR.

Science Museums

From hummingbirds to moose, nearly 500 Minnesota animals are on display at the University of Minnesota's **Bell Museum of Natural History** (10 Church St. SE, 612/624-7083, www.bellmuseum.org, 9 A.M.–5 P.M. Tues.–Fri., 10 A.M.–5 P.M. Sat., noon–5 P.M. Sun., $5 adults, free on Sun.). Equal parts art and science, the lifelike dioramas feature all of Minnesota's habitats from the prairie to the boreal forest. The kid-friendly Touch and See Room, overflowing with bones, hides, mounts, and live reptiles, lets you get up close and personal with nature. It was the first facility of its kind opened in the nation.

While the Bell looks at the natural world, **The Bakken** (3537 Zenith Ave. S., 612/926-3878, www.thebakken.org, 10 A.M.–5 P.M. Tues.–Wed. and Fri.–Sat., 10 A.M.–8 P.M. Thurs., $7 adults) tackles technology. Founded by Earl Bakken, inventor of the first wearable pacemaker and many other medical devices, the unique museum specializes in the history of electricity and magnetism in medicine and the life sciences. The galleries have hands-on displays about batteries, x-rays, magnets, and the like. Kids can participate in special programs on Family Science Saturdays; adults take over on the second Tuesday of every month, when the museum hosts Night Out at the Bakken with complimentary appetizers and wine, and scholars can peruse some 11,000 volumes in the library. It is all housed in an expanded 1928 Tudor-style mansion overlooking Lake Calhoun.

History Museums

Here in the Scandinavian-American heartland, the castle-like **American Swedish Institute** (2600 Park Ave. S., 612/871-4907, www.americanswedishinst.org, noon–4 P.M. Tues.–Wed. and Fri.–Sat., noon–8 P.M. Wed., 1–5 P.M. Sun., $6 adults), a tribute to a century and a half of the Swedish experience in America, attracts some 100,000 visitors a year. The museum's collection includes traditional outfits, folk art, the nation's largest collection of Swedish art glass, and original belongings carried from the old country by the state's early Swedish immigrants. Swan Turnblad, an immigrant newspaper publisher and self-made millionaire, built his 33-room home between 1904 and 1908 and spared no expense during construction: The ceilings are decorated with painted plaster sculpture, a third of the rooms have imported *kakelugnar* (porcelain tile stoves), and 18 craftsmen spent two years shaping the astounding woodwork.

Also filling a retooled, though much less grand, mansion is the little **Hennepin History Museum** (2303 3rd Ave. S., 612/870-1329, www.hennepinhistory.org, 10 A.M.–2 P.M. Tues., 1–5 P.M. Wed. and Fri.–Sun., 1–8 P.M. Thurs., $5 adults), with rotating exhibits of random artifacts from Minneapolis and its county.

You'll see 18 vintage fighter, transport, and spy planes, plus uniforms and other flight-related items at the **Minnesota Air Guard Museum** (612/713-2523, www.mnangmuseum.org, limited hours May–Sept., call first, free admission). It is located at the northeast corner of Minneapolis–St. Paul International Airport, off Highway 55.

Historic Buildings

The highlight of the Minneapolis Institute of Arts' world-famous Prairie School collection is the 1913 **Purcell-Cutts House** (2328 Lake Pl., 612/870-3131, hour-long tours by reservation only 10 A.M.–2 P.M. Sat. and noon–3 P.M. Sun., $5 adults), one of the country's most outstanding realizations of this uniquely American architectural style. Architects William Purcell and George Elmslie designed the house for Purcell and his family, though after a few years they moved to Philadelphia and sold the house to the Cutts family. The second owners, recognizing the significance of their purchase, made no major alterations during their 66-year residency. The exterior contains all the classic Prairie School elements and, while much of the furniture, such as lamps, bookcases, and a writing nook desk, was built-in, the MIA has exactingly reproduced the rest.

No longer much of a presence on the Minneapolis skyline, the 32-story Washington Monument–shaped **Foshay Tower** (821 Marquette Ave., 612/359-3030) still manages to stand out in a crowd. Wilbur Foshay, who earned his wealth in shady utilities dealings during the Roaring '20s, spent $3.7 million building the first skyscraper west of the Mississippi, and "The best address in the Northwest" opened to great fanfare in August 1929. Just two months after his grand opening the stock market crashed, and Foshay, whose fortune existed solely on paper, lost everything, including his beloved tower—a conviction for mail fraud sent him to Leavenworth for three years. Not until the 775-foot, 57-story IDS Tower went up in 1971 did the Foshay lose its status as the city's premier icon. Today, dwarfed by its many new neighbors, the tower is now the W Hotel, and Wilbur's 27th-floor office is a sleek bar. The **observation deck** (noon–9 P.M. daily, closed in bad weather, $8 adults) is still the best place to see all of downtown.

The cornerstone for the **Basilica of St. Mary** (88 17th St. N., 612/333-1381, 6:30 A.M.–5 P.M. Mon.–Fri., 8 A.M.–6:30 P.M. Sat., 6:30 A.M.–7:30 P.M. Sun., free tours after the 9:30 A.M. and 11:30 A.M. Sun. masses), the nation's first basilica and one of the finest examples of beaux arts architecture in the country, was laid in 1908. It took six years to complete the French and Italian Renaissance exterior with its 250-foot copper dome and monumental face. Another decade was spent on the phenomenal interior, which is filled with large stained-glass windows, carved stone, ornamental plaster, and an altar designed to be the finest in the land.

Costumed guides lead you around the quaint yellow **Ard Godfrey House** (28 University Ave. SE, 612/870-8001, www.ardgodfreyhouse.org, 1–4 P.M. Sat.–Sun. summer, free admission), the oldest surviving wood-frame house in Minneapolis. Franklin Steele, the man who laid the first claim to land at St. Anthony Falls, brought millwright Godfrey out from Maine in 1847 to build a dam and sawmill. Godfrey, impressed by the new settlement, sent for his family the next year and built his home with the first lumber sawn at his mill. Originally erected at Main Street and 2nd Avenue, it was moved four times before ending up in this park, just a stone's throw from its original site. The Woman's Club of Minneapolis has

© TRICIA CORNELL

Minneapolis City Hall is an impressive example of neo-Gothic architecture.

© BRUCE MANNING

The Como-Harriet Line, the last vestige of a once-extensive streetcar system, is open for pleasure rides.

restored and refurnished the property as it appeared in the 1840s.

At some point during your visit, be sure to stroll down to **Minneapolis City Hall** (350 5th St. S., 612/673-3000), a massive Romanesque building that took almost 20 years to build and nearly bankrupted the city before it was finished in 1905. *Father of Waters,* a Larkin Goldsmith Mead sculpture carved from the largest block of marble ever taken from Michelangelo's Carrara quarries, is Minneapolis's answer to Paul Bunyan. It sits surrounded by the marble and stained glass inside the 4th Street entrance's rotunda. Atop the building's 345-foot tower are the 14-foot hands of the four clock faces (larger than those surrounding Big Ben) and a 15-bell carillon. The bells are played from a Schroeder-sized keyboard in the rotunda at noon on holidays and summer Fridays. The best listening spots are in the plazas fronting the building. A tour brochure is available at the information desk, plus free guided tours are available on the third Wednesday of each month at noon.

Tourist Transit

Paradise Charter Cruises (612/378-7966 or 888/791-6220, www.twincitiescruises.com, $17.50–30) offers one to three cruises a day—including sightseeing, pizza, brunch, and cocktail cruises—on the *Minneapolis Queen* and the *Paradise Lady,* departing from Boom Island Park and heading down through the Upper Saint Anthony Falls Lock.

The **Como-Harriet Streetcar Line** (952/922-1096, www.trolleyride.org, 6:30 P.M.–dusk Mon.–Fri., 12:30 P.M.–dusk Sat.–Sun. May–Sept., weekend service first half of May and through early Nov., $2), part of a route between downtown Minneapolis and Lake Minnetonka that operated from 1880 to 1954, has been revived as a tourist attraction. Three beautifully restored classic cars, built between 1908 and 1946, run for a mile between Lake Harriet and Lake Calhoun. The 15-minute trips depart from the Linden Hills Station on the northwest shore of Lake Harriet at West 42nd Street. Free tours of the car barn (12:30–4:30 P.M. first and third Sun.

May–Sept.), where volunteers restore vintage streetcars, are available.

Historic Fort Snelling

Perched high above the confluence of the Mississippi and Minnesota Rivers, Fort Snelling (www.mnhs.org, 612/726-1171, 10 A.M.–5 P.M. Tues.–Sat., noon–5 P.M. Sun. Memorial Day–Labor Day, noon–5 P.M. Sat.–Sun. Sept. and Oct., $10 adults) was built by the U.S. Army's Fifth Regiment of Infantry between 1819 and 1825 to administer America's new Northwest frontier. When the land was opened to settlement, people branched out in both directions to found towns that would grow into Minneapolis and St. Paul. Today, after rebuilding the crumbling stone fortress in the 1950s, the Minnesota Historical Society runs a remarkable living-history museum. After brushing up on 19th-century current events in the Fort Snelling History Center you'll walk out to 1827, where costumed reenactors lead tours and demonstrate bygone skills. Plan on several hours to properly experience this National Historic Landmark.

Fort Snelling State Park

The historic fort only takes up a sliver of the 2,931-acre Fort Snelling State Park (612/725-2389, www.dnr.state.mn.us); most of the rest is bottomland forest extending down the Minnesota River. Though this is an urban corridor, wildlife is surprisingly abundant, and if you get out on the 18 miles of trail, you'll likely encounter some, even out on busy Pike Island separating the Mississippi and Minnesota Rivers. The easy **Pike Island Trail** skirts the island's edge, staying in sight of the rivers most of the time. Most of the rest of the trails, a mix of paved and gravel surfaces, run along the Minnesota River and connect to regional bike trails outside the park. Come winter, 12 miles of trails are groomed for cross-country skiing, and a trail through the center of Pike Island is packed for winter hiking. Paddlers can rent canoes to run the river or look for wildlife in Gun Club Lake. Other park facilities include historical exhibits in the visitors center and a swimming beach and accessible fishing pier on Snelling Lake. If you are driving here from Minneapolis or St. Paul, ignore the signs for Fort Snelling Historic Site, and take the Post Road exit off Highway 5. You can also walk downhill from the fort.

Minnehaha Park

Centered on the 53-foot waterfall made famous by Henry Wadsworth Longfellow's epic poem *The Song of Hiawatha* ("In the land of the Dacotahs/Where the Falls of Minnehaha/Flash and gleam among the oak-trees/Laugh and leap into the valley"), Minnehaha Park (Hiawatha Ave. and Minnehaha Pkwy.) is one of the city's most popular playgrounds. There are multiple overlooks of the falls, and the shady path through the glen below it is quite serene. The statue *Hiawatha and Minnehaha* stands on the island immediately above the falls.

A trio of historic buildings sits just west of the falls. Back in the 19th century, Minneapolis residents coming to the park detrained at the petite 1875 **Minnehaha Depot** (651/228-0263, 12:30–4:30 P.M. Sun. and holidays summer, free admission), so cute it was nicknamed "The Princess" by Milwaukee Road employees. The 1849 **John H. Stevens House** (612/722-2220, www.johnhstevenshouse.org, noon–4 P.M. Sat.–Sun. May–Sept., $3 adults) was the first settler's home built on the west bank of the Mississippi River. When the house was set to be razed, civic-minded citizens came to its rescue, and 7,000 children and a team of horses pulled it to the park. You can visit the interior of the home to see the period furnishings and historical displays.

The **Longfellow House** (612/370-4969, 8 A.M.–4:30 P.M. Wed.–Sat., noon–4 P.M. Sun., free admission) is a two-thirds-scale replica of the poet's Massachusetts home. The bright yellow building serves as an information center for the park and the Grand Rounds National Scenic Byway.

On the west edge of the park you can watch boats pass through **Lock and Dam #1** (612/724-2971, 8 A.M.–dusk daily Apr.–Oct.), actually the third in the series of 29 locks and dams along the Upper Mississippi River, from an elevated viewing area.

© BRUCE MANNING

Minnehaha Depot houses a tiny railroad museum.

Grand Rounds National Scenic Byway

The Grand Rounds (612/230-6446) is an urban byway like no other. The signed route runs right through downtown's St. Anthony Falls historic district and briefly passes the industrial northeast, but most of the 53-mile route follows the city's rivers and lakes—including the Mississippi River and the urban wilderness of **Theodore Wirth Park** (1339 Theodore Wirth Pkwy.)—along forest-lined boulevards. Pick up a map and information about recreational opportunities along the trail at the Longfellow House in Minnehaha Park, or let the many informational kiosks guide you.

NIGHTLIFE

There aren't many cities of comparable size that can match Minneapolis's after-hours entertainment offerings.

Rock

Few clubs anywhere in the world can boast a historic set list as impressive as **First Avenue** (701 1st Ave. N., 612/332-1775, www.first-avenue.com). This legendary venue—big names play the two-story main room while up-and-comers are relegated to the 7th Street Entry—has hosted just about every rock band that's ever mattered since it opened in 1970. Due to its strong support of local musicians and an impressively diverse calendar it remains, far and away, the best music venue in the city.

The **Fine Line Music Café** (318 1st Ave. N., 612/338-8100, www.finelinemusic.com) books a little of everything, including many of the biggest local acts; weekend headliners are usually mellower acts for a somewhat older crowd.

The hottest club for alternative acts these days is the **Triple Rock Social Club** (629 Cedar Ave. S., 612/333-7399, www.triplerocksocialclub.com), owned in part by Erik Funk, singer-guitarist of the band Dillinger Four. The bar has a commendable beer roster and a vegan-friendly menu.

Blues and R&B

The West Bank is Minneapolis's blues corner. The **Cabooze** (917 Cedar Ave. S., 612/338-6425, www.cabooze.com) is a neighborhood joint that just happens to pull in big names like George Clinton or Johnny Winter from time to time.

Many of the hottest local bands—mostly funk and R&B—have regular gigs across town at **Bunker's** (761 Washington Ave. N., 612/338-8188, www.bunkersmusic.com).

Famous Dave's BBQ & Blues (3001 Hennepin Ave. S., 612/822-9900, www.famousdaves.com) is a popular Uptown restaurant with live local and touring bands seven nights a week—though the weekends are reserved for blues, there's Cajun and Latin sounds other nights. Sunday features a blues brunch.

Country and Bluegrass

Lee's Liquor Lounge (101 Glenwood Ave., 612/338-9491, www.leesliquorlounge.com), a friendly beer joint complete with an Elvis shrine, is the best place in town to regularly hear country and rockabilly bands, though that's not all they book.

Jazz

Anybody who's anybody plays the **Dakota Jazz Club** (1010 Nicollet Mall, 612/332-1010, www.dakotacooks.com) when they are in town. This intimate space, with balcony seating and not a bad table in the house, has some mighty good food too.

Folk and International

The nonprofit **Cedar Cultural Center** (416 Cedar Ave. S., 612/338-2674, www.thecedar.org) hosts over 150 traditional musical (and a few dance) performances a year. The calendar spans the globe, from American folk to Afropop, and many of the biggest names in their genre, like Greg Brown and Baaba Maal, grace the stage. The sound is excellent, and there isn't a bad seat in the house; the only negative is that they close up each summer.

A trio of Irish-owned pubs host live music, but **Kieran's** (600 Hennepin Ave. S., 612/339-4499, www.kierans.com), with a famous Wednesday-night jam and bands through Saturday, is the best known.

Polka

Nye's Polonaise (112 Hennepin Ave. E., 612/379-2021), where 20-somethings mingle amiably with 80-somethings, is in a class by itself. Ruth Adams and The World's Most Dangerous Polka Band hold court Friday and Saturday night, as they have since 1967.

Dancing

Too many clubs come and go to pin down the dance floor du jour. No matter which way the winds of popularity are blowing, a safe bet is to head to downtown Minneapolis (more specifically: 1st Avenue between Washington Avenue and 6th Street) and follow the crowds. One club with some staying power is **The Lounge** (411 2nd Ave. N., 612/333-8800, www.theloungempls.com), which has endured since 1995, thanks to a loyal after-the-workday professional crowd and, at least in part, to some original programming. Pick your scene among the several rooms, each like a smaller club in itself and each spinning different music, from top-40 to underground electronica. Keep the dress code in mind—no white sneakers or white T-shirts, nothing saggy.

In a beautiful space that has housed a few clubs in its time, **Envy** (400 1st Ave. N., 612/673-9694, www.envnympls.com) has two scenes going on: serious dancing in the front and, most nights, electronica in the back. Be prepared for a crowd—Envy is packed, especially on Saturdays—and remember, no T-shirts, sports attire, or hats.

Comedy

The leading venue for stand-up is the Warehouse District's **Acme Comedy Company** (708 N. 1st St., 612/338-6393, www.acmecomedycompany.com). There's a popular open mic on Monday and touring headliners every Tuesday through Saturday.

ComedySportz (3001 Hennepin Ave. S., 612/870-1230, www.comedysportz.com) pits two teams in various improvisational, audience-directed games Thursday through Saturday.

Brave New Workshop (2605 Hennepin Ave. S., 612/332-6620, www.bravenewworkshop.com), the country's longest-running satirical review, started in 1958 and counts Al Franken and Louie Anderson as alumni. Besides the main show, they offer several nights of improv.

Eclectic

On any given night, the stage at the **Bryant Lake Bowl** (810 Lake St. W., 612/825-8949, www.bryantlakebowl.com) might be hosting film, music, dance, theater, performance art, trapeze, or shadow puppets. And, if the show is a dud, go knock down some pins. If that weren't enough, the Grain Belt beer sign fronting the building delivers on its promise of "Good Food;" we're talking organic roast chicken and pad Thai rather than anything typical of ten-pin alleys.

Taps and Taverns

Last call in Minneapolis is 2 A.M., but most kitchens close two to four hours before that.

Unlike the trendy nightspots the Warehouse District is best known for, **Runyon's** (107 Washington Ave. N., 612/332-7158, 10 A.M.–1 A.M. Mon.–Sat., 11 A.M.–midnight Sun.) comes pretty close to being a neighborhood bar and has some of the best buffalo wings you'll ever nibble on.

Tapping its first keg in 1981, **The Loon Café** (500 1st Ave. N., 612/332-8342, www.thelooncafe.com, 11 A.M.–2 A.M. Mon.–Fri., 10 A.M.–2 P.M. Sat., 11 A.M.–midnight Sun.), an attractive and oddly minimalist sports bar, helped revitalize the Warehouse District. The above-average meals (try one of their chilis!) means it's usually packed during lunch, and the proximity to the Target Center means you might not even get in the door before a Timberwolves game.

Minneapolis's Gluek Brewing Company opened their Bavarian-style beer hall in 1902, and though the interior woodwork and glass windows are reconstructions due to a fire, **Gluek's** (16 6th St., 612/338-6621, www.glueks.com, 11 A.M.–2 A.M. Mon.–Fri., noon–2 A.M. Sat., closed Sun.) retains its Old World charm. Among the many beers on tap is Gluek's, still brewed in the nearby town of Cold Spring. The highly regarded kitchen turns out everything from bratwurst to quesadillas.

Town Hall Brewery (1430 Washington Ave. S., 612/339-8696, www.townhallbrewery.com, 11 A.M.–1 A.M. Mon.–Thurs., 11 A.M.–2 A.M. Fri.–Sat., 11 A.M.–midnight Sun.) is a local brewpub with a national reputation. Not only are the food and brews consistently good, but the historic confines, trimmed with a mirrored back-bar, tile floor, and tin ceilings, offer a nice counterpart to the typical West Bank bar.

Northeast Minneapolis is known for its numerous neighborhood taps, and **Mayslack's** (1428 4th St. NE, 612/789-9862, www.mayslacksbar.com, 11 A.M.–2 A.M. Mon.–Fri., 10 A.M.–2 A.M. Sat.–Sun.) is a classic amongst classics. Once owned by professional wrestler Stan Mayslack, the tall wooden booths, pressed tin ceiling, garlic roast beef sandwiches, and live polka on Sunday nights add up to some wonderful Old World charm.

The **Herkimer** (2922 Lyndale Ave. S., 612/821-0101, www.theherkimer.com, noon–2 A.M. Mon.–Fri., 10 A.M.–2 P.M. Sat.–Sun.) is Uptown's only brewpub, and a noted game-day hangout for Green Bay Packers fans.

British Pubs

Step into **Brit's** (1110 Nicollet Mall, 612/332-3908, www.britspub.com, 11 A.M.–2 A.M. daily), and you've entered a classic pub atmosphere, though during the summer the best seats are on the upstairs patio surrounding the bowling green ($5 per person per hour). The "Bill of Fayre" hits the best and worst of British pub grub from fish and chips and tandoori chicken to scotch eggs, and they'll pull you a pint of half a dozen English ales.

What sets **The Local** (931 Nicollet Mall, 612/904-1000, www.the-local.com, 11 A.M.–2 A.M. Mon.–Fri., 10 A.M.–2 A.M. Sat.–Sun.) apart is the trio of almost museum-like Victorian pub decors. The food is fantastic, but in the evening they serve a lot more glasses of whiskey (more than any other pub in North America) and pints of Guinness than meals.

Wine Bars

Don't be fooled by the dark windows; **Bev's Wine Bar** (250 3rd Ave. N., 612/337-0102, 4:30 P.M.–1 A.M. Tues.–Fri., 6:30 P.M.–1 A.M. Sat., closed Sun.–Mon.) is very much open. The wine list isn't long, but it is carefully chosen and well priced. This is the perfect escape when a glass of peppery sangiovese and a plate of little cheeses in a quiet room is what you need.

Rather than dim and romantic, **Beaujo's** (4950 France Ave. S., 952/922-8974, www.beaujos.net, 11 A.M.–11:30 P.M. Mon.–Thurs., 11 A.M.–midnight Fri.–Sat., 3–10 P.M. Sun.) is cheery and suburban—the perfect place to rest your bags after a long day shopping at 50th and France. A nice perk for light drinkers: Wines are available by the bottle, the glass, and the half-glass.

With a well-known Twin Cities chef in the kitchen, **Toast** (415 1st St. N., 612/333-4305, 5–11 P.M. Tue.–Thurs., 5 P.M.–midnight Fri.–Sat., 5–11 P.M. Sun.) is a wine bar with something more to offer beyond the cheese and salami plates—excellent crostini, creative thin-crust pizzas, and hearty salads. It's a brighter and livelier space, rather than a dim and romantic one.

Lounges

The thing to do at **Bar Lurcat** (1624 Harmon Pl., 612/486-5500, www.cafelurcat.com, 5–10 P.M. Mon.–Thurs., 5 P.M.–1 A.M. Fri.–Sat., 5–9 P.M. Sun.) is to drape yourself over a vintage settee under a crystal chandelier and try to look as beautiful as the surroundings. Order small plates from a kitchen run by one of the best food outfits in town (D'Amico's) and choose from the extensive wine list (more than 40 served by the glass).

The whole of the **Chambers** (901 Hennepin Ave., 612/767-6900, www.chambersminneapolis.com) hotel, including both the rooftop and the lobby lounge (2–11 P.M. Sun.–Wed., 2 P.M.–midnight Thurs., 2 P.M.–1 A.M. Fri.–Sat.), is so sleek, so polished that it seems to glow. The walls hold hundreds of thousands of dollars worth of modern art. And the modern low couches hold well-heeled up-and-comers. Up on the roof there are striking views of Minneapolis. In years past, Chambers has built the country's only outdoor ice bar in the courtyard—that's ice not only in your drinks, but under your drinks and under your tush. The whole place is made of ice.

Gay and Lesbian Bars and Clubs

Serving the community since the 1950s, the unassuming **19 Bar** (19 W. 15th St., 612/871-5553, 3 P.M.–2 A.M. Mon.–Fri., 1 P.M.–2 A.M. Sat.–Sun.) is just your average neighborhood tavern with darts, pool tables, and a jukebox.

The Saloon (830 Hennepin Ave., 612/332-0835, 9 A.M.–2 A.M. daily), below the Hotel Amsterdam, is a wild pickup bar full of boys just wanting to be seen and DJs spinning most nights.

Way more chic and grown-up is **Jet Set** (115 1st St. N., 612/339-3933, www.jetsetbar.com, 5 P.M.–1 A.M. Tues.–Thurs., 5 P.M.–2 A.M. Fri., 6 P.M.–2 A.M. Sat., closed Sun.), just a single spare room in the Warehouse District with low-slung, backless leather benches that encourage lounging and schmoozing.

Gay 90's (408 Hennepin Ave., 612/333-7755) has been described as "the Mall of America of gay bars." There are three dance floors, seven bars, a restaurant, karaoke, strippers, the La Femme drag show, and a hidden back room. The DJs are excellent, so it attracts a large number of straight dancers and has become too mainstream for some gay men.

ENTERTAINMENT AND EVENTS

Theater

Minneapolitans love their theater. Around 100 companies fill the city's stages, and, outside of New York, no other American city has more live theater seats per capita than Minneapolis. Famed New York City–based director Sir Tyrone Guthrie founded the **Guthrie Theater** (818 S. 2nd St., 612/377-2224, www.guthrietheater.org) in 1963 to promote the level of creative development that Broadway theaters no longer could. It soon

© BRUCE MANNING

The Guthrie Theater fits comfortably among the old industrial buildings in downtown Minneapolis's milling district.

grew into a Tony Award–winning organization known far and wide for its innovative presentations of both classic and contemporary plays.

Recognized as the pioneer of theater for children and families, **The Children's Theatre Company** (2400 3rd Ave. S., 612/874-0400, www.childrenstheatre.org), which has also won a Tony, has been adapting classic literature—such as *The Hobbit, Charlie and the Chocolate Factory,* and Dr. Seuss's *Green Eggs and Ham*—since 1965.

Ostensibly for children, **In the Heart of the Beast Puppet and Mask Theatre** (1500 Lake St. E., 612/721-2535, www.hobt.org) delights all ages with larger-than-life-size puppets, marionettes, hand puppets, and multi-actor dragons that interact with live actors on fantastical, folk art–inspired sets. In the Heart of the Beast makes social issues understandable for the whole family.

The multicultural **Mixed Blood Theatre** (1501 4th St. S., 612/338-6131, www.mixedblood.com) has a reputation for breaking the rules. They stage their often cutting-edge work in a converted firehouse.

The highly acclaimed **Jungle Theater** (2951 Lyndale Ave. S., 612/822-7063, www.jungletheater.com) produces a wide variety of works in its modern home and is known for debuting new works.

For anything daring, gutsy, and yes, a little radical, from plays to puppetry to dance, look to **Bedlam Theatre** (1501 6th St. S., 612/341-1038, www.bedlamtheatre.org). The theater's digs include a main stage, lounge, and a restaurant and bar: the hip theater hangout.

A trio of historic theaters in downtown's brightly lit Hennepin Avenue Theater District host numerous touring shows, many making a final fine-tuning before debuting on Broadway. The **State, Orpheum,** and **Pantages** theaters opened between 1916 and 1921 as vaudeville stages and have been gorgeously restored to their former opulence. The box office for all three is at the State Theater (805 Hennepin Ave., 612/673-0404, www.hennepintheatretrust.org).

© TRICIA CORNELL

The Orpheum Theater sits at the heart of the Hennepin Avenue Theater District.

© TRICIA CORNELL

Free outdoor concerts, held every night during the summer at the Lake Harriet Bandshell on the Chain of Lakes, attract crowds.

Dance

Like theater, Minneapolis's dance scene is one of the country's strongest. The premier venues, which host top companies from around the world, are the U of M's **Northrop Memorial Auditorium** (84 Church St. SE, 612/624-2345, http://northrup.umn.edu), with the same "Balanchine Basketweave" stage as the New York City Ballet's stage at Lincoln Center, and the Walker Art Center's 385-seat **McGuire Theater** (1750 Hennepin Ave., 612/375-7600, www.walkerart.org), with the stage size and technology normally found in 1,000-seat spaces.

The Twin Cities' own **James Sewell Ballet** (612/672-0480, www.jsballet.org) combines innovative, award-winning dance at top venues.

Classical Music

The **Minnesota Orchestra** (612/371-5656, www.minnesotaorchestra.org), founded in 1903 and almost always ranked in the nation's top ten these days, performs over 200 concerts a year; most are held in the lovely and modern **Orchestra Hall** (1111 Nicollet Mall). The 95-member band performs both the classics and the contemporary, and conductor Osmo Vänskä has won national acclaim. The superb 200-voice **Minnesota Chorale** (612/333-4866, www.mnchorale.org), known for their innovative programming, often performs with the orchestra.

Freebies

Minneapolis's parks are busy all summer long with live performances. Something is happening almost daily over the lunch hour and early evening in **Peavey Plaza,** the fountain-filled park along Nicollet Mall. Bands are playing outdoors at **St. Anthony Main** every weekend night. **Loring Park** has Movies and Music on Monday nights during July and August—a band takes the stage at 7 P.M. and plays until dark, when a classic film rolls. Concerts are held nightly at the **Lake Harriet Bandshell** on the Chain of Lakes.

Cinema

Two U of M–area theaters managed by

© BRUCE MANNING

The highlight of the annual Aquatennial celebration is the milk carton-boat race.

Minnesota Film Arts (612/331-3134, www.mnfilmarts.org) have by far the most daring schedule around. The **Bell Auditorium** (10 Church St.) shows nonfiction films, while **Oak Street Cinema** (309 Oak St. SE) is noted for retrospectives, but just about any non-mainstream film might get screened.

The **Walker Art Center** (1750 Hennepin Ave., 612/375-7600) also shows occasional independent films.

Over in Uptown, the Landmark (612/825-6006, www.landmarktheatres.org) art-house chain runs the aging 900-seat **Uptown Theatre** (2906 Hennepin Ave. S.) and the modern five-screen **Lagoon Cinema** (1320 Lagoon Ave. S.).

All the biggest bombs and blockbusters out of Hollywood are available downtown at the **Crown Block E 15** (600 Hennepin Ave., 612/338-5900, www.crowntheatres.com) and **St. Anthony Main Theater** (115 Main St. SE, 612/331-4723, www.stanthonymaintheatre.com).

Spectator Sports

The National Football League's **Minnesota Vikings** (www.vikings.com) play in the aging **Hubert H. Humphrey Metrodome** (900 5th St. S, 612/338-4537). Although they are no longer the Purple People Eaters of the 1980s, the Vikes are still beloved by their fans, and tickets can be hard to come by.

The **Minnesota Twins** (612/375-1366, http://twins.mlb.com), who once shared the Dome with the Vikes, will throw out the first pitch of the 2010 season at the brand-new Target Field (3rd Ave. between 5th and 7th Sts., 612/375-1366), on the other side of downtown. Why the move? A yen to play ball under the open skies, even in Minnesota. The skyline views from some seats alone will be worth the price of admission.

The National Basketball Association's **Minnesota Timberwolves** (www.nba.com/timberwolves) take to the court at the **Target Center** (600 1st Ave. N., 612/673-1600) and tickets (612/673-0900) are priced as low as $10. Minnesota's WNBA affiliate, the **Lynx** (www.wnba.com/lynx) play at the Target Center during the men's off-season. Tickets start at $5 and are always available at tip-off.

The NCAA Division 1 **University of**

Minnesota Golden Gophers men's and women's hockey teams play in the WCHA conference and are perpetually among the best in the nation, while the football and men's and women's basketball teams usually put on a good show in the Big Ten conference. Few sports fans anywhere in the nation are more boisterous than the hockey backers at the **Mariucci Arena,** while the fanaticism is only a little more tempered across the street at **Williams Arena** ("The Barn") for the men's basketball games—both sports sell out well in advance. In 2009, the football team played its first game back on campus—in the brand-new **TCF Bank Stadium**—since it moved to the Metrodome in 1981. Tickets for all sports are available from the Minnesota Athletics Ticket Office (612/624-8080 or 800/846-7437, www.gophersports.com) in the Mariucci Arena.

Events

The **Minneapolis Aquatennial** (www.aquatennial.org) celebrates summer with dozens of free events across the city over 10 days at the end of July. Downtown hosts Grande Day and Torchlight parades and what is claimed to be the largest fireworks display west of the Mississippi. Out on the lakes there are sailing regattas, milk carton–boat races (the concept originated here), a sand-sculpture contest, and the Life Time Fitness Triathlon.

With well over 150 theater, comedy, spoken word, and dance acts taking the stage at nearly two dozen venues, the **Minnesota Fringe Festival** (www.fringefestival.org) has grown into the largest non-juried performing-arts festival in the nation. It is held over 10 days in early August, and many shows sell out.

Although activists march in it, Minneapolis's **May Day Parade** (www.hobt.org) is principally a mobile arts festival celebrating the arrival of spring. Oversized puppets, along with stilt walkers, musicians, costumed revelers, and other creative spirits, travel south along Bloomington Avenue to Powderhorn Park, delighting some 50,000 spectators.

The **Holidazzle** (612/376-7669, www.holidazzle.com) parades, made up of illuminated floats, storybook characters, musicians, and dancers, are so popular they run it two dozen times a year. The half-hour procession glides down the Nicollet Mall every Wednesday through Sunday at 6:30 P.M. between Thanksgiving and Christmas. If you want a spot in the heated skyway claim it early, or call for information about viewing the parade from the heated grandstand.

SHOPPING

Minneapolis's shopping central is **Nicollet Mall** downtown, and the best place to begin is at 7th Street, where you'll find a **Macy's** (still called Dayton's by some longtime residents) and the **City Center, IDS Crystal Court,** and **Gaviidae Common** shopping malls—the latter anchored by **Saks Off 5th** and **Neiman Marcus.**

There are a handful of exclusive antiques and interior-design galleries scattered around the Warehouse District. The **Minneapolis Farmers' Market** (312 East Lyndale Ave. N., 612/333-1718, www.mplsfarmersmarket.com, 6 A.M.–1 P.M. daily) blooms from late April through Christmas. Between May and October an adjunct market hits the Nicollet Mall on Thursdays.

On Saturday mornings, the **Mill City Farmer's Market** (704 2nd St. S., 612/341-7580, www.millcityfarmersmarket.org, 8 A.M.–1 P.M. Sat. mid-May–mid-Oct.) is the place to be, as much for the tasty eats, entertainment, and people watching as for the organic vegetables.

Start your tour of the **Northeast Minneapolis Arts District** on 13th Avenue, home to **Rogue Buddha** (357 13th Ave. NE, 612/331-3889, www.roguebuddha.com, noon–4 P.M. Wed.–Thurs., 3–8 P.M. Fri.–Sat., closed Sun.–Tues.) and nearly a dozen other galleries. Come the third weekend in May for **Art-A-Whirl,** or the top of each month for **First Thursdays in the Art District,** when galleries hold special events and hundreds of studios open their doors to the buying and browsing public.

The **Uptown** (www.uptownminneapolis.com) area has many wonderful one-of-a-

© BRUCE MANNING

The Bibelot in South Minneapolis sells tempting trinkets and elegant clothing.

kind shops, although chain stores like Victoria's Secret and NorthFace have come to the corner of Hennepin Avenue and Lake Street. The two main North-South axes are Hennepin and Lyndale Avenues, with Lake Street connecting them East to West.

The small-townish residential neighborhood of **Linden Hills** (43rd St. & Upton Ave. S.) is an unexpected place for a shopping destination, but at this intersection, you'll find about a dozen delightful stores—especially if you're shopping for children. Popular for grown-up treasures is **The Bibelot** (4315 Upton Ave., 612/925-3175, www.bibelotshops.com, 9:30 A.M.–8 P.M. Mon.–Fri., 9:30 A.M.–7 P.M. Sat., 11 A.M.–5 P.M. Sun.), which stocks everything from upscale housewares to gifts for children to women's clothing. There are four other locations throughout the metro area.

Bookstores

In our humble opinion, there is no better children's bookstore than **Wild Rumpus** (2720 43rd St. W., 612/920-5005, www.wildrumpusbooks.com, 10 A.M.–5 P.M. Mon. and Sat., 10 A.M.–8 P.M. Tues.–Fri., noon–5 P.M. Sun.), with its resident menagerie, well-worn comfy chairs, and an up-to-the-minute stock of the smartest of today's kids' literature.

Two enormous used book stores draw shoppers to Uptown. **Magers and Quinn** (3038 Hennepin Ave. S., 612/822-4611, www.magersandquinn.com, 10 A.M.–10 P.M. Sun.–Thurs., 10 A.M.–11 P.M. Fri.–Sat.) is more likely to have rare books and first editions. **Booksmart** (2914 Hennepin Ave., 612/823-5612) is more likely to have the current bestseller.

Twin landmarks on the Twin Cities' literary scene, **Uncle Edgar's Mystery Bookstore & Uncle Hugo's Science Fiction Bookstore** (2864 Chicago Ave. S., Uncle Hugo's 612/824-6347, Uncle Edgar's 612/824-9984, www.unclehugo.com, 10 A.M.–8 P.M. Mon.–Fri., 10 A.M.–6 P.M. Sat., noon–5 P.M. Sun.) are well known for staff that know their individual genres inside and out.

Bibliophiles might also want to stop by the **Open Book** (1011 Washington Ave. S.,

612/215-2650, www.openbookmn.org) literary arts center to see if any interesting exhibitions or events are going on.

Music

Music lovers have two not-to-be-missed stops in Minneapolis. The **Electric Fetus** (2000 4th Ave. S., 612/870-9300, www.electricfetus.com, 9 A.M.–9 P.M. Mon.–Fri., 9 A.M.–8 P.M. Sat., 11 A.M.–6 P.M. Sun.) has four decades of music history accreted on its storied racks, since it helped drive the birth of the Minneapolis sound.

Hymie's Vintage Records (3318 Lake St. E., 612/729-8890, 11 A.M.–7 P.M. Mon.–Sat., 1–6 P.M. Sun.) is like a museum tracing the evolution of popular sound from 45s to 78s to eight-tracks to cassette tapes to CDs, plus relevant books and videos.

RECREATION

Bicycling

The **Grand Rounds National Scenic Byway** (612/230-6446) is best seen on two wheels, and there are separate paths for bicyclists along most of the 50-mile route. The 12-mile Chain of Lakes segment (known to cyclists as the **Four Lakes Loop**) centered on Lake Calhoun is rightfully popular.

Another wonderful ride, especially during fall, is the seven-mile stretch along the **Mississippi River** between the Stone Arch Bridge and Minnehaha Park.

The **Midtown Greenway** (www.midtowngreenway.org) runs about six miles along a converted railbed between Chowen Avenue and West River Parkway, popular with both commuters and recreational cyclists. The western end of the Greenway hooks up to the South Loop of the **Southwest Regional LRT Trail** (763/559-9000, www.threeriversparkdistrict.org), if you want to extend your ride.

Rent bikes from **Calhoun Rental** (1622 Lake St., 612/827-8231, www.calhounrental.com, 9 A.M.–7 P.M. daily summer) on the north end of Lake Calhoun (they've also got inline skates) or from the **Freewheel Midtown Bike Center** (2834 10th Ave. S., 612/238-4447, www.freewheelbike.com, 6:30 A.M.–8 P.M. Mon.–Fri., 9 A.M.–6 P.M. Sat., 9 A.M.–5 P.M. Sun.) right on the greenway.

On the Water

The **Mississippi River** downstream of downtown runs through a deep tree-lined gorge, and it's easy to forget that you are in the midst of a major metropolis, though on the downside you will be sharing the scenery with a fair number of motorboats. The recommended run is to put in on the east bank of the river at the U of M and make a four-mile trip downstream to the Ford Dam before retracing your path. Many people sail and windsurf on Lake Calhoun and Lake Harriet, the largest of the **Chain of Lakes,** while the smaller Lake of the Isles, Cedar Lake, and Brownie Lake (connected by narrow channels) get plenty of paddling action. Canoe and kayak rentals are available at the pavilion on the northeast shore of Lake Calhoun and **Midwest Mountaineering** (309 Cedar Ave. S., 612/339-3433) on the West Bank, not far from the Mississippi.

Skating

If you want to ice skate, just find a park: The city freezes over 30 rinks and clears a patch on Lake of the Isles, and you can borrow skates at most. They also offer indoor skating at the **Parade Ice Garden** (600 Kenwood Pkwy., 612/370-4846, open year-round, $3).

Priced much higher, but with added character, is the gorgeous glass-enclosed **Depot Rink** (225 3rd Ave. S., 218/339-2253, open in winter, $7 adults). Both have skate rentals ($2 and $6 respectively). Lockers are available. Open-skate times are highly variable so call for details. **Peavey Plaza** (1111 Nicollet Mall, 612/371-5693) next to Orchestra Hall also has a rink, though no skate rental or warming shelter.

Skaters who prefer concrete to ice should follow the recommended bike routes above or, between November and April, head to the Metrodome stadium, which, for a few hours several days a week, becomes the **Rollerdome** (612/825-3663, www.roller-dome.com, $6.50 adults). You can speed down a pair of concourses on some remarkably smooth concrete. Skate rentals ($5) are available, and safety gear is free.

ACCOMMODATIONS

$50-100

The cheapest rooms downtown—with a fantastic location—are at the gay-owned and proudly gay-friendly **Saloon Hotel** (828 Hennepin Ave. S., 612/228-0459, www.saloonmn.com, $70)—right under the big pink triangle. Rooms are basic, and bathrooms are shared. Even if you're not planning to join the party at the club downstairs, you may find yourself listening to it.

A few dollars higher up the scale buys you a lot more class. A block from the river by the Guthrie Theater, **Aloft** (900 Washington Ave. S., 612/455-8400, www.alofthotels.com, $89) has nine-foot ceilings, platform beds, huge walk-in showers, funky furnishings (love the faux cowhide on the walls), and a Euro-inspired lobby lounge and bar.

On weekends, the **Hilton Minneapolis** (1001 Marquette Ave., 612/376-1000, www.hilton.com, $99) can be a steal: You get the marbled lobby to yourself while the business travelers are at home. Prices more than double during the week.

Another great weekend value is the **Marquette Hotel** (710 Marquette Ave., 612/333-4545, www.marquettehotel.com, $99), located in Minnesota's tallest building, the IDS Center. Rooms are extra large and comfortably appointed, with particularly broad and comfortable desks.

$100-150

The Depot (225 3rd Ave. S, 612/375-1700, www.thedepotminneapolis.com, $129) is actually two hotels in one, both by Marriott—The Depot Minneapolis, a Renaissance Hotel, and, for extended stays, Residence Inn at the Depot—just a block or so off the river and a short walk to the skyway system on the other side. The attached water park and winter skating rink attract families.

Right on the skyway, the **Grand Hotel Minneapolis** (615 2nd Ave. S., 612/339-3655, www.grandhotelminneapolis.com, $145) harks back to a time of great luxury and service. In fact, AAA has given it the highest rating of any Minneapolis hotel.

There are two good hotels in this price range near the University of Minnesota. The **Radisson University** (615 Washington Ave. SE, 612/379-8888 or 800/333-3333, $115) is as large and fancy as most of the downtown hotels in its class. There is a small on-site fitness center, and guests can also get a free pass to the superb university recreation facilities.

Over on the West Bank the **Holiday Inn** (1500 Washington Ave. S., 612/333-4646 or 800/448-2296, www.holidayinn.com, $105) has large rooms with great views. Overlooking downtown from the 14th floor is a small pool, whirlpool, sauna, and fitness center.

Over $150

Away from downtown's hustle and bustle, but still convenient, the **Nicollet Island Inn** (95 Merriam St. S., 612/331-1800, www.nicolletislandinn.com, $159) is the best place in town for a romantic getaway—which makes it the only downtown hotel whose rates go down instead of way up during the week.

Originally built as a bank in 1906, **The Hotel Minneapolis** (215 4th St. S., 612/340-2000, www.thehotelminneapolis.com, $169) still has original vaults in the lobby and in Restaurant Max. The rooms are spacious and equipped with modern toys like flat-screen TVs and iPod docking stations.

The Westin Minneapolis (88 6th St. S., 612/333-4006, www.westin.com, $189) offers the kind of sophistication you expect from this chain, and it is home to the critically beloved restaurant, Bank.

Chambers Minneapolis (901 Hennepin Ave. S., 612/767-6900, www.chambersminneapolis.com, $195) prides itself on its collection of contemporary art, from its very own art gallery to the lobby to the guest rooms. The contemporary rooms themselves show a careful attention to aesthetics, with clean, comfortable furnishings entirely by Room and Board.

Comfortable, unfussy luxury is the hallmark of the **Hotel Ivy** (201 11th St. S., 612/746-4600, www.thehotelivy.com, $199), from the cream-and-ivy color scheme to the elegant limestone bathrooms and the 400-thread-count sheets. And the Ivy Spa Club, right on the premises, offers top-of-the line fitness facilities and spa services.

Once Minneapolis's tallest building, the Foshay Tower is now **W Minneapolis - The Foshay** (821 Marquette Ave., 612/215-3700, www.starwoodhotels.com, $209), restored with a mixture of modern flare and cheeky historical detail (the boardroom is now a bar called Prohibition).

Sleek, sophisticated, and modern, **Graves 601** (601 1st Ave. N., 612/677-1100, www.graves601hotel.com, $250) offers a little bit of glamour during your stay in Minneapolis. It's connected to the skyway system and convenient to the Target Center, the Hennepin Theatre District, and central business district. Ask for an upper-level room with a view of the skyline.

Hostels and Bed-and-Breakfasts

The area's only hostel is the **Minneapolis Hostel,** in the same building as the **Historic King Inn** (2400 Stevens Ave. S., 612/874-0407, www.historickinginn.com, www.minneapolishostel.com). Hostel beds start at $28. Private rooms in the hotel run $35–125. Hostel guests must have out-of-town ID.

From the shady front porch to the tidy parlor to the three guestrooms (each with its own private bathroom), the **LeBlanc House Bed and Breakfast** (302 University Ave. N.E., 612/379-2570, www.leblanchouse.com, $60–108) feels like a step back in time to the Victorian period in which it was built. Perhaps the biggest bonus: Swedish pancakes with lingonberry jam for breakfast on weekend mornings.

By location and by design, **Wales House** (1115 5th St. S.E., 612/331-3931, www.waleshouse.com, $60, $70 with private bath) serves many University of Minnesota visitors. The 10 guest rooms—spare, homey, and comfortable—are a remarkable deal (rates go down for weekly and monthly rentals). Guests gather for an organic continental breakfast each morning and have use of the well-stocked kitchen, as well as three common areas.

FOOD

African

Tam-Tam's (605 Cedar Ave. S., 612/339-0854, www.tamtamsrestaurant.com, 11 A.M.–10 P.M. Sun.–Thurs., 11 A.M.–midnight Fri.–Sat., $9–15) serves a pan-African menu, with the *injera* (spongey bread) of the Horn of Africa, palm butter-based stews from Ghana, and peanut-based dishes from Eastern and Central Africa.

Red Sea (320 Cedar Ave. S., 612/333-3349, www.redseaclub.com, 11 A.M.–2 A.M. daily, $9–15) serves Ethiopian dishes—collections of meat and bean stews served communally with *injera*—alongside pub food like burgers and wings. There's live music and a dance club–like feel in the evenings, and there may be a cover.

American Casual

For the best sandwich in the Twin Cities,

Downtown Minneapolis's Nicollet Mall fills with restaurants' patio seating during the summer.

head to **Be'wiched** (800 Washington Ave. N., 612/767-4330, www.bewicheddeli.com, 8 A.M.–8 P.M. Mon.–Fri., 10 A.M.–6 P.M. Sat., closed Sun., $6–10) where everything from the pastrami to the turkey to the tuna confit to the bread is cured, smoked, or baked in house.

Humble spuds become gourmet meals at **Joe's Garage** (1610 Harmon Pl., 612/904-1163, www.joes-garage.com, 11 A.M.–10 P.M. Mon.–Wed., 11 A.M.–11 P.M. Sat., 10 A.M.–10 P.M. Sun., $8–15) when you stir in lamb meatballs, grilled ratatouille, or chipotle cream sauce—or any of the two dozen mix-ins. Beyond beef burgers, you'll find spicy Asian pork, lamb with chèvre, and black beans with falafel. Right on Loring Park, Joe's has a fantastic third-story patio.

The Wienery (414 Cedar Ave. S., 612/333-5798, www.wienery.com, 10 A.M.–7 P.M. Sun.–Thurs., 10 A.M.–8 P.M. Fri.–Sat., $2.75–$3.25), a little Bohemian West Bank dive, serves up top-quality bratwurst, polish sausage, and the like, all heaped with toppings of your choice. Veggie versions are available.

American Upscale

Hands down, the finest dining in the Twin Cities is at **La Belle Vie** (427 Groveland Ave., 612/874-6440, www.labellevie.us, 5–9 P.M. Sun.–Thurs., 5–10 P.M. Sat., $22–38). While you can order à la carte, La Belle Vie's tasting menus—five courses for $65 or seven for $80—shine. In the comfortable lounge you can fill up on not-so-small small plates, like a lamb burger or pappardelle with rabbit bolognese, for under $20.

Chef Lucia Watson, of **Lucia's** (1432 31st St. W., 612/825-1572, www.lucias.com, lunch 11:30 A.M.–2:30 P.M. Tues.–Fri., dinner 5:30–9:30 P.M. Tues.–Thurs., 5:30–10 P.M. Fri.–Sat., 5:30–9 P.M. Sun., brunch 10 A.M.–2 P.M. Sat.–Sun., closed Mon.) posts her menu online every Wednesday, based on local and seasonal ingredients. Next door, Lucia's Bakery serves weekend brunch and lunchtime crêpes and salads. Late-night bites are available on the bar menu.

The tables at **112 Eatery** (112 N. 3rd St., 612/343-7696, www.112eatery.com, 5 P.M.–midnight Mon.–Thurs., 5 P.M.–1 A.M. Fri.–Sat., 5–10 P.M. Sun., $18) fill quickly with diners hungry for a hearty egg sandwich with tangy *harissa,* meatballs made with foie gras, duck pâté in the crusty Vietnamese sandwich known as a *bành mì,* or a plateful of light-as-air parmesan gnocchi.

The menu at **Restaurant Alma** (528 University Ave. SE, 612/379-3030, www.restaurantalma.com, 4–9 P.M. Sun., 11 A.M.–9 P.M. Mon.–Thurs., 11 A.M.–10 P.M. Fri.–Sat., $25) is short, meticulously chosen, and constantly changing to reflect the best each season has to offer, from spring nettle soup to wild halibut. Despite critical acclaim, it still has the feel of a cozy neighborhood bistro.

The chef at **Heidi's** (819 50th St. W., 612/354-3512, www.heidismpls.com, 5–10 P.M. Tues.–Sun., closed Mon.) has cooked at Lespinasse and Le Bernardin and graced the cover of *Food & Wine*'s Best New Chefs issue in 2006. Now he serves butter-poached lobster and crispy chicken breast to his grateful South Minneapolis neighbors.

The first LEED-certified environmentally friendly restaurant in Minnesota, **Red Stag Supper Club** (509 1st Ave. NE, 612/767-7766, www.redstagsupperclub.com, 11 A.M.–2 A.M. Mon.–Fri., 9 A.M.–2 A.M. Sat.–Sun.) serves updated renditions of supper club classics, from mac and cheese with truffle oil to liver and onions with green garlic gravy. Friday is fish fry day, with an extensive menu of battered and fried in-season seafood.

Asian

It often surprises visitors just how many good Japanese restaurants there are here. After five decades, **Fuji Ya** (600 Lake St. W., 612/871-4055, www.fujiyasushi.com, 5–10 P.M. Tues.–Thurs., 5–10:30 P.M. Fri.–Sat., 5–9 P.M. Sun.) is still pulling in a young and hip crowd with its full sushi bar, tatami rooms, and authentic full Japanese dinners. Fuji Ya is also in St. Paul (465 Wabasha St. N., 651/310-0111, lunch 11:30 A.M.–2 P.M. Mon.–Fri., dinner 5–10 P.M. Mon.–Sat., closed Sun.).

At big and stylish **Nami** (251 1st Ave. N., 612/333-1999, www.namisushi.com, 11:30 A.M.–10 P.M. Mon.–Sat., closed Sun.), you can enjoy your sushi or bento box at a table for two in a quiet corner, somewhere closer to the rocking party going on at the bar, or right in front of the sushi chef.

Longtime favorite **Sawatdee** (118 N. 4th St., 612/373-0840, www.sawatdee.com, 11 A.M.–10 P.M. Tues.–Sun., 11 A.M.–9:30 P.M. Mon., $9–19) brings the Far East to the Midwest with walleye in ginger sauce and other flavorful favorites. There are also other branches (2650 Hennepin Avenue S., 612/377-4418, and 607 Washington Avenue S., 612/338-6451) in the city.

Quang (2719 Nicollet Ave. S., 612/870-4739, www.quangrestaurant.com, 11 A.M.–9 P.M. Mon. and Wed.–Fri., 10 A.M.–9 P.M. Sat., 10 A.M.–8:30 P.M. Sun., closed Tues.) is where big Southeast Asian families gather to celebrate and dine together. Heck, just about everybody eventually comes to bright and friendly Quang for their first or their 4,000th bowl of *phô.* (If you've had enough *phô,* have the fantastic barbecue pork salad.)

For upscale pan-Asian fusion fare, try celebrity chef Wolfgang Puck's **20.21** (1750 Hennepin Ave., 612/253-3410, www.wolfgangpuck.com, lunch 11:30 A.M.–2 P.M. Tues.–Sat., brunch 10 A.M.–2:30 P.M. Sun., dinner 5:30–10 P.M. Tues.–Thurs., 5:30–11 P.M. Fri.–Sat., closed Mon.) in the Walker Art Center. The menu spans Mongolian lamb to Cantonese duck to a Maine lobster with *shiso* and *yuzu.* The Sunday brunch buffet ($28) is unparalleled.

Bakeries and Coffeeshops

You are never more than a few blocks away from a good cup o' joe in Minneapolis. **Dunn Bros.** (www.dunnbros.com) is a local franchise with a blue million locations—always a good bet.

Uptown is packed with unique coffeehouses. Both **Spyhouse** (2451 Nicollet Ave. S., 612/871-3177, and 2404 Hennepin Ave. S., 612/377-2278, www.spyhousecoffeshop.com, 6:30 A.M.–midnight Mon.–Fri., 8 A.M.–midnight Sat.–Sun.) locations attract the laptop crowd and serve tasty sandwiches from their sister restaurant, The Bad Waitress.

I guarantee you won't soon forget the cinnamon buns at **Isles Bun & Coffee Co.** (1424 W. 28th St., 612/870-4466, www.islesbun.com, 6:30 A.M.–4 P.M. Mon.–Sat., 7 A.M.–3 P.M. Sun.).

Generations of Minnesotans have enjoyed treats and cakes from **Wuollet** (2447 Hennepin Ave., 612/381-9400, www.wuollet.com, 7 A.M.–6 P.M. Mon.–Sat., closed Sun.).

Madwoman Foods (4747 Nicollet Ave. S., 612/825-6680, www.madwomanfoods.com, 10 A.M.–7 P.M. Mon.–Sat., noon–5 P.M. Sun.) is a dream come true for the gluten-intolerant: A whole bakery, full of honest-to-goodness tasty baked goods, just for them.

Breakfast and Brunch

C Hell's Kitchen (80 9th St. S., 612/332-4700, www.hellskitcheninc.com, 6:30 A.M.–10 P.M. Mon.–Thurs., 6:30 A.M.–midnight Fri., 7:30 A.M.–midnight Sat., 7:30 A.M.–midnight Sun., $8–14) has no peers. There's a lot of silliness, but the food—eggs Benedict with bison sausage, lemon-ricotta hotcakes, and walleye BLTs—is seriously good. They now serve lunch and dinner with the same verve, but breakfast is still where the buzz is.

Eating at **Al's Breakfast** (413 14th Ave. SE, 612/331-9991, 6 A.M.–1 P.M. Mon.–Sat., 9 A.M.–1 P.M. Sun., $2–7), a 14-seat closet in Dinkytown, is a legendary Minneapolis experience. You'll have to decide if it's worth the wait, though anyone who's ordered a short stack or one of the creative omelets will tell you that it is.

French Meadow Bakery and Café (2610 Lyndale Ave. S., 612/870-7855, www.frenchmeadowcafe.com, 6:30 A.M.–9 P.M. Sun.–Thurs., 6:30 A.M.–11 P.M. Fri.–Sat.) is the original home of organic, vegan, gluten-free, sprouted-grain, natural-yeast, low-glycemic baking. But you'd never know it walking into this friendly, stylish café, where the bakery case is filled with tasty treats and the tables are filled with diners enjoying breakfast burritos and platter-sized pancakes. While French

Meadow has long lines at breakfast and lunch, it's something of a hidden gem for dinner.

Eclectic

With a wall of candles and cheeky sense of humor, **Chino Latino** (2916 Hennepin Ave. S., 612/824-7878, www.chinolatino.com, 4:30 P.M.–1 A.M. Sun.–Thurs., 4:30 P.M.–2 A.M. Fri.–Sat., $7–45) has long been one of the trendiest dining spots in the Cities, but it doesn't get by on attitude alone. Their open kitchen takes diners on a wonderful culinary tour of the vaguely equatorial "Hot Zone," as they have dubbed it. There's Philippine *paella,* Jamaican jerked chicken, and *chipotle* salmon sushi to name a few—they even have *cuy* (guinea pig) if you call 48 hours in advance. Most dishes are enormous and meant to be shared. The drinks list is just as much fun.

Dozens of locally owned independent food stalls, from Scandinavian to Somali and Chinese to Caribbean, fill the **Midtown Global Market** (920 E. Lake St., 612/872-4041, 7 A.M.–8 P.M. Mon.–Sat., 7 A.M.–6 P.M. Sun.), a centerpiece of the neighborhood's revitalization.

Bar and Café Lurcat (1624 Harmon Pl., 612/486-5500, www.damico.com, café 5–10 P.M. Mon.–Thurs., 5–11 P.M. Fri.–Sat., 5–9 P.M. Sun., bar open until 1 A.M. on weekends) is where you will find Minneapolis's beautiful people. The bar serves small plates like rave-worthy mini burgers and decadently golden fries. In the café, you'll find creative contemporary American fare with a touch of French influence—buckwheat crêpes, several cuts of steak, butter-poached prawns, and foie gras.

Ice Cream

Minnesotans love their ice cream. **Sebastian Joe's** (1007 Franklin Ave. W., 612/870-0065, and 4321 Upton Ave. S., 612/926-7916, 7 A.M.–11 P.M. daily) is the local favorite. The signature flavor is Pavarotti, an addictive blend of caramel, banana, and chocolate. But their raspberry chocolate chip has partisans as well.

A little jewel box of a restaurant, **Crema** (3403 Lyndale Ave. S., 612/824-3868, 8 A.M.–10:30 P.M. daily) serves Italian-style ice cream in flavors like cabernet chocolate chip and basil balsamic vinegar, as well as Italian-style sandwiches. When the weather cools off, Crema may restrict its hours to weekend evenings.

© BRUCE MANNING

Everyone loves Sebastian Joe's for its neighborhood atmosphere and creative ice cream flavors.

Italian

D'Amico Kitchen (901 Hennepin Ave., 612/767-6900, www.chambersminneapolis.com, 6:30 A.M.–2 P.M. daily, 5–10 P.M. Sun.–Thurs., 5–11 P.M. Fri.–Sat., $25) packed up its longtime reputation as the best expense-account restaurant in town and moved into the Chambers hotel in the summer of 2009. It serves classic Italian, from *antipasti* through *primi* and *secondi.*

The same people who wow the elite at D'Amico Kitchen please the masses at **D'Amico & Sons** (www.damicoandsons.com). The informal deli-cafés turn out good pastas and even better wood-fired pizzas at six Minneapolis locations, including downtown (555 Nicollet Mall, 612/342-2700, 11 A.M.–7 P.M. Mon.–Fri., noon–6 P.M. Sat., $6–8) and Uptown (2210

Hennepin Ave. S., 612/374-1858, 11 A.M.–9 P.M. Sun.–Thurs., 11 A.M.–10 P.M. Fri.–Sat., $7–10). Kids eat free on Sundays after 2 P.M.

At **Broder's Pasta Bar** (5000 Penn Ave. S., 612/925-9202, www.broders.com, 5–9:30 P.M. Mon.–Thurs., 5–10 P.M. Fri., 4:30–10 P.M. Sat., 5–9:30 P.M. Sun.) South Minneapolis diners cheerfully accept the no-reservations policy and line up for house-made pasta cooked to order and tossed to order with individually composed sauces (nearly two dozen choices, as a matter of fact, if you count the risotto). Across the street, at **Broder's Cucina Italiana** (2308 50th St. W., 612/925-3113), you can pick up pasta to cook at home (and maybe a slice of pizza to munch along the way) and other imported goodies.

Latin American and Spanish

Minneapolis has a large Mexican community and a number of authentic restaurants to match. Head down Eat Street or Lake Street east of the freeway to try your luck.

Masa (1070 Nicollet Mall, 612/338-6272, www.masa-restaurant.com, 11 A.M.–2:30 P.M. and 5–10 P.M. Mon.–Thurs., 11 A.M.–2:30 P.M. and 5–11 P.M. Fri., 5–11 P.M. Sat., closed Sun.) gives good old Mexican favorites the white-tablecloth treatment. Humble foods like tacos, *sopes,* and *pozole verde* still taste good when served by trained waiters on nice china.

Brasa (600 Hennepin Ave. E., 612/379-3030, www.brasa.us, 11 A.M.–9 P.M. Mon.–Thurs., 11 A.M.–10 P.M. Fri., noon–10 P.M. Sat., closed Sun.) is the mostly Latin version of a meat-and-three: Pick your protein (spit-roasted chicken or pork, both generously rubbed with spices) and your sides (fried yucca, creamed spinach, an ethereal muffin made with creamed corn, and more).

Gushing with Gaudiesque glitz, **Solera** (900 Hennepin Ave., 612/338-0062, www.solera-restaurant.com, 4 P.M.–1 A.M. Mon.–Thurs., 4 P.M.–2 A.M. Fri., 5 P.M.–2 A.M. Sat., 5–11 P.M. Sun., $9 small plates) offers 50 kinds of tapas and a heavily Spanish wine list in a massive, varied four-story space. The lush rooftop is among the best outdoor dining spots in the Twin Cities and shows movies during the summer.

Middle Eastern

People come from all over the Twin Cities and beyond to shop and eat at **Holy Land** (2513 Central Ave. NE, 612/781-2627, www.holylandbrand.com, 9 A.M.–9 P.M. Sun.–Thurs., 9 A.M.–10 P.M. Fri.–Sat., $8 buffet), a grocery store and restaurant. The all-you-can-eat buffet (sometimes including lamb and goat) is fantastic. The hummus is the best in town.

Classic techniques meet Middle Eastern flavors in the white-linen dining room at **Saffron** (123 3rd St. N., 612/746-5533, www.saffronmpls.com, 5–10 P.M. Mon.–Thurs., 5 P.M.–1 A.M. Fri.–Sat., closed Sun.). Enjoy lamb brains with tomato confit, for example, or carpaccio with crispy chickpeas.

Other European

There have only been superficial changes since **Nye's Polonaise** (112 Hennepin Ave. E., 612/379-2021, www.nyespolonaise.com, 11 A.M.–2 A.M. daily, $9–36) opened in 1949, and much of the clientele has regularly filled the booths all these many years. It's principally a supper-club menu of steak and seafood, with added Polish specialties like *pierogis* and pork hocks. A lounge singer holds court in the restaurant every night, and you can dance off the calories in the adjacent polka bar.

One block over is the equally venerable **Kramarczuk Sausage Company** (215 Hennepin Ave. E., 612/379-3018, www.kramarczuk.com, 7 A.M.–4 P.M. Mon., 7 A.M.–8 P.M. Tues.–Sat., 11 A.M.–4 P.M. Sun., $4–10), a traditional deli and cafeteria where you can get Ukrainian meatballs, Hungarian sausage, or pastrami sandwiches.

Lunch at **Vincent – A Restaurant** (1100 Nicollet Mall, 612/630-1189, www.vincentarestaurant.com, 11:30 A.M.–2 P.M. and 5:30–9 P.M. Mon.–Thurs., 11:30 A.M.–2 P.M. and 5:30–11 P.M. Fri., 5:30–11 P.M. Sat., closed Sun.) is French bistro fare: omelets, steak frites, buckwheat crêpes, and the fabulous short-rib and gruyère-infused Vincent burger. Dinner brings out the classic French pan sauces and high-end cuts of meat.

Everything at **Barbette** (1600 Lake

© TRICIA CORNELL

fine French dining on the sidewalk at Vincent - A Restaurant

St. W., 612/827-5710, www.barbette.com, 8 A.M.–1 A.M. Sun.–Thurs., 8 A.M.–2 P.M. Fri.–Sat.) is comforting, classically French, and frankly perfect, from the big plate of *pommes frites* with béarnaise sauce to the frisée salad with poached egg and lardons or a filled buckwheat crêpe. Save room for carrot cake.

Find the lighter, more Mediterranean side of Greek cuisine at **Gardens of Salonica** (19th 5th St. NE, 612/378-0611, www.gardensofsalonica.com, 11 A.M.–9 P.M. Tues.–Thurs., 11 A.M.–10 P.M. Fri.–Sat., closed Sun.–Mon., $8–17). Fill your table with small plates to share—hummus with pillowy Greek pita and olives, ultra-garlicky *skordalia* potato dip, pizzas built on pita bases, and the savory, flaky pastries they call *boughatsa*—or build a traditional three-course meal.

Pizza

Mock duck, barbecue chicken, and goat cheese are some of the more unusual of the fifty-plus toppings at **Pizza Lucé** (119 N. 4th St., 612/333-7359, www.pizzaluce.com, 11 A.M.–2:30 A.M. Sun.–Thurs., 11 A.M.–3:30 A.M. Fri.–Sat., $6–21), and they even offer a choice of vegan cheese alternatives. There are also other branches (3200 Lyndale Avenue S., 612/827-5978, and 2200 E. Franklin Ave., 612/332-2535) in the city.

At **Pizza Nea** (306 Hennepin Ave. E., 612/331-9298, www.pizzanea.com, 11 A.M.–9:30 P.M. Mon.–Thurs., 11 A.M.–10:30 P.M. Fri.–Sat., noon–9 P.M. Sun., $6–12), the thick and chewy pies are baked in a 900°F, wood-fired oven and fall somewhere between individual and sharing size. Toppings range from the basic Margherita with basil to an inspired pie with two fried eggs and sharp Parmesan cheese.

Seafood

Besides serving the Twin Cities' best seafood, flown in from both coasts and beyond, **Oceanaire Seafood Room** (1300 Nicollet Ave., 612/333-2277, www.theoceanaire.com, 5–10 P.M. Mon.–Thurs., 5–11 P.M. Fri.–Sat., 5–10 P.M. Sun., $18–99), in the Hyatt Regency, sets the standard for service. Reservations are required for the dining room, though walk-ins can still dine at the oyster bar.

From late spring through early fall, **Sea Salt Eatery** (4825 Minnehaha Ave., 612/721-8990, www.seasalteatery.com, 11 A.M.–7 P.M. Sun.–Mon., 11 A.M.–8 P.M. Tues.–Sat., Apr.–Oct., $7–15) fills the pavilion at Minnehaha Falls with the scent of fish tacos and lines of eager eaters. The menu—from oysters on the half shell ($26/dozen) to crab cakes ($9.95) to fried fish sandwiches and fish tacos—is ideal for a picnic on a warm summer evening.

On Lake Calhoun, in the classic park building, is the equally eagerly awaited **Tin Fish** (3000 Calhoun Pkwy. E., 612/823-5840, www.thetinfish.net, 11 A.M.–9 P.M. daily Memorial Day–Labor Day, reduced hours in April, May, Sept., and Oct., $6–15). The Tin Fish's specialty is the Mini Tin, a deceptively mammoth fried fish sandwich, but the shrimp tacos, the grilled mahi mahi, the flavorful burgers—heck, everything on the menu—are worth waiting for.

Steak Houses

For more than 60 years, the 28-ounce Silver Butter Knife Steak at **Murray's** (26 S. 6th St., 612/339-0909, www.murraysrestaurant.com, 11 A.M.–2 P.M. and 5–10:30 P.M. Mon.–Fri., 5–10:30 P.M. Sat.–Sun.) has been one of the classiest ways to say "I love you" to your meat-eating Minneapolis sweetheart.

You'll get the full four-star treatment at nationally renowned **Manny's** (821 Marquette Ave., 612/215-3700, www.mannyssteakhouse.com, 6:30 A.M.–10 P.M. daily) in the Foshay Tower. The steaks, the sides, and the wine list are all immense, and the room, while still upscale, is decorated with a little more casual humor than most steakhouses.

Vegetarian

In the laid-back and slightly hippy Seward neighborhood, the **Birchwood Cafe** (3311 25th Ave. E., 612/722-4474, www.birchwoodcafe.com, 7 A.M.–10 P.M. Mon.–Fri., 8 A.M.–10 P.M. Sat., 9 A.M.–8 P.M. Sun., $7–12) isn't strictly vegetarian, but vegetarians, vegans, and their fish- and poultry-eating friends will all find common ground in this cheery neighborhood gem. The atmosphere is casual—you order at the counter and the place is often teeming with kids—but pizzas, burgers, and light entrées are all a step above what you'd expect at a casual joint.

Spoonriver (750 2nd St. S., 612/436-2236, www.spoonriverrestaurant.com, lunch 11:30 A.M.–2 P.M. Tues.–Fri., brunch 10 A.M.–2 P.M. Sat.–Sun., dinner 5:30–10 P.M. Tues.–Thurs., 5:30–11 P.M. Fri.–Sat., 5–10 P.M. Sun., closed Mon.) is the elegant, urbane sister of Café Brenda, natural-food pioneer Brenda Langton's first restaurant. Right next to the Guthrie Theater, it's a popular choice for pre- or post-theater dining—you can't beat the wild mushroom and pistachio terrine or the smoked chicken quesadilla with mango. For dinner, the seafood *okisuki* (Japanese noodles in broth) is a big bowl of comfort. Weekend brunches (starting at 8 A.M. in the summer) are just a tiny bit more decadent, with omelets, French toast, and buckwheat crêpes.

INFORMATION AND SERVICES

Tourist Information

Meet Minneapolis (612/767-8000 or 888/676-6757, www.minneapolis.org), the city's tourism office, has a visitor information booth at the convention center (1301 2nd Ave., 612/339-0616, 11 A.M.–2 P.M. and 2:30–6 P.M. Mon.–Fri., closed Sat.–Sun.).

Post Office

The monstrous main post office (100 S. 1st St., 612/349-4715, 7 A.M.–8 P.M. Mon.–Fri., 9 A.M.–1 P.M. Sat., closed Sun.) is an art deco gem. Buy a stamp just for a chance to see the 1,000-foot lobby, lined by the longest brass light fixture in the country.

Internet Access

Most **Dunn Bros Coffee** (www.dunnbros.com) locations, of which there are many, have free computers for customer use. **Kinko's** (www.kinkos.com) has downtown branches at the IDS Center (80 S. 8th St., 612/343-8000) and convention center (1301 2nd

© BRUCE MANNING

The Minneapolis Central Library is a new architectural landmark on the north end of Nicollet Mall.

Ave., 612/339-0616) plus one on the U of M campus (612 Washington Ave. SE, 612/379-2452) and one in Uptown (1430 W. Lake St., 612/822-7700).

The **Minneapolis Central Library** (300 Nicollet Mall, 612/630-6000) is in a gorgeous new building, and visitors can access the Internet with any ID.

Car Rentals

Major car rental companies with downtown locations are **Avis** (829 3rd Ave. S., 612/332-6322 or 800/331-1212), **Budget** (229 10th St. S., 612/332-5218 or 800/527-0700), **Enterprise** (110 S. 10th St., 612/677-1319 or 800/261-7331) and **Thrifty** (1313 Nicollet Mall, 612/333-2050 or 800/847-4389).

You can travel in style with a Harley or Moskito Scooter rental from **Midwest Motorcycle** (215 Washington Ave. N., 612/338-5345 or 888/237-5853, www.midwest-motorcycle.com).

St. Paul

Those who paid attention in school will remember that St. Paul (pop. 288,000), not Minneapolis, is the capital of Minnesota. Political supremacy aside, the "Last City of the East" plays second fiddle to its larger sibling for all but its fiercely loyal residents. Yet when it comes to interesting attractions, St. Paul doesn't lag very far behind. Downtown has taken a sharp turn toward the modern in recent years, but it still has pockets of the European charm city boosters boast of, and the many structures from the city's past, most notably the historic homes along Summit Avenue, are popular destinations for tourists.

History

It has been said that the Mississippi River gave birth to the city, but Pierre "Pig's Eye" Parrant, a famously nefarious character, was its midwife. Parrant, an aging voyageur who got his nickname from his blind "marble-hued and crooked" eye, moved down the river from Fort Snelling in 1838, immediately after the land was opened to settlers, to run a ramshackle saloon. Others soon followed, some for the steady supply of whiskey and others to take advantage of the ideal steamboat landing: All took to calling the settlement Pig's Eye Landing. Unfortunately, in 1841 a pious French missionary named Lucien Galtier built a tiny log chapel here and pressured residents to adopt its name for the village.

St. Paul soon replaced Fort Snelling as the most important settlement on this stretch of the Mississippi, although it wasn't exactly a bustling metropolis yet; just 30 families, mostly French Canadians, called it home in 1845. In 1849 Minnesota became a territory and St. Paul its capital. Things changed virtually overnight when word reached the people of Minnesota. St. Paul nearly doubled in size in just three weeks, and by the fall of that year nearly 1,000 hopeful settlers had bought a one-way steamboat ticket. Some haughty boosters even predicted that St. Paul would become the new national capital. Back then, as today, Germans and Irish, in that order, made up the majority of the population, though the city is usually still thought of as an Irish enclave, in part because the Irish were dominant in politics from early on.

The first railroad came to St. Paul in 1862, connecting it with St. Anthony (now a part of Minneapolis), though it wasn't until the next decade that rail began to replace the paddlewheel. James J. Hill centered his railroad empire here and made St. Paul the gateway to and transportation center of the entire Northwest, and the city prospered along with him. Mark Twain visited in 1882 during his trip up the Mississippi River (that would be chronicled in *Life on the Mississippi*) and was impressed. "St. Paul is a wonderful town," he said. "It is put together in solid blocks of honest brick and stone, and has the air of intending to stay." Stay it did, of course; most new arrivals, though, did not. In the peak year of 1888, nearly 150 trains a day brought passengers through the city's Union Depot, but most people stopped only briefly before moving out to claim land on the Minnesota frontier.

The 20th century saw ups and downs as prohibition brought a horrible crime spree to the city, while the opportunities provided by the World Wars brought many of the city's poorest into the economic mainstream. During the Roaring '20s infamous gangsters like John Dillinger and Baby Face Nelson found St. Paul a safe haven; as long as they didn't commit crimes in the city (Minneapolis was fair game), Police Chief John O'Connor left them alone. The so-called O'Connor system worked for a while, but the city grew increasingly lawless, and kidnapping was a growth industry. By the early 1930s, law enforcement officials in Washington, D.C., had labeled St. Paul "poison spot of the nation," and a cleanup began. Not long after, Dillinger, then officially "Public Enemy Number One," famously shot his way past police and escaped from his apartment. On the morning of March 31, 1934, the city cracked down on other no-longer-welcome criminals and closed the brothels and gambling halls.

Little of note happened in St. Paul over the rest of the century, and while the city stagnated, Minneapolis gained its clear supremacy. Recent years, however, have brought billions of dollars in new development to downtown, including the RiverCenter convention complex, Xcel Energy Center arena, major housing developments, and office buildings. The changes have led to a rapid economic and attitudinal resurgence for the city.

Orientation

St. Paul stretches 29 miles around two sharp bends in the Mississippi River. **Downtown** sits on the steep north bank of the first bend and is centered on **Rice Park. Lowertown,** the eastern half of downtown, is a largely residential area with many artists occupying converted warehouses. The historic district surrounds the

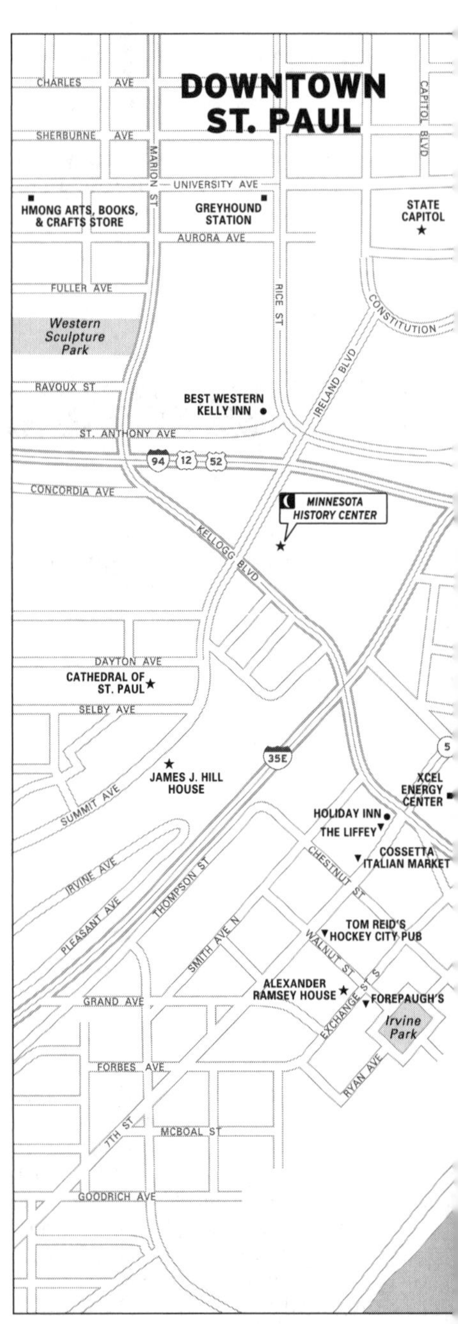

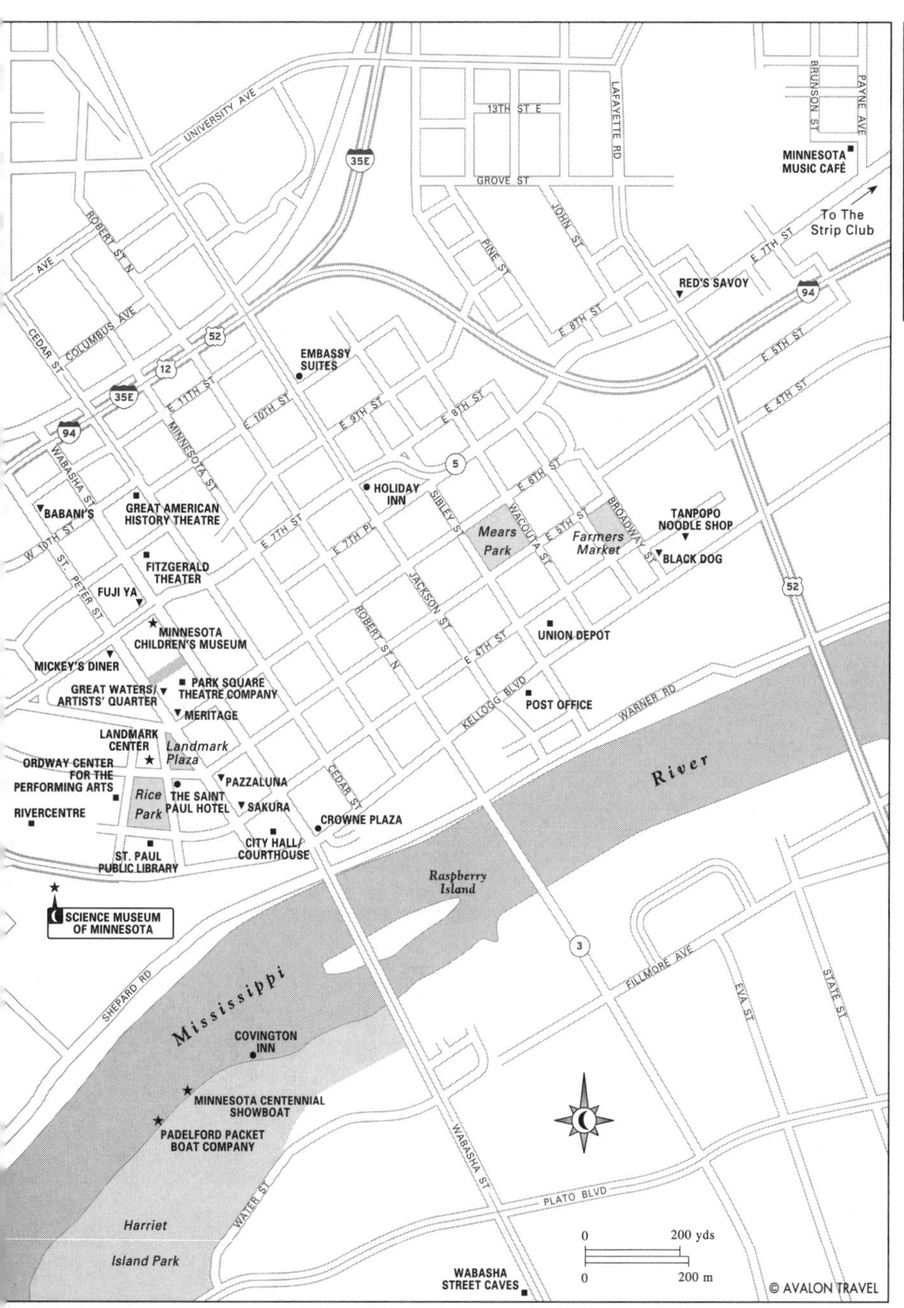

UNIVERSITY AVE
13TH ST E
LAFAYETTE RD
BRUNSON ST
PAYNE AVE
MINNESOTA MUSIC CAFÉ
GROVE ST
To The Strip Club
JOHN ST
PINE ST
E 7TH ST
RED'S SAVOY
ROBERT ST N
AVE
CEDAR ST
COLUMBUS AVE
E 8TH ST
EMBASSY SUITES
E 5TH ST
E 4TH ST
E 11TH ST
E 10TH ST
E 9TH ST
E 8TH ST
WABASHA ST
MINNESOTA ST
HOLIDAY INN
E 6TH ST
BABANI'S
GREAT AMERICAN HISTORY THEATRE
W 10TH ST
E 7TH ST
E 7TH PL
SIBLEY ST
Mears Park
WACOUTA ST
E 5TH ST
BROADWAY ST
Farmers Market
TANPOPO NOODLE SHOP
BLACK DOG
FITZGERALD THEATER
ST. PETER ST
FUJI YA
JACKSON ST
ROBERT ST N
MINNESOTA CHILDREN'S MUSEUM
UNION DEPOT
E 4TH ST
MICKEY'S DINER
GREAT WATERS/ ARTISTS' QUARTER
PARK SQUARE THEATRE COMPANY
KELLOGG BLVD
POST OFFICE
WARNER RD
MERITAGE
LANDMARK CENTER
Landmark Plaza
ORDWAY CENTER FOR THE PERFORMING ARTS
Rice Park
THE SAINT PAUL HOTEL
PAZZALUNA
SAKURA
CEDAR ST
River
RIVERCENTRE
CROWNE PLAZA
CITY HALL/ COURTHOUSE
ST. PAUL PUBLIC LIBRARY
Raspberry Island
SCIENCE MUSEUM OF MINNESOTA
SHEPARD RD
Mississippi
FILLMORE AVE
EVA ST
STATE ST
COVINGTON INN
MINNESOTA CENTENNIAL SHOWBOAT
PADELFORD PACKET BOAT COMPANY
WABASHA ST
WATER ST
PLATO BLVD
Harriet Island Park
0
200 yds
0
200 m
WABASHA STREET CAVES
35E
94
52
12
5
3

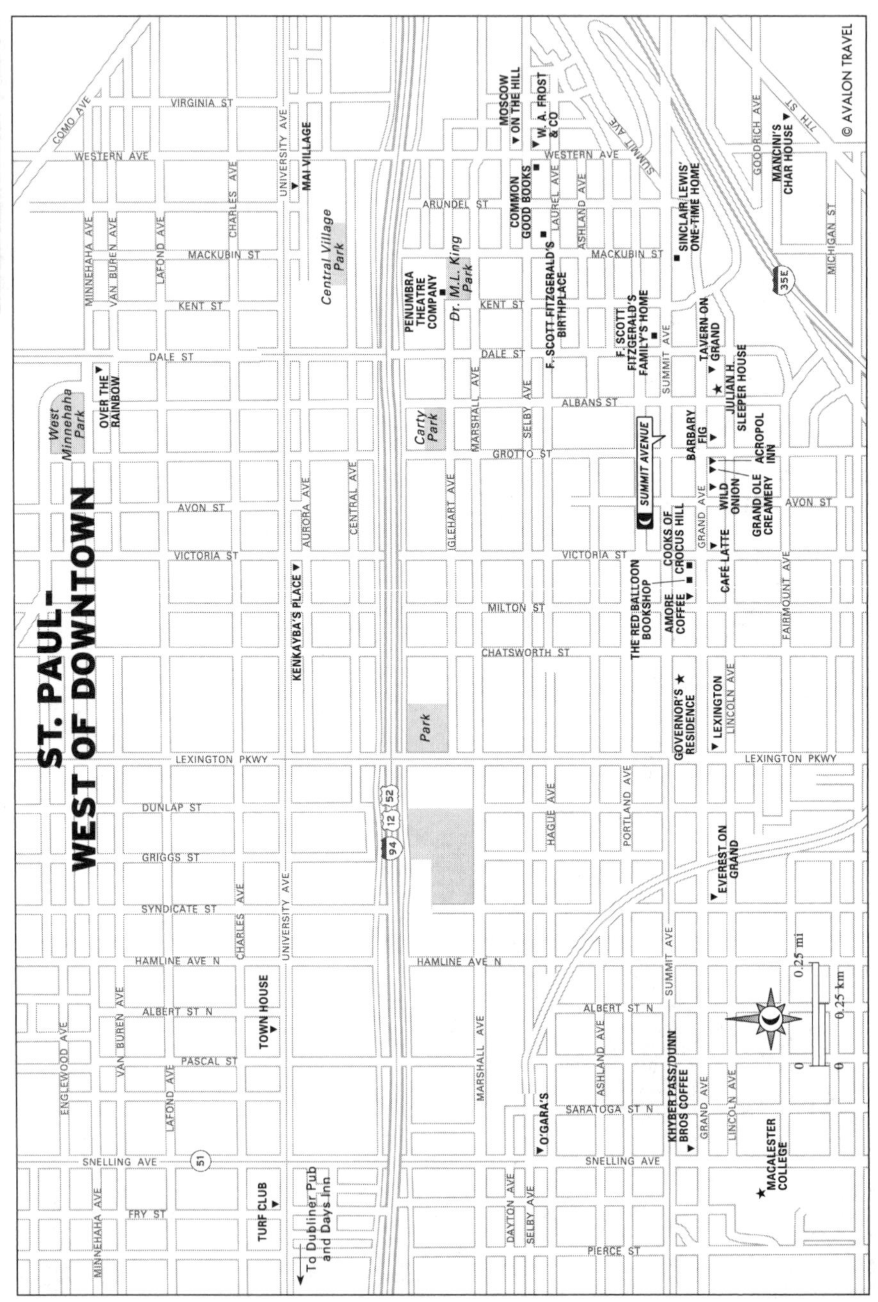
ST. PAUL–
WEST OF DOWNTOWN
COMO AVE
VIRGINIA ST
WESTERN AVE
UNIVERSITY AVE
MAI VILLAGE
CHARLES AVE
MINNEHAHA AVE
VAN BUREN AVE
LAFOND AVE
MACKUBIN ST
Central Village Park
KENT ST
DALE ST
OVER THE RAINBOW
West Minnehaha Park
AVON ST
AURORA AVE
CENTRAL AVE
VICTORIA ST
KENKAYBA'S PLACE
LEXINGTON PKWY
DUNLAP ST
GRIGGS ST
SYNDICATE ST
HAMLINE AVE N
ALBERT ST N
TOWN HOUSE
ENGLEWOOD AVE
PASCAL ST
SNELLING AVE
FRY ST
TURF CLUB
To Dubliner Pub and Days Inn
94
12
52
51
ARUNDEL ST
PENUMBRA THEATRE COMPANY
Dr. M.L. King Park
Carty Park
Park
MARSHALL AVE
IGLEHART AVE
MILTON ST
CHATSWORTH ST
GROTTO ST
ALBANS ST
SELBY AVE
HAGUE AVE
DAYTON AVE
MOSCOW ON THE HILL
W. A. FROST & CO
COMMON GOOD BOOKS
LAUREL AVE
ASHLAND AVE
F. SCOTT FITZGERALD'S BIRTHPLACE
F. SCOTT FITZGERALD'S FAMILY'S HOME
SUMMIT AVE
SUMMIT AVENUE
PORTLAND AVE
THE RED BALLOON BOOKSHOP
COOKS OF CROCUS HILL
AMORE COFFEE
GOVERNOR'S RESIDENCE
O'GARA'S
SARATOGA ST N
PIERCE ST
KHYBER PASS/DUNN BROS COFFEE
SINCLAIR LEWIS' ONE-TIME HOME
TAVERN ON GRAND
JULIAN H. SLEEPER HOUSE
BARBARY FIG
ACROPOL INN
WILD ONION
GRAND OLE CREAMERY
GRAND AVE
CAFÉ LATTE
LEXINGTON
LINCOLN AVE
EVEREST ON GRAND
MACALESTER COLLEGE
FAIRMOUNT AVE
GOODRICH AVE
MANCINI'S CHAR HOUSE
7TH ST
MICHIGAN ST
35E
0.25 mi
0.25 km
0
0
© AVALON TRAVEL

© BRUCE MANNING

Cathedral of St. Paul

tree-filled and stream-divided **Mears Park,** a great place to take lunch. A five-mile elevated indoor skyway system weaves across much of the area connecting hotels, restaurants, theaters, and the like. **West Seventh Street,** by Xcel Center, has several good bars and restaurants and is downtown's main entertainment district. Parking is rarely a problem.

Running west of downtown across the city are the Victorian mansions of **Summit Avenue** and the restaurants and specialty shops of **Grand Avenue.** The lovely neighborhood behind the Cathedral of St. Paul is known as **Cathedral Hill** and is home to several of St. Paul's top kitchens. Southeast Asian businesses line University Avenue between the Capitol and Lexington in an area known as **Frog Town.** West of Frog Town is the **Midway** neighborhood with some worthy restaurants, stores, and bars. The whole of University Avenue is still somewhat gritty, but the influx of Asians in the east and commuters in the west has put the area rapidly on the upswing. The upscale **Highland Park** neighborhood in the far southwest of the city has enough good restaurants to make it worth a visit. Head south of the river for south of the border flavor along Cesar Chavez Street in the **District del Sol,** the hub of St. Paul's Latino community.

SIGHTS

Summit Avenue

The longest stretch of Victorian homes in the nation runs over four miles from the edge of downtown to the Mississippi River along this stately avenue. The most fantastic mansions stand at the far east end, and though it's not an unbroken chain, the drive is lovely all the way across town. Beginning in the 1850s and peaking during the 1880s, the movers and shakers of Minnesota's moneyed class attempted to outdo each other with their elaborate designs, leading Frank Lloyd Wright to reportedly call it "the worst collection of architecture in the world." While many are excessively pompous you'll surely disagree with his assessment and enjoy the conceited legacy of St. Paul's elite. **Guided tours** (11 A.M. and 2 P.M. Sat. and 2 P.M. Sun. May–Sept., $8) of the neighborhood, consisting of a 90-minute walk, depart from the James J. Hill House (240 Summit Ave., 651/297-2555).

Perched high above downtown, right at the beginning of Summit Avenue, is the **Cathedral of St. Paul** (651/228-1766, 7:30 A.M.–6 P.M. Mon.–Thurs., 7:30 A.M.–4 P.M. Fri., 8 A.M.–8 P.M. Sat., 8 A.M.–6 P.M. Sun., free tours 1 P.M. Mon., Wed., and Fri.), an even more dominant landmark than the capitol. The nation's fourth-largest cathedral, modeled after St. Peter's in Rome, was built of St. Cloud granite between 1906 and 1915. Its domed steeple rises 306 feet and up to 5,000 people can attend services. The Shrines of the Nations surrounding the sanctuary feature the patron saints of the countries of origin of Minnesota's first settlers.

The **James J. Hill House** (240 Summit Ave., 651/297-2555, www.mnhs.org, 10 A.M.–3:30 P.M. Wed.–Sat., 1–3:30 P.M. Sun., $8 adults for tours, $2 just for art gallery), a National Historic Landmark, is truly something special. Hill constructed the Great Northern Railway (which earned him the nickname Empire Builder) and was one of the ten richest men in America when he spent nearly a million dollars on this home, which he only lived in about four months each year. Completed in 1891, the red sandstone mansion encompassed 36,000 square feet on five floors, making it to this day one of the largest private residences ever built in the Upper Midwest. But it is the fine detail, not the large scale, that makes the house so remarkable. Public rooms, including the 100-foot-long reception hall, are lined by stained glass, crystal chandeliers, and hand-carved woodwork. There is even artwork in the back of some of the 22 fireplaces. The pinnacle of elegance is the dining room, with a gold-leaf ceiling, hand-tooled leather wallpaper, and original furnishings built specifically for the home. Many clever and advanced (for the day) mechanical systems were employed in the design; one of them, Hill's personal pipe organ, is sometimes played on Saturdays. Ninety-minute tours of the home begin every 30 minutes.

To see how a more typical upper-class home looked during the Gilded Age, book a tour of the **Julian H. Sleeper House** (66 Saint Albans St. S., 651/225-1505, www.julianhsleeperhouse.com, tours by appt., $7). Seth Hawkins has turned his home into a museum of decorative arts and just about everything is authentic to the era. Eastlake furniture, oriental carpets, wall pockets, and over 500 owls fill the house, and during a visit you'll hear interesting stories about the how and why of 1880s interior design. A pair of rooms is set aside for Dr. Hawkins' other interests: One holds the largest collection of President James Garfield memorabilia outside of the museum in Garfield's Ohio hometown, while the basement houses an exhibition of Slovenian history and culture. Guided tours are available at just about any time, even evenings, though you need to call ahead.

Another house open for tours is the **Governor's Residence** (1006 Summit Ave., 651/297-2161, 1–3 P.M. first three Tues. in June, July, and Aug., free admission). Visitors can look around the suitably stately 1912 English Tudor mansion. The free tours last about 45 minutes.

Author F. Scott Fitzgerald, who echoed Wright's sentiments about the street, proscribing it "a mausoleum of American architectural monstrosities," resided in his family's apartment at 599 (which he described as "a house below the average on a street above the average") in 1919 while writing *This Side of Paradise.* Fitzgerald was born just a few blocks off Summit in the even more modest brick apartment building at 481 Laurel Avenue. Sinclair Lewis lived at 516 while writing his play *Hobohemia.*

Irvine Park Historic District

Not quite as grand an address as Summit Avenue, this historic district features many stately homes from the last half of the 19th century that are a very lovely sight nonetheless—especially those fronting the village green–style park. Most prominent is the **Alexander Ramsey House** (265 S. Exchange St., 651/296-8760, www.mnhs.org, 10 A.M.–3 P.M. Sat., noon–3 P.M. Sun. June–Aug., additional tours during the winter holiday season, $8 adults), one of the nation's best-preserved Victorian homes. Built by Minnesota's first territorial governor and second state governor, the 1872 Second Empire mansion remained in the family until 1964 when they turned it, and all original furnishings, over to the Minnesota Historical Society. Not only do you get to admire the walnut woodwork, crystal chandeliers, and other opulent embellishment, but you'll learn about life for the city's elite in the 1870s. Top-of-the-hour tours are led by actors portraying the family's servants. Hours are expanded between Thanksgiving and Christmas, when the house is decorated for the holidays.

Minnesota State Capitol

Topped by the world's largest unsupported marble dome, Minnesota's state capitol (75 Rev. Dr. Martin Luther King Jr. Blvd., 651/296-2881, 9 A.M.–4 P.M. Mon.–Fri., 10 A.M.–3 P.M. Sat., 1–4 P.M. Sun.) is a true architectural masterpiece. This, the state's third capitol, was designed in 1895 by Cass Gilbert (who also drew up the plans for the U.S. Supreme Court and New York City's Woolworth Building) and opened for business ten years later. It rises 223 feet and has an exterior of Georgian marble (a controversial choice) along with some Minnesota granite and sandstone. Its most unique feature is the gilded statue *Quadriga* (officially titled *The Progress of the State*) perched over the main entrance. The four horses, representing Earth, Fire, Water, and Air (nature), are reined in by two women symbolizing Industry and Agriculture. The charioteer riding into the future is Prosperity. The entire art-laden interior, from the grand rotunda to the painted hallway ceilings, is equally spectacular. Don't miss the Governor's Reception Room (yes, you can just walk right in), the most ornate part of the building. Before visiting any of it, though, pick up the self-guided tour brochure from the 1st-floor Information Desk. If you happen to come when the House or Senate is in action, you can watch from the 3rd-floor galleries. Free guided tours that take you up to see *Quadriga* (weather permitting) depart on the hour.

Minnesota History Center

The Minnesota History Center (345 Kellogg Blvd. W., 651/296-6126, www.mnhs.org) is a modern monumental building constructed primarily of Minnesota materials. Besides the library and offices of the Minnesota Historical Society, it houses gift and book shops with North Star State merchandise, the Café Minnesota, and the **History Center Museum** (10 A.M.–8 P.M. Tues., 10 A.M.–5 P.M. Wed.–Sat., noon–5 P.M. Sun., $10 adults), which examines the entire history of the state, from 3.6 billion-year-old geology to the present day. Exhibits focus more on telling stories than just displaying period artifacts, though there are, of course, plenty of the latter. Admission is free on Tuesday evenings.

Landmark Center

St. Paul's castle-like Landmark Center (75 W. 5th St., 651/292-3225, www.landmarkcenter.org, 8 A.M.–5 P.M. Mon.–Wed. and Fri., 8 A.M.–8 P.M. Thurs., 10 A.M.–5 P.M. Sat., noon–5 P.M. Sun., free admission) makes a dazzling backdrop to Rice Park. The 1902 Old Federal Courts Building, as lovely inside as it is out, has found new life as a cultural center. Take at least a few minutes to look around the grand atrium or learn the in-depth history of the building's construction, occupation, and preservation on a free 45-minute tour (11 A.M. Thurs. and 1 P.M. Sun.).

Four museums, all free, call the Landmark home. Down in the basement is the small **Schubert Club Museum of Musical Instruments** (651/292-3267, www.schubert.org, 11 A.M.–3 P.M. Mon.–Fri., 1–5 P.M. Sat.–Sun.), with a gamelan and lots of keyboards.

The **TRACES Center for History and Culture** (651/292-8700, www.traces.org, 9 A.M.–5 P.M. Tues.–Wed. and Fri., 9 A.M.–8 P.M. Thurs., 10 A.M.–5 P.M. Sat., noon–5 P.M. Sun.) examines POW camps and other Midwest-related WWII history.

The **American Association of Woodturners Gallery** (651/484-9094, www.woodturner.org, 11 A.M.–4 P.M. Tues., Wed., and Fri.,

© BRUCE MANNING

The Landmark Center is the cultural heart of downtown St. Paul.

11 A.M.–7 P.M. Thurs., noon–3 P.M. Sun.) showcases some pretty remarkable work. Finally, the **Ramsey County Historical Society Gallery** in the building's back lobby has displays about the Mississippi River.

Landmark Plaza memorializes former St. Paulite Charles Schulz with bronze statues of Charlie Brown, Snoopy, and the rest of the *Peanuts* gang. There is an ice rink and skate rental in the winter.

City Hall and Courthouse

The 1932 Saint Paul City Hall and Ramsey County Courthouse (15 W. Kellogg Blvd., 651/266-8266, 8 A.M.–4:30 P.M. Mon.–Fri., closed Sat.–Sun.) is an art deco masterpiece. Built during the depths of the Great Depression, the dramatic 20-story building was designed "to symbolize 20th century pride in progress, industry, and democracy." The ornate Zig-Zag Moderne interior is highlighted by the otherworldly Memorial Hall, where dark blue Belgian marble, bronze trim, and a mirrored ceiling surround *Vision of Peace,* a 36-foot Native American apparition carved from Mexican onyx by Swedish sculptor Carl Milles. The three-story lobby sits just inside the 4th Street entrance.

☾ Science Museum of Minnesota

Minnesota's most visited museum takes you on a journey from the ancient world to the future of high technology. The excellent collection at the Science Museum (120 Kellogg Blvd. W., 651/221-9444, www.smm.org, 9:30 A.M.–9 P.M. Mon.–Sat., noon–5 P.M. Sun. year-round except 5 P.M. closing Mon.–Wed. Sept.–May, $11 adults for exhibits, $7.50 Omnitheater, $17.50 for both) is chock-full of interactive exhibits of interest to both kids and adults. You can make a tornado, pilot a riverboat, experiment on cells, see dinosaur fossils, play the musical staircase, and much more. One of the most interesting sections is the often-overlooked Collections Gallery where the varied assortment of items includes a traditional Hmong house, pottery, a two-headed turtle, an Egyptian mummy, and quack contraptions from the late Museum of Questionable Medical Devices. The museum also hosts a **3D Cinema** and **Omnitheater** showing large-format IMAX films on a 70-foot-tall domed screen. The hours change frequently according to area school schedules, so be sure to call ahead.

Mississippi National River and Recreation Area

The National Park Service's Mississippi National River and Recreation Area possesses almost no land. Instead, they coordinate preservation, education, and recreation with various local agencies along a 72-mile stretch of the river between Anoka and Hastings. Their **Mississippi River Visitor Center** (651/293-0200, www.nps.gov/miss, 8 A.M.–4:30 P.M. Mon.–Fri., closed Sat.–Sun., free admission) at the Science Museum is the place to get information about recreational activities, historic sites, and events along the Mighty Mississippi (and there are a lot of them) and learn about the natural and cultural history of the entire river.

© BRUCE MANNING

The Science Museum of Minnesota is the state's most visited museum.

Minnesota Children's Museum

Kids can have a blast and learn something in the process at this museum (10 W. 7th St., 651/225-6000, www.mcm.org, 9 A.M.–5 P.M. Tues.–Thurs. and Sat.–Sun. plus summer Mon., 9 A.M.–8 P.M. Fri., $8.95) designed exclusively for them. Hands-on exhibits, aimed at toddlers to ten year olds, let kids make paper, shop in a market, and crawl through an anthill.

Jackson Street Roundhouse

The hodgepodge collection of railroad memorabilia at the Jackson Street Roundhouse (193 E. Pennsylvania Ave., 651/228-0263, www.mtmuseum.org, 10 A.M.–4 P.M. Wed. and Sat., $7 adults Wed., $10 adults Sat.) will excite rail fans. Housed in and around a 1907 steam locomotive maintenance shop are old rail cars, the original turntable, and various other bits of train memorabilia. Most interesting is the workshop where you can see engines in various states of repair and disassembly. Kids can take a ride on a miniature train.

Summit Brewing Company

Minnesota's favorite local brewery (910 Montreal Cir., 651/265-7800, www.summitbrewing.com, tours 1 P.M. Tues. and Thurs., 10:30 A.M. and 1 P.M. Sat., free) leads visitors through their small, modern bluff-top plant. At the end of the 45-minute tour you can sample what you've just watched them make. Reservations are required on Saturdays.

Parks

Harriet Island, a riverside park (no longer an island) across from downtown, hosts, among other things, an outdoor stage, restaurant, bed-and-breakfast, yacht club, and the Minnesota Centennial Showboat. It's also the home base of the **Padelford Packet Boat Company** (651/227-1100 or 800/543-3908, www.riverrides.com, noon and 2 P.M. daily summer, 2 P.M. Sat.–Sun. Sept., $16 adults), whose paddleboat sightseeing cruises run up the Mississippi to Fort Snelling. They also offer longer dining cruises, some of which pass through the locks.

Como Park is a 450-acre stretch of green surrounding Lake Como. The **Como Zoo** (651/487-8200, www.comozooconservatory.org, 10 A.M.–6 P.M. daily Apr.–Sept., 10 A.M.–4 P.M. daily rest of year, free admission) isn't the best of zoos, but most of the animals do have room to roam. The real gem of the park is the **Conservatory** (651/487-8200, www.comozooconservatory.org, 10 A.M.–6 P.M. daily Apr.–Sept., 10 A.M.–4 P.M. daily rest of year, $2 donation requested). The 100-foot-tall Palm Dome at the center of the massive greenhouse contains many palms, orchids, and other tropical foliage. A sunken garden and bonsai room are some of the displays branching off from the dome, while the lovely Como Ordway Japanese Garden sits outside. The 1914 **Cafesjian's Carousel** (1245 Midway Pkwy., 651/489-4628, www.ourfaircarousel.org, 11 A.M.–4 P.M. Tues.–Fri., 11 A.M.–6 P.M. Sat.–Sun. May–Labor Day, 11 A.M.–4 P.M. Sat.–Sun. Labor Day–Oct., also open Memorial Day and Labor Day, $1.50) is another popular attraction.

© BRUCE MANNING

Harriet Island Regional Park, along the Mississippi, is no longer an island.

Six large burial mounds, piled up some 2,000 years ago by the Hopewell peoples, sit on the highest point of the bluffs lining the river east of downtown. To get to **Indian Mounds Park** take 7th Street East to Mounds Boulevard and follow it south for about a mile and a quarter.

Everyone will likely find something they like at **Western Sculpture Park,** whether it's the giant picture frame or one of the other oversized statues residing across the freeway from the History Center.

NIGHTLIFE

There is no truth to the rumor that St. Paul has no nightlife, though this is one case where the capital envies Minneapolis.

Rock

A fancy country-and-western bar that opened at the end of World War II, the **Turf Club** (1601 University Ave., 651/647-0486, www.turfclub.net) took a chance and made a change to a rock format, letting up-and-coming bands play. The switch paid off and now even touring acts play on occasion.

Station 4 (2001 E. 4th St., 651/298-0173, www.station-4.com) in Lowertown is best known as the place to see heavy metal and hard rock bands.

Blues and Jazz

As popular as it has become, the **Minnesota Music Café** (499 Payne Ave., 651/776-4699, www.minnesotamusiccafe.com) still seems to be one of the Twin Cities' best-kept secrets. Great bands—usually blues or R&B—play seven nights a week and a large sunken dance floor ensures good viewing by all. The club's walls serve as a Minnesota music hall of fame.

Artists' Quarter (408 St. Peter St., 651/292-1359, www.artistsquarter.com), a downtown basement club with a movie-set-perfect ambience, features jams with local and touring acts six nights a week.

Folk

Have a craic with the best Irish bands and open jams at **The Liffey** (175 W. 7th St., 651/556-1420, www.theliffey.com), **Dubliner Pub** (2162 University Ave. W., 651/646-

5551, www.thedublinerpub.com), and **Half Time Rec** (1013 Front Ave., 651/488-8245, www.halftimerec.com). The classic main bar of the latter served as Slippery's in the movie *Grumpy Old Men,* and there's a bocce ball court in the basement. The original **Dunn Bros Coffee** (1569 Grand Ave., 651/699-2636), a relaxing space by Macalester College, has musicians nightly.

Dancing

Wild Onion (788 Grand Ave., 651/291-2525, www.wild-onion.net) is a casual bar and grill by day with a live DJ and small dance floor every night.

Crowds kick up their heels to the live big bands on Thursday (and occasionally Friday) "Swing Nights" at the **Wabasha Street Caves** (215 Wabasha St. S., 651/224-1191, www.wabashastreetcaves.com). The bands play 7–10 P.M., but if you are a neophyte come at 6:15 P.M. for a dance lesson.

Taps and Taverns

A game-day favorite is **Tom Reid's Hockey City Pub** (258 W. 7th St., 651/292-9916, www.tomreidshockeycitypub.com), owned by the current Wild color man.

O'Gara's (164 Snelling Ave. N., 651/644-3333, www.ogaras.com), a St. Paul institution, comes pretty close to being all things to all people. It's a neighborhood bar and grill with better-than-average pub grub and half a dozen of their own microbrewed beers, plus they host a variety of live bands in the adjoining wings. A young Charles Schulz lived upstairs.

Gay and Lesbian Bars and Clubs

The longest-running gay bar is the **Town House** (1415 University Ave. W., 651/646-7087, www.townhousebar.com), which, though it hosts karaoke, a piano bar, and a Thursday drag show, attracts a pretty mellow crowd.

Over the Rainbow (719 N. Dale St., 651/487-5070) is a simple neighborhood beer-and-shot joint with a dance floor upstairs and a mostly lesbian clientele.

ENTERTAINMENT AND EVENTS

Theater

The pageantry surrounding the **Ordway Center for the Performing Arts** (345 Washington St., 651/282-3000, www.ordway.org) begins with the liveried footmen greeting you at the lobby entrance and continues into the spectacular 1,900-seat Main Hall. They host everything from big-time Broadway and West End productions to children's puppet theater.

The beautiful **Fitzgerald Theater** (10 E. Exchange St., 651/290-1221, http://fitzgeraldtheater.publicradio.org) was one of the nation's premier theaters when completed in 1910 and is now best known as the sometimes home of Garrison Keillor's *A Prairie Home Companion* radio variety show. Advanced tickets to PHC are nearly impossible to come by (check www.prairiehome.org if you want to try), but you can always join the hopefuls out front for rush tickets ($15, cash only). It's best

The Fitzgerald Theater is the long-time home of the radio show *A Prairie Home Companion.*

© BRUCE MANNING

The Xcel Energy Center hosts Wild hockey games and other large events.

to be in line by at least noon to wait for the 4 P.M. sale, and you can only buy two.

The **Minnesota Centennial Showboat** (651/227-1100, http://showboat.umn.edu) is a 175-foot floating theater docked at Harriet Island. Plays are held year-round and crowds are encouraged to hiss the villain and cheer the hero at the summer melodramas produced by the U of M's theater department.

The **Great American History Theatre** (30 E. 10th St., 651/292-4323, www.historytheatre.com) makes the history of Minnesota and the Midwest exciting and entertaining.

The award-winning **Penumbra Theatre Company** (270 N. Kent St., 651/224-3180, www.penumbratheatre.org) is one of the nation's oldest and most respected African American theater companies. Two-time Pulitzer Prize winner August Wilson got his start here.

The **Park Square Theatre Company** (20 W. 7th Pl., 651/291-7005, www.parksquaretheatre.org) produces a classics repertoire and has a good reputation.

Classical Music

The **St. Paul Chamber Orchestra** (651/291-1144, www.thespco.org), founded in 1959, is the first and only full-time professional chamber orchestra in the United States and has been hailed as one of the world's best. They grace the stage at the Ordway and many other venues around the Twin Cities.

The Minnesota Opera (612/333-6669, www.mnopera.org) also puts on its lavish productions, both traditional and contemporary, at the Ordway.

Cinema

The **Grandview** (1830 Grand Ave., 651/698-3344, www.manntheatresmn.com) and the **Highland** (760 S. Cleveland Ave., 651/698-3085, www.manntheatresmn.com) are classic early 20th-century cinemas with the balconies converted into second screens.

The Science Museum's immense **Omnitheater** (120 W. Kellogg Blvd., 651/221-9444, www.smm.org) screens large-format IMAX films. Its convertible dome allows

© TRICIA CORNELL

The ice castle is the highlight of the St. Paul Winter Carnival, although it isn't built every year.

movies to be projected on a full-vision spherical screen or large flat screen when appropriate.

Spectator Sports

The National Hockey League's **Minnesota Wild** (http://wild.nhl.com) skate at the Xcel Energy Center. Tickets, starting at $15, can be bought in person at the box office or by phone through Ticketmaster (651/989-5151). The Wild have sold out every game since forming in 2000, though walk-up tickets are sometimes available on game day. Also playing at the "X" in the winter months are the **Minnesota Swarm** (www.mnswarm.com) of the National Lacrosse League. Tickets start at $12.

The **Saint Paul Saints** (www.saintsbaseball.com), part-owned by Mike Veeck (son of former White Sox owner Bill Veeck, "the greatest public relations man and promotional genius the game of baseball has ever seen") and Bill Murray (yep, that Bill Murray), play baseball in the American Association, an independent organization about the equivalent of AA minor-league ball. And all the special promotions, such as fireworks and theme nights (e.g., Star Trek, Disco, and Gilligan's Island) and the between-inning gimmicks, mean you don't need to enjoy baseball to enjoy a night at the ballpark. Home games are played in Midway Stadium. Tickets (651/644-6659) are no more than $10 and as little as $3, and you can usually buy them on game day.

Events

When a haughty New York City reporter claimed in 1885 that St. Paul was just "another Siberia, unfit for human habitation" in the winter, St. Paulites didn't protest with letters to the editor; they created the **St. Paul Winter Carnival** (www.winter-carnival.com) to prove him wrong. The 10-day festival, commencing the last Friday in January, features ice- and snow-carving competitions, parades, broomball tournaments, and softball on ice. Indoor activities include bonspiels, art exhibits, concerts, and a grand ball. Though the carnival is famous for its ice castles, they are built only occasionally. Another unique aspect is the reenacting of the festival's silly legend. Boreas (the King of Snows) battles Vulcanus Rex (the King of Fire) and his minions until spring ceremoniously triumphs over winter.

The **Minnesota State Fair** (www.mnstatefair.org) has everything other state agricultural fairs have—livestock shows, a carnival midway, washed-up rock stars on the grandstand, car races, and food on sticks—only a lot more of it than most; the 360-acre fairgrounds are the nation's largest. The Great Minnesota Get-Together runs for 12 days ending on Labor Day, and adult tickets cost $9.

St. Patrick's Day, Cinco de Mayo, and **Hmong New Year** are also large celebrations in St. Paul.

SHOPPING

Grand Avenue (www.grandave.com) is the city's most interesting shopping district. Most of the action is at the intersection of Grand and Victoria, but put on your walking shoes, because you've got two or three good miles of shopping to do. Although the occasional chain pops up (J. Crew has been here for years), mostly you'll find well-established, creative, local shops, like the delicious **Cooks of Crocus Hill** (877 Grand Ave., 651/228-1333, www.cooksofcrocushill.com, 10 A.M.–9 P.M. Mon.–Fri., 10 A.M.–7 P.M. Sat., noon–5 P.M. Sun.), a must for home cooks.

There are some quality antiques downtown along West 7th Street.

The covered open-air **St. Paul Farmers' Market** (290 5th St. E., 651/227-8101, 6 A.M.–1 P.M. Sat., 8 A.M.–1 P.M. Sun. Apr.–Nov. plus some winter Sats.) in Lowertown has been operating since 1853. Most days there is live music 9 A.M.–noon.

Minnesota's own hometown storyteller, Garrison Keillor owns **Common Good Books** (165 Western Ave. N., 651/225-8989, www.commongoodbooks.com, 10 A.M.–10 pm. Mon.–Sat., 10 A.M.–10 P.M. Sun.).

The Red Balloon Bookshop (891 Grand Ave., 651/224-8320, www.redballoonbookshop.com, 10 A.M.–8 P.M. Mon.–Fri., 9 A.M.–5 P.M. Sat., noon–5 P.M. Sun.) is a wonderful children's shop.

The Covington Inn is a floating bed-and-breakfast.

RECREATION

South of downtown it's mostly industrial, but the bluff-lined **Mississippi River** is quite beautiful to the west. It's a scenic trip by kayak or canoe, but you'll be sharing it with quite a few speedboats, which is why few people paddle it. Most active Twin Citians prefer to follow the river by bike, and paved trails follow both sides of the river all the way to Minneapolis. To make a really nice loop, head out from Harriet Island down to Fort Snelling and Minnehaha Park in Minneapolis, continue up the river, and return to downtown via Summit Avenue. It's about a 20-mile trip.

If you'd rather hike the river, go to **Crosby Regional Park** and the adjoining **Hidden Falls Regional Park,** which together have about seven miles of riverside trails. The 6.5 miles of hilly, wooded trails at **Battle Creek Regional Park,** half of them some pretty wild singletrack, offer some of the best mountain biking and cross-country skiing in the Twin Cities. The principal trailhead is off Winthrop Street by Afton Road.

The paved **Gateway State Trail** runs from Cayuga Street (not far from the capitol) to Pine Point County Park about four miles north of Stillwater. The scenery is urban for most of the route (punctuated by the **50-foot-tall snowman** along Highway 36 in North St. Paul), but eventually you escape to the countryside.

ACCOMMODATIONS

$50-100

You'll save money, especially on weekdays, by staying outside downtown.

The **Best Western Kelly Inn** (161 St. Anthony Ave., 651/227-8711 or 800/528-1234, www.bestwesternstpaul.com, $99) is out on the edge of downtown, but still within walking distance. You get an exercise room, sauna, whirlpool, and a rather large swimming pool, along with decent rooms and free parking.

The **Days Inn** (1964 University Ave. W., 651/645-8681 or 800/329-7466, $59) sits between St. Paul and Minneapolis and is just a couple blocks from the Amtrak station. Rooms are up-to-date, and there's a pool, whirlpool, and sauna.

Best Western Bandana Square (1010 Bandana Sq., 651/647-1637, www.bestwestern-minnesota.com, $89) is also equally convenient to the two downtowns. It shares a building with the **Twin Cities Model Railroad Museum** (651/647-9628, www.tcmrm.org). Even if you don't have the time to visit the museum, the old train tracks and the small exhibit in the lobby will amuse the little ones.

$100-150

Built in 1910 by the same people behind New York City's Grand Central Station, **The Saint Paul Hotel** (350 Market St., 651/292-9292 or 800/292-9292, www.stpaulhotel.com, $209) has no equal in the state for elegance. Rooms come with all the expected amenities and then some, plus high tea is served in the lobby under crystal chandeliers. There is a decent-sized fitness center up on the 12th floor with motivational views.

Also downtown, every room at the **Embassy**

© BRUCE MANNING

The Saint Paul Hotel is among the oldest and most elegant in Minnesota.

Suites (175 10th St. E., 651/224-5400 or 800/362-2779, www.embassystpaul.com, $139) is a two-room suite and faces the impressive palm-filled atrium, home to a family of ducks. Facilities include a pool, whirlpool, and exercise room. It is a very good value.

The **Holiday Inn** (175 7th St. W., 651/225-1515 or 800/465-4329, $112) sits right across the street from Xcel Energy Center and next to the area's bars and restaurants. There's a pool, whirlpool, and fitness center.

St. Paul's largest hotel, the **Crowne Plaza** (11 Kellogg Blvd. E., 651/292-1900 or 800/227-6963, $106), has 479 rooms, plus a fitness center, pool, and whirlpool.

The most unusual lodging in the city is the **Covington Inn** (100 Harriet Island Rd., 651/292-1411, www.covingtoninn.com, $140–200), a floating bed-and-breakfast docked at Harriet Island. The former towboat's four nautically themed rooms each have a private bath.

FOOD

African

Barbary Fig (720 Grand Ave., 651/290-2085, lunch 11 A.M.–2 P.M. Mon.–Sat., dinner 5:30–9 P.M. daily, $8–14) has a short menu of couscous, lentils, lamb, and other Algerian delights.

Kenkayba's Place (864 University Ave., 651/762-9451, lunch Tues.–Sun., dinner Mon.–Sat., $7–13) has a big menu of Ghanaian dishes, including many vegetarian choices such as peanut soup, and the delightful cook will gladly explain all the options to you—and even whip up some that didn't make the menu if she has time. They also serve soul food standards.

American Casual

Café Latte (850 Grand Ave., 651/224-5687, www.cafelatte.com, 9 A.M.–10 P.M. Sun.–Wed., 9 A.M.–11 P.M. Thurs., 9 A.M.–midnight, Fri.–Sat., $3–10) is a gourmet cafeteria and sweet shop, rightly the busiest restaurant on Grand Avenue. There's a separate pizza/wine bar in back, and high tea is served noon to 5 P.M. daily. Don't let the long lines scare you off; they move fast.

Worth a visit as much for the food and outdoor patio as their award-winning microbrewed beers, **Great Waters** (426 St. Peter St., 651/224-2739, www.greatwatersbc.com, 11 A.M.–2 A.M. daily, $6–24) has burgers and other pub food, but more typical menu items include a grilled portobello sandwich, penne arrabiata, jambalaya, and grilled duck breast. Some of these choices come infused with the house brews, as do their house mustards.

Tavern on Grand (656 Grand Ave., 651/228-9030, www.tavernongrand.com, 11 A.M.–10 P.M. Sun.–Thurs., appetizers available until midnight, 11 A.M.–midnight Fri.–Sat., $5–22) is a friendly neighborhood bar and grill with a Northwoods theme; they're rightly famous for their walleye.

Mickey's Diner (36 W. 7th St., 651/222-5633, open 24/7, $3–11) serves classic stick-to-your-ribs meals in a 1937 art deco dining car, one of just two listed on the National Register of Historic Places.

For an authentic New York–style Jewish delicatessen you'll have to head out to **Cecil's** (651 S. Cleveland Ave., 651/698-0334, www.cecilsdeli.com, 9 A.M.–8 P.M. daily, $4–13), a Highland Park institution since 1949.

American Upscale

W. A. Frost & Co. (374 Selby Ave., 651/224-5715, www.wafrost.com, lunch 11:15 A.M.–1:30 P.M. Mon.–Sat., 10:30 A.M.–2 P.M. Sun., dinner 5–10 P.M. Mon.–Thurs. and Sun., 5–11 P.M. Fri.–Sat., $18–38) fills a restored 1889 building and has been a St. Paul landmark since 1975. Dine on grilled red snapper or nibble on something from the cheese list in front of three fireplaces in the romantic dining room, at the historic and cozy bar, or on the huge, leafy patio. The liquor list is as impressive as the scenery.

You'll feel like a real mover and shaker when you sit down at **The St. Paul Grill** (350 Market St., 651/224-7455, www.stpaulgrill.com, 11 A.M.–10 P.M. Mon.–Fri., 11 A.M.–11 P.M.

© BRUCE MANNING

Open 24 hours a day, 365 days a year, Mickey's Diner is a favorite in downtown St. Paul.

Sat., 10:30 A.M.–10 P.M. Sun., $16–55), and many of your fellow diners probably are. The perfect companion to the posh Saint Paul Hotel in which it resides, the menu offers simple but superb delights such as pan-fried walleye and highly recommended steaks. The bar has the absolute best in scotch, bourbon, and vodka, not to mention an award-winning wine list. It's a popular spot for pre-theater dinners and Sunday brunch.

The venerable **Lexington** (1096 Grand Ave., 651/222-5878, www.the-lexington.com, 11 A.M.–10 P.M. Mon.–Thurs., 11 A.M.–11 P.M. Fri.–Sat., 10 A.M.–9 P.M. Sun., $16–37) served its first steak when prohibition was repealed and, with the white linens and chandeliers, it maintains a bit of an aura from that era. The menu has hot turkey dinners, walleye almondine, lamb chops, and other classics, and Sunday brunch is very popular.

The menu changes nightly at **Heartland** (1806 St. Clair Ave., St. Paul, 651/699-3536, www.heartlandrestaurant.com, 5:30–9:30 P.M. Tues.–Sun., closed Mon., $18–25), beloved by Twin Cities locavores. Two prix fixe menus—one vegetarian—are available each night.

Asian

You really can't go wrong with any of the many family-owned Vietnamese restaurants along University Avenue in St. Paul, though **Mai Village** (394 University Ave. W., 651/290-2585, 11 A.M.–9 P.M. Mon.–Thurs., 11 A.M.–10 P.M. Fri.–Sat., noon–8 P.M. Sun., $6–29) is a good choice, and not just because of the stunning dining room. If you've got a serious appetite try the Bo 7 Mon, their $17 seven-course beef dinner.

Two casual spots with sure-fire sushi are found downtown: **Sakura** (350 St. Peter St., 651/224-0185, www.sakurastpaul.com, lunch 11:30 A.M.–2:30 P.M. Mon.–Sat., noon–2:30 P.M. Sun., dinner 5–10:30 P.M. Mon.–Thurs., 5–11 P.M. Fri.–Sat., 4–9:30 P.M. Sun., $4–19) and **Fuji Ya** (465 Wabasha St. N., 651/310-0111, lunch Mon.–Fri., dinner daily, $4–22).

Tanpopo Noodle Shop (308 Prince

St. N., 651/209-6527, www.tanpoporestaurant.com, lunch 11 A.M.–2 P.M. Tues.–Fri., dinner 5:30–9 P.M. Mon.–Thurs., 5:30–10 P.M. Fri.–Sat., closed Sun., $6–11) serves Japanese comfort food: big bowls of rich broth, fat chewy noodles, enormous golden tempura shrimp. The serene atmosphere and spare decor are at least as comforting as the food.

A cross between northern Indian and Chinese, the Nepali and Tibetan cuisine at **Everest on Grand** (1278 Grand Ave., 651/696-1666, www.hotmomo.com, lunch 11:30 A.M.–2:30 P.M. and dinner 5–9 P.M. Mon.–Thurs., 11:30 A.M.–10 P.M. Fri.–Sat., 11:30 A.M.–9 P.M. Sun., $5–15) is based on lots of ghee and very mild spices. *Momos,* Tibetan dumplings served either steamed or fried, are the highlight of the menu and reason enough to come. The curries, *pakoras* (batter-fried vegetables), and samosas will feel like milder versions of familiar Indian favorites.

Bakeries and Coffeshops

The coffee shop of choice for hip Lowertown artists, the **Black Dog** (308 Prince St., 651/228-9274, www.blackdogstpaul.com, 7 A.M.–10 P.M. Mon.–Thurs., 7 A.M.–11 P.M. Fri., 7 A.M.–9 P.M. Sat., 8 A.M.–8 P.M. Sun., $4–11) has paintings on the wall, entertainment on stage, and good coffee and wine behind the counter. You can build your own sandwiches and pizza too.

With big chairs, board games, and jazz music, **Amore Coffee** (917 Grand Ave., 651/222-6770, www.amorecoffee.com, 6:30 A.M.–9 P.M. Mon.–Thurs., 6:30 A.M.–10 P.M. Fri.–Sat., 7:30 A.M.–9 P.M. Sun.) invites you to kick back and stay a while.

Ice Cream

The ice cream at **Grand Ole Creamery** (750 Grand Ave., 651/293-1655, www.grandolecreamery.com, 11:30 A.M.–11 P.M. Sun.–Thurs., 11:30 A.M.–midnight Fri.–Sat.) available in nearly 200 flavors, is so good there are sometimes lines down the sidewalk, even in January. Their creamy art is on many other restaurants' dessert lists.

Their St. Paul rival is **Izzy's Ice Cream Café** (2034 Marshall Ave., 651/603-1458, www.izzysicecream.com, 11 A.M.–10 P.M. Sun.–Thurs., 11 A.M.–10:30 P.M. Fri.–Sat.). Their signature is the "Izzy scoop," a melon ball–sized bonus. You could, for example, get a scoop of Norwegian chai with an Izzy scoop of dark chocolate zin.

Italian

Cossetta Italian Market (211 W. 7th St., 651/222-3476, 11 A.M.–9 P.M. Sun.–Thurs., 11 A.M.–10 P.M. Fri.–Sat., $3–9) opened as a grocery in 1911 and has expanded into the most popular Italian eatery in the city. Pizza, pasta, and hero sandwiches are served cafeteria style, and though it may look a little chaotic during the lunch rush, but don't be discouraged; the line moves plenty fast.

With its swank dining room and sometimes-whimsical ingredients, **Pazzaluna** (360 St. Peter St., 651/223-7000, www.pazzaluna.com, 5:30–10 P.M. Mon.–Thurs., 5:30–11 P.M. Fri.–Sat., 5:30–9 P.M. Sun.) is kind of Cossetta's evil twin, except that the food is also really good.

Winner of the You Can't Judge a Book by Its Cover award goes to Highland Park's **Ristorante Luci** (470 S. Cleveland Ave., 651/699-8258, www.ristoranteluci.com, 5–9 P.M. Tues.–Sat., $15–30). There aren't many restaurants where you can come in jeans and a T-shirt and order a $2,000 bottle of wine, but despite years as a nationally known kitchen Luci has not turned its back on its neighborhood roots. Like a real Italian trattoria, this fancy but unpretentious (they've got white linens, but never replaced the Pabst Beer sign from the building's previous incarnation) restaurant puts the emphasis on the food. If you want the elegant decor that usually comes with prices this high, just cross the street to **Luci Ancora** (2060 Randolph Ave., 651/698-6889, lunch 11:30 A.M.–2 P.M. Tues.–Fri., dinner 5:30–9 P.M. Sun.–Thurs., 5:30–10 P.M.

Fri.–Sat., $15–30), which takes a more creative turn in the kitchen.

Mexican

St. Paulites in the know head to the cafeteria in **El Burrito Mercado** (175 Cesar Chavez St., 651/227-2192, www.elburritomercado.com, 7 A.M.–9 P.M. daily, $2–7) grocery store for their Mexican fix. It's all simple but scrumptious.

The Frias family has been serving up class Mexican-American cuisine at **Boca Chica** (11 Cesar Chavez St., 651/222-8499, www.bocachicarestaurant.com, 11 A.M.–9 P.M. Mon., 11 A.M.–10 P.M. Tues.–Thurs., 11 A.M.–11 P.M. Fri.–Sat., 10 A.M.–9 P.M. Sun., $5–13) since 1964: flour and corn tacos, chiles rellenos, tamales, flautas, and tostados. Come hungry for the generous, filling lunchtime buffet.

Middle Eastern

Friendly **Babani's** (544 St. Peter St., 651/602-9964, 11 A.M.–9 P.M. Mon.–Thurs., 11 A.M.–10 P.M. Fri., 1–10 P.M. Sat., 3–9 P.M. Sun., $7–10) claims to be the first Kurdish restaurant in the nation, and, as improbable as it seems, they've made this out-of-the-way downtown location work since 1997. There is no need to be timid since everything is explained on the menu, and vegetarians have plenty of choices.

For some mighty tasty Afghan flavors there's **Khyber Pass** (1571 Grand Ave., 651/690-0505, www.khyberpasscafe.com, 11 A.M.–9 P.M. Mon.–Thurs. 11 A.M.–10 P.M. Fri.–Sat., closed Sun., $10–21).

Other European

Moscow on the Hill (371 Selby Ave., 651/291-1236, www.moscowonthehill.com, lunch 11 A.M.–2 P.M. Mon.–Fri., dinner 5:30–10 P.M. Mon.–Thurs., 5:30–11 P.M. Fri., 4–11 P.M. Sat., 4–10 P.M. Sun., $12–29) has Russian delicacies from across the empire, such as *pelmini, blini,* and *vareniki.* And lots of vodka, of course. The setting is beautiful, and the service is attentive.

Forepaugh's (276 S. Exchange St., 651/224-5606, www.forepaughs.com, lunch 11:30 A.M.–2 P.M. Mon.–Fri., dinner 5:30–9:30 P.M. daily, brunch 10:30 A.M.–1:30 P.M., $8–30), occupying an opulent 1872 Victorian mansion, offers a memorable dining experience. The service is impeccable, and for what you get (and where you get it), it's very reasonably priced.

A good dose of bonhomie and some of the best French food in Minnesota are what you'll find at **Meritage** (410 St. Peter St., 651/222-5670, www.meritage-stpaul.com, lunch 11 A.M.–2 P.M. Tues.–Fri., 10 A.M.–2 P.M. Sat.–Sun., dinner 5–9 P.M. Tues.–Thurs. and Sun., 5–11 P.M. Fri.–Sat., $18–29). From the two-bite appetizers to the proper starters (don't miss the baby beet salad) and the entrées (steak frites, roast chicken, sole Grenobloise), straight through to the marble-topped cheese cart, this is serious fine dining that doesn't take itself too seriously.

The Liffey (175 W. 7th St., 651/556-1420, www.theliffey.com, 6:30 A.M.–10 P.M. daily, appetizers until midnight, $9–17) is an Irish pub straight out of Dublin—literally, in fact, since the etched glass and dark wood were crafted on the island. Irish-born entrées include fish and chips, corned beef and cabbage, and shepherd's pie. Live bands play on weekends.

The **Acropol Inn** (748 Grand Ave., 651/298-0151, 11 A.M.–9 P.M. Mon.–Thurs., 11 A.M.–10 P.M. Fri.–Sat., closed Sun., $8–35), a classy landmark, has been getting rave reviews for their lamb shank, *papoutsaki, mousaka,* and breaded scallops for decades.

Pizza

Ask around about the best pizza in St. Paul and a majority of people will direct you to **Red's Savoy** (421 E. 7th St., 651/227-1437, 11 A.M.–10 P.M. Sun.–Thurs., 11 A.M.–midnight Fri.–Sat., $4–15), which, with red vinyl seats and an aquarium, is as classy as a hole-in-the-wall can be; the cheese-laden thin-crust pizzas really are good. They recently opened an outlet in Uptown (2329 Hennepin Ave. S., 612/377-3110, 11 A.M.–11 P.M. Mon.–Thurs., 11 A.M.–3 P.M. Fri.–Sat., noon–11 P.M. Sun.).

For a true Italian experience visit **Punch Neapolitan Pizza** (704 S. Cleveland Ave., 651/696-1066, www.punchpizza.com, 11 A.M.–9:30 P.M. Sun.–Thurs., 11 A.M.–10 P.M. Fri.–Sat., closed Mon., $8–13) in Highland Park, where they follow the rules of Vera Pizza Napoletana, a group of Naples pizzeria owners "dedicated to preservation of Neapolitan pizza." The flaky, wood-fired, brick oven–singed crust is topped with imported San Marzano tomatoes and fresh mozzarella. They are a little less conservative with the toppings, which include such options as arugula, cracked red pepper, and roasted eggplant. This, the original Punch Pizza, has table service, unlike the equally great location in Minneapolis (3226 Lake St. W., 612/929-0006, 11 A.M.–10 P.M. daily), where the prices are a little lower.

Steakhouses

The Strip Club (378 Maria Ave., 651/793-6247, www.domeats.com, lunch 11 A.M.–2 P.M. Tues.–Fri., brunch 9 A.M.–2 P.M. Sat.–Sun., dinner 4–10 P.M. Tues.–Thurs. and Sun., 4–11 P.M. Fri., 5–11 P.M. Sat., $14–35) serves up titillation of an entirely different sort: New York strip, filet, ribs—all of it local and grass fed. Pick your own sauce, from blue cheese to ginger and scallions. And those who want something more than a slab of meat on their plate can also put together a satisfying dinner from the long and innovative list of small plates, including catfish fries and walleye fritters.

Mancini's Char House (531 W. 7th St., 651/224-7345, www.mancinis.com, 4:30–10 P.M. Sun.–Thurs., 4:20–11 P.M. Fri.–Sat., $15–38) is *the* St. Paul steak house and has been since 1954. The dim lights and red vinyl booths transport you back to the set of a mobster movie in the heyday of Vegas.

INFORMATION AND SERVICES

Tourist Information

St. Paul tourism brochures are available at the Landmark Center, Science Museum, Children's Museum, Minnesota History Center, and the Capitol. You can also have any and all questions answered by the **St. Paul Convention and Visitors Bureau** (175 W. Kellogg Blvd., Ste. 502, 651/265-4900 or 800/627-6101, www.visitsaintpaul.com, 8 A.M.–5 P.M. Mon.–Fri., closed Sat.–Sun.).

Post Office

The city's main post office (180 Kellogg Blvd. E., 651/293-6034, 8:30 A.M.–5:30 P.M. Mon.–Fri., 9 A.M.–noon Sat., closed Sun.) is downtown.

Internet Access

If you show any library card you can get Internet access at the **St. Paul Public Library** (90 W. 4th St., 651/266-7000, www.sppl.org). Most **Dunn Bros Coffee** (www.dunnbros.com) locations, including the one downtown (367 Wabasha St., 651/767-0567) have free computers for customer use.

Car Rentals

You can rent a car from **Avis** (411 Minnesota St., 651/917-9955 or 800/331-1212), **Budget** (166 E. 7th St., 612/222-8562 or 800/527-0700), and **Enterprise** (395 E. 7th St., 651/225-9766 or 800/261-7331), all located downtown, or **Hertz** (730 Transfer Rd., 651/646-1702 or 800/654-3131) at the Amtrak station.

Metro South

Depending on your viewpoint, the towns below Minneapolis are the best or worst of suburbia. While you'll find street after street of strip malls, the area also holds some of the region's most popular attractions. In contrast to the amusement parks, malls, and casinos are some excellent historic sites, a traditional Japanese garden, and a 14,000-acre National Wildlife Refuge. With so much to offer it's not surprising that the southern suburbs are extremely popular places with locals and tourists alike.

THE MALL OF AMERICA

The Mall of America (60 Broadway E., Bloomington, 952/883-8800, www.mallofamerica.com, 10 A.M.–9:30 P.M. Mon.–Sat., 11 A.M.–7 P.M. Sun., opens at 9:30 A.M. Sat. in summer) is big. Really big. It could hold seven Yankee Stadiums, 32 Boeing 747s, or 24,336 school buses. It has its own zip code. You get the idea. It is also wildly popular. Not only do the more than one million annual visitors (more than Disney World, Graceland, and the Grand Canyon combined) make it far and away the most popular destination in Minnesota, it is, by some accounts, the third most popular tourist destination in America. Some people, particularly British, Scandinavian, and Japanese visitors, even come to Minnesota on package holidays just to shop the mall. The megamall is not just the largest shopping center in the United States; with a bank, post office, college campus, Chapel of Love (that's right, thousands of people have tied the knot here—call 800/299-5683 to be the next newlyweds), day care, and a church, it is almost like a city unto itself.

Some of the restaurants and attractions open earlier and close later than the mall hours given. Mall walkers are let in at 7 A.M. Grab a map the moment you get here; you'll need it.

For the lowdown on the mall stop by one of the **Guest Service Centers,** positioned at each of the main entrances on Level 1. Statewide tourism information is available at the **Explore Minnesota USA** store (N128; 952/854-8257). You can change many foreign currencies at **Highland Bank** (W322).

The **Hiawatha Line** light rail runs to downtown Minneapolis and the airport while express buses connect to downtown St. Paul.

Underwater Adventures

Over 4,500 sea creatures live beneath the Mall of America at Underwater Adventures (952/883-0202 or 888/348-3846, www.underwaterworld.com, 10 A.M.–8 P.M. Mon.–Thurs., 9:30 A.M.–8:30 P.M. Fri.–Sat., 10 A.M.–7 P.M. Sun., $15 adults). A tunnel through the 1.2 million gallons of aquarium displays lets you get eye to eye with denizens of Minnesota's deep such as sturgeon, alligator gar, and some enormous catfish, and ocean dwellers such as sharks, rays, moray eels, barracuda, and sea turtles. You'll also find touch ponds with sharks and stingrays, a virtual submarine ride, a pirate-ship playground, and can watch K.G. the octopus open a jar to get his meals. Certified scuba divers can swim with the sharks for $186: Tanks and weights are provided.

Other Sights

The Park at MOA (952/883-8600, 10 A.M.–9:30 P.M. Mon.–Thurs., 10 A.M.–10 P.M. Fri.–Sat., 10:30 A.M.–7:30 P.M. Sun.), the mall's 7.5-acre centerpiece, is the largest indoor theme park in the nation. The 20 rides include a roller coaster, seven-story Ferris wheel, log chute, bumper cars, and several kiddie rides. Other attractions include a climbing wall, arcade, and the X-treme trampoline. You can buy individual ride tickets or get a $25 wristband for unlimited thrills.

Part store, part art gallery, and part workshop, the **LEGO Imagination Center** (S164, 952/858-8949, 10 A.M.–9:30 P.M. Mon.–Sat., 11 A.M.–7 P.M. Sun., opens at 9:30 A.M. Sat. in summer, free admission) delights people of all ages and is one of the mall's must-sees.

Entertainment

Most of the 4th-floor bars and other diversions that once composed the Upper East Side Entertainment District have closed (and it's uncertain what will be replacing them), but the 14-screen movie theater is still there. You can fly an F/A-18 Hornet or P-51 Mustang at **A.C.E.S. Flight Simulation** (E340, 952/920-3519) or make a nonstop left turn at **NASCAR Silicon Motor Speedway** (S352, 952/854-7700).

Shopping

Ironically, the least interesting part of the Mall of America experience is the shopping, which stands out more for quantity than quality. That's not to say that you won't find something interesting; with 520-plus stores to browse it's sure to happen. Choices range from the anchor department stores Bloomingdale's, Macy's, Nordstrom, and Sears to specialty stores with stocks limited to nothing but magnets or belt buckles. The MOA became an even more beloved destination for young girls when American Girl Place, with a shop, café, doll hair salon, and birthday party rooms, opened in 2009.

Love From Minnesota (W380), **Minnesotah!** (E157 and N316), and **Minnesota Bound** (E132) all have various North Star State souvenirs. For a more far-flung cultural flavor there's **Sanrio** (N316) and **European Gifts** (W387).

Accommodations

Both the **Country Inn** (2221 Killebrew Dr., 952/854-5555 or 800/456-4000, $135) and **Days Inn** (1901 Killebrew Dr., 952/854-8400 or 800/329-7466, $73) are right across the street from the mall. The Days Inn's recreation area has a large pool, whirlpool, sauna, and video games. The Country Inn has two small pools, two whirlpools, and exercise equipment. While the former is a bit nicer, the latter is a better value. Both have free airport and mall shuttles.

Food

While most of the more than 50 restaurants are exactly the generic sort you would expect to find in a mall, there are a few tasty alternatives such as the southwestern-style burritos at **Baja Tortilla Grill** (S392), the award-winning ribs at **Famous Dave's Barbeque** (S320), and the sweet and savory wraps at **The Magic Pan Crepe Stand** (W114).

On the fancy end are a pair of formal restaurant chains operated by the same company; both specialize in California cuisine. The menu at the **Napa Valley Grille** (W220, 952/858-9934, daily, lunch $12, dinner $20) changes every other month or so, but almond-crusted walleye and beef rigatoni are typical. The **California Café** (S368, 952/854-2233, daily, lunch $12, dinner $20) has a broader menu running from wood-fired pizzas to beef satay.

BLOOMINGTON

Bloomington (pop. 85,000) is Minnesota's fifth-largest city and, as home to Mall of America, has made the Twin Cities' rivalry into a bit of a three-way affair. Despite the prevailing wisdom, the area is not all tills and thrills.

Sights and Recreation

Just seven miles west of Mall of America, but a whole world away, is the **Normandale Japanese Gardens** (9700 France Ave. S., 952/487-8145, www.normandale.edu/japanese-garden, sunrise to sunset daily, free admission). Islands, bridges, a waterfall, and meticulously manicured trees are positioned around a pond at the center of the two-acre site. Created and overseen by a garden architect from Tokyo, it follows traditional design elements, though most plants are heartier varieties that can withstand Minnesota winters.

Bloomington's 1,000-acre **Hyland Lake Park Reserve** (763/694-7687, www.threeriversparks.org) also has trails for biking, hiking, and cross-country skiing (4.5 km are lighted at night), but it is best known for the **Hyland Ski & Snowboard Area** (763/694-7800), with 14 short runs. You might see members of the Minnesota Ski Club flying off the 70-meter jump.

One of just four urban national wildlife

refuges in the country, the **Minnesota Valley National Wildlife Refuge** is a surprisingly wild place. The 14,000-acre preserve stretches 34 miles from Fort Snelling State Park upstream along the Minnesota River to Jordan. Despite the adjacent development, the myriad habitats are home to abundant animals, ranging from river otter to prairie skink, though the birds are most notable—the 120 or so nesting species include bald eagle, peregrine falcon, wild turkey, and scarlet tanager. The visitors center (3815 American Blvd. E., 952/854-5900, 9 A.M.–5 P.M. Tues.–Sun., free admission), which can give you the lowdown on hiking and wildlife-watching opportunities in the many units, is a mile east of Mall of America. The center also has an art gallery, interpretive exhibits, and free snowshoe rental.

Stevie Ray's Comedy Cabaret (7800 Normandale Blvd., 612/825-1832, www.stevierays.org, 8 P.M. Fri. and Sat., $15) at the Sheraton Hotel offers two nights of audience-led improv each weekend.

Accommodations

There are hotels next to Mall of America, but both the cheapest and the poshest lodgings in the area are down the freeway a bit.

The **Microtel Inn** (801 E. 78th St., 952/854-6600 or 800/771-7171, www.microtel.com, $48) has tiny rooms and a fitness center, plus a free airport and Mall of America shuttle.

At the other end of the spectrum is the **Hotel Sofitel** (5601 W. 78th St., 952/835-1900 or 800/763-4835, www.sofitel.com $80), where rooms have all the bells and whistles. It has a good fitness center and a pair of French restaurants.

The ☾ **Grand Lodge** (1700 E. American Blvd., 952/854-8700 or 866/472-6356, www.grandlodgeminnesota.com, $139), just minutes from the mall, surrounds the **Water Park of America** (952/698-8888, www.waterparkofamerica.com). The country's largest indoor water park has a wave pool, surf rider, water slides, and more, while hotel facilities include a fitness center, spa, shuttle service, and underground heated parking. All of the 403 rooms can sleep six (some more comfortably than others), so they are ideal for families.

Food

Despite being hidden away in a business park, **Da Afghan** (929 American Blvd. W., 952/888-5824, www.daafghan.com, lunch 11 A.M.–2:30 P.M. Thurs.–Fri., dinner 5–10 P.M.

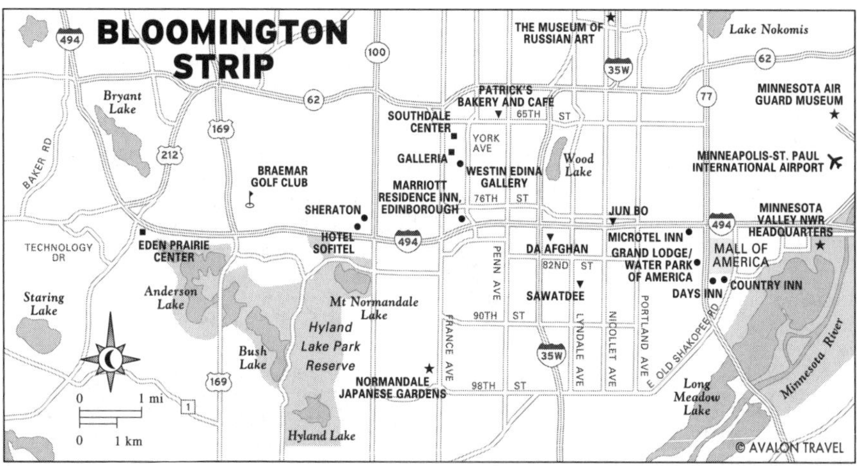

Tues.–Sat., 5–9 P.M. Sun., $8–15) has garnered a loyal following thanks to fantastic food, friendly service, and flavors you just can't find anywhere else. The lunch buffet ($7.95) is especially popular.

The unlikely **Jun Bo** (7717 Nicollet Ave., 612/866-6888, www.jun-bo.com, 11 A.M.–11 P.M. Mon.–Fri., 10 A.M.–11 P.M. Sat.–Sun., $6–16) serves some of the best authentic Chinese food in Minnesota, from dim sum (available all day every day) to Chinese hotpot.

For a taste of Thai, try the Bloomington branch of Minneapolis's popular **Sawatdee** (8501 Lyndale Ave. S., 952/888-7177, www.sawatdee.com, 11 A.M.–9 P.M. Sun.–Thurs., 11 A.M.–10 P.M. Fri.–Sat., $9–19).

SHAKOPEE

Somehow, the farm town of Shakopee ended up with the highest concentration of attractions in the state.

With over 75 rides, six roller coasters, and a water park, Shakopee's **Valleyfair** (1 Valley Fair Dr., 952/445-7600 or 800/386-7433, www.valleyfair.com, mid-May through Labor Day and weekends in Sept., $39 unlimited rides) is the biggest amusement park around. Also on the grounds is an IMAX theater and Challenge Park, with mini-golf and bumper boats.

Not far from Minnesota's largest amusement park is its largest "Amaizement Park." Each fall **Sever's Corn Maze** (next to Canterbury Park, 952/974-5000, www.severscornmaze.com, 11 A.M.–6 P.M. daily Sept.–Oct., $11) cuts miles of paths through a cornfield. Getting lost is fun enough, but live music, an exotic petting farm, pig races, and a hay-bale maze for the little ones lets you make an afternoon out of it. The maze is wheelchair accessible.

Just upriver from Valleyfair is **The Landing** (2187 E. Hwy. 101, 952/445-6901, www.threeriversparks.org, 10 A.M.–4 P.M. Mon.–Fri., 10 A.M.–5 P.M. Sat., noon–5 P.M. Sun. Apr.–Oct., 10 A.M.–4 P.M. Mon.–Sat., 11 A.M.–4 P.M. Sun. Nov., 10 A.M.–4 P.M. Sat., 11 A.M.–4 P.M. Sun. Dec., $8.50 adults summer weekends, $3 other days, $5 with guided tour), a 19th-century living-history museum spread out over 88 riverside acres. Nearly 40 restored and authentically furnished buildings are laid out in chronological order, from an 1844 fur-trading post to the 1893 town hall. Other structures you'll find in between

SHAKOPEE-MDEWAKANTON RESERVATION

- Total Area: 1 sq. mile
- Tribally Owned: 100 percent
- Total Population: 338 (in 2000)
- Native Population: 214
- Tribal Enrollment: 360

In the 1880s, a few of the Dakota who had been exiled from Minnesota after the 1862 Dakota Conflict began to return to their homelands near the upper reaches of the Minnesota River. In recognition of their ancestry the U.S. Government began purchasing land for them at this time, but when reservations were reestablished in the 1930s, the Shakopee band, with just a handful of families, was considered too small, and they were lumped in with the Lower Sioux. The tribe didn't earn official recognition until 1969. Their Mystic Lake casino, the second most successful Native American gaming enterprise in the nation by some estimates, lies just 25 miles from downtown Minneapolis and has made the Shakopee by far the wealthiest tribe in the state. While most of the thousands of daily players go home with lighter wallets, the tribe itself has hit the jackpot, and reportedly, most members are now millionaires. The community has made a significant charitable push, donating more than $75 million between 1997 and 2006 to both Native American and non-Native causes. While the reservation itself is just 250 acres, the tribe owns more than 2,800 acres in the area.

© TRICIA CORNELL

The Landing re-creates a settlement in 19th-century Minnesota.

include a general store, blacksmith shop, one-room schoolhouse, and homes representing different ethnic groups—Irish, German, Norwegian, and English to name a few. On weekends, costumed interpreters share their particular culture or demonstrate bygone skills like spinning yarn, making horseshoes, and baking bread—you can often try them yourself. It reopens in December for Folkways of the Holidays, a celebration of Christmases of various nationalities. Several 2,000-year-old Native American burial mounds lie at The Landing and next to it at **Veterans Memorial Park.**

In downtown Shakopee is the **Stans Historical Museum** (235 Fuller St. S., 952/445-0378, www.scottcountyhistory.org, 9 A.M.–4 P.M. Tues.–Wed. and Fri., 9 A.M.–8 P.M. Thurs., 10 A.M.–3 P.M. Sat., closed Sun.–Mon., $4 adults), which revolves around native son Maurice Stans. He served in several high government positions, including Secretary of Commerce under President Nixon, before being named finance chair of Nixon's Committee to Re-elect the President (CREEP) in 1972. The displays paint a rosy, hometown-proud picture of his Watergate shame. Much more interesting is Stans's African art collection, which spans the continent and was gathered during 19 visits. Next door is the house where Stans was born. No original furnishings remain, but Maurice himself restored the ground floor to the way he remembered it as a child.

It's far from the excess and glitter of Las Vegas, but Prior Lake's **Mystic Lake** (2400 Mystic Lake Blvd. NW, 952/445-9000 or 800/262-7799, www.mysticlake.com) is one of the largest casinos between Sin City and Atlantic City. The **Shakopee Mdewakanton Sioux Community Powwow** is held near here in late August. Gamblers can also play poker, the ponies, or the slots just up the road at **Canterbury Park** (1100 Canterbury Rd., Shakopee, 952/445-7223, www.canterbury-park.com).

The hundreds of knights, knaves, minstrels, and jesters frolicking around the 16th-century village that is the **Minnesota Renaissance Festival** (952/445-7361, www.renaissancefest.com, weekends mid-Aug.–Sept., $19.95

adults) guarantee a good time for all. There is lots of food to eat, crafts to buy, and people to watch between the jousting matches. The **Trail of Terror** ($15 adults), held weekend evenings during October on the Renaissance Festival grounds, has a trail of terror maze, haunted hay rides, and live music.

APPLE VALLEY

The sleepy berg of Apple Valley (pop. 50,000) is a growing commuting suburb full of cul-de-sacs. But it's also far enough from the central cities to have plenty of green space.

The **Minnesota Zoo** (952/431-9200, www.mnzoo.org, 9 A.M.–4 P.M. daily, until 6 P.M. during summer and weekends in May and Sept., $13 adults, $5 parking), in Apple Valley, is one of the nation's best. Over 2,100 animals from six continents live on the 500-acre compound, and a genuine effort is made to mimic their natural environment. Naturally northern creatures like caribou, Siberian tiger, and musk ox are a specialty, but the tropics area and aquatic hall are also excellent. The regular shark feedings and dolphin shows are crowd favorites. A monorail ride offers a bird's-eye (and climate-controlled) view of the outdoor animals. Also at the zoo is a jumbo-sized **IMAX Theatre** (952/431-4629, $9 adults, $20.50 combo ticket with zoo) with a six-story-tall movie screen.

The cross-country ski trails at **Lebanon Hills Regional Park** (860 Cliff Rd., Eagan, 651/554-6530, www.co.dakota.mn.us) are some of the metro's best, while the mountain bike trails are among the tops in the whole state. Short portages link seven of the lakes into a short canoe trail and rentals are available.

Considering it sits inside the metro area, the 93-site **Lebanon Hills Campground** (12100 Johnny Cake Ridge Rd., Apple Valley, 651/438-4636, May–Oct., $26 full hookup) is very good.

MENDOTA

Tucked into a riverbend just across from Fort Snelling, Mendota is a small commuting suburb.

The **Sibley House Historic Site** (1357 Sibley Memorial Hwy., 651/452-1596, www.mnhs.org, 10 A.M.–4 P.M. Fri., Sat., and Mon. plus 12:30–4 P.M. Sun. summer, only Sat.–Sun. May, Sept., and Oct., $5 adults), in the tiny riverside village of Mendota (a Dakota name for Meeting of the Waters), sits across from Fort Snelling at the confluence of the Minnesota and Mississippi Rivers and is the oldest permanent European settlement in the state. Fur traders, long familiar with the area, had established camps by the early 1800s, and in 1824 John Jacob Astor's American Fur Company built an outpost here. A decade later future first governor Henry H. Sibley was named the post's second director, and the house he erected in 1838 is the oldest stone residence in Minnesota. It was restored and refurnished in 1910 and has been open as a historic site ever since. A few other limestone-constructed structures from that era remain standing, including the home/inn built next door by the renowned fur trader Jean-Baptiste Faribault, which now houses some museum exhibits.

Metro West

The space between Minneapolis and Lake Minnetonka—including the relatively well-off first-ring suburbs of St. Louis Park, Edina, Hopkins, and Minnetonka—isn't very exciting, but it does have good shopping and dining.

SIGHTS AND RECREATION

It won't make most people's top 40 countdown, but most people will find something interesting at the **Pavek Museum of Broadcasting** (3515 Raleigh Ave., 952/926-8198, www.pavek-museum.org, 10 A.M.–6 P.M. Tues.–Fri., 9 A.M.–5 P.M. Sat., $6 adults) in St. Louis Park. You can watch TV on a screen the size of a doughnut or play a tune on a theramin, a musical instrument you don't actually touch. The jumbled collection contains over 1,000 radios, televisions, and phonographs from the first half of the 20th century; rows of historic vacuum tubes; a working 1912 rotary spark-gap transmitter like that used on the *Titanic;* and a 1960s radio studio where kids can broadcast their own show.

Heading west from Minneapolis, the two loops of the **Southwest Regional LRT Trail** (Trailheads on 8th Ave. N. in Hopkins and off Lake St. W. in Minneapolis, www.threeriversparkdistrict.org) are maintained by the Three Rivers Park District. The 10-foot-wide crushed limestone trails total over 30 miles. The North Loop begins in the near suburb of Hopkins, just north of Mainstreet, and ends in the tiny town of Victoria, 15 miles away, with great views of Lake Minnetonka along the way. The South Loop hooks right up to the end of Minneapolis's Midtown Greenway and ends 15.5 miles away in Chanhassen, passing along Minnehaha Creek and the Minnesota River Valley. Both Loops pass through several parks with picnic and restroom facilities. If all goes according to plan, the trails will share part of the corridor with a commuter light rail line from Minneapolis, through Hopkins and Minnetonka to Eden Prairie, currently slated to open in 2015.

Golfers might want to play a round at **Braemar Golf Club** (6364 John Harris Dr., Edina, 952/826-6799) or **Rush Creek Golf Club** (7801 Troy Ln. N., Maple Grove, 763/494-0400), two of the state's best.

ENTERTAINMENT

Plymouth Playhouse (2705 Annapolis Ln. N., Plymouth, 763/553-1600, www.plymouthplayhouse.com) in the Best Western hotel does comedies with a Minnesota flavor, such as the long-running and hugely popular *Church Basement Ladies* plays.

SHOPPING

A good variety of upscale shops and galleries form the **50th & France** area on the Edina–Minneapolis border.

If you enjoy shopping and history, spend a few dollars at Edina's **Southdale Center,** the first totally enclosed shopping center in the United States, which opened its doors in 1956. This 150-store center was also the birthplace of mall walking.

Across the street, **Galleria** is packed with posh shops like Coach and L'Occitane.

Kevin Smith's big-budget breakthrough movie *Mallrats* was filmed in the **Eden Prairie Center,** in Eden Prairie, but the mall has been so thoroughly remodeled that you'll barely recognize it anymore.

Around a dozen antiques stores line **Mainstreet** in downtown Hopkins.

ACCOMMODATIONS

Hotels along I-394 offer easy access to downtown Minneapolis. The **Sheraton** (12201 Ridgedale Dr., Minnetonka, 952/593-0000 or 800/325-3535, www.sheraton.com, $79), one of the poshest, overlooks a wildlife preserve. It has a small pool, whirlpool, fitness center, and sauna.

Convenient to the attractions of the southern suburbs and Minneapolis, the **Marriott Residence Inn, Edinborough** (3400

© TRICIA CORNELL

Mainstreet in Hopkins, a small town within minutes of downtown Minneapolis, is a popular destination for antiques shoppers.

Edinborough Way, Edina, 952/893-9300, www.marriott.com, $79) is uniquely situated in a one-acre indoor park with flowers, trees, a small waterfall, and a concert stage, along with an indoor pool, gym, and a three-story children's climbing structure called Adventure Peak. It's all attached to the hotel—along with a child-care center and senior citizens' residence—and guests get free entry. The park itself can be deafeningly loud, but the hotel is completely insulated from the noise.

The **Westin Edina Gallery** (3201 Galleria, Edina, 952/567-5000, www.westin.com, $99) is a fitting addition to the upscale shopping center, with a level of luxury unexpected in a suburban hotel.

FOOD

The fashionable 50th & France area, on the Minneapolis–Edina border, has plenty of quality dining. **Salut Bar Americain** (5034 France Ave. S., Edina, 952/929-3764, www.salutbaramericain.com, 11 A.M.–10 P.M. Mon.–Thurs., 11 A.M.–11 P.M. Fri.–Sat., 10 A.M.–5 P.M. Sun., $9–23) serves American food with a tongue-in-cheek French accent: "les cheesy puffs" and a "leetle beeg mac." Fortunately, the folks in the kitchen aren't kidding around: they actually know their way around both a croque monsieur and an excellent array of steaks. There is also a location in St. Paul (917 Grand Ave., 651/917-2345, 11 A.M.–10 P.M. Mon.–Thurs., 11 A.M.–midnight Fri.–Sat., 10 A.M.–10 P.M. Sun.).

Just up the road, the burgers, malts, and white-uniformed waitresses at the **Convention Grill** (3912 Sunnyside Rd., Edina, 952/920-6881, 11 A.M.–10 P.M. Sun.–Thurs., 11 A.M.–11 P.M. Fri.–Sat., $4–8) will take you back to the 1950s.

For an excellent breakfast in a lively atmosphere, bring the whole crowd to **Good Day Café** (5410 Wayzata Blvd., Golden Valley, 763/544-0242, 7 A.M.–3 P.M. daily, $6–9). Try their familiar classics with a few unexpected twists—like guacamole on one of the many eggs Benedict variations, for example, and beignets on a Midwestern menu.

Grown-ups and kids love **Yum!** (4000 Minnetonka Blvd., St. Louis Park, 952/922-4000, www.yumkitchen.com, 7 A.M.–8 P.M. daily, $7–13), where everybody can go as high-brow or low-brow as they want, from gooey, orange mac and cheese to tuna burgers and Szechuan green beans.

Aside from the strip-mall setting, it doesn't get much more French than **Patrick's Bakery and Café** (2928 66th St. W., Richfield, 612/861-7570, www.patricksbakery-cafe.com, 7 A.M.–9 P.M. Sun.–Wed., 7 A.M.–10 P.M. Thurs.–Sat., $7–13): ideal baguettes and boules, salads dressed to perfection, and, at dinner, coq au vin and osso bucco. You can find the same great menu inside Bachmann's garden shop (6010 Lyndale Ave. S., Minneapolis, 612/861-9277).

Lake Minnetonka and Chanhassen

This 14,310-acre Rorschach test has been a popular tourist destination since the 1860s. Tonka, as locals and regulars call it, has a multitude of long peninsulas and deep bays that sum to 105 miles of shoreline; some early explorers even named it Peninsula Lake. History has it that local Dakota dubbed it Minne-ho-Tonka, Water with a Big Voice (some historians dispute this), and Governor Ramsey shortened it to Minnetonka, which would translate to just Big Water. Tonka Toys got their start making trucks in a basement workshop in the lakeside community of Mound, and Minnetonka Moccasins took its name from the lake, though they began, and remain, a Minneapolis-based company.

Settlers came in 1852, immediately after the ratification of treaties with the Dakota, and fifteen years later James J. Hill's Great Northern Railroad passed Wayzata's (WISE-etta) lakeshore. From here, people boarded paddlewheel steamers to travel to luxurious resorts across the lake. Wildlife was abundant on the shore, and men could hunt and fish at will. At Minnetonka's peak during the 1880s, 90 boats loaded passengers at the Wayzata dock—the largest, the *Belle of Minnetonka,* carried 2,500 passengers—and the wealthy and famous from across the nation came to sample the good life here. Though today, with development along nearly all of the shore, it's no longer true, it's easy to understand why back then this was widely considered one of the most beautiful lakes in the state. By the turn of the 20th century the Eastern bigwigs found other playgrounds, and the gilded run ended, though Tonka tourism didn't die. Through the early 20th century most tourists were middle-class day-trippers lured out from Minneapolis and St. Paul by modern amusement parks. Though they continued to come through the Depression, they didn't spend enough money to keep the hotels, fun fairs, and other businesses going. Eventually the elite returned to build grand mansions and summer homes, and the numerous posh boutiques and top-flight restaurants catering to them have revived Tonka's status as a top weekend getaway. Fourteen communities front the lake, but just two small, busy cities, Wayzata (pop. 4,100) and Excelsior (pop. 2,400), see most of the action.

The city of Chanhassen, just below the lake, has a pair of Twin Cities favorites: the Minnesota Landscape Arboretum and the Chanhassen Dinner Theatres.

SIGHTS

The Twin City Rapid Transit Company's first streetcar tracks reached Lake Minnetonka in 1905. The line, which connected Minneapolis with Excelsior, served both tourists and the growing lakeside population. The rambling shoreline made expanding the lines prohibitively expensive, so the TCRT engineers built six boats to connect the rest of the lake's towns and resorts. The narrow 70-foot boats launched in 1906 were officially called Express Boats, but the public dubbed the double-deckers Streetcar

MINNESOTA LANDSCAPE ARBORETUM

People from across the Twin Cities make regular journeys to Chanhassen to stroll the 1,040 beautiful acres of the Minnesota Landscape Arboretum (3675 Arboretum Dr., Chaska, 952/443-1400, www.arboretum.umn.edu, 8 A.M.–8 P.M. or sunset, whichever comes first, daily, $9 adults, free after 4:30 P.M. on Thurs.), the northernmost of its kind in the United States. Find serenity in the traditional Japanese Garden or inspiration in the home demonstration gardens. The impressive perennial and annual flower gardens are packed with 20,000 plants; both peak in July. On the more natural side there's a bog walk and a prairie restoration. Most displays lie along a three-mile drive, though there are also trails to hike. Picnic areas are available during the summer, and six miles of trail are groomed for cross-country skiing in the winter. Though the public education and enjoyment missions have taken center stage, this remains a research facility under the direction of the Department of Horticultural Science at the University of Minnesota. Naturally, the focus is on cold-hardy species, and they have developed 80 species of fruit and ornamental plants since opening in 1908; apples remain a key focus. The Apple House, open in the fall and located about 1.5 miles away from the main grounds, sells as many as 50 varieties of apples developed and grown by the university, as well as honey and other local produce.

Tram tours run several times a day (10:30 A.M., noon, 1:30 P.M., and 3 P.M. May–mid-Oct., $2.50). Guided tours are available for groups of 15 or more. A variety of brochures for self-guided tours are available in the Snyder Building. Also in the Snyder Building are a conservatory, horticultural library, and gift shop with garden books, gifts, and supplies.

© TRICIA CORNELL

The Minnesota Landscape Arboretum has exhibits to interest adults and children.

Boats because both the land and water people movers were painted canary yellow and had the exact same seats. The service was popular, but short-lived. By the 1920s most travel to the lakes was by car, and the service ended in 1926. The boats were scuttled north of Big Island. The **Steamboat *Minnehaha*** (952/474-2115, www.steamboatminnehaha.org, weekends and holidays late May–mid-Oct., $12 and up) was raised from the lake's depths with the intention of putting it on display on dry land; however, others had grander ideas, and the restored boat made its second maiden voyage out of Excelsior in 1996.

Also boarding at the Excelsior dock is the modern ***Lady of the Lake*** (952/929-1209, www.ladyofthelakecruise.com, 1 P.M. Tues., Thurs., and Sun., $12), a 70-foot mock paddlewheeler with narrated 90-minute cruises around Big Island.

For a look at the lake's heyday, visit the **Excelsior-Lake Minnetonka Historical Society Museum** (305 Water St., Excelsior, 952/221-4766, www.elmhs.org, 3–6 P.M. Thurs., 10 A.M.–3 P.M. Sat., 1–4 P.M. Sun. May–Sept., free admission). It's worth a visit just to see the 1924 roller coaster car, which gives new meaning to the term thrill ride.

Boarding outside the museum is the **Excelsior Streetcar** (www.trolleyride.org, 2–6 P.M. Thurs., 10 A.M.–4 P.M. Sat., 1–4 P.M. Sun. and holidays May–Sept., Thurs. only through Oct., $2). Old No. 78, one of the oldest operating streetcars in the country, makes 15-minute trips across town.

While it's really just a decorative bus, Wayzata's shiny red **Towne Trolley** (Wayzata Depot, Mon.–Sat. May–Oct., free) is still fun. There are half-hour loops through town, and you can get on and off at will. Wednesdays at 1:30 P.M. the trolley leaves the city for a narrated hour-long tour ($5) around the lake.

The trolley rides start at the 1906 Wayzata Depot, which is also home to the little **Wayzata Depot Museum** (402 E. Lake St., Wayzata, 952/473-3631, noon–4 P.M. Wed. and Sat.–Sun. Apr.–Dec., free admission).

Outside town, the **Minnetonka Center for the Arts** (2240 North Shore Dr., Wayzata, 952/473-7361, 9 A.M.–9:30 P.M. Mon.–Thurs., 9 A.M.–5 P.M. Fri.–Sat., free admission) is primarily a large art education center with classes in many media, but there is often something interesting in the gallery.

Many people enjoy a stroll through the modest formal flower and shrub gardens at **Noerenberg Memorial County Park** just up the street from the art center, though picnics are prohibited.

ENTERTAINMENT AND EVENTS

The theater scene out here is truly superlative—largest and oldest to be precise. Having elicited giggles and guffaws since 1940 makes Excelsior's all-comedy **Old Log Theater** (5175 Meadville St., Greenwood, 952/474-5951, www.oldlog.com) the longest continually running professional theater in the country. Many people take advantage of their on-site restaurant for a pre-performance meal.

The out of the way location hasn't prevented **Chanhassen Dinner Theatres** (501 W. 78th St., Chanhassen, 952/934-1525 or 800/362-3515, www.chanhassentheatres.com) from growing into the nation's largest dinner theater. Serving as many as 1,000 guests a night also makes them the largest restaurant in the state and one of the largest in the nation. The Broadway of dinner theater has three stages, so at any one time you can choose from a musical, comedy, or drama.

The second weekend in September hosts two of the lake's biggest events. Wayzata's **James J. Hill Days** celebrates the man who first made this a tourist hotspot with a parade, arts and crafts fair, and dachshund races. Excelsior holds **Apple Day** that Saturday. Over 200 artists sell their wares on the lakeshore the second weekend of June during Excelsior's **Art on the Lake.** In early February over 1,000 duffers whack away at tennis balls on a pair of 10-hole golf courses out on Wayzata Bay during the **Chilly Open.**

SHOPPING

If shopping is your hobby you could spend a day exploring the streets of Excelsior and

Wayzata; without trying too hard you could max out a credit card or two. The best spot for antiques is the **Wayzata Home Center** (1250 E. Wayzata Blvd., Wayzata), a mall to the northeast of downtown now almost completely filled with antiques shops, though both cities have other good dealers.

If you need a read, try **Excelsior Bay Books** (36 Water St., Excelsior, 952/401-0932) and **The Bookcase of Wayzata** (607 E. Lake St., Wayzata, 952/473-8341, www.bookcaseofwayzata.com).

RECREATION

Excelsior's **Excel Marina** (141 Minnetonka Blvd., Excelsior, 952/401-3880) rents pontoons and kayaks and arranges fishing guides. Other boat rental options around the lake are **Howard's Point Marina** (5400 Howard's Point Rd., Excelsior, 952/474-4464), **Minnetonka Boat Club** (4850 Edgewater Dr., Excelsior, 952/472-1220), and **Rockvam Boat Yards** (4068 Sunset Dr., Excelsior, 952/471-9515).

ACCOMMODATIONS

Property values are way too high for any hotels to open on the lake, so lodging choices are limited. Of course, being so close to Minneapolis, the scarcity doesn't matter much. The only place right by the lake is the **Bird House Inn** (371 Water St., Excelsior, 952/474-0196, www.birdhouseinn.com, $159) bed-and-breakfast, a lovely and luxurious 1858 Italianate home in downtown Excelsior. Some of the five antiques-filled guestrooms have private baths and fancy touches, such as a claw-foot tub or hand-painted floors.

Over by the Chanhassen Dinner Theatres is the family-owned **Chanhassen Inn** (531 W. 79th St., Chanhassen, 952/934-7373 or 800/242-6466, www.chaninn.com, $72).

The classy **Country Inn and Suites** (591 W. 78th St., Chanhassen, 952/937-2424 or 800/456-4000, $89) has a small pool, whirlpool, and exercise room.

FOOD

Excelsior

The place to be seen in Excelsior is the boat-friendly **Maynard's** (685 Excelsior Blvd., 952/470-1800, www.maynardsonline.com, 11 A.M.–1 A.M. Mon.–Sat., 10 A.M.–midnight Sun., $8–29), where an expansive deck reaches out over the lake. You can still glimpse the water from the indoor tables, or sports fans can watch the game up by the bar. The menu has burgers, steak, portabella mushroom pasta, and fish tacos, and Sunday sees a stellar $15 brunch.

Two small Asian establishments downtown rarely disappoint: **Yumi's** (28 Water St., 952/474-1720, 5–9 P.M. Mon.–Thurs., 5–10 P.M. Fri.–Sat., closed Sun., $4–15) is best known for sushi while **Ming Wok** (205 Water St., 952/470-1010, 11 A.M.–9 P.M. Mon.–Sat., closed Sun., $5–17) does Chinese.

The namesake snack at **Adele's Frozen Custard** (800 Excelsior Blvd., 952/470-0035, www.adelescustard.com, 11 A.M.–9:30 P.M. daily, $3–5) is sinfully rich and delicious. There's also a location in Wayzata (888 Superior Blvd., Wayzata, 952/473-2838, 11 A.M.–9:30 P.M. daily).

The ***Queen of Excelsior*** (687 Excelsior Blvd., Excelsior, 952/474-2502, www.qecruise.com, May–Sept.) offers Sunday brunch ($29) and Tuesday night pizza and beer cruises ($25). Reservations are required.

Wayzata

Blue Point (739 E. Lake St., 952/475-3636, www.bluepointrestaurant.com, 4–9 P.M. Sun.–Thurs., 4–9:30 P.M. Fri.–Sat., closed Sun. in winter, $15–56) does everything right. From the setting to the service to the seafood this is one of the lake's best restaurants.

There is also plenty of seafood, plus steaks, sandwiches, and Caribbean flavors, at **North Coast** (294 Grove Ln. E., Wayzata, 952/475-4960, www.northcoastwayzata.com, 11 A.M.–10 P.M. Mon.–Wed., 11 A.M.–midnight Thurs.–Fri., 10 A.M.–midnight Sat., 10 A.M.–9 P.M. Sun., $11–34), which is in the beautifully renovated Minnetonka Boat Works. It has a large outdoor deck, and the interior design allows great lake views from most tables in the dining room.

Elsewhere

Perched on the middle of the lake since 1968, **Lord Fletcher's** (3746 Sunset Dr., Spring Park, 952/471-8513, www.lordfletcherslodge.com, 5–9:30 P.M. daily, lunch summer only, $9–50) is Tonka's most famous restaurant. With choices ranging from lobster tails served in the Old World–style dining rooms to burgers on a lakeside deck nearly big enough to land an airplane on, Fletcher's has something for most tastes. If you don't mind the high prices or the summer weekend mobs, you'll probably enjoy yourself here.

Nearby you'll find the classic **Minnetonka Drive-In** (4658 Shoreline Dr., Spring Park, 952/471-9383, 11 A.M.–9:30 P.M. daily Mar.–Oct., $2–4). They don't wear roller skates, but carhops still bring cheap ice cream, chilidogs, and chicken dinners right to your car.

Suburbs North and East

METRO NORTH

Though definitely part of the urban picture, the few worthy attractions in the northern suburbs have a rural personality. Because the hotels are away from the airport and Mall of America, rates tend to be lower up here.

Sights and Recreation

Jane and Heman Gibbs settled on this frontier farmstead in 1849, living in a sod house initially, and the family remained here for a century before the land was turned into the **Gibbs Museum of Pioneer and Dakotah Life** (2097 W. Larpenteur Ave., Falcon Heights, 651/646-8629, www.rchs.com, 10 A.M.–4 P.M. Tues.–Fri., noon–4 P.M. Sat.–Sun. Apr.–Nov., $6.50 adults). Costumed interpreters tell the Gibbses' pioneering story as they lead visitors through their 1867 house, farm buildings (home to sheep, chickens, pigs, and other barnyard residents), and the surrounding gardens—there's also a one-room schoolhouse. Jane had lived amongst the local Dakota as a child, and many of her native friends camped on the farm each year, so another part of the museum contains tepee and bark lodge imitations. Blacksmithing, Dakota dancing, doll-making, and other special events are held most weekends.

Now a tony suburb, the city of White Bear Lake was Minnesota's first resort community, with a lakeside hotel opening in 1853. Upward of 10,000 people a day made the trip from the Twin Cities at its peak around the turn of the 20th century, and in the 1930s it was a swinging getaway for artists like F. Scott and Zelda Fitzgerald and gangsters like Baby Face Nelson and Ma Barker. The resorts and amusement parks are gone, but this aspect of the past features prominently in the White Bear Lake Area Historical Society's tiny **Depot Museum** (4735 U.S. 61, White Bear Lake, 651/407-5327, www.wblareahistoricalsociety.org, 10 A.M.–1 P.M. Tues.–Wed. and Sat., 10 A.M.–4 P.M. Thurs.–Fri., free admission).

The **Roseville Skating Center** (2661 Civic Center Dr., Roseville, 651/792-7191, $5 open skating, $4 skate rental) has an indoor ice arena, as well as the **John Rose Minnesota OVAL,** the largest outdoor refrigerated ice surface in the country. The 400-meter track is the nation's only regulation-sized bandy (like field hockey on skates) sheet and is open November to March.

Not to be outdone, **Schwan's Super Rink** at the **National Sports Center** (1700 105th Ave. NE, Blaine, 763/785-5601, $3 open skating, $3 skate rental) has four Olympic-sized and four NHL-sized ice sheets under one roof. Also open to the public at the NSC is **Tournament Greens,** the mother of all miniature golf courses. The 18-hole putting course, designed by the PGA, uses real bent-grass greens.

The NSC is also home to the **Minnesota Thunder** (763/785-5600, www.mnthunder.com), which plays in the United Soccer League's First Division, one step down the

© BRUCE MANNING

The Gibbs Museum of Pioneer and Dakotah Life re-creates life in the 19th century.

hierarchy from Major League Soccer. The men's season runs April through September and about 3,000 people turn out for games in a stadium with a capacity of 8,500. Since the team's creation in 1990, it has won a single championship, in 1999, and reached the finals a handful of times. The 2005–2008 seasons have been particularly dispiriting, with the Thunder placing toward the bottom of the division every year. The team's mascot is a giant foam-suited Viking named Thor who waves his hammer on the sidelines during games and poses for pictures with soccer-loving kids.

Entertainment

The funky little **Heights Theater** (3951 Central Ave. NE, 763/788-9079, www.heightstheater.com), just over the border from Minneapolis in Columbia Heights, has been screening movies since 1926, and a Mighty Wurlitzer Organ recital still proceeds some weekend films.

Have a few good laughs at the **Minnesota Comedy Club** (4703 Hwy. 10, 612/961-4242, www.minnesotacomedyclub.com, 8:30 P.M. Fri.–Sat.) at Welsch's Big Ten Tavern in Arden Hills.

Shopping

White Bear Lake is one of the few suburban communities with any charm (or an actual downtown), and the flower-filled city center has a fair share of unique galleries, gift shops, and boutiques.

Accommodations

Roseville is a good lodging option because it's close to Minneapolis and convenient to St. Paul. Rooms at the **Radisson** (2540 Cleveland Ave. N., Roseville, 651/636-4567 or 800/333-3333, www.radisson.com, $89) have most of the bells and whistles of fancier downtown hotels and much better weekday prices. Recreational facilities include a large pool, jumbo whirlpool, sauna, fitness center, and game room, plus they offer shuttle service (for a fee) to both downtowns.

The **Motel 6** (2300 Cleveland Ave. N., Roseville, 651/639-3988 or 800/466-8356, www.motel6.com, $56) has the usual small and simple rooms as well as an outdoor pool.

Food

India Palace (2570 Cleveland Ave. N., Roseville, 651/631-1222, www.indiapalacemn.com, 11 A.M.–10 P.M. daily, $8–17) has won many awards, and some regard this as the best Indian restaurant in the Twin Cities.

You'll find a more authentically Russian experience than in the real Russian city at **St. Petersburg** (3610 France Ave. N., Roseville, 763/587-1787, www.myvodkabar.com, 5–11 P.M. Tues.–Thurs., 5 P.M.–1 A.M. Fri., closed Mon., $9–23), from *zakuski* through heavy Russian entrées and right onto the dance floor. By the way, Russians don't do casual. Come dressed to impress.

Families gather at **King's Fine Korean Cuisine** (1051 Moore Lake Dr. E., Fridley, 763/571-7256, www.kingsrestaurant.com, 11:30–9 P.M. Tues.–Sun.) for barbecue, sushi (yes, sushi), and more. After 9 P.M., King's becomes something entirely different: a karaoke-fueled nighttime hot spot.

METRO EAST

The eastern edge of the metro blends quickly into Stillwater and the St. Croix River Valley. But there are a few things to keep your eye out for after you leave St. Paul.

Two drive-in movie theaters survive in the rapidly expanding eastern suburbs. The **Cottage View** (9338 E. Point Douglas Rd. S., Cottage Grove, 651/458-5965, www.manntheatresmn.com) and the **Vali Hi** (11260 Hudson Blvd. N., Lake Elmo, 651/436-7464, www.valihi.com) screen double and triple features, respectively.

Lake Elmo Park Reserve (1515 Keats Ave. N., Lake Elmo, 651/430-8370, www.co.washington.mn.us, $5 day pass), one of the largest parks in the Twin Cities metro area, has a campground. The 80 sites in the main camp are shadeless and widely spaced and cost $20 for a full hookup. Pitching a tent in the grassy primitive camp area costs $14. Also scattered amongst the 2,165-acres of forest and grasslands are several lakes, with a swimming beach and fishing pier, plus 24 miles of trails for hiking, biking, and horseback riding. The park entrance is a mile north of I-94 on Keats Avenue North.

ST. CROIX VALLEY

Some of Minnesota's most scenic towns and best state parks are tucked away along this wild border river, so a drive through the valley is an engaging mix of natural scenery and country life. Stillwater, with its well-preserved downtown, elegant bed-and-breakfasts, and famous shopping, is by far the best known of the river towns, but it's really the smaller time-warped villages like Marine on St. Croix to the north and Afton to the south that give the valley its special character. They all get quite crowded on summer weekends and accommodation prices can nearly double, so plan a weekday visit if you can.

People who are particular about paddling will want to dip their oars in the upper stretches of the St. Croix or cinch up their spray skirts for some of the state's best white-water action on the St. Louis and Kettle Rivers.

PLANNING YOUR TIME

Getting to know this region requires a day for the historic towns of the south and at least a couple more for the wild parks in the north. It's all day-trip distance from the Twin Cities and Duluth, but **Stillwater** is such an appealing town that it's worth basing yourself there for at least part of your visit. And no matter how much fun you are having in Stillwater, make time to look over the villages of Afton and Marine on St. Croix.

Heading north, **Interstate State Park,** with its sheer cliffs and massive potholes, is the first must-see park. Continuing upstream, Wild River and **St. Croix State Park,** with superb hiking and canoeing, are similar enough that it makes sense to choose just one and take enough time to really enjoy it. The **North West**

HIGHLIGHTS

Stillwater: One of Minnesota's loveliest towns, Stillwater is rightly one of the state's most popular destinations. When you're not shopping for antiques or used books, the town's two specialties, you can pamper yourself in historic B&Bs and foodie-favorite restaurants (page 99).

Interstate State Park: The Dalles of the St. Croix River at the heart of this park has sheer pine-topped cliffs jutting 200 feet straight out of the river. Hundreds of glacially-carved potholes, including the world's deepest, top the cliffs, and paddlewheel tour boats cruise between them (page 107).

St. Croix State Park: This 32,000-acre park, part of the larger St. Croix National Scenic Riverway, offers some of the best paddling in the Midwest. The namesake river, with virtually no development along its 21 parkside miles, is mostly placid; white-water fans can get some in the Kettle River (page 110).

North West Company Fur Post: One of the state's best living-history reenactments takes you back to 1804 at this winter trading post (page 111).

Banning State Park: Unknown even to many Minnesotans, Banning straddles a mile-long gorge with rapids and waterfalls at its core. They are easily seen from riverside trails or, for the sufficiently skilled, from a kayak (page 112).

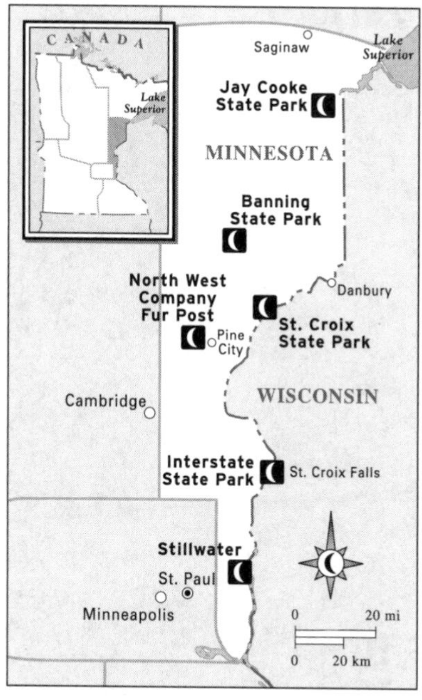

LOOK FOR TO FIND RECOMMENDED SIGHTS, ACTIVITIES, DINING, AND LODGING.

Jay Cooke State Park: With yet another wild river gorge, Jay Cooke is another can't-miss park (page 116).

Company Fur Post is one of the state's best living-history sites. Most people headed up the freeway drive right by **Banning State Park,** where the wild Kettle River cuts through a gorgeous gorge, but this is a mistake. Before checking out another wild gorge at **Jay Cooke State Park,** take a detour into Cloquet for a look at the Frank Lloyd Wright–designed gas station.

HISTORY

Though modern Minnesota was born at Fort Snelling, down where the Minnesota River joins the Mississippi, it grew up along the St. Croix. The Dakota occupied the valley when French explorer Daniel Greysolon, Sieur du Lhut—the man presumed to be the first European to visit—passed through in 1680. Swarms of fur traders, first the French and then later the English and Americans, weren't far behind. Though some trading posts were built, there could be no settlement until the Ojibwe, who had taken over the valley by force from the Dakota, relinquished their lands in 1837. The fur trade had largely gone bust by

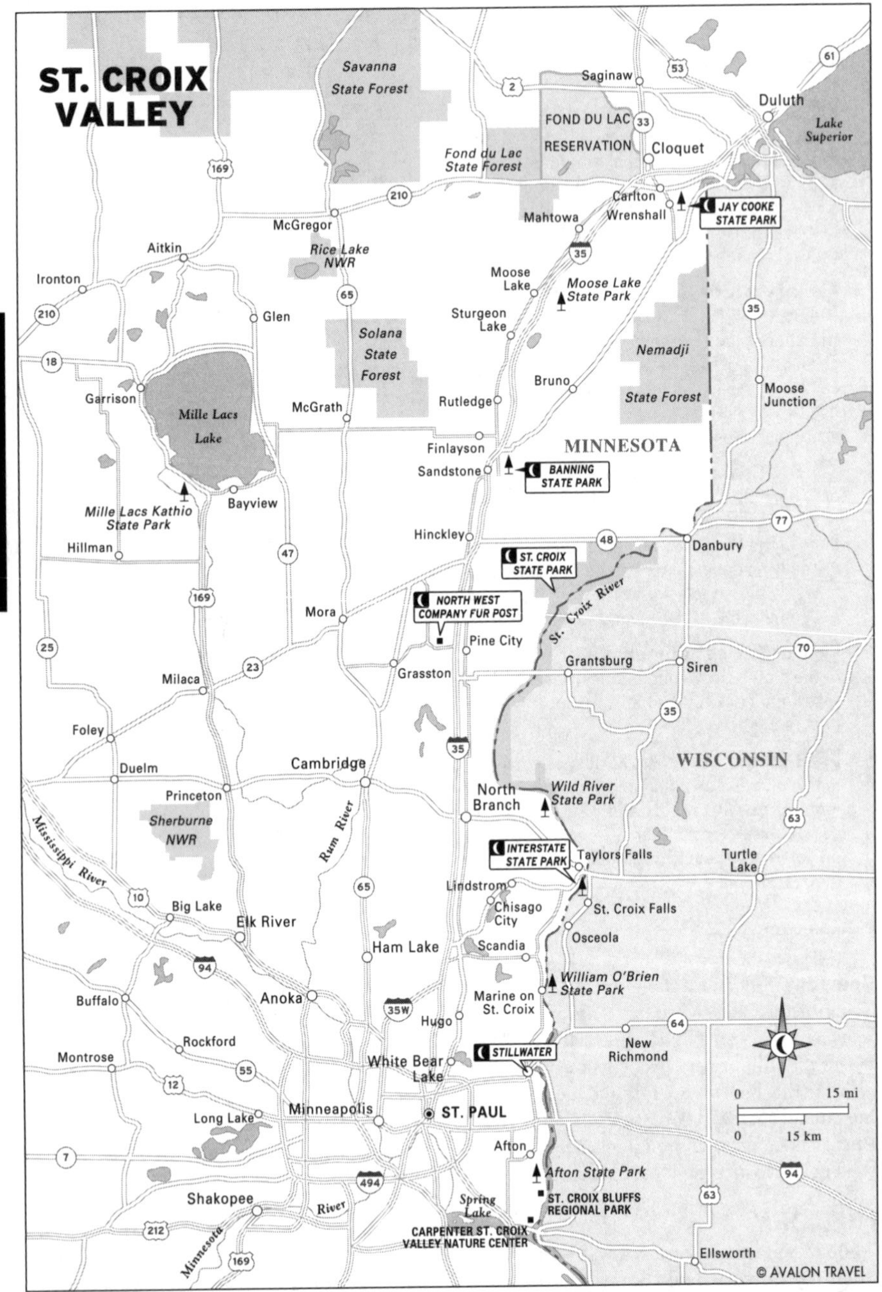
ST. CROIX VALLEY
Savanna State Forest
Saginaw
Duluth
Lake Superior
FOND DU LAC RESERVATION
Cloquet
Fond du Lac State Forest
Carlton
Wrenshall
JAY COOKE STATE PARK
Mahtowa
McGregor
Rice Lake NWR
Aitkin
Ironton
Glen
Moose Lake
Moose Lake State Park
Sturgeon Lake
Solana State Forest
Nemadji State Forest
Bruno
Moose Junction
Garrison
Mille Lacs Lake
McGrath
Rutledge
Finlayson
MINNESOTA
Sandstone
BANNING STATE PARK
Bayview
Mille Lacs Kathio State Park
Hillman
Hinckley
Danbury
ST. CROIX STATE PARK
St. Croix River
NORTH WEST COMPANY FUR POST
Mora
Pine City
Grasston
Grantsburg
Siren
Milaca
Foley
Duelm
Cambridge
Princeton
WISCONSIN
North Branch
Wild River State Park
Sherburne NWR
Rum River
Mississippi River
INTERSTATE STATE PARK
Taylors Falls
Turtle Lake
Lindstrom
Chisago City
St. Croix Falls
Big Lake
Elk River
Osceola
Ham Lake
Scandia
William O'Brien State Park
Buffalo
Anoka
Marine on St. Croix
Hugo
New Richmond
Rockford
STILLWATER
Montrose
White Bear Lake
Long Lake
Minneapolis
ST. PAUL
0 15 mi
0 15 km
Afton
Afton State Park
Shakopee
Spring Lake
River
ST. CROIX BLUFFS REGIONAL PARK
CARPENTER ST. CROIX VALLEY NATURE CENTER
Minnesota
Ellsworth
© AVALON TRAVEL

this time, though the river would soon transport another precious cargo. Lumberjacks moved in almost immediately after the treaty was signed, sending their logs downstream to the state's first sawmill in Marine on St. Croix and later to Stillwater, which quickly grew into the river's dominant lumbering center and one of the state's ranking cities.

Many of the earliest settlers in the valley were wealthy New Englanders, and several of the towns they built still bear a resemblance to their original homes. Wisconsin became the 30th state in 1848, leaving the St. Croix Valley, which had been a part of the previous Wisconsin Territory, in a political vacuum. A group of influential, though self-appointed, civic leaders hastily convened an August summit in Stillwater and elected American Fur Company director Henry Sibley to represent them in Congress. Though technically he had no right to a seat in Congress, and legally there wasn't even a white population large enough to form a territory, Sibley and his allies put the Minnesota Territorial Act on President Zachary Taylor's desk the next year.

The mills were largely silent and the logging camps empty by around 1915, but immigrant farmers tried to make a living off the land. The soil was far too sandy, however, and those who managed to get by struggled; others faced reality and gave up. As part of the relief effort during the Great Depression, the government bought out many of the farmers and reforested the land, leaving extensive state forests and parks along the river. In 1968 the St. Croix was one of the eight original rivers added to the National Wild and Scenic Rivers System, initiating a second period of preservation by both the National Park Service and the states of Minnesota and Wisconsin.

The Lower St. Croix

STILLWATER

If you want to relax and be pampered, spend a night in historic Stillwater: Book a table at a four-star restaurant, stroll along the riverfront promenade at sunset, take a moonlit gondola cruise, and count sheep at any of the grand bed-and-breakfasts. With Amish furniture, antique radios, and everything in between, Stillwater is also one of the best shopping locales in the state, and many people—bibliomaniacs and antiques fanatics in particular—come here just for a day of retail recreation.

History

Due to the aforementioned Territorial Convention of 1848, Stillwater boldly proclaims itself as the "Birthplace of Minnesota." The city's own birth came with the completion of the Stillwater Lumber Company's sawmill in 1844, and by 1848 Stillwater had become the river's largest community and the center of the lumbering industry. The census of 1850 listed a population of 620, second only to St. Paul. The next year the Territorial Legislature handed out the university to St. Anthony (which later became Minneapolis), the capital to St. Paul, and the penitentiary to Stillwater. In 1854 Stillwater and St. Paul became the territory's first two incorporated cities. With dreams of becoming the next Chicago, Stillwater thrived through the rest of the century and had 10 mills turning at its peak, but it suffered with the end of the logging era. The last log passed through the St. Croix Boom in 1914, and the city stagnated for decades, though never bottomed out thanks to the availability of jobs in the Twin Cities. The big turnaround came in the early 1980s when the historic buildings downtown were restored and empty storefronts hung signs for gift and antiques shops.

Sights and Recreation

The town itself is the most interesting attraction, and you should plan to spend a good deal of time admiring the 1931 **Stillwater Lift Bridge** (Chestnut St. E. and St. Croix

Trail) and wandering the well-preserved Main Street.

The Washington County Historical Society's **Warden's House Museum** (602 Main St. N., 651/439-5956, www.wchsmn.org, 1–5 P.M. Thurs.–Sun. May–Oct., $5 adults) was the home of the heads of the now closed Stillwater Prison. Though the house dates from 1853, the furnished rooms appear as they would have in the 1890s, while others hold lumber-era and similar historical displays. The prison room includes an exhibit on the most famous inmates, the Younger Brothers, the other half of the infamous James-Younger Gang.

Hear stories of the city's history on a half-hour walk through the **Joseph Wolf Caves** (402 Main St. S., 651/292-1220, 5 P.M. Thurs., 11 A.M. and noon Sat., 11 A.M. Sun., by appt. for groups of 25 or more, $5 adults), which were used to brew beer in the late 1800s, and have also served as a bomb shelter. The **Main Street Steps** next to the caves lead to a wonderful and oft-photographed view of the city and river.

Stillwater's architecture still reflects its shipping-industry past.

The Joseph Wolf Company once brewed beer in the caves on the shore of the St. Croix River. Now the caves are open for tours.

Explore the river on a pontoon rented from **Stillwater Boat Rentals** (575 Main St. N., 651/439-9000, www.stillwaterboatrentals.com, 8 A.M.–7 P.M. daily May 15–Sept. 30, from $255 half-day).

You can also ride smaller—much smaller boats—on the river, namely the two-passenger gondolas of **Gondola Romantica** (425 Nelson St. E. on the riverfront, 651/439-1783, www.gondolaromantica.com). Rides on the Venetian-style boats poled by burly men in striped sailor's shirts start at $95 for 45 minutes. Packages combining a ride with a meal at **The Dock Café** (425 Nelson St. E., 651/430-3770, www.dockcafe.com) are also available.

Entertainment and Events

If anything interesting is on stage, it's probably at the **Washington County Historic Courthouse** (101 Pine St. W., 651/275-7075). The popular **Valley Chamber Chorale** (651/430-0124, www.valleychamberchorale.org) performs there several times a year.

TAKE A RIDE

Watching the grand paddlewheelers cruise up and down the St. Croix River is one of the most enjoyable parts of a visit to Stillwater, but it's even better to be on one. **St. Croix Boat & Packet Company** (525 Main St. S., 651/430-1234, www.stillwater-riverboats.com, daily May-Oct.) offers a variety of lunch, dinner, and sightseeing cruises, priced from $18.

You can also take a much slower cruise in authentic Venetian gondolas with **Gondola Romantica** (425 Nelson St. E., 651/439-1783, www.gondolaromantica.com, daily May-Oct.). A 45-minute ride costs $95 for two people (the gondolas hold up to six people), and romantic meal packages are available.

The replica **Stillwater Trolley** (400 Nelson St. E., 651/430-0352, www.stillwater-trolley.com, daily May-Oct., $12.50) zips up and down city streets giving 45-minute narrated tours.

Hot air balloons are an increasingly popular way to take in the valley. **Aamodt's Hot Air Balloon Rides** (651/351-0101 or 866/546-8247, www.aamodtsballoons.com), **Stillwater Balloons** (651/439-1800, www.stillwaterballoons.com), and **Wiederkehr Balloons** (651/436-8172) all soar over the St. Croix from near Stillwater.

The city's heritage is celebrated during **Lumberjack Days** (www.lumberjackdays.com) with an 1860s-style baseball game, ice cream social, grand parade, and, of course, lumberjack competitions. The festivities take place over four days in late July. Another popular gathering is the **Fall Fine Art and Jazz Festival** the first weekend in October.

Shopping

Two of Minnesota's largest antiques stores—**Mill Antiques** (410 Main St. N., 651/430-1816, 10 A.M.–5 P.M. daily), in the 1870s Isaac Staples Sawmill and **Midtown Antique Mall** (301 Main St. S., 651/430-0808, www.midtownantiques.com, 10 A.M.–5 P.M. Mon.–Thurs., 10 A.M.–7 P.M. Fri.–Sat., 11 A.M.–6 P.M. Sun., open one hour later Mon.–Sat. in summer)—sit at opposite ends of Main Street, and about a dozen more sit in between. Prices are high, but so is the quality.

Books are the city's other consumer claim to fame. "King" Richard Booth of Hay-on-Wye in Wales officially proclaimed Stillwater North America's first Booktown (www.booktown.com) in 1994. Collectively, the city's outstanding bookshops have around half a million used titles on sale, about half of them at **Loome Theological Booksellers** (320 4th St. N., 651/430-1092, www.loomebooks.com, 9 A.M.–5 P.M. daily), the largest secondhand theology book dealer in the world—housed, appropriately enough, in an old church.

There is less volume but more variety at **Loome Antiquarian Bookstore** (201 Main St. S., 651/430-9805, noon–6 P.M. Sun.–Wed., 10 A.M.–6 P.M. Thurs.–Sat.) and **St. Croix Antiquarian Booksellers** (232 Main St. S., 651/430-0732, 11 A.M.–5 P.M. Mon.–Thurs., 11 A.M.–7 P.M. Fri.–Sat., noon–5 P.M. Sun.).

Accommodations

Stillwater has a host of historic and elegant inns, many in 19th-century lumber baron mansions, and choosing is easy because they are all excellent. Most are members of the **Stillwater Bed & Breakfast Association** (www.stillwaterbb.com).

Filled with the bounty from years of compulsive shopping in Southeast Asia, the exotic **Elephant Walk** (801 Pine St. W., 651/430-0359 or 888/430-0359, www.elephantwalkbb.com, $139–269) has as much character as any bed-and-breakfast in the state. It's like walking through a funky little museum. Each of the four guestrooms has a private bath, whirlpool, fireplace, and stocked refrigerator.

No detail is overlooked at the spectacular antiques-filled **Rivertown Inn** (306 Olive St. W., 651/430-2955, www.rivertowninn.com, $175–325), an 1882 Victorian mansion whose period decor is also of museum quality. The nine gorgeous guestrooms each have a private bath, whirlpool, and fireplace. Breakfast is served in the dining room, or you can eat outside in the gazebo.

Both of Stillwater's historic hotels have large rooms and antique furnishings. The ageless **Lowell Inn** (102 2nd St. N., 651/439-1100, www.lowellinn.com, $99) opened in 1927, and the rooms, though newly renovated, ooze character. The **Water Street Inn** (101 Water St. S., 651/439-6000, www.waterstreetinn.us, $129–229), just off the river, occupies a renovated and expanded 1890 commercial building and is equally charming.

The historic inns are a big part of the Stillwater experience, but you can save a lot by spending the night "up on the hill." Rooms at the **Super 8** (2190 Frontage Rd. W., 651/430-3990 or 800/800-8000, www.super8.com, $56–86) are the cheapest in town.

Food

Even natives of the Twin Cities—who are now spoiled for choice when it comes to fine dining—have been known to drive to Stillwater for a memorable meal. One particular destination is **Savories European Bistro** (108 Main St. N., 651/430-0702, www.savoriesbistro.com, 10:30 A.M.–9 P.M. Tues.–Fri., 8 A.M.–9 P.M. Sat.–Sun., $8–23). The menu changes every month or so but always features pizzas and pastas with a touch of luxury—whether its lobster or house-made sausage.

An equally luxurious meal can be had at **The Dock Café** (425 Nelson St. E., 651/430-3770, www.dockcafe.com, 11 A.M.–9 P.M. Mon.–Thurs., 11 A.M.–10 P.M. Fri.–Sat., 11 A.M.–8 P.M. Sun., $15–30), with the added bonus of a broad shaded patio right on the river. Although none of the fish itself comes from the St. Croix River, the location calls for a menu heavy on the seafood, from the local favorite walleye to scallops, shrimp, tuna, and salmon. Even if the weather isn't right for dining alfresco, the large plate glass windows in the dining room make every meal feel like outdoor dining.

Luna Rossa (402 Main St. S., 651/430-0560, 11:30 A.M.–10 P.M. daily, $9–23) brings the taste of southern Italy to its attractive dining room. The pizzas are cooked in a wood-fired oven, and there is create-your-own pasta during lunch.

Another great place to splash out on fine dining is at **Domacin Restaurant & Wine Bar** (102 2nd St. S., 651/439-1352, 4–10 P.M. Sun.–Tues., 4–11 P.M. Wed.–Thurs., 4–midnight Fri.–Sat., $16–24). Even if you don't want a big entrée, like paella or mustard-crusted salmon, you can enjoy one of their 300 kinds of wine with one of their small plates, like mini-burgers or a grilled cheese sandwich and green salad.

Both the **Water Street Inn** (101 Water St. S., 651/439-6000, www.waterstreetinn.us, 7 A.M.–9 P.M. Mon.–Fri., 8–10:30 A.M. and 5–9 P.M. Sat., 9 A.M.–2 P.M. and 5–9 P.M. Sun., pub open until 1 A.M.) and **Lowell Inn** (102 2nd St. N., 651/439-1100, www.lowellinn.com, breakfast 8–10:30 A.M., lunch 11 A.M.–2 P.M., dinner 5:30–9 P.M. daily) have well-regarded fine-dining restaurants.

The **Gasthaus Bavarian Hunter** (8390 Lofton Ave. N., 651/439-7128, 11 A.M.–9 P.M. Mon.–Fri., noon–9 P.M. Sat., noon–8 P.M. Sun., $10–19), a longtime favorite three miles west of town (follow Laurel Street, which becomes McCusick), serves authentic Old World recipes. Vegetarians need not fear, as they have a couple of meat-free options. An accordionist plays on Friday nights and Sunday afternoons; the occasional polka band heats things up at other times.

There's no reason you can't fuel your stroll through Stillwater with a more down-market, but entirely enjoyable, meal at **Chicago Dogs** (402 Main St. N., 651/323-7150, www.chicagodogsmn.com, 11 A.M.–9 P.M. daily Apr.–Nov.). Order your all-beef hot dog with all the right toppings from the window at this little nook in the Isaac Staples Sawmill.

It's always a party at **Nacho Mama's** (312 Main St. S., 651/439-9544, www.stillwaternachomamas.com, 11:30 A.M.–9:30 P.M. Mon.–Thurs., 11:30 A.M.–11 P.M. Fri., 9 A.M.–11 P.M. Sat., 9 A.M.–9:30 P.M. Sun., $10–15), with heaping portions and a colorful atmosphere. During lunch and dinner, the focus is on the dozen kinds of pancakes. Breakfast includes blue-corn pancakes and plays on huevos rancheros.

The **River Market Community Co-op** (215 Main St. N., 651/439-0366, 9 A.M.–9 P.M. daily, $3–7) has sandwiches, sushi, and smoothies to go.

The best pastries in Stillwater are found in a bike shop. **The Bikery** (904 4th St. S., 651/439-3834, www.thebikeryshop.com, 7 A.M.–7 P.M. Tues.–Sat., 8 A.M.–4 P.M. Sun., closed Mon.) makes European-style bread and galettes—and, yes, they sell bikes, too.

Information

Someone at the friendly **Greater Stillwater Chamber of Commerce** (106 Main St. S., 651/439-4001, www.ilovestillwater.com, 9 A.M.–4 P.M. daily) will have an answer to any question about the area.

Getting There

Metro Transit (www.metrotransit.org) bus #294 runs from downtown St. Paul to downtown Stillwater, but service is very limited and inconvenient. For those arriving by boat, there is public mooring at the **Stillwater Docks** (651/430-1234) and a trio of full-service marinas: **Wolf Marine** (514 Alder St. E., 651/439-2341, www.wolfmarine.net), **Sunnyside Marina** (6413 St. Croix Trail N., 651/439-2118, www.sunnysidemarina.com), and **Stillwater Yacht Club** (575 Main St. N., 651/439-9000, www.stillwateryachtclub.com).

AFTON

Highway 95 heads south along the St. Croix River and, except for a few quick glimpses of the water, is pretty ordinary until it hits Afton, a quaint village of 19th-century homes, several now housing restaurants and shops.

Sights and Recreation

The **Afton Historical Museum** (3165 St. Croix Trail S., 651/436-3500, 1–8 P.M. Wed. year-round, 1–4 P.M. Sun. summer, free admission), housed in an 1868 church, has a small collection of artifacts with an emphasis on farming, appropriately enough, since the first farm in Minnesota was established by Joseph Haskell just a mile west of the village in 1839.

Beyond Afton, scenic County Highway 21 veers away from the river and up a steep, wooded bluff, passing half a dozen orchards and farms where you can pick your own apples, strawberries, cherries, and the like. Four miles on is **Afton State Park** (6959 Peller Ave. S., 651/436-5391), established and managed for nature first and recreation second. The 1,700-acre park protects several deep, wooded ravines, some lined by sandstone outcrops that drop hundreds of feet down from the bluff tops to the St. Croix. With a mix of prairie and forest, Afton is a good park for bird-watchers. The primary reason for the park's overall peacefulness is that reaching most facilities requires a bit of a hike. The rocky beach and picnic area are half a mile downhill from the parking area. The only camping spots are the 24 widely spaced backpacking sites, reached by a long one-mile climb, and a single canoe site on the St. Croix. Most of the 20 miles of hiking trails have some long, steep climbs, but the effort is usually rewarded with great views, particularly the series of loops in the north end of the park. The riverside route along the south end of the park is also scenic, and the rocky beach makes a nice stroll when not busy with swimmers. Horses are allowed on one five-mile loop, and a four-mile paved bike path runs along the entrance road and down a short stretch of the river. Most of the trails are groomed for cross-country skiing, including 2.5 miles of level beginner trail.

Surrounded by, but independent of, the park is **Afton Alps** (6600 Peller Ave. S., 651/436-5245 or 800/328-1328, www.aftonalps.com), one of Minnesota's largest ski hills, with 48 trails, 18 lifts, a snowboard park, and a tubing hill. The rest of the year there is an 18-hole golf course and 7.5 miles of challenging mountain bike trails. Rentals are available.

A little farther down the road, **St. Croix Bluffs Regional Park** (10191 St. Croix Trail S., 651/430-8240, $5 day sticker) has one thing Afton State Park does not—a drive-in campground ($18–20 with electric and water hookups). With abundant shade, it's pretty good. The park also has hiking trails, boat access, and picnic sites.

In Afton itself, the large full-service **Windmill Marina** (16065 32nd St. S., 651/436-7744, www.windmillmarina.com) takes care of boaters' needs.

Practicalities

The **Afton House Inn** (3291 St. Croix Trail S., 651/436-8883 or 877/436-8883, www.aftonhouseinn.com, $79) was built in 1867 as a hotel, and a night here feels like a real escape. Most of the cozy rooms have fireplaces and/or whirlpools. Although there have been gaps in the lodging operation, a restaurant has operated here continuously since it opened, and currently they have a pair of them. The pasta, meat, and seafood menu in the **Wheel Room** averages over $20 for dinner, while the more casual **Catfish Saloon** is much cheaper. Both are open daily for lunch and dinner. You can also dine on the river between April and October on the Inn's Sunday brunch ($28) and Friday dinner ($35) cruises.

NORTH TO THE FALLS

Highway 95 up to Taylors Falls is heavily populated, but it's still not too shabby a drive and has some moments of true beauty.

Marine on St. Croix

Minnesota's lumber industry began here when the Marine Lumber Company cut its first pine board in 1839. Stillwater, just 11 miles to the south, didn't get its first mill for another six years, but it quickly grew into an important city while little Marine Mills, as it was then known, remained a scene right out of a New England postcard. Citizens and the post office rechristened their town Marine on St. Croix in 1917, though it took the U.S. Board on Geographic Names another 51 years to officially accept the change. Despite all the effort to get the longer name, most locals just call it Marine.

The foundation ruins of the **Marine Mill** can be seen in the little downtown park. Across the highway and up the hill, the 1872 town hall and jail now houses the little **Stonehouse Museum** (241 5th St., 651/433-3636, 10 A.M.–5 P.M. Sat.–Sun. May–Sept., free admission) and its assorted historical artifacts.

The **Asa Parker House** (17500 St. Croix Trail N., 651/433-5248, www.asaparkerbb.com, $129) bed-and-breakfast occupies a handsome 1856 home. The four guestrooms each have a private bath.

Grab a burger and a brew at the **Brookside Bar & Grill** (140 Judd St., 651/433-5132, 11 A.M.–9 P.M. Sun.–Thurs., 11 A.M.–10 P.M. Fri.–Sat.), and be sure to ask for a seat on the patio out back.

William O'Brien State Park

Just north of Marine on St. Croix is the popular and often busy William O'Brien State Park (16821 O'Brien Trail N., 651/433-0500). The original 180 acres were donated to the state by Alice O'Brien, daughter of the eponymous lumber baron, who purchased the land he had earlier cleared of trees. The park, which has since recovered, has expanded to 1,579 acres. Though it only composes a small part of the park, the most interesting area is the beautiful and wildlife-packed floodplain forest. The highly recommended **Riverside Trail,** a surfaced 1.5-mile loop with interpretive signs, offers up-close views of the river. Even better than walking along the water is getting right out on it. The easy paddle around Greenberg Island takes about an hour, though budget some extra time to poke around looking for wildlife and wildflowers. There are canoe rentals, and a shuttle service lets you explore more of the river. Many people are satisfied just taking it easy fishing, picnicking, or swimming in Lake Alice.

The rest of the 12-mile hiking trail system forms a series of loops across the mosaic of forest, prairie, oak savanna, and wetlands stretching atop the bluffs. All of the trails have some rolling hills, but few are especially challenging. The most interesting and least traveled are along the west edge of the park. The two-mile **Woodland Edge Trail** is mostly wooded, but as the name suggests, offers a look at the prairie as well, while the **Rolling Hills Oak Savanna Trail,** a mile-long loop through a savanna restoration, branches off the southern end of it. In winter most of these loops are groomed for cross-country skiing, both traditional and skating.

The pair of campgrounds, one down by the river and the other up on the hill, have 124 sites (61 electric) with a mix of shady and open choices in both; there is also a camper cabin. Overall, the last two loops of the Savanna Campground are the most peaceful and scenic options. The visitors center, open year-round, has nature displays and naturalist programs. For reservations, call 866/857-2757 or visit www.stayatmnparks.com.

Scandia

The state's first known Swedish immigrants settled here in 1850, and it was this general area that Swedish author Vilhelm Moberg described in his famous series of novels about famine-stricken peasants leaving the homeland to start a new life in Minnesota. The town, which chose the ancient name for Scandinavia as its own, clings tightly to its Swedish roots with cultural festivals, museums, and a few Dala horses decorating downtown.

The **Gammelgården** (20880 Olinda Trl., 651/433-5053, tours offered hourly 1–3 P.M. Fri.–Sun. May–Oct., gift shop open 10 A.M.–4 P.M. Mon.–Sat., 1 A.M.–4 P.M. Sun. year-round, $4 adults), on the south side of town, is a museum of Swedish immigration with half a dozen furnished buildings from the mid-19th century. These include an 1855 immigrant house, the oldest existing Lutheran church in Minnesota (built in 1856), and an 1879 barn filled with old farming tools. The historical park also hosts the Midsommar Dag (Midsummer Day) arts-and-crafts festival the fourth Sunday in June, Spelmansstämma music festival the third Saturday in August, a lutefisk dinner the third Thursday in November, and the traditional Lucia Christmas celebration on the Sunday closest to December 13th.

Just south of town, along Highway 3, is the **Hay Lake School Museum** (651/433-4014, www.wchsmn.org, 1–4 P.M. Sat.–Sun. May–Oct., plus Fri. in summer, $5 adults). When built in 1896 the redbrick one-room schoolhouse was quite fancy, which reflects the value the state's Scandinavian immigrants placed on education. The barn-shaped building in back is the Johannes Erickson Log Cabin, built in 1868 and now furnished as a Swedish immigrant might have done.

The Upper St. Croix

Lovely little Taylors Falls is the last town on the St. Croix in Minnesota. Beyond that, the river runs wild, with some of Minnesota's largest state parks protecting the shore.

TAYLORS FALLS

Taylors Falls mixes spectacular natural scenery with historic architecture to create one of the best quick getaways from the Twin Cities. The first two settlers here were the well-financed Benjamin Baker and his employee Jesse Taylor, who came in 1838 to open a sawmill. Baker died before the mill could be completed, and Taylor later sold his logging claims and moved on, but his name remained. The namesake falls are not the small rapids below the bridge, but a long, raging tumble that now lies buried behind the hydroelectric dam just upriver from the town. Though steamboat service began immediately (iron mooring rings from this era can still be seen along the river), the city didn't really begin to grow until 1850. In 1886, one of the largest logjams ever stretched seven miles upstream from the city.

Sights

Perched on the bluff above town is the **Angel's Hill District,** populated almost exclusively by

© WIKIMEDIA COMMONS

The Folsom House in Taylors Falls was constructed in 1854.

white Greek Revival homes with green trim; most were built in the 1850s and 1860s. The resemblance to a New England village is so remarkable that, according to some locals, transplants from out East sometimes visit to relieve bouts of homesickness. On your way up the hill you'll pass Minnesota's oldest schoolhouse (1852), second-oldest operating church (1861), and the simple but stately **Folsom House** (272 W. Government St., 651/465-3125, 1–4:30 P.M. daily except Tues. June–Oct., $5 adults). New England lumber baron W. H. C. Folsom came to Taylors Falls in 1850 and constructed this home four years later. It stayed in the family until 1968, at which time it and most of the original furnishings were acquired by the state. It also opens the two weekends following Thanksgiving to coincide with the city's Christmas-themed **Lighting Festival.**

There is always something interesting on display at **Franconia Sculpture Park** (29836 St. Croix Trail, Franconia, 651/465-3701, www.franconia.org, dusk–dawn daily, free admission). Dozens of works by artists from many countries grace the field along Highways 8/95, 2.5 miles southwest of town. Artists live and work communally while creating their art, which is then left on display for a year or two. Guided tours are given Sunday at 2 P.M.

Taylors Falls Scenic Boat Tours (651/465-6315 or 800/447-4958, www.wildmountain.com) of the St. Croix River begin by chugging through the Dalles of the St. Croix and then continue down the river, taking in more of the valley's beautiful scenery. There are up to four cruises a day from May to October, plus Wednesday and weekend dinner cruises. The shortest (three miles/30 minutes) trip is $11, while the most expensive dinner run is $37.75. The boat company is just off Highway 8 in downtown Taylors Falls; watch for signs at the only stoplight in town.

The same company operates **Wild Mountain,** seven miles north of town on Highway 16. In the summer you can get your thrills on five water rides, alpine slides, and a go-kart track. In the snowy season there are 25 downhill-ski and snowboard runs, the highest dropping 300 feet, and a tubing chute. You can ride the chairlift in the fall to take in the splendid color.

Located at Wild Mountain, **Taylors Falls Canoe and Kayak** (651/465-6315 or 800/447-4958, www.taylorsfallscanoe.com) rents boats ($10.50/hour or $42/day) and arranges shuttles.

Practicalities

The **Cottage Bed & Breakfast** (950 Fox Glen Dr., 651/465-3595, www.the-cottage.com, $120–140), perched on the edge of a bluff just outside town, offers serenity and phenomenal views from its private two-room cottage.

Conveniently located in town, the petite **Pines Motel** (531 River St., 651/465-3422, www.pinesmoteltaylorsfalls.com, $64) is older and very basic.

Five miles out of town, a mother-daughter team run the three-room **Country Bed and Breakfast** (17038 320th St., Shafer, 651/257-4773, www.countrybedandbreakfast.us, $85 single occupancy, $140 double) in a 130-year-old redbrick farmhouse that has been in their family since 1938. The whole house has a comfortable, lived-in feel, and the breakfasts are terrific.

Wild Mountain's **Wildwood RV Park and Campground** (20078 Lake Blvd., Shafer, 651/465-6315, $30 without hookup, $41 full hookup) is as far from wilderness camping as it gets. You can canoe on the river or swim in the heated pool; you can toss horseshoes or play mini golf.

In town, the **Old Jail** (349 Government St. W., 651/465-3112, www.oldjail.com, $140) has three large and distinctive self-contained suites with private entrances and a few funky touches. The namesake is in the 1884 jail, which retains the original exterior, including the iron cage door, but has been thoroughly modernized inside. In the house next to the jail are the Overlook Suite, with great views, and the ground-level Cave Suite, with its bath in an old beer cave extending into the bluff.

Carhops still bring you burgers and malts at **The Drive-In** (572 Bench St., 651/465-7831, 11 A.M.–9 P.M. Mon.–Fri., 11 A.M.–10 P.M. Fri.–Sat. May–Oct., $3–7).

With dishes like teriyaki-glazed Cornish game hen and whimsical decor, **Tangled Up In Blue** (425 Bench St., 651/465-1000, 5–9 P.M. Wed.–Thurs., 5–10 P.M. Fri.–Sat., 5–8 P.M. Sun., $17–31) is trying to take Taylors Falls up-market.

INTERSTATE STATE PARK

One of the smallest but most scenic and popular of Minnesota's state parks, Interstate (307 Milltown Rd., 651/465-5711, 866/857-2757 or www.stayatmnparks.com for reservations) sits right on the southern edge of Taylors Falls. The Dalles of the St. Croix, a gorge with sheer pine-topped cliffs jutting up to 200 feet straight out of the river, is one of the most beautiful sights in the state. By the early 1850s they had become a major tourist destination, with thousands arriving by steamboat and later railroad just to see them. That didn't stop businessmen from proposing to blast the cliffs into gravel, however. The citizens of Taylors Falls and St. Croix Falls, Wisconsin, pushed to preserve the Dalles as the centerpiece of a national park, but these dreams were dashed. Finally, the state of Minnesota set aside 298 acres as a state park in 1895, and Wisconsin opened its much larger share across the river five years later, creating the nation's first interstate park. Besides being beautiful, these cliffs are now the most popular rock-climbing destination in the state, with routes rated as high as 5.13. Naturally, the best sites in the 37-site (22 electric) campground are those abutting the river. Park stickers from either Minnesota or Wisconsin are valid on both sides on non-holiday weekdays.

Potholes

While the cliffs get the majority of oohs and aahs, the most interesting geological formations are the potholes. In many places the torrential water from the melting glaciers that cut the Dalles formed massive whirlpools. Sand and gravel trapped in the vortices carved shafts in the solid bedrock so symmetrical it's difficult to imagine nature doing it on its own. Over 200 potholes, including the world's deepest at 60 feet, are found in the two parks—a greater concentration than anywhere else.

Recreation

A small web of trails leads past and even into the potholes and atop the Dalles. Some of these form the **Pothole Trail,** a partly wheelchair-accessible quarter-mile route with interpretive panels along it. The **River Trail** leads for nearly 1.5 miles from the pothole area to the campground. It's an easy hike with great views, and even though it abuts the highway for part of the route, it is definitely worth your while. You can make a round-trip out of it by returning along the **Railroad Trail** on the other side of the highway. Across from the campground is the mile-long **Sandstone Bluffs Trail.** It has some great vista points, passes small Curtain Falls, and from mid-April through May the forest floor is carpeted by an amazing concentration of wildflowers. It requires a bit of a climb, but it's not too tough.

The best way to see the Dalles is from the water, and although you've got the option of the paddlewheel tour boats, the peaceful St. Croix is prime paddling territory. The river is part of the St. Croix National Scenic Riverway, and longer trips beyond the park are popular. Common day-trip options include the seven-mile float to Osceola and the 17-mile trip to William O'Brien State Park. Rental and shuttle service from **St. Croix River Canoe Rental** (651/465-6315 or 800/447-4958) are available. You can get additional information at the National Park Service's Riverway headquarters in downtown St. Croix Falls, Wisconsin.

WILD RIVER STATE PARK

Stretching 18 miles along a remote and beautiful stretch of the St. Croix River, this aptly named 6,803-acre park was created in conjunction with the St. Croix National Scenic Riverway. A remarkable abundance of wildflowers, including trillium and wild geranium, paint the forest floor each spring. The best spots for enjoying them are the **Trillium Trail,** which conveniently skirts the campground, and the **River Terrace Loop.** You can learn about the flowers and more at the **McElroy Visitor Center** (651/583-2925, 9 A.M.–5 P.M. Thurs.–Mon.), overlooking a wildflower garden and the St. Croix Valley.

The main park entrance is 10 miles north of Taylors Falls along Highway 95 and County Highway 12, though for a more scenic drive come via County Highway 16. The McElroy Visitor Center is about one mile from the park entrance; follow signs. The Sunrise River boat launch, along with its quiet picnic area, is in the west end along County Highway 9.

Recreation

Canoeing is obviously a top draw, and a pair of put-ins are spaced at a leisurely day-trip distance. Rentals and a shuttle service are available for the calm and easy 10-mile trip along the park or for longer journeys.

The canoeing is great, but Wild River is more than just the St. Croix. The 35-mile trail system stretches across most of the length of the park and has only the occasional steep hill. One of the most popular trails, and rightly so, is the **River Terrace Loop,** which circles the bottomland forest for 1.5 miles. Joining it at the Nevers Dam overlook (the dam was removed in 1955) is the **River Trail,** which follows the St. Croix south for the same distance. If you head up the hills you can make a loop out of it by following the **Old Logging Trail,** part of a three-mile paved route connecting the campgrounds and interpretive center. It is the only trail allowing bikes. Also in the southern section of the park is the three-mile **Amador Prairie Loops,** a pair of rings circling Wild River's prairie restoration. Two seldom-used trails, the five-mile **Sunrise Loop** and three-mile **Goose Creek Loop,** branch out through the bottomland forest in the north end of the park from the Sunrise River area. Both trails, particularly the latter, can be very wet but are also excellent places to encounter wildlife, as is the rolling **Sunrise Trail,** which continues along the river all the way back to the southern end of the park. A pair of easy mile-long self-guided nature trails, **Windfall** and **Amik's Pond,** begin at the visitors center and discuss forest and wetland ecology respectively; the latter passes a beaver pond and is a good bird-watching area.

Come winter, 30 miles of trail are groomed

ST. CROIX NATIONAL SCENIC RIVERWAY

Established in 1968 as one of the original projects in the National Wild and Scenic Rivers System, this 252-mile riverway begins in Wisconsin, where it also encompasses the entire 98-mile Namekagon River. The spring-fed St. Croix flows for 25 miles through the Badger State before becoming a border river. For the most part it's a narrow, shallow, lazy waterway winding through an often remote ribbon of wilderness – absolutely ideal canoeing territory. There are only occasional Class I rapids (a few of which can rise to Class II during high water), so it makes a leisurely trip, perfect for families. Thanks to the 60-foot-tall St. Croix Falls Hydroelectric Dam, the last 10 miles of the Upper St. Croix are now the Indianhead Flowage; because motorboats are common here most paddlers take out at Wild River State Park.

The river hits the sheer cliffs of the Dalles of the St. Croix at Taylors Falls and, after a short sprint through the narrow gorge, it spreads its banks and drops its bottom. For the next fifty miles, until it joins the Mississippi, the Lower St. Croix takes its time. The first twenty miles, down to the Apple River, are officially a "slow speed zone" for motorboats and so, despite substantial development along the shore, remain popular with canoes. Beyond the giant sandbar at the Apple's mouth the river grows some more, and large motorboats are the primary users. The river is so wide below Stillwater that it is known as Lake St. Croix, and sailboats join their gas-guzzling cousins on the water.

To prevent the spread of zebra mussels, boaters may no longer travel upstream past the High Bridge, about 3.5 miles north of Stillwater. Personal watercraft are also prohibited above Stillwater. Boaters should also read and heed the strict no-wake regulations posted at all landings.

CAMPING

While the canoeing is fantastic, the camping is even better. Over 100 free first-come, first-served campsites are stretched out along the Minnesota section of the riverway. All sites are marked by a sign and have a fire ring and a pit toilet; most also have a picnic table. The majority are individual sites that allow up to three tents and eight people, though a few designated group sites can accommodate twice as many.

Strict regulations have been enacted to protect the fragile river environment, and since these are always subject to change it is a good idea to inquire about them before heading out. Currently, campers must use designated sites above Taylors Falls, and there is a three-night limit at each. There are few campsites below Taylors Falls, but camping is allowed for up to seven nights anywhere on federal land (islands only between High Bridge and Stillwater) except the areas immediately south of the Dalles and around the towns of Osceola, Wisconsin, and Marine on St. Croix. Houseboaters may tie up for an overnight stay anywhere below Nevers Dam, but may not build fires or set up tents on the shore. Below Stillwater the riverway is managed collectively by the states, counties, and National Park Service (NPS), and there is little public land and no designated riverway campsites, though some state and county parks have campgrounds. The large delta at Wisconsin's Kinnickinnic State Park is a favorite with boaters.

INFORMATION

The **St. Croix Visitor Center** (401 Hamilton St. N., St. Croix Falls, 715/483-3284, 8 A.M.-4:30 P.M. daily June-Sept., weekdays rest of year) is located in St. Croix Falls, Wisconsin, just across the river from Taylors Falls. They can provide you with maps and information, including a complete list of area outfitters. Interpretive displays cover the St. Croix's human and natural history.

for cross-country skiing—the **Aspen Knob Loop,** a two-mile trail through the hilly southwest corner of the park, offers the biggest challenge—and the River Terrace Trail is packed down for winter hiking. Both skis and snowshoes are available to rent.

Accommodations

The campground has 96 (17 electric) mostly wooded campsites, each well screened from the others. Also in the camp area are two rustic camper cabins and a guesthouse with all the comforts of home, including air-conditioning, TV, VCR, and a fireplace. Horseback riders have their own rustic campground. The eight reservable backpacking sites are as little as a quarter mile, and no more than two miles, from park roads; only Buck Hill lets you camp in sight of the river. The park has another eight canoe-in campsites, and there are other National Scenic Riverway sites available. All canoe sites are first-come, first-served. Call 651/583-2125 for information, or visit www.stayatmnparks.com for reservations.

ST. CROIX STATE PARK

Minnesota's largest state park protects the scenic shore of not just its placid namesake river but also the writhing, boulder-strewn Kettle, the first state-designated Wild and Scenic River. In 1934, at the height the Great Depression, the National Park Service bought 18,000 acres of failing farms and over the next several years, aided by the Civilian Conservation Corps (CCC) and Works Progress Administration (WPA), helped restore the land and build public facilities, creating the park. Because most of the park's original design and historic buildings remain intact and in use, it has been declared a National Historic Landmark. Since then St. Croix State Park (30065 St. Croix Park Rd., 320/384-6591) has nearly doubled in size, and the hardwood forests, tamarack and black spruce bogs, meadows, marshes, and streams are home to an enormous diversity and abundance of flora and fauna.

Recreation

A 130-mile web of trails covers the park. Horseback riders can use well over half of them; though mountain bikers have access to 21 miles, the ride isn't very popular because the trails are rough and often sandy. Biking is quite good along the park roads, and a paved 5.5-mile trail connects the campground with the beach.

The best and most popular hiking trails are those along the rivers, particularly the three-mile **River Bluff Trail,** starting at the campground. The 3.5-mile **Kettle Rapids Trail** over in the west end of the park gets less use, even though it is arguably the most scenic. Not only does the nearby 2.75-mile **Two Rivers Trail** lead along both the St. Croix and the Kettle, but it is also the only riverside trail that forms a loop. The five-mile **Bear Creek Trail,** crossing through the heart of the park along its namesake waterway, is another worthy hike. The 11 miles of trail groomed for cross-country skiing offer several loops, most along the St. Croix, and all are level and easy. Snowshoes for exploring the rest of the park during the snowy season are available for rent.

Of course the canoeing is excellent, and together the two rivers offer something for paddlers of all stripes. Between them the two rivers have nine landings, allowing trips of almost any length and variety, from a nearly placid paddle with just a few Class I rapids along the entire 21 miles of the St. Croix to some moderate white water scattered along most of the Kettle. An outfitter in the park rents canoes and provides shuttle service for over 100 miles of river.

If you are looking for a more restful getaway, have a swim in Lake Clayton, climb the 100-foot fire tower, learn about geology (or just enjoy the scenery) at the **Kettle River Highbanks Overlook** perched atop the 50-foot cliffs, or cast a line into one of the trout streams emptying into the St. Croix. The **St. Croix Lodge,** an old log-and-stone CCC building overlooking the St. Croix River, houses human and natural history exhibits.

Camping

Canoe-in campsites on both the Kettle and St. Croix Rivers and two Adirondack-sheltered backpack sites, each miles from the trailhead, offer the park's most secluded camping. The main campground has 211 sites in three distinct sections. All of the park's 42 electric hookups are in the mostly open Riverview Campground, which is, naturally, where most of the RVs park. The park's four walk-in sites are over here too. The Old Logging Trail Campground loops are the most secluded of the three and, thus, the preferred choice for tent campers, while the Painted Rock Springs Campground is sort of middle ground. Five camper cabins (available May–Sept.) and two large, fully equipped guesthouses (open year-round) let you enjoy the park without roughing it. A separate horse camp can handle 100 horses. For reservations, visit www.stayatmnparks.com.

North to Duluth

It's a pleasant though fairly monotonous 150 miles from the Twin Cities to Duluth along I-35. The towns and parks along this route aren't quaint and remote like those on the St. Croix, but they are worthy of quick visits nonetheless—especially Banning State Park—so schedule a little extra time for your drive north if you can.

NORTH WEST COMPANY FUR POST

It's always 1804 at the North West Company Fur Post (12551 Voyageur Ln., 320/629-6356, www.mnhs.org/nwcfurpost, 10 A.M.–5 P.M. Thurs.–Sat. and Mon., noon–5 P.M. Sun. May through Labor Day, 10 A.M.–5 P.M. Fri.–Sat., noon–5 P.M. Sun. Sept.–Oct., $8 adults), and the voyageurs wintering here will share their lives with you at one of Minnesota's best living-history reenactments. During your visit to this small fortified outpost, authentically reconstructed on the exact Snake River site as the original, they will show you their quarters; barter for blankets, pots, and trinkets; challenge you to games; and try to con you into doing some of their chores. Outside, visit the summer-style wigwam to learn how the Ojibwe benefited from the fur trade, and check out the 25-foot birch-bark canoe and other exhibits in the visitors center. The annual **Fall Gathering** with music and demonstrations takes place in mid-September. The post is located just west of Pine City.

HINCKLEY

Halfway between the Twin Cities and Duluth, Hinckley makes a convenient pit stop, a role it has served since the 1850s when stagecoach service began between St. Paul and Superior, Wisconsin. Lumberjacks arrived in 1869 to begin clearing the surrounding stands of white pine, and the next year, when the Lake Superior and Mississippi Railroad connected St. Paul with Duluth, the town flourished. In 1894, the boom went bust in a big way. That summer remains one of the driest on record, and high winds on September 1 blew several small forest fires together, creating a raging firestorm that swept across the county, destroying Hinckley and five other towns in a matter of hours—over 400 people lost their lives. Though the city rebuilt, it never fully recovered.

The saving grace for the town has been the Mille Lacs Ojibwe's rapidly expanding **Grand Casino Hinckley** (777 Lady Luck Dr., 320/384-7101 or 800/472-6321). Of course there are slots and blackjack tables, but they also host big-name musical acts to draw people up from the Twin Cities. The **Grand Celebration Powwow** is held here in mid-June, and the Native American gift shop in the hotel lobby is small but good.

Few visitors make it to the little downtown, and really the only reasons to do so are to access the southern end of the paved **Willard Munger State Trail,** which runs 63 miles to Duluth, or visit the **Hinckley Fire Museum** (106 Old Hwy. 61, 320/384-7338, 10 A.M.–5 P.M. daily May–Oct., $5 adults). Besides telling the story of the deadly inferno, there are Native American, logging-era, and railroad displays.

Woodland Trails (40361 Grace Lake Rd.,

320/655-3901, www.woodlandtrails.net, $175–245) is a six-room bed-and-breakfast that feels like your own personal country lodge. A few miles out of town, it is surrounded by miles of hiking and skiing trails and has its own pond for boating.

If you are here to gamble it doesn't matter where you stay, since the casino runs a shuttle service to all of Hinckley's hotels, but you might as well sleep at the modern 281-room **Grand Casino Hinckley Hotel** (777 Lady Luck Dr., 320/384-7101 or 800/468-3517, www.grandcasinomn.com, $83). Facilities include a pool, whirlpool, and fitness center. There are also 222 RV campsites jammed together next to the casino.

The casino has half a dozen restaurants to choose from, including the all-you-can-eat **Grand Buffet** (lunch Mon.–Fri. $9, brunch Sat.–Sun. $11, dinner daily $13–21), with well over 100 choices.

Tobies (404 Fire Monument Rd., 320/384-6174, www.tobies.com, open 24/7, $4–12), along I-35, has been serving classic family fare to road-trippers and locals since 1920. The menu has burgers, salads, seafood, steak, and pasta, and there's a take-away counter for their popular bakery.

Jefferson Lines (888/864-2832, www.jeffersonlines.com) buses stop here on the Twin Cities–Duluth run.

SANDSTONE

A sandstone quarry was cut into the Kettle River bluffs here in 1885, and this city grew up alongside it. The town was completely wiped out by the same fire that destroyed Hinckley in 1894; most of the population rode out the inferno in the river. Highway 23, aka the **Veterans Evergreen Memorial Drive Scenic Byway,** leads from here all the way to Duluth and has long been the scenic route to Lake Superior.

The tiny **Sandstone History & Art Center** (402 Main St., 320/245-2271, 9:30 A.M.–1 P.M. Thurs., noon–4 P.M. Fri., 10 A.M.–2 P.M. Sat., $1 adults), built of local stone, features a diorama of the quarry and not much else.

You can walk around the real thing in **Robinson Park** on the east edge of town along 3rd Street. The self-guided trail map available at the museum gives a history of the site and details what remains after 50 years of cutting.

While the **Audubon Center of the North Woods** (54165 Audubon Dr., 320/245-2648 or 888/404-7743, www.audubon-center.org) specializes in group educational programs, visitors are warmly welcomed. The center rehabilitates animals for release into the wild and has seven resident raptors. There are several gentle trails around the center, and the shop is an excellent source of Northwoods information.

If twang is your thang, you'll want a ticket for the **Midwest Country Music Theater** (309 Commercial Ave., 320/245-2429, www.midwestcountry.com, $15–22), a 300-seat venue with weekend Grand Ole Opry–style shows.

If you are going to stick around a while, or are visiting nearby Banning State Park but not camping, consider the small and simple **61 Motel** (1409 Hwy 23 N., 320/245-5419, $40). It's so old it's now a classic, but it passes the white-glove test.

Jefferson Lines (888/864-2832, www.jeffersonlines.com) buses stop at the BP Convenience Store station along Highway 23.

☾ BANNING STATE PARK

Banning State Park's (61101 Banning Park Rd., 320/245-2668) 6,126 acres straddle the raging Kettle River, the first waterway officially designated Wild and Scenic by the state of Minnesota. White-water fanatics with sufficient skill and nerve shoot the mile-long gorge containing spectacular rapids like Dragon's Tooth and Hell's Gate, several of which can hit Class IV. The eight miles from the village of Rutledge to the take-out just before the Banning Rapids has nothing above Class I rapids and is an ideal canoe trip for beginners, though it gets pretty shallow after June.

Banning also contains several of the most rewarding hiking trails in the state. The trails of principal interest are those along the edge of the gorge, since they offer superb viewing of the river and the paddlers who brave it. The easiest is the two-mile **Quarry Loop Trail.** It follows an old railroad bed that was used, in part, to ship the stone from the quarry that operated here between 1892 and 1912. Today, most areas look quite natural, and even the ruins of the two remaining buildings are a scenic addition. Much more interesting than the man-made cuttings are the potholes carved into the rocks alongside the Kettle River during the last Ice Age. They can be found all along the river if you look carefully. The return half of the trail is scenic but not nearly as much so as the stretch along the river, so you may just want to backtrack instead of completing the loop. Continuing along the river south of the Quarry Loop are the **High Bluff Trail** and **Wolf Creek Trail,** which together lead for a little over a mile to Wolf Creek Falls. Beyond the falls the trail continues on to Robinson Park in the city of Sandstone. The **Hell's Gate Trail** and **Lower Hell's Gate Trail,** two short, scenic spurs right along the river, lead toward, but not actually to, Hell's Gate Canyon.

Few people bother with the rest of the 17-mile trail system, though the riverside half of the **Skunk Cabbage Trail,** blanketed by this large and somewhat foul-smelling flower in the spring (it generates enough heat to melt the snow and is the first plant to bloom in the spring), is very scenic. The upper half features more typical spring wildflowers. Branching off it is the three-quarter-mile **Trillium Trail,** another good spring wildflower walk. Both trails are level and easy, though the riverside half of the former can get wet in spots, and there is one long climb halfway through. **Big Spring Falls** at the far south end of the park is a lovely sight and a fun spot to explore. To get there, head to the village of Sandstone and take 3rd Street to Pine Street (the last turn before the bridge) and follow it to the small unmarked pull off. To get way off the beaten path, head up to the **Log Creek Arches,** large potholes worn away at the bottom, in the undeveloped northern half of the park. Come winter, 12 miles of trail, including the Quarry Loop and High Bluff trails along the gorge, are groomed for cross-country skiing.

The campground has 33 widely spaced drive-in sites (11 electric) and a camper cabin. Additionally, there are four first-come, first-served canoe-in sites along the river.

MOOSE LAKE STATE PARK

There is a Moose Lake nearby, but the focus of Moose Lake State Park (218/485-5420, www.stayatmnparks.com for information and reservations), both geographically and recreationally, is Echo Lake, with its picnic area and small swimming beach. Fishing is principally for largemouth bass, northern, and panfish. Rowboats and canoes can be rented from the park office. The campground, just east of the lake, has 33 mostly shady drive-in sites (20 electric), plus a pair of secluded walk-ins. This area is known for its abundance of agates, and the **Moose Lake Agate and Geological Interpretive Center** discusses and displays them. Collecting is not permitted in the park, but the office can direct you to some bounteous sites nearby. Five miles of seldom-used hiking trail and seven miles of groomed cross-country-ski trail lead over the gently rolling hills covering the rest of the park's 1,194 acres. Tops is the westernmost of the 2.5-mile **Rolling Hills Trail**'s three loops. It circles a pond and is the best spot to look for wildlife, including beaver and bald eagle, which have nested along it in recent years. With almost no development along the shore, the two-mile **Echo Lake Trail** also has its moments. Unfortunately you can't escape the hum of interstate traffic on any of them. For bikers, a paved spur of the **Willard Munger State Trail** leads 2.5 miles down to the park.

CLOQUET

Once the site of an Ojibwe village, this area's first European settlers came in 1870 when a sawmill was built at what was then known as Knife Falls. Many more people soon followed, and Cloquet had grown to 12,000 people (a bit larger than it is today) by 1918, when it and two dozen other area towns were almost completely wiped out by a forest fire. The blaze killed 453 people outright, and many more died from resulting injuries or disease.

This Frank Lloyd Wright-designed gas station in Cloquet still attracts architecture buffs.

Cloquet remains a lumber town at heart, and Carlton County's top private-sector employers, all based in Cloquet, are in the forest-product industries, including at the massive Sappi paper mill, with over 850 workers.

Although Frank Lloyd Wright defined himself with such important works of art as Fallingwater and New York City's Guggenheim Museum, he also designed the **Lindholm Service Station** (corner of Hwy. 33 and Cloquet Ave.). Though it was completed in 1958, Wright initially drew up the design as part of his Broadacre utopian city project in the 1930s. Only a compulsive fan of the famous architect would make the trip here just to see the somewhat run-down and frankly not all that interesting (though unmistakably Wright-designed) building, but if you are passing by it's worth a look.

Just down the street from the gas station is the **Carlton County History and Heritage Center** (406 Cloquet Ave., 218/879-1938, www.carltoncountyhistory.org, 9 A.M.–4 P.M. Tues.–Sat., 9 A.M.–8 P.M. Thurs., free admission). The small assortment of historical artifacts includes displays on the logging industry and the fire of 1918.

Two miles west of town at the Tribal Center is the **Fond du Lac Cultural Center and Museum** (1720 Big Lake Rd., 218/878-7582, 9 A.M.–noon and 1–4 P.M. Mon.–Fri., free admission). It's small, but there is some nice Ojibwe birch bark and beadwork. The tribe hosts the **Veteran's Powwow** in July in the nearby town of Sawyer.

Although at its lower reaches the Class V rapids of the St. Louis River offer a wild ride for experienced paddlers only, the 90 miles above Cloquet provide a scenic route with few rapids, all of which are easily portaged if necessary. A good number of campsites and put-ins are spread out between Highway 53 and Cloquet. The **Cloquet River,** a major tributary of the St. Louis River, which it joins just above the city, is an equally scenic and much wilder route. Above the Island Lake Reservoir it has many rapids and campsites, but this stretch is only runnable after heavy rains. Below the lake, water levels depend on the amount of water released by Minnesota Power and can

FOND DU LAC RESERVATION

- Total Area: 158 sq. miles
- Tribally Owned: 23 percent
- Total Population: 3,728
- Native Population: 1,353
- Tribal Enrollment: 3,965

French fur traders gave the name Fond du Lac (Head of the Lake) to the Ojibwe village they encountered at the mouth of the St. Louis River. The name stuck, and it was later applied to the reservation spread across St. Louis and Carlton Counties. The original boundaries cut the tribe off from their ricing and fishing lakes to the south, but through protest and pressure they successfully fought for redrawn property lines. The tribal headquarters is in the city of Cloquet.

By cooperating with outside governments the Fond du Lac band has found great success in both economic development and education. The tribe runs a pair of casinos including Fond du-Luth in the city of Duluth, the only casino in Minnesota located outside reservation boundaries. The Fond du Lac Tribal and Community College in Cloquet is also unique since it is the only combined tribal and state community college in the United States. Opened in 1987, the college concentrates on technology and computer training. In wonderful contrast to the college's high-tech ambitions, the architecture and landscape of its property illustrates ancient aspects of the Ojibwe culture. Campus buildings are laid out in the image of a bear paw, the Ojibwe archival library is shaped like a drum, and the traditional colors of red, black, white, and yellow are common throughout the campus.

One of the Fond du Lac's most famous sons is Jim Northrop, a writer known in and out of the state of Minnesota. His award-winning syndicated column *The Fond du Lac Follies* appears in several Native American publications, and his book *Walking the Rez Road* won a Minnesota Book Award.

be pretty low from July onward, but generally it's enough to scrape by.

One of the best ways to get out on the St. Louis River and on Lake Carlton is on a tour with **Minnesota White Water** (tours start at 3212 River Gate Ave., 218/384-4637, www.minnesotawhitewater.com, $40). They provide just about everything for the 2.5-hour tours except dry clothes—which you'll definitely need. Participants must be at least 12 years old.

The Fond du Lac operate **Black Bear Casino Resort** (1785 Hwy. 210, 218/878-7400 or 888/771-0777, www.blackbearcasinoresort.com) just south of town. The attached hotel ($74–135) has a pool, kiddie pool, two whirlpools, a sauna, fitness center, and game room.

During the warmer months the obvious choice for a meal is **Gordy's Hi-Hat** (415 Sunnyside Dr., 218/879-6125, 10 A.M.–9 P.M. daily Apr.–Oct., $3–6), just across the river on Highway 33. Their famous hamburgers, fishburgers, and malts are known near and far.

Jefferson Lines (888/864-2832, www.jeffersonlines.com) buses stop at Lake Superior Cleaners (12 2nd St., 218/879-2163) on their way between Duluth and the Twin Cities.

CARLTON

Instead of rushing on from Cloquet to Duluth along the freeway, consider taking the scenic route through Carlton. Though it has just 7 percent the population of its neighbor Cloquet, this city of 810 is the Carlton County seat. Carlton secured its dominion back in 1889 by stealing the county records and safes from the village of Thomson across the St. Louis River. The only reason to come to town is to follow one of the scenic routes out. The 15-mile stretch of the **Willard Munger State Trail** between Carlton and Duluth is easily the most scenic part of this popular paved bike trail. Highway 210 between Carlton and Highway 23 forms the **Rushing Rapids Parkway,** a winding drive along the wild St. Louis River.

© WIKIMEDIA COMMONS

the Swinging Bridge in Jay Cooke State Park

At nine miles it is the state's shortest official scenic byway, but one that truly deserves special recognition. Highway 23 will lead you right into Duluth.

JAY COOKE STATE PARK

Jay Cooke State Park (780 Hwy. 210, 218/384-4610, $20 non-electric, $24 electric) sprawls over nearly 9,000 acres, but most visitors are only interested in perusing the rugged St. Louis River and the deep gorge it has cut through the mangled bedrock. The best place to take in the gorge's splendid beauty is the **Swinging Bridge** (behind the River Inn Visitor Center) that spans it, but you don't even need to get out of your car to enjoy the spectacular scenery since Highway 210, the **Rushing Rapids Parkway,** hugs the torrential river for much of its route through the park. Experienced kayakers can tackle the challenging rapids: Adequate water flow is all but guaranteed all season long.

Hiking

The park's superb trail system extends 50 miles through all parts of the park. Naturally the trails along the river are the most popular, however, most park visitors don't get beyond the Swinging Bridge and the campground, so you won't encounter a crowd even on these. The **Carlton Trail** begins at the Swinging Bridge and hugs the south bank up to the north end of the park. It's an easy three miles in and out, or you could take the Willard Munger Bridge across the river and follow the **Thomson Trail** back through the forest. The three-mile **Silver Creek Trail** heads west from the Swinging Bridge and after about a mile turns in from the river and returns through the wooded hills. For some real solitude and a good chance of an animal encounter, strike out on the rolling, seldom-used loops branching off the Silver Creek Trail, like the **Bear Chase Trail, Lost Lake Trail,** and **Spruce Trail.** You can walk in history along the scenic **Grand Portage Trail,** a steep, narrow route north of the river that voyageurs used to bypass the rapids during the fur trade 300 years ago—head back along the river to complete a three-mile loop. Also north of the river, at Oldenburg Point, an easy paved path offers great valley views, and a long set of steps drops down to the river. The **Ogantz Trail,** a moderately hilly loop, is also scenic. The **Willard Munger State Trail,** a paved 63-mile route between Hinckley and Duluth, skirts the northern edge of the park, and about eight miles of trail branching off of it are open to horses and mountain bikes, including a spur to the campground. Thirty-two miles of trail are groomed for cross-country skiing, and most offer a good challenge. You can rent snowshoes at the park office to explore the rest of the park or, if you choose, stick to the ten miles of packed winter-hiking trails.

Camping

The park's campground has 79 (21 electric) widely spaced and mostly shady car-camping sites, plus three walk-ins for added seclusion and a heated camper cabin. The best camping is at the four backpacking sites south of the river.

THE ARROWHEAD

If Minnesota were to release a greatest hits album, most of the tracks would come from its northeast corner. Tucked in between Lake Superior and the Canadian border are some of the state's most interesting towns, best museums, oldest historic sites, and the deepest wilderness east of the Mississippi. The incomparable Boundary Waters Canoe Area Wilderness (BWCAW) encompasses the best of the best of Minnesota's lakes, and if you are even remotely interested in the outdoors you simply must dip a paddle into these enchanting waters at least once in your life.

In contrast to the placid borderland lakes, the waters of the North Shore rage through deep gorges and over massive waterfalls before emptying into Lake Superior. Places like Grand Marais, with its flourishing arts community, and the iconic Split Rock Lighthouse complete the North Shore mosaic. Duluth, which you'll inevitably pass through to get almost anywhere else in the Arrowhead, is perfectly pleasant in nearly every way, from its walkable size to its cool and comfortable weather.

Although it is defined by the city-sized scars left behind after more than a century of strip mining, these only serve to make the surprising Iron Range, stretched out across the heart of the Arrowhead, one of the most unusual places in the state. And spread across most of the region is the 4,680-square-mile Superior National Forest (SNF), which hosts every conceivable outdoor activity and then some. The Arrowhead is the Minnesota you've imagined, and—whatever the season—it just doesn't get any better than this.

HIGHLIGHTS

Canal Park and the Waterfront: Whether they're going nose to snout with a lake sturgeon at the Great Lakes Aquarium or watching gargantuan ships sail under the Aerial Lift Bridge, kids and adults find a day spent strolling Duluth's Lake Superior shoreline nothing less than enchanting (page 124).

Gooseberry Falls State Park and Split Rock Lighthouse State Park: These neighboring North Shore parks make a perfect pair (pages 146 and 147).

Palisade Head: If you're going to talk about the most beautiful sights in Minnesota or on Lake Superior, this 350-foot cliff climbing out of Lake Superior needs to be part of the conversation (page 149).

George H. Crosby Manitou State Park: The first Minnesota state park designed for backpackers is a quiet, beautiful, and little-visited wilderness escape (page 151).

Grand Marais: With a lovely lakeside setting and more cultural opportunities than many much larger towns, Grand Marais is a great base for exploring the surrounding wilderness (page 156).

Grand Portage: Relive the fur trade era at the Grand Portage National Monument, a re-creation of the North West Company's fortified 18th-century headquarters (page 164).

Paddling the Boundary Waters Canoe Area Wilderness: With over one million acres and nearly 1,200 lakes set aside for silent sports, this is one of the best canoeing destinations – not to mention one of the most beautiful places – in the world (page 170).

Dorothy Molter Museum: Dorothy Molter grew up in Chicago, but she dropped everything and moved deep into the wilderness of the Boundary Waters, where the "Root Beer Lady" spent the rest of her years. After her death, friends moved these two cabins and many of her belongings to Ely to open this remarkable memorial to a most remarkable woman (page 173).

Soudan Underground Mine State Park: Not for claustrophobics, tours of this retired iron mine take you half a mile down and nearly a mile into the deepest part of the mine (page 180).

Chisholm: This little town hosts the Iron Range's biggest attraction, Minnesota Discovery Center, which is the best place to learn about Minnesota mining (page 201).

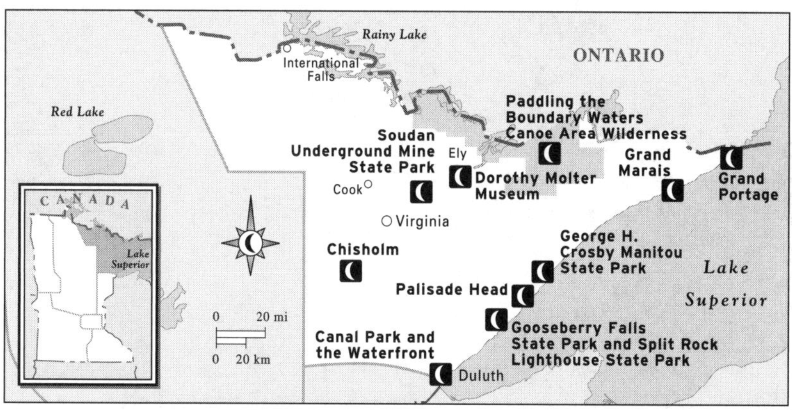

LOOK FOR TO FIND RECOMMENDED SIGHTS, ACTIVITIES, DINING, AND LODGING.

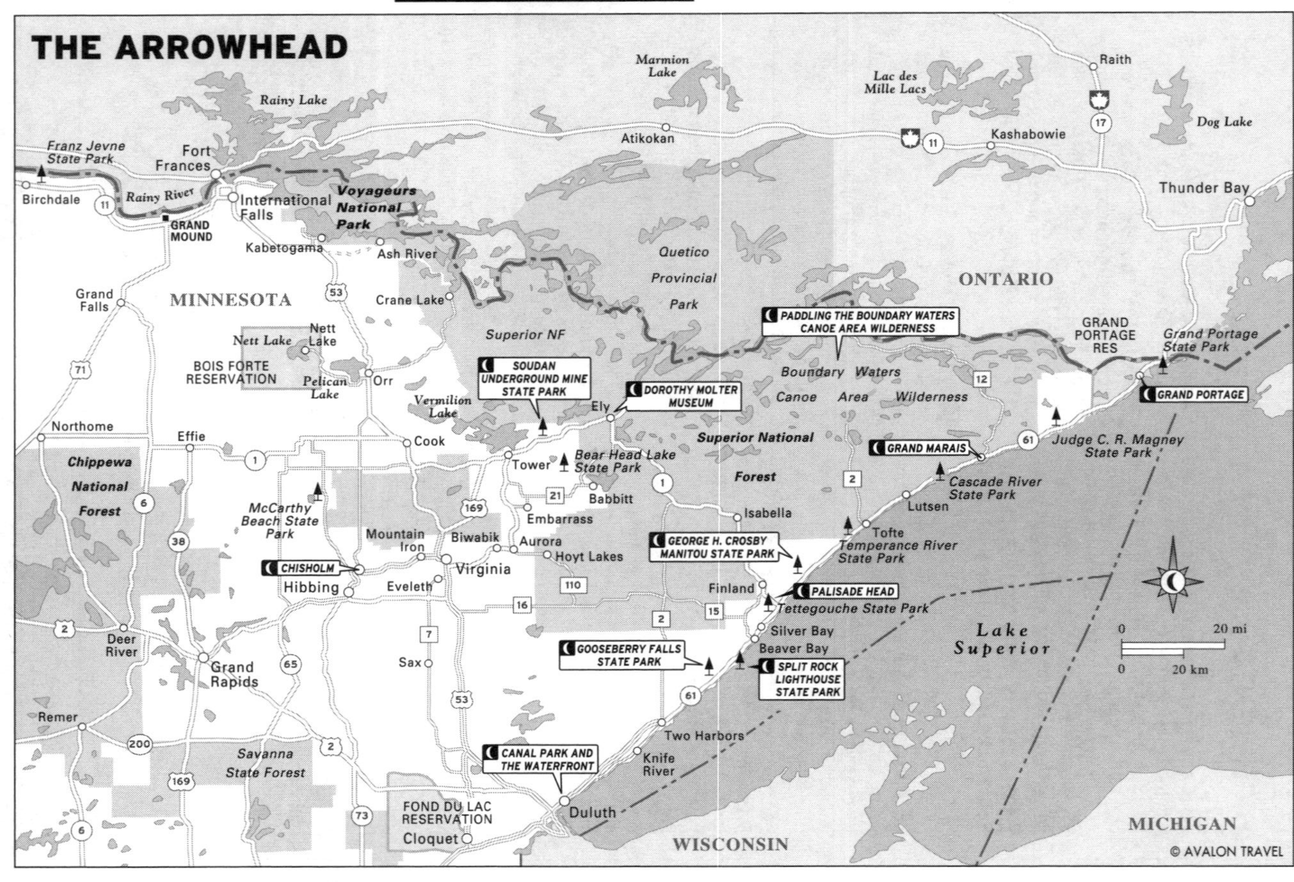

THE ARROWHEAD

PLANNING YOUR TIME

A week is enough time to circle through northeast Minnesota's four distinct regions, but if you love the outdoors even a month isn't enough time to really explore it. Duluth is a logical starting point, and though it's not centrally located, it could be used as a base for your entire visit. From **Hawk Ridge** to the **Aerial Lift Bridge** it's a fascinating city and deserves several days, but if your time is limited just make sure you at least poke around **Canal Park.** Two days is the minimum to properly do the North Shore, but if you've only got one you can easily get to **Two Harbors, Gooseberry Falls State Park,** and **Split Rock Lighthouse State Park** and still get back to Duluth. The abundance of outfitters and resorts around **Voyageurs National Park** and the **Boundary Waters Canoe Area Wilderness** means you don't need any outdoors experience to get deep into the remote, lake-littered Boundary Waters region, one of the most beautiful places on earth, and you're missing out if you don't spend at least one night on a remote lakeshore. Finally, don't cross the often-overlooked **Iron Range** without getting an up-close look at one of the massive open pit mines.

Duluth

Duluth is a city of many faces. It seamlessly blends small-town charm with a touch of big-city pizzazz, and though its 85,000 residents make it the third-largest city in Minnesota, it still has a wild side, as the resident bears and wandering moose will affirm. Ironically though, it is the gritty industrial side that attracts most visitors. While it sits 2,432 miles from the Atlantic Ocean, Duluth, along with Superior, Wisconsin, its neighbor to the south, is one of the busiest ports in the world and the top on the Great Lakes. Some of the world's largest grain elevators and ore docks dominate the shoreline, and more than 1,000 monstrous ships sail into the Twin Ports each year. Witnessing these leviathans up close and personal is a fascinating activity.

Although Duluth has something for everyone, those with children in tow will especially appreciate the city on the lake. Many people planning a first-time North Shore getaway just stop in Duluth briefly, only to regret not having budgeted more time. Don't make the same mistake; stick around for a few days and enjoy everything this wonderful city has to offer.

History

French voyageurs, who first arrived in the mid-17th century, called this area Fond du Lac (Head of the Lake) and, like the Native Americans before them, camped in the natural harbor for protection from Lake Superior's notoriously severe and sudden storms. Daniel Greysolon, Sieur DuLuth, a marine captain in the French army, landed on Minnesota Point in 1679 to promote peace between the warring Ojibwe and Dakota, and fur traders soon established a small outpost in Duluth's present-day Fond du Lac neighborhood. The enterprise succeeded, though never flourished, even after 1809 when John Jacob Astor's American Fur Company built a fort here. The station was abandoned in 1849, the same year Minnesota became a territory.

Rumors of copper in the area—later proven to be nothing but rumors—and the construction of the Sault Sainte Marie Locks brought settlers back in 1853. The next year, when the Treaty of La Point turned over most of the Ojibwe's land to the Americans, a true land rush began, and many predicted that a city here could rival Chicago. As a site for a city, the Head of the Lake couldn't be more ideal. The natural harbor is one of the best in the world, and, as the westernmost point on the Great Lakes, it is perfectly situated commercially. Wealthy land speculators from St. Paul and politicians from Washington threw money

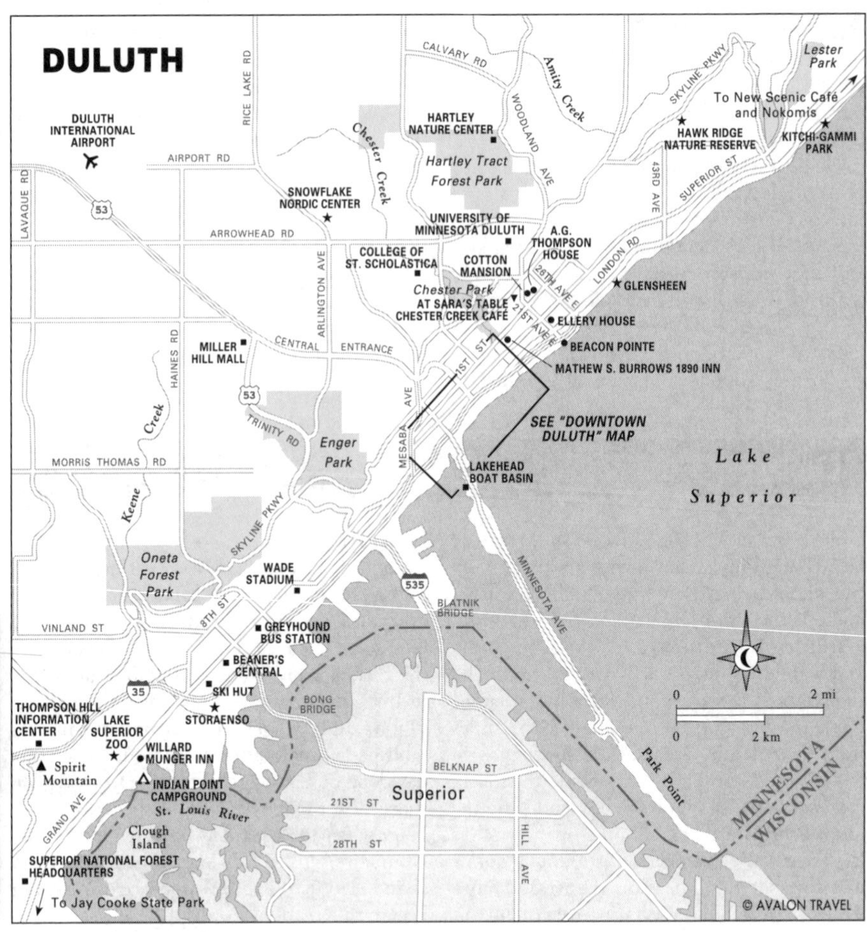

into development. Nearly a dozen small settlements, which eventually would merge into the present-day Duluth, sprang up below the steep hills on the north side of the bay, but most initial growth took place to the south on the broad plains of Wisconsin. Superior was the logical location for a great city, not only because of the level terrain, but it was also closest to the natural harbor entry, linked to St. Paul by a new military road, and a future rail line wouldn't need to span the St. Louis River. By 1857 Superior had swelled to around 3,000 people, while Duluth remained a backwater. The American Civil War began a few years later and put all plans for a new metropolis on ice.

It would be over two decades before anyone again dreamt of a great city here. That person was Eastern financier Jay Cooke, who came in 1868 and decided to bring his Lake Superior and Mississippi River Railroad north from St. Paul to Duluth instead of Superior. This was the first in a series of events that gave Duluth dominance and created a rivalry between the two cities that, to a small degree, still exists today. Even before the first train rolled into "Jay Cooke's town" in 1870, Dr. Thomas

The Aerial Lift Bridge spanning the Duluth Ship Canal is iconic to the Twin Ports.

Foster, publisher of the city's first newspaper, had declared Duluth "the Zenith City of the Unsalted Seas" and the population exploded from 14 in January of 1869 to 3,500 by the Fourth of July.

The bubble burst a second time in 1873 when Cooke's entire empire crumbled, inciting a stock market crash and national depression. The city officially lost its charter and most of its 5,000 citizens, but Duluth was just too strategically positioned and surrounded by too many natural resources not to fulfill its destiny. It took about a decade, but soon local logging and western wheat farming revived the Twin Ports' purpose and fueled construction of even more railroads to move these products here, plus the wharves, docks, and grain elevators needed to ship them to the East. By 1883 Duluth and its 14,000 residents were thriving, and the city, through further economic ups and downs, continued to grow. Shipping eventually made Duluth–Superior the second most important urban center in all of the Northwest and home to more millionaires per capita than any other city in the world.

As the 20th century rolled in, iron mining expanded on the Mesabi Range and Duluth–Superior became the busiest port on the Great Lakes. Many of the city's heavy industries shut down or moved on over the course of the century, but tourism and shipping, along with education and health care jobs, have kept the city moving forward.

Orientation

Duluth stretches 26 miles along Lake Superior and St. Louis Bay and is less than a mile wide most of the way. Downtown is tucked into the steep, rocky hills that parallel the shoreline, and a few streets here are as steep as any in San Francisco, though most everything of interest sits at the bottom along historic Superior Street. Most of the action for tourists is in the adjacent Canal Park, which is not a park at all but a reclaimed warehouse district brimming with shops, restaurants, and other diversions. Many more must-see attractions are just a short stroll away along the waterfront. The seven-mile finger of land jutting out beyond the city is Park Point (rarely referred to by its official name, Minnesota Point), the world's largest freshwater sandbar. Most of the city's bed-and-breakfasts lie just beyond downtown in the mansion-filled East End. Today most of the town's growth is inland along Highway 53, the area known as Miller Hill, but there is little reason for tourists to venture up this way.

SIGHTS

Canal Park and the Waterfront

The massive **Aerial Lift Bridge** spanning the Duluth Ship Canal is as iconic to the Twin Ports as the Golden Gate Bridge is to San Francisco, but much more unusual. Instead of your standard seesawing drawbridge, a 1,000-ton central span rises 138 feet like an elevator to let ships enter the harbor. Watching one of the massive ships pass under it is a mandatory part of a Duluth visit.

The **Lake Superior Maritime Visitor Center** (600 Lake Ave. S., 218/720-5260, www.lsmma.com, 10 A.M.–9 P.M. daily June–Oct., reduced hours rest of year, free admission) houses an excellent collection of Twin Ports and Great Lakes shipping past and present, including a giant steam engine (which the

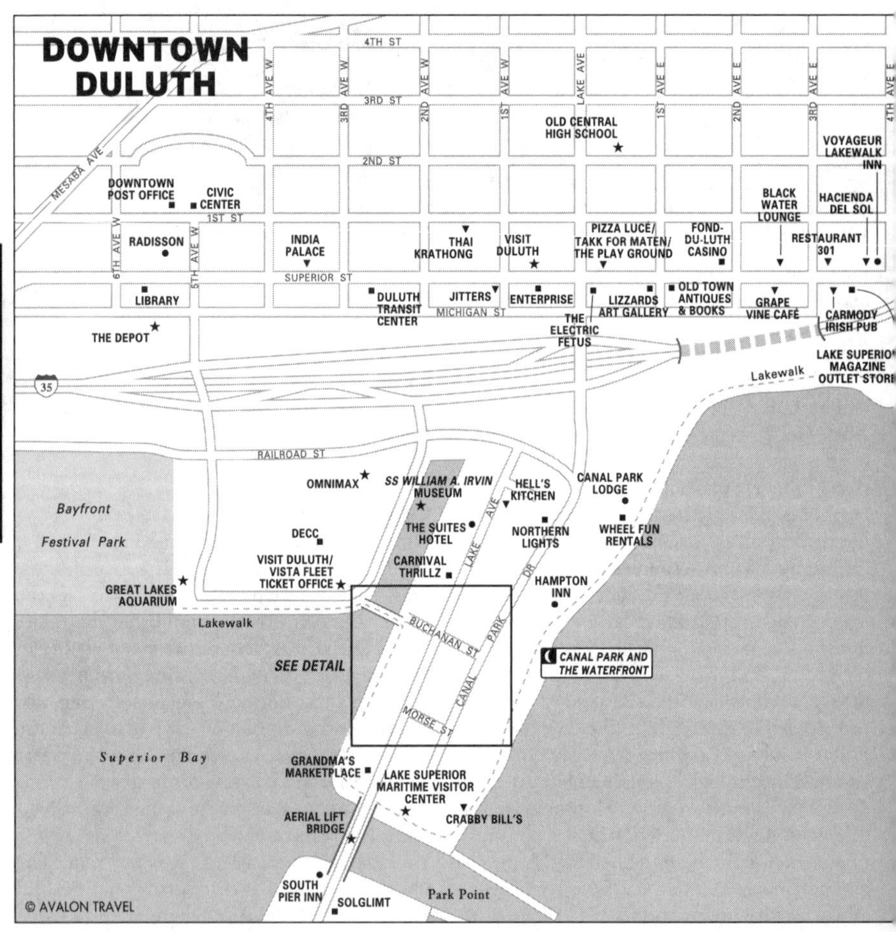

staff runs on request), a model of an ore dock, and lots of unique knickknacks. If you want to see a child's eyes light up, let her spin the wheel in the pilothouse mock-up. Computer screens post ship arrival and departure times, and telescopes let you examine ships out on the lake waiting for their dock to free up.

The **S.S. William A. Irvin Museum** (301 Harbor Dr., 218/722-7876, www.duluthfloatingmuseum.com, 9 A.M.–6 P.M. daily May–Sept., $9 adults) includes a pair of retired ships, the 610-foot *William A. Irvin* and the Coast Guard Cutter *Sundew.* The *Irvin,* the former flagship of U.S. Steel's Great Lakes Fleet, lets you see what takes place on board the monstrous ships you've been admiring in the port. During the hour-long tour of the former iron ore and coal vessel you'll see the 2,000-horsepower engines, elaborate guest quarters, pilothouse, and vast cargo hold. The *Sundew* was a Coast Guard workhorse that tended buoys, did search and rescue, and broke ice. For Halloween, the *Irvin* is transformed into the "Ship of Ghouls."

Vista Fleet Harbor Cruises (323 Harbor Dr., 218/722-6218, www.vistafleet.com, daily

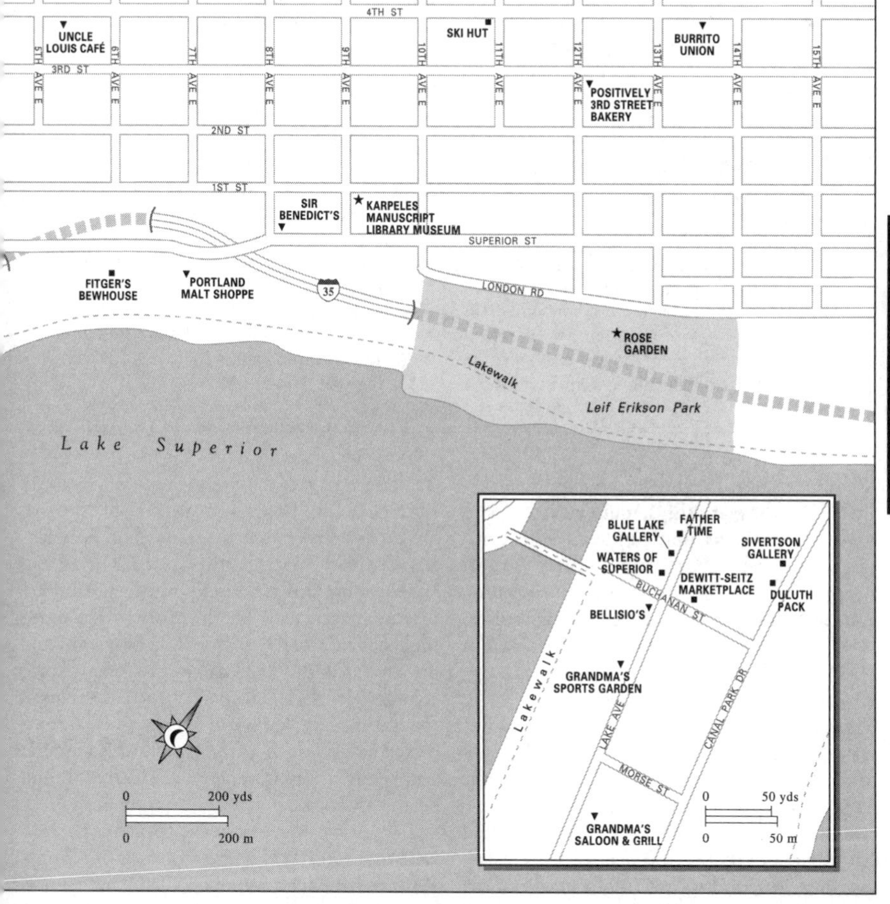

SHIP WATCHING

There is something almost magical about watching giant ships cruise in and out of port. Things that big, it seems, just shouldn't be so maneuverable, or even be able to float. Oceangoing "salties" stretch up to 730 feet long while the "lakers" can exceed 1,000 feet in length and weigh 100,000 tons when fully loaded – mostly with taconite, coal, and grain. The shipping season depends on the weather, but usually runs late March to mid-January. The **Boat Watcher's Hotline** (218/722-6489), a service of the U.S. Army Corps of Engineers, gives ship arrival and departure times for the Twin Ports and the North Shore. The wonderful ***Duluth Shipping News*** (www.duluthshippingnews.com), a free newsletter published daily during the summer, informs the curious of what cargo individual ships are carrying on that day along with their histories and statistics. Other articles offer an inside scoop on how the industry works and tell stories about the crews. You can pick it up just about anywhere in Canal Park or read it online.

The ultimate viewing spot is the **Duluth Ship Canal.** As the ships slip under the Aerial Lift Bridge they pass so close you can virtually reach out and touch them. The Lake Superior Maritime Visitor Center posts arrival and departure times. The viewing spot at the aquarium is farther away, but nearly just as good because it's at deck level. Also in Duluth, an elevated observation platform near the Duluth, Missabe, and Iron Range Railway Company's 2,000-foot-long **ore docks** lets you see the ships being loaded with taconite pellets. From South 40th Avenue West, just south of I-35, head east on Oneota Street and follow the signs. The **Vista Fleet Harbor Tours** take you past these and other docks in the harbor.

The **Harvest States grain elevators** (some of the largest in the world), across the bay in Superior, are the best place for an up-close look at boats in dock. You'll see them on the right as you come across the Blatnik Bridge and you can drive right up to them. You can also drive past the docks on **Connors Point,** a mile northwest of Superior's Tourist Information Center on U.S. Highway 53. Although it sees much less traffic than Duluth's canal, ships occasionally arrive and depart through the **Superior Entry.**

Moving up the North Shore your next best bet is **Two Harbors,** where you have unobstructed views of the ships pulling into Agate Bay and loading up at the ore docks. Ships can also be seen loading in **Silver Bay** and at **Taconite Harbor** much further northeast along the coast.

May–Oct., $14) let you get up close and personal with the giant ships, grain elevators, and ore docks in the harbor, and, weather permitting, you'll even get to cruise under the Lift Bridge. The standard tour takes 90 minutes, and they also offer a variety of dining cruises.

The **Great Lakes Aquarium** (353 Harbor Dr., 218/740-3474, www.glaquarium.org, 10 A.M.–6 P.M. daily, $14.50 adults, $8.50 children 3–16), the nation's largest freshwater aquarium (though traveling exhibits are often oceanic), puts you face to face with the native residents of Lake Superior, such as the five-foot lake sturgeon in the 103,000 gallon Isle Royale tank and the bizarre paddlefish, long-nose gar, and slimy sculpin in one of the 22 other tanks. Not all of the aquarium's creatures have fins. Besides 70 species of fish there are turtles, snakes, salamanders, mud puppies, frogs, ducks, and playful otters. The Great Lakes Aquarium is actually much more than just an aquatic zoo. There are also often-overlooked historical, ecological, geological, and artistic exhibits about the world's largest lake, spanning its glacial creation to current environmental threats. Plenty of interactive exhibits aimed at kids, such as the stingray touch tank and virtual submarine, let them learn without even realizing it.

East down the Lakewalk is picnic-perfect **Leif Erikson Park,** home to a stunning **Rose Garden** filled by over 3,000 bushes and a

© BRUCE MANNING

The Great Lakes Aquarium in Duluth is the largest freshwater aquarium in the country.

half-sized replica of the **Viking ship** that Leif Erikson sailed to North America. In 1926 this very boat retraced the route from Norway before ending up here.

Downtown

Officially it's the St. Louis County Heritage and Arts Center, but everyone calls it **The Depot** (506 Michigan St. W., 218/727-8025 or 888/733-5833, www.duluthdepot.org, 9:30 A.M.–6 P.M. daily summer, 10 A.M.–6 P.M. Mon.–Sat., noon–6 P.M. Sun. rest of year, $10 adults), after the imposing 1892 Chateau-style structure's original purpose. Today it houses four museums, with the **Lake Superior Railroad Museum** (218/722-1273, www.lsrm.org, 10 A.M.–5 P.M. Mon.–Sat., 1–5 P.M. Sun.) being the top draw. The outstanding collection of classic rolling stock includes an 1861 wood-burning steam engine, railway post office, and rotary snowplow, plus kids love the locomotive simulator.

The hands-on **Duluth Children's Museum** (218/733-7543, www.duluthchildrensmuseum.org, 9:30 A.M.–6 P.M. daily summer, 10 A.M.–5 P.M. Tues.–Sat., 1–5 P.M. Sun., closed Mon. rest of year, $6.75 adult, $4 children, $2 ages 3–5, ages 2 and under free), entered by descending through a giant tree trunk, focuses on natural history and world cultures.

The displays of the **St. Louis County Historical Society** (218/733-7586, www.thehistorypeople.com, 8 A.M.–4:30 P.M. Mon.–Fri., closed for lunch noon–1:30 P.M., closed Sat.–Sun.) look back at northeastern Minnesota.

The tiny **Duluth Art Institute** (218/733-7560, www.duluthartinstitute.org, 9:30 A.M.–6 P.M. daily summer, 10 A.M.–5 P.M. Mon.–Sat., 1–5 P.M. Sun. rest of year) has rotating exhibits.

Seemingly out of place in far-off Duluth, the **Karpeles Manuscript Library Museum** (902 1st St. E., 218/728-0630, www.rain.org/~karpeles, noon–4 P.M. Thurs.–Sun., free admission) is one of the largest collections of historical documents in the world, and Duluth native David Karpeles wanted one of his seven branch museums to be located here. Displays are rotated every three months so you never know what you will find, but his collection includes original copies of such landmarks as the

HISTORIC TOURS

Superior Street, Duluth's historic main drag, is lined with gorgeous turn-of-the-20th-century buildings, and you should take some time to admire the classic architecture of a bygone era: They don't build them like this anymore – and unfortunately Duluth no longer preserves them like they used to. The free ***Downtown Duluth: Architecture and Public Art*** brochure, available at the downtown tourist office, points out dozens of historic buildings on Superior Street and elsewhere. The one building not to miss, though it would be difficult to do so, is **Old Central High School.** This 1892 Romanesque Revival brownstone has gargoyles and a 230-foot clock tower with chimes patterned after London's Big Ben. Beyond downtown, the ***Walking Tour of Duluth's Historic East End*** brochure details two dozen historic houses on Superior and 1st Streets between 21st and 24th Avenues.

For a more in-depth look at the city's past, hop aboard the Port Town Trolley for **Historic Architecture Tours** (218/727-8025, 10 A.M. every other Sun. June-Oct., $32). The 3.5-hour tours, led by a storytelling guide in period costume, start at The Depot and cross Canal Park, downtown, the East End, and Fitger's; plus the price includes a brunch buffet at Bennett's on the Lake and free admission to The Depot. You can also buy an entertaining CD ($12) of the tour at The Depot, Visit Duluth offices, and many stores.

Bill of Rights and Emancipation Proclamation, letters from Darwin and Galileo, Disney contracts, and Wagner's *Wedding March.* It can be fascinating to see history with changes written in the margins.

East Duluth

Self-made millionaire Chester Congdon spared no expense in building his opulent estate on Lake Superior, and little has changed inside the 39-room Jacobean-style **Glensheen** (3300 London Rd., 218/726-8910 or 888/454-4536, www.glensheen.org, 9:30 A.M.–4:30 P.M. daily May–Oct., 9:30 A.M.–4 P.M. Sat.–Sun. rest of year, $13 adults standard tour, $5 grounds pass) mansion since it was completed in 1908. A variety of tours take you past the wealth of custom-designed furniture, hand-carved woodwork, leaded art-glass windows, and the formal gardens in the surrounding 7.5-acre grounds.

The modern **University of Minnesota Duluth** (UMD) campus is home to the best art museum in the northland, the **Tweed Museum of Art** (1201 Ordean Ct., 218/726-8222, www.d.umn.edu/tma, 9 A.M.–8 P.M. Tues., 9 A.M.–4:30 P.M. Wed.–Fri., 1–5 P.M. Sat.–Sun., free admission), with works from around the globe in the permanent collection. The **Marshall W. Alworth Planetarium** (1023 University Dr., 218/726-7129, www.d.umn.edu/planet, 7–8 P.M. Wed., free admission) has free public shows each week.

On your way out of town on Scenic Highway 61 is **Kitchi-Gammi Park,** an excellent place to enjoy the cooling breezes off the lake, with picnic areas, grills, a swing set, and a WPA-built fire shelter.

A few minutes up the road, you'll hit the DNR's **French River Fish Hatchery** (5357 North Shore Dr., 218/525-0867, 8 A.M.–4:30 P.M. Mon.–Fri., free admission), where trout are raised. There is a small visitors center with a video explaining the operation and a glass viewing window—best time to look is April and early May just before the yearlings are ready for release.

Next is **Tom's Logging Camp** (5797 North Shore Dr., 218/525-4120, www.tomsloggingcamp.com, 9 A.M.–5 P.M. daily May–Oct., $4 adults, $3 children.), with the ultimate kitschy gift shop, replica buildings from the heyday of lumbering, such as a blacksmith shop, and bunkhouse. Kids love feeding the goats and llamas. Right across from Tom's is the **Stoney Point** wayside, a noted storm-watching site.

West Duluth

Residents of the **Lake Superior Zoo** (7210 Fremont St., 218/733-3777, www.lszoo.org,

© TIM BEWER
The Depot

10 A.M.–5 P.M. daily Apr.–Sept., 10 A.M.–4 P.M. rest of year, $9 adults) come from around the globe, but the focus is fittingly on northern species. The zoo has had some hard times—including losing its Association of Zoos and Aquariums accreditation in 2006—and it shows in the condition of some of the exhibits. But the facility is on the mend again after the city of Duluth ceded management to a private nonprofit in early 2009.

StoraEnso (100 N. Central Ave., 218/722-6024) offers fascinating one-hour **paper mill tours** (9 A.M., 10:30 A.M., 1 P.M., and 3 P.M. Mon., Tues., and Fri. summer, free) in their high-tech facility. You'll get a video overview of the process and then see (and hear!) the giant rolls being wound. You must call in advance to reserve the free tickets. Open-toed or high-heeled shoes and children under 10 are not allowed.

Scenic Train Rides

Rail fans hit the jackpot in Duluth, which has two scenic excursions chugging out of the city. The **North Shore Scenic Railroad** (506 Michigan St. W., 218/722-1273 or 800/423-1273, www.northshorescenicrailroad.org) at The Depot skirts Lake Superior on either a 90-minute excursion (12:30 P.M. and 3 P.M. daily May–Oct., plus 10 A.M. Fri.–Sun. summer, $14 adults) or a six-hour trip all the way to Two Harbors (10:30 A.M. Fri. and Sat. May–Oct., $25 adults). Other options include murder mysteries and a pizza train. Both trips travel in vintage passenger cars pulled by classic engines. Friday morning passengers can combine a ride with an overnight at the Lighthouse Bed and Breakfast in Two Harbors, if arranged in advance.

Heading in the opposite direction is the **Lake Superior and Mississippi Railroad** (6930 Fremont St., 218/624-7549, www.lsmrr.org, 10:30 A.M. and 1:30 P.M. Sat.–Sun. June–Oct., $10.50), which follows the St. Louis River for 12 miles along the original rail line connecting Duluth with the Twin Cities. They like to call their train ride a "nature walk on rails," which pretty much sums it up. You can ride in their vintage coaches, but the best views come from the completely open "Safari Car." Trains depart across from the zoo.

Skyline Drive

This scenic 25-mile drive stretches right across the top of the city. The marked route roughly follows the ancient Lake Superior shoreline some 600 feet above today's lake surface. Though the central portion of the drive passes through the city, most of the parkway leads through forest and past rushing rivers and waterfalls. You can access the east end from Superior Street at Lester Park and the west end at Becks Road near Gary–New Duluth. The popular eastern section is known as **Seven Bridges Road,** a narrow unpaved route with not seven but nine stone-arch bridges and the most scenic of the roads many scenic overlooks.

Also along the eastern portion is the **Hawk Ridge Nature Reserve** (Skyline E. & 52nd Ave. E., 218/428-6209, www.hawkridge.org), a 315-acre hilltop natural area. People flock from all over the country beginning in mid-August, when tens of thousands of migrating raptors follow the air currents along the Lake Superior

THE DULUTH LYNCHINGS

In June of 1920, four black men were falsely accused of rape. Three were lynched by a mob of nearly 3,000, and the fourth was convicted in a mockery of a court trial. At the time, the lynchings earned headlines in newspapers across the country. But memories receded to the point where most Minnesotans were unaware of the crime. Court records were burned, and the Duluth Historical Society discouraged research into the event. In 1992, the play *The Last Minstrel Show* premiered at Penumbra Theatre and helped resurrect the tragedy. Since then, the play has been reprised, the Minnesota Historical Society Press published Michael Fedo's *The Lynchings in Duluth* and Warren Read's *The Lyncher in Me*, and Duluth has erected a memorial to Elias Clayton, Elmer Jackson, and Isaac McGhie, the three men who were murdered.

shoreline on their way south for the winter. Over 100,000 broad-winged hawks were once counted in a single day. The best viewing is usually from early September through October between about 9 A.M. and 4 P.M., and some still pass by as late as December. During the migration, Hawk Ridge naturalists conduct research and offer free educational programs for the general public. The rest of the year it's still a worthwhile destination for the 2.5 miles of hiking trails.

Enger Park (16th Ave. W. & Skyline Dr.), near the middle of the parkway at 18th Avenue West, should also not be missed. A historic rock observation tower rises five stories from the city's highest point, and a Japanese garden, picnic area, and several secluded overlooks surround it.

ENTERTAINMENT AND EVENTS

For the full scoop on what's on during the week, scan The Wave section from Friday's ***Duluth News-Tribune*** or the ***Reader Weekly,*** both of which are distributed free around town.

The biggest touring acts that make it to the Twin Ports, from Broadway musicals to circuses, play at the **DECC** (Duluth Entertainment Convention Center, 350 Harbor Dr., 218/722-5573, www.decc.org).

Both **UMD** (www.d.umn.edu) and the **College of St. Scholastica** (www.css.edu) have full cultural calendars.

Nightlife

Several of Duluth's best restaurants have music most nights. **Black Water Lounge** (231 Superior St. E., 218/740-0436, www.blackwaterlounge.com) hosts smoky jazz perfectly suited to its high-style atmosphere every Tuesday and Wednesday, 7:30–10:30 P.M.

It's generally bluegrass, Celtic, and similar at **Sir Benedict's** (805 Superior St. E., 218/728-1192, 11 A.M.–1 A.M. daily).

Folk artists play at **Amazing Grace Bakery & Café** (394 Lake Ave. S., 218/723-0075, 7 A.M.–10 P.M. Sun.–Thurs., 7 A.M.–11 P.M. Fri.–Sat.).

It could be anything at **Beaner's Central** (324 Central Ave. N., 218/624-5957, 6:30 A.M.–8 P.M. Mon.–Tues. and Thurs., 6:30 A.M.–11 P.M. Wed. and Fri., 7 A.M.–11 P.M. Sat., 8 A.M.–7 P.M. Sun.) in West Duluth.

Pizza Luce (11 Superior St. E., 218/727-7400, www.pizzaluce.com, 8 A.M.–1:30 A.M. Sun.–Thurs., 8 A.M.–2:30 A.M. Fri.–Sat.) finds unusual bands to suit its funky atmosphere.

There's music all over the place in the several bars in the Fitger's complex, with **Fitger's Brewhouse** (600 Superior St. E., 218/279-2739, 11 A.M.–10 P.M. Sun.–Thurs., 11 A.M.–11 P.M. Fri.–Sat.), a particularly popular draw.

Carmody Irish Pub (308 Superior St. E., 218/740-4747, www.carmodyirishpub.com, 3 P.M.–1 A.M. daily) sometimes has Irish music on weekends.

Grandma's Sports Garden (425 Lake Ave. S., 218/722-4724) in Canal Park clears the floor for dancing Wednesday, Friday, and Saturday nights.

Classical Music and Dance

The **Duluth-Superior Symphony Orchestra** (218/733-7575, www.dsso.com) performs more or less year-round at the DECC.

The Duluth-based **Minnesota Ballet** (218/529-3742, www.minnesotaballet.org) also puts on a few performances there each year.

The **Lake Superior Chamber Orchestra** (218/726-8877) holds five Wednesday-evening concerts at UMD each summer.

Theater

The **Duluth Playhouse** (218/733-7555, www.duluthplayhouse.com), entertaining the masses since 1914, is the state's oldest community theater group. They stage regular shows for adults and children year-round at The Depot (506 Michigan St. W.).

The small **The Play Ground** (11 Superior St. E., 218/733-7555, www.duluthplayground.org) mixes theater, live music, independent films, and other special events.

Cinema

The **Duluth 10** (300 Harbor Dr., 218/722-1573, www.marcustheatres.com), gets all the big Hollywood movies.

The large-format **OMNIMAX** (350 Harbor Dr., 218/727-0022, www.decc.org/attractions/omni) is also downtown.

Spectator Sports

The **UMD Bulldogs** compete in a full slate of NCAA Division II athletics, but for the fans it is pretty much all about hockey. Despite the school's small size, the men's team is a regular contender in the Division I WCHA conference and counts Brett Hull among the dozens of alumni who have skated in the NHL. Order tickets through the UMD Ticket Office (218/726-8595 or 877/221-8168, www.umndbulldogs.com).

The **Duluth Huskies** play in the Northwoods League, made up of Division I college baseball players who get minor-league experience while keeping their college eligibility. Home games are played at historic **Wade Stadium** (34th Ave. W. & Grand Ave., 218/786-9909, www.duluthhuskies.com). Tickets start at $6.

Many of the world's best curlers compete for the **Duluth Curling Club** (218/727-1851, www.duluthcurlingclub.com), whose home ice is at the DECC. The bonspiel season runs November to March, and they have introductory clinics if you want to throw some stones of your own.

Events

So much more than just a race to Duluthians, mid-June's **Grandma's Marathon** (www.grandmasmarathon.com) is one of the most anticipated dates on the city's calendar. Though the racers compete on Saturday morning, live entertainment and a health expo run all weekend, plus the post-race party is free and open to the public. Runners start near Two Harbors and continue along scenic route 61, finishing in Canal Park, outside the namesake restaurant—you can see the finish line year-round. The race, a Boston Marathon qualifier, registers runners on a first-come, first-served basis. The men's record is 2:09:37, and the women's is 2:27:05.

A slightly smaller crowd—an estimated 4,000 spectators—converges on Duluth on the last Sunday in January for the **John Beargrease Sled Dog Marathon** (218/722-7631, www.beargrease.com). Run since 1981, the marathon is the longest sled dog race in the lower 48 and is an Iditarod qualifier race. Mushers race north from Duluth almost to the Canadian border and back. The mid-distance race, about 100 miles, starts in Duluth and finishes on the shore of Lake Superior in Tofte. The race is named for the son of an Ojibwe chief who helped the communities of the North Shore survive and grow by delivering mail by dog sled in the late 19th century.

Four thousand skaters follow the same route as Grandma's in September during the **Northshore Inline Marathon** (www.northshoreinline.com), the largest inline race in the country and an official World Cup event.

The **Bayfront Blues Festival** (www.bayfrontblues.com) has the whole town swinging the second weekend in August. Dozens of acts perform on three stages in Bayfront Festival Park, and many area clubs get in on the action as well. Recent headliners have included Buddy Guy and Blues Traveler.

SHOPPING

Whether you're looking for a souvenir T-shirt or a piece of fine art, the place to start in Duluth is Canal Park. And, after you've made the rounds there, head to Superior Street.

Shopping Centers

A great place for one-stop shopping is **DeWitt-Seitz Marketplace** (394 Lake Ave. S., www.dewitt-seitz.com, 10 A.M.–9 P.M. Mon.–Fri., 10 A.M.–8 P.M. Sat., 11 A.M.–5 P.M. Sun.), a beautifully converted warehouse with 11 stores, including **Northern Waters Smokehaus** (218/724-7307, www.nwsmokehaus.com), with highly regarded fish and gourmet cheeses; **Art Dock** (218/722-6410, www.art-dock.net), a consignment gallery for hundreds of regional artists; and **J. Skylark** (218/722-3794), an independent toy store with a real sense of what it means to be a kid.

© TRICIA CORNELL

The Fitger's Brewery Complex near downtown Duluth is a one-stop destination for shopping and dining.

Just on the edge of downtown is the **Fitger's Brewery Complex** (600 Superior St. E., www.fitgers.com), a renovated 1885 brewhouse with a surprising selection of upscale shopping, including clothing and shoes and the highly recommended **The Bookstore at Fitger's** (218/727-9077, www.fitgersbookstore.com, 10 A.M.–9 P.M. Mon.–Sat., 10 A.M.–5 P.M. Sun.). While there, stop by the free **Fitger's Museum** (hours vary) which displays various bits of brewing memorabilia around one of the original copper kettles.

Most Duluthians do their day-to-day shopping along Central Entrance and Highway 53 where the **Miller Hill Mall** (1600 Miller Trunk Hwy., 218/727-8301, www.miller-hill-mall.com, 10 A.M.–9 P.M. Mon.–Fri., 10 A.M.–7 P.M. Sat., 11 A.M.–6 P.M. Sun.) holds more than 100 stores.

Art and Antiques

For fine art with a true Northland touch, check out **Sivertson Gallery** (361 Canal Park Dr., 218/723-7877 or 888/815-5814, www.sivertson.com, 10 A.M.–6 P.M. Mon.–Sat., 11 A.M.–5 P.M. Sun.). You'll find photos by National Geographic photographer Jim Brandenburg and works by many Native Americans.

Waters of Superior (395 Lake Ave. S., 218/786-0233, www.watersofsuperior.com, 10 A.M.–9 P.M. Mon.–Sat., 10 A.M.–8 P.M. Sun.) has a Scandinavian vibe, with jewelry, clothing, and ceramics.

Slightly lower prices, though just as fine a selection of art, can be found at **Blue Lake Gallery** (395 Lake Ave. S., 218/725-0034, 10 A.M.–8 P.M. Mon.–Sat., 11 A.M.–4 P.M. Sun.).

Lizzards Art Gallery (11 Superior St. W., 218/722-5815, www.lizzards.com, 10 A.M.–5 P.M. Mon.–Wed., 10 A.M.–6 P.M. Sat., closed Sun.) features the work of dozens of regional artists.

Father Time (395 Lake Ave. S., 218/625-2379, 11 A.M.–5:30 P.M. Mon.–Thurs.,

11 A.M.–7 P.M. Fri., 11 A.M.–8 P.M. Sat., 11 A.M.–6 P.M. Sun.) has the largest selection of antiques.

While **Old Town Antiques & Books** (102 Superior St. E., 218/722-5426, 10 A.M.–6 P.M. daily) has mostly the former, it is also worth a browse for the latter.

Other Shops

Book-lovers and anyone looking for a literary take on the region should stop by **Northern Lights** (307 Canal Park Dr., 218/722-5267 or 800/868-8904, www.norlights.booksense.com, 9 A.M.–6 P.M. Mon.–Thurs., 9 A.M.–8 P.M. Fri.–Sat., 10 A.M.–6 P.M. Sun., extended hours during summer), which has an excellent Minnesota section in a small but well-curated space.

For a sure-fire coming-home present, head to **Grandma's Marketplace** (501 Lake Ave. S., 218/727-5885, www.grandmasrestaurants.com), where you'll find a classier collection of Duluth-themed gear, Thymes-brand soaps and lotions (a Minnesota company), and whole sections devoted to moose and black bears.

Souvenirs of a different kind can be found at the **Lake Superior Magazine Outlet Store** (310 Superior St. E., 888/244-5253, www.lakesuperior.com, 8:30 A.M.–5:30 P.M. Mon.–Fri., closed Sat.–Sun.), which sells wall maps, nautical maps, books, gear, and furnishings all related to the Lake.

A "Duluth Pack," in regional parlance, is a heavy-duty rectangular canvas backpack with a fold-over top. The original 1882 design was known as a "Poirier pack," after the inventor. **Duluth Pack** still makes the bags, along with school bags and heavy-duty luggage, and sells them at their only retail outlet (365 Canal Park Dr., Duluth, 218/722-1707, www.duluthpack.com, 10 A.M.–8 P.M. Mon.–Sat., 10 A.M.–6 P.M. Sun.) along with other high-quality outdoor gear.

The Electric Fetus (12 Superior St. E., 218/722-9970, 9 A.M.–9 P.M. Mon.–Fri., 9 A.M.–8 P.M. Sat., 11 A.M.–6 P.M. Sun.) is an outpost of the Twin Cities store that helped launch the Minneapolis sound in the 1980s. Look for indie music, clothes, and gifts.

WHERE'S THE THERMOSTAT?

"The coldest winter I ever spent was a summer in Duluth."

While Mark Twain never uttered this frequently misattributed quote, Duluth does fashion itself as "The Air-Conditioned City." Lake Superior, with an average temperature of just 39 degrees, cools the surrounding air, making the climate pleasant during all but the fiercest heat waves. If the winds blow out of the east it can keep the city's temperature down by as much as 15 degrees over the temperature just a mile inland. The lake has the opposite effect in the winter, when it serves as a three-quadrillion-gallon radiator.

RECREATION

On Land

Though the wilderness north of Duluth beckons, don't overlook the 11,000 acres of green space right in the city's backyard. Twenty-three rivers and creeks rush down the hills of Duluth in a long series of waterfalls and rapids before emptying into Lake Superior. The rivers are truly wild in the spring, while later in the year they can slow to not much more than a trickle, but the settings are gorgeous anytime. These wild waterways form the core of some of the city's best parks, and the hiking trails following them offer a near-wilderness experience. The trails are often steep, of course, but generally easy to follow. From east to west, some of the best hikes are the **Lester Park Trail** (Superior St. & Lester River Rd.), **Congdon Park Trail** (Superior St. & 32nd Ave. E.), **Chester Park Trail** (4th St. & 14th Ave. E.), **Lincoln Park Trail** (3rd St. & 25th Ave. W.), and **Kingsbury Creek Trail** (behind the zoo). For a scenic hike of a different nature, follow the wooded four-mile **Park Point Trail** at the end of Minnesota Avenue past sand dunes and a ruined lighthouse. Bird-watchers will have a field day out here during the spring and fall migrations.

Hartley Nature Center (3001 Woodland

© TRICIA CORNELL

The Lakewalk runs between the train tracks and the shore of Lake Superior near downtown Duluth.

Ave., 218/724-6735, www.hartleynature.org, visitor center 9 A.M.–4 P.M. Mon.–Fri., 10 A.M.–5 P.M. Sat., closed Sun.) has 10 miles of hiking trails, most of which are also open to mountain bikers and skiers. The forested paths are particularly popular with birders. The visitor center is a great place to visit with small children.

Duluth's 4.2-mile **Lakewalk** is a remarkable urban trail. Separate walking and biking lanes hug the shore from the Great Lakes Aquarium to beyond Leif Erikson Park. It not only connects many of the city's most popular attractions, but with such fantastic scenery, it's a top attraction itself.

Wheel Fun Rentals (436 Canal Park. Dr., 218/260-7140, www.wheelfunrentals.com, 9 A.M.–7 P.M. daily summer, 10 A.M.–sunset Sat.–Sun. Sept.–Oct., $7 hourly, $20 half-day, $30 day) near Canal Park Lodge rents mountain and touring bikes, as well as multi-passenger surreys.

After the Lakewalk, the city's most popular bike routes are the **Western Waterfront Trail,** a five-mile gravel and grass path along the St. Louis River, and the 14-mile segment of the **Willard Munger State Trail** (www.mungertrail.com) leading to Jay Cooke State Park. The Munger trail continues all the way to Hinckley and will eventually connect the Twin Ports with the Twin Cities. Both trails are best accessed at a parking area just south of Grand Avenue on 75th Avenue West. The nearby **Willard Munger Inn** (7408 Grand Ave., 218/624-4814 or 800/982-2453, www.mungerinn.com) rents bikes and offers shuttle service.

Skyline Drive also makes for a great bike ride.

On Water

Duluth's **charter fishing** docks are located alongside the William A. Irvin, while a few captains are also docked out on Park Point. Check with Visit Duluth (800/438-5884, www.visitduluth.com) for referrals or other information.

UMD Recreational Sports Outdoor Program (199 Sports and Health Center, UMD campus, 218/726-7128 or 218/726-6134, www.umdrsop.org) leads sea-kayaking and rock climbing trips around Duluth and beyond; no experience is necessary.

Because the water is shallow, and thus warm, the most popular place for a swim is the **Park Point Recreation Area** (45th St. & Minnesota Ave.), which has lifeguards and changing rooms. There is another public beach on Park Point just five blocks south of the bridge at South 12th Street. You can also take a quick dip at the rocky beaches in **Canal Park** and Brighton Beach in **Kitchi Gammi Park** at the far east end of town along Highway 61, though locals warn of a tricky undertow.

Winter Sports

Spirit Mountain (9500 Spirit Mountain Pl., exit 249 off I-35, 218/628-2891 or 800/642-6377, www.spiritmt.com) has 22 runs (the biggest drops 700 feet) for skiers and snowboarders, who can also shred the half-pipe and massive terrain park. A one-day lift ticket is $40. Cross-country skiers enjoy 14 miles of

THE GREATEST OF THE GREAT LAKES

To call Lake Superior big is to make a colossal understatement. Just look at the numbers: The lake's surface area covers 31,280 square miles – almost the same size as South Carolina – making it the largest lake in the world. It stretches 350 miles at its longest and 160 miles at its widest, has 2,726 miles of shoreline, and its deepest point sinks 1,279 feet below the surface. Its three quadrillion (that's 15 zeros) gallons of water constitute one-eighth of the world's fresh water supply and is enough to cover all of North and South America one foot deep. Only Lake Baikal in Russia and Lake Tanganyika in East Africa, both much smaller but deeper lakes, contain more. It isn't just the volume of water that makes this lake special, it also happens to be some of the purest and cleanest in the world.

Though the lake is usually enchanting, it also has a dark side. During the worst storms waves can rage over 30 feet high. Superior has sent at least 350 ships to its bottom, including the *Edmund Fitzgerald,* which famously snapped in half near Sault Ste. Marie, Michigan, on November 10, 1975. All 29 crew members aboard the 729-foot ore carrier died. It's easy to see why those who are intimately familiar with her will tell you that Superior deserves as much respect as admiration.

groomed, double-tracked trails with an eight-foot skating lane through beautiful woods; a half-day trail pass is just $7.

The city grooms another 27 miles of cross-country trail (call 218/723-3678 for trail conditions) in local parks, including the intermediate-level nine-mile **Magney-Snively Ski Trail** starting just off Spirit Mountain along the Skyline Parkway.

One third of the nine miles of the **Lester-Amity Trail,** with beginner to advanced loops in Lester Park, are lighted during early mornings and late into the evening.

The **Chester Bowl Trail** is just 2.5 miles long, but it's the most challenging route in the city. The park also has a 175-foot-tall downhill run with a chairlift ($5) and an ice-skating oval.

The private **Snowflake Nordic Center** (4348 Rice Lake Rd., 218/726-1550, www.skiduluth.com, $7 adult day pass) has nine miles of trails groomed for classic and skating—a third are lighted at night—plus a biathlon range. Snowflake has rentals, instruction, a chalet, and even a sauna for after the trails. And the lake effect causes snow to come earlier and stay longer here than even some other areas around Duluth.

Ski Hut (1032 4th St. E., 218/724-8525, and 5607 Grand Ave., 218/624-5889, 9 A.M.–7 P.M. Mon.–Fri., 9 A.M.–5 P.M. Sat., 11 A.M.–5 P.M. Sun., www.theskihut.com) rents cross-country skis and snowshoes.

Positive Energy Outdoor (Ed)Ventures (218/391-0147 or 218/428-5990, www.outdooredventures.org) leads dogsled trips, as well as sleigh and wagon rides and summertime fun like kayaking and rock-climbing.

Epic Sleddog Adventures (218/721-3692, www.dogmusher.com) will take you mushing. Two-hour trips costs $90 and you'll get to drive at the end.

Other Diversions

Carnival Thrillz (329 Lake Ave. S., 218/720-5868, 11 A.M.–9 P.M. Mon.–Thurs., 11 A.M.–10 P.M. Fri.–Sat., 11 A.M.–8 P.M. Sun.) has video games, laser tag, mini golf, a trampoline jump, climbing wall, and indoor amusement park rides. A little dingy, it's recommended mostly for getting in out of the rain or cold.

Enger Park (1801 Skyline Blvd. W., 218/723-3451, www.engerpark.golfinduluth.com) and **Lester Park** (1860 Lester River Rd., 218/525-0828, www.lesterpark.golfinduluth.com) each have public golf courses overlooking Lake Superior and 18-hole games starting at $29.

Downtown's **Fond-du-Luth Casino** (129 Superior St. E., 218/722-0280 or 800/873-0280, www.fondduluthcasino.com) is run by the Fond du Lac Ojibwe.

ACCOMMODATIONS

The Duluth area has nearly 5,000 hotel rooms, but they can all fill up on some summer weekends. Visit Duluth can help you find rooms on short notice. If you are here to ski, check with Spirit Mountain about ski-free specials they have with area hotels.

Hotels and Motels

CANAL PARK

No hotel is better situated than the **South Pier Inn** (701 Lake Ave. S., 218/786-9007 or 800/430-7437, www.southpierinn.com, $127), on Park Point just across from Canal Park. Most rooms look up at the Lift Bridge, and you can watch ships pass through the harbor from a private balcony. Most of the 29 rooms are whirlpool suites, and there is a two-night minimum on weekends.

Four large hotels at varying price points line the lakeshore on Canal Park. They all have spacious lakeside patios right on the Lakewalk and great views of the water. The swankest is the recently remodeled **Canal Park Lodge** (250 Canal Park Dr., 218/279-6000 or 800/777-8560, www.canalparklodge.com, $170). Its decor is modern-rustic, with comfy public areas, an indoor pool and whirlpool, and spacious rooms.

Most rooms at the **Inn on Lake Superior** (350 Canal Park Dr., 218/726-1111 or 888/668-4352, www.theinnonlakesuperior.com, $173) have a private lake-view balcony or patio, plus there is a pool, whirlpool, and sauna.

Two less expensive choices, with older decor but the same great location, are **Hampton Inn** (310 Canal Park Dr., 218/720-3000, $125) and **Comfort Suites** (408 Canal Park Dr., 218/727-1387, $129).

The Suites Hotel (325 Lake Ave. S., 218/727-4663 or 800/794-1716, www.thesuitesduluth.com, $104), the only Canal Park hotel not on the lakeshore, is a lovely warehouse conversion incorporating some of the original building features into the design. All rooms have kitchens, and guests have use of the pool, whirlpool, sauna, and fitness center. Some of the cheapest rooms don't have windows.

DOWNTOWN

The friendly **Voyageur Lakewalk Inn** (333 Superior St. E., 218/722-3911 or 800/258-3911, www.voyageurlakewalkinn.com, $45) is an older but well-kept hotel and all rooms are more modern than the exterior would lead you to believe.

The **Radisson** (505 Superior St. W., 218/727-8981 or 800/395-7046, www.radisson.com, $149), in the heart of downtown, has a pool, whirlpool, sauna, fitness center, and great views from upper-level rooms.

The fanciest hotel in town is the nationally recognized **Fitger's Inn** (600 Superior St. E., 218/722-8826 or 888/348-4377, www.fitgers.com, $145), part of a restored lakeside brewery complex. The more expensive suites are very large and well appointed, and all guests can use the fitness center.

EAST

Just two miles north of Canal Park on the Lakewalk, **Beacon Pointe** (2100 Water St., 877/462-3226, $99–169) is a surprisingly good deal. The smaller guestrooms are just as stylishly appointed as the suites, and among the best-priced waterfront rooms in Duluth. You could, of course, choose to pay much more for a penthouse.

The **Edgewater Resort & Waterpark** (2400 London Rd., 218/728-3601 or 800/777-7925, www.duluthwaterpark.com, $109) features a 30,000-square-foot water park with waterslides, a kiddie play area, and more. The 297-room hotel also has a pool, whirlpool, sauna, arcade, miniature golf course, free bikes, and nicely appointed rooms. It's not directly on the shore, but it has easy access to the Lakewalk and great views from lakeside rooms.

The **College of St. Scholastica** (1200 Kenwood Ave., 218/723-6000) has two- and three-bedroom apartments with private baths ($164) and two-bedroom suites ($95) available to the public June through mid-August. They also rent out dorm rooms ($37 single, $58 double).

WEST

You can generally save a good chunk of change by sleeping on the west side of town, although most of the properties are pretty basic. The exception is the friendly, family-run **Willard Munger Inn** (7408 Grand Ave., 218/624-4814 or 800/982-2453, www.mungerinn.com, $59.95), which has modern rooms right by the Willard Munger and Western Waterfront Trails (and it's only half a mile from Spirit Mountain). Guests get free use of bikes, in-line skates, canoes, and kayaks and can grill out in the rock garden at night. The whirlpool or fireplace suites are a good value, and off-peak prices are a steal.

Bed-and-Breakfasts

If you fancy bed-and-breakfasts, then Duluth, with a dozen in beautifully restored historic homes, is your kind of town. The Historic Bed and Breakfast Inns of Duluth website (www.duluthbandb.com) lists most of them, and competition for opulence and hospitality holds them to high standards. Most require a two-night minimum stay on weekends in the high season.

A stunner inside and out, the **Cotton Mansion** (2309 1st St. E., 218/724-6405, $135–265) has seven guest rooms in a 16,000-square-foot Italian Renaissance mansion built for the powerful Duluth lawyer Joseph Cotton in 1908. Marble, carved wood, and exquisite furnishings fill every room. The Terrace Suite has it's own private terrace.

From the gingerbread exterior to the opulent decor full of stained glass and carved woodwork, the storybook **Mathew S. Burrows 1890 Inn** (1632 1st St. E., 218/724-4991 or 800/789-1890, www.1890inn.com, $95) also has a spectacular atmosphere. The five guestrooms have private baths.

Although it is in a grand 1890 Victorian home, the **Ellery House** (28 S. 21st Ave. E., 218/724-7639 or 800/355-3794, www.elleryhouse.com, $109–189) has a very homey atmosphere. Each of the four guestrooms has a private bath, and two of the rooms overlook Lake Superior, which is just two blocks away. The Halquist family is known for serving hearty baked egg dishes at breakfast.

Over on Park Point, you can watch boats pass through the canal from the beach and back porch at **Solglimt** (828 Lake Ave. S., 218/727-0956 or 877/727-0596, www.solglimt.com, $165). The contemporary house is full of art and one of the three guestrooms has a Kandinsky theme. One room has a fireplace, another its own private deck, and the third overlooks the lake.

Stately and elegant, **A. G. Thompson House** (2617 3rd St. E., 218/724-3464, www.thomsonhouse.biz, $139–299) mixes old-time luxury with modern amenities. All rooms have fireplaces and most have giant whirlpool bathtubs.

Campgrounds

The best camping in the area is at nearby **Jay Cooke State Park** (780 Hwy. 210, 218/384-4610, $20) in Carlton.

As far as municipal campgrounds go, the 70 sites along the St. Louis River at the **Indian Point Campground** (902 S. 69th Ave. W., 218/628-4977 or 800/982-2453, www.indianpointcampground.com, $32 full hookup) are really good.

Snowflake Nordic Center (4348 Rice Lake Rd., 218/726-1550, www.skiduluth.com, $15) has tent sites.

FOOD

While it's very easy in Duluth to accidentally find oneself eating the kind of heavy, mediocre fare usually foisted on tourists and college kids, the city is also home to a few of the state's best creative restaurants.

American

Hungry diners have been known to drive up from the Twin Cities for a meal at the **New Scenic Café** (5461 North Shore Scenic Dr., 218/525-6274, www.sceniccafe.com,

© TRICIA CORNELL

Crabby Bill's serves up smoked fish, mini doughnuts, and other snacks in Duluth's Canal Park.

11 A.M.–9 P.M. daily, $10–23), which serves an ever-changing menu of refined locally focused dishes in a casual atmosphere. Be prepared for a crowd and a wait, especially at dinner.

Just two miles up the road, the newer **Nokomis** (5593 North Shore Scenic Dr., 218/525-2286, www.nokomisonthelake.com, 11 A.M.–10 P.M. daily summer, noon–10 P.M. Wed.–Sun. rest of year, $14–23), started by picking up some of those overflow diners and now attracts its own following. The menu changes seasonally, with the walleye po'boy, elk burger, white fish cakes, and coq au vin all getting national raves. A seat on the deck with a view of the lake across scenic Highway 61, is an essential part of the experience.

Even more great food, this time with a cheeky twist, is to be found at the Twin Cities export **Hell's Kitchen** (10 Lake Ave. S., 218/727-1620, 8 A.M.–9 P.M. Mon.–Thurs., 9 A.M.–10 P.M. Fri.–Sat., 9 A.M.–8 P.M. Sun., $11–15). Although it built its reputation on breakfast—lemon ricotta pancakes, quarter-inch-thick bacon, wild rice porridge—it's also great for lunch and dinner, with casual eats like barbecue ribs and bison burgers.

Duluth does have more traditional white-tablecloth dining. In the Fitger's complex, **Midi** (600 Superior St. E., 218/727-4880, www.midirestaurant.com, 7 A.M.–10 P.M. Sun.–Thurs., 7 A.M.–11 P.M. Fri.–Sat., $13–26) has the feel of a wine cellar and prides itself on fine service. Unique on the menu are the German sausages and roulades, but otherwise you can expect the usual steak, seafood, and chicken.

Restaurant 301 (301 Superior St. E., 218/336-2705, www.restaurant301.com, 7 A.M.–10 P.M. daily, lounge open until midnight, $16–28) dazzles with fancy presentations of upscale meats and seafood. You can't beat the Sunday tasting menu: same great cooking, but just $15 for three courses.

At Sara's Table Chester Creek Café (1902 8th St. E., 218/724-6811, 7 A.M.–9 P.M. Mon.–Sat., 7:30 A.M.–4 P.M. Sun., $6–22) is a casual place near UMD where walls of books invite you to stay awhile. The regular menu has basics like a veggie burger and Caesar salad, while the daily specials, based on organic and free-range ingredients and often seasoned with herbs from their own herb garden, get more creative. At breakfast, the huge pancakes get raves.

Another favorite local place for breakfast is **Uncle Louis Café** (520 4th St. E., 218/727-4518, 6 A.M.–2:45 P.M. Mon.–Fri., 7 A.M.–2:45 P.M. Sat.–Sun., $5–10), where the spots at the bar are coveted, and the short-order cook slings out hearty omelets and heaping plates of potatoes.

For breakfast, lunch, dinner, live music, or just a cup of coffee, **Amazing Grace Bakery and Café** (394 Lake Ave. S., 218/723-0075, www.amazinggracebakery.com, 7 A.M.–10 P.M. Sun.–Thurs., 7 A.M.–11 P.M. Fri.–Sat.), is the spot. This little bohemian basement space with a shady outdoor patio serves up largely local and organic sandwiches and soups, with plenty of choices for vegans and vegetarians.

Grandma's Saloon & Grill (522 Lake Ave. S., 218/727-4192, 11:30 A.M.–11:30 P.M. daily, $7–25), covered in unique antiques and collectibles, is a Northland institution. The please-everyone menu covers such options as curried wild rice Cajun shrimp, turkey burgers, and lasagna.

If you can't bear to go inside on a beautiful Duluth day, **Crabby Bill's** (504 Canal Park Dr., www.crabbybillsduluth.com, $3–8) is a 35-foot tugboat in Canal Park. Out its service window come delicious battered seafood, wild rice bratwurst, and bear-battered French fries.

Asian

The excellent lunch buffet and seemingly thousands of curry choices, including lamb and seafood, at **India Palace** (319 Superior St. W., 218/727-8767, www.duluthindiapalace.com, 11 A.M.–3 P.M. and 5–9 P.M. Mon.–Thurs., open until 10 P.M. Fri.–Sat., closed Sun., $12–30) make this longtime gem one of the city's best restaurants.

Duluth's only Thai dining is the friendly **Thai Krathong** (114 1st St. W., 218/733-9774, www.thaikrathong.com, 11 A.M.–10 P.M. Sun.–Thurs., 11 A.M.–11 P.M. Fri.–Sat., $10–20), with curries of all sorts perfectly prepared—the seafood comes particularly recommended—though if you want it spicy, you need to beg. There's a weekday lunch buffet.

Taste of Saigon (394 Lake Ave. S., 218/727-1598, 11 A.M.–8:30 P.M. Sun.–Thurs., 11 A.M.–9:30 P.M. Fri.–Sat., $5–13) serves Vietnamese fare (and a little Chinese too) adapted for American palates in a comfortably casual atmosphere.

Italian

The excellent and eclectic **Pizza Luce** (11 Superior St. E., 218/727-7400, www.pizzaluce.com, 8 A.M.–1:30 A.M. Sun.–Thurs., 8 A.M.–2:30 A.M. Fri.–Sat., $6–13) is far from your average pizzeria. Roasted eggplant, barbecue chicken, and goat cheese are some of the more unusual of their fifty-plus toppings, and they even offer a vegan cheese alternative. Take-away slices are available and they deliver. Pizza Luce is also a surprisingly great choice for both breakfast and late-night live music.

At classy **Bellisio's** (405 Lake Ave. S., 218/727-4921, 11:30 A.M.–10 P.M. daily, $7–29) the atmosphere is romantic and the wine list impressive.

Mexican

A great atmosphere—more polished pub than south-of-the-border—a great list of beers on tap, and creative takes on Tex-mex classics make **Burrito Union** (1332 4th St. E., 218/728-4414, www.burritounion.com) a favorite with local college students. The Rasputin (a murderously huge burrito) and the Fat Capitalist (a particularly filling one) are all part of the joint's obsessive russo/sovietophilia.

Hacienda Del Sol (319 Superior St. E., 218/722-7296, www.hacienda-del-sol.com, 11 A.M.–9 P.M. Mon.–Thurs., 11 A.M.–11 P.M. Fri.–Sat., closed Sun., $7–12) isn't exactly a south-of-the-border experience, but it is still some of the best Mexican in the northland. The secluded, shady deck in back is a wonderful place for a warm-weather meal.

Mediterranean

With a warm and welcoming Greek family in the kitchen, **Grape Vine Café** (220 Superior St. W., 218/464-4027, www.grapevinecafeduluth.com) serves excellent souvlaki, lamb chops, meze plates, and other home-style Greek specialties.

Scandinavian

The sleek and modern **Takk for Maten** (11 Superior St. E., 218/464-1260, 7 A.M.–3 P.M. Mon.–Fri., 8 A.M.–2 P.M. Sat., closed Sun., $3–6) serves lingonberry pancakes and other Scandinavian specialties during the day, then becomes **Kippis** (5–11 P.M. Tues.–Thurs., 5 P.M.–1 A.M. Fri.–Sat., $3–16) (Finnish for "cheers") at night. Get $5–6 small plates like pepper-smoked salmon, rye bread with mild Finnish cheese, and catfish pate, as well as northern-inspired cocktails.

Snacks and Coffeeshops

There are snack stands all over Canal Park, but it is worth a trip over to the cute **PortLand Malt Shoppe** (716 Superior St. E., www.portlandmaltshoppe.com). The constant crowds hovering in front of it tell you how good it is.

The small, worker-owned **Positively 3rd Street Bakery** (1202 3rd St. E., 218/724-8619, www.positively3rdstreetbakery.com, 8 A.M.–5:30 P.M. Mon.–Fri., 10 A.M.–4 P.M. Sat., 11 A.M.–4 P.M. Sun., $1–4) uses mostly organic ingredients in its wonderful cookies, bars, and breads, yet they still manage to price them ridiculously low.

Jitters (102 Superior St. W., 218/720-6015, 6:30 A.M.–7 P.M. Mon.–Fri., 8 A.M.–5 P.M. Sat., closed Sun.) downtown serves a good cup o' joe in a small and relaxed environment.

INFORMATION AND SERVICES

Tourist Information

Visit Duluth (218/722-4011 or 800/438-5884, www.visitduluth.com) staffs a pair of information centers. Their **main office** (21 Superior St. W., 8:30 A.M.–5 P.M. Mon.–Fri., closed Sat.–Sun.) is downtown, while their busy **Waterfront Center** (323 Harbor Dr., 218/722-6024, 9:30 A.M.–7:30 P.M. daily June–Sept., 11:30 A.M.–3:30 P.M. daily May and Oct.) is at the DECC.

The **Thompson Hill Information Center** (8525 Skyline Pkwy. W., 218/723-4938, 9 A.M.–5 P.M. daily), west of town off I-35, has statewide travel information.

Media

The city's daily paper, the ***Duluth News Tribune*** (www.duluthnewstribune.com), isn't bad, though for national and world coverage pick up one of the Twin Cities dailies, which are widely available.

It's worth checking in occasionally to see what's playing on **KUMD** (103.3 FM, www.kumd.org), the university's student radio station, since it could can from Mingus to Motorhead at the top of the hour.

Post Office

The downtown post office (515 1st St. W., 218/722-1681, 8 A.M.–4 P.M. Mon.–Fri., closed Sat.–Sun.) is in the Civic Center.

GETTING THERE

By Air

Duluth International Airport (4701 Grinden Dr., 281/727-2968, www.duluthairport.com), just off Highway 53 on the northwest edge of town, handles **Delta Airlines** (800/221-1212, www.delta.com) flights to the Twin Cities and Detroit. You'll find most major rental car companies here.

By Boat

Transient dockage is available at the full-service **Lakehead Boat Basin** (1000 Minnesota Ave., 218/722-1757, www.lakeheadboatbasin.com) just south of the Lift Bridge.

By Bus

The **Greyhound** (800/231-2222, www.greyhound.com) station (4426 Grand Ave., 218/722-5591) is on the west side of town. Each day there is an express to Minneapolis ($29.50).

GETTING AROUND

By Bus

The Duluth Transit Authority bus system offers a fairly extensive service for a market this small (buses even go to Park Point and Spirit Mountain). The fare is $1.25 on weekday mornings and afternoons and $0.60 all other times. Most routes pass the downtown **Duluth Transit Center** (214 Superior St. W., 218/722-7283, 9 A.M.–5 P.M. Mon.–Fri.), where you can get schedules and information. Route information is also available online at www.duluthtransit.com.

As enjoyable as it is convenient, the **Port Town Trolley** (11 A.M.–7 P.M. summer, $0.50) travels between Canal Park and downtown every half hour.

By Taxi

Allied Taxi (218/722-3311) and **Yellow Cab** (218/727-1515) have 24-hour service.

Car Rentals

Five major rental car companies have offices at the airport: **Alamo** (218/727-7426, www.alamo.com, 7:30 A.M.–11:30 P.M.

Mon.–Fri., 9 A.M.–11:15 P.M. Sat., 8:30 A.M.–11:15 P.M. Sun.), **Avis** (218/727-7233, www.avis.com, 7:30 A.M.–11:30 P.M. Mon.–Fri., 8:30 A.M.–4:30 P.M. Sat., 8:30 A.M.–11:30 P.M. Sun.), **Budget** (218/727-7685, www.budget.com, 7:30 A.M.–11:45 P.M. Mon.–Fri., 8:30 A.M.–11:45 P.M. Sat.–Sun.), **Hertz** (218/722-7418, www.hertz.com, 7:30 A.M.–12:30 A.M. Mon.–Fri., 8:30 A.M.–4:30 P.M. Sat., 9 A.M.–12:30 A.M. Sun.), and **National** (218/727-7426, www.nationalcar.com, 7:30 A.M.–11:30 P.M. Mon.–Fri., 8:30 A.M.–11:30 P.M. Sat.–Sun.).

Enterprise (301 East Central Entrance, 218/722-5800, www.enterprise.com, 7:30 A.M.–6 P.M. Mon.–Fri., 9 A.M.–noon Sat.) is located just minutes from the airport and will arrange a shuttle to pick you up when you land.

North Shore

Minnesota's North Shore is one of those places that truly deserves all the accolades so freely heaped on it. Officially an All-American Road, the 150 miles of Highway 61 from Duluth to the Canadian border is about as rewarding as a drive can be. Tucked in between Lake Superior and the worn-down remnants of the ancient Sawtooth Mountains you'll find improbably tall shoreline cliffs, countless waterfalls, lighthouses, myriad moose, and much more. You need several days to do it justice.

This is a popular place, so it's wise to make weekend reservations as far in advance as possible during summer and fall. Even weekday reservations are a near necessity during July and August and then again for fall color. Two-night minimum stay requirements are common on peak weekends, and prices drop very low during the shoulder seasons.

If you want to get right up to Two Harbors, stay on four-lane Highway 61, otherwise take the exit after Kitchi-Gammi Park and follow North Shore Drive as it hugs the lake for the next 20 miles.

KNIFE RIVER

Though copper prospectors came a half century earlier, Knife River was platted in 1899 following the construction of a logging railroad. Like most North Shore towns it made the switch from logging to fishing when the forests were cut over. Today it is one of the few that retains a commercial fishing industry, though just a handful of people along the entire North Shore (down from 450 in the 1920s) are able to make it their livelihood. Nevertheless, tiny Knife River is still famous for its aquatic bounty, and many North Shore residents and regular visitors stop here when passing by to pick up some of the famous smoked fish. Many swear by the smoked and cured salmon, trout, herring, and more from **Russ Kendall's Smokehouse** (149 Scenic Hwy. 61, 218/834-5995, 9 A.M.–6 P.M. daily).

If you want to get your fish the hard way, the Knife River is chock-full of trout in the spring (be careful though, the Ojibwe chose the river's name because of the numerous sharp stones in it), or call the full-service **Knife River Marina** (115 Marina Rd., 218/834-6076, www.knife-river-marina.com, 8 A.M.–4:30 P.M. daily, open until 6 P.M. in the summer) for charter captain recommendations.

The shady deck at **Emily's** (218 Scenic Hwy. 61, 217/834-2501, www.emilyseatery.com, 11 A.M.–7:30 P.M. Tues.–Thurs. and Sun., 11 A.M.–9 P.M. Fri.–Sat., closed Mon., $8–10) sits right over the mouth of the Knife River. The casual sit-down menu includes sandwiches, light entrees, and the de rigeur walleye. Emily's wild rice soup is a classic of the genre.

Get dessert or a midday pick-me up at **Great! Lakes Candy** (223 Scenic Hwy. 61, 218/834-2121, www.greatlakescandy.com, 10 A.M.–7 P.M. daily summer, reduced hours in fall) across the street. They make their own fudge, caramel, and "agate" lollipops.

A few miles up the road, stop in at the

© TRICIA CORNELL

The North Shore of Lake Superior is beloved by Minnesotans and visitors alike.

Burton Forge Gallery (Scenic Hwy. 61, www.burtonforge.com, 1–5 P.M. Thurs.–Mon. summer, Sat.–Sun. Sept.–Dec.) to see remarkable examples of a dying art: wrought iron, including architectural pieces, furniture, and home accents.

TWO HARBORS

With over 3,600 residents, Two Harbors is the largest community on the North Shore—after Duluth, of course. The city promotes itself as the trailhead to the North Shore, and realistically the spectacular lakeside scenery and most interesting sights do begin just beyond town. Most businesses are centered along Highway 61 (7th Ave.), though most places of interest are down along Agate Bay, the more industrial of the twin bays. Two Harbors actually began as two communities—Agate Bay and Burlington—each named for the natural harbors on which they sat. Though the first settlers arrived in 1855, the towns didn't really blossom until iron ore was found on the Vermilion Range. This was the shortest route to Lake Superior from the Soudan Mine, and the railroad hauled its first ore to a waiting boat on Agate Bay in 1884. Ore shipments peaked in 1945, but to this day more ore is shipped out of Two Harbors than any other Great Lakes Port.

Sights

The 1892 **Two Harbors Lighthouse** (1 Lighthouse Point Dr., 218/834-4898, www.lighthousebb.org, 9 A.M.–5 P.M. Mon.–Sat., 10 A.M.–4 P.M. Sun. May–Oct., $2.50 adults) is the oldest lighthouse still in operation on the North Shore. You can climb the tower and see the two 1,000-watt bulbs spinning and tour the assistant keeper's house, now operated as a bed-and-breakfast by the Lake County Historical Society. Also located on the grounds is a restored pilothouse from the wrecked oreboat *Frontenac,* with displays about Lake Superior shipwrecks and fishing.

The Lake County Historical Society looks at the rest of the county's past in the **Depot Museum** (520 South Ave., 9 A.M.–5 P.M. Mon.–Sat., 10 A.M.–4 P.M. Sun. May–Oct., $2.50 adults), with a historical hodgepodge in the 1907 Duluth & Iron Range Railroad depot—the building used in the movie *Iron Will.* Outside is a pair of steam locomotives, including the 569-ton Mallet, one of the largest train engines ever built.

Docked below the depot is the **Edna G. Tugboat** (9 A.M.–5 P.M. Mon.–Sat., 10 A.M.–4 P.M. Sun., $2.50 adults), a coal-fed, steam-powered tugboat. Built in 1896, she served Two Harbors for nearly a century, and you can now tour her from the captain's quarters down to the engine room.

The tiny **3M Museum** (201 Waterfront Dr., 12:30–5 P.M. Mon.–Fri., 9 A.M.–5 P.M. Sat., 10 A.M.–4 P.M. Sun. May–Oct., $2.50 adults) commemorates the founding of Minnesota Mining & Manufacturing, which started here in 1902. Initially they tried to mine corundum, a durable mineral used to make grinding wheels, but couldn't find it where they expected to. After nearly going bankrupt they invented sandpaper, moved to St. Paul, and became one

MY WAY OR THE HIGHWAY

There are many ways to travel the North Shore besides Highway 61. The **Superior Hiking Trail** is the greatest thing to happen to the North Shore since the Ice Age. Sticking primarily to the ridgeline on its 205-mile run from Two Harbors to near the Canadian Border, it has frequent vistas of Lake Superior to complement the waterfalls, gorges, and other up-close scenery. It connects seven state parks (all but Grand Portage) and many of the Superior National Forest's scenic highlights, plus it joins with the Border Route Trail at the east end, letting you continue on for another hundred miles across the Boundary Waters Canoe Area Wilderness. Work is underway to connect the trail with Duluth. It's no surprise that readers of *Backpacker* magazine recently ranked it as the second-best long-distance trail in the country. Most access points are between five and ten miles apart, so the trail is ideal for day trips. No matter how long you are hiking, you can travel between most trailheads with the Superior Shuttle (218/834-5511, www.superiorhikingshuttle.com). The 12-person van runs on a set schedule Friday through Sunday (plus holiday Mondays) from mid-May to mid-October. In general the cost is $15 for the first stop and $5 for each additional, with a maximum cost of $60. Transport outside these times can be arranged for about twice the normal rate. Though not necessary, reservations are a good idea, especially on holiday weekends and during fall color. Many area resorts will also drive their guests to trailheads. Eighty-one free, first-come, first-served backcountry campsites – with latrines, fire rings, and room for two or three tents at most – are spread out along the trail. Another overnight option is Lodge to Lodge Hiking, arranged by Boundary Country Trekking (800/322-8327, www.boundarycountry.com). The Superior Hiking Trail Association (731 7th Ave., 218/834-2700, www.shta.org) in Two Harbors can answer any and all questions about the trail. They also publish the detailed *Guide to the Superior Hiking Trail,* sell maps, and lead guided hikes.

Though it won't be finished until around 2011, the **Gitchi-Gami State Trail** is already earning rave reviews. The 86-mile paved path, open to bikers, in-line skaters, cross-country skiers, and other non-motorized travelers, will run from Two Harbors to Grand Marais, connecting the towns and parks in between. The route generally hugs the highway, but often runs down to the lake and up through the adjacent forest. Currently about 26 miles of the trail are paved and open to the public, including a 13-mile stretch between Gooseberry Falls State Park and Beaver Bay and three miles along Temperance River State Park. Check with the Gitchi-Gami Trail Association (www.ggta.org) for trail updates.

Up behind the bluffs, the rugged **North Shore State Trail** (218/834-6626) runs all the way from Duluth to Grand Marais. The 146-mile path is used primarily by snowmobilers, though the rest of the year it offers a remote and seldom-used mountain bike route. The 70 miles through the Finland State Forest and Superior National Forest are the best bet for biking since the western half often has long stretches of standing water. Camping shelters are spaced out along the entire route.

More and more sea kayakers are discovering the joys of the North Shore and the still-developing **Lake Superior Water Trail** (www.lswta.org) offers a campsite or rest area every three-or-so miles for most of the journey between Two Harbors and Grand Marais. Remember, lake conditions can change from placid to rough in a matter of minutes and the cold water means small mistakes can be deadly. Beginning paddlers should take a guide or at least stay very close to shore.

With safe harbors at nearly a dozen spots and full-service marinas in Duluth, Knife River, Silver Bay, Grand Marais, and Grand Portage, traveling by boat is fairly easy. Anyone boating on Lake Superior should not set out without a copy of Bonnie Dahl's *Superior Way: The Cruising Guide to Lake Superior* at the helm. Its 400-plus pages are filled with harbor maps, wilderness charts, and GPS coordinates. If you don't have your own boat, sailing and fishing charters operate out of several North Shore towns.

of the globe's largest corporations. The handful of displays recalls the company's past and promotes its current products. The collection of historic Scotch Tape containers is about as exciting as it gets.

Paul Van Hoven Park, next to the tug, is the closest you can get to the boats loading taconite at the three massive (1,300 feet long and seven stories high) **ore docks;** the breakwater by the lighthouse is another good viewing point. Arrival and departure times are posted at the Visitor Center and Depot Museum. The rocky beach at the **Flood Bay Wayside,** a mile northeast of town, is excellent for agate hunting.

Entertainment and Events

The city hosts several wonderful events during the summer. Two Harbor's biggest festival is **Heritage Days** (www.theheritagedays.com), the weekend after the Fourth of July, with a car show, kiddie parade, and lutefisk toss.

Later in the month is the **Knife River Music Festival** (www.kniferivermusicfestival.org) with three days of music.

There are races, clinics, and demos during the **Two Harbors Kayak Festival** (www.kayakfestival.org) the first weekend of August.

Shopping

At **Buddy's Mercantile** (720 7th Ave., 218/834-3303, 10 A.M.–5 P.M. Mon.–Sat., closed Sun., summer hours sometimes longer), you'll find a huge selection of local honey and jams, as well as quilts and old-timey souvenirs. This is one of the best places to buy local wild rice.

Agate City (721 7th Ave., 218/834-2304, 9 A.M.–5 P.M. Mon.–Sat., 10 A.M.–4 P.M. Sun.) sells rocks (polished and unpolished) and fossils from around the world, including, of course, plenty of Lake Superior agates.

As many as ten sellers stock the 5,000-square-foot **Harbor Antiques** (601 1st Ave., 218/834-0836, 9 A.M.–4 P.M. daily) with collectibles, furniture, and primitive arts.

Honey-smoked salmon is the specialty at **Lou's Fish House** (1319 Hwy. 61, 218/834-5254, www.lousfish.com, 9 A.M.–5 P.M. Mon.–Fri., 9 A.M.–7 P.M. Sat.–Sun.), but they also sell lots of other fish, beef and turkey jerky, and Wisconsin cheese.

About 11 miles north of town, **Northwoods Pioneer Gallery and Gifts** (2821 Hwy. 61, 218/834-4175, www.pioneercrafts.com, 9 A.M.–5 P.M. daily summer, Fri.–Sun. only Oct.–Dec., Sat.–Sun. only rest of year) is a long-lived co-op stocking the handiwork of 55 local craftspeople, including jewelry, candles, ceramics, textiles, woodworking, and more.

Recreation

The short, easy loop of the **Sonju Harbor Walking Trail** behind the Two Harbors Lighthouse is a surprisingly scenic stroll. A paved stretch of the trail heads along the shore up to Burlington Bay.

If you want to hit the trails or the water, **The Canoeist** (710 7th Ave., 218/834-3523, www.thecanoeist.com, 7 A.M.–9 P.M. Mon.–Sat., noon–5 P.M. Sun.) will arrange hiking, canoeing, and fishing trips, with or without a guide. Whether you want to be out for a few hours or several days, they'll take care of all the equipment and transport. You can get your BWCA permit here, too.

Accommodations

Easily the top option for spending the night, if you can get a room, is the **Lighthouse Bed & Breakfast** (1 Lighthouse Point Dr., 218/834-4814 or 888/832-5606, www.lighthousebb.org, $135) in the restored Two Harbors Lighthouse. The three guestrooms, filled with period furnishings, share a bath, and a full breakfast is served in the morning. All proceeds are used for lighthouse maintenance.

The other bed-and-breakfast right in town is the remarkably unfussy **B & B Whistlestop** (505 8th Ave., 218/834-5571, www.bnbwhistlestop.com, $100), housed in a 1901 Arts and Crafts built from a catalogue kit. Four rooms share a bathroom, and the third-floor loft has private half bath.

The family-run **Voyageur Motel** (1227 7th Ave., 218/834-3644, www.voyageur-motel.net, $50) has small, basic rooms, but they are clean and a good value.

The newer **Country Inn of Two Harbors** (1204 7th Ave., 218/834-5557 or 877/604-5332, www.countryinntwoharbors.com, $100) offers a pool, whirlpool, sauna, and miniature golf course.

For something unique, stay in a boxcar at **Northern Rail Traincar Suites** (1730 Hwy. 3, 218/834-0955 or 877/834-0955, www.northernrail.net, $147). Rooms are in actual train cars, though you only notice this from the outside and the hallway connecting them.

Superior Shores Resort (1521 Superior Shores Dr., 218/834-5671 or 800/242-1988, www.superiorshores.com, $99) just outside town has a wide variety of rooms ranging from standard hotel units to decked-out lake homes. Facilities include indoor and outdoor pools, hot tub, sauna, and tennis courts.

Ten miles beyond town, on the site of Minnesota's first cabin resort, **Grand Superior Lodge** (2826 Hwy. 61, 218/834-3796 or 800/627-9565, www.grandsuperior.com, $119) sits on a scenic stretch of shoreline. Most units, whether the hotel rooms in the lodge or the large log homes near the shore (one is actually right on it) have fireplaces and whirlpool tubs, plus spectacular views. There's a small pool, large whirlpool, sauna, exercise room, and a bevy of board games. The restaurant, Splashing Rock, attracts diners from outside the resort, as well.

South of town, **Stonegate on Superior** (box 411–412 Scenic Hwy. 61, 877/229-4949, www.stonegateonsuperior.com, $125–149) is a charming collection of log cabins on a woodsy outcropping directly over Lake Superior. The kitchens come fully equipped, but you won't find any TVs or electronic toys here.

The most sought-after campsites in Two Harbors are at the municipal **Burlington Bay Campground** (Hwy. 61 & Park Rd., 218/834-2021, www.ci.two-harbors.mn.us, mid-May–mid-Oct., $20 primitive, $28 with hookup), right on the water. The 66 sites are packed in, but you'll be too busy enjoying the lake to bother about your neighbors.

Food

What began as a wayside fish shack has grown into the legendary **Betty's Pies** (1633 Hwy. 61 E., 218/834-3367 or 877/269-7494, www.bettyspies.com, 7 A.M.–9 P.M. daily, $6–16), which now has a full menu. Locals and regular visitors alike continually sing its praises, and it is not just hype—these pies are amazing. Expect a long wait for a table.

The homey **Vanilla Bean Bakery & Cafe** (812 7th Ave., 218/834-3714, www.thevanillabean.com, 7 A.M.–7 P.M. Sun.–Thurs., 7 A.M.–8:30 P.M. Fri.–Sat. May–Oct., reduced hours rest of year, $4–16) serves thin Swedish pancakes and a variety of omelets for breakfast and a full selection of favorites for lunch and dinner, from pasties and Swedish meatballs to smoked salmon and herring.

To keep a big group happy, head to **Black Woods** (612 7th Ave., 218/834-3846, www.blackwoods.com, 8 A.M.–10 P.M. daily), a big restaurant with an even bigger menu, including burgers, steaks, and pasta dishes. This is a good place for a hearty breakfast.

The fanciest dining is at **Kamloops** (218/834-5671, 7 A.M.–9 P.M. Sun.–Thurs., 7 A.M.–10 P.M. Fri.–Sat., $10–29) at the Superior Shores Resort. The menu has steak, seafood, and pasta, much of it with a Minnesota touch. The dining room overlooks the lake, and there is an outdoor deck.

South of town, you can get a good cup of coffee and a nice, light sandwich at **Mocha Moose** (543 Scenic Hwy. 61, 218/834-6299, www.mochamoose.com, 7 A.M.–5 P.M. Mon.–Thurs., 7 A.M.–6 P.M. Fri., 8 A.M.–6 P.M. Sat., 8 A.M.–3 P.M. Sun.). This is a convenient North Shore–themed gift shop, as well.

Information

Right on the main drag, the visitor center inside **Sawtooth Mountain Trading Post** (802 7th Ave., 218/834-5592, 10 A.M.–5 P.M. Mon.–Thurs., 10 A.M.–6 P.M. Fri., 10 A.M.–4 P.M. Sun.) is large, friendly, and well equipped to help you plan your trip as you head north, including making hotel and campground reservations. There's a great selection of books and maps, as well as T-shirts and souvenirs.

The **Superior Hiking Trail Association**

© TRICIA CORNELL

The North Shore Scenic Railroad runs between Duluth and Two Harbors.

(731 7th Ave., 218/834-2700, www.shta.org, 9 A.M.–5 P.M. Mon.–Fri., 10 A.M.–4 P.M. Sat., noon–4 P.M. Sun. May–Oct., 9 A.M.–4:30 P.M. Mon.–Fri. rest of year) offices have maps and any other information you could want to know about one of the best long-distance hiking trails in the nation, plus books, clothing, and related items for sale.

As you head out of town, the **R. J. Houle Visitor Information Center** (1330 Hwy. 61, 218/834-6200 or 800/777-7384, 9 A.M.–5 P.M. Sun.–Thurs., 9 A.M.–6 P.M. Fri.–Sat.), housed in a historic CCC log building just east of town, has brochures for all of northeast Minnesota and will help find hotel vacancies during busy event weekends.

Getting There

You can visit Two Harbors with the **North Shore Scenic Railroad** (520 South Ave., 218/722-1273 or 800/423-1273, www.northshorescenicrailroad.org), which travels here from Duluth and lays over for two hours every Friday and Saturday May through October. Arrangements for an overnight stay on Friday can be made with the Lighthouse Bed and Breakfast (218/834-4898).

GOOSEBERRY FALLS STATE PARK

With your first glimpse of Gooseberry Falls you'll quickly understand why this is Minnesota's most popular state park (218/834-3855). (So popular, you should plan to arrive very early on summer weekends if you want to find parking.) The swift Gooseberry River shoots around a narrow bend, drops over Upper Falls into a rocky gorge, blankets the 100-foot-wide rock wall forming Middle Falls, and plunges over the split Lower Falls before calmly marching on to Lake Superior. Though nearly 600,000 people gaze upon these scenes each year—the whole 90-foot drop sits just a short stroll down a wheelchair-accessible trail—a relatively small number of them venture through the rest of the 1,675-acre park.

A pair of excellent hiking trails follows the river down to Lake Superior. The **River View Trail** starts below the falls and climbs up a ridge with a superb view of Lower and Middle Falls before hitting lovely Agate Beach. The **Gitchi-Gami Trail** (www.gitchigamitrail.com) follows the much higher ridge across the river looking down upon the river's mouth from above; it's rather noisy when circling back by the highway so consider retracing your steps instead of completing the two-mile loop. Both trails have a few climbs, but steps make them pretty easy overall. Heading upstream, the two-mile **Fifth Falls Trail** (part of the North Shore–length **Superior Hiking Trail**) hugs the river as it climbs to its namesake cascade and returns on the opposite shore. Another 12 miles of trail, most of them open to mountain bikes, wind through the park's hills. Come winter most of the trails are groomed for cross-country skiing, while the Gitchi-Gami and Fifth Falls trails are available for winter hiking. The campground has 70 well-spaced nonelectric sites, and there is also a kayak site on Lake Superior.

SPLIT ROCK LIGHTHOUSE STATE PARK

On November 28, 1905, a great gale whipped Lake Superior into such a rage that half a dozen ships were wrecked within 12 miles of the Split Rock River. In response, the **Split Rock Lighthouse** (3713 Split Rock Lighthouse Rd., 218/226-6372, grounds open 8 A.M.–sunset daily year-round, tours 10 A.M.–6 P.M. daily May–Oct., $8 adults) was built atop this magnificent 130-foot cliff; it began operations in 1910. Its 370,000-candlepower beacon steered ships away from the treacherous shore for 59 years before onboard navigational equipment made it obsolete. The Minnesota Historical Society has restored the gorgeous facility to its pre-1924 appearance, and when you tour the lighthouse, fog-signal building, and keeper's home, costumed interpreters share tales of their isolated pre-road lives. Exhibits in the visitors center (10 A.M.–6 P.M. daily during tour season, 11 A.M.–4 P.M. Sat.–Sun. rest of year) discuss the lives of the families who lived here, how the light station was built, and other North Shore topics.

Though many visitors don't realize it, Split Rock is much more than just a lighthouse, and

© TRICIA CORNELL

Split Rock Lighthouse is among the most popular North Shore attractions.

the rest of the park's 2,103 acres shouldn't be overlooked. This is one of the best spots on the North Shore to explore by kayak, and there are put-ins near both ends of the park's 6.25-mile shoreline, the longest of any Minnesota park on the North Shore. Divers can explore the wreck of the tow barge *Madeira,* one of the ships lost in the 1905 storm, near Gold Rock Point. Register in the park office.

About half of the park's 12 miles of trail stick to the shore side of the highway, and these are available for hiking and mountain biking, and groomed for cross-country skiing or snowshoeing (snowshoe rentals are available). There are many wonderful lakeside overlooks, but none compare to the view from the peak of the 1.25-mile **Day Hill Trail.** The easier **Little Two Harbors Trail** connects Day Hill with the lighthouse. Turning inland, the stretch of the **Superior Hiking Trail** following the waterfall-rich Split Rock River is a challenging, but rewarding, walk.

Split Rock's campground is one of the best on the North Shore. All 20 cart-in sites are secluded and most come with lake views; none is more than 2,000 feet from the parking area. Though the sites lack electricity, there is a modern shower building. Another four backpacking sites—two are bluff-top and two sit lakeside—and a kayak-only site on Crazy Bay offer even more solitude.

BEAVER BAY

A group of German and Swiss families who arrived on a steamboat in 1856 were Beaver Bay's first settlers. A nationwide financial panic the very next year caused the abandonment of all the other fledgling towns between Duluth and Grand Portage, but these hardy immigrants remained. A sawmill provided the livelihood for most of the town's first residents, and soon several Ojibwe families moved here to join them in the lumbering business. About two dozen, including John Beargrease, a legendary North Shore resident who is famous for delivering the mail by dogsled before any roads or trails existed in these parts, were laid to rest in the traditional **burial ground** behind town. There's little to see here since it is left in a natural state, but if you want to visit, take the first left off County Highway 4.

Shopping

The **Beaver Bay Agate Shop** (1003 Main St., 218/226-4847, www.beaverbayagate.com, 9 A.M.–5 P.M. daily) is worth a look even if you don't want to buy.

Accommodations

Half a mile before town is **Cove Point Lodge** (4614 Hwy 61, 218/226-3221 or 800/598-3221, www.covepointlodge.com, $128 rooms, $209 cottages), a great hotel in a great setting on 150 acres. All rooms in the lodge, built and decorated in the classic Northwoods style, face the lake, as do the large two- and three-bedroom cottages. Guests can use the pool, whirlpool, sauna, and canoes, but lazily watching the lake appears to be the most popular activity. A spur trail connects the lodge to the Superior Hiking Trail.

The plain-Jane **Inn at Beaver Bay** (1017 Main St., 218/226-4351, www.innatbeaverbay.com, $55–130) is on the main drag, away from the lake, but very close to hiking and ATV trails. If you plan to spend most of your time outside anyway, this is an affordable choice. Not all rooms have air-conditioning.

Food

The inimitable **Northern Lights Roadhouse** (Hwy. 61, 218/226-3012, 10 A.M.–8 P.M. Sun.–Thurs., 10 A.M.–9 P.M. Fri.–Sat., summer hours sometimes longer) serves big platters of Northwoods game and Scandinavian specialties in a dining room full of outdoor gear and on a patio surrounded by wildflowers.

Get a quick sandwich or a sweet treat at **Wits' End Corner Country Store and Bakery** (Hwy. 61, 218/226-4074, www.witsendcorner.com, 8:30 A.M.–5 P.M. Tues.–Sat., closed Sun.–Mon.), where they bake bread, cookies, cakes, and more daily. It's also stocked with deli meats and cheese, a few meals to take home, and gifts.

SILVER BAY

Rocky Taconite welcomes you to the youngest town on the North Shore. Silver Bay was built from scratch by the Reserve Mining Company in 1951 to house workers for its new taconite processing plant, the first in North America. While the mine near Babbitt once shipped more than five million tons of iron pellets down the Great Lakes each year, economic hard times shut it down indefinitely in 2009.

Sights and Recreation

The **Visitor Information Center** (218/226-3143, 10 A.M.–4 P.M. Mon.–Sat., noon–4 P.M. Sun. summer, Sat.–Sun. Sept.–Oct.), a half-mile up the hill on Outer Drive, has a small historical display. Just beyond it (follow the signs) is a **scenic overlook** with signs identifying the various taconite buildings and explaining the process.

Keep going from the scenic overlook and you'll find yourself on the **Twin Lakes Trail,** a 6.8-mile loop with spectacular views over Bean and Bear Lakes. Be prepared for fairly serious climbing.

Silver Bay is the eastern end of the 59-mile **Superior National Forest Scenic Byway,** which connects the North Shore to the Iron Range.

The **Silver Bay Marina** (218/226-3121, www.silverbay.com/marina, 8 A.M.–6 P.M. daily May–Oct., reduced hours after Labor Day) is a great place to stop and take a walk out over the rocky breakwater. Ask at the marina office for charter fishing recommendations.

Accommodations

Rooms at the **Mariner Motel** (46 Outer Dr., 218/226-4488, $55) are large and clean, and since the town itself isn't much of a tourist destination, this is a good place to look for last-minute bookings.

Ten miles northeast of Silver Bay, the **Baptism River Inn** (6125 Co. Hwy. 1, 218/353-0707 or 877/353-0707, www.baptismriverinn.com, $86–189) bed-and-breakfast sits in 32 acres of forest on its rushing namesake. The energy-efficient log home has a bright mix of art and Northwoods decor, and each of the three guestrooms have private baths with large whirlpool tubs; two have balconies. After hiking or using their snowshoes you can relax in the sauna.

The **Whispering Pines Motel** (5763 Hwy. 61, 218/226-4712, www.whisperingpinesmotel.com, $65–165) is nothing fancy, but has plenty of charm and a great location. In addition to 15 motel rooms, there is one honeymoon cabin, removed from the rest of the sites by a little footbridge, and a suite that sleeps six and has its own fully-stocked kitchen.

PALISADE HEAD

Arguably the most beautiful site in the state, Palisade Head's ruddy cliff climbs 350 feet straight out of Lake Superior. A slim road at mile marker 57 snakes to the top, where you can walk along as much of the rim as your fear lets you—needless to say, be careful. Even severe acrophobes should make the trip just to take in the wonderful scenery in the distance. Shovel Point, another rhyolite lava headland, crawls out of the lake to the north, and Wisconsin's Apostle Islands are visible on the horizon. Palisade Head is a part of Tettegouche State Park, the main entrance of which is just 1.5 miles away, though no state park sticker is required for visits of less than an hour. Rock climbers need free permits from the park office.

TETTEGOUCHE STATE PARK

By far the largest state park on the North Shore, Tettegouche's (5702 Hwy. 61, 218/226-6365) 9,346 acres are just an hour from Duluth, but make a wonderful wilderness escape. Palisade Head and Shovel Point, stunning cliffs climbing straight out of Lake Superior, make the coastal scenery some of the best on the lake, though most of the park sits atop the Sawtooth Range, where six lakes are nestled between the steep hills, and the Baptism River leaps over a succession of waterfalls and rapids. Established in 1979, Tettegouche (TET-uh-gooch) is one of Minnesota's newest state parks, but it's also one of the North Shore's earliest protected areas. The Alger-Smith Lumber Company set up a logging camp in the park at the end of the 19th century and gave many area lakes Algonquin names since the men were mostly from New Brunswick, Canada. In 1910, after having cleared the area's red and white pine, they sold the land to a group of Duluth businessmen who created a fishing camp. Though it changed hands a few times, all subsequent owners stewarded the land, allowing today's beautiful park.

Tettegouche's 23 miles of hiking trail, including a 12-mile stretch of the **Superior Hiking Trail,** are generally hilly, though the myriad scenic vistas make the lung-chugging climbs worthwhile. The most popular destination is **High Falls,** a 70-foot drop on the Baptism River. The tallest waterfall entirely in Minnesota is just an easy half-mile round-trip from the campground, but the most scenic route follows the **Baptism River Trail** 1.5 somewhat difficult miles up from Highway 61, passing two more waterfalls along the way. A series of interconnected loops winds around the interior lakes offering many scenic overlooks—Palisade Valley is arguably the most beautiful.

SUPERIOR NATIONAL FOREST

Stretching 150 miles across Minnesota's Arrowhead, the Superior National Forest (SNF) is home to two of the nation's premier recreation destinations: the Boundary Waters Canoe Area Wilderness and the Superior Hiking Trail. Though the forest is best known for these two heavyweights there are few outdoor activities that you can't enjoy here. The forest's three million acres surround over 2,000 lakes, 2,250 miles of stream, some almost-mountain-like hills, and an extensive boreal forest ecosystem. All mammals typical of the Northwoods inhabit the forest, but the roughly 400 gray wolves roaming Superior are the real stars and the 155 breeding bird species are more than any other national forest. Not surprisingly the American Bird Conservancy chose this as one of its Globally Important Bird Areas.

Most of the campgrounds sit lakeside and are peacefully rustic, though if you aren't into roughing it, many of the state's best resorts and most charming towns border the forest, so after taking in the scenery during the day you can retire to elegant quarters and a gourmet meal. The Superior is so vast that for the purposes of this book the five administrative districts are treated as individual places and spread throughout this chapter. The Boundary Waters Canoe Area Wilderness spans four districts and has its own section. If you are coming in September and October, call the Forest Service's **Fall Foliage Hotline** (800/354-4595) to get the up-to-the-minute scoop on autumn's annual exhibition.

RECREATION

The Superior National Forest's nearly 500 miles of hiking trail range from quarter-mile strolls to weeklong wilderness treks with some of the best backpacking east of the Rockies, including much of the 205-mile **Superior Hiking Trail,** which hugs the North Shore. Mountain bikers are largely limited to forest roads and old logging roads, though the Tofte District's **Superior Mountain Bike Trail System** has something for everyone. Mountain bikes are not allowed anywhere in the BWCAW or on the Superior Hiking Trail.

Come winter 290 miles of trail are groomed for cross-country skiing, with most of these spread across the Tofte and Gunflint Districts. This includes the **North Shore Ski Trail,** which combines for 120 miles along the hills between Tofte and Grand Marais. The Laurentian District has additional groomed miles, while most of the trails in the Kawishiwi and LaCroix Districts extend into the BWCAW – where snowmobiles are banned – and so are ungroomed. In total, snowmobilers have nearly 700 miles of groomed trail to ride.

Paddling is principally about the BWCAW, where you can explore over 1,000 lakes and streams, but it's not the only option. Another 13 designated lake and river portage routes lie

A mature forest covers the park's lake area, and there are even scattered old-growth white and red pine stands, such as Conservancy Pines on Mic Mac's east shore. Down at Lake Superior the popular **Shovel Point Trail** is a fairly easy walk out along its namesake cliffs; interpretive displays discuss the park's geology. In the winter the Shovel Point Trail is designated for snowshoeing, and the office rents shoes. Fifteen more trail miles are groomed for cross-country skiing, with most offering a bit of a challenge. Experienced rock climbers scale Palisade Head and Shovel Point (a free climbing permit is required); paddlers can rent canoes from the park office to explore the portage-linked Mic Mac and Nipisiquit Lakes, while anglers take trout from Bear and Bean Lakes and the Baptism River.

Tettegouche's varied overnight options make the park one of the best places to spend the night on the North Shore. The 34 sites (no electric, six walk-in) in the Baptism River Campground are widely spaced. Down on Lake Superior (and unfortunately right next to the highway) are 14 cart-in sites—none are more than half a mile from the parking lot and about half have lake views. There are also five backpack sites along the Superior Hiking

outside the Wilderness, and not only do they have great scenery, but relatively few people follow them. Another bonus to these lesser-known trips is that permits and fees are not required. Even though most are short enough to run in a day, campsites facilitate overnight trips. Obviously, with 695 square miles of surface water, fishing is popular here. The Gunflint and Tofte Districts are rumored to have the best angling opportunities, though you can't really go wrong wherever you cast a line. Many people fish the BWCAW for the serenity, and because more big fish live to maturity, some smallmouth aficionados believe world-record bass swim these waters.

CAMPING

Superior has 23 developed campgrounds. All sit on a lake or river and the majority lie in the eastern end of the forest with access from the North Shore. Only Whiteface Reservoir by Hoyt Lakes and Fall Lake near Ely have electric hookups, and only the latter has showers and flush toilets. Individual campsites all have a picnic table, fire grate, and tent pad. In general the camps are fully operational from mid-May into September. In the off-season some of the campgrounds are gated and have no water or other services, but camping is allowed. About half take reservations (877/444-6777, www.reserveusa.com, $10 nonrefundable fee), though all have some first-come, first-served sites available. Surprisingly, except for summer weekends the camps rarely fill up – and even on summer weekends it is usually possible to show up and get a site somewhere. Summer rates range $10-20 depending on amenities provided; there is usually no charge after the water is shut off. There are also 17 rustic campgrounds with fewer facilities that tend to be very peaceful (none have more than eight sites) and more remote. All of these free camps are in the Tofte District, except for one nearby in the Gunflint District.

Many remote backpacking and canoe-in sites with fire grates and latrines dot the forest's lakes and trails. For more information on these free sites inquire at one of the district offices. Forest Service rules also permit you to camp anywhere on National Forest land outside the BWCAW, as long as you're 100 feet from any trail or water source and observe Leave No Trace (www.lnt.org) outdoor ethics. Though registration isn't required for backcountry camping, checking in at a ranger station before heading out is always a good idea, especially to find out about fire restrictions.

INFORMATION

The **Forest Headquarters** (8901 Grand Avenue Pl., 218/626-4300 or 218/626-4399 TTY, www.fs.fed.us/r9/superior, 8 A.M.-4:30 P.M. Mon.-Fri.) is in Duluth, though information on specific facilities is best requested from the appropriate district ranger station.

Trail and kayak-accessible sites for those paddling the shore.

The **Tettegouche Camp** has four classic log cabins ($80) from the early 1900s on Mic Mac Lake, a 1.7-mile walk, bike, or ski in from the nearest road. Three cabins sleep six, while the other is wheelchair accessible and has room for two people. The cabins have electricity but no running water; however, a modern shower building means you don't really have to rough it all that much. Meals are cooked on a hotplate or campfire, and there is also a small fridge. Each cabin comes with a canoe.

Further up the Baptism River, the modern **Illgen Falls Cabin** has all the conveniences of home for $130 per night. It's a fully accessible two-bedroom home with a back deck overlooking the 45-foot waterfall.

GEORGE H. CROSBY MANITOU STATE PARK

Crosby Manitou (7 mi. north of Finland on County Rd. 7, 218/226-6365, $20 campsite) is one of the best, but least-known, wilderness escapes on the North Shore—in part because getting there requires a long detour off Highway 61. This was the first Minnesota state park designed for backpackers, and 21 wonderful campsites are scattered about the 6,682 acres, mostly along the Manitou River. The 24 miles of hiking-only trails are generally steep and rugged, but they reward the adventurous with overlooks of the gorge and excellent wildlife and fall-color viewing. Arguably the most beautiful path is the **West Manitou River Trail,** which hugs the river through most of the park and, at the north end, passes the only waterfall accessible by trail. A recommended loop combines the River Trail with the **Middle Trail, Yellow Birch Trail,** and **Misquah Trail.** It's about a 3.5-mile hike and features four fantastic overlooks. The park's easiest hike is the mile-long boardwalk around Benson Lake. The North Shore–length **Superior Hiking Trail** follows parts of each of these trails through the park for five miles. Anglers appreciate the small lake because trout are abundant and motors are prohibited. Even the less energetic should consider a picnic along Benson Lake, or just come up for the lovely drive along the Baptism River.

SCHROEDER

The **Cross River Heritage Center** (7932 Hwy. 61 W., 218/663-7706, www.crossriverheritage.org, 10 A.M.–4:30 P.M. Tues.–Sat., noon–4 P.M. Sun. June–Oct., free admission) is a surprising gem of a history museum. Learn about Olympic skier Cindy Nelson and the Miracle on Ice and visit period rooms. This is a good place for classier souvenirs, like photographs, knitwear, and Swedish fabric.

Just over the river—and its long, lovely cascade—is **Father Baraga's Cross,** a granite monument replacing the original wooden marker the missionary placed here in 1846.

Six miles north of Schroeder on Highway 61 is the **Sugarloaf Cove Nature Center** (218/525-0001, www.sugarloafnorthshore.org). Once home to a logging operation, the 34 acres surrounding the cove are now dedicated to preserving the area's natural beauty. The small interpretive center—with hours that vary—has nature and history exhibits and hosts free programs throughout the summer. Signs along the mile-long trail share information about the geology, wildlife, and history of the museum. It winds past a logging camp, a rare wetland, and a stony beach.

TEMPERANCE RIVER STATE PARK

If you are short on time or energy, Temperance River State Park (218/663-7476, $24 campsite with electricity) is a great stop because you can get a quick taste of the best of the North Shore—wild waterfalls and rugged coast. The 539-acre property is centered on the river, so named because, unlike other North Shore rivers, there was no gravel "bar" at its mouth. In less than a mile you can stroll an easy riverside path down to Lake Superior's rocky beach and jagged cliffs and then head upriver along an impossibly narrow, corkscrewing gorge to Hidden Falls. Along the river look for deep potholes carved into the soft lava during the last Ice Age. Many more trails run beyond the park through the adjacent Superior National Forest, including the **Superior Hiking Trail,** which leads to **Carlton Peak,** one of the highest points on the North Shore and a popular spot for hikers and rock climbers—a free permit from the park office is needed by the latter. The 924-foot summit, where the Superior views stretch on seemingly toward infinity, is 2.8 miles in from the heart of the park, though it can be reached in a three-mile round-trip from the trailhead on County Highway 2. For an unobstructed view of Carlton Peak, scramble up the comparatively dinky **Britton Peak,** just a quarter-mile round-trip from the County Highway 2 trailhead. The twin campgrounds sit unfortunately close to the highway, but on the plus side, many of the sites come with lake views. The 55 campsites are shady and well spaced, with all 18 electric and 3 cart-in sites in the upper camp.

TOFTE

Sights and Recreation

The best reason to stop in this little town is to tour the **North Shore Commercial Fishing Museum** (7136 Hwy. 61, 218/663-7804 or 888/616-6784, www.commercialfishingmuseum.org, 9 A.M.–5 P.M. daily, $3 adults). Housed in a replica fish house, the displays engagingly explain the who and how of Lake Superior's fishing industry through old equipment—including a fish table that received heavy use, as the scales still embedded in it will attest—and fascinating photos. The museum is also the office of the helpful **America's North Coast Travel Planner** (www.americasnorthcoast.org).

Tofte is linked to the BWCAW via County Highway 2 (aka the Sawbill Trail), and an outfitter at each end can set you up with everything you need to paddle it.

In town is **Sawtooth Outfitters** (7213 Hwy. 61, 218/663-7643, www.sawtoothoutfitters.com, 7 A.M.–7 P.M. daily), which also has mountain bikes, sea kayaks, and cross-country skis.

Sawbill Canoe Outfitters (4620 Sawbill Trl., 218/663-7150, www.sawbill.com, 7 A.M.–9 P.M. daily) is right up at the Sawbill Lake Entry.

Accommodations and Food

Composing seemingly half the town is the oft-lauded **Bluefin Bay Resort** (7192 Hwy. 61 W., 218/663-7296 or 800/258-3346, www.bluefinbay.com, $145). Some of their topflight amenities include a fitness center, tennis courts, two saunas, indoor pool, and a year-round outdoor pool and hot tub. They also offer movie nights, guided sea kayak and snowshoe tours, sailing trips (you need not be staying at the resort for these), and will shuttle you to Lutsen Mountains or area trailheads. The 133 diverse lakeside units range from studios to three-bedroom condos, and most have fireplaces, decks, and whirlpools. Add the lake views and it's a great romantic getaway. Two-day rentals are required on weekends.

Bluefin Bay also runs both of Tofte's restaurants. **Bluefin Grille** (7192 Hwy. 61 W., 218/663-6200, 8 A.M.–9 P.M. Sun.–Thurs., 8 A.M.–10 P.M. Fri.–Sat., $8–46) is a very popular place. Enjoy cinnamon wild rice pancakes, roast duck, and one of dozens of wines with great lake views from the dining room or deck.

Just up the road, **Coho Café & Bakery** (7126 Hwy. 61, 218/663-8032, 7 A.M.–9 P.M. daily summer, 7 A.M.–2 P.M. Sun.–Thurs., 7 A.M.–9 P.M. Fri.–Sat. rest of year, $7–18) has fancy deli sandwiches, pasta, and pizza.

Information

You can get Superior National Forest information at the **Tofte Ranger Station** (7355 Hwy. 61, 218/663-7280, 7 A.M.–5 P.M. daily).

Pick up local books, along with lots of outdoor gear, at **WatersEdge Trading Co.** (7124 Hwy. 61 W., 218/663-7021, www.watersedgetrading.com).

LUTSEN

Lutsen is just barely a town, but it is still one of the North Shore's busiest destinations.

Recreation

Lutsen Mountains (467 Ski Hill Rd., 218/663-7281, www.lutsen.com), a mile to the south, is the Midwest's largest downhill ski area, with 90 ski runs and a 986-foot drop, in addition to 17 miles of challenging cross-country ski trails. But it is more than just a winter destination, with 20 miles of mountain bike trail, horseback riding, an alpine slide, and a gondola ride that's ideal for viewing fall color. An unlimited day pass for the summer activities costs $33 (cheaper options are available), and bikes are available for rent. They also organize canoeing, kayaking, and rock climbing trips.

Big-name bands from the Twin Cities often play **Papa Charlie's** (467 Ski Hill Rd., 218/663-7281, 11:30 A.M.–11 P.M. daily peak summer and winter seasons, reduced hours rest of year), Lutsen Mountains' restaurant and bar.

Lutsen Rec. (245 Ski Hill Rd., 218/663-7863, www.lutsenrec.com, hours vary), halfway up the hill, rents skis, snowboards, and snowshoes in the winter and offers paintball, miniature golf, and RC car racing the rest of the year.

Finally, **Superior National** (5731 Hwy. 61, 218/663-7195, www.superiornational.com, sunrise–sunset, $72 18 holes with cart) has 27 of the loveliest holes you'll ever golf.

Accommodations

There is plenty of quality lodging in the area. Down on a gorgeous 1,000-foot Lake

Superior pebble beach is **Lutsen Resort** (5700 Hwy. 61, 218/663-7212 or 800/258-8736, www.lutsenresort.com, $99 lodge, $260 log cabins). The Swedish-style main lodge has 31 rooms, and there are also larger cottages and condos. Some of their many amenities include a pair of pools, whirlpools, and saunas, as well as shuffleboard and a par-3 golf course. There are many naturalist and other kids' programs. Their lovely dining room (breakfast, lunch, and dinner daily, $8–33) is the most highly regarded kitchen in the area. The menu is mostly steak and seafood, and there are cheaper sandwiches and the like in their Poplar River Pub ($8.50–18).

The 11 units at **Thomsonite Beach Resort** (2920 Hwy. 61 W., 218/387-1532 or 888/387-1532, www.thomsonite.com, $68–181) have cozy wood paneling and basic furniture and sleep four to six people; the larger ones have kitchens. On a rocky outcropping and down a slight hill from the highway, it's a lovely location.

Solbakken Resort (4874 Hwy. 61 W., 218/663-7566, $50–230) welcomes visitors year-round to stay in cabins and motel units with up to three bedrooms. The tidy porches lead directly down a grassy slope to the lake.

Eagle Ridge Resort (565 Ski Hill Rd., 218/663-7284 or 800/360-7666, www.eagleridgeatlutsen.com, $99) is the closest resort to the ski hill, but what really sets it apart is the heated indoor/outdoor pool, which stays at 85 degrees right through the winter. Many of the varied rooms have a fireplace or whirlpool.

Next door, **Caribou Highlands Lodge** (371 Ski Hill Rd., 218/663-7241 or 800/642-6036, www.caribouhighlands.com, $90), another ski-in ski-out property, has a mix of lodge rooms and large log condos. Facilities include indoor and outdoor pools, tennis courts, a sauna, game room, and a Kids Camp with varied activities.

Lutsen's most affordable rooms are at the **Mountain Inn** (360 Ski Hill Rd., 218/663-7244 or 800/686-4669, $65), a standard but well-run hotel with a whirlpool and sauna.

Food

The **Lockport Store** (1273 Hwy. 61, 218/663-7548, breakfast and lunch daily) is a local favorite with tons of character. Housed in a converted gas station convenience store and decorated with outdoor gear, it serves up classic pasties (hand pies) and an all-you-can-eat plate of sourdough pancakes.

Moondance Coffee House (5335 Hwy. 61 W., 218/663-7915, www.moondancecoffeehouse.com, 7 A.M.–6 P.M. Mon., 7 A.M.–1 P.M. Tues.–Thurs., 7 A.M.–5 P.M. Fri.–Sat., 7 A.M.–1 P.M. Sun.) is serious about its coffee and how it's roasted. The vibe is urban, and live music plays on Monday nights.

CASCADE RIVER STATE PARK

The Cascade River drops 900 feet during the last three miles of its journey, tumbling over a pair of waterfalls right before running into Lake Superior. The 5,550-acre park (3481 Hwy. 61 W., 218/387-3053) surrounding this aptly named waterway also stretches along three miles of Lake Superior shoreline, and its 18 miles of trail let you stroll or ski along the rugged coast or climb up into the Sawtooth Range for some spectacular scenery both near and far. It's less than half a mile round-trip along the **Cascade River Trail** to reach Cascade Falls and The Cascades. The **Superior Hiking Trail** continues along both banks of the river gorge into the adjacent Superior National Forest and up to County Highway 45, offering a 7.7-mile loop. Down another branch of the SHT is **Lookout Mountain.** The popular overlook on the east side is a steep but worthy 1.75-mile climb, and you can continue on to complete a 3.7-mile loop around the peak. The easy **Lake Trail** skirts two miles of gorgeous shoreline, but suffers highway hum. Five backpacking campsites ($18) with Adirondack-style shelters are scattered about the park, and an otherwise good 40-site semi-modern campground is situated unfortunately close to the highway.

If a night under the stars isn't your thing, consider **Cascade Lodge** (3719 Hwy. 61, 218/387-1112 or 800/322-9543, www.cascadelodgemn.com, $75 rooms, $99 cabins), a North Shore fixture that sits right by the park entrance and is directly connected to its trail system. Many of the guestrooms in the 1930s log lodge come with lake views, while the cabins, most with fireplaces, are oozing Northwoods charm. Naturally, due to its location, the lodge caters to outdoor sports enthusiasts, so outdoor gear, including mountain bikes, is available for rent.

SUPERIOR NATIONAL FOREST – TOFTE DISTRICT

The Tofte District, running up from the North Shore into the Boundary Waters, features many of the best day hikes in the forest and several good non-BWCAW canoe routes. Rangers run a busy summer interpretive program with morning hikes, evening campfires, and more every Tuesday through Saturday; though most events take place at area resorts, all programs are open to the public. The district is also known as a blueberry mecca, and the Forest Service has management areas dedicated to increasing production and a brochure with maps directing pickers to prime sites.

Recreation

The district's most popular hike is the **Oberg Mountain Trail,** a not-too-strenuous 2.4-mile climb with views of Lake Superior and Oberg Lake waiting at the top. The 3.4-mile **Leveaux Trail** also has great ridge-top views, though it gets much less traffic. These are some of the best fall-color hikes on the North Shore, and Oberg gets almost as busy as Highway 61 at this time. Both loops are connected to the **Superior Hiking Trail** and start on Forest Road 336 between Tofte and Lutsen.

The little-known **Hogback Lake Trail** on Forest Road 172 between Tofte and Isabella has six miles of peaceful loops along six small and slender lakes. It is only half a mile in to the gorgeous ridge-top views between Hogback and Scarp Lakes. Trout are stocked in these waters, and there are some great backpacking campsites on the shore. West of Isabella, the **Flathorn Lake Trail**'s main summer route is a two-mile loop around its namesake, but come winter people head off to ski the 15 miles of groomed intermediate-level trails—known as Flathorn-Gegoka—branching deeper into the forest. There are also pleasant and easy hikes at the **Divide Lake, McDougal Lake,** and **Ninemile Lake** campgrounds.

Mountain bikers will want to stop by the Lutsen-Tofte Tourism Association for maps of the **Superior Mountain Bike Trail System,** 200 marked miles of everything from casual road routes to wild single-track. Cross-country skiers will also want to pick up a regional map of the **North Shore Ski Trail,** whose 120 miles spread across the Tofte and Gunflint Districts. Two of the most popular sections are the **Sugarbush** and **Moose Fence** trails, both of which lie north of Tofte along County Highway 2 (the Sawbill Trail), with 36 miles of easy to difficult loops.

Timber-Frear, 15 miles northwest of Tofte, is the most traveled of the district's four non-BWCAW portage canoe routes. The nine-mile loop covers six lakes, and on weekends all 12 campsites might be occupied. Although they are primarily used as day paddles, there are also a few campsites along the five-mile **Crescent Lake-Rice Lake,** three-mile **Crooked Lake Area,** and six-mile **Island River** routes. Canoeing into Scarp Lake around the Hogback Trail is also scenic and enjoyable.

You can learn about natural history as you drive up the **Temperance River Watershed Tour,** a roundabout route to the Sawbill Lake Campground; the roadside interpretive signs are only kept up spring through fall. More signs are put up for a **Fall Color Tour.**

Camping

Sawbill Lake, the district's largest campground, has 51 sites right on the edge of the BWCAW, and it rarely fills up. If you want to paddle into the wilderness or take a shower, **Sawbill Canoe Outfitters** (4620 Sawbill Trl., 218/663-7150, 7 A.M.–9 P.M. daily) is right next door. There are 32 more sites nearby at **Crescent Lake.** The nine sites, several riverside, at **Temperance River,** halfway between Tofte and Sawbill Lake along County Highway 2 (the Sawbill Trail), also don't fill up very often. Sites at the campgrounds are $16 per night. Call 877/444-6777 or go online at www.reserveamerica.com.

The other four developed camps lie on a line west of Tofte. The closest and thus busiest is **Ninemile Lake** (located off County Rd. 7 northwest of Schroeder), with 26 sites and good bird-watching in the surrounding forest. With just three sites, **Divide Lake** (east of Isabella on Forest Rd. 172) is more peaceful, and it has a lovely two-mile trail around the lake. The 11 riverside sites at **Little Isabella** (located off Hwy. 1, 4.5 miles west of Isabella) are noted for their serenity. Nearby and also in a beautiful setting is **McDougal Lake** (Forest Rd. 106, 10 miles west of Isabella, sites from $12), with 21 sites, a mile-long hiking trail, and a swimming beach. Twelve small **rustic campgrounds** are spread across the district. These more remote and less developed sites are available free of charge.

Information

The **Tofte Ranger Station** (7355 Hwy. 61, 218/663-7280, 7 A.M.–5 P.M. daily May–Sept., 8 A.M.–4:30 P.M. Mon.–Fri. rest of year) is located on the edge of Tofte.

Maps and brochures can also be picked up at the **Isabella Work Station** (3989 Forest Service Dr., 218/323-7722, 7:30 A.M.–4 P.M. Wed.–Sun. May–Sept.).

GRAND MARAIS

Grand Marais is not your average small town. This bustling village of 1,400 people has more cultural offerings than many much larger cities. Artists and progressive thinkers have been arriving for decades, and today their work fills galleries and keeps the stages stirring throughout the year.

The name Grand Marais, or Big Swamp, comes from the French version of the Ojibwe name for the area, though some historians claim they did a poor translation and the actual name was Place Beside the Duplicate Waters. Trading posts and fishing camps were established here previously, including one for John Jacob Astor's American Fur Company, but a permanent community didn't take hold until 1871, when explorer and prospector Henry Mayhew came looking for iron, copper, and silver. He never found great mineral wealth, but the town he founded prospered with fishing and logging. Today Grand Marais is a good base for exploring the surrounding wilderness and a great destination on its own.

Sights

The **Cook County Historical Museum** (8 Broadway S., 218/387-2883, 11 A.M.–4 P.M. Tues.–Sat. June–Sept., by appt. rest of year, free admission) occupies an 1896 lighthouse keeper's home. Most of the small but interesting collection of artifacts and photos relate to past industries, such as logging and farming, but there are some Native American and geological displays as well.

Just down the street is the **Johnson Heritage Post Art Gallery** (115 Wisconsin St. W., 218/387-2314, 10 A.M.–4 P.M. Wed.–Sat.,

AN EDUCATIONAL VACATION

The abundance of artists in and around Grand Marais has resulted in some special opportunities for visitors, so you might want to see what is on schedule at the following organizations before planning your trip.

The wonderful **North House Folk School** (500 Hwy. 61 W., 218/387-9762 or 888/387-9762, www.northhouse.org) promotes and preserves knowledge and skills from the past. You can try your hand at making brick-oven breads, pine-needle baskets, knives, longbows, moose-hide mukluks, and birch-bark canoes. You can also learn sailing and outdoor skills.

Classes of a different nature are on offer through the **Grand Marais Art Colony** (120 3rd Ave. W., 218/387-2737 or 800/385-9585, www.grandmaraisart-colony.org), which has led workshops in a variety of media since 1947. You can even get university credit for some of them.

© TRICIA CORNELL

Vacationers relax in the broad, quiet park along the bay in Grand Marais.

1–4 P.M. Sun. summer, 1–4 P.M. Thurs.–Sun. rest of year, free admission), with exhibitions by local and regional artists. Even if art isn't your thing, stop by just to admire the hand-hewn log building, a replica of a 19th-century trading post that once stood here.

In 1907 a forest fire destroyed most of the community of Chippewa City, which overlooked Lake Superior a mile east of present-day Grand Marais. **St. Francis Xavier Church** (1–4 P.M. Sat. July–Aug., free admission), built as a mission for the local Ojibwe, survived the blaze and, after extensive restoration, is now open to visitors. Both the unique interior construction and the photographs of its congregation back in 1895 when it was constructed are worth a look. The church, known locally as the Chippewa City Church, is one mile north of Grand Marais on Highway 61.

The Cook County Historical Society, which maintains the above three properties, also has a small **Commercial Fishing Museum** (7136 Hwy. 61, 218/663-7804, 9 A.M.–5 P.M. daily, $3 adults) down by the campground.

A stroll along the breakwater to the **Grand Marais Lighthouse** (3 blocks south of the stoplights on Hwy. 61) and past the forested cliffs of **Artist Point** is an essential trip. While tiny in size, Artist Point's beauty is immense—pack a picnic and you can easily spend half a day here. Unfortunately, everybody and her sister knows about it. You can often find solitude by walking out to **Sweetheart's Bluff** across the bay. The short, easy trail starts at the far west end of the campground, behind the blue gate.

Anderson Aero (80 Skyport Ln., 218/387-1687, 8 A.M.–nightfall daily, weather permitting, starts at $60) offers sightseeing flights, including guaranteed moose-viewing rides.

For something a bit different, you can visit a sawmill. Tours of the **Hedstrom Lumber Company** (1504 Gunflint Trl., 218/387-2995, www.hedstromlumber.com, 12:30 P.M. Tues. Memorial Day–Labor Day, free), five miles up the Gunflint Trail, are offered once a week.

In 2010 the Gunflint Trail Historical Society plans to open the **Chik-Wauk Museum and Nature Center** (28 Moose Pond Rd., www.gunflinttrailhistoricalsociety.org) on Saganaga Lake.

The 1930s stone cabin will house artifacts encompassing the area's history—from the Native Americans to the voyageurs to the resort owners. The 50-acre grounds are laced with trails and teeming with wildlife.

Entertainment and Events

The focus of Grand Marais cultural life is the **Arrowhead Center for the Arts** (51 5th St. W., 218/387-1284, www.arrowheadcenterforthearts.org). The $3.5 million complex—hosting theater, concerts, and more—has made locals proud and many other cities a little envious. The **Grand Marais Playhouse** (Broadway & 5th St., 218/387-1284, www.grandmaraisplayhouse.com) is a big part of the performance schedule, with a fall season packed with community theater favorites.

Since 1947, the **Grand Marais Art Colony** (120 3rd Ave. W., 218/387-2737, www.grandmaraisartcolony.org, 10 A.M.–4 P.M. Mon.–Sat.) has proved a creative haven for area artists. Housed in a white clapboard church, it offers workshops in everything from painting to glass blowing and hosts exhibitions open to the curious public.

If you plan ahead, you can combine your trip with a class at the **North House Folk School** (500 Hwy. 61 W., 218/387-9762, www.northhousefolkschool.org). People come from all over the country to learn woodworking, outdoor skills, textile arts, and much more.

For nightlife your best bet is the cozy **Gun Flint Tavern** (111 Wisconsin St. W., 218/387-1563, www.gunflinttavern.com, 11 A.M.–1 A.M. daily), which has a rollicking round of live blues, jazz, and reggae on weekends and an open stage on Wednesdays. They keep a dozen microbrews on tap and serve wine by the glass.

You can rack your brain over a pizza during the Thursday-night trivia contest at **Sven and Ole's** (9 Wisconsin St. W., 218/387-1713, www.svenandoles.com, 11 A.M.–9 P.M. daily, $3–21).

During the **Fisherman's Picnic,** held the first weekend in August, the townsfolk battle it out in log sawing, rock skipping, and loon calling, while gorging themselves on fish burgers.

Field trips and speakers during the **Boreal Birding Festival,** held the first weekend of June, center around the returning migration.

Lake Superior gets a touch of color the last weekend of July during the **North Shore Dragon Boat Festival** (218/387-2372, www.northshoredragonboat.com).

Shopping

Jim Brandenburg's photography and Betsy Bowen's woodcut prints are available at **Sivertson Gallery** (14 Wisconsin St. W., 218/387-2491 or 888/880-4369, 10 A.M.–5 P.M. daily), which sells "Art of the North" by regional, Canadian, and Alaskan artists, including many Native Americans.

You might see Bowen at her press at **Betsy Bowen Studio** (301 1st Ave. W., 218/387-1992, www.woodcut.com, 11 A.M.–5 P.M. Tues.–Sat.), a converted 1903 church where many other artists sell their work.

Another great art gallery for shopping and admiring is the **Johnson Heritage Post** (115 Wisconsin St., 218/387-2314, 10 A.M.–4 P.M. daily summer, 1–4 P.M. Thurs.–Sun. rest of year), which sells pieces by regional artists and has a permanent exhibit of works by a local artist from the turn of the 20th century, Anna Johnson.

Birchbark Gallery (11 1st Ave. W., 218/387-2315, 7 A.M.–9 P.M. daily summer, hours vary rest of year) is a massive gift shop with a fantastic selection of Minnesota and North Shore books.

Drury Lane Books (12 Wisconsin St., 218/387-3370, www.drurylanebooks.com, 10 A.M.–8 P.M. Mon.–Sat., 10 A.M.–4 P.M. Sun.) also has many regional titles.

For lower-brow shopping, pick up delicious fudge and some kitschy T-shirts at **Beth's Fudge and Gifts** (11 Broadway S., 218/387-2081, 10 A.M.–5 P.M. Mon.–Sat., 11 A.M.–5 P.M. Sun., closed Sun. in winter).

The **Dockside Fish Market** (418 Hwy. 61 W., 218/387-2906, 9 A.M.–7 P.M. Sat.–Thurs., 9 A.M.–8 P.M. Fri., closed Jan.–March), better known as the fish house, is the Toftey family's commercial fishing operation, which sells smoked and fresh fish direct to the public.

If you need any camping gear you'll probably find it at the **Lake Superior Trading Post** (10 S. 1st Ave. W., 218/387-2020, www.lstp.com, 9 A.M.–8 P.M. Mon.–Sat., 9 A.M.–6 P.M. Sun.).

Recreation

SUMMER

With the BWCAW so close, some people overlook the fantastic paddling available on Lake Superior, but not **Superior Coastal Sports** (20-B E. 1st St., 218/387-2360 or 800/720-2809, www.superiorcoastal.com, 7 A.M.–5 P.M. Mon.–Sat., 8 A.M.–4 P.M. Sun. summer, reduced hours in winter), who do sales and rentals for those with experience and lessons and guided trips ($39 half-day) for those without. SCS also offers sailing lessons and charters.

The **North House Folk School** (500 Hwy. 61 W., 218/387-9762, www.northhousefolkschool.com, 9 A.M., 11:30 A.M., 2:30 P.M., 5 P.M. Thurs.–Mon. June–Oct., weather permitting, $45 adults) has two-hour sailing trips.

To explore on land, rent a mountain bike, road bike, or tandem from **Superior North Outdoor Center** (13 S. Broadway, 218/387-2186, www.superiornorthoutdoor.com, 10 A.M.–5 P.M. Mon.–Fri., 10 A.M.–2 P.M. Sat.–Sun. summer, hours vary Nov.–Mar., $30 day, $38 mountain bike, $60 tandem, hourly rates also available) right in downtown Grand Marais. They also lead regular group rides and can provide a private guide. Ask about rock and ice-climbing trips.

The nine-hole **Gunflint Hills Golf Course** (1181 Golf Course Rd., 218/387-9988, 7 A.M.–7 P.M. daily summer) has sweeping views of Lake Superior. The moose are in play.

WINTER

Bear Track Outfitting (2011 Hwy. 61 W., 218/387-1162 or 800/795-8068, www.beartrack.com, 9 A.M.–5 P.M. daily) rents skis and snowshoes in the winter and offers fly-fishing clinics in the summer.

Devils Track Nordic Ski Shop (922 Gunflint Trl., 218/387-3373, www.devilstracknordic.com, hours vary by season) also has winter rentals.

When the lakes are frozen, several companies, including **Arleigh Jorgenson Sled Dog Adventures** (60 Frank's Way, 218/387-1107 or 800/884-5463, www.dogmushing.com), offer mushing trips. For around $320 you can drive your own team for a full day. Overnight trips through the BWCAW and Superior National Forest offer the option of camping or staying in cabins.

Accommodations

Right downtown, **East Bay Suites** (21 Wisconsin St., 218/387-2800 or 800/414-2807, www.eastbaysuites.com, $149), has a great lakeside location and rooms ranging from studios to three bedrooms. Most have fireplaces, whirlpool tubs, and lake balconies or porches with Superior views.

Just down the beach is the **Shoreline Inn** (20 Broadway S., 218/387-2633 or 800/247-6020, www.gmhotel.net, $109), where the lobby is full of games, puzzles, and books to enjoy in your room or in front of the fireplace.

The same owners run the **Aspen Lodge** (310 Hwy. 61 E., 218/387-2500 or 800/247-6020, $139), where most rooms have a lake view. There is a sauna, whirlpool, and the only hotel swimming pool in town.

The **Harbor Inn** (207 Wisconsin St., 218/387-1191, www.bytheharbor.com, $135) has another fantastic location, facing the harbor and just a few blocks from the lighthouse and other attractions. Many rooms have balconies, and they all have a cozy, paneled, nautical feel.

The little **Gunflint Motel** (101 5th Ave. W., 218/387-1454, www.gunflintmotel.com, $79), built in 1966 with five kitchenette units, has some of the cheapest rooms in town.

Grand Marais has many bed-and-breakfasts. **Superior Overlook** (1620 Hwy. 61 E., 218/387-9339, www.superioroverlookbb.com, $105–170) has just two guestrooms on a secluded outcropping just north of downtown. One has a private deck, and one has it's own living room with a fireplace.

The **MacArthur House** (520 2nd St. W., 218/387-1840 or 800/792-1840, www.macarthurhouse.com, $74–179) was purpose-built as a bed-and-breakfast and has five large rooms and a two-room whirlpool suite, all with private bath.

Antler Inn (118 3rd Ave. W., 218/387-3131) is like a bed-and-breakfast without the latter. A homey bungalow with five bedrooms sharing three bathrooms, it can be rented by the room or all at once. It's next door to the Grand Marais Art Colony and down the road from the North House Folk School.

The city-owned **Grand Marais RV Park & Campground** (Hwy. 61 and 8th Ave. W., 218/387-1712 or 800/998-0959, $35 full hookup) on the west side of town has 300 sites. Despite its waterfront location, it is a very uninspiring campground. Camp at a nearby state park or in the Superior National Forest if you can.

Food

Grand Marais's most beloved eatery is the **Angry Trout Cafe** (416 Hwy. 61 W., 218/387-1265, www.angrytroutcafe.com, 11 A.M.–8 P.M. Sun.–Thurs., 11 A.M.–9 P.M. Fri.–Sat., May–Oct., $9–22), which serves fresh and smoked fish right out of Lake Superior, in addition to salads and sandwiches made from as many organic and local ingredients as possible.

Across the street at **Chez Jude** (411 Hwy. 61 W., 218/387-9113, www.chezjude.com, 11 A.M.–10 P.M. Tues.–Fri., 8 A.M.–10 P.M. Sat.–Sun., closed Mon., $8–50), chef and owner Judi Barsness serves French-influenced bistro fare based on local ingredients. During the winter, the restaurant is open only one week a month—when there's a full moon. During the other three weeks, Barsness offers cooking classes in her kitchen.

A relative newcomer attracting its own following of foodies is the **Crooked Spoon Café** (17 Wisconsin St. W., 218/387-2779, www.crookedspooncafe.com, lunch 11 A.M.–3 P.M., dinner 4:30–8 P.M. daily, $19–20). It feels like a French bistro and serves up food to match, from big plates of juicy mussels to pan-roasted duck. Kids are welcome, too, and the menu for them goes beyond the usual.

In a log mansion dating to the 1800s, the atmosphere and views at the **Birch Terrace Supper Club** (6th Ave. W. on Hwy. 61, 218/387-2215, 4–10 P.M. daily, $15–25) can't be beat. The menu includes local favorites like lake trout and walleye, as well as ribs and steaks.

The Pie Place (2017 Hwy. 61 W., 218/387-1513, 7:30 A.M.–8:15 P.M. Tues.–Sun., closed Mon., $7–24), while specializing in the obvious, also serves up mouthwatering made-from-scratch meals. The menu changes weekly, and they even do free delivery.

Sven and Ole's Pizza (9 Wisconsin St. W., 218/387-1713, www.svenandoles.com, 11 A.M.–9 P.M. daily, $3–21) is a North Shore institution and, for many, a mandatory stop after canoeing the BWCAW. The Pickled Herring Pub in back has a wide selection of local microbrews and imported beers. They deliver.

A popular locals' hang-out, **My Sister's Place** (410 Hwy. 61 E., 218/387-1915, www.mysistersplacerestaurant.com, 11 A.M.–8 P.M. Sun.–Thurs., 11 A.M.–9 P.M. Fri.–Sat., $6–13) specializes in creative and bountiful toppings on burgers and hot dogs.

It doesn't take much imagination to figure out the specialty of **World's Best Donuts** (10 Wisconsin St. E., 218/387-1345, www.worldsbestdonutsmn.com, 7 A.M.–4 P.M. Mon.–Sat., 7 A.M.–2 P.M. Sun. Memorial Day–mid-October)—and the crowds agree.

Another sweet seasonal treat is **Sydney's Frozen Custard** (14 Broadway S., 218/387-2693, 10 A.M.–10 P.M. daily summer, reduced hours rest of year).

Little **Java Moose** (218 Wisconsin St. W., 218/387-9400, 6 A.M.–8 P.M. Mon.–Sat., 7 A.M.–6 P.M. Sun. summer, 6 A.M.–6 P.M. Mon.–Fri., 7 A.M.–5 P.M. Sat.–Sun. rest of year) is the city's top choice for a caffeine fix.

Information and Services

The **Grand Marais Visitor Information Center** (13 Broadway N., 218/387-2524

© TRICIA CORNELL

Great frozen treats are a must in any good resort town.

or 888/922-5000, www.grandmarais.com, 9 A.M.–5 P.M. Mon.–Sat., 10 A.M.–2 P.M. Sun. June, 9 A.M.–5 P.M. Mon.–Thurs., 9 A.M.–6 P.M. Fri.–Sat., 10 A.M.–2 P.M. Sun. July–Oct., 10 A.M.–4 P.M. Mon.–Sat., 10 A.M.–2 P.M. Sun. Nov.–May) will help you find a vacancy, recommend a fishing charter captain, or answer any other questions about the area. They also stock information about other North Shore destinations in Minnesota and Ontario.

The **U.S. Forest Service Gunflint Ranger Station** (2020 Hwy. 61 W., 218/387-1750, 7 A.M.–5 P.M. daily May–Sept., 8 A.M.–4:30 P.M. Mon.–Fri. rest of year) can give you the lowdown on recreation in the Superior National Forest.

Superior Coastal Sports (20 1st St. E., 218/387-2360 or 800/720-2809, www.superiorcoastal.com) has computers with Internet access.

All of the city's banks and many businesses exchange Canadian dollars. If you are arriving by boat the **Grand Marais Marina** (Hwy. 61 & 8th Ave. W., 218/387-1712 or 800/998-0959) has 22 slips.

GUNFLINT TRAIL

County Highway 12, better known as the Gunflint Trail, runs 63 resort-lined miles through the Superior National Forest from Grand Marais to Saganaga Lake on the Canadian border. You can paddle into the BWCAW, roam the endless trails, and maybe spot some of the myriad moose.

Recreation

There is no shortage of outfitters ready to send you out into the BWCAW. Two well-known and highly experienced operators, **Voyageur Canoe Outfitters** (189 Sag Lake Trl., 218/388-2224 or 888/226-6348, www.canoeit.com, 7 A.M.–7 P.M. daily summer) and **Way of the Wilderness** (12582 Gunflint Trl., 218/388-2212 or 800/346-6625, www.wayofthewilderness.com, 8 A.M.–8 P.M. daily), sit at the far end of the road and have lodging available on-site.

Boundary Country Trekking (11 Poplar Creek Dr., 800/322-8327, www.boundarycountry.com, 7 A.M.–10 P.M. daily) specializes in inn-to-inn trips for bikers, hikers, and paddlers, plus offers yurt cross-country ski touring and dog-sledding. It also has on-site lodging.

Accommodations

One of the first resorts up the trail is also one of the best. Each of the ever-so-cozy cabins at **Bearskin Lodge** (124 E. Bearskin Rd., 218/388-2292 or 800/338-4170, www.bearskin.com, $230) are widely spaced along East Bearskin Lake and come with a fireplace, grill, and private dock. Amenities include a whirlpool and sauna that can be reserved for private use.

Famous for its friendliness, the **Gunflint Lodge** (143 Gunflint Lake S., 218/388-2294 or 800/328-3325, www.gunflint.com, $220) has been run by the Kerfoot family since 1927. All of the two dozen cabins have fireplaces, many have whirlpool tubs, and most have private saunas. There's a busy schedule of activities for young and old, including horseback riding. Both resorts offer boat and canoe rentals and some of the state's best cross-country skiing is right out your door. They are expensive, but low-season rates are more reasonable.

Another year-round destination with an enthusiastic following is **Hungry Jack Lodge** (372 Hungry Jack Rd., 218/388-2265, www.hungryjacklodge.com, $99–499). The beautiful setting offers a wide variety of cabins—from rustic to almost luxurious, in a Northwoods sort of way, sleeping from two to 20 people—and both tent and RV sites. It has boats for rent on-site and is just a mile from the BWCA.

Food

Gunflint Lodge serves excellent food, but you should have at least one meal at **Trail Center Lodge** (7611 Gunflint Trl., 218/388-2214, 8 A.M.–9 P.M. Sun.–Thurs., 8 A.M.–10 P.M. Fri.–Sat., closed Apr. and Nov., $4–36), which is as close to a neighborhood tap as you can have in these parts. The menu has all the usual, but also choices like peanut butter and mayo burgers, Italian fried chicken, and a popular peppermint schnapps malt. Not only is the food great, but so are the Northwoods atmosphere and friendly service.

Way of the Wilderness (12582 Gunflint Trl., 218/388-2212 or 800/346-6625, www.wayofthewilderness.com, 8 A.M.–8 P.M. daily) runs the **Trail's End Café** (8 A.M.–8 P.M. daily, May–Oct.), with pizza, burgers, and the like.

Information

For more area information contact the **Gunflint Trail Association** (800/338-6932, www.gunflint-trail.com). They run the **Gunflint Trail Information Center** (218 Wisconsin St. W., 218/387-3191, 8 A.M.–5 P.M. Mon.–Sat., 8 A.M.–3 P.M. Sun. June, 8 A.M.–7 P.M. daily July–Aug., 9 A.M.–5 P.M. Mon.–Sat., 9 A.M.–3 P.M. Sun. rest of year) in Grand Marais and keep a vacancy list.

SUPERIOR NATIONAL FOREST – GUNFLINT DISTRICT

The forest's easternmost reaches surround the Gunflint Trail (County Highway 12), making most recreational facilities easily accessible to those who want to head out into the wilderness by day and relax with all the comforts of home at a resort by night.

Recreation

Just about all of the district's trails are on or near the Gunflint Trail highway. The first trailhead you pass, just a mile up from Grand Marais, is for the **Pincushion Trail System** (www.pincushiontrails.org), a side loop of the **Superior Hiking Trail.** The 15-mile nest of loops is generally level in the front with some good climbs toward the back, and there are some great views, especially from the Pincushion Mountain Loop at the far end. Pincushion is the most popular cross-country skiing in the area (out of seven trails offering 221 groomed miles) and offers the only mountain biking trails in the district, though other off-road opportunities exist on old logging roads.

The next two paths are the often-muddy **George Washington Memorial Pines Trail,** an easy three-mile loop through a tall stand of pines with a swamp at the back end, and the **Northern Light Lake Overlook,** a steep half-mile climb to a sweeping vista atop Blueberry Hill. Even though your odds of seeing the lumbering giants from the observation deck at the end of the **Moose Viewing Trail** aren't much better than just driving along the road, if you do find some you can observe them in a much more intimate setting—it's about a half-mile round-trip.

There are more fantastic vistas at the ends of the ten-mile **Lima Mountain Trail** and **Honeymoon Bluff Trail and Overlook,** not to mention beautiful scenery along the way: From the summit of Lima Mountain, a 1.5-mile walk, you'll be rewarded with 360-degree forest and lake views; the Honeymoon Bluff Overlook is a half-mile loop leading to a sunset-ready overlook of Hungry Jack Lake. Both trails have steep climbs and good bird-watching. The **Central Gunflint Trail System,** impeccably maintained by Bearskin Lodge and Golden Eagle Lodge, is some of the best cross-country skiing in the state. There is terrain for all abilities, and about half of the 46 groomed miles can accommodate skate-skiers. The Central Gunflint Trails connect to the remote 29-kilometer **Banadad Trail** to offer a full spectrum of skiing choices.

Right near the end of the Gunflint is the remarkable Magnetic Rock, a house-sized behemoth that deflects compass needles. The fairly easy 1.5-mile hike to the rock, naturally called the **Magnetic Rock Trail,** is a great berry-picking route. Plenty more Gunflint area hikes cross into the BWCAW, and these trails are detailed with that section.

Naturally the BWCAW is the primary paddling destination in these parts; however, for a short trip that is sure to be crowd-free, dip an oar in the three- to five-mile **Pine-Kemo-Talus-West Twin** canoe route about a third of the way up the Gunflint. It has four short portages and a pair of campsites.

If you are driving up the Gunflint Trail and want to learn more about the blowdown, pick up the brochure ***A Changing Forest*** at the ranger station in Grand Marais.

Camping

All but three of the district's campgrounds lie along the Gunflint Trail. First in from Grand Marais is **Kimball Lake** (2 miles east on Forest Rd. 140 from Gunflint Trl.). The namesake lake is stocked with trout, so the camp's 10 sites are popular with anglers, and there is a swimming beach nearby. Reservations are not accepted.

East Bearskin Lake (124 Bearskin Rd. E., 218/388-2292, www.reserveamerica.com, $18) and **Flour Lake** (468 Clearwater Rd., 877/444-6777, www.recreation.gov, $18) campgrounds have 33 and 37 sites respectively and are the best places to look for a last-minute spot. They also offer some great paddling, both inside and outside the BWCAW.

Though not far off the highway, **Iron Lake** (36 miles north of Grand Marais off County Rd. 12, 218/388-2212, www.reserveamerica.com, $16) has a real middle-of-nowhere feel, and despite having just seven sites it also tends to not fill up.

All the way at the end of the Gunflint Trail is **Trails End** (12582 Gunflint Trl., 218/388-2212, www.reserveamerica.com, $16) with 32 gorgeous and widely spaced sites, some of which have water hookups for RVs. This is a great base for short explorations of the BWCAW, and Way of the Wilderness Outfitters is right next door.

Devil Track Lake (off County Rte. 57, $15) is the forest campground closest to Grand Marais, and most of its 16 sites sit lakeside. Reservations are not accepted.

Also in a beautiful setting nearby are **Two Island Lake** (218/387-1750, $15), 15 miles northwest of Grand Marais on County Road 27, with 38 first-come, first-served sites, and the four-site **Cascade River** (3481 Hwy. 61 W., 218/387-3053, $18) rustic campground.

Information

The **Gunflint Ranger Station** (2020 Hwy. 61 W., 218/387-1750, 7 A.M.–5 P.M. daily May–Sept., 8 A.M.–4:30 P.M. Mon.–Fri. rest of year) is located in Grand Marais.

JUDGE C. R. MAGNEY STATE PARK

Before the Brule River flows into Lake Superior, it thrashes through a mass of volcanic rock in a fit of white water fury within Judge Magney

State Park (4051 Hwy. 61 E., 218/387-3039). At **Devil's Kettle Falls** a pinnacle splits the river, sending the eastern half on a 50-foot plunge while the western section cuts its way through a seemingly bottomless pothole. It is an awesome and intriguing sight and arguably the best hike on the North Shore. The 2.5-mile round-trip to the falls is steep with a long set of steps near the end. In total, nine miles of hiking trail, including a stretch of the **Superior Hiking Trail,** follow the Brule River and Gauthier Creek through the 4,674 acres of forest. Twenty-seven well-spaced campsites ($18) are available during the summer in the shady campground.

Accommodations

The one-of-a-kind **Naniboujou Lodge** (20 Naniboujou Trl., 218/387-2688, www.naniboujou.com, May–Oct., some weekends in winter, $74–109) is inside the park, on the lake side of the river. It is as much a work of art as a hotel. It was built in 1928 as an exclusive private club for such luminaries as Babe Ruth and Jack Dempsey, but thanks to the stock market crash the following year it didn't last long. The building languished for decades, but has been lovingly restored with modern amenities added—though the lack of phones and TVs in the rooms ensures your stay is truly relaxing.

Even if you aren't staying here, do yourself a favor and have a breakfast, lunch, dinner, or even high tea in the Great Hall dining room (8 A.M.–8:30 P.M. daily, $8–23), which is painted in a kaleidoscope of Cree Indian designs and centered on a massive stone fireplace. Dinner options include cranberry pork tenderloin and seafood pasta; the lunch menu has sandwiches and salads, and take-away box lunches are available.

GRAND PORTAGE

The last town before the Canadian border, the little village of Grand Portage, on the Grand Portage Ojibwe reservation, has a surprising array of offerings for visitors. The last five miles of Highway 61 are a beautiful drive.

Recreation and Events

The **Grand Portage Lodge and Casino** (70 Casino Dr., 218/475-2401, www.grandportage.com, open 24 hours) has 15,000 square feet of gaming space, plus a bingo hall, 500 slot machines, and more. Because it is on Native American land, smoking is permitted. If you'd like to gamble without the smoke, the Trading Post across the highway is smoke free.

An excellent hike leads to the **Mt. Josephine Lookout** with panoramic views in all directions, including Lake Superior's **Susie Islands,** important for the typically arctic plants they harbor. The fairly challenging 1.5-mile climb starts a mile east of the National Monument on County Highway 17.

Grand Portage Isle Royale Transportation (Hat Point Marina, 218/475-0024 or 218/475-0074 May–Oct., 651/653-5872 or 888/746-2305 Nov.–Apr., www.grand-isle-royale.com) takes passengers to Michigan's remarkable Isle Royale National Park.

Day trips on the ***MV Wenonah*** (8:30 A.M. Wed.–Sun., June–Sept., $51) allow 2.5 hours on Isle Royale plus fantastic scenery—including the sacred Witch Tree at the tip of Hat Point, seen on countless postcards—along the way.

The **Grand Portage Rendezvous Days and Powwow,** held the second weekend of August, re-creates the summer gathering held annually during the post's existence.

Grand Portage National Monument

Grand Portage National Monument (170 Mile Creek Rd., 218/475-0123, www.nps.gov/grpo, Museum 9 A.M.–5 P.M. daily late May–early Oct., Heritage Center 8:30 A.M.–6 P.M. daily summer, 8:30 A.M.–5 P.M. daily rest of year, $3 adults) is an excellent living-history museum. From 1784 to 1803 the Scottish-run North West Company, the most profitable fur trade operation on the Great Lakes, had their inland headquarters here, and Native Americans and Europeans came from across the region to buy and sell pelts. Grand Portage was one season's journey from Montreal, and goods

GRAND PORTAGE RESERVATION

- Total Area: 76 sq. miles
- Tribally Owned: 95 percent
- Total Population: 557
- Native Population: 322
- Tribal Enrollment: 1,115

The Grand Portage Reservation sits along 18 miles of Lake Superior shoreline at the tip of Minnesota's Arrowhead. It is named after the 8.5-mile portage trail developed by early Native Americans to bypass the waterfalls and rapids on the lower Pigeon River. Both the Ojibwe and the French arrived here about 1730 and made the portage a vital link in the inland fur trade. In those days many Ojibwe worked with the fur traders and later at the commercial fishing station opened by the American Fur Company.

Residents and the tribal government have cooperated with the State of Minnesota and the Environmental Protection Agency on wildlife habitat and resource protection, and in 1996 the tribe became the first in the nation to be certified by the EPA as having the technical capability to monitor its own water quality. They have played an active role in restoring and protecting Lake Superior's fish populations.

John Beargrease, a northland legend (and the man for whom the Sled Dog Marathon is named) for his years of service as the mailman before a road led up the North Shore, was a Grand Portage member, though the most famous tribal member goes by the name Manito Geezhigaynce, or The Little Spirited Cedar Tree. For 300 years this gnarled, windblown cedar has clung to the rocky cliffs at Hat Point on Lake Superior. Though it technically lives off the reservation, this tree has played such a vital role in the spiritual lives of tribal members that they have bought the land, and guides must accompany visitors.

transported between the coast and the interior—the French Voyageur Highway extended far into northwest Canada—were exchanged here with Montreal men ("pork-eaters") wintering in the city and the North men remaining in the wilderness. To get here from the west they carried 180 pounds of "soft gold" over the 8.5-mile Grand Portage, bypassing a long stretch of waterfalls and rapids on the lower Pigeon River. The cedar-picket palisade and many of the buildings have been reconstructed and furnished in the 1797 style. In and around the stockade you will find exhibits on the fur trade and Native American heritage, historic gardens, and massive birch-bark canoes. Guides in period costume tell stories and demonstrate traditional skills.

The more adventurous can retrace the steps of the voyageurs along the **Grand Portage Trail,** a long but fairly level walk through the woods to the site of Fort Charlotte. Register with the park service if you wish to camp there.

The short but steep **Mount Rose Trail** climbs 300 feet from the parking lot with a couple of good vistas along the way.

The beautiful **Heritage Center** opened in 2007 to accommodate year-round visitors and expand on the monument's educational offerings—as well as to fulfill a 50-year-old promise from the federal government to the band of Ojibwe that had donated the land. The 16,000-square-foot building houses exhibits on Ojibwe culture—with a life-size diorama—as well as a bookstore and classroom.

Grand Portage State Park

Tucked up against the Canadian border is one of Minnesota's smallest but most beautiful state parks (9393 Hwy. 61 E., 218/475-2360). The state's highest waterfall, **High Falls** (aka Pigeon Falls), drops 120 feet at a narrowing of the Pigeon River. It's no Niagara, but to call the scene awe-inspiring is not an overstatement. A half-mile paved trail and boardwalk lead to a pair of overlooks of the falls, one of which is wheelchair accessible. To get here in the winter, consider renting a pair of snowshoes from the park office. It's 3.5-miles round-trip along the Pigeon River to smaller Middle Falls.

To see High Falls from the Canadian side, park at the Ontario Travel Information Center and follow the mile-long trail under the bridge. It's a bit rough and wet in a few places, but worth it since you can island hop in the rocky river right above the falls.

Accommodations

About halfway between Grand Marais and Grand Portage, the secluded **Hollow Rock Resort** (7422 Hwy. 61 E., 218/475-2272, www.hollowrockresort.com, $230–370 for a two-night minimum stay) has five unique cabins sleeping two to eight people overlooking Superior. All the cabins have kitchens.

The **Grand Portage Lodge and Casino** (70 Casino Dr., 218/475-2401, www.grandportage.com, $90) has 95 rooms in a lovely modern lodge with an indoor pool, sauna, and a remarkable common room with a fireplace reaching up three stories. Their restaurants serve both guests and visitors.

Information

The state-run **Grand Portage Travel Information Center** (218/475-2592) on Highway 61 is open May to October.

Boundary Waters Canoe Area Wilderness

With 1.3 million acres and nearly 1,200 lakes, the Superior National Forest's Boundary Waters Canoe Area Wilderness is an unrivalled dreamscape for outdoor lovers. Stretching 150 miles along the Canadian border, it is the largest wilderness east of the Rockies and one of the most beautiful spots in North America. *National Geographic Traveler* included the Boundary Waters, along with the Taj Mahal, Grand Canyon, and Venice, in its "50 Places of a Lifetime" issue.

Streams and portages connect the myriad lakes, allowing unlimited canoe travel, and not surprisingly 99 percent of visitors journey on the water; however, the wilderness surrounds some of Minnesota's best hiking trails too. Motorboats are allowed on 19 periphery lakes, but that was a necessary part of the compromise to get the wilderness protection in the first place, and they won't impede on your experience if you are here to paddle. For the ultimate in isolation, plan part of your trip through one of the Primitive Management Areas. Previously established portages and campsites are no longer maintained on these 299,760 acres, so reaching the lakes they surround requires a bit of bushwhacking. There is no limit on day use, but only one group can camp in each zone each night.

With over 200,000 visitors each year, this paddlers' paradise is also the most heavily used wilderness area in the country; however, a strict permit system protects the beauty, solitude, and wildlife and ensures a quality wilderness experience.

NATURAL HISTORY

Geology

Sitting on a low plateau at the southern end of the Canadian Shield, an ancient slab of rock stretching from the Great Lakes up to the Arctic Ocean, the Boundary Waters are a unique Ice Age relic. The glaciers that swept south over the last two million years bulldozed right down to the bedrock, and since they last retreated some 10,000 years ago, only a very thin skin of soil—six inches on average—has formed. In many places, particularly lakeshores, the eroded bedrock is still exposed, lending a unique beauty to the area. This Precambrian crust is estimated to be 2.7 billion years old, making it some of the oldest exposed rock in North America. The gouging glaciers left a noticeable (if you look on a map) northeast "grain" across most of the area.

Glacial meltwater filled these long, narrow basins, forming the myriad lakes that cover nearly a quarter of the BWCAW's area.

Flora and Fauna

The BWCAW lies in a transition zone between the temperate deciduous forest and the coniferous northern boreal forest, though the latter predominate. This mixed "North Woods forest" features white and red pine surrounded by spruce, balsam, jack pine, aspen, and birch, and because of the early limits on logging, there are still many old-growth stands. Summer is berry time, and blueberries, a favorite of both humans and black bears, ripen throughout most of July and early August. Wild raspberries peak about the same time, while wild strawberries are ready weeks earlier. The odd, dead-looking plants clinging to nearly every large rock in the forest are lichens, a symbiotic union of fungus and algae. Of course, the storm of 1999 has changed the forest considerably, and it will be decades before anyone knows exactly how.

As you'd expect, this wild corner is one of Minnesota's best wildlife-watching destinations, but the most enduring animal memories are usually not the ones seen, but those heard. The common loon is surprisingly common on these lakes—nearly all have a nesting pair—and their echoing wails on a still summer night are reason enough to pitch a tent. The territories of several wolf packs extend into the BWCAW, and if you're lucky, their plaintive howls will float past your campsite too. White-tailed deer and moose are a wolf's primary prey, and spotting the latter grazing in streams and shallow bays is not a rare event. Beaver and otter are common in the water, while bald eagles frequently soar above it, and you will probably see several large-eared woodland deer mice scavenging around your campsite at night. Other common critters include great blue heron, herring gull, spotted sandpiper, broad-winged hawk, ruffed grouse, gray jay, white-throated sparrow, a variety of ducks, snowshoe hare, and the chattery red squirrel. You'd be very lucky to see a mountain lion, bobcat, lynx, fisher, pine marten, mink, northern flying squirrel, star-nosed mole, spruce grouse, black-backed woodpecker, boreal chickadee, or red-backed salamander, but they are all out there. In total there are around 200 species of bird, 45 mammal, 12 amphibian, and 7 reptile in the BWCAW.

Bears deserve special mention. Hundreds of the lumbering giants roam the BWCAW and, unfortunately, the place you are most likely to see them is in camp. Keep your site clean, however, and you probably don't have to worry about them crashing your party.

HUMAN HISTORY

The Boundary Waters' early history mirrors that of the state. The first inhabitants were nomadic Paleo-Indians who followed the melting glaciers north hunting large game such as mastodon, musk ox, and giant beaver. The first French-Canadian fur traders—the very first may have been Jacques de Noyon in 1688—shared these waterways with the Dakota, but by the time the fur trade began in earnest in the mid-18th century, the Ojibwe had taken control. The fur traders continued to paddle and portage these waters until the dwindling beaver populations and changing European fashions crashed the industry in the 1840s.

Following World War I a national interest in outdoor recreation emerged, and the profusion of automobiles brought a great influx of vacationers to the Superior National Forest, prompting the conflicts between recreationists and commercializers that continues today. Before 1919 scant regard was given to public use of national forests, though in that year the U.S. Forest Service hired Arthur C. Carhart as a landscape architect to develop multiple-use policies. He initiated the first serious discussions within the Forest Service of protected wilderness, and one of his earliest acts was a management plan for what would become the BWCAW. Acting on Carhart's recommendations, Secretary of Agriculture William Jardine signed a plan for the unnamed wilderness in 1926 that prohibited roads and other development across 1,000 square miles and required loggers to leave "tree screens" around lakes.

THE BLOWDOWN

On July 4, 1999, a fierce storm with straight-line winds in excess of 90 miles per hour whipped across northern Minnesota, and though it lasted only 20 minutes its effect will be felt for a lifetime. The hurricane-strength maelstrom toppled 600,000 acres of forest across Minnesota and Ontario, more than half of it in the Boundary Waters Canoe Area Wilderness. The storm's ground zero was a 4- to 12-mile-wide and 30-mile-long swath right along the Canadian border between Ely and the end of the Gunflint Trail – 80 percent of the trees in this area were knocked over or snapped in half. It was one of the largest blowdowns ever recorded in North America. Though the scale of the devastation brought tears to the eyes of many, it must be remembered that these events, however extraordinary, fit in a forest's natural ecological cycle. The sunlight, once blocked by the mature trees, will allow new trees to grow and this emerging forest is actually beneficial to much wildlife, including moose, lynx, and wolf.

The biggest problem is fire. The additional fuel available to burn increases not only the likelihood of wildfires, but also the severity. Millions of dollars have already been spent on storm recovery, and fire mitigation, including prescribed burns, will continue for several years. Blowdown area-related closures and campfire restrictions have been reduced in recent years, but will continue – always check on these before beginning a trip. Also, don't pitch a tent under damaged or leaning trees. In some BWCAW campsites there are no longer trees, so bear-proof food storage containers are highly recommended. While many paddlers, understandably, now try to avoid blowdown areas, this is not entirely necessary since even in the hardest-hit spots some stands of trees were not toppled, especially on shorelines – scientists suspect that growing up with more winds strengthened these trees – and so out on the lakes you might not even notice the damage. The Forest Service or your outfitter will be able to tell you what to expect in specific locales.

Thanks to noted conservationists like Sigurd Olson and Ernest Oberholtzer, a series of state and federal laws during the 1930s, '40s, and '50s solidified and expanded these protections, and the debate helped shape the landmark Wilderness Act of 1964. Beginning in 1948 the federal government began buying out private resort- and homeowners in what was then called the Superior Roadless Primitive Area. One person who stayed was Dorothy Molter, known to most as the Root Beer Lady. She lived deep in the wilderness of Knife Lake between 1934 and her death in 1986. Her nursing skills and immense popularity prompted the Forest Service to grant her a lifetime exemption, allowing her to remain at her home. Her house was removed after her death and is now a museum in Ely; by all means, visit it.

Restrictions on incompatible uses such as fly-ins, mining, and snowmobiles came piecemeal and not without opponents fighting every step in court; a few even resorted to violence against preservationists. The most contentious period in its history surrounds the 1978 passage of the BWCA Wilderness Act, which established the present boundaries and codified the regulations. To the chagrin of the wilderness backers, motorboats remained permissible on many periphery lakes. This was, however, far from the final word, and there are still serious efforts to roll back most of the wilderness protection.

PLANNING AND PRACTICALITIES

Though you can just show up and head right out into the wilderness, there are numerous factors—not the least of which is the quota system—that make advanced planning for an overnight journey a good idea. A night under the stars is the ultimate Boundary Waters experience, though day trips can still be pretty amazing too, and they require much less advance thought.

When to Visit

There is no best time to experience the Boundary Waters, but three-quarters of visitors set out during June, July, and August, leaving the beautiful-weather months of May and September crowd free. September also gets you fall colors. The peak tourist season runs mid-July though mid-August, though even then you can find solitude. Ice-out usually comes at the end of April, while the first snow falls and the lakes refreeze around the end of October, and there are always some who paddle right up against these limits. Blackflies are at their worst the first two weeks of June, while mosquito swarms are gone by the end of July. Late May to early June, as well as September, tend to offer the best fishing. Winter visitors are a hardier bunch, but skis, snowshoes, and dogsleds are an excellent way to experience the Boundary Waters.

Permits

Between May 1 and September 30 the BWCAW operates under a quota system, and all overnight visitors, plus daytime motorboaters, must get a permit before entering. The cost is $16 per adult per trip (children as well as Golden Age and Golden Access card holders are $8), plus a nonrefundable $12 reservation fee. A $44 deposit will be collected regardless of the group size, and the rest must be paid (or the difference will be refunded if you are traveling solo) when picking up the permit. A seasonal fee card ($40 adults, $20 youth) covers permit costs for the whole year, but does not eliminate the reservation fee or deposit.

While not required, reservations are a very good idea since you cannot count on just showing up and finding a route that suits your desires. Reservations are handled by the **BWCAW Permit Reservation Center** (877/550-6777 or 877/833-6777 TDD, www.bwcaw.org). Reservations for the coming year may be submitted beginning November 1, and those received before January 15 will join a lottery. Following the lottery, reservations are accepted on a first-come, first-served basis. Permits can be picked up at all Superior National Forest ranger stations, the forest headquarters in Duluth, and 66 other locations, including resorts and outfitters. These cooperating permit stations only accept credit cards for payment, and some charge a small service fee. If an outfitter is arranging your trip they will probably secure your permit for you.

Overnight visitors between October 1 and April 30, plus non-motorized day-trippers throughout the year, must fill out a self-issuing permit form, which is available at the ranger stations and most entry points. No reservations are required, and there are no limits on the number of visitors. An overnight in a Primitive Management Area, regardless of the season, requires first-come, first-served authorization in person from a Forest Service office.

Outfitters

An outfitter—a good one, anyway—is not just a company that rents canoes and camping gear. They are, as the Ely Chamber of Commerce puts it, "biologists, historians and woods-wise guides whose knowledge and love of this area will add immensely to the pleasure you'll have on your canoe trip." They can plan a route that ideally fits your abilities and desires, and their intimate knowledge of the area (your map will be marked with scenic and historic highlights, good wildlife-viewing territory, prime fishing spots, the best campsites, or anything else that interests you) is often worth the price of your gear rental. And with all the portaging you'll probably be doing, it pays to use their lightweight equipment. Complete outfitting includes just about everything you need for your trip from toilet paper to the tent. Most companies can also arrange transportation to the entry point and pre- and post-trip accommodation. Many will even guide your trip if you are unsure of your outdoor skills.

There are dozens of outfitters and guides to choose from in the surrounding communities, and all of those listed in this book are highly regarded, though they are far from the only good ones out there. Before choosing an outfitter be sure to talk with them. They should begin by asking you questions about the type of trip that you want to do and be willing to give you references. Also, remember that a higher price usually means better and lighter equipment, so ask specifically what you are getting for your money.

Rules and Etiquette

The BWCAW's strict regulations, which will be detailed when you get your permit, are meant to maximize people's wilderness experiences while minimizing their impact. First and foremost, everyone must observe Leave No Trace (www.lnt.org) principals. Maximum group size is nine people and four watercraft. One rule that catches some people off guard is the ban on cans and glass bottles, though fuel, insect repellant, medicine, and personal hygiene products in their original containers are allowed. Food and drink may be stored in plastic containers, but these must be packed out.

For those traveling by water, camping is restricted to designated sites, except for people with Primitive Management Area authorization forms. Those following hiking trails are strongly encouraged to use the designated sites, but it is not a requirement. Winter visitors should set up camp out on the ice and make only one trail connecting camp with the shoreline. If you build a fire, burn only dead and down wood collected well away from your campsite—it is, of course, illegal to cut live vegetation. Tree vandalism is a serious problem in the BWCAW and even minor damage adds up over time. Canoes must be licensed in Minnesota or your home state. Motorboats are only allowed on 19 lakes, and your wilderness permit must specifically designate motorized use. Portage wheels are only permitted over a handful of portages.

One final thing to remember is to be quiet. Voices carry surprisingly far across the lakes, especially on still evenings, and loud noises not only disturb other visitors but scare off wildlife. Barking dogs do the same thing, so they are best left at home. If you must bring Fido, keep him on leash at landings and portages.

Information

Your best sources of information are the Superior National Forest ranger stations or an experienced outfitter. On the Web, check out www.fs.fed.us/r9/forests/superior/bwcaw and www.canoecountry.com.

Naturally, with the labyrinth of lakes you'll be traveling, a good map is essential. USGS topographic maps are excellent for detailing the lay of the land, though they do not show portages and campsites, so it is best to buy BWCAW-specific maps. The most popular maps are the Fisher F-Series, which use a scale of 1.5 inches per mile, while others prefer MacKenzie Maps with their larger 2 inches to 1-mile scale. Both are excellent, waterproof, and readily available; you may want to make your map decision based on the number of maps needed since a single map by one company may cover your entire route as opposed to two or three maps from the other. Also, keep in mind that no maps are perfect and will show portages and campsites that no longer exist, which is one more reason to discuss your trip with the Forest Service or an outfitter.

Exploring the Boundary Waters by Daniel Pauly is an invaluable resource for route planning. First-time paddlers should also look at *Boundary Waters Canoe Camping* by Cliff Jacobson. This comprehensive book covers everything from paddling, camping, and orienteering basics to how to follow a moose trail.

PADDLING

With 56 entry points and 1,200 miles of canoe route, recommending where to paddle is simply not possible in this book; for that you will need to rely on a Boundary Waters–specific guidebook or, much better, get local advice. But, before deciding where you want to go, you must determine what sort of trip you want, and there are as many possibilities as there are lakes. Some people will want to pick a single base camp and spend a weekend there. Others may want to head out for 10 days of exploration, packing up and heading to a new camp every day. Many come with a single purpose, such as seeing the northern lights, spotting a moose, or casting for trout. Whatever kind of trip you choose, it can't be stressed strongly enough that when poring over maps or discussing routing with an outfitter you need to be realistic about your strength and skills. It is wise to plan a couple of layover days. Regardless of whether you use these to relax or cover more territory (there is less gear to haul over portages), they will keep you on schedule if rough weather slows you down.

You don't have to head deep into the wilderness to enjoy the BWCAW's beauty, but during the summer this is a near necessity for finding solitude. The best advice for getting away from other paddlers is to portage often—the longer the better. Most portages are a quarter mile or less, though some are over a mile. Don't forget that, unlike most other paddling trips, weight matters here. Also, remember that elevation change rather than distance is usually a better indication of a portage's difficulty. Portage lengths are usually given in rods; one rod equals 16.5 feet. The number of permits available for each entry point (the quota corresponds to the number of campsites available) is also a good general rule for determining the number of other canoes you will encounter, but there is not a direct correlation since some people won't portage, and there is no limit on day-trippers. Generally there are more bugs and portages on the smaller lakes, so the more willing you are to "sweat and swat" the more privacy you will get. The other bonus from the smaller lakes is that most people consider them more beautiful. On lakes where motors are still allowed, you can use a towboat service to get you out to the edge of the real wilderness faster.

HIKING

The Boundary Waters isn't just for boating: There are also many hiking trails, including short, easy trails on the edge of the wilderness and long-distance treks through its heart. Remember that hikers and backpackers are subject to the same permit and quota system as boaters.

Long-Distance Trails

These rugged and remote routes have downed trees, beaver dam crossings, streams to wade, and other challenges, so they are not for inexperienced hikers. Though the trails are marked, a topographic map and compass are essential. Campsites are spread out along each of them.

The **Kekekabic Trail** runs 38 gently rolling miles across the heart of the Boundary Waters from the end of County Highway 18 east of Ely to the end of County Highway 12 (the Gunflint Trail) west of Grand Marais. This trail was constructed in the 1930s for firefighting access and left abandoned until the Kekekabic Trail Club (www.kek.org) formed in 1989 to reclaim the route for recreation, though this is such a remote route that maintenance is still only intermittent. The **Snowbank Trail** is an easier 24-mile loop that starts out along the east end of "The Kek" and then heads north around its namesake lake, passing many more lakes along the way. It is an exceptionally scenic route with mature pine stands, shoreline bluffs, and some hilltop overlooks at the north end. The **Old Pines Trail** is a similarly beautiful S-curve off the east end that, with a return along the Kekekabic, can be added on to Snowbank to double the mileage.

As the name suggests, the **Border Route Trail** sticks close to Canada for most of its 75 miles. The fairly difficult route runs along the north side of County Highway 12 (the Gunflint Trail), with over half of that passing through the BWCAW. Besides the river and lake scenery—some of the Boundary Waters' best—there are many rock ledges and stands of old-growth pine along the way. The BRT connects to the Superior Hiking Trail at the east end, and the Magnetic Rock Trail can be used as a connector with the Kek, leaving just about a quarter-mile road walk: The section follows the route of the **North Country National Scenic Trail.**

Two other abandoned trails revived by the Kekekabic Trail Club are the 29-mile **Pow-Wow Trail** and the 32-mile **Sioux-Hustler Trail,** both very rugged and seldom-followed loops. Pow-Wow passes though prime moose and wolf habitat and features many old-growth pines. The trailhead is 17 miles north of Isabella on Forest Road 377. Sioux-Hustler originates

29 miles east of Orr on County Highway 116 near the Forest Service's Lake Jeanette Campground and is noted for the many granite outcrops along it. It is the only long-distance trail not affected by the blowdown.

Ely Area

Generally a backpacking trip, the rugged and sometimes challenging **Angleworm Trail** can be hiked in a day if you get an early start. The 14-mile loop around Angleworm and other lakes passes ridge-top overlooks and mature red and white pine stands, plus moose are often spotted in the Home Lake area. There are nine lakeside campsites, and this is a relatively popular winter camping destination. The trailhead is 17 miles northwest of Ely on County Highway 116 (the Echo Trail).

All the way up by Crane Lake is the 15-mile **Herriman Lake Trail** with various loops linking four lakes. Less than half a mile down the trail, before entering the BWCAW, is a picnic site on the Echo River. Further in, on various hilly branches, you will find three lakeside campsites, a sandy beach, and many scenic overlooks. Herriman and Knute Lakes are good fall-color destinations.

Gunflint Trail Area

It's a seven-mile round-trip to the state's highest point along the **Eagle Mountain Trail.** Most of the hike is pretty easy, though it's fairly rugged and strenuous over the last half mile to the endless views atop the 2,301-foot granite summit. The trailhead is on Forest Road 170, 17 miles northwest of Grand Marais.

The six-mile **Brule Lake Trail** is a little-used alternate route to the summit starting to the west on Forest Road 326. There are two campsites on Whale Lake right below the hill.

All other area trails lie along County Highway 12 (the Gunflint Trail). The **Daniels Lake Trail** is an easy 1.5-mile round-trip stroll from near the end of County Highway 66 to the shore of its namesake lake. Much more challenging is the 3.5-mile **Caribou Rock Trail,** starting two miles up County Highway 65. Within the first 0.75 mile, you'll get beautiful overlooks of West Bearskin and Moss Lakes before entering the BWCAW and passing more lakes and a handful of campsites. Both of these trails link up with the Border Route Trail.

WINTER

At 18 miles, the easy-to-intermediate **Banadad Trail** near the end of the Gunflint Trail is the Boundary Waters' longest ski trail and its only groomed route (use of snowmobiles to groom the trail was grandfathered into the wilderness legislation), though because it is so remote it can be a rugged trip even with grooming. It also has the distinction of offering yurt-to-yurt skiing through Boundary Country Trekking. Although the trail is not groomed, cross-country skiers appreciate the wilderness scenery of the **South Farm Trail,** a generally easy five-mile route eight miles east of Ely on County Highway 16 that crosses its namesake lake and loops through a spruce swamp at the back end. Skiers are also the primary users of the **North Arm Trail** 13 miles north of Ely; take County Highway 116 (the Echo Trail) to County Highway 644. Most of the 16 ungroomed loops are intermediate level, though beginners and experts will find appropriate routes along the 26 total miles. Other popular winter ski destinations are the Herriman Lake, Angleworm, and Sioux Hustler Trails, and the **Hegman Lake Pictographs** north of Ely, which is one of the finest examples of this style of Native American rock art in North America.

If you've never experienced dog sledding before, there is no better place to give it a try. Outfitters in Ely and Grand Marais will let you take the reins across the frozen lakes on trips ranging from a few hours to a week.

Ely

On the map, Ely appears to be at the end of the road. For people who love wilderness and beauty and solitude, on the contrary, it's at the center of the world.

– Charles Kuralt

Charles Kuralt named Ely his "number one vacation destination" and made several trips here annually in his later years, though the gentleman journalist certainly isn't the only one to laud Ely. Travel and sports magazines like *Midwest Living* and *Canoe Journal* regularly honor this little town set conveniently near the middle of nowhere. Five hundred lakes lie within 20 miles of Ely and this is the most popular gateway to the Boundary Waters Canoe Area Wilderness. Though most people are here to explore the outdoors, if the surrounding two million acres of public forest were to suddenly disappear, the unique museums and fantastic amenities would still make this town of 3,724 a wonderful destination.

History

While modern-day boosters have dubbed Ely the "Canoe Capital of the World," it was once the "Capital of the Vermilion Range." Like most other range cities, Ely began as a rough-and-tumble mining town—filled with taverns, casinos, and brothels—in the 1880s and was especially festive in the spring when thousands of lumberjacks poured in to blow the money they had earned over the winter. When the flamboyant fundamentalist preacher Billy Sunday passed through during the summer of 1900 he quipped: "The only difference between Ely and Hell is that Ely has a railroad into it."

Between 1888 and 1967, miners hauled over 80 million tons of ore out of the city's five iron mines. By 1897 the average miner took home $2 a day, and though unions eventually brought safety and justice to the miners, working the pits was never an easy life. Ely sent more men per capita to World War II than any other community in the United States, because for many joining the infantry was preferable to going underground. Tourism, the principal industry today, began back in the 1910s, and the remote fly-in resorts attracted many gangsters and bootleggers in the 1930s. Today, besides the short-term visitors, Ely's remoteness attracts many artists and explorers who have added to the city's already singular character.

SIGHTS

Dorothy Molter Museum

The Dorothy Molter Museum (2002 Sheridan St. E., 218/365-4451, www.rootbeerlady.com, 10 A.M.–5:30 P.M. Mon.–Sat., noon–5:30 P.M. Sun. summer, Sat.–Sun. only May and Sept., $6 adults) celebrates a most remarkable woman. In 1934, at the age of 27, this Chicago nurse dropped her life and moved to the deep wilderness of Knife Lake up near the U.S.-Canadian border to help run the Isle of Pines Resort. She soon became a self-sufficient wilderness expert living in a large canvas tent for most of the year, only moving to more solid quarters for the winter. Known to many as the Root Beer Lady, as many as 7,000 canoeists would stop each summer to chat and get a drink—chilled with ice she had cut during the winter and packed in sawdust and moss. The U.S. Forest Service had added her property to the Wilderness Area, but due to her popularity and vital nursing skills (she was also known as the "Nightingale of the Wilderness"), Molter was allowed to stay. Though she could no longer conduct business out there, nobody was prevented from making a free-will donation in exchange for a cold root beer. When she died in 1986, two of her cabins were hauled out piece by piece by dogsled and reassembled in Ely, and they form the majority of the museum. The interior of her winter cabin remains just as she left it, while the Point Cabin, formerly used by guests, holds various photos and other personal effects. Though small, the museum deserves plenty of your time, since most of the

© TIM BEWER

The Dorothy Molter Museum celebrates the woman known as the Root Beer Lady.

guides knew Dorothy and have decades' worth of stories to share.

International Wolf Center

Considering that Ely lies in the heart of the largest population of wolves in the Lower 48, and that Dr. David Mech (one of the world's foremost wolf experts) did much of his pioneering wolf research here, it is only natural that the International Wolf Center (1396 Hwy. 169, 218/365-4695 or 800/359-9653, www.wolf.org, 10 A.M.–7 P.M. daily July–Aug., 10 A.M.–5 P.M. daily May–June and Sept.–Oct., 10 A.M.–5 P.M. Sat.–Sun. rest of year, $8.50) opened their education center here. For most people the highlight is the resident wolf pack living in the 1.25-acre enclosure behind the center. Though the wolves can and sometimes do hide out in the forest, they tend to roam and rest up front, allowing close-up views through the massive windows. The other exhibits are also excellent and should not be missed. You'll learn about vocalizations and behaviors, understand the social structure of the pack, see inside a den, and hear about legend and lore back to the Middle Ages. Children can follow a wolf pup through its first year in the Little Wolf room. They also offer behind-the-scenes tours, short off-site tracking and howling trips, and extended adventure programs where you can accompany researchers into the field.

North American Bear Center

Building on the success of the International Wolf Center, the North American Bear Center (1926 Hwy. 169, 218/365-7879, www.bear.org, 9 A.M.–7 P.M. daily summer, 10 A.M.–4 P.M. Fri.–Sat. rest of year, $8.50 adults) opened in 2007. The large indoor display hammers hard on the idea that bears have been unfairly demonized in folklore, and the media and reports of their danger to humans have been exaggerated. Other exhibits include a children's play area and a movie about the work of local bear researchers.

From a raised observation deck, visitors can watch the three captive bears Honey (a female born in 1996), Ted (a male born in 1997), and Lucky (a male born in 2007) play. Only about half of their two-acre enclosure is visible from

© TRICIA CORNELL

Two male bears play in the viewing area at Ely's North American Bear Center.

the deck, so they do have a chance to step out of the limelight when they feel like it.

The center hosts free educational programs on everything from bear language to the ecology of the area. Photographers can pay an additional $25 to (safely) get up close and personal with the bears.

Other Sights

Over at Vermilion Community College, the **Ely-Winton History Museum** (1900 Camp St. E., 218/365-3226, www.vcc.edu/ewhs, 10 A.M.–4 P.M. Mon.–Fri. year-round., $3 adults) has a small but well-presented local history collection. Exhibits cover mining, logging, Native American history, the women of Ely, and the Boundary Waters Canoe Area Wilderness.

A few other historic sites will be of interest to some. The **Pioneer Mine Headframe** sits on the north edge of what was then an open pit iron mine, but is now Miner's Lake. It may be opened for tours in the future.

On the northeast side of town, near the junction of 13th Avenue East and Main Street, is a hunk of exposed volcanic Ely Greenstone. It can be found by following Trezona Trail (3 blocks north of Sheridan St.). Known as **Pillow Rock,** the undulating lava solidified underwater and really does look soft.

There is history of a different sort at the **Ely Steam Bath** (127 S. 1st Ave. E., 218/365-2984, 4–10 P.M. Wed., Fri., and Sat., $6/day public, $8/hour private). Miners, loggers, and, more recently, paddlers have been coming for a good sweat at the Finnish-style sauna since 1915. Remember, the top bench is for experts only.

To see some historic sites beyond town, reserve a seat with **Burntside Heritage Tours** (2755 Burntside Lodge Rd., 218/365-5445, www.burntsidetours.com, $30). The two-hour pontoon tours of Burntside Lake cover geological and historical sites, including Sigurd Olson's Listening Point.

ENTERTAINMENT AND EVENTS

Thanks to a bit of good fortune, Ely has an active arts scene. In 1988 a painting that hung inconspicuously in the Ely Public Library for over 50 years was discovered to be *Breakfast in the Garden,* a long-lost masterpiece by American impressionist Frederick Frieseke. A New York collector bought the painting for over $500,000, and the city used the proceeds to create the Donald G. Gardner Trust. Besides funding the library, much of the money goes to the **Northern Lakes Arts Association** (218/365-5070, www.elyarts.org), which sponsors a wide variety of theater, music, dance, literary, and visual arts events throughout the year, including summer concerts in Whiteside Park.

The city's biggest celebration is the **Blueberry Arts Festival** (www.ely.org), held the last weekend in July. Besides the 250 arts and crafts exhibitors, there are copious children's activities and food vendors. The Blueberry Arts Festival is so successful that Ely repeats it the weekend after Labor Day as the **Harvest Moon Festival.**

The **Boundary Waters Blues Fest** (www.elyblues.com) blows into town every

AURORA BOREALIS

You have to go another 800 miles or so north to reach prime viewing territory, but northern Minnesota is still close enough to regularly see the Northern Lights. This unparalleled evening show, caused by the interaction of oxygen and nitrogen atoms in the upper atmosphere with charged particles emitted by the sun, leaves a deep impression on all who see it. Auroral displays can be seen almost any time, but around here your best bet is during the summer months. Displays tend to be most intense around the equinoxes. The colorful lights dance for anywhere from just a few minutes to several hours.

year in late July or early August, bringing with it national acts.

The **Ely Winter Festival,** starting the first Thursday in February, is focused on snow sculpture, but there's much more to see and do.

SHOPPING

Naturally, with all the tourists descending on town, there is no shortage of Northwoods-themed shops selling loon coffee mugs and the like, though thankfully many shops lie beyond the generic. Internationally renowned nature photographer Jim Brandenburg lives in Ely when not traveling the globe for *National Geographic,* and much of his Boundary Waters work is sold at the **Brandenburg Gallery** (11 Sheridan St. E., 877/493-8017, www.jimbrandenburg.com, 10 A.M.–5 P.M. Mon.–Sat., 10 A.M.–4 P.M. Sun.).

Dozens of local and regional artists not lucky enough to have their own galleries sell their creations at the **Kess Gallery** (130 Sheridan St. E., 218/365-5066, www.kessgallery.com, 9 A.M.–5 P.M. Mon.–Sat., 11 A.M.–4 P.M. Sun.).

Crafted from moose hide using a Cree design, **Steger Mukluks** (33 Sheridan St. E., 218/365-3322, www.mukluks.com, 9 A.M.–5 P.M. Mon.–Thurs., 9 A.M.–6 P.M. Fri.–Sat., 9 A.M.–4 P.M. Sun., reduced hours in the off-season) are not only half the weight and twice as warm as regular winter boots, but they are fashionable enough for *Elle* and *Mademoiselle* magazines.

For the rest of your body take a look at **Wintergreen Designs** (205 Sheridan St. E., 218/365-6602, www.wintergreendesigns.com, 9 A.M.–8 P.M. Mon.–Sat., 9 A.M.–5 P.M. Sun. summer, 9 A.M.–5 P.M. Mon.–Sat., 11 A.M.–4 P.M. Sun. rest of year). They stock anoraks and other outdoor apparel with a distinctive ribbon edging made in Ely since the 1980s.

To outfit your own sauna and pick up local souvenirs, stop by **Mealey's Gift and Sauna** (124 Central Ave. N., 218/365-3639, www.mealeysinely.com, 10 A.M.–5 P.M. Mon.–Thurs., 10 A.M.–6 P.M. Fri.–Sun.).

Lisa's Second-Floor Bookstore (105 Central Ave. N., 218/365-6745, 6 A.M.–8 P.M. daily summer, 9 A.M.–5 P.M. daily winter) at the Piragis Northwoods Company has an immense selection of outdoor-related titles.

Chapman Street Books & Prairie Fire Tobacco (139 Chapman St. E., 218/365-2212, 10 A.M.–5:30 P.M. Tues.–Fri., 11 A.M.–5 P.M. Sat., closed Sun.–Mon.) is a decent used book store and also sells imported tobacco.

RECREATION

The primary reason for Ely's popularity is that recreational opportunities in the surrounding wilderness are nearly limitless. The four-mile **Trezona Trail** is a generally easy paved route around Miner's Lake. A spur at the east end connects it to the International Wolf Center. Trezona's south side follows an old rail line and is part of the new **Mesabi Trail** (www.mesabitrail.com, www.boundarycountry.com) that will someday stretch 132 miles across the Iron Range from Ely to Grand Rapids. As of late 2009, 102 miles were complete.

Some mountain bikers ride the rough-surfaced **Taconite State Trail** that stretches 165 miles to Grand Rapids, although it's principally a snowmobile trail. The **Hidden Valley Recreation Area** has 12 miles of hilly loops

© TRICIA CORNELL
Kawishiwi Falls, outside Ely, is an easy hike.

through a mix of birch stands and pine plantations just a mile east of town off Highway 169. Though designed for cross-country skiing, the trails are open to mountain bikers in the summer. Maps are sometimes available at the trailhead, but it would be best to pick one up at the chamber of commerce. In fact, the chamber distributes maps for most area ski and bike trails.

Spirit of the Wilderness (2030 Sheridan St. E., 218/365-3149 or 800/950-2709, 6 A.M.–9 P.M. daily May–Oct.) rents mountain bikes.

Follow the bridges for a scenic walk around the rocky islets at **Semers Park.** Though the swimming season is short, the park also has a sandy beach for those summer days when you need to cool off. Semers is on the shore of Shagawa Lake, just west of town.

The **Kawishiwi Falls Hiking Trail** offers a pretty big pay-off for not a lot of effort. The trail is less than a mile long and leads to an up-close view of the dramatic falls. While the trail is easy, the ledge over the falls is unprotected, so this might not be the best hike for small children. To get there, take Highway 169 northeast from downtown Ely until it turns into Fernberg Road, and watch for signs on your left.

At last count there were over 20 outfitters in town, all waiting to set you up with everything you need for a Boundary Waters canoe trip. About half are members of Ely Outfitters, whose helpful website (www.canoecapital.com) lets you choose an outfitter from a map or a comparison chart. The following three, each conveniently located right in town, are some of the most highly recommended. Ely's very first canoe company, **Wilderness Outfitters** (1 Camp St. E., 218/365-3211 or 800/777-8572, www.wildernessoutfitters.com, 6 A.M.–9 P.M. daily May–Oct.) started leading travelers into the wild in 1921.

Piragis Northwoods Company (105 Central Ave. N., 218/365-6745 or 800/223-6565, www.piragis.com, 6 A.M.–8 P.M. daily summer, 9 A.M.–5 P.M. daily winter) also operates a large outdoors store, so you can test a canoe on your trip before purchasing it.

Voyageur North Outfitters (1829 Sheridan E., 218/365-3251 or 800/848-5530, www.vnorth.com) has their own bait shop.

It seems a shame to spend any time golfing when you are so close to such wonderful wilderness, but if you must, the nine-hole course at the **Ely Golf Club** (901 Central Ave. S., 218/365-5932, 7 A.M.–8 P.M. daily, $18 for 9 holes, $25 for 18 holes) is there for you.

Winter Recreation

Although canoeing dominates the Ely outdoors scene, **dogsledding** is the area's fastest growing sport, and half a dozen companies—more than any other town in the world, according to Ely's Chamber of Commerce—can take you out for a canine adventure. Trips run anywhere from a few hours to a week, and even if you've never seen a sled dog before, you'll get to mush your own team of huskies through the BWCAW, though you can always take it easy and just ride in the basket. For overnight options you can choose to experience true winter solitude and beauty with a camping trip, or pick a deluxe lodge-to-lodge option and refresh yourself each night with four-star meals. Remote yurt camps offer a middle option.

The first name mentioned with Ely area dogsledding trips is almost always Paul Schurke, who runs the **Wintergreen Dogsled Lodge** (1101 Ringrock Rd., 218/365-6022 or 877/753-3386, www.dogsledding.com, 3- and 4-day packages from $600/person Dec.–Mar.). The noted arctic explorer—part of the first confirmed team to reach the North Pole overland without resupply—has a reputation for not only offering top-notch fun and adventure, but also leading the most educational trips around.

Also recommended are **White Wilderness** (218/235-1300 or 800/701-6238, www.whitewilderness.com) and **White Wolf** (2141 Hwy. 1, 218/365-6815 or 888/804-0677, www.whitewolfdogtrips.com, $200 adults half-day trip).

No matter who you choose, expect to pay $150–200 for a day-long trip and a whole lot more for lodge-to-lodge or camping trips. In most cases, appropriate winter clothing can be rented through the trip provider.

ACCOMMODATIONS

One of the loveliest resorts in all of Minnesota—and surely the most photographed—**Burntside Lodge** (2755 Burntside Lodge Rd., 218/365-3894, www.burntsidelodge.com, May–Sept., $150/night, $1,061/week one-bedroom), six miles northwest of Ely, got its start as a hunting camp in the early 1900s. Many of the ultra-cozy cabins overlooking island-studded Burntside Lake were built in the 1920s, and each is unique. The National Park Service, noting both its age and architecture ("a remarkable architectural achievement in an outstanding state of preservation"), has added it to the National Register of Historic Places. Resort amenities include a marina renting everything from kayaks to pontoons (personal watercraft are prohibited), a pair of sandy beaches, a Finnish sauna, a cappuccino bar, and one of the area's best restaurants.

Twenty miles east of Ely on the north shore of Lake One, right on the edge of the BWCAW, is **Kawishiwi Lodge** (3187 Fernberg Rd., 218/365-5487, www.elycanoerentals.com, May–Sept., $20/person bunkhouses, plus non-refundable $50 deposit, $625/week cabins), a paddle-only resort. Most of the 16 one- to four-bedroom housekeeping cabins have screened porches and their own dock; a few can only be reached by water. Each rental includes a canoe, and they offer full outfitting for overnight trips. There are also hiking trails nearby, and guests can unwind in the sauna after a busy day.

Seven miles east of Ely on Farm Lake, one of the area's best fishing waters outside the BWCAW, is the friendly **Timber Trail Lodge** (629 Kawishiwi Trl., 218/365-4879 or 800/777-7348, www.timbertrail.com, $1,300/week two-bedroom cabin, $69/day room), an excellent choice for families. Guests have use of the sauna, there is a game room and fireplace in the small log lodge, and kids' activities are scheduled during the summer. They also offer complete outfitting and have fishing guides who work right out of the resort. Timber Trail is one of the minority of Ely resorts to remain open year-round; off-season discounts are substantial, and cabins are available for daily rental outside the summer.

Back on the quieter end of Farm Lake is the funky and artsy **Blue Heron Bed & Breakfast** (827 Kawishiwi Trl., 218/365-4720, www.blueheronbnb.com, $135), where the north-facing lake views are phenomenal. Blue Heron is located on the edge of the BWCAW, so day-tripping right out the door, either by land or water, is wonderful. Guests have free use of canoes and snowshoes and can unwind in the wood-fired sauna. The five inviting guestrooms, all with private bath, usually require a two-night minimum stay most of the summer and fall.

Close to downtown and right on the lake is the **Grand Ely Lodge** (400 Pioneer Rd. N., 218/365-6565, www.grandelylodge.com, $119–279). The dramatic lodge is built so that all 61 rooms—furnished with a little Northwoods flair—have lake views.

Log Cabin Hideaways (1321 Hwy. 21 N., 218/365-6045, www.logcabinhideaways.com,

$475/week) offers nine scattered and secluded cabins, most right on the edge of the BWCAW. Though they are rather plush in most other regards, the log cabins do not have electricity or indoor plumbing, and all but one is reached by paddling, hiking, or skiing. Only the cheapest lacks a wood-fired sauna. They can sleep anywhere from two to ten people. During the summer, you need to rent by the week, otherwise there is a three-month minimum stay.

Houseboats are available from a pair of companies on contorted Birch Lake, 15 miles south of Ely by Babbitt: **Kinsey Houseboats** (2718 Birch River Rd., 218/827-3763 or 888/827-3763, www.kinseys.com, $700 three-day stay) and **Timber Bay Houseboats** (1 mile east of Babbit on County Rd. 70, 218/827-3682 or 800/846-6821, www.timberbay.com, $690 three-day stay).

The city's best lodging value is in town at **Adventure Inn** (1145 Sheridan St. E., 218/365-3140, www.adventureinn-ely.com, $50 economy, $70 deluxe). The large "deluxe rooms," individually decorated in a Northwoods theme, have four beds, and some have kitchenettes.

Also in town, the older **Canoe on Inn** (110 N. 2nd Ave. W., 218/365-4590, www.canoeoninn.com, $50) is a clean, no-frills motel with friendly hosts.

Paddle Inn (1314 Sheridan St. E., 218/365-6036 or 888/270-2245, www.paddleinnely.com, $80) is very similar, but also offers a sauna.

If you're looking to save money but don't want to camp, check with the chamber of commerce about **bunkhouse** availability. Many outfitters keep these simple hostel-like rooms available for groups heading to and returning from the BWCAW and will sometimes rent them to individuals. Expect to pay about $15 per bed.

FOOD

Many, if not most, diners choose the **Burntside Lodge** (2755 Burntside Lodge Rd., 218/365-3894, www.burntside.com, breakfast 8–10 A.M. Sat.–Sun., dinner 6–10 P.M. nightly, bar opens at 5:30 P.M., $10–23) for dinner because of the fantastic setting—the dining room in the historic main lodge surrounds a fireplace and has excellent lake views—but no one goes home disappointed in the meal. Steak, walleye, and pasta highlight the creative menu, and Burntside is the only seasonal restaurant in the state to earn *Wine Spectator* magazine's Award of Excellence.

The deck overlooking Shagawa Lake at the **Stony Ridge Café** (60 Lakeview Ave., 218/365-6757, 7 A.M.–8 P.M. Mon.–Sat., 7 A.M.–noon Sun. May–Sept., $7–16) is where locals go for burgers—all 33 varieties. Get the Elyite—made with a sausage patty.

Yet another great lodge restaurant is the **Evergreen** (Grand Ely Lodge, 218/365-6565, www.grandelylodge.com, 6 A.M.–10 P.M. daily, $15–20). From a humble burger to a pan-fried walleye filet to a giant surf and turf platter, there's something here for everyone—except vegetarians.

The **Ely Steak House** (216 Sheridan St. E., 218/365-7412, 11 A.M.–10 P.M. daily, $4–30), a casual local favorite that's as well known for their walleye as the steaks, sits downtown at the top of the hill. The menu also includes club sandwiches, shrimp Alfredo, and roasted chicken, and the evenings feature karaoke, trivia, and open-mic jams.

Oriental Orchid (506 Sheridan St. E., 218/365-7502, 11 A.M.–9 P.M. Mon.–Fri., noon–9 P.M. Sat. year-round, 4–8 P.M. Sun. summers only, $6–16) is a better-than-average counter-service Chinese restaurant.

A departure from the usual surf-and-turf, **Chocolate Moose** (101 Central Ave. N., 218/365-6343, $7–15) attracts crowds who love the chili and the wild rice–crusted walleye. Seats on the tiny porch are great for people-watching but are highly sought after.

Tops for java is **Front Porch** (343 Sheridan St. E., 218/365-2326, 7 A.M.–7 P.M. Mon. and Wed.–Sat., 7 A.M.–9 P.M. Tues., 7 A.M.–5 P.M. Sun. summer, 8 A.M.–4 P.M. daily rest of year, $3–7), where the coffee, tea, and cocoa are fair trade and organic. They have computers with Internet access and make box lunches for the lake or trail.

The pasties from **Zup's** (303 Sheridan St. E., 218/365-3188, www.zups.com, 7 A.M.–8 P.M.

Mon.–Thurs., 7 A.M.–9 P.M. Fri.–Sat., 7 A.M.–6 P.M. Sun.) grocery store make a good BWCAW meal.

INFORMATION

The very helpful and friendly staff at the **Ely Information Center** (1600 Sheridan St. E., 218/365-6123 or 800/777-7281, www.ely.org, 9 A.M.–5 P.M. Mon.–Sat., noon–3 P.M. Sun. summer, 9 A.M.–5 P.M. Mon.–Fri. rest of year) know just about everything about the area. They also do vacancy searches, and there's an RV dump station in the parking lot.

There is no better way to catch the pulse of Ely than to tune in to **WELY** (94.5 FM). Music ranges from bluegrass to New Age, while other programs include the *End-Of-The-Road Trading Post* and *Birding with Bill.* The true gems of the broadcast day are the personal and emergency messages. Anyone looking for lost glasses, a ride to Minneapolis, a fourth member for a bowling league, or to invite their friends who live beyond the range of telephone service to a birthday party can spread the word to the entire listening audience.

TOWNS AND PARKS AROUND ELY

Bear Head Lake State Park

With the spectacular scenery of the BWCAW beckoning, it's understandable that some people bypass Bear Head Lake State Park (9301 Bear Head State Park Rd., 218/365-7229 or 866/857-2757, www.dnr.state.mn.us, $24 electric site), but its 4,523 wild and rugged acres are definitely worth a visit. The park touches the shores of nine pine-rimmed lakes, and most visitors head for the water. Anglers seek walleye, bass, crappies, and trout. The easiest paddling (rental boats and canoes are available) is in the sheltered North Bay of the 674-acre namesake lake, while the more adventurous can portage out to smaller lakes. Boats are allowed on Bear Head, but a 10-mph speed limit is enforced. Bear Head Lake also has a swimming beach.

The 10 miles of hiking trail, each named for the lakes they circle, quickly get you into the wild. The three-mile **Norberg Lake Trail** is the easiest and most popular hike, while most of the remote campsites lie along the challenging **Becky Lake** and **Blueberry Lake** Trails, both of which are rather hilly. Most miles are groomed for cross-country skiing in the winter, and the Taconite State Trail, a popular snowmobile route, links the park with Ely and Grand Rapids. Although seldom used, the portion through the park makes for a decent warm-weather hike. Bald eagles nest on Bear Head Lake each summer, so if you spend some time here sightings are almost guaranteed. The camping is excellent too. The 73 (26 electric) sites in the campground are shady and fairly secluded, while you can truly get away from it all at the six backpack and canoe-in campsites scattered along the shores of several lakes. There is also one camper cabin and a fully-appointed three-bedroom guesthouse, both open year-round, for those who don't want to rough it.

Soudan Underground Mine State Park

The opening of the Soudan Mine in 1882 heralded the beginning of Minnesota's iron mining industry, and over the next 80 years nearly 16 million tons of ore were shipped down to Two Harbors and on to Eastern steel mills. Known as "The Cadillac of Mines" for its modern safety features, this National Historic Landmark has been left almost exactly as it was when operations shut down in 1962. On the Historic Underground Mine Tour, you begin your journey toward the center of the earth by donning a hardhat and climbing into the cage for the half-mile descent. At level 27 you board a railcar and journey three quarters of a mile into the last and deepest area mined at Soudan, where you will learn about the former operations. Although ore is no longer extracted, the mine has buzzed with activity of a futuristic kind since 1980 when the University of Minnesota opened a **High Energy Physics Lab.** Currently, physicists are searching for dark matter and trying to measure the mass of neutrinos. The mine tours run several times daily, and the physics tours (10 A.M. and 4 P.M. daily, Memorial Day–mid-Oct.) run twice a day. Both cost $10. Bring warm clothes since the mine temperature stays at about 50°F at all times.

There is plenty to see and do above ground while waiting for your tour to begin. The visitors center (1379 Stutz Bay Rd., 218/753-2245) contains exhibits on Soudan's geological and mining history, and several surrounding mine buildings are open to explore. Elsewhere on the park's 1,300 acres is a 2.5-mile hiking trail that passes other mining sites and some decent Northwoods scenery.

A beautiful place to spend the night in the area is just down the road from the mine, at **McKinley Park Campground** (5563 Hoodoo Point Rd., Tower, 218/753-5921, www.mckinleypark.net, $25 campsite, $38 with hookup). Campers at the 70 sites are treated to a beautiful vista of Lake Vermilion, nearby hiking and biking trails, access to showers, laundry, and a small convenience store.

Tower

The Minnesota Gold Rush of 1865 brought the first settlers to the Lake Vermilion area, though the prospectors packed up and left the next year after the only nuggets they uncovered were fool's gold. The village of Tower began in 1882 as a shantytown supply center for the Soudan Mine and was named after Charlemagne Tower, one of the men who fronted money to open the mine. The town was initially founded at the end of the Vermilion Trail, a rugged path three days from Duluth by horse and wagon; the railroad soon arrived and facilitated not only mining but logging, and by the end of the decade Tower was a thriving city. Today it sees large numbers of tourists passing through on their way to Ely and serves as a supply center for those visiting the Soudan Mine State Park or Lake Vermilion. Vermilion, Minnesota's fifth-largest lake and one of the most popular in the state for anglers and boaters, sprawls over 40,557 acres, but because of its many twists and turns there are still some places where it feels intimate. Wildlife remains abundant—at last count some 25 pairs of bald eagle nested around the lake, and one of the 230 resident loons will sing you to sleep at night. Many of the lake's 365 islands have picnic sites and campgrounds.

If you don't have your own boat, and don't want to rent one, you can hop on the mailboat at **Aronson Boat Works** (6143 Pike Bay Dr., 218/753-4190, 9 A.M. Mon.–Sat. summer, $18 adults), located on Pike Bay two miles west of town, for the 80-mile, 3.5-hour trip. Reservations are recommended.

To see Vermilion—or any of the thousands of other Boundary Waters area lakes—from a different angle call **Van Air** (218/753-2331, www.flyvanair.com) for an aerial tour in their five-seat floatplane. A basic 20-minute flyover costs $45 per person, though longer options are also available. Call to schedule your flight.

From mid-April to mid-May you can visit the **Pike River Fish Hatchery** (1429 Grant Momahan Blvd., 218/753-5692, 8 A.M.–4 P.M. Mon.–Fri., closed Sat.–Sun., free), where millions of walleye are raised before being stocked into Vermilion and other lakes. Morning is the best time to visit. It is located west of town by the Pike River Dam: Head north on County Highway 77, and take the first right past the dam.

Right in town is the **Tower Train Museum** (404 Pine St., 800/869-3766, 10 A.M.–4 P.M. daily summer, free), a wee collection of historical photos and artifacts housed in a rail coach car. A gift shop and area tourism information can be found in the adjacent depot.

There are dozens of resorts on Lake Vermilion. The busiest is the Bois Forte Band of Ojibwe's **Fortune Bay Resort Casino** (1430 Bois Forte Rd., 218/753-2611 or 800/555-1714, www.fortunebay.com, $125) on the south shore, which has 169 rooms, 36 RV sites, and a steady stream of people hoping to beat the odds. Among the many amenities are a pool area, fitness center, 18-hole golf course, and marina.

While this resort is the future of the tribe, you can get a look at their past in the **Bois Forte Heritage Center** (1500 Bois Forte Rd., 218/753-6017, www.boisforte.com,

BOIS FORTE RESERVATION

- Total Area: 212 sq. miles
- Tribally Owned: 32 percent
- Total Population: 657
- Native Population: 464
- Tribal Enrollment: 2,990

The French called this band of Ojibwe the "Strong Men of the Forest," and the name Bois Forte stuck. Today most reservation lands lie around Nett Lake, and the tribal headquarters is in the small village of the same name. The tribe also controls a special reserve on Lake Vermilion, and this is where they constructed the successful Fortune Bay Resort Casino. Wetlands cover half of the reservation, though it is also marked with great timber stands, and four Indian-owned logging firms operate in the area. Nett Lake, covering 7,300 acres, is the largest wild rice-producing lake in the United States, and most of the harvest is consumed locally rather than being sold since this is considered a superior product to what can be bought in most stores. Sitting in the middle of the lake is Spirit Island, sometimes called Picture Island, a beautiful spot covered with hundreds of human, animal, and geometric petroglyphs. Though it was carved thousands of years before the Ojibwe moved into this region, many people still believe it is a sacred site, so they leave offerings of tobacco, clothing, and food.

10 A.M.–5 P.M. Tues.–Sat., closed Sun.–Mon., $5). The collection is small but well presented and includes a wigwam, fur-trading post, and historical and cultural artifacts. Outside is a tepee and short nature trail that passes one of the old gold mines.

West of Tower, at the end of Pike Bay, is the much more relaxing **Pike Bay Lodge** (9422 Hearthside Dr., 218/753-2430 or 800/474-5322, www.pikebaylodge.com, $180/night, $900/week). Once the summer estate of mining tycoon A. B. Coates, the original home, boathouse, and three other buildings have been converted into cozy cottages, and there are also four massive modern cabins that can sleep 10 to 12 people.

To completely immerse yourself in lake life, call **Vermilion Houseboats** (9482 Angus Rd., 218/753-3548 or 800/262-8706, www.vermilionhouseboats.com). They offer midweek, weekend, and weeklong packages, and prices vary considerably with what you rent. A 40-foot Explorer, which sleeps five people, is $765 for a weekend, while a week in the luxurious 60-foot Executive sleeps 14 and will set you back $5,500.

If you want to stay in town there is the **Marjo Motel** (712 Hwy. 169, 218/753-4851, $45). It has changed little since 1956, when it was built by the same family that runs it today, though the price of the large clean rooms has risen from $2.50.

The popular city-run **Hoodoo Point Campground** (5788 Hoodoo Point Rd., 218/753-6868, www.hoodoopoint.com, $25 campsite, $35 with hookup) has 85 sites. Ones without a lake view are a little cheaper.

Zup's (315 Main St., 218/753-2725, 7 A.M.–8 P.M. Mon.–Thurs., 7 A.M.–9 P.M. Fri.–Sat., 7 A.M.–6 P.M. Sun.) grocery store has pasties in their deli case.

If you're not catching and frying up your own crappies, the local watering hole is **Good Ol' Days Bar and Grill** (316 Main St., 218/753-6097, 6 A.M.–10 P.M. Mon.–Sat., 8 A.M.–10 P.M. Sun.). Decorated with bits of local area history, it serves up contemporary sandwiches and pizza. Fridays are fish-fry days.

For just a cup of coffee or a quick sandwich, there's **Sulu's Espresso Café** (Main St., 218/753-5610, 7 A.M.–7 P.M. Mon.–Sat., 9 A.M.–3 P.M. Sun.).

Cook

Cook, a busy Highway 53 pit stop, has a few restaurants, gift shops, and even the oldest continuously operating movie theater in the state (since 1939) to keep you busy for a short while, but the real action is north of town on the small end of Lake Vermilion. The gorgeous **Ludlow's Island Lodge** (8166 Ludlow Dr., 218/666-5407 or 877/583-5697, www.ludlows-resort.com, May–Oct., $2,100/week), eight miles west of Cook on County Highway 540, is the fanciest, and most of their 22 deluxe cabins are on a private island. Besides the usual facilities there are racquetball and tennis courts, and they host a multitude of activities, including scavenger hunts and amphibious car rides. If you want a vacation during your vacation they have a separate camping island nearby.

A little more traditional, but no less relaxing, is **Pehrson Lodge Resort** (2746 Vermillion Dr., 218/666-5478 or 800/543-9937, www.pehrsonlodge.com, May–Sept., $125/day, $950/week), with 27 cabins spread along 2,000 feet of shore, out on Pamahan Island, or tucked up on the hillside. There is free use of canoes, windsurfers, and sailboats—personal watercraft are prohibited. Pehrson's is six miles north of town on County Highway 24.

On the west end of Lake Vermilion, **Voyageur Cove Resort** (2600 Wakely Rd., 218/666-6058, www.voyageurcove.com, $225/night, weekly rates available) is open year-round. Eight fairly rustic cabins are spread out along the lakeshore. Six have private docks.

In town, the award-winning **Vermilion Motel** (320 Hwy. 53 S., 218/666-2272, $58) has large, new rooms plus RV campsites ($15 full hookup); all guests have use of the sauna.

The Montana Café (29 River St. S., 218/666-2074, 6 A.M.–7 P.M. Mon.–Thurs. and Sat., 6 A.M.–8 P.M. Fri., 8 A.M.–2 P.M. Sun.) is a sweet little café with it's own bakery, serving three meals a day.

Antiques-filled **Comet Coffee** (102 River St. S., 218/666-5814, 8 A.M.–6:30 P.M. Mon.–Sat., 9 A.M.–3 P.M. Sun.), part of the aforementioned movie theater, serves fair-trade coffee. Folk and similar artists sometimes perform here.

Although it's on a peninsula, not an island, the only direct access to the **Black Bay Trail** is via water, so the six-mile route on the north end of the lake is an excellent place for wildlife-viewing. If you don't mind getting up long before the crack of dawn you can witness the fascinating mating dance of the male **sharp-tailed grouse.** The spectacle takes place during April at about 4:15 A.M., and you need to arrive at the site well before the birds. The observation blinds are on private land; call the DNR (218/744-7448) for information.

Besides dispensing information about the forest, the **Superior National Forest – LaCroix District Office** (320 Hwy. 53 N., 218/666-0020, 7 A.M.–5 P.M. daily summer, 8 A.M.–4:30 P.M. daily Sept., 8 A.M.–4:30 P.M. Mon.–Fri. rest of year) has a display of Northwoods wildlife, sells nature-related items, and is stocked with area tourism brochures. Outside, a short nature trail circles a pond.

Embarrass

Tiny Embarrass, regularly one of the coldest towns in the state, was settled in the 1890s by Finns who wanted to farm instead of mine. It took its name from the Embarrass River, which had been christened by French voyageurs (the name comes from a word meaning "to hinder") who had trouble navigating it due to the many downed trees. It wasn't until the 1950s that non-Finns began arriving in significant numbers. (According to the *WPA Guide to the Minnesota Arrowhead Country,* published in 1941, the entire township's "population of 652 includes only two persons who are not Finns.")

The Finnish heritage remains strong today, and to preserve their roots and attract tourists, the community has opened the **Embarrass Visitor Center** (7503 Levander Rd., 218/984-2084, 8 A.M.–3 P.M. Mon.–Thurs.) along Highway 135 and started the caravan-style **Heritage Homestead Tours** (1 P.M. Thurs.–Sat., $6 adults), which visit several early-20th-century farmsteads and other historic sites around the town each summer. The knowledgeable guides share stories of the pioneers' lives and explain some of the clever construction methods they used to make their log structures. While some of the sites are on private property, you can visit a pair of them on your own. The **Hanka**

Homestead is 1.5 miles north of the village on County Highway 21, one-quarter mile west on County Highway 26, one-quarter mile north Pylka Road, and then east at the first driveway. The **Pyhala Homestead** is on Salo Road, just east of the campground.

There are several relocated Finnish structures in the village along County Highway 21, and nearby is **Timber Hall,** which locals believe is the largest freestanding log building in the United States. Regardless of its rank, at 144 feet by 60 feet it is worth a look.

The **Finnish-American Summer Festival,** held the first Saturday in June, is a daylong celebration of all things from the motherland, including food, crafts, music, dance, and pesäpallo, a Finnish game that resembles baseball as it would be played if the writers of *Mad Magazine* made the rules.

Experience a little of the life of those Finnish farmers at **Northern Comfort Bed and Breakfast** (4776 Waisanen Rd., 218/984-2014, www.northerncomfortmn.com, $65–90). Secluded and not overly fancy—the old farmhouse has a real Finnish sauna, and your hosts are happy to offer evening wine and cheese in addition to breakfast.

The **Heritage Park Campground** (4789 Salo Rd., 218/984-2084, $18 with electric and water), half a mile east of Country Road 21 on Salo Road, has 20 shady campsites. Hiking trails and a bog walk lead from the campground through the forest along the Embarrass River.

SUPERIOR NATIONAL FOREST – KAWISHIWI DISTRICT

Being centered on Ely, the most popular entryway into the Boundary Waters, surely makes Kawishiwi the forest's busiest district. There is no shortage of solitude though, especially for canoeists who travel outside the BWCAW and for hikers.

Recreation

The district's most popular hike is along the beautiful **Bass Lake Trail,** six miles north of Ely on County Highway 116 (the Echo Trail). The gorge holding Bass and Low Lakes was once filled by much larger lakes, but in 1925 the glacial ridge separating the pair gave way, dropping the water level 55 feet in just hours. It's six miles around Bass and Dry Lakes, but most hikers just head to the waterfall, about a mile in on Bass's north shore. There are campsites on Bass and several surrounding lakes.

Also highly recommended is the **Secret/Blackstone Trail,** out near the end of County Highway 18. The five-mile path has a pair of loops around its namesake lakes. The longer and steeper back loop has numerous ridge-top vistas of lakes and bogs and a cliff well known by area rock climbers. There is a campsite just a short walk in on Blackstone Lake. The seldom-followed 0.8-mile portage into **Agassa Lake** passes through thick-forested hills and crosses a bog, making it a beautiful hike and a good wildlife-watching destination.

There are also short, easy hikes at the **Fenske Lake** (2229 Echo Trl., 218/235-1299) and **South Kawishiwi River** (12208 Hwy. 1, 218/235-1299) campgrounds. Mountain bikers should get maps of the Forest Service's four recommended routes that follow little-traveled forest roads.

Naturally, most paddlers are here to hit the BWCAW, but canoe routes on lakes and rivers outside the wilderness do not require permits or fees and are equally beautiful. One of the most scenic and peaceful options is the 20-mile, seven-portage Fenske and Bass Lakes route, which begins 11 miles north of town along County Highway 116. The dozens of backcountry campsites on this and other waterways are free of charge. Part of the forest's **Discovery Tour** auto route runs along County Highway 116.

Camping

Fall Lake (14197 Fall Lake Rd., 218/365-2963, $22 full hookup), the campground nearest to Ely (five miles east on County Hwy. 18), is the forest's largest and most developed. Many of the 66 sites have electric hookups, and this is the forest's only campground with showers and flush toilets. There is also a swimming beach and direct access to the BWCAW.

Also popular, **Fenske Lake** (2229 Echo Trl., 218/235-1299, $10) 10 miles up the Echo Trail, has 16 well-spaced sites, and access to the BWCAW is nearby.

South of town are the 32-site **South Kawishiwi River** (12208 Hwy. 1, 218/235-1299, $10) and 30-site **Birch Lake** (3060 Echo Trl., 218/235-1299, $10) camps—both very popular with anglers—which rarely fill up. Reservations are accepted for all four campgrounds.

Information

From May through September contact the **Kawishiwi Forest Service Office** (1393 Hwy. 169, 218/365-7561, 7 A.M.–5 P.M. daily May–Sept.), in the lobby of the International Wolf Center.

The rest of the year stop by the **Kawishiwi Ranger Station** (118 S. 4th Ave. E., 218/365-7600, 8 A.M.–4:30 P.M. Mon.–Fri., closed Sat.–Sun.).

Voyageur Country

Minnesota's only national park brings hundreds of thousands of visitors to these remote forests and waters, but communing with wild bears at the Vince Shute Wildlife Sanctuary is reason alone to make the drive. The gateway community of International Falls is also a worthy diversion.

INTERNATIONAL FALLS

Famous for its frequent mention on TV weather reports as the Lower 48's cold spot, temperatures in the Icebox of the Nation often dip in to the minus 30s Fahrenheit during the long winters: The all-time low is minus 46°. The 6,000 hardy souls who live here are rather proud of their frigid lifestyles, though you are very unlikely to encounter any of these extremes. The local Convention and Visitors Bureau, hoping to attract more visitors outside the summer months, doesn't discuss the cold very much, though they will quickly point out that the mean high temperature from June through August is an idyllic 77°. While they stay mum on the winter weather to tourists, they actively promote the frozen north to companies who need to do cold-weather product testing.

As the name suggests, International Falls is tucked up along the border with Canada, though the long series of rapids that provided the second half of the name lies buried behind the hydroelectric dam. Founded in 1895 as Koochiching, the town was nearly wiped out by a fire in 1902, and the rebuilt community renamed itself the next year. Its original Algonquin moniker means Mist Over the Water, referring to the thick rainbow-filled cloud the waterfall threw up as the lake emptied into the river. Though the cold put the town on the map nationally, it is paper and tourism that keeps it going. The dam went up in 1908, and it powers a paper mill on each side of the border. Boise Paper Solutions employs 850 in town, and you won't just see how immense their operations are, you'll probably smell it too—don't worry, you get used to it quickly. Also important to the local economy are the tens of thousands of people stopping by on their way to Voyageurs National Park, which begins about ten miles to the east.

Ranier, a quaint village with a historic Rainy Lake waterfront and lift bridge, sits three miles to the east on Highway 11 (turn at the giant Voyageur statue) and should be a part of any visit here.

Sights

Tours of **Boise Paper Solutions** (400 2nd St., 218/285-5011) let you see one of the world's largest and fastest papermaking machines—it turns out about 1,500 tons of paper per day. The free 75-minute tours (8:30 A.M., 11 A.M., and 1:30 P.M. Mon.–Fri.) are available during the summer. No open-toed shoes or children under age 10 are allowed, and reservations are recommended.

HOKEY SMOKE!

International Falls was the real-life inspiration for **Frostbite Falls,** home of TV stars Rocky the Flying Squirrel and Bullwinkle J. Moose. In one episode, Rocky is taken to Koochiching County Hospital.

The **Koochiching County Historical Society** (214 6th Ave., 218/283-4316, 9 A.M.–5 P.M. Mon.–Fri., closed Sat.–Sun., $4 adults) runs a pair of side-by-side museums. The excellent **Koochiching County Historical Museum** begins with the first Paleo-Indians and continues through the modern day with interesting discussions of past industries such as gold mining, fishing, and the fur trade. Highlights of the collection include a birch bark canoe, beaver felt hat, Native American crafts, and Jesuit rings. A visit here is a great way to round out your Voyageurs National Park experience.

International Falls' most famous son is commemorated in the **Bronko Nagurski Museum.** Often considered the greatest football player ever, the inaugural Pro Football Hall of Famer played both fullback and defensive tackle during nine years with the Chicago Bears in the 1930s and '40s and was the only player to ever win All-American honors at two positions in the same year. After retirement from football and professional wrestling, he farmed and ran a gas station in town. Exhibits include his size-22 Hall of Fame induction ring and a copy of his first contract (for $5,000), and you can watch his exploits in a 14-minute video. Out in front of the museums, a 26-foot-tall **Smokey Bear** with two cubs at his feet greets visitors—locals dress them up for the winter with earmuffs, gloves, and scarves and give them fishing gear in the summer.

The private **Sportsmen's Service Wildlife Museum** (424 3rd Ave., 218/283-2411, 7:30 A.M.–5:30 P.M. daily, $1) has about 150 Minnesota mammal and bird mounts on display, including moose, wolves, lynx, lots of owls and ducks, and an albino skunk. There are also a few Native American and other historical displays.

Entertainment and Events

What could be more appropriate in International Falls than **Icebox Days.** Held each January, the wintry events include turkey bowling, snow sculpting, a polar bear dip, and the Freeze Yer Gizzard Blizzard 10K and 5K races.

The **International Falls Bass Championship** (www.ifallsbass.com) offers a lot more than fishing. For three days in late August, locals and visitors enjoy entertainment into the evening, a car show, an art fair, kiddie games and rides, and more.

Shopping

Spruce Street Landing, a handful of small stores linked by a boardwalk in Ranier, is a fun place to stroll and shop.

The **Koochiching Museums' gift shop** (214 6th Ave., 218/283-4316, 9 A.M.–5 P.M. Mon.–Fri., closed Sat.–Sun.) has authentic Native American arts and crafts and an excellent regional book selection.

If you forgot to pack anything for a Voyageurs National Park trip you can probably find it at **The Outdoorsman's Headquarters** (1100 3rd Ave., 218/283-9337, 5 A.M.–9 P.M. Mon.–Sat., 5 A.M.–6 P.M. Sun.).

Border Bob's (200 2nd Ave., 218/283-4414, www.borderbobs.com, 9 A.M.–6 P.M. daily summer, closed mid-fall–mid-May) bills itself as the "last building in the U.S." You can pick up U.S. or Canadian souvenirs, pack the fish you caught in dry ice, or—if they weren't biting—buy some walleye filets to take home.

Recreation

Based in Ranier, Chris Hemstad of **Boreal Explorations EcoAdventures** (2111 Spruce St., 218/286-5487, www.borealexplorations.com) offers guided and unguided trips in and around Voyageurs National Park via foot, sailboat, kayak, skis, or snowshoes. The focus of your adventure will be tailored to your interests, whether you want to hear a wolf howl or add a boreal owl to your life list. He also has fishing and sailboats for rent.

You can pedal, skate, walk, or ski from International Falls to Ranier and Voyageur National Park's Rainy Lake Visitor Center, a 12-mile trip, along the paved **Rainy Lake Bike Trail.**

Tara's Wharf (2065 Spruce St., 218/286-5699, 11 A.M.–9 P.M. daily summer), on the waterfront in Ranier, rents bikes, canoes, and paddleboats.

If you are here on a hot summer day and want to cool off, **City Beach** is located on the east side of Ranier, and there is another small, unsupervised swimming beach right in Ranier itself.

The 18-hole course overlooking the Rainy River at the **Falls Country Club** (Golf Course Rd. off Hwy. 71, 218/283-4491, 7 A.M.–dusk daily, $35) is one of northern Minnesota's best links.

Accommodations

Most of International Falls' hotels line Highway 53, though the fanciest is the **Holiday Inn** (1500 Hwy. 71, 218/283-8000 or 800/331-4443, www.hiifalls.com, $107), over on the shores of the Rainy River. Guest amenities include a pool, kiddie pool, hot tub, sauna, game room, and exercise room, plus there are whirlpool suites with river views.

Also above average is the **Days Inn** (2331 Hwy. 53 S., 218/283-9441 or 800/329-7466, www.daysinn.com, $74), on the south end of town, which has a whirlpool, sauna, and exercise room.

Among the many small, inexpensive, family-run places along the highway leading into town, **Hilltop Motel** (2002 2nd Ave. W., 218/324-2400, $55) is among the best.

The wonderful **Rainy Lake Inn and Suites** (2065 Spruce St., 218/286-5699 or 877/724-6955, www.taraswharf.com, $85) in Ranier sticks right out over Rainy Lake. All five guestrooms have private baths and kitchens, and all but one has its own balcony or deck. For breakfast, you get a coupon for an area restaurant such as Grandma's Pantry just a block down the street. If you want to add a night of camping in Voyageurs National Park, Tara can arrange equipment and transport.

Right across the street in Ranier, **F. R. Woody's Rainy Lake Resort** (3481 Main St., 866/410-5001, www.fairlyreliable.com, $500/three nights, weekly rates available)—the F. R. stands for "fairly reliable"—looks a little ramshackle on the outside—but inside there are eight modern condo units with living rooms and fully equipped kitchens. Woody's also has two cabins out on a private island in Rainy Lake. The whole operation is geared toward anglers and staffed by people who love fishing, themselves. After a day on the lake, a beer in Woody's pub hits the spot.

Food

Asking local advice on where to eat usually elicits a recommendation to drive east and dine with a view at any Rainy Lake resort. In town there are some decent views at the Holiday Inn's **Riverfront Grill** (1500 Hwy. 71, 218/283-4451, 6 A.M.–2 P.M. and 5 P.M.–9 P.M. Sun.–Fri., 6–11 A.M. and 5–9 P.M. Sun. summer, reduced hours rest of year, $7–18), which overlooks the Rainy River and a flower garden. It has a typical family-fare menu with burgers, pasta, steak, and seafood.

The Northwoods-themed **Chocolate Moose** (2501 2nd Ave., 218/283-8888, 6 A.M.–10 P.M. daily, $5–17) has a pretty similar menu with generally lower prices.

The Spot (1801 Hwy. 53 S., 218/283-2440, lunch 11 A.M.–2 P.M., dinner 4–10 P.M. Tues.–Sat., closed Sun.–Mon., $8–28) has the classiest dining room in town—in an old-style supper club kind of way. The menu is mostly steak and seafood—with many combinations of the two—though the lunch menu has several sandwiches.

With house-roasted coffees from around the world and the work of local artists on the walls, **Coffee Landing Metro** (444 3rd St., 218/283-8316, www.coffeelanding.com, 6 A.M.–3 P.M. Mon.–Fri., 8 A.M.–2 P.M. Sat.–Sun., $3–8) brings a little big city to The Falls. Besides caffeine, they serve bakery items, full breakfasts, and some sandwiches.

Tara's Wharf (2065 Spruce St., 218/286-5699, 11 A.M.–9 P.M. daily summer) on Ranier's waterfront is a popular stop for ice cream cones.

Hearty, friendly, home cooking is on the menu at **Grandma's Pantry** (Ranier, 218/286-5584, 7 A.M.–7 P.M. Mon.–Fri., 7 A.M.–10:30 P.M. Sat., closed Sun.), including massive wild rice pancakes.

Information and Services

The enthusiastic **International Falls Area Convention and Visitors Bureau** (301 2nd Ave., 218/283-9400 or 800/325-5766, www.rainylake.org, 8 A.M.–5 P.M. Mon.–Fri., closed Sat.–Sun.) can find last-minute vacancies, recommend fishing guides, or answer just about any question you might have.

Coffee Landing Metro (444 3rd St., 218/283-8316, 6 A.M.–3 P.M. Mon.–Fri., 8 A.M.–2 P.M. Sat.–Sun.) has a computer with free Internet access for their customers. All banks and many stores will change Canadian currency.

Getting There and Around

Falls International Airport (3214 2nd Ave. E., 218/283-4461, www.internationalfallsairport.com) just south of town, is served by **Delta Airlines** (800/221-1212), which flies to the Twin Cities several times a day. If you are coming from or heading on to Canada, there is scheduled air and bus service from Fort Frances across the river. **Avis** (218/285-7799), **Ford** (218/283-8486), and **National** (218/283-3471) have car rental offices at the airport.

The U.S. **Port of Entry** (2 2nd Ave., 218/283-2541) is staffed 24 hours a day. You will need your passport to enter Canada and to reenter the United States. Keep in mind that Canada places limits on the importation of alcohol and live bait. Anyone with a criminal record (including drunk driving) may be prohibited from entering Canada.

WEST ON HIGHWAY 11

Highway 11 hugs the sandy-banked Rainy River for most of its run through this sparsely populated and occasionally scenic border region. Although maps show a number of towns along the road between International Falls and Baudette, all but a few of them exist in name and memory only.

Grand Mound

Seventeen miles out of International Falls, at the junction of the Rainy and Big Fork Rivers, is the largest Native American burial mound in the Upper Midwest. The site of the 28-foot-tall gravesite is permanently closed to the public out of respect.

Franz Jevne State Park

Peace and quiet are the main features of this diminutive park. Tucked into a small bend of the Rainy River, Franz Jevne (State Hwy. 11, 218/783-6252) encompasses just 118 acres, but this is one of the more scenic stretches of the river. Bear, wolf, and moose have all been known to wander through on occasion, and in the summer you might see sturgeon splashing at the surface. A small picnic area overlooks Sault Rapids, and anglers have foot and boat access for their search for walleye and northern. An easy 2.5-mile hiking trail (groomed for cross-country skiing in winter) follows the Rainy before it loops back through the forest. The 18 sites (two electric, three walk-in) in the rustic campground are shaded and well spaced; several have covered picnic tables.

Basshenge

As you approach the turnoff to Franz Jevne State Park from the east, keep your eyes open for Basshenge, though you can't really miss it. With a name like this in the Land of 10,000 Lakes you would expect a monument to fish, but instead this work of art was the dream of Joseph Guastafeste, one time principal double bassist with the Chicago Symphony who has a cabin near here. He laid out 21 steel sculptures of string basses in the pattern of a bass clef.

VOYAGEURS NATIONAL PARK

Befitting of the Land of 10,000 Lakes, Voyageurs National Park is dominated and defined by water. The park is centered on four large lakes—Rainy, Kabetogama (cab-eh-to-ga-ma), Namakan, and Sand Point—and water covers nearly 40 percent of its 218,200 acres. Water isn't just part of the scenery, it's the primary means of transportation too. Except for those leading up to the four entry points, there are no roads in the park. To witness the hundreds of lopsided islands and slender bays or explore the rugged 75,000-acre Kabetogama Peninsula at the heart of the park, you'll have to travel by boat.

Visually, Voyageurs is similar to the BWCAW, which sits just to the east, but it comes without the serenity of official wilderness designation. Most people enjoy the scenery from a fishing boat, houseboat, or pontoon, and the many motors—either the rumbling boats in the summer or whining snowmobiles in the winter—might affect the tranquility of your adventure. On the other hand, Voyageurs is one of the least visited national parks—more people visit Alaska's Denali National Park during the month of June than come to Voyageurs during the entire year—so it is still easy to commune with nature in peace, especially if you head out to the Kabetogama Peninsula or spend a night under the stars.

Human History

The French-Canadians for whom Voyageurs National Park is named first paddled these waters in the late 17th century, following routes shown them by the area's Dakota inhabitants. The first European arrival is presumed to be Jacques de Noyon, an independent fur trader who may have paddled up from Lake Superior in 1688 and built a winter outpost on Rainy Lake—though some doubt he really came. Others followed, though the fur trade didn't truly flourish in these remote parts until the Canadian-born Pierre Gaultier de Varennes, Sieur de La Verendrye, and his party arrived on the scene in 1731. La Verendrye opened Fort St. Pierre and, over the next three decades, established a string of forts and trading posts from Rainy Lake to Winnipeg. Shortly after his arrival the Ojibwe, close allies of the French, drove the Dakota out in order to monopolize the most productive trapping lands.

While Native Americans procured the beaver and other pelts, the voyageurs transported them back to Montreal in birch-bark canoes—strong and maneuverable, but light enough to be portaged around the many waterfalls and rapids. Whole fleets would paddle in from Montreal each spring bringing trade goods like guns, pots, fabric, and beads and return with their 35-foot vessels stacked high with up to two tons of bundled furs. The roughly 1,000 miles from Montreal to Grand Portage, on the western shore of Lake Superior, was as far as they could travel in a season and still make it back before winter, so other groups of men (known as *hivernauts*) overwintered in the northwest and journeyed in from the western outposts, meeting up at Grand Portage to exchange cargoes. This far more demanding western route, passing through what is now the park, eventually expanded so deep into Canada that it also needed to be broken up, so the North West Company built Fort Lac la Pluie across the river from International Falls. All the other major fur-trading companies, including Hudson's Bay, XYZ, and American Fur Company, also based operations here at one time or another. In fact, the voyageurs' influence was so strong in these parts that the 1783 treaty ending the American Revolution specified that the American–Canadian border would follow their "customary waterway" between Lake of the Woods and Lake Superior.

The fur trade died out by 1850, due mostly to a combination of changing European fashions and the near extirpation of beaver from this part of North America. Gold fever hit Rainy Lake in 1893, and though the finds were real, the costs of extracting the ore made it a short-lived enterprise. The mine on Little American Island, the only profitable one of the seven in the area, lasted until 1897. A few years later lumberjacks moved in to fell the valuable white pine. Commercial fishing, most notably for sturgeon eggs to be sold as caviar, and commercial blueberry picking also started around the turn of the 20th century, and both were very profitable. None of these industries, however, were practiced in a sustainable manner, and they all died out around the time of the Great Depression. Another short-lived but very profitable enterprise at this time was smuggling alcohol in from Canada during Prohibition. Resorts catering to anglers sprung up early in the century, and as the land healed, more tourists arrived. Congress made Voyageurs Minnesota's first and the nation's 36th national park in 1971.

Natural History

Voyageurs lies at the southern end of the Canadian Shield, and across Minnesota's border lakes region much of this 2.7-billion-year-old bedrock—some of North America's oldest exposed rock—lies bare along the park's shorelines. The last glacier to sweep south across North America scraped away large quantities of this Precambrian layer, gouging out the area's many lakebeds. The thin layer of soil that has accumulated over the 10,000 years since the last glaciation naturally supports a transitional boreal forest, though, as a legacy of logging, aspen remains the dominant tree in the park's relatively young forest. Scattered marshes, swamps, and bogs (home to insectivorous pitcher plant and sundew) sit between the many hills and outcrop ridges. Summer sees a profusion of wild berries, with strawberries ripening in early July and blueberries filling out around the end of the month—most years you can pick some of both on the same trip.

Voyageurs is home to just about every animal species typical of the Northwoods. Spotting a beaver is almost guaranteed, while black bear and moose are most likely to be seen deep in the heart of the Kabetogama Peninsula. You'd have to be pretty lucky to happen upon a gray wolf, though around 35 roam these woods, so you might hear one howling at night. Few of Voyageurs' over 240 bird species are as beloved as the bald eagle, and the nation's symbol is frequently spied perched in trees alongside or soaring over the park's largest lakes. Out on the lakes you'll likely see common loon, great blue heron, hooded merganser, common tern, belted kingfisher, a variety of ducks, and large flocks of ring-billed and herring gulls, while spruce grouse, pileated woodpecker, boreal chickadee, scarlet tanager, ruby-throated hummingbird, and around 25 species of warbler reside across the inland forests. This is one of the best places in Minnesota to look for boreal forest birds.

Orientation and Information

Voyageurs National Park follows the Minnesota–Ontario border for 55 meandering miles. Access for most visitors is through one of the four resort areas on the park's periphery. Rainy Lake is at the northwest corner, not far from International Falls, while Crane Lake is on the far southeast end. Kabetogama and Ash River sit in the middle. Each gateway offers lodging, food, fishing guides, water taxis (prices depend on the length of trip and number of people, but expect to pay about $50 for a short trip), and just about anything else you could need during your trip. The western three each have visitor centers, while Crane Lake has a sporadically open ranger station. The **Ash River Visitor Center** (9899 Meadwood Rd., 218/374-3221, 9 A.M.–5 P.M. daily late May–Sept.) is housed in the historic Meadwood Lodge, a 1935 log building, while the **Kabetogama Lake Visitor Center** (9940 Cedar Ln., 218/875-2111, 9 A.M.–5 P.M. daily late May–Sept.) has some wildlife exhibits.

The **Rainy Lake Visitor Center** (1797 Town Rd. 342, 218/286-5258, www.nps.gov/voya, 9 A.M.–5 P.M. daily late May–Sept., 10 A.M.–5 P.M. Wed.–Sun. rest of year) is the only one open year-round. There are no fees for visiting Voyageurs, though all overnight visitors require free permits. Get them at park visitors centers or self-registration stations at most boat launches.

Historic and Natural Attractions

Though the red and white **Kettle Falls Hotel** (12977 Chippewa Trl., 218/240-1724, www.kettlefallshotel.com) sits 16 miles from the nearest road, people come from all corners of the park to stroll the grounds, have a meal or a drink in the Lumberjack Saloon, or just relax

© TIM BEWER

deep in the heart of Voyageurs National Park on the Kabetogama Peninsula

on the endless veranda. The simple, antiques-filled lodge facing south toward Canada was erected on this remote border site around 1910. It is rumored to have started as a brothel and did a thriving business during Prohibition, but soon it became a fashionable getaway attracting the rich and famous such as Charles Lindbergh and John D. Rockefeller. Just a short walk from the hotel is the **Dam Tender's Cabin,** a restored 1912 log home that will be opened for tours in coming years.

Gold fever struck Rainy Lake in July of 1893 when prospector George Davis hit pay dirt on **Little American Island.** You'll learn the whole story of the Rainy Lake Gold Rush along the short wheelchair-accessible trail, which takes you past a mineshaft, tailings piles, and other mining remnants from the only area mine that produced significant ore. Another mine can be seen on the south shore of nearby **Bushyhead Island,** and the Park Service intends to open the Kabetogama Peninsula site of Rainy Lake City, a short-lived mining boomtown, to the public in the future. For a glimpse of another Rainy Lake industry stop by **Oveson's Fish Camp** (accessible by water, ask directions at the the Rainy Lake Visitor Center) where an ice house, fish processing house, and camp home in use between 1958 and 1985 stand at the water's edge.

Ellsworth Rock Gardens on the north shore of Kabetogama Lake features 52 terraced flower beds and over 150 geometric and animal-themed sculptures assembled out of the local granite. Built by Chicago contractor and regular summer visitor Jack Ellsworth between 1944 and 1965, this singular spot makes an ideal picnic ground.

The cliffs on the Canadian side of **Namakan Narrows,** a channel at the southeast end of Namakan Lake, feature moose, human, canoe, and other ancient pictographs. Another popular natural attraction near Crane Lake are the pinkish granite **Grassy Bay Cliffs.**

You don't need your own boat to see the park. **Pontoon Tours** (888/381-2873, June–Sept., $17–41) of Kabetogama, Rainy, and Namakan Lakes, some stopping at Kettle Falls Hotel and Ellsworth Rock Gardens, depart from the visitors center. Most resorts also do tours for their guests, and you can get information on the ranger talks and canoeing programs at park visitors centers.

Well outside the park, but certainly worth a stop if you are driving by, is the 16-foot-long **Lake Kabetogama Walleye.** Climb up into the saddle for a one-of-a-kind photo-op. It sits at the junction of Highway 53 and County Highway 122.

Boating

Most park visitors get around in a motorboat of some kind (personal watercraft are forbidden), though some boaters choose to sail. The most important advice for boaters is to be sure you understand the U.S. Coast Guard buoy system and can read navigation maps, which are sold at the visitors centers. Use great care if motoring beyond the buoys since many rocks and reefs are unmarked, plus water levels change considerably over the summer.

There are marinas, rentals, and free public boat ramps in each of the four gateways. The average cost of a small fishing boat is around $70 per day, while a pontoon goes for about $150. Several Crane Lake resorts have rentals docked on Mukooda Lake, an inland lake only accessible by a short portage.

Paddling

If you want to paddle through deep wilderness without another soul around, you are probably better off dipping your oar in the nearby Boundary Waters Canoe Area Wilderness than at Voyageurs. That said, you do not have to be a horsepower addict to enjoy the park, and there really is some excellent paddling here—*Canoe and Kayak* magazine named it one of the top-ten sea kayaking destinations in the country. Plus, some of the BWCAW's drawbacks don't come into play here: There are few portages, and with no permits or quotas, you can just show up and go. Most paddlers start at Ash River because it has the easiest access to quiet back bays, though the north end of Kabetogama Lake, directly accessible from the Woodenfrog Campground, has lots of small islands and relatively few boaters. A 75-mile circumnavigation of the Kabetogama Peninsula—possible with two short portages—takes about a week.

Canoe rentals are available at each of the four gateways, plus outfitters at Kabetogama and Crane Lake can set you up with everything you need for an extended trip: **Anderson's Canoe Outfitters** (7255 Crane Lake Rd., 218/993-2287 or 800/777-7186, www.anderson-outfitters.com, 5:30 A.M.–7 P.M. Sun.–Thurs., 5:30 A.M.–8 P.M. Fri.–Sat.) at Crane Lake lets you easily fold the BWCAW into your trip.

One of the best ways to experience the park with a paddle is by taking advantage of the **Boats on Interior Lakes** program. The Park Service has placed canoes and rowboats on nine Kabetogama Peninsula lakes (Locator, Quill, Ek, Cruiser, Cranberry Creek, Little Shoepack, Shoepack, Brown, and Peary), and the first-come, first-served boats can be used for day trips or overnight journeys. Reservations (by phone or in person, Kabetogama Lake 218/875-211, Rainy Lake 218/286-5258, Ash River 218/374-3221, $10/party per day) can be made up to a week in advance. You must bring your own life jacket—if you aren't traveling with one you can rent one for a couple of bucks from area resorts.

Hiking

Voyageurs is all about the water, but if you prefer to travel by foot you will not be disappointed here. The **Cruiser Lake Trail,** Voyageurs' most adventurous hike, cuts 9.5 miles across the east end of the Kabetogama Peninsula and, together with its adjoining trails, passes a dozen lakes and nearly as many campsites—this is the best backpacking destination in the park. Though hilly, the route is only moderately challenging; still, because of the peninsula's remoteness you should have some basic outdoors skills before venturing out here. The primary path connects Kabetogama Lake's Lost Bay (about a three-mile paddle with one short portage from the Ash River Visitor Center) to Rainy Lake's Anderson Bay, climbing ridges for remarkable panoramas and dropping down to cross beaver dams, trout streams, and berry patches.

Wildlife abounds on this remote peninsula, and you might spot any of the park's most exciting species. Peary, Brown, Cruiser, and Ek Lakes are all represented in the Boats on Interior Lakes program. Cruiser Lake, near the trail's midpoint, makes a good day-trip destination. Several other paths with similarly stunning scenery branch off the Cruiser Lake Trail, including the highly recommended **Anderson Bay Trail** at the northeast end. The two-mile loop leads atop the Anderson Bay Cliffs, which rise 70 feet above the water, for some magnificent long-distance views.

Over on the west end of the peninsula are the **Locator Lake Trail** and the **Beaver Pond Trail.** The former starts on Kabetogama Lake and crosses two miles of beautiful country inhabited by countless beaver. The moderately difficult (very difficult if you are shouldering a canoe) path climbs a ridge and drops through a ravine before reaching its namesake, part of a long, narrow chain of lakes through the heart of the peninsula. There's a day-use picnic area and rental boats at the end. You can probably figure out what's at the end of the Beaver Pond Trail, a 1.25-mile-long round-trip starting near the Rainy Lake Visitor Center. Many of the peninsula's portage trails, particularly **Gold, Cranberry Creek,** and **Ryan Lake,** cross through some beautiful scenery.

Over on the mainland the 26-mile **Kab-Ash Trail,** which links the Kabetogama Lake and Ash River gateways, accounts for over half of all the park's trail miles, and a variety of forest types and wetland boardwalks make for great wildlife-viewing. There are also some short trails at each of Voyageurs' four gateways. Rainy Lake's option is the **Oberholtzer Interpretive Trail,** an easy 1.5-mile route that covers a cattail marsh, pine forest, and scenic views of Black Bay; the first half is wheelchair accessible. The slightly hilly 2.5-mile **Echo Bay Trail,** a few miles northwest of the Kabetogama Lake Visitor Center, loops through a mix of aspen and conifer stands. You'll pass many areas flooded by beavers and might spot wolf tracks. The Ash River area's **Blind Ash Bay Trail** is arguably Voyageurs' most beautiful short mainland path. The hilly 2.5-mile round-trip follows a rocky ridge—there are some great views of Kabetogama Lake from atop it—and ends up looking out over the narrow namesake bay.

Winter Recreation

Very few visitors come when there is snow on the ground, and most of those are here to snowmobile, since this is one of the few national parks where snowmobiles are allowed. Over 110 miles of well-marked trail wind over the park's frozen lakes and connect to the extensive trail system extending beyond the park; trail maps are available from the Rainy Lake Visitor Center or any area resort. Sleds are not allowed anywhere on land except for marked safety portages and the popular, though ungroomed, Chain of Lakes Trail cutting across the Kabetogama Peninsula. The speed limit on the lakes is 45 mph—it is enforced!

Despite the predilection for horsepower, silent sport lovers are not completely overlooked. The principal cross-country ski route is the **Black Bay Trail,** a six-mile series of groomed loops for all abilities on the northwest corner of the Kabetogama Peninsula—drive the **Rainy Lake Ice Road** to the trailhead. Also starting near the Rainy Lake Visitor Center is the Koochiching State Forest's **Tilson Creek Trail,** a challenging 10-mile set of loops. The Park Service packs three winter hiking trails: The Blind Ash Bay and Oberholtzer trails are open year-round and **Sullivan Bay Trail,** an easy 1.5-mile path starting just south of the Ash River Visitor Center, is open in the winter only. The Rainy Lake Visitor Center rents skis and snowshoes.

Camping

Your Voyageurs experience will be excellent during the day, but it isn't complete without a night under the stars. All of the over 200 campsites are accessible only by boat, and most are equipped with a fire ring, picnic table, privy, tent pad, and bear-proof food locker. The first-come, first-served sites are only intended for use by a single party and can accommodate two tents (some larger ones can handle four).

A fully accessible campsite on Namakan Lake can be reserved through the Kabetogama Lake Visitor Center. You are also allowed to pitch a tent at undeveloped sites elsewhere in the park as long as you stay 200 yards from any official campsites and a quarter mile from any other developed site. Camping is free, though each party must fill out a self-registration overnight permit. While it should be standard practice anywhere in Minnesota's Northwoods, it is especially important to keep a clean camp at Voyageurs so as not to attract bears—if no food locker is available be sure to properly hang all food-scented items in a tree (ten feet up and four feet from the trunk).

If you are staying on the mainland, many area resorts have RV parking, though the pair of state forest campgrounds are your best bet. The beautiful and popular **Woodenfrog Campground** (Co. Rd. 122, 218/365-7229, $12) has 61 widely spaced sites on Lake Kabetogama. Also on-site are a swimming beach, two-mile nature trail, and picnic ground. The **Ash River Campground** (Co. Rd. 129, 218/365-7229, $12) has nine far less scenic sites.

Houseboats

This increasingly popular option for exploring Voyageurs lets you enjoy the wilderness with all the comforts of home. No experience (or license) is needed and the rental company will set you up with everything from food to maps. The NPS maintains designated mooring sites with fire rings throughout the park, or you can overnight at one of the resort areas. Four companies can set you up with a floating cabin, and according to the National Park Service, all are tightly run operations. **Voyagaire Houseboats** (7576 Gold Coast Rd., 218/993-2266 or 800/882-6287, www.voyagaire.com, prices start at $260 one day) at Crane Lake is the largest, while **Ebel's Voyageur Houseboats** (10326 Ash River Trl., 218/374-3571 or 888/883-2357, www.ebels.com, $290 one day) operates out of Ash River. Both **Northernaire Houseboats** (2690 County Rd. 94, 218/286-5221 or 800/854-7958, www.northernaire-houseboats.com, $249 one day) and **Rainy Lake Houseboats** (2031 Town Rd. 488, 218/286-5391 or 800/554-9188, www.rainy-lakehouseboats.com, $560 three-day minimum) operate on Rainy Lake. Prices range anywhere from about $249 a day for the basic boat, which sleeps 2–4 people comfortably, to over $5,500 a week for the most luxurious model with private bedrooms for a dozen people, hot tubs, entertainment centers, air-conditioning, and other top-notch touches. Spring and fall discounts are as high as 20 percent, plus Ebel's and Rainy Lake have substantial midweek discounts during the summer.

Accommodations

A night in the historic **Kettle Falls Hotel** (12977 Chippewa Trl., 218/240-1726 or 218/875-2070 winter, www.kettlefallshotel.com, May–Sept., $60 rooms, $160 cabins) is a highlight for many park visitors. The 12 antiques-filled rooms in the main lodge share three baths, plus there are modern cabins that sleep up to six—the cabins usually require a three-day minimum stay. Canoes, kayaks, boats, and everything an angler could need is available, and a shuttle service runs from the mainland.

Dozens of other lodging options sit on the periphery of the park. The casual **Thunderbird Lodge** (2170 Co. Rd. 139, 218/286-3151 or 800/351-5133, www.thunderbirdrainylake.com, $89 lodge, $280 cabins), out near the tip of the peninsula, has great Rainy Lake views from most of its lakeside lodge rooms and cabins—during the summer cabin rentals require a three-day minimum stay. There is a marina with boat rental on-site, and all cabins have their own docks.

Kabetogama's **Arrowhead Lodge** (10473 Waltz Rd., 218/875-2141 or 866/847-7118, www.arrowheadlodgeresort.com, $165/day and $945/week cabins, $35/person lodge rooms) is a simple, family-friendly fishing resort. The 10 cabins, several on the shore and all with at least some lake view, are centered on an atmospheric log lodge built around the 1920s, and its screened porch is a popular place to dine. They have a full-service marina (they'll even clean your fish) and rent fishing boats, pontoons, canoes, and kayaks.

Sandy Point Lodge (10606 Gamma Rd., 218/875-2615 or 800/777-8595, www.sandypointlodge.com, $135/day and $620/week cabins, $95/day lodge rooms, $45/day RV campsites), out at the end of the road, is similar. They've got a sauna and sandy beach.

Ironically, the largest of the dozen resorts around Crane Lake is also one of the most peaceful. **Nelson's Resort** (7632 Nelson Rd., 218/993-2295 or 800/433-0743, www.nelsonsresort.com, May–Sept., $1,100/week one-bedroom), family-run since 1931, has 28 classic log cabins along 1.5 miles of private lakeshore over on the quiet end of Crane Lake. Facilities include a wonderful swimming beach, hiking trail, sauna, shuffleboard, and a vegetable garden used to prepare the Thursday Swedish Smorgasbord ($20, open to the public) and other dinners.

The little **Pine Ridge Motel** (7258 Crane Lake Rd., 218/993-2265 or 888/310-4225, www.pineridgemotel.com, $69 rooms, $35/person three-bedroom cabin) is completely modern inside, but looking at the log exterior you can still imagine it as the trading post–fish shop–bar that it was back in the 1950s when this was still a truly wild corner of the country. There is also a bunkhouse (no shower, bring a sleeping bag and pillow, $16) with beds.

There is no single resort association for the park's four gateways, so if you want additional lodging information contact the **Crane Lake Visitor & Tourism Bureau** (800/362-7405, www.visitcranelake.com), **Ash River Trail Commercial Club** (www.ashriver.com), **Kabetogama Lake Association** (800/524-9085, www.kabetogama.com), or **International Falls Area Convention & Visitors Bureau** (800/325-5766, www.rainylake.org).

ORR

Far from Voyageurs National Park, Orr is nevertheless the gateway to these famous waters since Highway 53 shuttles just about every park visitor through the surprisingly busy town of 250 people.

Vince Shute Wildlife Sanctuary

The Vince Shute Wildlife Sanctuary (218/757-0172, www.americanbear.org, 5 P.M.–dusk Tues.–Sun. summer, $7 adults) is one of Minnesota's most surprising attractions. Vince ran a logging camp in these remote woods starting in the 1930s, and like most others living in the wilderness at the time, he routinely shot bears. Eventually though, he figured out that the lumbering giants weren't vicious, just hungry, so he started feeding them in a clearing outside the camp. Soon the "Bear Man," as he became known, had earned a special relationship with the bears, and they no longer feared each other's presence. As Vince's health deteriorated he sought a way to protect his bears' future, and the American Bear Association was formed to not only protect this 360-acre refuge but "to promote the well-being of the black bear through a better understanding of its behavior, biology, and habitat needs." From the elevated viewing deck you can watch the 30–50 black bears who come to eat the food provided for them here and, though it seems somewhat zoo-like, these are truly wild bears who only tolerate the presence of humans within the two-acre clearing at the heart of the sanctuary. Trained naturalists are always on hand to answer your questions. To reach the reserve, head 13 miles west on County Highway 23 and follow the signs. Sundays are the best day to visit since it has by far the smallest crowds. It does not open during heavy rains.

Accommodations

Most other local tourism activity is focused on 10,945-acre Pelican Lake. About a dozen small, family-run resorts (www.pelicanlakeresorts.com) sit on Pelican's wild shore, and the friendly **Deer Lodge** (4487 Deer Lodge Rd., 218/757-3134 or 888/592-7151, www.deerlodgeresort.com, $1,450/week two-bedroom) at the lake's quiet back end is as good as any. It has five large log cabins, and there are boats and ice houses for rent.

The fanciest lodging in the area is the

lakeside **AmericInn** (4675 U.S. 53, 218/757-3613 or 800/860-3613, $125) just north of town. The hotel features a mini indoor water park with slide, pool, whirlpool, and sauna. Suites with whirlpools, fireplaces, and balconies are available.

Families will feel right at home in the cabins at **Grey Wolf Lodge** (4411 Pelican Lake Rd., 800/840-9653, www.greywolflodge.com, $615–915 weekly, 3- and 4-day rates also available) right on Pelican Lake. With a sauna, volleyball court, small mini golf course and, of course, the whole expanse of the lake in front of you, you may feel you never need to leave.

If bed-and-breakfasts are more your style there's the **Hundred Acre Woods** (5048 Old Hwy. 53, 218/757-0070, www.voyageurcountry.com/HundredAcreWoods, $89–115), a modern home about three miles north of town. One of the pair of Northwoods-themed guestrooms has a sauna while the other has a double whirlpool tub.

Food

T. Pattenn Café (4557 Hwy. 53, 218/757-3908, 4:30 A.M.–8 P.M. Mon.–Sat., 5 A.M.–8 P.M. Sun.), right on Pelican Lake serves breakfast all day, as well as other homey basics.

Right by the Vince Shute Wildlife Sanctuary, **The Dam Supper Club** (4247 Hwy. 53, 218/757-3985, 11 A.M.–midnight Tues.–Thurs., 11 A.M.–1 A.M. Fri.–Sat., 11 A.M.–midnight Sun., $4–10) is a popular local watering hole with a game room and offers all-you-can-eat walleye on Fridays.

Information

The **Orr Travel Information Center** (4429 U.S. 53, 218/757-3932 or 800/357-9255, 9 A.M.–5 P.M. daily summer, 10 A.M.–4 P.M. Thurs.–Sat. rest of year) is a convenient place to get national park and other regional tourism information, and they have many animal mounts on display. It is also the site of the **Orr Bog Walk,** a half-mile boardwalk through a variety of wetland habitats, including a tamarack swamp and a black spruce bog.

SUPERIOR NATIONAL FOREST – LACROIX DISTRICT

The forest's most overlooked district runs along the Canadian border in the forest's remote northwest corner.

Recreation

Two trails near the Crane Lake resort area, one of the gateways to Voyageurs National Park, lead to wonderful spots on the Vermilion River. The namesake destination of the **Vermilion Gorge Trail,** a three-mile round-trip starting behind Voyagaire Houseboats, features sheer granite cliffs with white-water rapids hitting Class V during high water. The fairly easy path is surfaced with gravel most of the way, and interpretive panels discuss the area's human history. Further up the river is a small picnic area and accessible overlook of **Vermilion Falls,** where the river shoots through a ten-foot crack in the rock. From the parking lot, a half-mile trail hugs the river past some wild rice beds and "the chute," a stretch of white water—this walk is as scenic, if not more so, than the view of the falls. The six-mile **Astrid Lake Trail** starting at the Lake Jeanette Campground skirts five lakes, crosses a black spruce bog filled with carnivorous pitcher plants, passes some huge boulders dropped here during the last Ice Age, and features half a dozen lakeside campsites.

Besides the BWCAW there is fantastic paddling on the **Vermilion River,** which flows 39 miles along the western edge of the forest from Lake Vermilion up to Crane Lake. There are many rapids, including some unrunnable waterfalls (well-worn portages take you around), along this wild, cliff-lined waterway, though these lie between long stretches with a barely perceptible current. The campsites and scenery make it a great choice for overnight trips. For some easier paddling, put in to the **Johnson Lake** canoe route, 23 miles northeast of Orr at the end of Forest Road 203. The only access is a half-mile portage, but after that streams connect the trio of narrow, winding lakes, with seven campsites on their islands and shorelines. There are two more campsites a few miles down the road on little Franklin Lake, reached by a mile-long portage.

You can also portage along the Astrid Lake hiking trail to connect those lakes with the namesake river of the **Hunting Shack** canoe route.

If you prefer seeing nature from behind a windshield, stop by the ranger stations in Cook or Ely and pick up the ***Discovery Tour*** booklet. It will guide you on a pair of auto tours—one focusing on the Crane Lake area and the other following the Vermilion River and County Highway 116 (the Echo Trail) down to Ely—pointing out historic and natural sites along the way.

Camping

The LaCroix District's two campgrounds lie along County Highway 116 (the Echo Trail) in the vicinity of Crane Lake. Both are very good and accept reservations. Because most of its 12 campsites (including the two walk-ins) overlook the lake and most are right next to the shore, **Lake Jeanette** has the highest occupancy rate in the forest. The **Echo Lake** (Echo Trl., www.recreation.gov, $10) camp has 24 sites plus a beach, dock, and playground and rarely fills up.

Information

The **LaCroix Ranger Station** (320 U.S. 53 N., 218/666-0020, 7 A.M.–5 P.M. daily summer, hours vary rest of year) is located in Cook.

The Iron Range

Though not the only iron range in Minnesota, the Mesabi Range gave up far more ore than the Vermilion and Cuyuna combined and is the only one still worked. This is a land pocked by massive open pit scars and enormous rusty scrap hills, and many people dismiss the Iron Range as a tourist destination when, in fact, it is one of Minnesota's most interesting regions. Today the mining industry employs about 3,500 people, a far cry from the 15,000 working here as recently as the 1980s, and former miners talk about how many years they would have had on the job if they hadn't been laid off. Some parents still give their children the same old advice that they and their grandparents heard in their younger years—get a good education so you can leave—but things are changing. The population's strong work ethic has attracted new industries like call centers to the Range in recent years, and now there is talk of copper, nickel, and zinc mines; new power plants; and modern "electric minimills" to produce steel right here at the source. Some people believe these new plants could make the Iron Range the center of the steel world. Despite the changes, regional unemployment remains above the state average, and city populations continue to decline.

The operational and retired mines have become fascinating tourist attractions, and you can watch 37-cubic-yard shovels loading 240-ton production trucks at the working pits. Environmentalists might cringe, but even the most ardent Luddites are likely to be awed by the scale of it all. Back in the early 20th century the new mining jobs attracted immigrants from across Europe, making the Range nearly as diverse a melting pot as New York City, and that ethnic heritage remains strong here as the various festivals, churches, and menu items will attest.

A new travel option, the **Mesabi Trail** (www.mesabitrail.com), will stretch 132 miles between Grand Rapids and Ely, making it one of the longest paved recreational trails in the world. At the end of 2009, 102 miles were complete, with a 75-mile chunk running from Grand Rapids through Hibbing, Chisholm, Mountain Iron, and Virginia to McKinley. A two-day ($5) or annual ($15) Wheel Pass is required for adult users and can be purchased at area businesses or self-service stations at trail access points.

The **Iron Range Tourism Bureau** (403 1st St. N., 218/749-8161 or 800/777-8497, www.ironrange.org, 8 A.M.–5 P.M. Mon.–Fri., closed Sat.–Sun.) based in Virginia is one of the best-run tourism organizations in the state, and if you have a particular interest in something—like bird-watching or fishing or shopping—they've probably got a brochure and/or a webpage about it.

HIBBING

Hibbing's a good ol' town.

– Bob Dylan, *My Life in a Stolen Moment*

With just over 16,000 residents, Hibbing, "The Iron Ore Capital of the World," is by far the largest Iron Range city. Frank Hibbing founded his town in 1893 on the spot where he discovered iron ore, but with money and people pouring into nearby Virginia, Hibbing got off to a very slow start. The roads were poor, drinking water was scarce, and a nationwide financial panic put most people out of work. A couple years later, however, several mines were operating around the village and its existence was secure, but the location was not. By 1915 Hibbing was home to 20,000 people and had a thriving downtown, but the mines were eating their way toward the city from several directions. The Oliver Mining Company decided the town had to be moved. Beginning in 1919 most of the city was transferred two miles south to the present site. As a payoff, the company developed the new downtown; provided low interest loans to families; and built many civic buildings, including a hospital, Village Hall, and high school.

Many famous people have called Hibbing home, including Roger Maris, Kevin McHale, and Vincent Bugliosi, but by far the city's most famous former resident is Robert Allen Zimmerman, known to the rest of the world as Bob Dylan. Bob was born in Duluth in 1941 and his upper-middle-class family moved to Hibbing to run an appliance store when Bob was five years old. After graduating from Hibbing High School in 1959, he moved to Minneapolis and briefly attended the University of Minnesota before ending up in New York City, where he melded folk and rock music, reinventing both in the process. Dylan rarely discusses his Minnesota past, and except for his 10-year high school reunion and the occasional funeral, he has rarely returned—one local theory attributes this to being ashamed of the many lies he told about his boyhood when he first gained fame. Though the city has done little to promote its Dylan history, a slow trickle of fans still makes a pilgrimage here. Plans for a Bob Dylan museum have been proposed several times before, and it is certain to happen someday. Ironically, his biggest fans are surely hoping that they can't visit it for a long time since Bob has specifically requested that it wait until after his death.

Sights

Hibbing's **Hull Rust Mahoning Mineview** overlooks the world's largest operational open pit iron ore mine. Since the first ore was shipped in 1895, more than 1.5 billion tons of earth have been removed, creating a cavity over 3.5 miles long, 1.5 miles wide, and over 500 feet deep. At its WWII peak, around one quarter of all the ore mined in the United States came out of the 30 separate mines that composed the "Grand Canyon of the North."

The Mesabi Range's first strip mine remains one of the few in operation, and the Hibbing Taconite Company still extracts eight million tons of ore a year. Volunteers, including some retired miners, staff the little **visitors center** (401 Penobscot Rd., 218/262-4166, 9 A.M.–5 P.M. daily summer, free admission) and love to answer questions. Old mining equipment, including a truck that could haul 170 tons—the trucks in the mine today carry 240—is on display outside. To reach the National Historic Landmark, follow 3rd Avenue East north from downtown for two miles. You'll pass the old city center on the way. Two-hour mine tours ($5) are available on Tuesdays and Thursdays during the summer. They depart at noon from Minnesota Discovery Center in nearby Chisholm, and reservations (218/254-7959 or 800/372-6437) are required. Children must be age 10 or older.

© TRICIA CORNELL

Robert Zimmerman, better known as Bob Dylan, graduated from Hibbing High School in 1959.

The **Hibbing Historical Museum** (400 E. 23rd St., 218/263-8522, 9 A.M.–4 P.M. Mon.–Fri. summer, 9 A.M.–3 P.M. Mon.–Thurs. rest of year, $4 adults) is small, but definitely worth visiting to see the scale model of Hibbing as it was in 1913, shortly before the move.

While there, pick up the Historical Walks brochure, which details two dozen noteworthy buildings around downtown. One of these is **Hibbing High School** (800 E. 21st St.). Education was a priority for the immigrant miners and, as part of the payoff for relocating the city, citizens demanded the best school possible. Construction on the castle-like structure began in 1920; three years and $3,927,325 later the "Palace in the Wilderness" was complete. The remarkable edifice features marble floors, brass railings and doorknobs, murals, statuary, and other ornate interior details, though the coup de grace is the 1,800-seat auditorium—a nearly exact replica of New York City's Capitol Theater, the city's grandest opera house of that age. Its Barton vaudeville organ has 1,949 pipes and is one of just two left in existence, while the crystal chandeliers are valued at $250,000 each. During the summer the building is generally open during the day, and you can just pop in anytime to look around—the auditorium is in the south wing, and the janitors are used to pointing people the right way. You can usually take a look during the school year too, but stop by the principal's office first.

In 1914 Carl Wickman began shuttling people between Hibbing and the new community of Alice for 15 cents in his Hupmobile car. This simple two-mile route was the beginning of Greyhound Bus Lines, and the whole story is told in the **Greyhound Bus Museum** (1201 Greyhound Blvd., 218/263-5814, www.greyhoundbusmuseum.org, 9 A.M.–5 P.M. Mon.–Sat., 1–5 P.M. Sun. May–Sept., $4 adults) near the mineview. The collection includes everything from historic baggage tags and belt buckles to one bus from each decade up to the 1980s, including Wickman's original car.

There are a handful of **Bob Dylan sites** that fans will want to seek out. For most of his life in Hibbing, Bob lived in the same large square house (2425 7th Ave. E.); the family is used to people stopping by for a look, but that doesn't mean it's okay to ring the bell and ask to see inside. You may get that chance down the road though, since the current owners plan to open the house as a bed-and-breakfast someday. The closest thing to a museum is the **Bob Dylan Exhibit** in the basement of the Hibbing Public Library (2020 5th Ave. E., 218/262-1038, 9 A.M.–8 P.M. Mon.–Thurs., 9 A.M.–5 P.M. Fri.–Sat., closed Sun. summer). There is a timeline, and many posters, records, and news clippings are on display. Another shrine of sorts, and a worthy stop for Dylanphiles, is **Zimmy's** (531 E. Howard St., 218/262-6145, www.zimmys.com), a restaurant decorated with Dylan photos and posters: The tattered, autographed Los Angeles Lakers cap, donated by Bob's mom, is their pride and joy. The library distributes a Dylan **walking tour brochure,** but it doesn't include the **Moose Lodge** (421½ E. Howard St.) where some of Bob's early bands like The Golden Chords performed. To see inside, and maybe play the same piano Bob did, attend a Friday-night fish fry.

Entertainment and Events

The **Paulucci Space Theatre** (1502 E. 23rd St., 218/262-6720, $4) at Hibbing Community College presents large-format films and planetarium shows on a 40-foot-diameter domed screen, plus free planetarium presentations on Wednesday nights. **Zimmy's** (531 E. Howard St., 218/262-6145, www.zimmys.com) often has singer-songwriters performing on weekends.

Dylan Days (www.dylandays.com) is held the week of May 24th (Bob's birthday) and features Dylan trivia, karaoke, and art works; a poetry contest; and a tour of Dylan haunts.

The city's biggest bash is the **Mines and Pines Jubilee** (www.hibbing.org/minespines), held for nine days over the middle of July. Events include a parade, fireworks, arts and crafts fair, and ice cream social.

Shopping

Antiques on Howard (404 E. Howard St., 218/362-8449, 10:30 A.M.–4:30 P.M. Mon.–Fri., 10:30 A.M.–3:30 P.M. Sat., closed Sun.) is large and reputable.

Howard Street Booksellers (115 E. Howard St., 218/262-5206, 10 A.M.–5:30 P.M. Mon.–Fri., 11 A.M.3 P.M. Sat.–Sun.) has new and used books, including a good Minnesota section and plenty of Dylan merchandise.

Recreation

Carey Lake Park (25th St., 218/263-8851), four miles east of town, has 10 miles of trails looping around and along the undeveloped lake. They are open for hiking and biking in the summer, but are used primarily by cross-country skiers. Ski and snowshoe rentals are available on winter weekends. The park also has a beach, fishing pier, and some nice picnic spots.

Accommodations

There aren't a lot of options in Hibbing itself. The very nicest is the **Mitchell-Tappan House** (2125 4th Ave. E., 218/262-3862 or 888/662-3862, www.mitchell-tappanhouse.com, $75), a large, bright, and friendly bed-and-breakfast in an 1897 home originally built for the superintendent of the Oliver Iron Mining Company. (It was moved here from the old town.) One of the five antiques-filled guestrooms has a private bath, and the others share two. The attic rooms have a separate sitting area and make a good family suite; children are welcome.

South of town is the very serviceable **Super 8** (1411 40th St. E., 218/263-8982 or 800/800-8000, www.super8.com/Hibbing, $64). Otherwise, you're limited to some rundown rooming houses in town.

Food

More than just a Dylan shrine, **Zimmy's** (531 E. Howard St., 218/262-6145, www.zimmys.com, 11 A.M.–1 A.M. Sun.–Thurs., 11 A.M.–2 A.M. Fri.–Sat., $5–17) serves the best food in town. The wide-ranging selection includes burgers and pizza, but Caribbean chicken and garlic steak set it apart from the competition.

Bach Yen (2510 1st Ave., 218/263-3647, 11 A.M.–9 P.M. Mon.–Sat., closed Sun., $7–13) is one of the best Chinese restaurants outside of the Twin Cities.

It's just a hole in the wall bar, but many locals swear by the hamburgers at **Tuffy's** (2314 1st Ave., 218/262-1021, 11 A.M.–9 P.M. daily, $3–6).

Visit **Sunrise Bakery** (1813 3rd Ave. E., 218/263-4985, 6 A.M.–4:30 P.M. Mon.–Fri., 7 A.M.–noon Sat., closed Sun.) for pasties, potica, porketta, ravioli, and other tastes of the Iron Range. This Hibbing tradition, opened in 1913, also makes deli sandwiches, and most of their food is surprisingly cheap.

Information

Hibbing's **Tourist Information Center** (1202 E. Howard St., 218/262-4166, 9 A.M.–5 P.M. Mon.–Sat. summer, 10 A.M.–4 P.M. Mon.–Fri. rest of year) is staffed by retired women who love to share stories about the town's old days and are your best source of area information.

You can also pick up some brochures at the **Hibbing Area Chamber of Commerce** (211 E. Howard St., 218/262-3895 or 800/444-2246, www.hibbing.org, 8 A.M.–5 P.M. Mon.–Fri.). The Hull Rust Mahoning Mineview and the library also stock area tourism brochures.

Getting There and Around

The **Chisholm-Hibbing Airport** (11038 Hwy. 37, 218/262-3451) is served by **Delta/Northwest** (800/225-2525) a couple of times a day. For a cab, call **Hibbing Shalloe's Taxi** (218/263-5065).

AROUND HIBBING

Chisholm

If Walt Disney had been an iron miner instead of a cartoonist, Disneyland might have looked a little like **Minnesota Discovery Center** (801 SW Hwy. 169, 218/254-7959 or 800/372-6437, www.mndiscoverycenter.com, 10 A.M.–5 P.M. Tues.–Wed. and Fri.–Sun., 10 A.M.–9 P.M. Thurs., $8 adults). (Known as Ironworld to generations of Minnesota school children who have come here on field trips, the museum recently changed its name.) Overlooking the massive Glen Mine, this is the best place to get the full story on the history and methods of mining in Minnesota—museum displays start at the geological formation of the state

© TRICIA CORNELL

The Iron Man Statue in Chisholm honors the region's miners.

and proceed to the present—but the exhibits also look at the Range's rich ethnic heritage. Costumed interpreters demonstrate bygone customs and traditions at a fur trapper's cabin and traditional sod-roofed Sami home, and there are festivals throughout the year and daily music performances and craft demonstrations. Also at the park you can research your roots in the Iron Range Research Center (open year-round), one of the Upper Midwest's largest genealogical and local history collections; visit a well-done Civilian Conservation Corps museum; ride a genuine electric trolley; and finish the day off with a round at Pellet Pete's 19-hole miniature golf course. In late 2009 the Discovery Center closed due to budget difficulties and staff were working out the details of whether, when, and in what form to reopen.

The **Mesabi Trail** (www.mesabitrail.com) runs right by the Discovery Center, with a trailhead is accessible from the parking lot.

Across Highway 169 is the 81-foot **Iron Man Statue,** which is the third-largest freestanding statue in the nation, behind the St. Louis Arch and the Statue of Liberty. The miner, holding a pick and shovel, honors those who worked the Mesabi, Vermilion, and Cuyuna Ranges.

Often overlooked by visitors to Chisholm, and understandably so, is the **Minnesota Museum of Mining** (701 Lake St. W., 218/254-5543, 9 A.M.–5 P.M. Mon.–Sat., 1–5 P.M. Sun. summer, $4 adults), which doesn't appear to have changed much since it opened in 1954. The small castle-like building houses most of the mining displays, while outside is a simulated underground mineshaft. The surrounding park is a mining graveyard of sorts, with all kinds of vehicles and implements lying about. There is also a collection of various historical items, from old farm tools to old fire engines. Fans of the artist Francis Lee Jacques will want to take a look at the model railroad diorama he designed.

As you approach or depart town from the east along Highway 169 look for the **Bruce Mine Headframe,** the last of its kind on the Mesabi Range. The rusting tower lowered and raised the cages that carried miners and ore from the 300-foot-deep mine.

The only hotel in town is the pleasant **Chisholm Inn** (501 Iron Dr., 218/254-2000 or 877/255-3156, www.chisholminn.com, $85) across from Minnesota Discovery Center. Extras include a pool, hot tub, sauna, bike rentals, and large breakfast buffet.

McCarthy Beach State Park

Though McCarthy Beach State Park (7622 McCarthy Beach Rd., 218/254-7979) spreads across 2,311 acres, most facilities and visitors are found on the narrow isthmus between Side and Sturgeon Lakes. A wide, shallow beach stretches deep into the latter and you can rent a canoe or fishing boat from the park office to further explore the lakes or maybe snare some trout and walleye. Elsewhere, 18 miles of decent though unspectacular hiking trails (most open to mountain bikes and horses and half groomed for cross-country skiing) follow the park's ridges through red and white pine stands. **Pickerel Lake** is the one noteworthy destination, and a trail follows its shore. There are also some nice views of Sturgeon Lake along the **Ridge Trail** that heads north from Pickerel. The main campground has 86 sites in three loops along Side Lake—so get up early for that sunrise view. The upper loop is the most secluded and, since all 18 electric sites are in the lower loop, the middle one is also a quiet option. The most peaceful campground is tucked away on Beatrice Lake in the north end of the park. It has 30 sites (three walk-in, $18) and few facilities.

VIRGINIA

Like the other Iron Range cities, Virginia was a boomtown, built following the discovery of iron in the area, but it also became one of northern Minnesota's most important lumber towns. At one point early in its history, Virginia had both the world's largest white pine sawmill, the Virginia and Rainy Lake Mill, and the largest iron mine, Missabe Mountain. The dual industry city, platted in the middle of virgin wilderness (hence the name, though it helped that one of the promoters of the new town was originally from the state of Virginia), swelled to 5,000 people in its first year of existence. That same year, 1893, the town was wiped out by a forest fire, and though locals rebuilt, it took a second citywide blaze seven years later to convince Virginians to build with brick, stone, and concrete. Because of its wealth and grandeur Virginia became known as "The Queen City of the North," a moniker it retains today. Its central location and variety of services make it the best base for visiting the Iron Range.

Sights and Recreation

The city's main draw, the **Mineview in the Sky** (Hwy. 53, 218/741-2717, 9 A.M.–6 P.M. daily May–Sept., free admission) offers a panoramic view of the Rouchleau Mine. The massive cavity, cut right along the eastern edge of Virginia, stretches nearly three miles long, a half-mile wide, and 450 feet deep, though the bottom 200 feet are now filled in by water. It produced 300 million tons of ore before closing in 1977. You'll also find a 240-ton capacity production truck and a few other mining vehicles parked at the overlook, and any mining questions can be answered by the staff of the information center. You can get another view of the Rochleau pit at the **Oldtown-Finntown Overlook** (east end of 3rd St. N.).

The **Olcott Heritage Museum** (800 9th Ave. N., 218/741-1136, 11 A.M.–4 P.M. Thurs.–Sat., $1) in Olcott Park is very well presented. Because there are so many mining exhibits in surrounding towns, this museum focuses on logging and also has a good display about the city's twin fires. Relics of the bygone days, such as a foot-operated dentist's drill, are housed in a 1910 Finnish log cabin and 1930s tourist cabin (back then a night cost just $1.50). Next to the museum is the **Olcott Park Greenhouse,** and you'll find a **giant loon** (21 feet long) floating in nearby Silver Lake.

Mesabi Recreation (720 9th St. N., 218/749-6719, www.mesabirecreation.com, 9:30 A.M.–6 P.M. Mon.–Fri., 9:30 A.M.–4 P.M. Sat., noon–4 P.M. Sun.) can set up active travelers with bike, canoe, kayak, snowshoe, and cross-country ski rentals.

If you are looking to explore the Range's crystal-clear mine pits, you should talk to the people at **Tall Pine Divers** (416 Chestnut St., 218/749-1561). They do sales, service, classes, and air fills.

Accommodations

The **Pine View Inn** (903 17th St. N., 218/741-8918 or 866/263-0535, $49) on the north side of town is a good value. The rooms are old but pass the white-glove test, and a sauna is available on a first-come, first-served basis so you don't have to share.

Also a bargain is the more centrally located **Lakeshor Motor Inn** (404 6th Ave. N., 218/741-3360 or 800/569-8131, www.lakeshor.com, $49), which overlooks Virginia (aka Bailey's) Lake.

You get a pool, whirlpool, sauna, and free pass to the nearby Quad Cities Optimal Fitness Center at the **Coates Plaza Hotel** (502 Chestnut St., 218/749-1000 or 800/777-4699, www.coatesplazahotel.com, $59), Virginia's best hotel.

Out on the highway, the **Americinn** (5480 Mountain Iron Dr., www.americinn.com, 218/741-7839, $129) offers spacious rooms and great service.

Food

There is a wonderful atmosphere in the historic **Rainy Lake Saloon** (209 Chestnut St., 218/741-7665, 11 A.M.–1 A.M. daily, $6–22). The menu is the most varied in town and includes some Mexican, Italian, and Cajun besides the expected American fare.

Also popular is **Grandma's Saloon and Grill** (1302 12th Ave. S., 218/749-1960, www.grandmasrestaurants.com, 11 A.M.–2 A.M. daily, $7–16). Wild Cajun chicken with wild rice is typical of their somewhat spiced-up American menu.

You can get a filling pub meal with an Iron Range twist at **Adventures** (5475 Mountain Iron Dr., 218/741-7151, www.adventuresrestaurants.com, 11 A.M.–1 A.M. daily, $8–18), from burgers to wild rice meatloaf to breaded walleye.

Despite the name, the menu at the **Saigon Cafe** (111 2nd Ave. N., 218/741-6465, 11 A.M.–8 P.M. Mon.–Thurs., 11 A.M.–9 P.M. Fri., 4–9 P.M. Sat., $6–17) is mostly Chinese, though there are Vietnamese and Thai options.

If you want a Chinese buffet head to **Jue's** (312 Chestnut St., 218/741-7695, 11 A.M.–9 P.M. Mon.–Thurs., 11 A.M.–10 P.M. Fri.–Sat., $6.25 lunch, $8.25 dinner).

The coffee shop and deli tucked into the back corner of the **Natural Harvest Food Co-op** (505 3rd St. N., 218/741-4663, www.naturalharvestcoop.com, 8 A.M.–8 P.M. Mon.–Fri., 9 A.M.–9 P.M. Sat., 10 A.M.–3 P.M. Sun., $3–5) has a deck overlooking Virginia Lake.

The **Italian Bakery** (205 1st St. S., 218/741-3464, 6 A.M.–5 P.M. Mon.–Fri., 6 A.M.–3 P.M. Sat., closed Sun., $0.50–2) opened for business in 1905 and it is still turning out Iron Range specialties like pasties and potica.

They've lost a lot of the atmosphere by adding a gift shop, but **Canelake's** (414 Chestnut St., 218/741-1557, www.canelakes.com, 9 A.M.–5 P.M. Mon.–Wed. and Fri.–Sun.,

9 A.M.–8 P.M. Thurs.) still make handmade candies as they have since 1905.

Other Practicalities

Regional tourism information is available at the Mineview in the Sky. When they are closed, stop by the **Iron Range Tourism Bureau** (403 1st St. N., 218/749-8161 or 800/777-8497, www.ironrange.org, 8 A.M.–5 P.M. Mon.–Fri., closed Sat.–Sun.) at the corner of 2nd Street North and 4th Avenue West.

You can get around with **C&M Taxi** (218/749-4000).

AROUND VIRGINIA

Mountain Iron

The first iron of the Mesabi Range was discovered here in 1890, and two years later the Mountain Iron Mine shipped the first load of ore to Duluth. This town of just under 3,000 residents—and shrinking—has since proudly proclaimed itself the "Birth Place of the Mesabi Iron Range." Mountain Iron is still home to North America's most productive active taconite mining operation, the **Minntac Mine,** which turns out 18 million tons of ore annually. You can get up close and personal with the whole process, every detail of which is overwhelmingly massive, on a free tour led by former Minntac employees. The 90-minute tours begin at an overlook of the East Pit (if you're lucky you'll get to see a blast) and follow the same route as the rocks until the finished pellets are loaded onto the trains. Along the way you will visit the half-mile-long concentrator building where the iron is separated from the rock. Tours (218/749-7300, 10 A.M. and 1 P.M. Fri. summer) depart from the Mountain Iron Senior Center on Main Street and no children under 13 years of age are allowed. You can get a quick look at the Minntac Mine, and several smaller abandoned ones, from the **Wacootah Overlook** just east of downtown across from the mine entrance.

In town, directly across from the Senior Center, is a 10-foot-tall statue of Leonidas Merritt, the man who found the "Mountain of Iron," as he called it. You can also admire some taxidermied **albino animals** nearby at Mac's Bar. One block north is an overlook of the **Mountain Iron Mine,** a National Historic Landmark, which crept right up to the edge of downtown before exhausting itself. A 1910 Baldwin steam locomotive and some old mining equipment are parked here.

Eveleth

Like Hibbing, iron ore was discovered directly under Eveleth, and in 1900, just eight years after it was founded, the city moved about a mile northeast from its original location. Two mines wrap around the town, and you can get a distant view of the work going on in the pair, now known as the Thunderbird Mine, from the **Leonidas Overlook,** a mile west of town on Fayal Road. Eveleth, like many northern Minnesota towns, has a long hockey history, so it makes sense that they have erected the **world's largest hockey stick**—110 feet, 10,000 pounds—downtown in Big Stick Plaza. A 700-pound puck waits for Paul Bunyan's slap shot.

A pilgrimage for hockey fans, the **United States Hockey Hall of Fame Museum** (801 Hat Trick Ave., 218/744-5167, www.ushockeyhallmuseum.com, 9 A.M.–5 P.M. Mon.–Sat., 10 A.M.–3 P.M. Sun. Memorial Day–Labor Day, noon–5 P.M. Fri., 9 A.M.–5 P.M. Sat., 10 A.M.–3 P.M. Sun. rest of year, $8 adults) honors more than 100 hockey greats and displays their jerseys and other memorabilia. Enthusiasts can climb aboard a zamboni or lace up their skates and head out onto the replica rink.

To see the town and its history on foot, pick up a copy of the ***Captains' Homes and Immigrant Halls*** self-guided walking tour brochure from the Laurentian Chamber of Commerce. Most of the dozen buildings are now in private hands, including the old Italian-American Hall, Slovenian Hall, Finnish Hall, and homes of the captains of industry.

Seven miles south of town on County Highway 95, just 2,000 feet from the place where the U.S. Senator died in a plane crash, is the solemn **Paul Wellstone Memorial and Historic Site.** It has short trails through the forest lined by historical markers.

SAX-ZIM BOG

More than a few Minnesota bird-watchers will tell you that the 200-square-mile Sax-Zim Bog, a mix of spruce, tamarack, and northern white cedar, is the best bird-watching site in the state. Nesting species include upland sandpiper, great gray owl, gray jay, and LeConte's sparrow. Look for snowy and northern hawk owls, northern goshawk, snow bunting, and hoary redpoll in the winter.

Even if birds aren't your thing it's a beautiful area. Black bear are common and some of the state's more elusive mammals like wolves and pine marten might be spied here. Also look for fascinating bog plants like the carnivorous pitcher plant, stemless lady's slippers, and leatherleaf.

Numerous County Highways cross the bog, which is centered on the abandoned town of Sax. One of the reasons Sax-Zim is so loved is that roadside bird-watching is excellent. A couple of noted hotspots are County Highways 202 and 203 for coniferous species like boreal chickadees and Connecticut warblers, the junction of County Highways 208 and 52 for sharp-tailed grouse, and County Highway 319 a mile and a half east of County Highway 7 for yellow rails. If you venture into the bog on foot heed any No Trespassing signs – and expect to get muddy. The DNR office in Eveleth (218/744-7447) can provide additional advice.

The family-run **Koke's Motel** (714 Fayal Rd., 218/744-4500 or 800/892-5107, $49) near downtown has simple but spotless rooms and a ski-wax room.

K&B Drive-Inn (218/744-2772, 11 A.M.–8 P.M. daily, $5–15), 1.5 miles south of town on Highway 53, still has old-fashioned carhop service, and if you want your sloppy Joe and root beer float clipped to your window in subzero weather you can—they stay open all year long, though most people use the smoke-free indoor dining area in the winter. They are quite proud of their authentic Texas BBQ menu items.

Near the Hockey Hall of Fame, **Goodfellas Bar and Grill** (501 Hat Trick Ave., 218/744-9974, 11 A.M.–midnight daily, $5–11) serves up crowd-pleasing pastas, pizzas, and burgers in a room filled with hockey memorabilia.

Gilbert

Gilbert, a small village next to Lake Ore-Be-Gone, is home to the **Iron Range Off-Highway Vehicle Recreation Area** (7196 Pettit Rd., 218/748-2207, 8 A.M.–7:30 P.M. daily May–Sept., 8 A.M.–1 hour before sunset Thurs.–Sat. rest of year), with over 30 miles of trails for motorcycles, ATVs, and 4x4 trucks, but the best reason to come here is to eat.

The **Whistling Bird** (101 Broadway N., 218/741-7544, 5 P.M.–1 A.M. Tues.–Thurs., 4 P.M.–1 A.M. Fri.–Sun., $8–25) draws diners from across the Range for its Caribbean flavorings like Jamaican jerk chicken, but they also have steak, seafood, and international pastas.

Biwabik

Named from the Ojibwe word for valuable, Biwabik was founded in 1892 when iron was discovered in the area. Within a few years the population soared to 3,000 as miners from around the world arrived to work the city's seven mines, the last of which closed in 1956. Today the population is well under 1,000 and falling fast. The number of tourists, however, continues to climb thanks to Giants Ridge, which sits five miles outside of town. Recognizing that tourism was their future, Biwabik began a Bavarian theme back in the 1980s, which now includes the city hall and most downtown buildings. Continuing in the German vein, the annual **Weihnachtsfest** (Christmas Lighting Fest), held the first Saturday in December, is one of the city's biggest events. Following a day of food, crafts, music, and fireworks, the Christmas lights are turned on in Carl Schuster Park (home to a statue celebrating **Honk the Moose** and the classic children's story he inspired) and the rest of downtown. The lights stay on through March.

Preceding the evening fireworks on the Fourth of July is the city's century-old **Calithumpian parade,** with dozens of clowns and floats judged on humor.

What began as a local ski hill in the 1950s has grown into the multifaceted **Giants Ridge Golf & Ski Resort** (6325 Wynne Creek Dr., 218/865-3000 or 800/688-7669, www.giantsridge.com), which is regularly listed as one of the Midwest's best by both ski and golf magazines. Besides the downhill runs and terrain park, snowy-season visitors can use a snowshoe trail climbing to the top of the Laurentian Divide and 35 miles of world-class cross-country ski trails—initially developed for the U.S. Ski Team—through the adjacent Superior National Forest. As for golf, The Legend and The Quarry are widely considered the state's best public golf courses. Other summer diversions include mountain biking the ski trails and letting one fly from atop the ski run on the disc golf course. Rental equipment is available for all of these activities. A shuttle connects Giants Ridge to town so you can drink safely in the half-dozen bars on Main Street.

Giants Ridge has Play & Stay packages available with hotels across the region, though you might as well stay right on-site at the excellent **Lodge at Giants Ridge** (6373 Wynne Creek Dr., 218/865-7170 or 877/442-6877, www.lodgeatgiantsridge.com, $149). Ideal for families, condominiums with 1–4 bedrooms are available, and on-site facilities include a large pool, hot tub, game room, exercise room, and ski storage/waxing room.

Next door the **Sports Dorm** (6325 Wynne Creek Dr., 218/865-3000, $70) has simple rooms with twin bunks.

Just down the road are the fancier **Villas at Giants Ridge** (6266 Giants Ridge Rd., 218/865-4155 or 800/843-7434, www.villasatgiantsridge.com, $136), with lakeside condos and cabins ranging from studios to four bedrooms—most come with full kitchens, fireplaces, and whirlpool baths. There's an outdoor pool, private beach, and tennis courts on the grounds.

The city-owned **Vermillion Trail Park Campground** (6040 Vermillion Trl., 218/865-6705, $18 with electricity), just west of town on Embarrass Lake, has 44 shady and well-spaced sites.

Alden's Restaurant (209 Main St., 218/865-6371, 7 A.M.–2 P.M. Sun.–Wed., 7 A.M.–7 P.M. Thurs., 7 A.M.–9 P.M. Fri., 7 A.M.–8 P.M. Sat., $5–17) has home-cooked meals and all-you-can-eat specials in a simple smoke-free dining room.

Vi's Pizza (215 Main St., 218/865-4164, dinner daily) is just a kitchen attached to a bar, but they do a decent thin-crust pie.

The somewhat fancy **Timbers Restaurant** (6373 Wynne Creek Dr., 218/865-7170, 8 A.M.–9 P.M., $5–21) at Giants Ridge has an outdoor deck and choices such as honey pecan walleye and fettuccini Alfredo.

SUPERIOR NATIONAL FOREST – LAURENTIAN DISTRICT

This two-part district running north of the main Iron Range communities and over toward Beaver Bay on the North Shore was named after the north–south continental divide, aka the Laurentian Divide, that runs the length of the forest. In this part of the state, rain falling south of the divide flows into the Atlantic Ocean via the Great Lakes, while to the north it heads up to Hudson Bay.

Recreation

Straddling the Laurentian Divide on Highway 53/169 four miles north of Virginia are the **Lookout Mountain Trails.** The series of loops extends 15 miles back toward a fantastic vista—great for fall-color viewing—though unfortunately you have to walk pretty far in to get away from the highway noise. There is a mile-long fitness trail and a brief interpretive trail at the front end, while geological markers in the parking lot present the area's unique geology. The 10 groomed miles are some of the area's most challenging cross-country ski trails. Another well-known ski path is the **Sturgeon River Trail,** nine miles north of Chisholm on Highway 73, with 23 mostly easy (the Jean Lake Loop is somewhat hilly) miles groomed. It's a beautiful summer hike, especially the parts that follow the river, though parts get pretty wet at times. Other worthy and easy hiking opportunities in this portion of the district include the two-mile, river-fronting **North Dark River Trail** on County Highway 688 near the Sturgeon River Trail, and the 2.5-mile **Pfeiffer Lake Trail** at its namesake campground. The latter includes a short interpretive trail. The 20 miles of the **Big Aspen Trail** are open to multiple users, including ATV, horse, and mountain bike riders in the summer and cross-country skiers in the winter. There are some steep hills leading to scenic vistas, but for the most part these three trails are pretty easy.

Several more trails lie just off the 61-mile **Superior National Forest Scenic Byway,** which runs through the forest from Aurora to Silver Bay connecting the Iron Range to the North Shore. The main trailhead of the **Bird Lake Trail** lies five miles southeast of Hoyt Lakes and leads to a rolling two-mile loop with a bog boardwalk on the east side of the namesake lake. There is also a nice picnic site here. The majority of the 11-mile trail leads back to town on the south side of the highway, and portions are too wet to hike in the summer but groomed for cross-country skiing in winter. Just south of the Cadotte Lake Campground on Forest Road 416 is the **Otto/Harris Trail** with a path linking loops around these two quiet fishing lakes. The easy 2.8-mile loop around Otto Lake stays quite close to the shore and is the most scenic part of the eight-mile trail; there are two campsites along it. At the **White Pine Picnic Area** on County Highway 2, just north of the byway, a thousand-foot interpretive trail surfaced with gravel circles through a stand of white pines where a 150-foot giant is still standing.

For an easy walk with a payoff for history buffs at the end, visit the **Longyear Drilling Site** (206 Kennedy Memorial Dr., 218/225-2344, www.boartlongyear.com) in Hoyt Lakes. Look for an information booth in the parking lot and signs to the quarter-mile path. The walk leads to the 1890 drill site where the multinational corporation got its start, with original equipment in place.

Camping

The Laurentian District has three lakeside campgrounds (218/229-8800 or 877/444-6777); all have beaches and take reservations. With 52 sites in four loops, **Whiteface Reservoir,** south of Hoyt Lakes, is one of the forest's largest camps and one of just two with electric hookups. Quieter are the 27 sites nearby at **Cadotte Lake. Pfeiffer Lake**'s 16 sites are located between Tower and Cook.

Information

The **Laurentian Ranger Station** (318 Forestry Rd., 218/229-8800, 8 A.M.–4:30 P.M. Mon.–Fri.) is located in Aurora.

CENTRAL LAKES

This is Minnesota's backyard. A quick glance at a map shows why the north-central slice of the state is where the average Minnesotan comes to unwind: Lakes are abundant (even by Minnesota standards), the forests vast, wildlife is seemingly everywhere, and the mighty Mississippi River runs right down the middle of it all. Of course, the other factor in its popularity is that you can find all of this just a couple of hours outside the Twin Cities, which is why on summer weekends it seems just about every other car on the major highways is pulling a camper or a boat—or a camper *and* a boat. Although forests cover most of the region, the southern tier is pure farm country: Garrison Keillor's fictional Lake Wobegon tales stem from his time living in a farmhouse near St. Cloud.

PLANNING YOUR TIME

This is a big area, so count on a week if you want to see all its highlights. If you are heading up from the Twin Cities, you're probably eager to hit the Northwoods, but there are several worthwhile stops before the farms turn into forest. You can try your hand at 1850s farming techniques at **Oliver H. Kelley Farm** and see how Sinclair Lewis was raised at his home in Sauk Centre. If you have an interest in Native American history, then the **Pope County Historical Museum** is worth the trip. Everyone will like **Munsinger and Clemens Gardens** in St. Cloud.

If you've brought kids or golf clubs along for the trip, you might want to set up shop in the Brainerd Lakes area for a few days. Regardless, visit the excellent **Mille Lacs Indian Museum** before heading out.

HIGHLIGHTS

Munsinger and Clemens Gardens: St. Cloud's Clemens Garden is laid out in the formal European style, while its neighbor Munsinger twists around a mature pine grove fronting the Mississippi River. It's a delightful combination (page 213).

Oliver H. Kelley Farm: Costumed farmers work the fields here using the same techniques farmers used back in the middle of the 19th century. Visitors are welcome to lend a hand (page 221).

Mille Lacs Indian Museum: The best Native American museum in Minnesota looks at Ojibwe culture, past and present (page 237).

Charles A. Lindbergh House: Lucky Lindy's modest summer home just outside Little Falls remains almost exactly as he left it before striking out to see the world, while the museum next door details his extraordinary life (page 240).

Itasca State Park: Minnesota's first state park is famous for harboring the Mississippi River's humble headwaters, but there is also a wealth of history and gorgeous scenery (page 253).

Forest History Center: Meet lumberjacks from 1900 in Camp #1 of the Northwoods Logging Company (page 271).

Savanna Portage State Park: This wild, remote, and diverse tract is a great place to really get away from it all (page 273).

Big Bog State Recreation Area: A mile-long boardwalk leads through one of the largest bogs in North America. It's a unique and impressive place, though if you don't appreciate the subtleties of ecology you may not want to make the long drive (page 276).

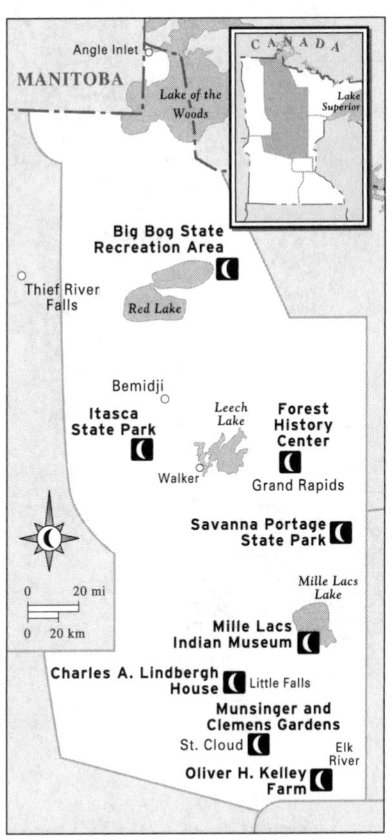

LOOK FOR [icon] TO FIND RECOMMENDED SIGHTS, ACTIVITIES, DINING, AND LODGING.

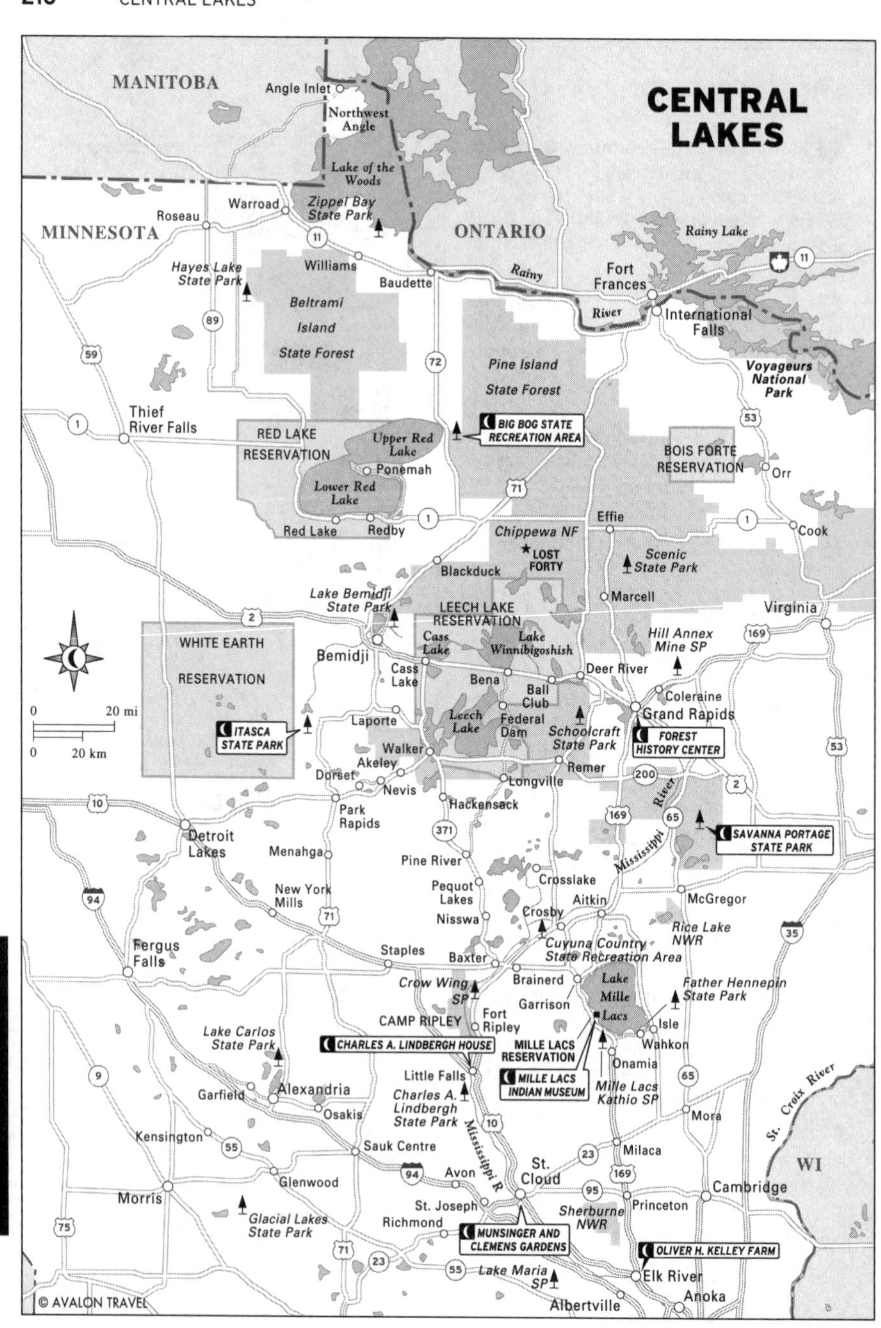

CENTRAL LAKES

North of Brainerd there is nature on a national order. **Itasca State Park,** surrounding the humble headwaters of the Mississippi River, deserves at least a full day, and the surrounding cities of Bemidji and Park Rapids are pleasant places. Next door is the Chippewa National Forest, with abundant wildlife, especially bald eagles, and weeks' worth of outdoor recreation. In and around the forest are some superb state parks such as **Savanna Portage State Park** and **Big Bog State Recreation Area.** East of the forest, Grand Rapids is still a logging town at heart, so it's an appropriate home for the excellent **Forest History Center.**

St. Cloud

The first city of consequence along the Mississippi River is home to four large colleges and universities, and students make up a big chunk of its 66,000 residents. Like any decent college town, St. Cloud is a fun place with more than its fair share of good restaurants and nightspots, and a downtown back on the upswing adds to the city's pleasant character. Because it is located in the heart of the state, St. Cloud rests at the junction of many highways (hence the chamber of commerce's "All roads lead to St. Cloud" slogan), so there is a good chance you'll be passing by.

History

St. Cloud was born in 1856 when three separate communities, the creatively named Lower Town, Middle Town, and Upper Town—each settled just a few years earlier—merged. A sawmill was the first industry, and later the city supplied and serviced the new settlements emerging in the wilderness west of the Mississippi River. It was granite, however, that put St. Cloud on the map. The first quarry opened in 1863, and eventually over 30 more were cut in the area. Minnesota granite, noted for its strength, was used to construct the State Capitol and the Cathedral of St. Paul, as well as other buildings around the nation. The solid rock features prominently in downtown St. Cloud as well. Cold Spring Granite is still one of the world's largest granite producers.

Orientation

Downtown St. Cloud lies west of the Mississippi River along St. Germain (sometimes called Mall Germain, but rarely St. Germain Street), and parking is cheap and easy to find. The St. Cloud State University (SCSU) campus is just to the south. About one quarter of the city lies east of the Mississippi River, though most recent growth is to the west around the Crossroads Center shopping mall.

St. Cloud began in a three-for-one deal, and today history has essentially repeated itself as the city has grown right up against its neighbors Waite Park (pop. 6,700) and Sauk

© TRICIA CORNELL

Downtown St. Cloud retains its historic character.

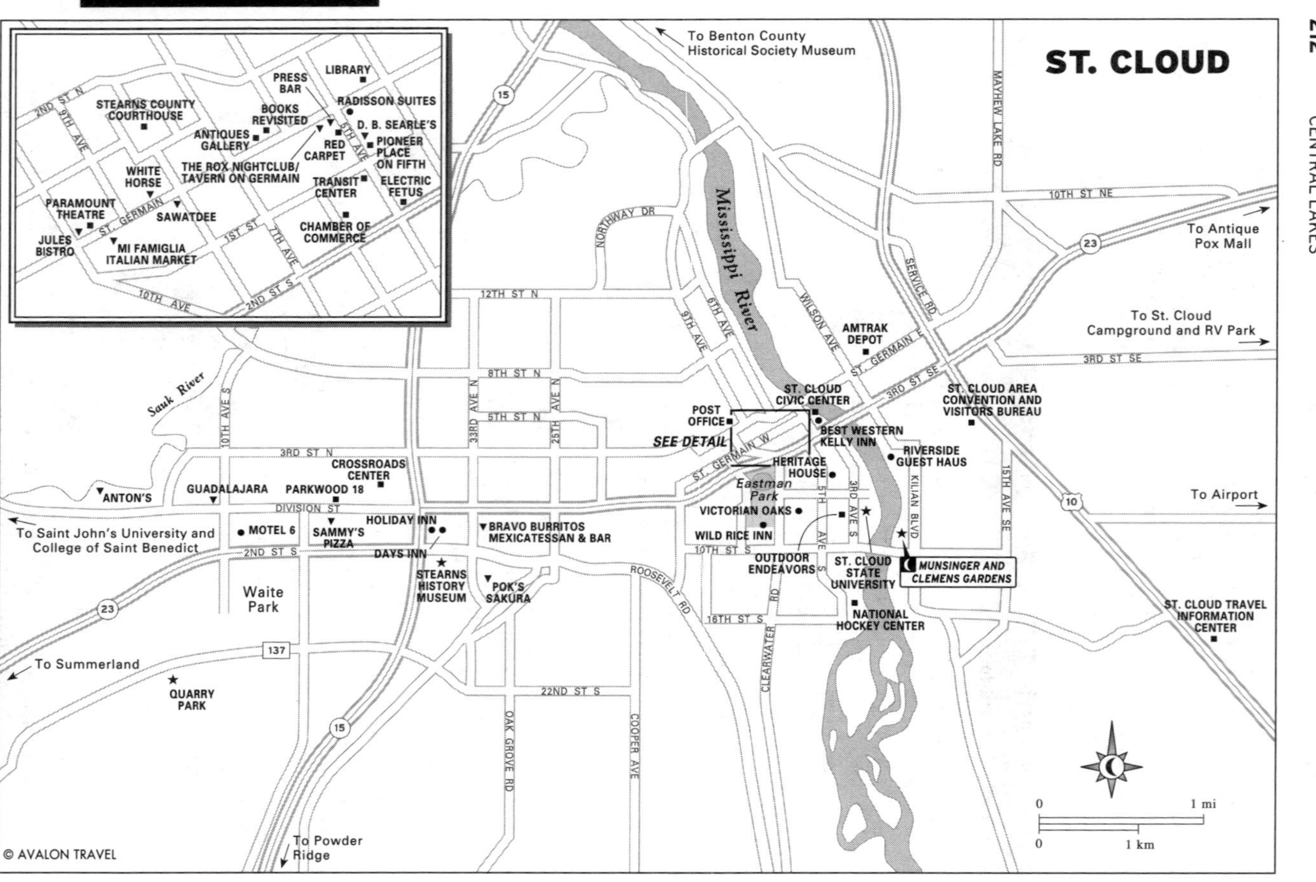

ST. CLOUD
To Benton County Historical Society Museum
MAYHEW LAKE RD
10TH ST NE
To Antique Pox Mall
To St. Cloud Campground and RV Park
3RD ST SE
To Airport
SERVICE RD
NORTHWAY DR
Mississippi River
WILSON AVE
AMTRAK DEPOT
ST. GERMAIN E
3RD ST SE
9TH AVE
6TH AVE
12TH ST N
8TH ST N
5TH ST N
3RD ST N
33RD AVE N
25TH AVE N
10TH AVE S
Sauk River
ST. CLOUD CIVIC CENTER
POST OFFICE
SEE DETAIL
BEST WESTERN KELLY INN
ST. CLOUD AREA CONVENTION AND VISITORS BUREAU
RIVERSIDE GUEST HAUS
ST. GERMAIN W
HERITAGE HOUSE
Eastman Park
5TH AVE S
3RD AVE S
KILIAN BLVD
15TH AVE SE
VICTORIAN OAKS
WILD RICE INN
10TH ST S
OUTDOOR ENDEAVORS
ST. CLOUD STATE UNIVERSITY
MUNSINGER AND CLEMENS GARDENS
NATIONAL HOCKEY CENTER
16TH ST S
CLEARWATER RD
ROOSEVELT RD
ST. CLOUD TRAVEL INFORMATION CENTER
CROSSROADS CENTER
PARKWOOD 18
GUADALAJARA
ANTON'S
DIVISION ST
HOLIDAY INN
MOTEL 6
SAMMY'S PIZZA
BRAVO BURRITOS
MEXICATESSAN & BAR
DAYS INN
2ND ST S
STEARNS HISTORY MUSEUM
POK'S SAKURA
To Saint John's University and College of Saint Benedict
Waite Park
To Summerland
QUARRY PARK
22ND ST S
OAK GROVE RD
COOPER AVE
To Powder Ridge
0
1 mi
0
1 km
© AVALON TRAVEL
PRESS BAR
LIBRARY
RADISSON SUITES
2ND ST N
9TH AVE
STEARNS COUNTY COURTHOUSE
BOOKS REVISITED
D. B. SEARLE'S
ANTIQUES GALLERY
RED CARPET
5TH AVE
PIONEER PLACE ON FIFTH
WHITE HORSE
THE ROX NIGHTCLUB/ TAVERN ON GERMAIN
TRANSIT CENTER
ELECTRIC FETUS
PARAMOUNT THEATRE
ST. GERMAIN
SAWATDEE
JULES BISTRO
MI FAMIGLIA ITALIAN MARKET
1ST ST
7TH AVE
CHAMBER OF COMMERCE
10TH AVE
2ND ST S

© TRICIA CORNELL

Munsinger and Clemens Gardens are an urban oasis.

Rapids (pop. 13,000). The latter still has its own personality, but you can only tell the former apart by the "Welcome to Waite Park" sign on Division Street and the confusing change in addresses. St. Cloud is also at the junction of three counties, and while it is the Stearns County seat, parts of the city also lie in Benton and Sherburne Counties.

SIGHTS

☾ Munsinger and Clemens Gardens

The most pleasant way to spend an hour—or half a day—is strolling through these two distinct but complementary gardens (320/255-7216, www.munsingerclemens.com, 7 A.M.–10 P.M. daily spring, summer, and fall, closed winter, free admission), on the eastern side of the river, where 13th Street SE crosses Killian Boulevard SE and Riverside Drive. Clemens Gardens are laid out in the formal European style and the nearly 1,200 rose bushes, the 24-foot Renaissance Fountain (the tallest in any Minnesota public garden), and the English-style White Garden are the highlights of the six geometrically precise plots. On the east bank of the Mississippi River are the wilder Munsinger Gardens, first planted in the 1930s. The flowers, bushes, and lily pond lie at the foot of a mature pine grove, creating a rather shady floral experience. You can continue a Mississippi stroll to the north through **Riverside Park** where geese and ducks congregate, or you can stop at the **Clemens Gardens Gift Shop** (1399 Killian Blvd., 320/258-0381, May–Oct.) for ice cream, coffee, snacks, and a kitschy garden-related trinket.

Museums

The well-executed **Stearns History Museum** (235 33rd Ave. S., 320/253-8424 or 866/253-8424, www.stearns-museum.org, 10 A.M.–5 P.M. Mon.–Sat., noon–5 P.M. Sun., $5 adults, $2 children 5 and over) covers pre-settlement times to the present. The two most popular stops are the replica granite quarry and the mint 1919 Pan automobile, which was manufactured in St. Cloud.

Kids will surely get a kick out of the

LAKE WOBEGON

Located about 20 miles north-northwest of St. Cloud and eight miles from Millet, near Holdingford, the "Gateway to Central Minnesota" sits on the western shore of its namesake lake. The Mist County seat is a one-traffic-light town with quiet streets lined by small white frame houses. Time seems to pass slower in Lake Wobegon than in other places and it embodies a stereotypical Americana that only exists in legend, but still rings true to countless people.*

Up until recent years the only outsiders who came to this small (pop. 942) town on the edge of the prairie were those who knew somebody living here or made a wrong turn off the highway and got lost. These days, ever since local boy Garrison Keillor made it big by sharing news and personal observations about his hometown ("Where all the women are strong, all the men are good-looking, and all the children are above average") on his *A Prairie Home Companion* radio show, a great many people want to come and see what it is all about. Those who find it – Lake Wobegon is still not on maps due to a series of surveyors' errors that omitted the fifty-square-mile quadrangle that is Mist County – rarely stay very long, often not even getting out of the car, and they almost always find themselves thankful they don't live here.

HISTORY

For a town where so little out of the ordinary happens, Lake Wobegon has a long, interesting history. A few meandering voyageurs had previously stumbled up the shallow Lake Wobegon River (really just a small stream) from the larger Sauk River to what they called Lac Malheur (Misfortune Lake), though the first recorded history of the area is from 1836 when the Italian Count Carlo Pallavicini camped for a night on the lakeshore. Upon reaching the lake, Pallavicini momentarily believed that he had found the headwaters of the Mississippi River, but he quickly realized that this couldn't possibly be correct. It wasn't until much later that he learned Henry Schoolcraft had identified Lake Itasca as the true source four years earlier. In 1850 a small band of Unitarian missionaries from Boston came in a failed attempt to convert the Ojibwe to Christianity using interpretive dance. The next year Henry Francis Watt, a member of that original party, convinced Benjamin Bayfield, a wealthy New England coffee broker, to return with him to found a city on the lake. New Albion, as the investors named it, though built on a swamp in the middle of nowhere, was promoted as the Boston of the West and attracted many speculators who bet that the St. Paul & Manitoba Railroad would pass through – they even built a train depot and laid out an extra wide Main Street in anticipation. The town almost went bust during the Panic of 1857, and the railroad never arrived because the officials couldn't find it on the map. A spur line was mistakenly built in 1885, but it stopped just short of the town when the error was discovered. Though the original settlers were New Englanders, the town grew on the strength of Norwegian Lutherans and German Catholics. The Norwegians had hoped to settle along Lake Agassiz in North Dakota, but found out that it was a prehistoric lake long since vanished. The Germans were initially headed to the Moorhead area, but misread their maps and stopped here – once they discovered the error they stayed put rather than admit their mistake. The Norwegians pushed for changing the name to Lake Wobegon, which, in the

Ojibwe language, means "we sat all day in the rain waiting for [you]."

SIGHTS

The lovely spring-fed Lake Wobegon covers 678.2 acres and is the town's main attraction. A sandy **beach** with a floating dock to dive off lies just two blocks down from Ralph's Pretty Good Grocery, and the best fishing, any local will tell you, is in weedy Sunfish Bay. The **Statue of the Unknown Norwegian** has looked toward the lake from the bend in Main Street since it was carved in 1896. There wasn't enough money to build a pedestal for the granite lad so the plaque honoring the town's early Norwegian settlers that belongs with the statue is on display in the **Mist County Historical Society Museum.** The assorted historical artifacts include a display of old underwear and Norwegian crafts. The most unique item on display is the small, black Lake Wobegon Runestone, which, like the more credible and famous Kensington Runestone in Alexandria, purports to prove that Vikings explored the area in 1381. This block, discovered along County Highway 2 in 1921 by a Professor Oftedahl (some say it was Ostenwald) from Chicago, reads "8 of [us] stopped & stayed awhile to visit & have [coffee] & a short nap. Sorry [you] weren't here. Well, that's about [it] for now." The museum is in the musty basement of the town hall and is open normal business hours; get the key from the town clerk. Admission is free. Many fans of the radio show want to get a look at the 1878 **Our Lady of Perpetual Responsibility Catholic Church,** which sits on McKinley Street just off Main – you can't miss it. The opulent interior has marble pillars, gold-flecked mosaics in the maroon tile floor, and ornate stained-glass windows tucked inside its large stone columns and arches. It's a long, steep climb to the top of **Adams Hill** behind the school, but you will be rewarded with a panoramic view of the town and lake. If you are arriving or departing from the east you can stop at the **Pet-the-Tame-Deer Park** along U.S. Highway 10.

PRACTICALITIES

If for some reason you need to stay, your only option is **Art's Bait & Night O'Rest Motel,** on the lake outside of town; rooms are cheap but it is not really recommended. The small, aging cabins have uncomfortable furniture, exposed nails on the floor, and the owner is notoriously cranky. Locals crowd the **Chatterbox Café** on Main Street for home cooking away from home or a bottomless cup of coffee ($0.85 cents for the morning or $1.25 all day). Pot roast and tuna hot dish are the specialties, while the hot beef sandwich, liverwurst sandwich, and BLT are other typical menu items. No matter what you order you'll get a heaping platter for just a few dollars. The closest thing to entertainment in town is listening to the pre-rock 'n' roll classics on the orange-and-purple jukebox at the **Sidetrack Tap,** a dark, stale beer-scented dive on Main Street where you'll feel right at home if you like to talk about fishing or transmissions. The town's biggest bash is summer's **Toast N' Jelly Days,** which has a toast toss, a dunk-the-pastor booth, and a hotly contested creative Jell-O contest. The winner of the toast-cooking contest wins the coveted "Toast of the Town" award. On **Flag Day** (June 14th) Wobegonians don red, white, and blue caps and form a living flag.

***In case you didn't already know, Lake Wobegon is not a real place. This all sprang from Keillor's imagination.**

horse-drawn school bus fitted with skis at the little **Benton County Historical Museum** (218 1st St. N., 320/253-9614, 10 A.M.–4 P.M. Mon.–Fri., free admission), across the river in Sauk Rapids.

St. Cloud State University

With around 17,000 students, SCSU is Minnesota's second-largest public university. The main diversion here is visiting the pair of small art galleries. The **Kiehle Gallery** (320/308-4283, 8 A.M.–4 P.M. Mon.–Fri., closed Sat.–Sun., free admission) is open during the school year while the **Atwood Gallery** (320/255-2205, 8 A.M.–7 P.M. Mon.–Fri., 7 A.M.–5 P.M. Sat.–Sun. during the school year, closed Sat.–Sun. summer, free admission) stays open year-round.

Granite

For a look at the industry that built St. Cloud, visit 643-acre **Quarry Park** (County Rd. 137, 320/255-6172, 8 A.M.–30 min. after sunset daily, $4 per car). Hiking and mountain biking trails lead past 30 abandoned granite quarries last worked in the 1950s. Today the deep pits are filled with water, and many are stocked with trout. Swimming is allowed in one (it's a half-mile walk there), and local dive shops offer scuba outings in another of the crystal-clear pits. Some areas are reserved for rock climbing; purchase a permit at the gatehouse when you enter.

ENTERTAINMENT

St. Cloud has a rich and growing arts scene and visitors should never lack options. The best source for what's on is the "Up Next" section of Thursday's *St. Cloud Times.*

The beautifully renovated 1921 **Paramount Theatre** (913 St. Germain W., 320/259-5463, www.paramountarts.org) is the focal point of the city's arts scene. Both resident companies and touring acts perform in the ornate theater, and the building is home to a host of organizations, including the **St. Cloud Symphony Orchestra, The Troupe Theatre,** the **St. Cloud Civic Theatre,** the **Great River Educational Theatre,** and more. Beyond the performing arts, the **Visual Arts Center** offers classes and support for local artists, while the **Paramount Gallery** offers them a place to display and sell their work.

© TRICIA CORNELL

The Paramount Theatre is St. Cloud's arts hub.

Pioneer Place on Fifth (22 5th Ave. S., 320/203-0331 or 800/851-3935, www.ppfive.com), an elegant structure originally built as an Elks Lodge in 1913, mounts seven or eight shows a season by professional theaters from St. Cloud, the Twin Cities, and beyond, as well as the resident Pioneer Players.

St. Cloud State University (320/308-3223 for music, 320/308-3229 for theater and dance, www.stcloudstate.edu) hosts a full range of theater, arts, and music. Not too far west of St. Cloud, the **College of Saint Benedict** and **Saint John's University** jointly run a wonderful fine-arts series (320/363-5777, www.csbsju.edu/finearts) that brings an eclectic mix of music, dance, and theater groups.

Just about once a month, **Art Crawl St. Cloud** (www.www.artcrawlstcloud.com) organizes an evening of art and eats up and down St. Germain.

You'll find mainstream movies at the

Parkwood 18 (1533 Division St., 320/253-4328, www.marcustheatres.com) in Waite Park.

Nightlife

Around a dozen downtown bars and clubs put bands and/or DJs on stage, most near the junction of St. Germain and 5th Avenue. The biggest rock, reggae, and blues bands play the neon-happy **Red Carpet** (11 5th Ave. S., 320/251-4047, www.redcarpetnightclub.com), and there are also comedians some nights. You've also got nine bars, a martini lounge, and outdoor deck spread over three stories to explore for other diversions.

Around the corner the **Press Bar** (502 St. Germain W., 320/251-5911, 5 P.M.–2 A.M. Mon.–Thurs., 7 P.M.–2 A.M. Fri.–Sat., closed Sun.) is another St. Cloud music landmark graced mostly by heavy metal and hard rock bands.

The Rox Nightclub (506 St. Germain St., 320/259-6807, www.roxtav.com) hosts a huge variety of bands, from bluegrass to rock to hip hop.

Acoustic musicians take the stage at the mellower **Tavern on Germain** (506 St. Germain W., 320/259-6807, www.roxtav.com).

For late night eats, you can satisfy just about any appetite at **White Horse** (809 St. Germain W., 320/257-7775, www.whitehorsemn.com, 11 A.M.–2 A.M. Mon.–Sat., 2 P.M.–2 A.M. Sun., $10–17), which serves pizza, wings, chili, Thai dishes, and more until midnight.

Spectator Sports

The **St. Cloud State Huskies** compete in a full slate of athletics, but it's the Division 1 men's hockey team that gets all the attention. Home ice is the National Hockey Center, which seats 5,763 screaming fans—though getting tickets (320/255-2137 or 877/727-8849, www.stcloudstate.edu/athletics) is no small feat.

The **St. Cloud River Bats** play in the Northwoods League, made up of Division I college baseball players who get a minor-league experience while keeping their college eligibility. Home games are played at **Joe Faber Field** (5001 Veterans Dr., 320/240-9798, www.riverbats.com, $6).

SHOPPING

St. Cloud is the commercial hub of central Minnesota, so you can get just about anything you need here. The main shopping mall is **Crossroads Center** (4101 Division St., www.crossroadscenter.com, 10 A.M.–9 P.M. Mon.–Sat., 11 A.M.–6 P.M. Sun.), but the commercial build-up sprawls along most of Division Street and beyond.

Get away from the malls by strolling the few historic downtown blocks on St. Germain. **Antiques Gallery** (619 St. Germain W., 320/202-9068, www.antiquesgallerysc.com, 10 A.M.–4 P.M. Mon.–Sat., closed Sun.) has a good selection downtown, but the **Antique Pox Mall** (5114 Marson Dr., 320/251-2550, 10 A.M.–5 P.M. Mon.–Sat., 11 A.M.–4 P.M. Sun.) hidden away in Sauk Rapids, four miles east along Highway 23, is much bigger.

Books Revisited (607 St. Germain W., 320/259-7959, www.booksrevisited.com, 10 A.M.–6 P.M. Mon.–Fri., 10 A.M.–5 P.M. Sat.) has an outstanding used selection and a second location at Crossroads Center.

St. Cloud also has its own outpost of the Minneapolis institution, the **Electric Fetus** (28 5th Ave. S., 320/251-2569, www.electricfetus.com, 9 A.M.–9 P.M. Mon.–Fri., 9 A.M.–8 P.M. Sat., 11 A.M.–6 P.M. Sun.). Find music, local art, and a few funky tchotchkes.

RECREATION

The **Beaver Islands Trail** roughly follows the Mississippi River south from downtown for three paved miles, though it only has river views along the northern half, and even these are pretty limited.

While St. Cloud isn't quite resort territory yet, you can get a taste of it at **Summerland** (Hwy. 23 E., 320/251-0940, www.summerlandfunpark.com, 11 A.M.–10 P.M. daily), with mini golf, batting cages, a waterslide, go karts, and more fun stuff.

Outdoor Endeavors (720 4th Ave. S., 320/308-3772, www.stcloudstate.edu/campusrec/outdoorendeavors, 3–8 P.M. Mon.–Wed. and Fri., 9 A.M.–2 P.M. Sat.) in Halenbeck Hall at SCSU has canoe and kayak rentals and offers shuttle service on both the Mississippi and Sauk Rivers.

The 4.3 miles of groomed cross-country ski trails at **Quarry Park** (320/255-6172, 8 A.M.–11 P.M. daily during ski season, $4 per car) are lighted for night skiing.

Downhill skiers have 15 runs and a tubing hill at **Powder Ridge** (320/398-5295 or 800/348-7734, www.powderridge.com), the highest dropping 290 feet. Powder Ridge is located 16 miles south of St. Cloud on Highway 15; then follow the signs. Hours depend on conditions, so call ahead.

Eagle Trace (1100 Main St., Clearwater, 320/558-4653 or 800/842-4386, www.eagletracegolf.com), with 18 holes tucked up against the Mississippi River, is both the most challenging and most scenic golf course in the vicinity.

ACCOMMODATIONS

Hotels

The **Motel 6** (815 1st St. S., 320/253-7070 or 800/446-8356, www.motel6.com, $50) out in Waite Park isn't fancy, but it's a good value.

The **Holiday Inn** (75 37th Ave. S., 320/253-9000 or 800/465 4329, www.holidayinn.com, $95), with several pools and whirlpools, a sauna, fitness center, volleyball court, and more indoors, is a good choice for families.

So is the **Days Inn** (70 37th Ave. S., 320/253-4444 or 800/329-7466, www.daysinn.com, $55), which has a kiddie pool, hot tub, and two-story waterslide.

St. Cloud's fanciest hotel is the downtown **Radisson Suites** (404 St. Germain W., 320/654-1661 or 800/395-7046, www.radisson.com/hotels/st_cloud, $129). Facilities include a pool, whirlpool, sauna, and fitness center, plus its 103 well-appointed suites are connected to the Civic Center by a skywalk.

Also joined to the Civic Center is the less flashy **Best Western Kelly Inn** (100 4th Ave. S., 320/253-0606, www.bestwesternstcloud.com, $80). With similar amenities, their rooms are a much better value.

Bed-and-Breakfasts

Victorian Oaks (404 9th Ave. S., 320/202-1404 or 866/842-6257, www.vicoaks.com, $90–140) is an 1891 Second Empire house—the city's finest in it's time—that's just as stunning inside as out, from the extensive woodwork to the antique furnishings. The floor plan is original, so the bathrooms are shared between the three guestrooms.

The 1904 Queen Anne Victorian **Heritage House** (402 6th Ave. S., 320/656-5818 or 888/547-4422, www.heritagehousebbmn.com, $100) near the SCSU campus is fancy but homey. The redbrick building features stained-glass windows, hand-carved woodwork, a wraparound porch, and octagonal tower.

Overlooking the Mississippi River, not far from Munsinger and Clemens Gardens, is the **Riverside Guest Haus** (912 Riverside Dr. SE, 320/252-2134 or 888/252-2134, www.riversideguesthaus.com, $150). The River Room, with a limited Mississippi view, is the favorite choice, but the real gem is the Garden Room, with garden-encased balcony. Each has a private bath.

A good value halfway between downtown and St. Cloud State, near Lake George, is **Wild Rice Inn** (1016 8th St. S., 320/259-0178, www.wildriceinn.com, $62–89). This 1891 yellow-brick house has two guest rooms with private bathrooms.

Campgrounds

The **St. Cloud Campground & RV Park** (2491 2nd St. SE, 320/251-4463 or 800/690-7045, www.stcloudcampground.com, $31.95 full hookup) is a typical family-style RV park and the only camping available right near the city. It has 102 largely shadeless pull-through sites.

FOOD

American

Anton's (2001 Frontage Rd. N., 320/253-3611, www.antonsrestaurant.com, 11 A.M.–10 P.M. Mon.–Thurs., 11 A.M.–11 P.M. Fri.–Sat., 4–9 P.M. Sun., $13–25) in Waite Park opened as a speakeasy during Prohibition. They are still going strong in the same riverside log cabin, and though they have added on considerably to meet demand, the fun Northwoods atmosphere remains intact. Seafood is their specialty, but they also serve up a flavorful steak.

D. B. Searle's (18 5th Ave. S., 320/253-0655, www.dbsearles.com, 5–9 P.M. Mon.–Thurs., 5–9:30 P.M. Fri.–Sat., bar only 5–9 P.M. Sun., $7–20) fills four floors of one of the city's most beautiful historic buildings. Burgers, grilled salmon, shrimp scampi, and filet mignon are representative of the broad menu.

Bo Diddley's (216 6th Ave. S., 320/255-9811, 10 A.M.–2 A.M. daily, $3–7) serves up subs and pita pockets plus dozens of microbrewed and imported beers in a simple pub-style atmosphere.

Jules Bistro (921 St. Germain, 320/252-7125, www.julesbistrostcloud.com, 10 A.M.–10 P.M. Mon.–Thurs., 10 A.M.–11 P.M. Fri.–Sat., closed Sun., $4–10) is a refreshing change from the hunk-of-meat-heavy dining elsewhere, though the menu is more ladies-who-lunch than French bistro. There's a long list of creative sandwiches and salads, as well as 12-inch pizzas topped with feta, goat cheese, and the like.

Veranda Lounge (22 5th Ave. S., 320/203-0331, www.verandalounge.com, 6:30 A.M.–midnight Mon.–Fri., 8 A.M.–midnight Sat.–Sun.) occupies the lobby and porch of the Pioneer Place on Fifth theater, but is a great casual dining location in its own right, with breakfast burritos, and soups and sandwiches for lunch. In the evening, it morphs into a swank wine bar with live music.

Asian

Sawatdee (800 W. St. Germain, 320/240-1135, www.sawatdee.com, 11 A.M.–9 P.M. Sun.–Thurs., 11 A.M.–10 P.M. Fri.–Sat., $7–17), a branch of the successful Twin Cities Thai empire, has one of the most difficult-to-decide menus in town because it's all so good.

Hong Kong (37 33rd Ave. N., 320/251-5907, 11 A.M.–9 P.M. Mon.–Sat., closed Sun., $5–13) is hidden away just off Division Street. The atmosphere is a little fancier, and the menu has all the standard Chinese-American options plus a few fancy tropical drinks.

Pok's Sakura (266 33rd Ave. S., 320/656-0044, 11 A.M.–8 P.M. Tues.–Thurs., 11 A.M.–9 P.M. Fri.–Sat., closed Sun.–Mon., $5–12) serves St. Cloud's most popular sushi, as well as other Japanese dishes.

Italian

Mi Famiglia Italian Market (912 St. Germain W., 320/217-6002, 10 A.M.–6 P.M. daily) is a delightful little deli selling Italian cheeses, sausages, and other groceries, as well as gelato, sweets, coffee, and pastry. Right next door **Mi Famiglia Ristorante** (912 St. Germain W., 320/217-6000, 11 A.M.–10 P.M. Mon.–Fri., 4–10 P.M. Sat., closed Sun., $11) serves hearty Italian American favorites.

Students and families love the huge pizzas, sandwiches, and pasta dishes at **Sammy's Pizza** (58 Division St. W., 320/252-4540, www.pizzasince1956.com, 11 A.M.–2 P.M. and 5–9 P.M. Mon.–Thurs., $8–11) in Waite Park. The buffet is an especially good deal when you're famished.

Mexican

The only authentic Mexican in town is dished up at **Guadalajara** (1001 Division St., 320/654-9020, 11 A.M.–10 P.M. daily, $6–15) in Waite Park. Everything on the massive menu is excellent, in part because they make their own chorizo, guacamole, and other staples.

Bravo Burritos Mexicatessan & Bar (68 33rd Ave. S., 320/252-5441, 11 A.M.–9 P.M. Sun.–Thurs., 11 A.M.–10 P.M. Fri.–Sat., $5–11) serves a fantastic burrito stuffed with your choice of eight meats. Even if you order the mini you're going to be full.

INFORMATION AND SERVICES

Tourist Information

There are several places to pick up maps and brochures and ask questions: the **St. Cloud Area Convention and Visitors Bureau** (525 U.S. 10 S., 320/251-4170 or 800/264-2940, www.granitecountry.com, 8 A.M.–4:30 P.M. Mon.–Fri., closed Sat.–Sun.), the **St. Cloud Area Chamber of Commerce** (110 6th Ave. S., 320/251-2940, www.stcloudareachamber.com, 7:30 A.M.–4:30 P.M. Mon.–Fri., closed Sat.–Sun.), and the **St. Cloud Travel Information Center and Rest Stop,** just to the south on U.S. Highway 10, which has statewide travel information.

Media

The daily ***St. Cloud Times*** (www.sctimes.com) does a good job of local coverage, but for news from around the state and beyond they just can't compete with either of the Twin Cities papers, both of which are available.

It's worth checking in to see what's playing on **KVSC** (88.1 FM, www.kvsc.org), SCSU's student radio station, since it could change from Marvin Gaye to the Meat Puppets at the top of the hour.

Post Office

St. Cloud's main post office (915 2nd St. N., 320/251-8220, 8:30 A.M.–5 P.M. Mon.–Fri., closed Sat.–Sun.) is downtown.

Internet Access

Besides the **St. Cloud Public Library** (405 St. Germain W., 320/650-2500, 10 A.M.–9 P.M. Mon.–Thurs., 10 A.M.–6 P.M. Fri., 10 A.M.–5 P.M. Sat., closed Sun.), visitors can get on the Web at **Copy Central** (211 5th Ave. S., 320/257-2679, 7 A.M.–7 P.M. Mon.–Fri., 10 A.M.–4 P.M. Sat., closed Sun.) and **FedEx Office Print and Ship Center** (2423 Division St., 320/259-1224, www.fedex.com, 6 A.M.–10 P.M. Mon.–Fri., 9 A.M.–10 P.M. Sat., closed Sun.).

GETTING THERE

The **St. Cloud Regional Airport** (1550 45th Ave. SE, 320/255-7292, www.stcloudairport.com) is four miles east of downtown on County Highway 7. **Delta Airlines** (800/221-1212) makes the short hop to the Twin Cities up to five times a day.

Amtrak (800/872-7245, www.amtrak.com) heads west at 12:40 A.M. and east at 5:14 A.M. from the historic depot (555 East St. Germain). Tickets to or from St. Paul cost $11.

Greyhound (800/231-2222, www.greyhound.com) buses stop at the city's downtown Transit Center (510 1st St. S., 320/251-5411) three times a day in each direction on the Minneapolis–Fargo run. One-way to Minneapolis is $14.

Lakes Express (218/855-6973 or 866/955-6973, www.lakesexpress.com, $35) and **Executive Express** (320/253-2226 or 888/522-9899, www.executiveexpress.com) run shuttles to the Minneapolis–St. Paul International Airport from the Holiday Inn (75 37th Ave. S.) up to six times a day.

GETTING AROUND

St. Cloud's **Metro Bus** buses offer pretty good coverage. Most routes converge at the downtown Transit Center (510 1st St. S., 320/251-7433, www.stcloudmtc.com). The regular fare is $0.90 plus $0.25 for a transfer. There is a fare-free zone downtown, but it's so small you might as well just walk.

The free **Downtown Trolley** (10 A.M.–6 P.M. Mon.–Sat. June–Sept.) regularly runs between downtown and the Munsinger and Clemens Gardens.

If you need a taxi there's **Yellow Cab** (320/251-5050), and if you need a car **Avis** (2239 Roosevelt Rd., 320/252-4012, 8 A.M.–5:30 P.M. Mon.–Fri., 9 A.M.–noon Sat., 10 A.M.–noon Sun.), **Enterprise** (3630 Division St. W., 320/240-9000, 10 A.M.–4 P.M. Mon.–Fri., 9 A.M.–noon Sat.), and **Hertz** (3104 Division St., 320/229-0409, 7:30 A.M.–6 P.M. Mon.–Fri., 9 A.M.–noon Sat.) are there for you.

AROUND ST. CLOUD

Lake Maria State Park

Lake Maria (ma-RYE-uh) State Park (11411 Clementa Ave. NW, Monticello, 763/878-2325, www.dnr.state.mn.us/state_parks/lake_maria), a 1,590-acre remnant of the Big Woods—a maple, oak, and basswood forest that once spread across southeast Minnesota—is one of the nearest wilderness experiences to the Twin Cities. While many people are drawn by the secluded campsites and cabins, most of which overlook the 10 small lakes scattered among the rolling, wooded hills, Lake Maria is worth a visit even if you just want to take it easy. There is a lakeside picnic site, and the drive to the back end of the park is very beautiful. This is also a great spot for viewing spring wildflowers and fall colors. The park is known for its population of state-threatened Blanding's turtles—one of four kinds of turtle residing here—easily identifiable by the bright yellow spots on its shell.

The 14 miles of hilly hiking trails (six open to horseback riders) weave a web of interconnected loops across the eastern half of the park. The 5.5-mile **Big Woods Loop** passes more lakes than any other trail, and the three-mile **Anderson Hill Loop** offers a wonderful hilltop vista and has some prairie for variety. The 1.5-mile **Kettle and Kame Trail** is the most rugged trail in the park, while two-mile **Bjorkland Lake Trail** is the most popular. Each winter the trails are groomed for cross-country skiing, a three-mile path is packed down for winter hiking, the cabins are stocked with firewood, and a skating rink is lighted in the evening. Snowshoes are available for rent, as are canoes in the summer. None of the three log cabins or 17 backpack campsites is more than a mile's walk from the parking area. The simple cabins have bunks for six people, a table, benches, and a wood-fired stove, but no other facilities.

Oliver H. Kelley Farm

Oliver Hudson Kelley, originally from Boston, moved to this Mississippi River homestead two miles south of Elk River in 1850 and taught himself to farm. He quickly became an expert in the emerging field of scientific farming and in 1867 founded the first successful national farmers' organization, the Order of the Patrons of Husbandry (better known as the Grange), to share new ideas and information among farmers. The Minnesota State Historical Society has revived his farm (15788 Kelley Farm Rd., 10 A.M.–5 P.M. Wed.–Sat., noon–5 P.M. Sun. June–Aug., 10 A.M.–5 P.M. Sat., noon–5 P.M. Sun. May, Sept., and Oct., $8 adults), now a National Historic Landmark, and hires costumed guides to work the fields using methods from the 1850s to 1870s. The authenticity is impressive in all aspects, right down to the many nonhybridized crops the family planted and unique livestock breeds they raised. The staff can answer just about any questions you have, including how it would be done today, or show you how to do something if you want to give it a try. There's ox-driven plowing in the spring and threshing in the fall, while the pigs always need slopping. You can also try your hand at the women's work (remember, this is the 19th century) such as churning butter and canning vegetables. Beyond the fields are a pair of nature trails through a restored prairie and along the wooded banks of the Mississippi, while the visitors center (763/441-6896, same hours as farm plus 9 A.M.–4 P.M. Mon.–Fri., free admission) has videos and exhibits on the Kelley family, the Grange, and 19th-century farming methods. Many special events take place here throughout the year, and some, such as an old-fashioned Independence Day celebration and a barn dance, don't involve farming.

Sherburne National Wildlife Refuge

Though just an hour outside Minneapolis, the 30,700-acre **Sherburne National Wildlife Refuge** (17076 293rd Ave., Zimmerman, 763/389-3323, www.fws.gov/midwest/sherburne) is a pretty wild place. The refuge was established in 1965, and much effort has been put into restoring the wetlands, prairie openings, and oak savanna straddling the St. Francis River. Well over 200 species of bird have been recorded here, and visitors have a good chance of spying bald eagle, ruffed grouse, wild turkey, trumpeter swan, sandhill crane, common loon, and many neotropical migrants such as scarlet tanager and chestnut-sided warbler. Mammals like beaver, otter, and fox are here, but harder to find. Your best bet for seeing the varied landscapes and spotting critters is along the 7.3-mile **Prairie's Edge Wildlife Drive** (Apr.–Oct.). Along the way you'll pass lakes and ponds filled with waterfowl, wildlife observation decks with powerful spotting scopes, a wildflower demonstration area, informational panels, and three easy half-mile trails. Near the refuge headquarters (8 A.M.–4:30 P.M. Mon.–Fri.), along County Highway 9, are two longer hiking trails. Both the three-mile **Mahnomen Trail** and five-mile **Blue Hill Trail** are a series of interconnected loops winding mostly through oak woods with some oak savanna and prairie openings too. Neither is difficult. Canoes are allowed on limited sections of the St. Francis River and Battle Brook. The **Sand Dunes State Forest** (763/878-2325) immediately south of the refuge has a primitive campground on Ann Lake.

Alexandria and Vicinity

From Norse to Native American to the Nobel Prize, there is a lot of history in this lake-filled region.

Big Ole, a 28-foot-tall Viking dressed in full battle regalia, greets visitors to Alexandria. To some residents, the slogan "Alexandria, Birthplace of America" displayed prominently on his shield is no joke. Despite overwhelming evidence to the contrary, many steadfastly believe that the famous Kensington Runestone is authentic, and the local chamber of commerce shamelessly promotes this view to keep the curious crowds coming. Even without the stone, Douglas County's 247 lakes and roughly 50 resorts draw thousands of visitors a week during the summer, and most of them pass through "Alex," as the nearly 12,000 locals call their home.

SIGHTS

Alexandria's famous rock is displayed in the **Runestone Museum** (206 Broadway, 320/763-3160, www.runestonemuseum.org, 9 A.M.–5 P.M. Mon.–Fri., 9 A.M.–4 P.M. Sat., closed Sun. May–Oct., 10 A.M.–4 P.M. Mon.–Sat., closed Sun. rest of year, $6 adults). The Viking section of the museum promotes, rather than examines, the stone's authenticity, even going so far as to show invented maps of the travel route, but this is actually a small part of a rather good museum. Other historical displays include an excellent Native American collection with lots of beadwork and taxidermy from around the state. Out back the collection of 19th-century buildings, grandly named **Fort Alexandria,** includes a log cabin and one-room schoolhouse, plus a large building full of antique tractors.

Behind the Runestone Museum, between Lake Henry and Lake Winona, is the **Minnesota Lakes Maritime Museum** (205 3rd Ave. W., 320/759-1114, www.mnlakes-maritime.org, 10 A.M.–5 P.M. Tues.–Fri., 10 A.M.–4 P.M. Sat., noon–4 P.M. Sun. May–Oct.). Get up close and personal with beautifully crafted boats from many Minnesota manufacturers, but especially the Alexandria Boat Works, for which they have one example from each decade, starting with the inaugural 1902 model through the 1950s when the company stopped production. There are also displays on fishing and resort history.

The two-ton **Big Ole** stands overlooking Broadway near the Runestone Museum. He was built of fiberglass in 1964 to accompany the runestone to the World's Fair in New York for the "Minnesota, Birthplace of America" display. An equally huge **replica runestone** sits east of town along Highway 27 (take 6th Avenue E. if you want to stop and take a closer look).

The Douglas County Historical Society offers half-hour tours of the **Knute Nelson House** (1219 Nokomis St., 320/762-0382, 10 A.M.–3 P.M. Mon.–Fri., $2). Though born in Norway and raised in Wisconsin, Knute Nelson served Minnesota in Congress, as governor, and most prominently for 28 years as a maverick Republican U.S. Senator. He built his home shortly after arriving in Alexandria in 1871, though he modified it considerably over the years. The bedrooms and living room retain the original furnishings. Those wishing to use the archives for genealogical and historical research are welcome to do so for $7.50 per day.

You can sample a range of grape and apple

© TRICIA CORNELL

Big Ole greets visitors to Alexandria.

wines at the **Carlos Creek Winery** (6693 County Rd. 34, 320/846-5443, www.carloscreekwinery.com, 11 A.M.–6 P.M. Mon.–Sat., noon–6 P.M. Sun.), two miles north of town. Quick tours of the winemaking facility are available on the hour, and in mid-September the winery hosts the popular **Grape Stomp and Fall Festival.** You can also see Arabian horses, wander an elm-tree maze, and hear live music daily for much of the summer and weekends year-round.

ENTERTAINMENT AND EVENTS

The respected **Theatre L'Homme Dieu** (1875 County Road 120 NE, 320/846-3150, www.tlhd.org, $17.50) has been performing summer theater at their home on Lake Le Homme Dieu since 1961.

The Alexandria Area Arts Association's **AAAA Theatre** (618 Broadway, 320/762-8300, www.alexandriaareaarts.org, $15 adults) hosts a variety of concerts and plays throughout the year. On the last Sunday in June the **Vikingland Band Festival** attracts dozens of marching bands and drum and bugle corps from across the Midwest.

Sports fans who think heart matters more than cash will appreciate the **Alexandria Beetles** (www.alexandriabeetles.pointstreaksites.com), part of the Northwoods League, which puts top college baseball players on the roster while letting them keep their NCAA eligibility. Games take place at **Knute Nelson Memorial Stadium** (503 5th Ave. W., 320/763-8151, $8).

The biggest crowds are found Saturday nights at the **Viking Speedway** (Douglas County Fairgrounds, 320/762-1559, www.vikingspeedway.net, $11) for car races on the half-mile dirt oval.

SHOPPING

Serious shoppers could spend half a day at the half-dozen antiques stores downtown. **Yesterday's** (517 Broadway, 320/762-8990, 9 A.M.–6 P.M. Mon.–Fri., 9 A.M.–5:30 P.M. Sat., noon–4 P.M. Sun.) and **Now & Then** (601 Broadway, 320/763-6467, 10 A.M.–5 P.M. Mon.–Sat., noon–4 P.M. Sun.) are the largest.

Used-book lovers will find the **Vikingland Book Trader** (605 Broadway, 320/762-8722, 10 A.M.–5 P.M. Mon.–Sat., closed Sun.) worth a browse.

Even more than browse, **Cherry Street Books** (503 Broadway, 320/763-9400, 10 A.M.–5:30 P.M. Mon.–Sat., noon–4 P.M. Sun., closed Sun. Jan.–Mar.) invites you to come in, take a seat, and spend some time. There's even story time Saturdays at 10 A.M.

If you came here to enjoy Minnesota's Scandinavian heritage, you'll find plenty of tempting (sometimes pricy) stuff at the **Scandinavian Gift Shop** (604 Broadway, 320/763-6363, www.scandinaviangifts.com, 9 A.M.–5:30 P.M. Mon.–Fri., 9 A.M.–5 P.M. Sat., closed Sun.). They stock Marimekko, Iitala, Arabia, Aarika, and other iconic brands.

RECREATION

Alex lies along the **Central Lakes Trail,** a 55-mile paved bike trail stretching through 55 miles of countryside between Fergus Falls

GULLIBLE'S TRAVELS

Eight Goths and 22 Norwegians on exploration journey from Vinland over the West We had camp by 2 skerries one days journey north from this stone We were and fished one day After we came home found 10 men red with blood and dead Ave Maria Save from evil.

On November 8, 1898, Swedish immigrant Olaf Ohman and his 10-year-old son Edward were pulling stumps on the family farm about three miles northeast of Kensington. Edward, as the story goes, noticed strange markings on a rock he found under a poplar tree. The 202-pound sandstone slab measured 31 by 16 by 6 inches and bore the above text on its smooth face, while "Have 10 of our party by the sea to look after our ships 14 days journey from this island Year 1362" was carved on an edge. If the runic inscriptions were genuine it would show that Vikings were exploring what is now Minnesota at least as early as 1362, 130 years before Columbus sailed the ocean blue.

After Ohman cleaned it up, the stone was displayed in a bank window in Kensington, but when newspapers reported the story the next year it was sent to the University of Minnesota and Chicago's Northwestern University where Scandinavian scholars unanimously declared it a fake. Interest quickly died and Ohman used it as a doorstep. The legend got a second wind in 1907 when Hjalmar Holand, a Norwegian-born historian from Wisconsin with an interest in Scandinavian settlements, bought the stone and became its greatest champion. Holand gave speeches, wrote books and articles, and took the stone to Europe. Constant Larson urged a group of ten Alexandria businessmen to chip in $200 apiece to buy the stone back and then his daughter Lorayne took the stone on a nationwide tour during the 1930s. In 1948, after pressure by Minnesota's Congressional delegation, the rock ended up on display at the Smithsonian – which labeled it with "might be one of the most important pieces of evidence for pre-Columbian European exploration of North America" – making it a national phenomenon. The stone continues to travel, though it now spends most of its time in Alexandria's Runestone Museum.

Not letting evidence or logic get in the way, amateur sleuths have used the stone's 70 words to create a fanciful history. Although exactly which lake is detailed in the carving remains a topic of debate amongst Runestone proponents, the generally accepted story has the 30 Vikings, including English astronomer Nicolas of Lynn as navigator, sailing from Vinland (a proven Norse settlement in Newfoundland circa 1000) up to Hudson Bay, where Nicolas discovered the magnetic North Pole. They then took the Nelson River to Lake Winnipeg, headed south along the Red River, and followed a now-extinct chain of lakes and streams south to Sauk Centre where they performed some religious ceremony at a massive stone altar. For some reason they remained behind and lived out their days with Mandan Indians in the Dakotas.

Not only is the entire legend preposterous on its face, but to believe it you have to ignore a mountain of contrarian evidence. Despite their initial endorsement, an embarrassed Smithsonian now considers the rock a fraud, and though they do not hold an "official" position the Minnesota Historical Society has spent considerable effort investigating and subsequently denouncing it. In fact, no reputable historian, archaeologist, or linguist backs the stone's validity – those who do are self-taught or work in unrelated fields. Although the reasons are many, the primary factors pointing to a hoax are the lack of any other legitimate archaeological evidence suggesting that Vikings traveled through the continent's interior and the fact that nearly half of the runes on the rock didn't exist in the 14th century.

It's highly unlikely that seafaring people who enriched themselves plundering coastlines would end up on the Minnesota prairie, a place where it just so happens that masses of Scandinavians would settle five centuries later. Historians also point out that the idea of Vikings traveling for the sake of exploration is absurd – they would not have headed inland without an economic incentive. Even taking the giant leap that Norsemen would or could have journeyed here, the anachronistic message they supposedly left behind gives the prank away. Looking at the runic forms, vocabulary, and grammar, nearly half of the text could not have come from the 14th century. As one scholar has stated, the text "is the way my grandfather would write, not my ancestors from the 1300s."

Not that they are needed, but there are plenty of other facts working against the reality of the runestone, including: the face is only barely weathered; Ohman was a stone mason; like all other boys his age in Sweden he learned runes in school; Ohman's extensive library contained several books on Swedish history that would have aided him in carving the stone; neighbors remembered Ohman, who had little education but was very smart, expressing a desire to put one over on "them that was educated"; geological surveys show lake levels were not significantly different 500 years ago than they are today; and the Minnesota Historical Society has taped interviews with people who claim their father admitted assisting Ohman to pull off the hoax.

For the most part, runestone believers have just one strategy to rely on: claiming the experts are wrong. They contend the language of the text really was in use back in the 14th century, there are just no surviving examples, and the dozens of 14th-century Norse artifacts found in this part of the country and dismissed by archaeologists are in fact real. Supporters also frequently cite the discovery of many "mooring rocks" across this part of Minnesota. The boulders with triangular-shaped holes cut into them – in order to fasten anchor pegs for their boats – are similar to those used by Vikings along the Norwegian coast; however, these holes have been clearly shown to have been drilled by modern inhabitants for blasting.

More "proof" of the stone's authenticity came in 2001 when a 2,200-pound granite boulder bearing more runes was found on an island a quarter mile from where the Kensington Runestone was unearthed. The AVM stone bears the year 1363 leading to the speculation that the Vikings stuck around the area. Members of the Kensington Runestone Scientific Testing Team presumed the new find genuine; however, instead of being the smoking gun advocates had hoped for, the big breakthrough was revealed as the work of five University of Minnesota graduate students in 1985. Their goal at the time was to see if runestone believers would accept their "obviously false" carvings.

Whether the Kensington Runestone was a record of Vikings in Minnesota during the 14th century or a well-executed hoax perpetrated by clever immigrant farmers was once a hot topic of discussion in the state – any mention in a newspaper resulted in a flood of letters from both sides – though there is relatively little interest in the topic today. New translations and theories continue to pop up regularly and these still often earn a headline, but most people now accept that it is nothing more than a monument to Scandinavian immigrant humor.

and Osakis. **The Bike & Fitness Company** (805 1st Ave. E., 320/762-8493, www.bikeandfitnessco.com, 10 A.M.–7 P.M. Mon.–Fri., 10 A.M.–5 P.M. Sat., noon–4 P.M. Sun. summer, 10 A.M.–6 P.M. Mon.–Fri., 10 A.M.–5 P.M. Sat. rest of year) sits next to the trail and rents bikes, including tandems and recumbents (and recumbent tandems), and cross-country skis. They also run a limited shuttle service.

Casey's Amusement Park (1305 Nokomis St. N., 320/763-7576, 10 A.M.–11 P.M. daily May–Oct.) has go karts, mini-golf, and more.

Arrowwood Resort hosts **The Big Splash** (320/762-1124) indoor water park. **Arrowwood Stables** (320/762-1124) charges $24.95 for a 45-minute trail ride.

The Arrowwood Resort's **Atikwa Golf Course** (320/298-4253, $42 18-holes) and **Geneva Golf Club** (4181 Geneva Golf Club Dr., 320/762-7089, www.genevagolfclub.com, $33 18-holes) are two good 18-hole public courses near town.

PGA pro Tom Lehman, who has a summer home here, golfs at the **Alexandria Golf Club** (2300 North Nokomis St. NE, 320/763-3605, www.alexandriagolfclub.com). Though it's a private club, the public is often allowed to play.

Winter enthusiasts have 15 ski runs, a terrain park, tubing hill, and 15 kilometers of cross-country ski trail at **Andes Tower Hills** (4505 Andes Rd. SW, Kensington, 320/965-2455 or 877/542-6337, all-day lift tickets $35 adults), 15 miles west on Highway 27.

For fun on the water, **Fun Rentals** (1405 Scenic Heights Rd. NE, 320/491-6028) can rent you just about any vehicle you need, from speed boats to pontoons, canoes, and tubes. They even deliver and pick up.

For fun under the water, **Diver's Clubhouse** (1123 3rd Ave. E., 320/759-1999, www.diversclubhouse.com) gives scuba lessons and leads dives in local lakes and quarries.

ACCOMMODATIONS

The **Skyline Motel** (605 30th Ave. W., 320/763-3175 or 800/467-4096, $46) looks like the set of a 1950s movie, though its 12 rooms have been kept up to date inside.

The classiest bed-and-breakfast in town is the **Cedar Rose Inn** (422 7th Ave. W., 320/762-8430 or 888/203-5333, www.cedarroseinn.com, $100). This antiques-filled 1903 Tudor revival with original stained glass and other ornamentation has four lovely guestrooms with private bath, plus a sauna and mountain bikes. Guests also have access to a private 95-acre nature preserve nearby.

You can get the B&B experience in a newly built home right on the lake at **Lake L'Homme Dieu Bed and Breakfast** (441 South Le Homme Dieu Dr. NE, 320/846-5875, www.llbedandbreakfast.com, $145–175), just three miles out of town. The four unfussy rooms all have whirlpools, and there's a hot tub on the deck for guests' use.

The biggest, fanciest, and best-known resort in the area is **Arrowwood** (2100 Arrowwood Ln. NW, 320/762-1124 or 866/386-5263, www.arrowwoodresort.com, $149). Its 200 varied rooms come with all the amenities you'd expect at this price. The 450-acre grounds have, among many other things, a golf course, stables, indoor water park, marina, day spa, and Camp Arrowwood for the kids. It is located on Lake Darling, four miles northwest of town.

But Arrowwood isn't the only game in town. The lakes are teeming with small, family-run resorts with fewer amenities but plenty of charm. **Woodland Resort** (13270 E. Lake Miltona Dr. NE, 218/943-5191 or 877/699-6637, www.vacationminnesota.com, $725/week) has eight well-kept lakeshore cabins, ten miles north of town on Lake Miltona.

On Lake Geneva, the family-friendly **Geneva Beach Resort** (105 Linden Ave., 877/891-3200, www.genevabeachresort.com, $568–2353 weekly) has a varied range of units available, from a large six-bedroom house, to cozy connected studios. All have fully-equipped kitchens, and guests can enjoy the sandy beach, boats, playground, and bonfire pit.

Another popular way to vacation is to park the RV at a campground all summer long—returning year after year to the same spot. **Big Food Resort and RV Park** (8231 Hwy. 114 SW, 320/283-5533 or 888/239-2512, www.bigfootresort.com, $560–1,300 weekly cabins, $170 weekly RVs) attracts that clientele and has ten cabins facing a big beach to offer as well. As at nearly all resorts, rates vary with the season and the number of guests. Nightly rates are also available.

FOOD

Part of a successful family of four Minnesota restaurants, **Doolittles Woodfire Grille** (4409 Hwy. 29 S., 320/759-0885, 11 A.M.–midnight Mon.–Sat., 11 A.M.–11 P.M. Sun., $9–17) is among your best bests for fine dining. The menu is packed with stick-to-your-ribs choices, like prime rib, chicken and ribs cooked in a wood fire, and parmesan-crusted walleye.

Watch the chefs grill, sauté, broil, toss, and plate your meal in the central open kitchen at **Weston Station** (4417 Hwy. 27, 320/763-6677, www.westonstation.com, 5–9 P.M. Mon.–Thurs., 5–10 P.M. Fri.–Sat., closed Sun., $10–30). The menu is huge and hearty, and Sonny's walleye—a kind of walleye piccata—is said to be among the best preparations of the beloved state fish.

For a lighter meal or just a glass or two of good wine with a plate of bruschetta, the absolute best bet in town is **Sixth Avenue Wine and Ale** (115 6th Ave. E., 320/759-2277, www.sixthavenuewineandale.com, 4–10 P.M. Tues.–Wed., 4–11:30 P.M. Thurs.–Sat., $8.50–14). Primarily a wine bar (though beer lovers aren't neglected—they have 50 choices as well), Sixth Avenue also has a few full entrees on the menu, like pasta with roasted vegetables and roast chicken.

The city's oldest restaurant, the **Traveler's Inn** (511 Broadway, 320/763-4000, 6 A.M.–8 P.M. Mon.–Sat., 6 A.M.–3 P.M. Sun., $3–9) opened in 1928 and is still going strong. The reasonably priced American fare—think classic meatloaf and roast turkey—is complemented by a couple of Italian plates. Weekends have all-you-can eat fish and prime rib.

If you want to go completely casual, have a burger or walleye sandwich at **Fat Daddy's** (115 30th Ave. E., 320/763-6565, 11 A.M.–10 P.M., $7–16).

Information and Services

The **Alexandria Lakes Area Chamber of Commerce** (206 Broadway, 320/763-3161 or 800/235-9441, www.alexandriamn.org, 8:30 A.M.–5 P.M. Mon.–Fri. year-round, plus 9 A.M.–4 P.M. Sat., 11 A.M.–4 P.M. Sun. May–Oct., 10 A.M.–4 P.M. Sat. rest of year) office is at the Runestone Museum, and they will help you find lodging vacancies.

Getting There and Around

Greyhound (800/231-2222, www.greyhound.com) buses stop at Viking Auto Parts (308 3rd Ave E.). This is quite far from downtown, so you may need to call **Viking Taxi** (320/808-5000). **Executive Express** (320/253-2226 or 888/522-9899, www.executiveexpress.biz) runs a shuttle to the Minneapolis–St. Paul International Airport from the Country Inn (5304 Hwy. 29 S.) several times a day.

The public transport system in Douglas, Stevens, and Todd Counties is known as **Rainbow Rider** (320/283-5061, www.rainbowriderbus.com, 6 A.M.–8 P.M. Mon.–Fri., 8 A.M.–4 P.M. Sat., closed Sun.). Call ahead to arrange door-to-door trips. All buses are wheelchair accessible. You pay by the length of the trip: $2 up to 5 miles, $4 up to 10 miles, $5 up to 20 miles, and $2 for every 10 miles beyond that.

LAKE CARLOS STATE PARK

Lake Carlos State Park (2601 County Rd. 38 NE, 320/852-7200, www.stayatmnparks.com) hugs the north end of its eponymous lake. Most visitors find their enjoyment in or on the water, so the trails offer a great escape, especially in the quiet western half. Fourteen miles of hiking and nine miles of horseback trails lead through the hardwood forests, over the steep glacial hills, and past small hidden lakes. In winter five miles of trail are groomed for cross-country skiing, and snowshoes can be rented at the park office to explore the rest of the 1,236-acre park. Campers will find 125 sites (81 electric) in two campgrounds; the Upper Campground, especially the northern loop, is far more secluded and also has a walk-in site.

Horseback riders have their own campground where four of the seven sites have electricity.

Just outside the park on the northeast side, **Lake Carlos Marina** (9490 South Park Dr. NE, 320/852-7575, 8 A.M.–8 P.M. daily mid-May–Labor Day) serves boaters who want to rent pontoons and fishing boats, stock up on supplies, and get gas for their own boats or for camping. It also rents boat slips seasonally.

OSAKIS

The line of cars exiting the highway at Osakis likely belong to antiquers. The town of 1,600 has a handful of great shops—the kind that are especially fun to dig through for being a little off the beaten path (for now).

Downtown Osakis—just a few square blocks—sits right on the lake of the same name. Founded in 1866, the town most likely got its name from the Ojibwe word for "place of the Sauk:" oh-za-kees.

Start your antiquing at **Grandpa's Attic and Gifts** (210 1st Ave. E., 320/859-5575, 10 A.M.–5 P.M. daily), a Victorian house so stuffed with furniture, kitchenware, Amish baskets, and more that it all overflows out onto the lawn.

Around the corner, **Antiques Osakis** (26 Main St. W., 320/859-3200, 10 A.M.–5 P.M. May–Oct.) is home to 25 dealers on two floors.

Jacob's Lefse Bakery (28 Main St., 866/995-3373, www.gotlefse.com, 10 A.M.–5 P.M. Mon.–Fri., 10 A.M.–4 P.M. Sat., closed Sun.) alone is a great reason to get off the highway. Jacob's makes lefse—a flat Scandinavian bread usually reserved for holidays—year-round and sells a beautiful selection of Swedish and Norwegian textiles and knickknacks. You can order lefse and lefse-making supplies online.

Do a little more shopping, and get a cup of coffee and a light lunch at **Just Like Grandma's Tea Room** (113 Main St., 320/859-4504, 10 A.M.–5 P.M. daily May–Oct.), a 1904 Victorian house.

When the kids are tired of being dragged through shops, take them to **Erickson's Petting Zoo** (11890 Hope Rd., 320/762-0184, www.ericksonpettingzoo.com, 10 A.M.–4 P.M. Mon.–Sat., noon–4 P.M. Sun., $4) to visit the alpacas, rabbits, poultry, peacocks, miniature horses, sheep, and more.

The **Osakis Chamber of Commerce** (11 Main St. E., 320/859-3777, www.visitosakis.com, 9 A.M.–5 P.M. Mon.–Fri. year-round, plus 9 A.M.–3 P.M. Sat., 10 A.M.–2 P.M. Sun. May–Oct.) has information for visitors. The trailhead for both the **Central Lakes Trail** and the **Lake Wobegon Trail,** which meet here, is behind the office, toward the lake.

SAUK CENTRE

Though you may never have heard of Sauk Centre, in the 1920s it was the most famous small town in America thanks to native son Sinclair Lewis. America's first winner of the Nobel Prize for literature based his 1920 novel *Main Street* on his hometown, and though he called it Gopher Prairie the veil was very thin. The book attacked the simple-mindedness of small town America, and while local residents were outraged, it was both a popular and critical sensation nationally. Ever since then sociologists and journalists have come to Sauk Centre to take the pulse of Middle America. Surprisingly, many residents, especially those who knew the families of the real people behind the characters, still harbor resentment over Lewis's book, though by now most have either forgiven or forgotten—and most who haven't keep quiet while the city capitalizes on his fame.

Sights

The **Sinclair Lewis Interpretive Center** (320/352-5201, www.saukcentrechamber.com, 8:30 A.M.–4:30 P.M. Mon.–Fri. year-round, plus 8:30 A.M.–4:30 P.M. Sat.–Sun. summer, free admission), at the junction of I-94 and Highway 71, greets visitors arriving from the south. Besides providing an in-depth look at Lewis's life, the center presents a brief history of the town and is home to the chamber of commerce. On the same grounds is the restored **Little Red Schoolhouse,** built in the 1870s and operated until the 1960s, open for tours only by appointment.

In town, the **Sinclair Lewis Boyhood**

The Little Red Schoolhouse stands on the grounds of the Sinclair Lewis Interpretive Center.

Home (810 Sinclair Lewis Ave., 320/352-5359, 1–5 P.M. Tues.–Sat. summer, $5 adults), a quaint 1884 East Lake cottage where Lewis lived from 1889 to 1902, has been restored to the way it looked when he was growing up and is now a National Historic Landmark. Many of the events in his books actually took place in this house, and you will hear about several during the half-hour guided tours. Lewis was born in the smaller red-and-white house across the street at number 811, and his ashes are buried in the family plot in Greenwood Cemetery (from the main entrance, it is three rows in and eight monuments to the left) a mile east of downtown on Sinclair Lewis Avenue.

There is a wee collection of photos and artifacts in the **Sauk Centre Area Historical Society Museum** (430 Main St. S., 320/351-8777, noon–4 P.M. Mon.–Fri., $3) in the basement of the library, though none specifically about Lewis.

Recreation

The paved **Lake Wobegon Trail** (www.lakewobegontrails.com) runs 50 miles from Sauk Center southwest St. Joseph along an old rail bed. It also heads north a few miles to Osakis, where it meets up with the Central Lakes Trail, for a beautiful and popular ride through forests, farms, and parks. The trail passes through the centers of the small towns of Melrose, Freeport, Albany, and St. Joseph, allowing for plenty of interesting stops along the way. A short spur heads north from Albany to Holdingford.

To explore on water rather than on land, call **Minnewaska Kayaks** (320/239-5925, www.minnewaskakayak.com, $40/day), which will deliver kayaks, life jackets, and paddles in the Alexandria Lakes and Lake Minnewaska area.

Greystone Golf Club (10548 Andrews Dr., 320/351-4653, www.greystonegc.net, $43 18 holes) got 4.5 stars out of 5 from *Golf Digest* and won a place on their Best Place to Play list.

Practicalities

The cheapest beds in town are at the clean and cozy **Hillcrest Motel** (965 Main St. S., 320/352-2215 or 800/858-6333, $43).

You've seen his homes, his museum, and his grave, now, if you're carrying your own shelter, you might as well stay at the **Sinclair Lewis Campground** (320/333-9546, $18 full hookup) just northwest of downtown, where 70 sites are crammed up against Sauk Lake.

In a town obsessed with Sinclair Lewis, it's not surprising that the most popular hotel and dining spot also has a connection. The writer did in fact work at (and get fired for reading and sleeping on the job) the **Palmer House** (500 Sinclair Lewis Ave., 320/351-9100 or 866/834-9100, www.thepalmerhousehotel.com, $65). Rooms in the 1901 redbrick hotel are small but atmospheric. The ground-floor restaurant (7 A.M.–9 P.M. daily, $5–19) has a classic look but a much more contemporary menu. Teriyaki-glazed salmon and beer-battered walleye are typical entrees.

Get hearty breakfasts and homemade soups and sandwiches at **Main Street Coffee Company** (604 Main St., 320/351-8000, 7 A.M.–5 P.M. Mon.–Sat., 8 A.M.–4 P.M. Sun., $4–7), once a private home, now packed from front porch to back door with knickknacks for sale.

Executive Express (320/253-2226 or 888/522-9899, after-hours call 612/726-9157, executiveexpress.biz) runs a shuttle to the Minneapolis–St. Paul International Airport from the Country Inn and Suites (5304 Hwy. 29 S.) several times a day.

GLENWOOD

The city of Glenwood (pop. 2,000) hugs the northeast edge of 7,110-acre Lake Minnewaska, Minnesota's 13th-largest body of water.

Sights and Events

Splendid views over the lake and town can be had from **Mt. Lookout** (Hwy. 55 at 14th Ave. NE), a 90-foot bluff-top overlook, and **Indian Mounds Park,** where Princess Minnewaska and Chief White Bear are buried. Take Highway 28/29 to County Highway 24 and look for the sign.

Nearby is the **Glenwood Hatchery** (23070 Lakeshore Dr. N., 320/634-4573, 8 A.M.–4:30 P.M. Mon.–Fri., closed Sat.–Sun., free admission) where hundreds of thousands of walleye are raised each spring.

More Native American lore is on display at the excellent **Pope County Historical Museum** (809 Lakeshore Dr. S., 320/634-3293, www.popecountyhistory.com, 10 A.M.–5 P.M. Tues.–Sat., $3). The Helbing Gallery of Indian Arts and Crafts is good enough to have attracted the attention of the Smithsonian Institute, but Cleora Helbing, a Glenwood native who gathered this priceless collection as director of education for the Bureau of Indian Affairs, wanted it displayed in her hometown. The museum also houses displays of old industry and recreation in the large exhibition hall. Out back are a couple of log homes, a one-room schoolhouse, and a building filled with farm machinery, and a two-headed cow, among other things.

The 1913 Craftsman-style **Ann Bickle Heritage House** (226 Minnesota Ave. E., 320/634-4687, open by appt., free admission) was Glenwood's fanciest when built and has a lovely English garden in the backyard. The garage is now an art gallery (10 A.M.–1 P.M. Wed.–Sat. summer, free admission).

Twelve miles south of town on Highway 104 is the 1903 **Terrace Mill** (320/268-3545, www.terracemill.org, 5–8 P.M. Wed., noon–8 P.M. Thurs.–Sat., noon–3 P.M. Sun. July–Aug., Sat.–Sun. only June and Sept., closed rest of year, $1), now restored and, along with an 1870s log cabin, the miller's house, and the Norwegian Heritage House, open for tours. Several musical events, including a fantastic fall fiddle contest, are held here annually.

Glenwood residents have staged the **Waterama** (www.waterama.org) festival since 1956, making it one of the oldest community festivals in Minnesota. The three days of family fun takes place the last full weekend in July and include a lighted pontoon parade, sand castle contest, water-ski shows, and fireworks.

Practicalities

On Lake Minnewaska, the **Scotwood Motel** (340 County Rd. 21 S., 320/634-5105, $72) has a pool and a hot tub.

A little farther out of town, on Minnewaska and Lake Pelican, there are a handful of small resorts. **Green Valley Resort** (17532 Pelican Lake Rd. N., 320/766-2359, www.minnewaskamn.com/greenvalley, $462–953 weekly, nightly rates and off-season discounts available) has a dozen cabins and four dozen hookups for RVs ($25/day) on a small beach.

Hunts Resort and RV Park (23306 Lakeshore Dr. N., 320/634-3322, www.huntsresort.com, $655–1,655 weekly, two- and three-night rates available) is open year-round for ice fishing and snowmobiling. Nine basic cabins ring the beach, and 13 shaded RV sites sit behind them.

Little Glenwood has several good dining choices. Every table, indoors and out, at **Lakeside Steak & Chop House** (180 Lakeshore Dr. S., 320/634-0307, 11 A.M.–1 A.M. Mon.–Fri., 8 A.M.–1 A.M. Sat.–Sun., $7–29) overlooks Lake Minnewaska. It is attached to the Lakeside Ballroom (the original, destroyed by fire in 2003, hosted a who's who of orchestras back in the day, and photos of many of the performers hang on the walls), which has occasional weekend entertainment, including big-band dances on Sundays.

Café Bella (9 Franklin St. N., 320/634-3371, lunch 11 A.M.–2 P.M. Wed.–Fri., dinner 5–10 P.M. Wed.–Sat., $6–24) has a full Italian menu and the area's best wine list. There is live jazz on occasion.

GLACIAL LAKES STATE PARK

Although the name celebrates the park's geology, Glacial Lakes (25022 County Rd. 41, 320/239-2860) is actually one of the state's best prairie experiences. Kettle lakes sit nestled in valleys surrounded by rolling fields of big and little bluestem, pasqueflower, and goldenrod. From atop the bare hills, which appear as if they long to be mountain ranges, you can gaze out across a very pristine landscape. Both the biology and the geology of the 1,880-acre park are discussed along the half-mile **Prairie-Woodland Interpretive Trail,** which has a beaver lodge along it. The epicenter of park activity is the remarkably pure 56-acre Mountain Lake, the park's largest, where swimming, fishing, and boating (canoes, kayaks, and rowboats are available for rent) are big draws on summer weekends; during the week the park can be nearly deserted.

The 38 campsites (14 electric) and a camper cabin are nestled in the shade of an oak grove, while six backpack sites are scattered down the 16 miles of hiking trails that cross the warped terrain. Horseback riders have their own camp at the head of the nine miles of trail open to them.

Brainerd Lakes

In this region, it's all about a week at the lake. Minnesota's most popular vacation destination spans five counties and five hundred lakes. Brainerd is the unofficial gateway to "Up North," and for the most part, people spend their time here fishing, golfing, and shopping. There's also a lot of history to explore, from ancient Native American burial mounds to Charles Lindbergh's boyhood home. Since it all sits just a couple hours outside the Twin Cities, the weekend crowds can be a little maddening at times, especially on the roads. Half of all resort revenue for the entire state comes out of this little area, and the lakes suffer—or enjoy—more second-home development than anywhere else in Minnesota. For a fun family getaway, the Brainerd Lakes area can't be beat—but if you're looking for a peaceful wilderness escape, then keep on driving.

BRAINERD

Brainerd is an If You Build It They Will Come success story. For over a century, Crow Wing, a town built by fur traders, was the northernmost European settlement on the Mississippi River. Naturally Crow Wing's 700 residents expected that the new Northern Pacific Railroad would come through their home, but in 1870 the railroad decided to bridge the river 10 miles north, and Brainerd was born. The railroad also chose to build their repair yards here and by 1873 21 stores, 18 hotels, 15 saloons, and five churches had sprung up to serve the new residents, while Crow Wing was already nearly a ghost town. Though a nationwide financial panic that year hit the new town hard, it soon recovered. The Northern Pacific was the town's largest employer, and their facilities, still standing east of downtown, were valued at $2 million in 1888. The 1880s were also the peak of the area's logging industry, and some 8,000 lumberjacks would descend on town on payday to drink, gamble, whore, and fight away their salary. Still, town boosters boasted of Brainerd's chivalry and claimed that women were safe on the streets at any hour of the day. The forests were finally cut over by around 1910, but the immense railroad operations, the influx of tourists to area lakes, and the discovery of iron in the nearby Cuyuna Range kept the city moving forward. The massive rail yards are now just a shadow of their former selves, and the last paper mill is a pretty small operation, leaving tourism as the lynchpin of the economy.

Brainerd and its western neighbor Baxter have grown right up against each other and are essentially one city; the most noticeable difference between the two is that Brainerd has an actual downtown. Just about all commercial development is stretched out along Highways 210 and 371, which are the roads people drive down to get to the area lakes.

Sights

If you're like me, you can't hear the name Brainerd without fond memories of Steve Buscemi uttering the name in the movie *Fargo.* The film also featured a giant statue of Paul Bunyan looming over the highway, though it was built just for the movie. Brainerd's actual giant Paul Bunyan statue resides at **Paul Bunyan Land** (17553 Hwy. 18 E., 218/764-2524, www.thisoldfarm.net, 10 A.M.–6 P.M. daily summer, $12.95), seven miles east of town. (There is another giant statue of Paul Bunyan, along with his sidekick Babe the Blue Ox, outside the Paul Bunyan Bowl at the junction of Highways 371 and 210 in Baxter and a couple of smaller Pauls at the town's two visitors centers.) After the meet and greet with the 26-foot-tall Paul, who waves and welcomes kids by name, you can take a spin on the amusement rides and enjoy Dick Rademacher's immense private collection of antiques and collectibles. His "hobby gone mad" encompasses over 20,000 items ranging from antique chainsaws to dancing raisin figurines, and much of the collection is housed in historic buildings, including a one-room schoolhouse, log cabin, and the train depot used in the movie *Iron Will.* The buildings come to life during Show Days, the second weekend in August, and you can lose yourself in the 15-acre corn-maze during September and October.

Brainerd's 1917 jailhouse now houses the **Crow Wing County Historical Museum** (320 Laurel St., 218/829-3268, 10 A.M.–3 P.M. daily year-round, $3 donation requested). Naturally, much of the collection is related to the logging era, though railroad, mining, and Native American artifacts are also featured, plus a couple of the old cells were left intact. A highlight is the 1890s all-wood oxcart. Tours of the sheriff's quarters, restored and furnished as they were in the early 20th century, are given on request.

Anglers may enjoy ogling the inductees' shrines at the **Minnesota Fishing Hall of Fame** (14275 Edgewood Dr., 218/828-1736, www.minnesotafishinghalloffame.com, 9 A.M.–9 P.M. Mon.–Fri., 8 A.M.–9 P.M. Sat., 10 A.M.–6 P.M. Sun., free admission) inside the massive Gander Mountain sporting goods store. The 30 or so Minnesota men who have all made a "significant contribution to angling" have donated memorabilia, photos, and mounted fish.

Crow Wing State Park

Considering its location—just nine miles south of Brainerd along Highway 371—you'd expect Crow Wing State Park (3124 State Park Rd., 218/825-3075) to be overflowing with visitors,

© TRICIA CORNELL

The Crow Wing County Historical Museum is housed in a 1917 jailhouse.

but in their rush to get up to the lake most people drive right on by, leaving the park nice and peaceful. Allan Morrison established a trading post here at the junction of the Mississippi and Crow Wing Rivers in 1823. The town, also named Crow Wing, that grew up around it was for half a century the northernmost European settlement on the Mississippi, and many of the state's most influential early citizens settled here. Clement Beaulieu came in 1847 to run the American Fur Company's operations, and he built what was in its day a stately mansion. Crow Wing's population reached 600, but when the Northern Pacific Railroad chose to cross the Mississippi ten miles north, where the city of Brainerd now stands, Crow Wing quickly died. Today a boardwalk with signs discussing life in that era leads through the old village site, though all that remains is the Greek Revival **Beaulieu House** and a couple of cemeteries—the church was built in 1968. A section of the Woods Trail, traveled by oxcart caravans between St. Paul and Winnipeg from the 1840s to 1860s, also remains.

After visiting the modest historic site, be sure to explore the rest of the 2,871-acre park. The park lies at a spot where the state's three primary biomes—deciduous forest, coniferous forest, and prairie—merge, and the varied habitats make for good wildlife-viewing. The 18 miles of hiking trail (six miles are groomed for cross-country skiing) are at their best where they hug the Mississippi, especially at the Chippewa Lookout, just a short climb from the boat launch. There are some rolling hills, but the trails are generally very easy. The paddling is excellent here too, and with calm waters it's ideal for families. Most people just canoe around the park, though longer trips on either river are excellent, especially the 10 undeveloped miles of the Mississippi downstream to the Nokasippi River. The park office has canoes and rowboats for rent, and there is a canoe-in campsite on the Mississippi. The shady campground has 59 sites (12 electric) and a camper cabin.

Camp Ripley

Nine miles south of Brainerd, Camp Ripley (15000 Hwy. 115, 320/616-2699) is one of the largest National Guard facilities in the United States, and around 230,000 troops train here annually, many in winter skills. Visitors can pick up a self-guided tour brochure, which leads you around the base, but the main reason to stop is the **Minnesota Military Museum** (320/632-7374, 10 A.M.–5 P.M. daily summer, 9 A.M.–4 P.M. Thurs.–Fri. rest of year, free admission). It houses several absorbing displays about all aspects of conflict from weapons to war bonds. Artillery, tanks, helicopters, and the like are displayed outside. The displays are so well done that even the most ardent pacifist will find them interesting. The best time to visit the base is mid-September of odd-numbered years for **Community Appreciation Day,** when the public are offered tours, demonstrations, and vehicle rides.

Entertainment and Events

There are many bars downtown on and around Laurel Street with nighttime diversions such as live music, comedy, dancing, sumo wrestling, and poker tournaments. **Coco Moon** (601 Laurel St., 218/825-7955, 6:30 A.M.–7 P.M. Mon.–Sat., 9 A.M.–4 P.M. Sun.) has a Thursday-night bluegrass jam.

The hottest tickets in town are for the races at **Brainerd International Raceway** (5523 Birchdale Rd., 218/824-7220 or 888/444-4455, www.brainerdraceway.com) seven miles north of town. Stock cars, superbikes, and muscle cars race on the three-mile, ten-turn track between May and September. The raceway's **NHRA Nationals** in mid-August is far and away the town's biggest event.

The **Brainerd Lakes Area Lunkers** (www.lunkersbaseball.com, $8) play in the Northwoods League at Stewart C. Mills Field (Q St. NE). Their games, June through mid-August, make for a fun evening of small-town baseball just steps from Rice Lake.

The **Brainerd Jaycees Ice Fishing Extravaganza** is the world's largest ice-fishing tournament, with thousands of anglers drilling holes on Gull Lake. The $150,000 in prizes are up for grabs the third Saturday in January.

Shopping

Chain stores cluster along Highway 210, including **Westgate Mall** (14136 Baxter Dr., Baxter, 218/828-1668, www.thewestgatemall.com, 10 A.M.–9 P.M. Mon.–Fri., 10 A.M.–6 P.M. Sat., noon–5 P.M. Sun.), a midsize mall anchored by Herberger's department store.

There is a varied handful of shops on and around Laurel Street downtown. **Cat Tale's** (609 Laurel St., 218/825-8611, 10 A.M.–5 P.M. daily, a little later Thurs.–Fri.) carries new and used books, and it has a good Minnesota section and many Paul Bunyan titles.

Antiques & Accents (214 S. 7th St., 218/828-0724, 10 A.M.–5 P.M. Mon.–Sat., closed Sun.) is the city's principal antiques store, though there are many others on the roads around town.

The classrooms at the old Franklin Junior High School, now the **Franklin Arts Center** (1001 Kingwood St., 218/833-0416, 9 A.M.–5 P.M. Mon.–Fri., closed Sat.–Sun.), hold artists' studios and galleries. It is just east of downtown along Highway 210.

Recreation

The **Paul Bunyan State Trail** runs north all the way up to near Walker, where it joins the Heartland State Trail for nearly 120 miles; the majority of it is paved. You can rent a bike or arrange shuttle service at **Easy Riders** (415 Washington St., 218/829-5516, www.easyridersbikes.com, $23/day). They also rent in-line skates, canoes, kayaks, cross-country skis, and snowshoes.

If you'd rather ride a horse than a bike, call **Outback Trail Rides** (12210 Pillsbury Forest Rd., Pillager, 218/746-3990, www.outback-ranch.com), who take riders of all abilities through the Pillsbury State Forest; a one-hour ride costs $25.

The **Northland Arboretum** (14250 Conservation Dr., 218/829-8770, $3) covers nearly 500 acres of forest, marsh, and prairie and is best known for its 12 miles of ski trail (three miles are lighted at night). The trails are open to hikers the rest of the year. The Nature Conservancy protects a 160-acre jack pine

BRAINERD LAKES LINKS

With 32 courses, the Brainerd area has grown into Minnesota's premier golfing area, and *Golf Digest* has rated this one of the world's top 50 golf destinations. Acclaimed creators such as Robert Trent Jones Jr., Joel Goldstrand, and Arnold Palmer have carved out many world-class holes that, while not cheap, are veritable bargains when compared with courses of similar quality in better-known places.

An informal survey resulted in the following list of central Minnesota's best courses: **Deacon's Lodge, Golden Eagle, The Classic** (the state's only five-star public course in *Golf Digest*'s most recent Places to Play ranking), **The Legacy courses at Cragun's, The Pines, The Preserve,** and **Whitefish Golf Club.**

savanna within the preserve, one of just five remaining examples of this rare ecosystem in the state. There is also a garden and reflecting pond based on Monet's garden in Giverny, France, and a native tree trail. The entrance is on NW 7th Street right behind the Westgate Mall. The chamber of commerce distributes a free packet with maps of other ski and hiking trails around town.

Downhill skiers and snowboarders have 14 runs on the west shore of Gull Lake at **Ski Gull** (2533 Baxter Dr., 218/963-4353, www.skigull.com, lift tickets start at $20).

A great way to get out on the water, even beyond the lakes, is to take a Sunday brunch cruise on the paddle-wheel boat the ***Mississippi Belle*** (14935 Hwy. 210 E., 218/828-3503, www.brainerdboat.com, $30). The 2.5-hour cruise departs Rice Lake at noon every Sunday from June through September and heads out to the Mississippi River.

Another unique way to enjoy the water is scuba diving with the **Minnesota School of Diving** (712 Washington St., 218/829-5953, www.mndiving.com), which offers classes (including a pre-certification introductory class for just $25), rents equipment, and can arrange private divemasters.

More low-key thrills can be had at **Pirate's Cove** (17944 Hwy. 371, 218/828-9002, www.piratescove.net, 10 A.M.–11 P.M. daily, call for hours before Memorial Day and after Labor Day), with elaborate mini golf and go karts.

Accommodations

A pair of the state's largest and fanciest resorts, **Madden's** (11266 Pine Beach Peninsula, 218/829-2811 or 800/642-5363, www.maddens.com, Apr.–Oct., $197) and **Cragun's** (11000 Craguns Dr., 218/825-2700 or 800/272-4867, www.craguns.com, $99–179), sit next to each other on the south shore of Gull Lake eight miles west of Brainerd, and both are very similar. Both have beaches, spas, tennis courts, marinas with boat rentals, and a busy schedule of activities ranging from horseback riding to bonfires, while their golf courses—The Classic and The Legacy, respectively—are two of the state's best. Lodging options run the gamut from hotel rooms to lakeside cabins, and there is normally a two- or three-night minimum stay on summer weekends. Madden's shuts down for the winter while Cragun's stays open for skiers, ice fishers, and even those looking to escape the cold with a little luxury.

For something quieter, try **Whiteley Creek Homestead** (12349 Whiteley Creek Trl., 218/829-0654, www.whiteleycreek.com, May–Oct., $95), one of the funkiest bed-and-breakfasts in the state. The three quirky cottages and two whimsical rooms, all with private baths and antique furnishings, sit on 35 acres just 2.4 miles past the East Brainerd Mall. They have a walking trail, canoes for paddling the namesake creek, and a massive screened porch, lined by birdfeeders, for lounging. A mostly organic breakfast is served in an 1890 railroad car.

If you just want an ordinary hotel you'll find all the expected chains along Highway 371, but also the simple **Rodeway Inn** (7836 Fairview Rd., 218/829-0391, $60), near the junction of Highway 210, which offers good value.

The U.S. Army Corps of Engineers' **Gull Lake Recreation Area** (10867 E. Gull Lake Dr., 218/829-3334 or 877/444-6777, $26) on County Highway 125 three miles west of Highway 371 has 39 shady and well-spaced campsites, all with electric hookups. Also onsite are a beach, boat launch, and a dozen ancient Native American burial mounds.

Food

Prairie Bay Restaurant (15115 Edgewood Dr., Baxter, 218/824-6444, www.prairiebay.com, 11 A.M.–9 P.M. daily, $16–30) serves surprisingly good and creative food, including wood-fired pizza and reimagined homey classics like tuna casserole with ahi tuna and soba noodles. Oddly, the dining room is nowhere near as fancy as the food, but it has proven popular nonetheless.

Iven's on the Bay (19090 Hwy. 371 N., 218/829-9872, www.ivensonthebay.com, 5–10 P.M. Mon.–Sat., 5–9:30 P.M. Sun., $10–36) specializes in upscale seafood. Comparatively inexpensive sandwiches, like the angus burger and the walleye sandwich, let you enjoy the formal dining room (think white tablecloths and high-back leather chairs) and the view of North Long Lake without breaking the bank. Or you can splash out on king crab, lobster tail, and New York strip.

The malts at the 1950s-style **371 Diner** (14901 Edgewood Dr., 218/829-3356, 6 A.M.–9 P.M. daily, $5–10) north of town along Highway 371 are worth going out of your way for, as evidenced by the steady stream of patrons coming through the door for nothing else.

The Barn (711 Washington St., 218/829-9297, 5:30 A.M.–4 P.M. Mon.–Fri., 5:30 A.M. 3 P.M. Sat., $2–6) is a simple lunch counter with Maid Rite loose-meat sandwiches and the best pie around.

E Squared Café (123 Washington St. NE, 218/838-7806, www.esquaredcafe.com, 10 A.M.–10 P.M. Tues.–Thurs., 10 A.M.–midnight Fri., 6 P.M.–midnight Sat., closed Sun.–Mon., $5–7) feels like a coffee shop or college hangout, but it has a good wine and beer list and serves the kind of casual, flavorful sandwiches and pizza that hits the spot when you don't want to end the day with a heavy steak.

Your best bet for coffee and a taste of coffeehouse atmosphere is **Coco Moon** (601 Laurel St., 218/825-7955, 6:30 A.M.–7 P.M. Mon.–Sat., 9 A.M.–4 P.M. Sun.).

Information and Services

The **Brainerd Lakes Area Welcome Center** (7393 Hwy. 371 S., 800/450-2838, www.explorebrainerdlakes.com, 9 A.M.–5 P.M. Mon.–Thurs., 9 A.M.–6 P.M. Fri., 10 A.M.–4 P.M. Sat.–Sun. summer, 9 A.M.–5 P.M. Mon.–Fri., 10 A.M.–2 P.M. Sat., closed Sun. rest of year) is seven miles south of the city. They maintain a vacancy list for their 185 or so members, which can be very handy on summer weekends.

You can also get some information in town under the historic water tower at the **Brainerd Lakes Area Chamber of Commerce** (124 6th St. N., 218/829-2838, 7:30 A.M.–5 P.M. Mon.–Fri., 7:30 A.M.–noon Sat.–Sun. summer, 8 A.M.–5 P.M. Mon.–Fri., closed Sat.–Sun. rest of year) offices.

The **Brainerd Public Library** (416 5th St. S., 218/829-5574, 9 A.M.–8 P.M. Mon.–Thurs., 9 A.M.–6 P.M. Fri., 9 A.M.–4 P.M. Sat., closed Sun.) is also a good resource.

Getting There and Around

The **Brainerd Lakes Regional Airport** (16384 Airport Rd., www.brainerd.com/airport) is just 2.5 miles northeast of town along Highway 210. **Delta Airlines** (800/221-1212, www.delta.com) makes the short hop to the Twin Cities several times a day.

Amtrak (1st Ave. NE and 4th St. NE, Staples, 800/872-7245, www.amtrak.com) service is half an hour west of Brainerd in Staples.

Jefferson Lines (888/864-2832, www.jeffersonlines.com) buses stop well south of downtown at the Econo Lodge (11617 Andrew St.).

Lakes Express (218/855-6973 or 866/955-6973, www.lakesexpress.com) runs a shuttle to the Minneapolis–St. Paul International Airport six times a day, and they will pick you up and drop you off at any hotel.

Executive Express (320/253-2226 or 888/

522-9899) has similar service from the Red Roof Inn (215 S. 6th St.) in Brainerd and the Country Inn (15058 Dellwood Dr.) in Baxter.

Enterprise Rent-a-Car (14695 Edgewood Dr., 218/828-0200, www.enterprise.com, 7:30 A.M.–6 P.M. Mon.–Fri., 9 A.M.–noon Sat., closed Sun.) and **National Car Rental** (16384 Airport Rd., 218/829-7321, www.nationalcar.com, 10 A.M.–10:30 P.M. Sun., 8:30 A.M.–10:15 P.M. Mon.–Fri., 9 A.M.–6:30 P.M. Sat.) have branches here. **Brainerd Area Taxi** (218/828-1111) operates 24 hours a day.

MILLE LACS

At 207 square miles, Lake Mille Lacs is an angler magnet. Hundreds of thousands of walleye, a surprising number of them trophy size, are caught yearly making it the top catch, but muskie, smallmouth bass, and northern pike are all enormous and abundant. Marinas, bait shops, and public landings ring the lake, though the easiest way for the occasional angler to land a lunker is to join a launch. These large boats, long a part of Mille Lacs history, depart from many area resorts. The action doesn't let down even a little in the winter when over 6,000 fish houses, linked by plowed roads and regular shuttle service, form the temporary city of Frostbite Flats. You can rent one of these fish houses, decked out with propane heaters and electrical generators for lights and television, from area resorts by the day or overnight.

Though it often seems like it, fishing isn't the only diversion here. Nature lovers will love Mille Lacs Kathio State Park, and there is plenty of room on the lake for sailing and windsurfing. If you just want a scenic country drive, the less-developed north and east shores deliver.

Mille Lacs Indian Museum

The Ojibwe tell their own story at the Mille Lacs Indian Museum (320/532-3632, 11 A.M.–4 P.M. Wed.–Sat. summer, by reservation only rest of year, $7 adults), a project of the Minnesota Historical Society. The museum traces their history and displays let you learn about their fantastic beadwork, the significance of what you'll see at a powwow, and modern sovereignty issues. The heart of the center is the Four Seasons Room, where life-sized dioramas show what life was like here 200 years ago. Cooking, craft demonstrations, and other cultural programs are held daily during the regular season and occasionally at other times of the year. You can shop for authentic Native American crafts at the restored 1930s **Trading Post** next door. The museum is located along U.S. Highway 169, eight miles south of Garrison.

Father Hennepin State Park

The smaller of two state parks on the lake's southern shore, the 320-acre Father Hennepin State Park (41294 Father Hennepin Park Rd., 320/676-8763, www.stayatmnparks.com, $20) near Isle is used primarily for its two campgrounds (103 sites, 41 electric) and for access to the lake at its beach, fishing piers, and boat launches. It's also worth spending some time searching for albino deer along the four miles of rolling hiking trails, half of which are groomed for cross-country skiing in the winter.

Mille Lacs Kathio State Park

The lake's much larger park, Mille Lacs Kathio State Park (15066 Kathio State Park Rd., 320/532-3523, $16) is 10,585 beautiful acres of steep forested hills and deep lakes. While a quick look at a map explains why the French dubbed the region Thousand Lakes (only later was it applied to Spirit Lake, as the Dakota called it), Kathio, as this spot on the southwest shore is known, is a name without meaning. The Dakota called it Izatys, and so did French explorer Daniel Greysolon, Sieur du Lhut, in 1679 after he became the first European to travel here. Someone mistranscribed the "Iz" in his journal to a "K," and later mispronunciations resulted in Kathio. Izatys was an important civic and religious site for the Dakota before they were driven out by the Ojibwe in the Battle of Kathio, a legendary three-day fight that not all historians are convinced really occurred. The archaeological record here actually extends back 9,000 years to the earliest nomadic Paleo-Indians, and more than 40 significant

MILLE LACS RESERVATION

- Total Area: 103 sq. miles
- Tribally Owned: 6 percent
- Total Population: 4,704
- Native Population: 1,171
- Tribal Enrollment: 3,824

During the forced migration of Minnesota's Ojibwe to the White Earth Reservation in the mid-19th century, only a few people remained on their native homelands. One such group, the Non-Removal Mille Lacs Chippewa Band, as they became known to U.S. government officials, resisted and stayed put around Lake Mille Lacs despite the resulting oppression and persecution. Although most of their native lands were cleared for lumber and then turned into dairy farms, eventually the reservation – albeit a diminished one – was restored thanks to the few hundred resilient members left behind. Most tribal lands lie on the south side of the lake, though other parcels are scattered widely across Pine and Aitkin Counties. Tribal headquarters are in Onamia.

Thanks to its location on a large lake and its proximity to the Twin Cities, the tribe has been very successful and uses much of its tourism and gaming revenue to buy more land. In the process, their gaming enterprises (they run casinos in Onamia and Hinckley) have drastically reduced the tribe's unemployment rate. Tourism, however, is a double-edged sword as the influx of visitors drives up property values, making the purchase of land more expensive for the tribe.

The area's native singing and drumming once caught the ear of Grateful Dead member Mickey Hart. Two songs by the tribe's own Little Otter Singers were included on the *Honor the Earth Powwow: Songs of the Great Lakes Indians* album recorded for Hart's "The World" music series. The well-known song and drum group has other releases available too.

archaeological sites have been uncovered so far, leading to designation of the park as a National Historic Landmark. The whole human history, as well as ecological topics, are presented at the park's informative **Kathio Interpretive Center** (10 A.M.–4 P.M. Sat.).

The park's most popular walk is the **Touch the Earth Trail,** a self-guiding mile-long loop behind the Interpretive Center. It passes through a variety of forest types, including a tamarack bog via a boardwalk. The wonderful three-mile **Landmark Trail** combines history and scenery. Just a short distance from the parking area the trail passes ancient burial mounds and the site of a former Dakota village; signs explain how life was once lived here. The trail continues past lovely lake views and over the interior hills. The rest of the park's 35 miles of hiking trail (27 of which are shared with horseback riders) can get pretty remote, and since maples are abundant they are absolutely wonderful for fall color. You'll find the steepest hills along the northernmost loops, while the seldom-used trails south of the river are less hilly overall, though far from flat. In winter 20 miles of trail are groomed for both beginner and expert skiers and are often mentioned as Minnesota's best. Both skis and snowshoes are available for rent, and there is a popular sledding hill. Mille Lacs Kathio also has a vertigo-inspiring 100-foot **fire tower** to climb, a swimming pond, and canoes and rowboats are available for rent if you want to paddle the Rum River or the lakes along it.

Just about every site in the two campgrounds is shaded and secluded, plus there are four backpack sites. The Petaga Campground has 41 regular campsites (22 electric) plus five camper cabins with heat, electricity, and screened porches and three secluded walk-in sites. Much more peaceful are the 26 sites in the primitive Ogechie Campground. Horse riders have their own camp.

Other Sights and Recreation

The **Mille Lacs Lake Museum** (405 Main St.

W., 320/676-3945, 2–6 P.M. Fri., 10 A.M.–4 P.M. Sat., 1–3 P.M. Sun. summer, free admission) in Isle has a small local-history hodgepodge in a pair of old one-room schoolhouses. The highlight is the Model T modified to run as a snowmobile.

Of interest to serious bird-watchers are Hennepin and Spirit Islands, two rocky islets in the south end of the lake, that together compose **Mille Lacs National Wildlife Refuge** the nation's smallest NWR. Though they cover just over half an acre, the islands are nevertheless a vital nesting habitat for the state-threatened common tern and are used by many other migrating species unusual to the area, such as arctic loons and Baird's sandpipers. Bring a good pair of binoculars since the islands are closed to the public and visitors are requested to approach no closer than 100 feet. You don't need to boat out to the islands for good bird-watching though: Some 230 species of birds have been recorded around the lake, and bald eagles are frequently spotted soaring overhead.

The **Rum River** spills out of Mille Lacs's southwest end and can be paddled all the way to Anoka where it feeds the Mississippi, a trip of 148 miles. The first eight miles to Onamia cuts across Mille Lacs Kathio State Park and flows through three lakes. It's an easy day trip. Downstream from Onamia all the way to Princeton the Rum is shallow and rocky with a few small rapids and may need to be waded at times. Another recommended day trip (though a campsite allows this to be an overnighter too) is the 15 miles from U.S. Highway 169 to Milaca. The wildest and most scenic part of the river is the winding stretch between Princeton and Cambridge. If you want to be guided down the river, call **Lundeen's Tackle Castle** (38752 Twilight Rd., 320/532-3416, www.lundeens.com, 6 A.M.–8 P.M. Mon.–Fri., 5 A.M.–8 P.M. Sat.–Sun.) in Onamia.

Eleven miles of the **Soo Line Trail** between Onamia and Isle are paved for bike riders.

Finally, don't forget to get your picture taken with the **giant walleye sculptures** in Garrison and Isle.

Entertainment and Events

Besides gambling, the **Grand Casino Mille Lacs** (777 Grand Ave., 320/532-7777 or 800/626-5825, www.grandcasinomn.com), operated by the Mille Lacs Band Ojibwe, also hosts big-name entertainment a couple times a month. The Mille Lacs Band holds the **Mille Lacs Band Powwow** the third weekend of August.

Shopping

Scattered antiques stores and generic gift shops pop up all around the lake, but **Someday Isle** (250 Main St. W., 320/676-1962, 10 A.M.–4 P.M. daily) offers something different. Operated by a dedicated bunch whose enthusiasm is infectious, it sells work by dozens of local artists, including many hand-woven rugs made on-site—visitors can often take a seat at a loom and give it a try. There is also workspace for artists, many of whom tutor local children.

Accommodations

There are over three dozen resorts on the lake, mostly aging family-run fishing establishments. On the other end of the spectrum is **Izaty's Golf and Yacht Club** (40005 85th Ave., 320/532-4574, www.izatys.com, $79), a popular getaway for Twin Citians on the lake's south shore, with a 120-slip marina. Other amenities on the 650 acres include a pair of 18-hole golf courses (two of the state's best), tennis courts, indoor and outdoor pools, a beach, and boat rental. The lodging, as fancy as the surroundings, span hotel rooms to four-bedroom lakeshore townhouses with kitchens and fireplaces.

Much simpler and more fishing focused is the tribal-owned **Eddy's Lake Mille Lacs Resort** (41334 Shakopee Lake Rd., 320/532-3657 or 800/657-4704, www.eddysresort.com, $90) along U.S. Highway 169 about five miles north of Onamia. In addition to the 79 hotel rooms, Eddy's has a pool, whirlpool, sauna, large marina, launch and guide service, and a free shuttle to the casino.

Filling a needed niche between chain hotels

and home-away-from-home lakeside resorts is the comfortable **Garrison Inn and Suites** (9243 Hwy. 169, 320/692-4050, www.garrisoninnsuites.com, $79–119) in Garrison. There's a small indoor pool and some rooms have a Jacuzzi, but this is more about a quiet place to stay than the amenities.

The **Northern Inn** (125 Main St. N., 320/495-3332, www.northerninnbymillelacs.com, $66) in Wahkon has new rooms and is a good value for the area.

Food

You won't find much fine dining in the area. Eating out is all about casual, hearty, and fun: from steaks to walleye and back again. The **Blue Goose Inn** (9347 Hwy. 169 S., 320/692-4330, www.bluegooseonmillelacs.com, 7 A.M.–10 P.M. daily, $7–18) in Garrison is pretty typical. The original inn, built in 1923 was a landmark. It burned down in 1993 and was rebuilt immediately. This is a great place for a big breakfast before hitting the lake and a big burger when you come in off it again.

The home cooking at **Svoboda's Spotlite** (111 Madison, 320/692-4692, 6 A.M.–3 P.M. Mon.–Thurs., 6 A.M.–9 P.M. Fri.–Sat. summer, 6 A.M.–3 P.M. Mon.–Sat., closed Sun. rest of year, $4–13) in Garrison is a family tradition for many locals. The food is scrumptious, portions large, and prices low.

The **Sunrise Coffeehouse** (245 Isle St. W., 320/676-9965, 7 A.M.–3 P.M. Mon.–Sat., 8 A.M.–1 P.M. Sun.), a block south of Main Street in Isle, serves sandwiches, bakery items, and a good cup o' joe in front of a fireplace.

Information

You can get tourism information at the **Mille Lacs Lake Tourism Office** (Hwy. 47, north of Isle, 320/532-5626 or 888/350-2692, www.millelacs.com, 9 A.M.–3 P.M. Mon.–Fri. May–Sept., 10 A.M.–4 P.M. Mon.–Sat. rest of year) in Onamia's renovated depot. There is also a little tourist information hut (11 A.M.–7 P.M. Thurs.–Mon. May–Sept.) under the giant walleye by the lake in Garrison.

LITTLE FALLS

Charles A. Lindbergh Jr., who grew up in Little Falls, put this Mississippi River town on the map. When Lucky Lindy landed his single-engine *Spirit of St. Louis* in Paris in 1927, he immediately became one of the most famous people in the world, but he never forgot his hometown. He made several return visits over the rest of his life and wrote longingly of his life there in several books. Little Falls, likewise, continues to celebrate its most famous son.

French traders named these rapids Painted Rocks, and Lieutenant Zebulon Pike, who wintered in a small fort here in 1804, called it "a remarkable rapid in the river, opposite a high piney island." Sadly, visitors today can only imagine what a wonderful scene it must have been, since the falls now lay buried behind a hydroelectric dam. The rapid drop in the river was a natural spot to develop early industry, and the first dam and sawmill were built in 1849. Many more mills followed, making Little Falls a very prosperous city in its day, as evidenced by the solid downtown business district and many fine homes around it.

Charles A. Lindbergh House

Lindbergh spent all of his boyhood summers in this modest house south of town, and he lived here permanently from 1917 to 1920 to run the family farm. Now a National Historic Landmark, the Charles A. Lindbergh House (1620 Lindbergh Dr. S., 320/616-5421, www.mnhs.org, 10 A.M.–5 P.M. Tues.–Sat., noon–5 P.M. Sun. summer, $7 adults) remains almost exactly as he left it when he departed to study engineering at the University of Wisconsin. Next to the home is the Lindbergh History Center, dedicated in 1973 by Charles himself, commemorating the whole Lindbergh family. There is also a 23-minute movie about Lucky Lindy's life, warts and all, and a replica of the *Sprit of St. Louis* cockpit.

The Lindbergh home sits at the entrance to the 436-acre **Charles A. Lindbergh State Park** (1615 Lindbergh Dr. S., 320/616-2525), named for the more-famous Lindbergh's father, whose family donated the land in his

© TIM BEWER

The Charles A. Lindbergh House remains almost exactly as he left it.

honor. The elder Lindbergh was a progressive Republican congressman (his anti-World War I stance cost him later elections for U.S. Senate and Minnesota governor) and pioneering conservationist. Although the park is small, walking the seven miles of hiking trails or dipping a paddle in Pike Creek will satisfy nature lovers. Canoes are available for rent in the summer, as are snowshoes in the winter. Snowy-season visitors will also find five miles of groomed cross-country ski trails, and **Pap's Sport Shop** (64 Broadway E., 320/632-5171, 9 A.M.–5:30 P.M. Mon.–Fri., 9 A.M.–2 P.M. Sat.) has ski rentals.

Other Sights

The Morrison County Historical Society's **Charles A. Weyerhaeuser Memorial Museum** (2151 Lindbergh Dr. S., 320/632-4007, www.morrisoncountyhistory.org, 10 A.M.–5 P.M. Tues.–Sat., free admission) is named for, but not specifically about, the great lumber baron. It is a small, well-presented collection with some interesting items from the logging era and an actual beaver top hat, the fashionable item that spawned the North American fur trade. The museum is just south of the Lindbergh House, and a wooded trail along the Mississippi connects them.

Pack thousands of rods, reels, lures, motors, and similar objects into a large room and you've got the **Minnesota Fishing Museum** (304 Broadway W., 320/616-2011, www.mnfishingmuseum.com, 10 A.M.–5 P.M. Tues.–Sat. year-round, noon–4 P.M. Sun. May–Sept., $4, $1 Tues.). Highlights of the impressive collection include artistic spearing decoys, intricate flys, and old boat engines dating back to 1902—and you don't have to fish to find the history interesting.

The best part of **Pine Grove Park** (1200 Broadway W., 320/616-5595, www.pinegrovezoo.com) is the stand of old-growth white pines hovering over the picnic area. The modest zoo (10 A.M.–6 P.M. daily Apr.–Oct., $5 adults) has mostly Minnesota animals like gray wolves and cougars, plus a few exotics, including tigers.

The **Burton-Rosenmeier House** (606 1st St. SE, 320/616-4959 or 800/325-5916, www.littlefallsmn.com, 9 A.M.–5 P.M. Mon.–Fri., closed Sat.–Sun., free admission), a 1903

Classical Revival mansion, houses the Little Falls CVB, and several upstairs rooms are decorated with period furnishings.

Accommodations

The stunning **Waller House Inn** (301 3rd St. SE, 320/632-2836, www.wallerhouseinn.com, $109–159) is not just your nicest lodging choice, it's also one of the most beautiful homes in the area. The Queen Anne was built in 1897 and now has five lovingly restored guest rooms with private baths, as well as plenty of comfortable lounge areas, including a wrap-around porch.

A few national chains, including the **Country Inn** (209 16th St. NE, 320/632-1000 or 888/201-1746, $85), which has a pool and whirlpool, are east of town at the junctions of Highways 10 and 27.

The excellent campground at **Lindbergh State Park** (1615 Lindbergh Dr. S., 320/616-2525) has 38 (15 electric) wooded and well-spaced sites. For even more seclusion there is a backpack site that can be reached by foot or canoe.

Food

For a meal, most locals will direct you to the **Black & White Hamburger Shop** (116 1st St. SE, 320/632-5374, www.attheblacknwhite.com, 7 A.M.–3 P.M. Sun.–Tues., 7 A.M.–8 P.M. Wed.–Thurs., 7 A.M.–9 P.M. Fri.–Sat., $7–24), a local landmark and a fun place to dine. Besides burgers, the menu features steak, walleye sandwiches, and a roasted vegetable plate.

For a snack or sandwich you can't do any better than **Pete & Joy's Bakery** (121 Broadway E., 320/632-6388, 6 A.M.–5 P.M. Mon.–Fri., 6 A.M.–3 P.M. Sat., closed Sun.), where the doughnuts, pies, and bread are all fantastic and cheap. The bakery is known for its peanut brittle and has sold as much as 39,000 pounds in a year. No matter where you decide to dine, consider getting your order to go and eating it in Maple Island Park, just south of downtown, where you can enjoy the flowers and fresh air and watch the Mississippi River race by.

Other Practicalities

The **Little Falls Convention and Visitors Bureau** (606 1st St. SE, 320/616-4959 or 800/325-5916, www.littlefallsmn.com, 9 A.M.–5 P.M. Mon.–Fri., closed Sat.–Sun.) is housed in the Burton-Rosenmeier House.

Jefferson Lines (888/864-2832, www.jeffersonlines.com) buses stop at McDonald's, east of town along U.S. Highway 10. **Lakes Express** (218/855-6973 or 866/955-6973, www.lakesexpress.com) shuttles to the Minneapolis–St. Paul International Airport stop at the Perkins restaurant (201 16th St. NE), and **Executive Express** (320/253-2226 or 888/522-9899, www.executiveexpress.biz) uses the Country Inn (209 16th St. NE).

CROSBY

Crosby sits on the edge of the narrow Cuyuna Iron Range, named for homesteader Cuyler Adams, who first found iron here in 1904, and his St. Bernard, Una. Though much smaller than the Mesabi and Vermilion Ranges, over 100 million tons of ore were extracted between 1908 and 1984.

Sights

The range's heyday is remembered at **Croft Mine Historical Park** (8th St. and 2nd Ave., 218/546-5466, 10 A.M.–6 P.M. Fri.–Sun. summer, $7 mineshaft, exhibits free), on the north side of town. On your hour-long guided tour you'll get to see and touch old mining equipment—the Croft was worked from 1916 to 1934—and learn a lot about the history of mining from knowledgeable guides. The highlight is a re-created mineshaft, while the rest of the park has a ho-hum museum filled mostly with old photos, a few historic buildings, and some rusting mining equipment.

There's more mining memorabilia plus other historical artifacts at the small **Cuyuna Range Historical Museum** (101 1st St. NE, 218/546-6178, 10 A.M.–4 P.M. Tues.–Sat. summer, donations requested), housed in a 1910 Soo Line Depot.

Recreation

The **Cuyuna Country State Recreation Area** (218/546-5926) covers 5,000 largely undeveloped acres and encompasses over 20 lakes—15 of which are deep mine pits now filled with water—and 25 miles of shoreline. Another interesting feature are the up-to-200-foot-high piles of excess rock now covered with trees that, like the man-made lakes, look natural at first glance. Anglers come for the 50,000 trout stocked annually, and scuba divers have discovered the clear water of the pits.

The first five paved miles of the **Cuyuna Lakes State Trail,** which will eventually reach Brainerd, cut through the park, and an extensive mountain bike trail system is in the works. With just short portages between the lakes, paddlers can easily reach isolated waters, and the staff can recommend a loop route that avoids private property. The campground has 17 rustic and mostly shadeless campsites on the northwest side of Portsmouth Mine Pit Lake, available on a first come, first served basis.

Cycle Path & Paddle (115 3rd Ave. SW, 218/545-4545, www.cyclepathpaddle.com, 9 A.M.–6 P.M. Mon.–Fri., 9 A.M.–5 P.M. Sat., 10 A.M.–4 P.M. Sun.) rents bikes, in-line skates, canoes, kayaks, and more.

If you are here the second Saturday in June make a quick detour north to the village of Cuyuna for the annual **Wood tick Races.**

Shopping

Crosby bills itself "The Antique Capital of the Lakes Area," and there were ten stores along the main drag at last count. Two of the best known and largest sit across from each other but are part of the same enterprise. **Abbey House Antiques** (27 West Main St., 218/678-3286, www.hallett-abbey.com, 9:30 A.M.–5:30 P.M. daily) and **Hallett Antique Emporium** (28 West Main St., 218/546-5444, 9:30 A.M.–5:30 P.M. daily) together house more than 40 individual dealers of all eras.

Accommodations

One of the state's most unusual lodging options calls Crosby home. The over-the-top **Nordic Inn** (210 1st Ave. NW, 218/546-8299, www.vikinginn.com, $65) isn't just another bed-and-breakfast, it's a Medieval Brew and Bed. Owner Richard Schmidthuber is a self-taught scholar of Viking history, and to live out his Norse dream he converted an old church into a Viking realm. At night, for an added fee, you can dress in Viking attire and join in interactive dinner theater or just relax in the Valhalla room with its hot tub and grill.

Seven miles south of town on Highway 6 is **Ruttger's** (25039 Tame Fish Lake Rd., 218/678-2885 or 800/450-4545, www.ruttgersresort.com, Apr.–Oct., $164), one of the first resorts in the state. With a pair of links, Ruttger's is known as a golfers' destination, but they have all the other amenities that you would expect from a top-of-the-line facility like this. Zig's is an excellent dining room, and many area residents come here to eat.

Food

For a family-style meal at a good price you can't do any better than the **Heartland Kitchen** (131 Main St. W., 218/546-5746, 7 A.M.–4 P.M. daily, $5–16).

AITKIN

William Aitkin, for whom the city and county are named, was a prominent fur trader who opened a school for the local Ojibwe here in 1832. An actual town wasn't established, however, until 1871 when the arrival of the railroad facilitated logging. Steamboat service ran up and down the Mississippi River between Aitkin and Grand Rapids until the 1920s, and when river levels are low the ribs of sunken steamers still rise to the surface. The city became not only a major supply center for the logging camps, but a major release valve for the lumberjacks working in them who arrived with pockets full of cash to drink, gamble, whore, and fight before heading back to work. The money, from both the legitimate and illegitimate businesses, soon made the town prosperous, and it remains healthy today despite the dwindling fortunes of most of the surrounding Cuyuna Range towns.

Sights and Events

Aitkin's main claim to fame is the **Fish House Parade.** The day after Thanksgiving, residents pull their dolled-up ice-fishing shanties and similarly unique and humorous floats down Minnesota Avenue.

The **Jaques Art Center** (121 2nd St. NW, 218/927-2363, www.jaquesart.com, 11 A.M.–4 P.M. Tues.–Sat., closed Sun., free admission) is named for Francis Lee Jaques, former Aitkin resident and one of America's premier wildlife artists, best known for his work at the American Museum of Natural History in New York City. It contains many of the prolific artist's paintings and a pair of his three-dimensional "duoramas," an art form he invented. The center also hosts bimonthly exhibits from other artists.

The **Depot Museum** (20 Pacific St., 218/927-3348, 10 A.M.–4 P.M. Wed., Fri., and Sat. May–Sept., plus Tues. summer, $2 adults) has railroad, logging, riverboat, and other historical memorabilia.

You might also want to catch a flick in the **Rialto Theatre** (220 Minnesota Ave. N., 218/927-2824), a 1937 movie house with a funky marquee and a psychedelic art deco interior. In its day this was as fancy as they came.

Practicalities

Best bet for spending the night is the spic-and-span **40 Club Inn** (950 2nd St. NW, 218/927-2903 or 800/682-8152, $90), with a pool and hot tub. The county also maintains seven **campsites** (218/927-7364 $12) on the Mississippi River.

The **Beanery** (209 Minnesota Ave. N., 218/927-7811, 7 A.M.–7 P.M. Mon.–Thurs., 7 A.M.–9 P.M. Fri., 7 A.M.–3 P.M. Sat., 8 A.M.–1 P.M. Sun., $5) has coffee, wraps, and bagels, plus musicians on weekends and computers for checking your email.

Rice Lake National Wildlife Refuge

One of Minnesota's oldest national wildlife refuges covers 18,300 acres around its namesake lake. Surrounding the refuge area like a giant horseshoe are a series of glacial hills that trap much of the water that accumulates here, and as the low-lying areas fill with sediment and vegetation they become floating peat bogs. This build-up of decaying vegetation creates a nutrient-rich growing environment that, in part, accounts for the vast beds of wild rice in the lake, which are still harvested by Native Americans each fall. The lake's plentiful food sources also attract waterfowl in staggering numbers during the fall migration—the refuge is most famous for hosting over 150,000 ring-necked ducks at a time. Bald eagles nest on the refuge, and songbirds like LeConte's sparrow, Connecticut warbler, and yellow rail are common in the uplands. In total around 240 species of bird have been recorded here. Lucky visitors might spot a black bear or gray wolf, though white-tailed deer and beaver are more common.

Almost everything of interest to visitors is found along the 9.5-mile auto tour (generally open to vehicles May though November) that cuts through the heart of the refuge. A brochure discusses the history of this area and points out ancient Native American burial mounds. A seven-mile chain of hiking trails crosses forest and field, and the 0.75-mile **Twin Lakes Trail,** which skirts Twin Lakes, a bog, and a flower-filled field, is arguably the most scenic. In winter, about half of the trails are groomed for cross-country skiing. The observation tower near the end of the drive lets you truly appreciate how large and shallow the lake is, while North Bog Road, branching off the auto tour, offers close-up views of a peat bog in various stages of succession. The visitors center (36298 Hwy. 65, 218/768-2402, 8 A.M.–4 P.M. Mon.–Fri., closed Sat.–Sun.) has a few nature displays.

NISSWA

Highway 371, once a Native American footpath and later a lumber-wagon route known as the Leech Lake Trail, funnels thousands of people to area lakes every day during the summer, and the action doesn't let up much in the winter. Nisswa, Pequot Lakes, and Crosslake are busy shopping and supply centers for those recreating at the abundant resorts and second homes.

© TIM BEWER

Nine historic buildings make up the Nisswa Pioneer Village.

Early settlers in Nisswa chose the name Hill's Crossing for their growing village in 1898, but since there was already another town with that name, the post office chose the name of the man who submitted the denomination petition and dubbed it Smiley. Ten years later citizens chose the Ojibwe word *nisswa* (three), in reference to the three main lakes around town, known today as Roy, Nisswa, and Clark. This reasonably attractive town is pretty much all about shopping—well over half the businesses in town are gift shops of some sort—and this helps make it the busiest destination in the Brainerd Lakes area.

Sights and Events

Nine historic buildings moved to the edge of downtown make up the **Nisswa Pioneer Village** (intersection of Cullen Dr. and Nisswa Ave., 218/963-3570, 10 A.M.–4 P.M. Wed.–Sat. summer, $1). The furnished buildings include a one-room schoolhouse, bank, and several log homes, while railroad relics are kept across the street in the old caboose and train depot.

If you can, visit Nisswa on a summer Wednesday to watch the weekly **turtle races.** The sluggish sprints are held rain or shine downtown, and around 500 kids participate each week. The first heat of the day is at 2 P.M., and the event lasts for about an hour. There is no entry fee, though turtle rental is $3.

The whole town turns out for two days of Scandinavian folk music and dance during early June's **Nisswa-Stamman Festival** (www.nisswastamman.org). And, when the winter cold comes, they all turn out again for the **Nisswa Winter Jubilee** in February, with snow sculptures music, games, parades, and a broomball tournament.

Recreation

The **Paul Bunyan State Trail** (www.paulbunyantrail.com), a former railroad bed between Brainerd and Hackensack, parallels busy Highway 371 for most of its 110-mile paved route from Guthrie to Bemidji. Thankfully, the route sidesteps the nonstop sprawl along the highway south of Nisswa, and, since development tails off to the north, it's a fairly scenic ride despite the highway. Bike rental is available in many trailside towns.

If you're a bird-watcher, pick up the ***Birds of the Byway*** brochure at any area tourism office. It points out 15 top spots on the Paul Bunyan National Scenic Byway, a 54-mile signed drive along area roads, and with the variety of habitats it passes, 100-species days are not unheard of.

If you didn't bring your own wheels, rent a ride downtown at **Trailblazer Bikes** (Nisswa Sq., 218/963-0699, 9 A.M.–6 P.M. Mon.–Sat., 10 A.M.–4 P.M. Sun.) or **Martin's Sport Shop** (25451 Main St., 218/963-2341, 9 A.M.–9 P.M. Mon.–Fri., 9 A.M.–6 P.M. Sat., 10 A.M.–4 P.M. Sun.)—the former has tandems available, and the latter also leases in-line skates, cross-country skis, and snowshoes.

Rent jet skis, boats, pontoons and more at **Lake Fun Rentals** (7993 Interlachen Rd., 218/961-000, www.brainerdboatrentals.com) on Gull Lake.

Accommodations

The little **Nisswa Motel** (5370 Merril Ave., 218/963-7611 or 800/254-7612, $72) is right downtown. Three-night minimums apply on July weekends, and bicyclists get a 10 percent discount during the week.

Grand View Lodge (23521 Nokomis Ave., 218/963-2234 or 800/432-3788, www.grandviewlodge.com, $245), just to the west of town on Gull Lake, opened in 1919. The original log lodge, surrounded by thousands of flowers, is still at the center of things, but they've since expanded over 550 acres. Most of that is taken up by their four excellent golf courses. Other top-notch facilities include a day spa, seven Laykold tennis courts, an indoor pool area with a waterslide, 1,500-foot sandy beach, boat rentals, and six restaurants. There's a multitude of kids' programs available day and night, while activities for adults run the gamut from horseback riding to cooking classes. With all the various facilities and special packages they offer it's tough to pin down a price, but the two-bedroom options range $245–715, and there are often multi-night minimum stay requirements. These prices include breakfast, dinner, and use of most facilities.

Food

Locals are quick to recommend the steak and seafood (though there are also burgers and grilled cheese) at the **Bar Harbor Supper Club** (8164 Interlachen Rd., 218/963-2568, www.barharborsupperclub.com, 11 A.M.–10 P.M. daily, bar until 1 A.M., $6–28) 4.5 miles west of town on the north shore of Gull Lake. Back in its heyday this was such a renowned club that it attracted the likes of Duke Ellington and Tommy Dorsey to play for the Chicagoland gangsters and others who came out for the night. The grand original burned down in 1968, but it's still tough to beat a table on the lakeside deck of this, the third incarnation. Lounge singers still perform on weekends.

Stone House Coffee (Nisswa Sq., 218/961-2326, www.stonehousecoffe.com, 7 A.M.–6 P.M. Mon.–Sat., 8 A.M.–5 P.M. Sun.) roasts fair-trade organic beans daily and bakes its own pastries.

Information

Nisswa Chamber Welcome Center (25532 Main St., 218/963-2620 or 800/950-9610, www.nisswa.com, 9 A.M.–5 P.M. Mon.–Fri., 10 A.M.–4 P.M. Sat., 11 A.M.–3 P.M. Sun. summer, 9 A.M.–4 P.M. Mon.–Fri., 10 A.M.–4 P.M. Sat. rest of year) is your best bet for information.

PEQUOT LAKES

This town was founded as Sibley Siding in 1894, but postal officials eventually insisted that the name be changed because there was already another Sibley in the state. It became Pequot six years later, and Lakes was added in 1940. One legend of the name says that O-Pequot was a daughter of a White Earth Ojibwe chief who let the first settlers gather for Sunday services in her home, while another says that it just happened to be the first Indian-sounding word (the Pequot were a small tribe from Connecticut) that popped into the mind of the postal official charged with making the choice. The town has the inevitable concentration of gift and antiques shops, but Pequot is less a tourist trap than Nisswa.

Sights and Events

Little Pequot's most obvious claim to fame is the fishing-bobber water tower. Legend has it that Paul Bunyan got it caught in the scaffolding and he just let the town keep it.

At the foot of the bobber in a 1937 WPA building, the **Pequot Lakes Area Historical Society Museum** (4285 Tower Sq., 218/568-5708, noon–4 P.M. Sat. summer, $1) has a small collection of artifacts from the Great Depression and World War II, plus photos of outhouses.

Anyone with a fear of heights won't even want to look up at the **Pequot Lakes Fire Tower,** but everyone else can scramble to the top of the 100-foot steel spire for some superb forest views. It is located half a mile east of town on County Highway 11, and it's a steep climb uphill from the parking lot.

Pequotians also celebrate the area's logging heritage with **Bean Hole Day.** On the first Tuesday after the Fourth of July (sometimes it's held a week later), 150 gallons of baked beans are buried in a rock-lined pit and then dug up the next day at noon to feed the assembled masses. The old logging camp tradition was revived in 1935 and today 2,500 people take a bite. An arts and crafts fair and other events are held concurrently.

A pair of area stables, **Benvelle Equestrian Center** (4828 Treefarm Rd., 218/568-4826, www.benvelleequestriancenter.net) and **Pine River Riding Stable** (County Rd. 2 W., 218/587-5807 or 218/587-4844, www.pineriverstable.com), offer trail rides through the surrounding forest.

Accommodations

The combination of big rooms and little touches makes the **AmericInn** (32912 Paul Bunyan Trl., 218/568-8400 or 888/568-8400, www.upnorthlodge.com, $129) one of the best small hotels in all of Minnesota—and they've got the awards to prove it. There is a pool, whirlpool, and sauna indoors; volleyball, a patio ringed by birdfeeders, and more in the large backyard; and par 3 and miniature golf courses next door. These Northwoods-themed rooms two miles north of town along Highway 371 require a two-night minimum stay on summer weekends.

Five miles east of Pequot on Pelican Lake is the enormous **Breezy Point Resort** (9252 Breezy Point Dr., 218/562-7811 or 800/432-3777, www.breezypointresort.com, $139), with a pair of 18-hole golf courses and an ice arena among the top-flight amenities available to those staying in the 350 varied rooms and cottages. An Elvis impersonator performs on summer Saturdays.

Food

Some of the best—and biggest—restaurants in town are at **Breezy Point Resort** (9252 Breezy Point Dr., 218/562-7811 or 800/432-3777, www.breezypointresort.com). Antlers ($13–33), a remarkable dining room with a vaulted ceiling and overlooking the golf course, is for top-of-the-line special-occasion dining, with steaks, lobsters, and creamy pastas. Marina II ($10–16) is on the water and a lot more casual, serving upscale burgers and pasta. The Dockside ($9–11) is as casual as Breezypoint gets, with burgers and fries, pizzas, and a great outdoor patio.

Norway Ridge Supper Club (34757 County Rd. 39, 218/543-6136, www.norwayridge.com, Apr.–Dec. $17–32) serves up a similarly surf-and-turf (and similarly pricy) menu in a 1948 pine cabin on Kimble Lake. The difference is in the history: They make their barbecue sauce from scratch from the original recipes and smoke their own ribs, as they always have. As in most of this part of the state, vegetarians will feel left behind.

Timberjack Smokehouse (4443 County Rd. 168, 218/568-6070, 11 A.M.–close Tues.–Sun., $7–29) two miles south on Highway 371 is best known for ribs, though they also smoke shrimp, game hen, and more out back. Wednesday is meat raffle night.

Information

The **Trailside Information Center** (Hwy. 371 N., 218/568-8911 or 800/950-0291, www.pequotlakes.com, 9 A.M.–4:30 P.M. Mon.–Fri., 10 A.M.–2 P.M. Sat.) is housed in a renovated depot.

© TIM BEWER

The Uppgaard Wildlife Management Area is used as a landscaping-for-wildlife demonstration area.

CROSSLAKE

The Crosslake Logging Company opened a camp here in the 1870s and 1,400 men lived at the "Old Headquarters" during its peak. The company moved on in 1912, but around the same time many tourist camps chose to open on the back end of the Whitefish Chain of Lakes for the sunset views, and so the little village on the eastern shore of Cross Lake survived. Today this tourism-dependent city straddles County Highways 66 and 3 for many miles and has just about everything a vacationer could want, from birch-bark lampshades to boat rentals to miniature golf.

Sights and Recreation

Down by the junction, the closest thing there is to a downtown, is the **Historic Log Village** (218/692-5400, 11 A.M.–4 P.M. Sat.–Sun. summer, free admission), with a half-dozen old log buildings and a replica general store filled with historical artifacts.

About three miles west of town along County Highway 16 is the unique **Uppgaard Wildlife Management Area** (218/828-2228). The 110-acre tract surrounds two lakes and is used as a landscaping-for-wildlife demonstration area. Even if you have no interest in this subject, it's a scenic walk (guided tours 9 A.M. Wed. summer), and there's a good chance of spotting wildlife along the easy 1.5-mile trail.

Paddlers will enjoy the 19-mile trip to the Mississippi along the **Pine River,** a little known but very scenic paddling stream. It's a very easy run with just a few small rapids.

Accommodations

Pine Terrace Resort (35101 Pine Terrace Rd., 218/543-4606 or 800/950-1986, www.pineterrace.com, $785/week) is exactly what a family resort should be: small and peaceful with a great view right out your cabin. There are no other resorts and only a few houses on scenic Star Lake, and no personal watercraft or large boats are allowed. The twelve spic-and-span cabins, ten on the lake and two perched up on the hill, each come with a boat, dock, and grill.

Although it looks modern, **Manhattan Beach Lodge** (39051 Hwy. 66, 218/692-3381, www.mblodge.com, $69–139) was actually built in the 1920s and hosted many Chicagoland gangsters soon after. Each of the 18 rooms has a sunset view over Big Trout Lake, and facilities include a small beach, whirlpool, sauna, and exercise room.

The U.S. Army Corps of Engineers' **Crosslake Recreation Area** (35507 Hwy. 66, 218/692-2025 or 877/444-6777, $18 non-electric, $24 electric) at the junction of County Highways 3 and 66 is about as good as a 125-site RV campground can be. All sites are shaded, and there is also a public beach and boat launch here.

Food

Whether you come by boat or by car, you'll find **Moonlite Bay** (37627 County Rd. 66, 218/692-3575, www.moonlitebay.com, $9–22) packed with people there not just to have dinner but to make a night of it with music and dancing. Vacationers have been coming here since 1933 (although the original building burned down). The menu is typically neo-Northwoods—burgers, steaks, walleye.

For fine dining try **Manhattan's** at the Manhattan Beach Lodge (39051 Hwy. 66, 218/692-3381, www.mblodge.com, 11 A.M.–10 P.M. daily summer, hours vary rest of year, $8–28), whose eclectic menu includes chicken pecan pasta, prime rib, and Thai walleye. Vegetarians will find more choices here than at most Northwoods restaurants.

For mostaccioli, lasagna, peppery hot sausage, pizza, and other Italian favorites, try **Maucieri's** (34650 Hwy. 3, 218/692-4800, www.maucieris.com, 11 A.M.–9 P.M. daily, open until 10 P.M. summer, $5–22) south of town. Bands play on weekends.

Information

The **Crosslake Area Welcome Center** (218/692-4027, 10 A.M.–4 P.M. Mon.–Sat. summer, by chance rest of year) is at the junction of County Highways 3 and 66.

Headwaters

When Henry Rowe Schoolcraft stepped onto the shore of Lake Itasca in 1832, he not only identified the source of the Mississippi River, but also ensured that generations of visitors would follow in his footsteps. Half a million people are drawn to the region annually, and not just to amble across the mighty river's meager headwaters at Itasca State Park, but also to visit family-friendly Park Rapids, the surprisingly artsy college town Bemidji, and a collection of quirky tourist-trap villages. They're all set in a legendary forest, big enough to give birth to Paul Bunyan.

PARK RAPIDS

The "Gateway to Itasca State Park" centers around a bustling, old-fashioned downtown and its unique center-of-street parking, a legacy of logging days when streets were built extra wide to accommodate oxcarts making U-turns. Logging was the early mainstay of the local economy, with several mills operating on the Fish Hook River, but tourism, fueled by the establishment of Itasca State Park in 1891 and aided by the arrival of the railroad that same year, gained its foothold early. The hordes of visitors drawn by a wealth of outdoor recreation—not just in the state park, but also on the Heartland State Trail and dozens of nearby lakes—have not drained this city of its down-to-earth personality.

Sights and Recreation

Two museums, the **Hubbard County Historical Society** (301 Court Ave., 218/732-5237, 11 A.M.–5 P.M. Tues.–Sun. May–Sept., free admission) and the **North Country Museum of Arts** (301 Court Ave., 218/237-5900, 11 A.M.–5 P.M. Tues.–Sun. May–Oct.), share a home in the original Hubbard County

Courthouse. On the bottom floor, local history is showcased in typical fashion: rooms stuffed with artifacts including old typewriters, farm tools, and women's clothing dating back to the 1880s. There's also a replica classroom from a circa-1905 school and a cabin interior showing the quality of local life when residents were pioneers on a challenging frontier.

The **Heartland State Trail** starts in downtown Park Rapids and continues 49 paved miles north on an abandoned railroad grade to Cass Lake, passing many lakes along the way. **Northern Cycle** (501 1st St. E., 218/732-5971, 9 A.M.–5 P.M. Mon.–Sat., 11 A.M.–5 P.M. Sun.) rents bikes and in-line skates.

Entertainment and Events

Summer stages are very busy in Park Rapids. The **Northern Light Opera Company** (11700 Island Lake Dr., 218/237-0400, www.northernlight-opera.org) produces operettas—a lot of Gilbert and Sullivan and Rogers and Hammerstein—in the Park Rapids high school.

Long Lake Theater (12183 Beacon Rd., 218/732-0099, www.longlaketheater.net) has its own building in nearby Hubbard, where it stages mostly contemporary comedies and hosts visiting performers and open-mic nights.

Jasper's Jubilee Theater (17339 Hwy. 34 E., 218/237-4333, www.jasperstheater.com), is a popular "Branson-style" musical revue.

Lakes, Loons, and Legends, an art and music festival held the second weekend in August, is one of the largest of Park Rapids' many events. There's also a loon-calling contest and beer garden. Menahga, 12 miles south of Park Rapids, hosts one of the state's largest **St. Urho's Day** events on March 16—a popular and entirely made-up Finnish-American holiday celebrating the fictional "saint" who supposedly drove the grasshoppers out of Finland.

Shopping

Summerhill Farm (218/732-3865, 10:30 A.M.–5 P.M. Mon.–Sat., 11 A.M.–4 P.M. Sun. summer), six miles north of town on U.S. Highway 71, is a small shopping complex on a former dairy farm selling everything from women's clothing to gourmet chocolate. The blue-painted farm buildings are only open during the summer.

Rich's (409 Park Ave. S., 218/732-3949, 9 A.M.–5 P.M. Mon.–Sat., 10 A.M.–4 P.M. Sun.) and **Six-Toed Cat** (2083 Hwy. 34, 218/732-8919, 10 A.M.–5 P.M. Wed.–Sat., closed Sun.) are two antiques stores worth a look.

Accommodations

There are many good bed-and-breakfasts in and around Park Rapids. Right in town, the **Red Bridge Inn** (118 Washington Ave. N., 218/237-7337 or 888/733-7241, www.redbridgeinn.com, $125) is a big, funky pink house perched on the edge of the lovely Fish Hook River near its namesake walkway. It could have been called the River View Inn since all six guestrooms overlook the river, as does the enormous backyard deck. All guestrooms also have a private bath and are tastefully filled with antique furnishings.

The **Lady Slipper Inn** (51722 270th St., 218/573-3353 or 800/531-2787, www.ladyslipperinn.com, $125) between Park Rapids and the Tamarack National Wildlife Refuge sits on 160 acres with two spring-fed ponds and a cedar bog. There are trails on the property, and guests have free use of snowshoes, as well as canoes and paddleboats.

LoonSong (17248 LoonSong Ln., 888/825-8135, www.loonsongbedandbreakfast.com, $99–125) is a homey lakeside log cabin with four rooms decorated with cozy, comfy Americana.

Jewel of the Northwoods Bed & Breakfast (39050 Twin Lakes Rd., 218/564-6162, www.jewelofthenorthwoods.com, $50–100) in Menahga is homey and run by a very solicitous and welcoming family (as well as their resident cats and dogs!). There are three rooms, including the spacious April Francesca suite, which has a private balcony overlooking the lake.

Newer hotels include the **C'mon Inn** (1009 1st St. E., 218/732-1471 or 800/258-6891, www.cmoninn.com, $90), which has a pool, hot tub, and game room, and the **Super 8** (1020 1st St. E., 218/732-9704 or 877/274-

3040, www.parkrapidssuper8.com, $82), which has a sauna and a hot tub.

Food

The **Rapid River Logging Camp** (15073 County Rd. 18, 218/732-3444, 7:30 A.M.–9 P.M. daily, $7.95 breakfast, $11.95 lunch and dinner), six miles north of town (take U.S. 71 to County Highway 18 and follow the signs), offers a unique dining experience in the bygone spirit of logging-camp mess halls. An all-you-can-eat set menu is served on tin plates and cups at wooden tables and benches in a log hall. There is some old logging equipment on the grounds and a big gift shop.

The **Schwarzwald Inn** (122 Main St. S., 218/732-8828, 7 A.M.–8 P.M. daily, $3–11) specializes in German cuisine, though most of the menu, including the huge breakfast platters, is American-style. There's a small but good wine list and fun decorations around the dining room.

Bella Caffe (116 3rd St. W., 218/732-7625, 7 A.M.–8 P.M. Mon.–Thurs. and Sat., 7 A.M.–8 P.M. Fri., 9 A.M.–4 P.M. Sun., $5–7) is a small space known for its wine and espresso. They also serve panini sandwiches during lunch.

The **MinneSoda Fountain** (205 Main St. S., 218/732-3240, 11 A.M.–8 P.M. Mon.–Sat., noon–5 P.M. Sun., $4–10) has a huge selection of ice cream goodies, as well as sandwiches and subs. The checkerboard floor and counter stools lend nostalgic ambience.

Information and Services

The **Park Rapids Area Chamber of Commerce** (1204 Park Ave. S., 218/732-4111 or 800/247-0054, www.parkrapids.com, 7 A.M.–5 P.M. Mon.–Fri. year-round, plus 9 A.M.–4 P.M. Sat. summer) offers information on Park Rapids and surrounding communities.

WEST OF PARK RAPIDS

Three unique little towns, each boasting a world-class tourist trap, lie between Park Rapids and Walker, and the **Heartland State Trail** bike path links them all.

Dorset

Tiny Dorset's claim to be "The Restaurant Capital of the World" seems preposterous at first glance, but the numbers don't lie. With four restaurants and a population of just 26, there probably isn't any place that can beat the per-capita average. With four gift shops, plus an old-time photo studio, it could probably compete for a world gift shop title too. Downtown Dorset is really just a single block, surrounded by quiet fields, where shops and restaurants line up along Old West–style boardwalks and the community ethos has distinctly more to do with play than work.

Of course, a town of such culinary fame must have a food festival, and the annual **Taste of Dorset** is held the first Sunday in August. You can sample foods on the boardwalk or enter the minnow races, though the day's highlight is the election of the mayor of Dorset; the only qualification to be a candidate is the ability to plunk down $1.

Besides a good Minnesota section, **Sister Wolf Books** (20471 Hwy. 226, 218/732-7565, www.sisterwolfbooks.com, 10 A.M.–9 P.M. daily May–Sept.) has an espresso bar.

The town's 1920 schoolhouse has been converted to a homey inn, which makes an interesting mix of styles. The six guestrooms (in the old classrooms) at the **Heartland Trail B&B** (20220 Friar Rd., 218/732-3252, www.heartlandbb.com, May–Nov., $80) all have 12-foot ceilings, a fireplace, and a private bath, plus guests can make themselves at home on two outdoor decks or in the library and TV area. The bed-and-breakfast is located right next to its namesake, and offers bike rentals ($20/day, half-priced for guests).

None of Dorset's restaurants will be gracing the pages of *Gourmet* magazine, but they are friendly enough—and Dorset itself is picturesque enough—to attract diners from miles around. The **Dorset Café** (20456 Hwy. 226, 218/732-4072, 4:30–10 P.M. Mon.–Sat., noon–8 P.M. Sun., Apr.–Oct., closed Mon.–Tues. rest of year, $6–18) features family fare like roasted chicken, baked lemon-pepper cod, and steak.

Cute little **La Pasta** (20470 Hwy. 226, 218/732-0275, 7:30 A.M.–9 P.M. daily

THE LARGER-THAN-LIFE LUMBERJACK

Paul Bunyan is the pinnacle of American tall tales. His early years are lost to time, but it is assumed that the first stories of the extraordinary lumberjack circulated through the logging camps of Minnesota, Wisconsin, and Michigan in the late 1800s, though apparently they were not very widespread. The immigrant lumberjacks, whose sense of humor was as vast as the new land they conquered, created a colleague so large that his meals were cooked on a griddle greased by men using hams as skates, so strong that he could fell 20 trees in a single stroke, so fast that he could blow out his lantern and jump into bed before the room became dark, and so smart that he trained beavers to build dams for him. The flamboyant lumberjack has since starred in a Disney movie, been featured on a U.S. postage stamp, and had an acclaimed opera written about him.

Paul's over-the-top stories may have originated in lumber camps, but they didn't gain a popular audience until after most of the forests of his birthplace had been cleared. James MacGillivray, a *Detroit News* reporter, first put the legendary lumberjack in print in 1910 with a brief mention in the story "The Round River Drive." Four years later Minneapolis ad man and former Minnesota lumberjack William Laughead put the myth in the national spotlight with a series of illustrated pamphlets sharing the exploits of Paul as well as extolling the virtues of the Red River Lumber Company for whom they both worked. In 1922 Laughead expanded the tales in *The Marvelous Exploits of Paul Bunyan as told in the camps of the white pine lumberman for generations, during which time the loggers have pioneered the way through the north woods from Maine to California, collected from various sources and embellished for publication*. The book became so popular that Red River began publishing annual editions and gave away over 100,000 of them over the next two decades. The popularity of these stories led to serious analysis by university professors and an endless stream of children's books.

In Minnesota, Paul Bunyan lives on in more than just legend. His name graces everything from bowling alleys to bike trails to Internet service providers – ironically, there is even a Paul Bunyan Nature Center – and many old logging towns like Bemidji honor him and his contemporaries with giant statues. The most widespread reminders of Paul are Minnesota's many lakes which, according to legend, are the footprints of his partner, Babe the Blue Ox, who "weighed more than the combined weight of all the fish that ever got away."

May–Sept., $6–20) serves American breakfasts, burgers, and pastas for lunch, and a full Italian menu at dinner.

The **Dorset House Restaurant & Soda Fountain** (20415 Hwy. 226, 218/732-5556, 11 A.M.–10 P.M., closing time varies throughout year, $8.95 dinner buffet) has pizzas and dairy treats with an all-you-can-eat dinner buffet.

For more information about Dorset, pick up the annual **Dorset Daily Bugle,** a tongue-in-cheek local rag, or check out their website (www.dorsetmn.com).

Akeley

As the Heartland State Trail enters Akeley from the west, it passes over a trestle above the Crow Wing River, which flows out of the 11th lake in the Crow Wing Chain, a system of lakes popular with canoeists and a central factor in the town's history. Akeley was once an important logging town that boomed when the Red River Lumber Company, who popularized the legend of Paul Bunyan, opened a sawmill here in 1898. Over the next 19 years they cut up eight million trees before packing up and moving their operations to California. The town continued to grow for another decade, peaking with a population of 4,512 people in 1930. Since then the town has slowly declined, and today there are 4,100 fewer residents.

There is no shortage of Paul Bunyan statues in Minnesota, but since Akeley claims to be

Paul's birthplace it's appropriate that the **tallest Paul Bunyan statue** resides here. Located right on Main Street, Akeley's Paul bends down on one knee, allowing visitors to take a seat on his outstretched palm. The statue is only 25 feet tall, but he'd be twice this if he stood up.

Right behind him, the **Akeley Paul Bunyan Historical Museum** (noon–4 P.M. daily summer, free admission) has a hodgepodge of local historical items, including logging tools and photographs spanning the town's history.

The **Red River Museum** (440 Broadway E., tours 10 A.M. Tues.–Sat. May–Oct., $4 adults), attached to Bunyan's gas and convenience store on the highway, represents one man's fascination with the history of logging, specifically the Red River Lumber Company. Nels Kramer has amassed 6,000 square feet of memorabilia.

Akeley is also home to the summertime **Woodtick Musical Theater** (65 Broadway St. E., 218/652-4200 or 800/644-6892, www.woodticktheater.com, shows at 3 P.M. Wed.–Thurs. and 8 P.M. Wed.–Sat. mid-June–mid-Sept., $15.50 adults), which presents a two-hour Grand Ole Opry–like stage show with a satirical Minnesotan touch.

One of the area's best-known restaurants lies a little west of town. **Brauhaus** (28234 Hwy. 34, 218/652-2478, 4–10 P.M. Wed.–Sat., noon–10 P.M. Sun. Apr.–Oct., $11–22) features German specialties such as plum-glazed duck and *rinderbraten* (roast beef), plus American dishes such as buffalo steak. There's a large selection of imported wine and beer, and the staff is garbed in traditional German costumes.

ITASCA STATE PARK

Established in 1891, Itasca was Minnesota's first state park, and it remains one of the best loved. At over 32,000 acres, harboring the humble headwaters of the Mississippi River and a wealth of history, Itasca is a state park with national significance; in fact, it's a National Natural Landmark. One could easily spend a week here getting to know the shores of Lake Itasca, learning about the history of exploration and conservation in the park, spotting wildlife in a landscape covered by towering pine forests and over 100 deep glacial lakes, and staring in awe at the diminutive inauguration of North America's greatest river.

History

Though he wasn't the first white man to pass through, explorer Henry Rowe Schoolcraft did identify this as the source of the Mississippi River in 1832. He was accompanied here by the Ojibwe guide Ozawindib and created the name Itasca for the lake from which the river flows by combining the middle syllables of the Latin phrase *Veritas caput,* meaning "true head." Subsequent decades saw various challenges to Schoolcraft's claim, but in the late 1800s Jacob V. Brower—a historian, anthropologist, and land surveyor—largely put the matter to rest. Though Lake Itasca is fed by five tributaries, Brower determined that its outflow is the first point where the volume of water is great enough to truly be called a river. It was Brower who spearheaded efforts to establish Itasca State Park and thus protect the virgin pine stands from Minnesota's burgeoning logging industry. On April 20, 1891, the proposal squeaked through the Minnesota state legislature. An era of wilderness tourism had begun, and today Itasca preserves the majority of Minnesota's 15,000 remaining acres of virgin pine forest.

Jacob V. Brower Visitor Center

Itasca's visitor center (218/266-2100, 8 A.M.–8 P.M. daily summer, open to skiers daily but not always staffed winter) has varied historical and ecological displays, though the best place to start is the short orientation film. The excellent gift shop is stocked full of nature- and history-related books. Other places to pick up information are the campground office, the North Entrance station, and Douglas Lodge.

Mississippi Headwaters

Though it leaves Minnesota as a mile-wide behemoth, here in Itasca the Mississippi River is just a small stream tumbling over a pile of rocks. And, though tiny, the Mississippi here flows with purpose, running fast right from the

© TIM BEWER

Itasca State Park harbors the headwaters of the not yet mighty Mississippi.

start. A raindrop falling into Lake Itasca will reach the Gulf of Mexico 2,552 miles and 90 days later, dropping 1,475 feet along the way. Given that the Father of Waters drains two-thirds of the United States and holds a cherished place in the American imagination, it's no surprise that almost everyone who comes to Itasca wants to stroll over it. A 600-foot accessible trail leads to the small, man-made rock dam marking the clear outflow from the lake—if you don't want to get your feet wet there's also a nearby bridge to take you across. Outdoor display panels and exhibits in front of the Mary Gibbs Mississippi Headwaters Center discuss the river and detail the expeditions of Henry Rowe Schoolcraft and other explorers.

Wilderness Drive

A good way to tour to get a taste of the park is along **Wilderness Drive,** a 10-mile one-way route shared by cars and bicycles that circles the 2,000-acre **Itasca Wilderness Sanctuary.** The **Forestry Demonstration Area** is a CCC plantation with interpretive markers detailing the basics of forest management. **Minnesota's largest red and white pines** are each a short distance off the road. Near the red pine is the **Bison Kill Site** where Native Americans hunted buffalo 8,000 years ago. The restored 1917 **Nicollet Cabin** is less than a mile down the Nicollet Trail, and a good place for a picnic.

The route passes **Elk Lake,** sometime contender for the headwaters title, before ending up back at the Douglas Lodge area. The **Aiton Heights Fire Tower** near the end of the drive is reached by hiking about three-quarters of a mile from the parking area on Wilderness Drive or via the 1.5-mile Deer Park Trail, which starts at Douglas Lodge. The 110-foot tower can be climbed (except during the winter), and interpretive signs detail forest canopy wildlife and the history of fire towers.

Other Sights

Across the main park drive from the visitors center, **Douglas Lodge** anchors a small village of historic buildings on the south end of Lake Itasca. Completed in 1906, the log-and-stone structure's large lobby has a stone fireplace and wicker furniture, and it's worth a peek inside even if you aren't sleeping or eating here.

Nearby, the 1940 **Forest Inn** is the most significant contribution of the CCC workers who labored in Itasca during the Great Depression. It features a large, cathedral-ceilinged meeting room and houses a summer-only gift shop.

Many other historic log structures—including the **Dormitory, Clubhouse,** and **Fireplace Rooms**—were renovated during the 1980s and '90s. Pick up the *Historic Buildings Tour* brochure for more information on the construction and renovation of these buildings.

A quarter-mile down the Dr. Robert's Trail, which leaves from the pier below Douglas Lodge, the **Old Timer's Cabin** is worth a look for its almost comical construction: It's a small cabin built of logs so enormous that it only took four to complete each wall.

Heading north from Douglas Lodge (which you can do by car, bike, or foot), there are two prime lookout spots on the east shore of Lake Itasca. **Preachers' Grove** is a stand of 250-year-old pines, named for preachers' conventions once held there, and the **Peace Pipe Vista** is a wooden platform a mile or so farther north.

The small, summer-only **Itasca Museum** focuses on the park's early history and the **Wegmann Store Ruins** mark the spot where Theodore Wegmann, the park's first game warden, and his wife, Johanna, ran a small store and post office in the park's early days. Alongside the ruins of their cabins, a reconstructed version of their homestead gives a sense of what the original was like. The Wegmanns and 12 others are buried in the nearby **Pioneer Cemetery,** where graves date to 1898. The nearby **Indian Cemetery** is a series of Native American burial mounds.

Trails

The 33 miles of hiking trail in Itasca range from short bog boardwalks to isolated paths along remote lakes. Three of the easiest trails, each half a mile in length, branch off the west side of Wilderness Drive. The **Landmark Interpretation Trail** affords access to a deer exclosure, while the **Blowdown Trail** is known as a bird-watching loop and also gives a close-up look at wind-damaged trees. The **Bohall Trail** leads out to Bohall Lake and is the only trail that goes into the Itasca Wilderness Sanctuary. Also starting from Wilderness Drive, the 2.5-mile **Two Spot Trail** and 3.8-mile **Nicollet Trail** are both great places to spot wildlife in Itasca's wild interior.

The **Dr. Roberts Trail** is an accessible two-mile loop near Douglas Lodge that starts out as a bog boardwalk—great for orchid-viewing—before reaching the Old Timer's Cabin and continuing along Lyendecker Lake. The **Deer Park Trail,** also highly recommended, is 3.1 miles long, wide and grassy, and leads past many small lakes and several hike-in campsites—beaver and otter are often spotted here.

Hugging the shore of Lake Itasca, the two-mile **Brower Trail** is an excellent way to travel between Bear Paw Campground and the Douglas Lodge area. It passes **Peace Pipe Vista** and **Preachers' Grove** along the way and frequently serves up bald eagle and loon sightings. The mile-long **LaSalle Trail** passes through a pine regeneration area where you might see woodcock peenting in the spring. The Ozawindib Trail and Eagle Scout Trail are both really parts of the **North Country National Scenic Trail,** which leads from North Dakota to New York. Itasca's 13 miles of this 4,200-mile route pass through the southwest quadrant, the park's most undisturbed corner.

A five-mile paved **bike trail** runs along the east shore of Lake Itasca, connecting the Mississippi Headwaters with Douglas Lodge. It is gently rolling along most of its length and cross-country skiers use it in wintertime. Bikers can continue around the Wilderness Drive for another 10 miles. Other trails used by cross-country skiers include Aiton Heights, Deer Park, DeSoto, Eagle Scout, Nicollet, North Country Trail, and Red Pine—31 miles are groomed in total.

Other Recreation

Canoeists favor Itasca's four main lakes: Itasca, Elk, Mary, and Ozawindib. In spring, some canoeists take on the Mississippi River, but this becomes impossible later in the year when the water level drops. Motorboats are also permitted on the four main lakes with a 10-mph speed limit.

Itasca Sports Rental (15441 Main Park Dr., 218/266-2150, www.itascasports.com, 7 A.M.–9 P.M. daily May–Oct.) rents a wide selection of outdoor equipment, including bikes, canoes, kayaks, motorboats, and paddleboats. They also offer fishing licenses, bait, fish-freezing, and battery-charging. Snowshoes can be rented at the visitors center.

There's a **swimming beach** by the Brower Inn.

Accommodations

Itasca lodging facilities are open Memorial Day to mid-October, and reservations (866/857-2757 or www.stayatmnparks.com) are essential (though you might get lucky and find openings on short notice during the week).

The 1905 **Douglas Lodge** ($69) is a lovely log building with leafy views of Lake Itasca from its deck and dining room. Most guestrooms have double beds and shared baths, but there are also several two-bedroom suites with private baths.

There are also a variety of **cabins** available for rent in Itasca. Near Douglas Lodge, 15 cabins ranging from one to three bedrooms are scattered along the lakeshore. All have living rooms, and some have fireplaces and screened porches. Prices range $100–195 depending on size and number of guests.

Also near Douglas Lodge are the modern **Itasca Suites** ($115), which can sleep four. Housekeeping cabins ($103) near the Bear Paw Campground sleep four people and have full kitchens, but no private showers (guests can use the campground showers). Four **fireplace rooms** ($90)—essentially motel units in a CCC-era building—have fireplaces and screened porches.

Another lodging option—equally appealing, and much less expensive—is the **Mississippi Headwaters Hostel** (27910 Forest Ln., 218/266-3415, $27), housed in another historic log building that once served as park headquarters. The Hostelling International–affiliated facility offers 31 beds, a kitchen and dining area, living area with fireplace, and an outside fire ring. The basic, cozy amenities are used more often by families than the expected twenty-something backpackers, though all are welcome. They are closed for much of the spring and fall.

Camping

Itasca has two campgrounds (866/857-2757) with full facilities. With 223 sites (100 electric), **Pine Ridge** is the larger of the two and stays open year-round. The northern loops—Poplar and Pine—have more widely spaced sites and lack electricity, so they are the most peaceful in the park. **Bear Paw,** right on the lakeshore, has 68 campsites (35 electric), and 11 of these are cart-in sites. Itasca also has 11 **backpack sites** on or very near the park's smaller lakes. Call for reservations at either.

Food

Douglas Lodge (8 A.M.–8 P.M. daily June–Oct., $3–21) has a full-service restaurant with lovely views from the picture windows or from the outside deck in back. Choices include buffalo burgers, steak, and wild rice hot dish. Try the wild rice pancakes for breakfast. The snack bar at the **Mary Gibbs Mississippi Headwaters Center** (breakfast and lunch daily June–Oct.) offers inexpensive sandwiches, salads, desserts, and beverages.

BEMIDJI

Stretched along the shore of 6,765-acre Lake Bemidji and energized by an infusion of thousands of college students, the "First City on the Mississippi" (pop. 13,500) has a sophisticated feel that belies its size. Bemidji is an art-friendly place with an excellent history museum and enough good restaurants and other diversions to distract you from outdoor activities for a day or two.

The city takes its name from the Ojibwe phrase Bemiji-gau-maug ("cutting sideways through"), which describes the diagonal path the Mississippi River takes across the lake. A trading post and sawmill opened in the late 1800s and settlers, mostly Scandinavians, soon followed. As the town grew throughout the 1890s, logging established itself as the area's primary industry, and it remains important today. Tourists arriving en masse during visits to the Chippewa National Forest and Itasca State Park have given the city an economic mix that ensures its vitality.

Sights

You can't miss Bemidji's most famous attraction: the giant statues of **Paul Bunyan and Babe the Blue Ox.** The Northwoods folk heroes stand on the downtown waterfront greeting visitors as they arrive in town. Built in 1937 for a winter carnival, Paul and Babe graced the pages of *Life* magazine that same year and soon inspired the whole trend of oversized sculptures in Minnesota. Right next to the statues, the CVB has a hokey display of Paul's personal effects, including a giant toothbrush and boxer shorts. There's also a fireplace built with stones from 48 states and the Canadian provinces. A Native statue of Chief Bemidji, just as tall as Paul, waves at them from across the street.

Bemidji is something of an artist's haven, and its credentials include a **sculpture walk** around the downtown. Twenty public sculptures are on display, and a brochure available at several spots around town points you to their locations. There are some new ones every year, and the sculptures are available for sale.

The **Bemidji Community Art Center** (426 Bemidji Ave. N., 218/444-7570, www.bcac-mn.org, noon–5 P.M. Tues.–Fri., noon–4 P.M. Sat., free admission) is a gallery space located in a historic Carnegie Library that showcases changing exhibits by regional artists.

The attractive lakeside campus of **Bemidji State University** (218/755-3735), just north of downtown, has two tiny art galleries with student and other work: The **Talley Gallery** (9 A.M.–9 P.M. Mon.–Thurs., 9 A.M.–4 P.M. Fri.–Sat., closed Sun., free admission) is in the Education Art Building and the **Touche Gallerie** (8 A.M.–7 P.M. Mon.–Fri., closed Sat.–Sun., free admission) is in the Hobson Memorial Union. Both are open only during the school year.

The **Beltrami County History Center** (130 Minnesota Ave. SW, 218/444-3376, 10 A.M.–4 P.M. Mon.–Sat., closed Sun., $5) is housed in the beautifully restored 1912 Great Northern Depot. It's small, but unlike most local history museums, it is professionally curated, using photographs, maps, and artifacts to tell stories about the area's past. A telegrapher's station and a collection of Native American artifacts (including some wonderful bandolier bags) are on permanent display, while other exhibits change regularly.

The **Headwaters Science Center** (413 Beltrami Ave., 218/444-4472, www.hscbemidji.org, 9:30 A.M.–5:30 P.M. Mon.–Sat., 9:30 A.M.–8 P.M. Thurs., 1–5 P.M. Sun., $5) is a kid-oriented museum featuring many hands-on exhibits. Visitors can study a living stream, climb into a bear den, and shoot their friends with an air cannon, plus the staff conducts demonstrations on various topics ranging from stone tools to cryogenics.

For something on the opposite end of the entertainment spectrum, drop a few bucks at the little **Paul Bunyan Amusement Park** (Paul Bunyan Dr. N. and 2nd St., 10 A.M.–dusk daily summer), with a mini golf course, Ferris wheel, tilt-a-whirl, and a couple of other rides.

A couple of miles east on Highway 2, **Paul Bunyan Animal Land** (3857 Animal Land Dr. SE, 218/759-1533, www.paulbunyansanimalland.com, 10 A.M.–6 P.M. daily, Memorial Day–Labor Day, $6.95) is a private zoo with more than 100 wild animals, from kangaroos to Siberian tigers.

Recreation

Headwaters Canoe Outfitters (12404 Land End Ln. SE, 218/751-2783, 8 A.M.–8 P.M. daily May–Oct.) rents canoes, arranges shuttles, and offers half- and full-day guided trips departing from Itasca Park.

Located 12 miles north of town on County Highway 15, **Buena Vista Ski Village** (119276 Lake Julia Dr. NW, 218/243-2231 or 800/777-

RED LAKE RESERVATION

- Total Area: 1,260 sq. miles
- Tribally Owned: 100 percent
- Total Population: 5,162
- Native Population: 5,071
- Tribal Enrollment: 9,294

More than just about any tribe in the United States, the Red Lake Ojibwe has done things its own way. The band lives collectively on land that has never been subdivided: Oregon's Warm Springs tribe is the only other in the United States that also successfully resisted allotment. In the late 19th century, as members struggled against outside pressure to subdivide their Rhode Island-sized home, they chased off surveyors, missionaries, and other outsiders who might pose a threat. With no land in private hands, none can be sold to outsiders without the approval of all and thus, unlike the checkerboard reservations of other Minnesota tribes, the Red Lake band still owns all of the land (excepting a few small chunks sold to a railroad) within its borders. Red Lake is also one of the nation's few "closed" reservations, meaning that except for a few federal matters, the reservation retains total control over all criminal and civil affairs. Consistent with its fierce independence, Red Lake is also the only Ojibwe band that does not belong to the Minnesota Chippewa Tribe Federation.

The Red Lake Reservation encompasses all of Lower Red Lake, the largest lake within Minnesota, as well as much of Upper Red Lake, and this land, much of it wetland, is one of the most pristine environments in the state. The reservation also includes the majority of the Northwest Angle and scattered parcels across nine counties. Tribal headquarters are located in Red Lake, an important Dakota village during the French fur-trade era, while the little villages of Redby, Little Rock, and Ponemah are the reservation's three other communities. The latter is one of the most traditional Native towns in the Lower 48, and English remains a second language for many adult residents across the reservation.

Though Red Lake suffers economically because of its isolation, it has managed to succeed in several natural-resource industries, including logging and gravel mining. The Red Lake Fisheries Association, the oldest Native-controlled marketing cooperative in North America, began in 1929 and had 300 members until their excessive netting of walleye caused the population to collapse. Thanks to intensive efforts by the tribe and the state, walleye are recovering. Cranberries and wild rice are still small industries, but with tens of thousands of acres suitable for cultivation they have great potential. The tribe's Seven Clans Casinos operate in Red Lake, Warroad, and Thief River Falls.

7958, www.bvskiarea.com) has 16 runs for downhill skiing and snowboarding, plus a terrain park and tubing hills, built around a historic village. You can also take a sleigh ride when it's snowy or a covered wagon ride during the fall-color season. Buena Vista hosts the **Finlandia Ski Marathon** (218/751-0041, www.minnesotafinlandia.com), with three days of events in mid-February.

Lake Bemidji State Park

Only five miles north of town, Lake Bemidji State Park (3401 State Park Rd. NE, 218/308-2300) is a popular place. Most people come to enjoy the lakefront—an accessible fishing pier, public boat access, and boat rentals make the park a good place for fishing, and there is a sandy swimming beach below the visitors center—though nature lovers are well served too. With its various habitats, including upland red and white pine forests, jack pine barrens, and scattered wetlands, the 1,688-acre park is home to diverse flora and fauna. The park's premier hike is the **Bog Walk,** a 1,200-foot boardwalk leading through a spruce-tamarack bog before winding up at isolated Big Bog Lake. Interpretive signs along the way discuss the formation of bogs and the flora visible from the trail, including the insectivorous sundews and pitcher plants and myriad orchids—most bog flowers bloom in late spring and early summer. The wheelchair-accessible boardwalk is reached via a one-mile gravel path. The Bog Walk connects to a 15-mile network of longer trails across the park, including the 3.6-mile **Old Logging Trail** and 2.5-mile **Pinewood Trail,** which wind through mixed pine and aspen forests. Flowers are also abundant along the **Sundew Pond Boardwalk,** an easy mile-long walk down the **Fish Hawk Trail.** The mile-long **Rocky Point Trail** near the visitors center climbs a bluff overlooking the lake. Off-road bikes are allowed on five miles of trail, while the northern trailhead of the **Paul Bunyan State Trail** is also located at the park—currently the northern end is only paved for the first six miles, though when completed it will run 110 miles south to Brainerd. Winter brings 11 miles of groomed trail for cross-country skiing and snowshoe rentals. The 98-site (43 electric) campground is quiet and shady, though not very secluded.

Entertainment and Events

Bemidji State University (1500 Birchmont Ave. NE, 218/755-2001, www.bemidjistate.edu) hosts a full spectrum of theater and music, including a two-day jazz festival in February.

The **Bemidji Symphony Orchestra** (218/444-7914, www.bemidjisymphony.org) performs in the Bemidji High School building (2900 Division St. W.). Look for their frequent family concerts.

The **Paul Bunyan Playhouse** (314 Beltrami Ave., 218/751-7270, www.paulbunyanplayhouse.com), one of the oldest professional summer theaters in the nation, stages drama, comedy, and musicals.

There's something going on every night of the week at **Brigid's Cross** (317 Beltrami Ave. NW, 218/444-0567, www.brigidsirishpub.com, noon–11 P.M. Mon.–Wed., noon–1 A.M. Thurs.–Sat., closed Sun.), whether it's trivia, games, auditions, or professional Irish music.

Bemidji has a busy schedule of events, starting with January's **Brrrmidji Polar Daze,** a weeklong celebration of winter with ice golf, a 5K run, and swimming in Lake Bemidji.

In February, Buena Vista Ski Area hosts **Logging Days,** where participants relive the historic logging era with demonstrations, sleigh rides, and a stump-pulling contest.

Shopping

The **Bemidji Woolen Mills Factory Store** (301 Irvine Ave. NW, 218/751-5166, 8 A.M.–5:30 P.M. Mon.–Sat., 10 A.M.–5 P.M. Sun.) offers some of their locally made clothes, such as heavy-duty voyageurs jackets, but also similar items from many other companies. It is quite a popular destination.

Across the street, **Gallery North** (502 3rd St. NW, 218/444-9813, 10 A.M.–5 P.M. Mon.–Sat., closed Sun.) sells affordable works by local artists in just about any media, and some of the people are often working on-site.

Grandma's Attic (502 3rd St. NW, 218/759-8931, 10 A.M.–5 P.M. Mon.–Sat., closed Sun.), in the same building, is the largest area antiques mall.

Book World (316 Beltrami Ave. NW, 218/444-5523, 9 A.M.–8 P.M. Mon.–Fri., 9 A.M.–6 P.M. Sat., 10 A.M.–5 P.M. Sun.) has a good Minnesota section.

Accommodations

Your only bed-and-breakfast choice in Bemidji, **Villa Calma** (915 Lake Blvd. NE, 218/444-5554, www.villacalma.com, $89–139) is a restored 1910 with beautiful views of Lake Bemidji. The four guest rooms are all exceedingly comfortable, and the common areas are welcoming, as well.

The award-winning **Hampton Inn** (1019 Paul Bunyan Dr. S., 218/751-3600 or 800/426-7866, $125) sits on 650 feet of private beach on Lake Bemidji's south shore. Canoes, paddleboats, and boats are for rent at their two docks. On land there are separate pools for adults and children, a sauna, exercise room, arcade, and an all-seasons indoor-outdoor hot tub.

Taber's Historic Log Cabins (2404 Bemidji Ave. N., 218/751-5781, www.taberslogcabins.com, May–Oct., $59–89) offers a more rustic experience in 1930s log cabins. The site is convenient to downtown, but near the lakeshore, and feels secluded. Most cabins have full kitchens and special features include antique, handcrafted log furniture. Right next door is the landmark Taber's Bait and Tackle, Bemidji's oldest bait shop.

Ruttger's Birchmont Lodge (7598 Bemidji Rd. NE, 218/444-3463 or 888/788-8437, www.ruttger.com, $59 rooms, $148 cottages) on the lake's north shore is Bemidji's premier entry in the large resort category, and they offer a variety of lodging options from the basic, good-value rooms in the historic Main Lodge to modern cottages with all the extras. Ruttger's has an appropriately fancy restaurant on-site, a marina that rents boats, indoor and outdoor pools, tennis courts, and a private sandy lakeshore.

Food

Ho-hum on the outside, but ultra-elegant on the inside, **Sparkling Waters** (824 Paul Bunyan Dr. S., 218/444-3214, www.sparklingwatersbemidji.com, 11 A.M.–10 P.M. daily, $10–32), on the south end of Lake Bemidji, serves white-tablecloth favorites, including walleye meuniere and a "Nisswa" salad. The prix fixe menus at lunch and dinner are actually quite good deals.

With two locations, **Keith's Pizza** (1425 Paul Bunyan Dr. NE, 218/751-7941, 11 A.M.–10 P.M. Mon.–Sat., noon–5 P.M. Sun.; 110 Paul Bunyan Dr. SE, 218/751-7940, 11:30 A.M.–11 P.M. Mon.–Sat., 4–10 P.M. Sun., $5–16) does brick oven–baked pizza and features a garlic white sauce, as well as more traditional pies. They also do pastas and sandwiches.

Your best choice for breakfast—and creative burgers and hot sandwiches later in the day—is the **Minnesota Nice Café** (414 Beltrami Ave., 218/444-6656, 6 A.M.–4 P.M. Mon.–Thurs., 6 A.M.–8 P.M. Fri.–Sat., closed Sun., $4–6).

Locals linger over coffee and conversation at **Raphael's Bakery Cafe** (319 Minnesota Ave. NW, 218/759-2015, 6 A.M.–5:30 P.M. Mon.–Fri., 6 A.M.–2 P.M. Sat., closed Sun. $3–5). They serve breads, pastries, and cakes, plus very inexpensive soups and sandwiches in an old-fashioned atmosphere. If you only sample one thing here, make it the wild rice bread.

Both **The Cabin Coffeehouse and Cafe** (214 3rd St., 218/444-2899, 8 A.M.–9 P.M. Mon.–Fri., 8 A.M.–8 P.M. Sat., 8 A.M.–6 P.M. Sun., $4–6) and **Wild Hare Bistro and Coffeehouse** (523 Minnesota Ave., 218/444-5282, www.wildharebistro.com, 7 A.M.–5 P.M. Mon.–Fri., 9 A.M.–3 P.M. Sun., $3–9) serve organic, fair-trade coffees and gourmet create-your-own sandwiches. The latter has a shady little patio in back plus some scrumptious breakfast burritos.

Information and Services

Bemidji Tourist Information Center (300 Bemidji Ave., 800/458-2223, www.visitbemidji.com, 8 A.M.–6 P.M. Mon.–Fri., 9 A.M.–5 P.M. Sat., noon–4 P.M. Sun. summer, 8 A.M.–5 P.M. Mon.–Fri., 10 A.M.–2 P.M. Sat. rest of year) next to the Paul and Babe statues offers a wealth of information, including hotel and resort vacancy listings.

Dunn Bros Coffee (501 Paul Bunyan Dr. S., 218/444-5252, 6 A.M.–7:30 P.M. Mon.–Fri., 6 A.M.–8 P.M. Sat., 6 A.M.–7 P.M. Sun.) has computers with Internet connections for customer use.

Getting There and Around

The **Bemidji/Beltrami County Airport** (3824 Moberg Dr. NW, 218/444-2438) is west of town on U.S. Highway 2. **Delta Airlines** (800/221-1212) makes the hour-long flight to the Minneapolis–St. Paul airport four times a day. **National** (218/751-1880, www.nationalcar.com, 6 A.M.–9 P.M. Mon.–Fri., 8 A.M.–8 P.M. Sat.–Sun.) and **Enterprise** (218/759-9960, www.enterprise.com, 8 A.M.–5 P.M. Mon.–Fri., closed Sat.–Sun.), both located at the airport, rent cars.

Jefferson Lines (888/864-2832, www.jeffersonlines.com) buses stop at Golden Eagle Transportation (905 Midway Dr. S).

Chippewa National Forest

Encompassing three of the state's largest lakes, plus the infant Mississippi River and thousands of acres of forest and wetland, the Chippewa National Forest is absolutely packed with recreational opportunities. Established in 1908, this preserve became the first national forest in the eastern United States. Well over half of the forest's 667,000 acres are lakes, streams, and wetlands, including Leech Lake and Lake Winnibigoshish, the third- and fourth-largest lakes in Minnesota. In total there are 1,300 lakes within the forest boundaries. Most campgrounds sit lakeside, and there is accommodation for all tastes.

The Chippewa is home to one of the highest percentages of breeding bald eagles in the Lower 48 and most years there are about 180 pair. Federal Dam on Leech Lake, Winnie Dam on Lake Winnibigoshish, and Knutson Dam on Cass Lake are all productive fishing grounds for eagles and thus good places to spot them, especially during the winter since the churning water doesn't freeze below the dams. The birds also frequently soar over the Mississippi, so a canoe trip or a drive along U.S. Highway 2 often yields sightings. Just about all other Northwoods wildlife resides in the forest too, including osprey, common loon, northern goshawk, black-backed woodpecker, deer, pine marten, wolverine, fisher, black bear, bobcat, cougar, lynx, and wolf. In total, nearly 250 species of bird have been recorded here.

Towns within the forest—Walker is the largest—got their start as lumbering centers, but rely mostly on tourism these days. The Leech Lake Ojibwe Reservation sits within the forest, as does the north–south continental divide, also called the Laurentian Divide. Rain falling to the south of the line flows to the Gulf of Mexico via the Mississippi River, while water to the north enters the ocean via Hudson Bay. Historical sites include a CCC-era camp and several stands of old-growth pine, preserved by fortunate error and forward-thinking conservationists.

Recreation

The Chippewa has over 160 miles of trails for hikers with routes ranging in length from the half-mile walk around Elmwood Island to a 68-mile portion of the **North Country National Scenic Trail,** which stretches from New York to North Dakota. Most of the hiking trails in the forest (the North Country and Shingobee Trails are notable exceptions) are also open to off-road bicycles. Most are easy or moderate, though those looking for a challenging ride will find it—Suomi Hills is considered the most difficult mountain bike route in the forest. There are also hundreds of miles of unpaved forest roads, most fairly rough, that bikers looking to get off the beaten path can explore at will; bring a map and compass. Snowmobilers can take advantage of 315 miles of groomed trails and many forest roads, including a third of the 148-mile **Soo Line North Trail,** the longest recreation trail for motorized vehicles in Minnesota, which connects Cass Lake to Moose Lake along an abandoned rail bed.

There is good fishing right across the state, but the Chippewa National Forest encompasses some of the best of the best. These nationally recognized fishing waters provide ideal habitat for a wide variety of species. Deep basins like Benjamin Lake, Bee Cee Lake, and Diamond Lake harbor rainbow and lake trout, while more shallow, nutrient-rich lakes, including Blackduck, Winnibigoshish, Cass, and Leech, are home to walleye, muskie, northern pike, bass, and panfish. Facilities and services for anglers abound throughout the forest, and there are seemingly as many bait shops as there are lakes. There are launch services on Leech Lake, Cass Lake, and Lake Winnibigoshish.

Canoeists and kayakers have loads of water to choose from too. Nine designated routes of varying lengths and difficulties cover the forest's largest lakes and most secluded streams. There's a two-mile route on the slow-moving Shingobee River, highly recommended for

NORTH COUNTRY NATIONAL SCENIC TRAIL

When completed, the North Country National Scenic Trail will stretch 4,400 miles across seven states from Lake Sakakawea in central North Dakota to Lake Champlain in eastern New York. It will be the longest hiking trail in the nation. Currently, nearly 1,800 miles have been certified by the National Park Service since the trail's inception in 1980, and hundreds more are now hikable.

Minnesota's 850-mile slice enters from the east near Jay Cooke State Park and then turns north and merges with the Superior Hiking Trail to follow the North Shore past an abundance of waterfalls and ridgetop views of Lake Superior before turning inland near the Canadian border and crossing the remote and rugged Boundary Waters Canoe Area Wilderness along the Border Route and Kekekabic Trails. From Ely the trail heads west through public and private lands to Grand Rapids, Lake George, and then through the Chippewa National Forest – a beautiful and wild 68-mile stretch across the southern border. New trail is being built through Paul Bunyan State Forest and Itasca State Park, linking to completed trails through Tamarac National Wildlife Refuge, Maplewood State Park and into North Dakota at Breckinridge.

For more information, including trail condition reports, contact the North Country Trail Association (866/445-3628, www.northcountrytrail.org).

families, while the Turtle and Mississippi are other easy paddles with good eagle-viewing opportunities. More-difficult routes follow the Big Fork River, which has some white water, and the 120-mile Chippewa Headwaters Loop connecting Lake Winnibigoshish, Leech Lake, and Cass Lake via the Mississippi and other waterways. Canoeing on the large lakes is dangerous in high winds, so use caution and get weather information before setting out. Many of the forest's rivers have primitive campsites facilitating multi-day excursions.

Fall colors normally reach their peak around the third week in September. Call the Forest Service's **Fall Foliage Hotline** (800/354-4595) to get the up-to-the-minute scoop.

Camping

The Chippewa has 21 campgrounds on or near the forest's major lakes. Most are officially open May to September and some allow access into November; however, there will be no water or facilities available in the off-season. Each campsite has a picnic table, fire grate, tent pad, and parking spot. Beyond that, facilities vary, though three—Norway Beach, O-Ne-Gum-E, and Stony Point—have electric hookups, flush toilets, and showers. Nine of the larger, more developed campgrounds take reservations (877/444-6777, www.reserveusa.com, $9 non-refundable fee). Camping rates in summer range $14–20, depending on how developed the campground is.

Nearly 400 "dispersed" backpacking sites are sprinkled throughout the forest. For more information on these free and typically very primitive options, as well as more developed hike- and canoe-in sites, inquire at one of the district offices. Forest Service rules also permit you to camp anywhere on public land, as long as you're 100 feet from any water source or trail and observe Leave No Trace (www.lnt.org) outdoor ethics. Though registration isn't required for backcountry camping, checking in at a ranger station is always a good idea, especially to find out about any current fire restrictions.

Information

There are three ranger districts in the Chippewa: Walker, Blackduck, and Deer River. For convenience, the latter is divided into two areas. The **Forest Headquarters** (200 Ash Ave. NW, 218/335-8600 or 218/335-8632 TTY, www.fs.fed.us/r9/forests/chippewa, 7:30 A.M.–5 P.M. Mon.–Fri. May–Oct., 8 A.M.–4:30 P.M. Mon.–Fri. Nov.–Apr., closed

Sat.–Sun.) in Cass Lake can give general information, but district offices and seasonal visitors centers are the best places to get advice.

Cass Lake

Though not actually within the forest, Cass Lake is a regular stop for visitors because it lies right along U.S. Highway 2 near many of the most popular forest destinations. The body of water for which this sleepy town was named was originally dubbed Red Cedar Lake, a translation of the Ojibwe name. During his 1832 expedition to find the source of the Mississippi River, Henry Rowe Schoolcraft renamed it in honor of his friend, Lewis Cass, who as Territorial Governor led an expedition here 12 years earlier and errantly declared this the great river's source. The area's logging industry was centered here in the late 1800s and was so large that the city's population exceeded 7,000 at the turn of the 20th century. These days, Cass Lake has about ten percent that total, and its downtown is largely boarded up.

Lyle's Logging Camp and Museum (Lyle Chisholm Dr., 218/335-6723 or 800/356-8615, 10 A.M.–6 P.M. Thurs.–Mon. summer, $4) features an evocative reconstruction of a logging camp as it would have appeared during the timber industry's early 20th-century heyday. Lyle Chisholm, who had worked in a similar camp starting at age 11, built the authentic bunkhouse, mess hall, tool shop, and other buildings, and these are enhanced by recorded narratives. The museum, in a former railroad depot, houses wildlife and local history exhibits. There is a **traditional Ojibwe garden** across the road.

Known as the Log Palace, the remarkable **Chippewa National Forest Headquarters** (200 Ash Ave. NW, 218/335-8600, 7:30 A.M.–5 P.M. Mon.–Fri., closed Sat.–Sun.) was the largest log structure in Minnesota when built in 1935. Constructed from giant red pine, the three-story structure surrounds a 50-foot-high fireplace built from glacial boulders. The Finnish-style log construction uses only grooves and notches to fit the logs together, no nails, while handcrafted interior features include gnarled stair railings, split-log steps, and hand-hammered ironwork. Also inside are a few Forest Service and natural history exhibits. The **Heartland State Trail** is paved all the way to Park Rapids, 49 miles to the southwest, though there are no bike rentals in town. You can rent a fishing or pontoon boat from **Sailstar Marina** (741 Sail Star Dr. NE, 218/335-2316, 8 A.M.–6 P.M. Mon.–Sat. 9 A.M.–6 P.M. Sun.). Cass Lake **powwows** are very popular. Three take place every summer—Memorial Day, Fourth of July, and Labor Day—at the Veterans Memorial Grounds near the Palace Casino.

About 30 family- and fishing-focused resorts sit on the surrounding lakes, with about half of those on Cass Lake itself. **Sah-Kah-Tay Resort** (16348 60th Ave. NW, 218/335-2424 or 800/232-3224, www.sahkahtay.com, $96 daily, $480 weekly), north of town on Cass Lake's west shore, is typical. There are 11 two- to five-bedroom housekeeping cabins near the shady lakefront, and guests have access to a good beach, sheltered harbor, outdoor fireplace, and boat rental.

The large **Palace Casino Hotel** (6280 Upper Cass Frontage Rd. NW, 218/335-8935 or 800/442-3910, www.palacecasinohotel.com, $55) at the Leech Lake Band Ojibwe's casino has a pool, hot tub, and a game room. They also have a few RV campsites.

The **Cass Lake Information Center** (16599 69th Ave. NW, 218/335-2250 or 800/356-8615, www.casslake.com, 8 A.M.–4:30 P.M. Mon.–Fri., closed Sat.–Sun.) lies along U.S. Highway 2. They can help you find hotel and resort vacancies on short notice.

Jefferson Lines (888/864-2832, www.jeffersonlines.com) buses stop at the Che-Wa-Ka-E-Gon Gift Shop (115 6th St. NW).

WALKER DISTRICT

By far the biggest and busiest town in the forest, Walker (pop. 1,200) bustles with visitors tramping between the restaurants and gift shops. It sits on the western arm of busy Leech Lake—Minnesota's third largest with 122,610 acres of water and 154 miles of shoreline. Though this part of the forest is more heavily developed than the rest, the activity isn't overwhelming.

LEECH LAKE RESERVATION

- Total Area: 1,310 sq. miles
- Tribally Owned: 3 percent
- Total Population: 10,205
- Native Population: 4,561
- Tribal Enrollment: 8,917

The Mississippi and Pillager Ojibwe bands first arrived in the wooded and swampy areas of north central Minnesota around the mid-18th century, originally making their homes on the small islands of Leech Lake. The reservation was created in a series of treaties and executive orders between 1855 and 1874, and an 1864 resettlement plan developed by the U.S. Government called for moving all of Minnesota's Ojibwe here, though the relocation effort was redirected to the White Earth Reservation three years later. It was at Sugar Point – now known as Battle Point – on the northeast shore of Leech Lake that the Ojibwe Chief Bug-Oh-Nay-Geshig and his followers successfully fought off the army that had been sent to arrest him on trumped-up charges. Their goal was to intimidate the Ojibwe into giving up their land and timber rights. The Battle of Sugar Point, fought in 1898, is sometimes described as "the last deadly battle in the United States between the American military and the American Indian."

Today, the reservation expands over parts of Beltrami, Cass, Hubbard, and Itasca Counties, and 75 percent of the Chippewa National Forest is land that had once been part of the reservation. Itasca State Park, surrounding the headwaters of the Mississippi River, was another portion taken out of Ojibwe control.

Tribal headquarters are located in Cass Lake, with other key native settlements at Onigum, Ball Club, and Bena. Leech Lake-run casinos operate at Cass Lake, Deer River, and Walker. While tourists bring much income to the tribal community, locals also harvest wild rice on some 40 lakes to sell locally as well as on the international market.

Sights and Events

The highlight of the **Cass County History Museum** (201 Minnesota Ave. W., 218/547-7251, 10 A.M.–5 P.M. Tues.–Fri. May–Sept., $4 adults) is the Native American display with its exquisite and unusual beadwork from several tribes. There's also a birch-bark canoe inside and a 1912 one-room log schoolhouse on the grounds.

Fifteen miles northwest of town is **Forestedge Winery** (35295 Hwy. 64, 218/224-3535, 10 A.M.–5:30 P.M. Tues.–Sat., noon–5 P.M. Sun. May–Dec.), which crafts wines out of rhubarb, blueberries, cranberries, plums, and other fruits that can easily withstand harsh northern winters.

In Walker, the Leech Lake Ojibwe provide nonstop gaming action, entertainment, and a hotel at their **Northern Lights Casino** (6800 Y Frontage Rd. NW, 218/547-2744 or 800/252-7529, www.northernlightcasino.com).

Leech Lake is considered one of the world's best walleye factories, but Walker is best known for celebrating a big-headed, spotted fish that's so ugly it's cute. The **Eelpout Festival** (www.eelpoutfestival.com) one of Minnesota's best-known community celebrations, is held the second weekend of February and features fishing tournaments, a fish-house parade, and lots of cold-defying outdoor revelry to close out the ice-fishing season. The eelpout, a flatheaded freshwater cod, is also known as a burbot or lawyer. Normally reviled by anglers, it's actually a tasty catch and the 10,000 or so people who descend on the town for the festivities can sample it boiled, barbecued, or battered and fried.

Recreation

Walker lies very near the mid-point of the 49-mile **Heartland State Trail,** a wide paved path running from Park Rapids to Cass Lake, though there is no bike rental available in town.

While there is a lot to do on land in and around Walker, most people come here to get out on the lake. The easiest way to do that is with **City Dock Launch Service** (309 5th St., 218/547-1662, 8 A.M.–noon daily summer, $60), which runs daily trips in the summer for anglers seeking walleye and muskie. They rent poles and will fillet and freeze your catch if you get lucky.

Leech Lake is one of the state's top sailing waters, and you can rent a boat or take a lesson at **Fleet Sails** (6913 Hwy. 371, 218/547-1188, 10 A.M.–sunset) south of town.

Leech Lake takes up much of the Walker District, and most land-based recreation is scattered around the area to its south. **Shingobee Recreation Area** is five miles southwest of Walker off Highway 34 and was developed as a downhill ski area during the CCC era of the early 1930s. Today it's a favorite of cross-country skiers, hikers, and canoeists.

The six-mile **Shingobee National Recreational Trail** winds through the area's cedar, spruce, and balsam woods. Rolling topography provides scenic vistas and a couple of places for sledding. The **North Country National Scenic Trail** also passes through Shingobee, and the slow-moving **Shingobee River** provides a beautiful, easy canoe route.

Lake Erin is another family favorite with a half-mile interpretive trail around the lake and wetland areas that provide good wildlife-spotting opportunities. The 12-mile **Goose Lake Trail** crosses wetlands and is groomed for skiing in winter.

The 23 miles of the **Boy River** between Leech and Iguadona Lakes is favored by canoeists for its excellent bird-watching. The eight-mile **Pike Bay Connection** is a more difficult canoe route with a number of portages.

Federal Dam, where Leech Lake empties into the Leech Lake River, is a well-known eagle-watching site.

Accommodations

Over fifty resorts sit on the shore of Leech Lake, and **Adventure North** (4444 Point Landing Dr. NW, 218/547-1532 or 800/294-1532, www.adventurenorthresort.com, $150/night, $750/week) is one of the fanciest. Seven large cabins—including one that can sleep 24—have a prime location on Pine Point. There's a nice stretch of beach, a heated outdoor pool, and covered docks.

Friendly **Embracing Pines** (32287 Mississippi Rd., 218/224-3519, www.embracingpines.com, $120) bed-and-breakfast has lovely views of the Kabekona River. There is a sauna and canoes and bikes for guest use, but you might just find yourself lounging on the pier with a book. One of the three guestrooms has a private bath. It is five miles out of town on County Highway 38.

Right across the road from City Park, the **Lakeview Inn** (107 Minnesota Ave., 218/547-1212 or 800/252-5073, $48) is clean and cozy, and 6 of the 13 rooms have kitchenettes.

Camping

Stony Point ($23), a 44-site campground that juts into Leech Lake northeast of Walker, is very popular due to its scenic location, electric hookups, and modern facilities (showers and flush toilets). There's also a boat ramp and swimming beach, and the grassy sites are surrounded by old-growth forest with some trees over 200 years old. Reservations are accepted. **Mabel Lake** ($14), with 22 sites near the Boy River and a beach, and **South Pike Bay** ($16), with 24 sites and access to the Pike Bay Connection canoe route, are more secluded and primitive. Both have boat ramps. For reservations, call 877/444-6777 or go online at www.recreation.gov.

Food

The variety of dining options in Walker far exceeds all other forest towns. The ever-popular **Ranch House Supper Club** (9420 Hwy. 371 NW, 218/547-1540, 4:30–10 P.M. Mon.–Sat., 11:30 A.M.–10 P.M. Sun., $5–25) in a secluded setting four miles north of town has nightly all-you-can-eat specials served in covered-wagon booths. The regular menu includes ribs, steaks, seafood, and pasta. And you shouldn't pass up the chance to try their house specialty: honey-buttered popovers.

White tablecloths meet Northwoods decor at semi-formal **The Boulders** (8363 Lakeland Trl. NW, 218/547-1006, www.theboulderrestaurant.com, 5–9 P.M. daily summer, reduced hours rest of year, $13–28), a mile north of Walker on Highway 371. Lemon-pepper walleye, paella, and rack of lamb typify the menu.

In addition to the Americanized Mexican dishes at **Café Zona Rosa** (101 5th St. N., 218/547-3558, 11 A.M.–9 P.M. Mon.–Sat., noon–9 P.M. Sun. summer, reduced hours rest of year, $6–17), you can order a BLT wrap, fettuccine Alfredo, prime rib, and New York Strip. The cantina specializes in margaritas, and the outdoor deck is a pleasant place to dine.

Information and Services

The **Leech Lake Chamber of Commerce** (205 Minnesota Ave. W., 218/547-1313 or 800/833-1118, www.leech-lake.com, 8:30 A.M.–4:30 P.M. Mon.–Fri. year-round, plus 9 A.M.–1 P.M. Sat. summer) has information on Walker and the rest of the region. They can also find you a last-minute vacancy, not always an easy thing to do around here.

The **Walker Ranger Station** (201 Minnesota Ave. E., 218/547-1044, 7:30 A.M.–4:30 P.M. Mon.–Fri., closed Sat.–Sun.) is located on the south edge of town.

For those who don't have their own wheels, **Jefferson Lines** (888/864-2832, www.jeffersonlines.com) buses stop at the Super 1 (701 Michigan Ave.).

BLACKDUCK DISTRICT

Blackduck

Just north of the forest, Blackduck is a tidy community of 700 named after the lake just west of town. In the Ojibwe's days, 2,700-acre Blackduck Lake was a favorite feeding place for ducks, and so many descended that they obscured the water surface and inspired the name. The town honors its namesake birds with two giant **black duck statues.** One is in a small park along U.S. Highway 71, and the other sits near the fire station on Main Street. Dozens of whittlers come to town the last Saturday in July to show off their work during the **Woodcarvers Festival.**

The **Drake Motel** (172 Pine Ave., 218/835-4567 or 888/253-8501, www.drakemotel.com, $45) is a simpler and smaller option with a smaller black duck statue in front.

The **Countryside Restaurant** (240 Summit Ave. W., 218/835-3333, 6 A.M.–7 P.M. daily, $4–17) has inexpensive burgers, steaks, pizza, omelets, Hawaiian chicken, and a salad bar.

The **Hillcrest Supper Club** (20250 Tepee Hill Ln. NE, 218/835-4250, dining room 5:30–9 P.M., bar 3 P.M.–midnight Tues.–Sun., $6–33) two miles west of town (take Summit Avenue past the golf course) is similar in some regards, but has views of Blackduck Lake and a menu leaning more toward the higher end, with plenty of steak, seafood, and Polynesian ham.

Ten Section Area

The Blackduck District contains many of the forest's most popular historic and natural areas. Many of these fall within the Ten Section Area, a stand of old-growth pines east of Cass Lake that was the first area protected by law in 1902 and is thus the historical heart of the forest.

The **Norway Beach Recreation Area,** on the east shore of Cass Lake, is one of the forest's most heavily visited spots. People are drawn by the developed campground and the beach, as well as the **Norway Beach Visitor Information Center** (200 Ash Ave. NW, 218/335-8600, noon–5 P.M. Tues.–Sat. May–Sept.). The CCC-era building houses interpretive displays, and there are naturalist programs each summer.

The paved, 19-mile **Migizii Trail** leads into town, circles Pike Bay of Cass Lake, and follows the shore through Norway Beach Recreation Area; a two-mile **nature trail** gives a close-up look at the huge red pines there.

Out on Cass Lake itself **Star Island** contains a very unusual feature: 195-acre Lake Windigo, featured in *Ripley's Believe It or Not!* as the "lake in the island in the lake." Hiking the six-mile **Star Island Trail** is a good way to see most of the 1,000-acre island, named for its four-point shape. Many local resorts offer Star Island tours in the summer.

Other Recreation

Pennington Bog, a 107-acre cedar swamp 14 miles northeast of Cass Lake on County Highway 39, is a great place to see rare orchids—early to mid-summer is the best time to visit. Another bog walk, this one part of the six-mile **Webster Lake** trail system, has interpretive panels discussing the bog's carnivorous pitcher plants. The trailhead is at the Webster Lake Campground, seven miles south of Blackduck on County Highway 39, and then three miles southeast on Forest Roads 2207 and 2236.

The **Blackduck Lookout Tower,** three miles south of town on County Highway 39, then a short drive west down County Highway 300, was in use from the mid-1930s until 1970; unfortunately you can no longer climb it.

Further north, the famous **Lost Forty** is a 144-acre section of virgin pine, spared from logging by a surveyor's error in 1882. There's a one-mile trail through the enormous trees, many of which are up to 350 years old and harbor bald eagles and other wildlife—the largest pines are on the area's east end. From Blackduck take County Highways 30, 13, and 29 about 25 miles east to Dora Lake, and head north on County Highway 26 for two miles to Forest Road 2240. Then follow that for about 1.5 miles.

Nearby, Island Lake contains **Elmwood Island,** an undeveloped island with a half-mile trail through a stand of upland cedar. Occupied by CCC workers from 1935 to 1941, **Camp Rabideau** is six miles south of Blackduck on County Highway 39. A one-mile interpretive trail highlights the 17 original buildings remaining here from which CCC workers—the "Tree Army"—conducted forest management and construction projects during the Depression. Designated a National Historic Landmark because of the enormous legacy of the CCC, Rabideau is under restoration to preserve what were originally meant to be temporary structures. Guided tours are available during summer.

The Chippewa Discovery Tour runs 50 miles between Cass Lake and Blackduck taking in many of the sights listed above. It is a great way to get acquainted with the layout of this part of the forest and to learn about the natural and human history. Most of the route follows Highways 10 and 39, and part of it also forms the state-designated **Ladyslipper Scenic Byway** (www.ladyslipperscenicbyway.org).

The **Turtle River, Mississippi River,** and **Pike Bay Connection** are designated canoe routes: Pike Bay is considered a historic route and is fairly difficult, with six portages in eight miles.

Camping

The **Norway Beach Recreation Area** has four separate campground loops with 170 sites. There are flush toilets and showers, and the Chippewa and Norway Beach loops are two of only four campgrounds in the forest with electricity. Reservations are accepted. Another large campground by Blackduck is named **Winnie** since it sits on the west shore of Lake Winnibigoshish. It has 35 sites in a stand of large red and white pines and a boat ramp.

Knutson Dam has 14 sites on the north side of Cass Lake and is known both for good fishing and its Mississippi River canoe access. **Noma Lake,** also noted for fishing, has 14 sites in a stand of birch and a boat launch. **Webster Lake** has 15 sites among large red pines, plus a boat ramp and direct access to some of the district's best hiking. The tiny **Star Island** campground, with three free sites but no drinking water, provides a spectacular location. Contact Chippewa National Forest (218/335-8600) for information.

Information

The **Blackduck Ranger Station** (417 Forestry Dr., 218/835-4291, 8 A.M.–4:30 P.M. daily) is located on the south side of Blackduck along U.S. Highway 71. There is also the handy **Norway Beach Visitor Information Center** (200 Ash Ave. NW, 218/335-8600, noon–5 P.M. Tues.–Sat. May–Sept.).

MARCELL AREA

The only town of consequence in this chunk of the forest, **Marcell** is an outpost of about 50 souls. Settled in 1901 on the shores of Turtle Lake to support the logging industry, the town's buildings were moved south to the railroad tracks in 1911 when the industry had finally cut over the whole area. Marcell remains a logging town, and with gas, groceries, and sporting goods it makes a good supply stop.

The **Timber Wolf Inn** (Hwy. 38 Jack the Horse Rd., 218/832-3990, $70) two miles north of town has 12 rooms in a modern log building and a sandwich, steak, and seafood restaurant (lunch and dinner daily, $5–27).

Buckhorn Resort (45101 Buckhorn Resort Rd., 218/832-3723 or 800/450-6628, www.buckhornoncaribou.com, $600/week) south of town has an exceptional setting on Caribou Lake, one of Minnesota's deepest and clearest. There are five older red chalet-style cabins along the shore and three beautiful modern four-bedroom log lodges—all of which come with a fishing boat.

Scenic State Park

The name says it all. This 3,360-acre park (218/743-3362), right on the edge of the national forest, protects virgin pine shorelines on half a dozen lakes. Along with the huge trees, other park highlights include fishing, swimming, paddling, a bog walk (currently closed for repairs), and a hike along **Chase Point,** a long esker dividing Coon and Sedgwick Lakes. The history of the CCC is told in the historic log pavilion with its grand stone fireplace and original log-and-branch furniture. In total there are 10 miles of hiking trail and five of them are groomed for cross-country skiing each winter. Boat and canoe rentals are available.

There are a variety of lodging opportunities. Ninety-five drive-in campsites (20 electric) are divided between **Chase Point Campground,** on a hill above Coon Lake, and **Lodge Campground,** near the beach and fishing pier—the latter is a bit more convenient, though the former is generally more scenic and secluded. There are also two backpack sites about a mile in from the parking area and five lakeside canoe sites—four of which can be reached on foot as well. Finally, a rustic CCC-built cabin (mid-Apr. through Oct.) has a fireplace, and a four-bedroom guesthouse comes with a boat and a canoe.

Recreation

This area is characterized by many smaller lakes and dispersed camping, making it one of the more secluded corners of the forest. Several areas have been set aside for nonmotorized use and contain beautiful opportunities for hiking, biking, and backpacking.

The **Trout Lake Recreation Area,** 16 miles south of Marcell off Highway 38, contains 11 lakes in its 6,000 nonmotorized acres. There are five miles of hiking and biking trails (groomed for skiing in the winter) and Spider Lake has over two dozen primitive campsites on its shore. The **Joyce Estate,** reached by a short hike, was a hunting camp, built by a wealthy logging family in 1924, with 40 buildings (nine remain), including a main lodge, servant's cabins, and outdoor facilities like a golf course and greenhouse. Many of the buildings were Adirondack style, with log architecture and stickwork. You can wander the grounds and admire the plushness of the Joyces' version of roughing it.

Suomi Hills Recreation Area, also nonmotorized, covers an area of rolling hills on the west side of Highway 38. Twenty-one miles of trail accommodate hikers, bikers, and skiers and are accessible from two marked trailheads along the highway. Mountain bikers consider this the choicest ride in the whole forest. With enough miles of trails and few enough visitors to ensure solitude among the numerous small lakes, this area is ideal for camping. A CCC camp on the north end of Suomi Hills was used to house prisoners of war during World War II. Suomi (the Finnish word for Finland) is known as a fall-color destination, and hikers will find morel mushrooms and blueberries in season. Within Suomi Hills the **Miller Lake Geologic Area** is reached by a short hike from a fire road off Highway 38. Miller Lake, a "disappearing lake," broke through an earthen levy at its south end in 1982; beavers subsequently built a dam at the breach, but that too washed away in 1993, once again sending the lake into oblivion. More beaver activity is visible today.

The short **East Lake Pines Trail** (accessible by boat only) loops through old-growth red pines on the north shore of East Lake and explains how glaciers created kettle lakes. Near **Thydean Lake** on Forest Road 2180, not too far north of Marcell, is a meadow noted for its bounty of butterflies.

Three driving tours feature highlights of the area. The **Edge of the Wilderness National Scenic Byway,** a favorite fall leaf-peeping route, covers 47 miles of Highway 38 between Grand Rapids and Effie. Its 14 stops include Trout Lake, a tamarack bog, and the Laurentian Divide. The **Chippewa Adventure Tour** is 17.5 miles and focuses on wildlife-viewing opportunities (bald eagles, wetland birds, beaver, and ruffed grouse in particular) and various kinds of forest and marsh habitats. A 39-mile **Fall Color Tour** includes the Chippewa Tour and adds a long stretch of Highway 38.

Camping

The two developed campgrounds in the Marcell Area have swimming beaches and are named for the noted fishing lakes they sit on. **Clubhouse Lake** has 48 sites, a boat ramp, and accepts reservations. The **North Star** camp has 38 generally quieter sites. For information on either, call the Marcell Ranger District (218/832-2161).

Information

The seasonal **Marcell Area Visitor Center** (49554 Hwy. 38, 218/335-8600, 8 A.M.–4:30 P.M. Mon.–Fri., closed Sat.–Sun.) is located next to the post office in Marcell.

DEER RIVER AREA

Most people stop at **Deer River** (pop. 923) for supplies or to gaze at the car-sized **northern pike statue.** Other than gas, food, lodging, and the photogenic fish, the nonprofit **White Oak Society** (33155 Hwy. 6, 218/246-9393, www.whiteoak.org), where members reenact the Great Lakes voyageur days of 1798 at their reconstructed fur post, is the principal reason to come to town. The society hosts the **White Oak Sled Dog Classic** in January, **Living History classes** ($10) in May, and the **White Oak Rendezvous** ($6) the first full weekend of August. During the latter, you can watch demonstrations and join workshops in things like blackpowder shooting, wilderness survival, clay-oven cooking, birch-bark canoe building, basket making, and quill calligraphy. The gift shop, open only during events, is a historically accurate company trading post with such items as fabrics, tomahawks, and copper kettles.

The Leech Lake Ojibwe's little **White Oak Casino** (45830 Hwy. 2 W., 218/246-9600 or 800/653-2412, www.whiteoakcasino.com) is just west of town.

The **White Oak Inn** (201 4th Ave. NW, 218/246-9400 or 877/633-5504, www.whiteoakinnandsuites.com, $89) has a pool, kiddie pool, whirlpool, exercise equipment, tanning bed, and video games.

Shelly's (220 Hwy. 2 E., 218/246-8500, 6 A.M.–9 P.M. daily, $5–16) serves family fare plus ice cream and some scrumptious bakery goods.

Lake Winnibigoshish

Not quite the tongue twister it appears to be, Winnibigoshish is pronounced just like it is spelled, using a hard "O." If that's too intimidating just call it "Big Winnie" like everyone else does. Big it certainly is—with 116 miles of shoreline (less than 5 percent developed) and 70,000 acres, Minnesota's fourth-largest lake dominates this part of the forest. Because storm winds can churn up the lake's muddy bottom, the long name the Ojibwe bestowed upon it means "miserable wretched dirty water," but the scores of anglers and boaters who flock to its shores are enough proof that Winnibigoshish is a misnomer.

A third of the National Forest campgrounds are bunched around the northeast end of the lake, and over a dozen resorts sit on its shore. A good family-friendly choice is **Eagle Nest Lodge** (58671 Eagle Nest Rd., 218/246-8701 or 800/356-3775, www.eaglenestlodge.net, May–Oct., $142 daily, $710 weekly, winter $50 daily, $150 weekly) at the lake's northeast end (on a large bay known as Cut Foot Sioux Lake). With 15 housekeeping cabins, some with fireplaces, and a beautiful stretch of sandy beach, the resort is a tidy, relaxing escape. Naturalist programs, a game room, sailboats, and canoes are some of the many on-site activities and facilities, plus visitors can rent fishing boats.

The **Gosh Dam Place** (38589 Hwy. 46, 218/246-8202, $35/person) has 21 basic motel rooms popular with anglers. Their restaurant (7 A.M.–10 P.M. daily, $5–21) serves pizza, burgers, and other family fare.

Bena

Sitting smack-dab in the middle of the forest is the friendly, family-run **Big Fish Supper Club** (456 Hwy. 2 NE, dinner Wed.–Sun. May–Aug., Fri.–Sun. rest of year, $9–16), with a classic meat and potatoes menu—the chicken and ribs combo is very popular—but the food isn't the main reason to stop: It's the 65-foot-long, 14-foot-tall tiger muskie sitting next to it that the restaurant took its name from. Built as a drive-in in 1958, the fish itself—in serious disrepair and on the Preservation Alliance of Minnesota's list of ten most endangered historic places—now just serves as storage space, but that doesn't take away the magic for curious road-trippers. It even made it into the classic tourist trap montage at the beginning of *National Lampoon's Vacation.* They have five little log cabins ($30/person) in back and rent ice-fishing shanties.

Recreation

The **Cut Foot Sioux Trail** is a 22-mile loop that follows the Laurentian Divide and passes numerous small lakes. The trail passes a fire tower (climbing it is not allowed) and leads through the Cut Foot Experimental Forest, a forest-management laboratory. Starting at the same place is the **Simpson Creek Trail.** Thirteen miles of nonmotorized path give access to a cedar swamp, red and white pine stands, glacial eskers, and eagle-watching spots on the shore of Cut Foot Sioux Lake. Both trails are used by hikers, bikers, and skiers. The **Cut Foot Sioux Visitor Center** (44623 Hwy. 46, 218/246-8233, 9 A.M.–4:30 P.M. Mon.–Sat., closed Sun.), 16 miles northwest of Deer River on Highway 46, houses local and natural history exhibits.

Nearby, the original **Cut Foot Sioux Ranger Station** is one of the oldest surviving structures in the U.S. Forest Service's eastern region. Built in 1908, it was used as a ranger station, honeymoon cabin, and tool shed over the years until it was restored in the 1990s. It's decorated the way it was in 1911, when a ranger and his wife called it home. Guided and self-guided audio tours are available each summer.

The U.S. Highway 2 bridge over the Mississippi River, eight miles east of Deer River, is a noted spot for viewing bald eagles. Lake Winnibigoshish, including the Cut Foot Sioux Lake and Little Ball Club Lake, are top fishing spots.

Camping

The area's drive-in campgrounds are clustered on Cut Foot Sioux Lake, an isolated offshoot of Lake Winnibigoshish, and most have boat ramps. Both **O-Ne-Gum-E** and **Deer Lake** have 48 sites: The former has electricity and is one of the busiest campgrounds in the forest, while the latter has a swimming beach. Smaller (none have more than 23 sites) and generally quieter are **Mosomo Point** and **West Seelye Bay,** both angler favorites; **Williams Narrows,** with good bald eagle viewing; and **East Seelye Bay**—all have boat ramps, and the latter two have beaches. **Tamarack Point** has 32 sites on Winnie's south shore. **Cut Foot Horse Camp,** the forest's only horse-rider campground, has 34 campsites and is surrounded by over 120 miles of rideable road and trail. All but West Seelye Bay, East Seelye Bay, and Tamarack Point take reservations. Contact Deer River Ranger District (218/246-2123, www.fs.fed.us/r9/chippewa/camp/deeriver.htm) for more information.

Information

The **Marcell/Deer River Ranger Station** (1037 Division St., 218/246-2123, 8 A.M.–4:30 P.M.

Mon.–Fri., closed Sat.–Sun.) is located along Highway 46 north of Deer River. You can also get information at the **Cut Foot Sioux Visitor Center** (44623 Hwy. 46, 218/246-8233, 9 A.M.–4:30 P.M. Mon.–Sat., closed Sun.), 16 miles northwest of Deer River on Highway 46.

Grand Rapids and Vicinity

GRAND RAPIDS

Founded on the riches of the forest, this lumber town (pop. 9,700) got its start in 1870, but it took 20 years and the arrival of the railroad before it blossomed into a real village. The initial transport was via steamboats that ran up the Mississippi River from Aitkin to the namesake rapids, a wild half-mile drop now buried behind the Blandin Dam. The journey took about a day if conditions were good, but when water levels dropped passengers often had to help push the boat over shoals. The remains of wrecked boats still poke out of the river when water levels are low. Despite its unpredictability, steamer service didn't completely die out until the 1920s.

Though Grand Rapids sits on the edge of the Mesabi Iron Range, it never became a mining center. Lumbering and papermaking became the city's economic foundation, and they are still the lynchpins today. U.S. Highways 2 and 169, two busy cross-state routes that converge here, are the principal reasons people pass through town; however, the hometown of Judy Garland has several worthwhile attractions, and its small-town friendliness makes them all the more appealing.

Forest History Center

The Minnesota Historical Society's Forest History Center (2609 County Rd. 76, 218/327-4482, 10 A.M.–5 P.M. Thurs.–Sat., noon–5 P.M. Sun. summer, trails 9 A.M.–4 P.M. Mon.–Fri. rest of year, $8 adults) is a well-executed living-history museum re-creating Camp #1 of the Northwoods Logging Company. After learning about the history of logging in Minnesota in the museum (don't miss the short film of Minnesota's last log drive), you'll be led back to the year 1900 in the logging camp. Camp employees will explain their duties, answer questions, and share stories—such as the cook's efforts to sneak prunes into the lumberjacks' meals to keep them regular. Visits to the bunkhouse, horse barns, and blacksmith's shop offer a good taste of what a lumberjack's life was like. Down on the Mississippi River you'll visit the wanigan, a floating cook shack that fed the men who traveled downstream with the logs. Reforestation is discussed in the 1934 Forest Service patrolman's cabin, and you'll learn about fire spotting at the top of the 100-foot-tall lookout tower.

Other Sights

For a look at the modern lumber industry, take a tour of the **Blandin Paper Mill** (122 3rd St. W., 218/327-6682, 10 A.M.–3 P.M. Wed.–Fri. summer, free admission). The massive complex dominates the downtown business district and turns out magazine papers for publications such as *Time* magazine and the Lands' End catalog. No open-toed shoes or children under 12 are allowed.

The **Judy Garland Museum** (2727 Hwy. 169 S., 218/327-9276 or 800/664-5839, www.judygarlandmuseum.com, 10 A.M.–5 P.M. daily summer, closed Sun. Apr.–May and Sept.–Oct., open Fri.–Sat. only rest of year, $7) is a loving shrine to the star of *The Wizard of Oz,* who lived here until she was four. Born in 1922, she was Frances Ethel Gumm when she crashed her older sisters' performance at their parents' Grand Rapids theater, making it through *Jingle Bells* before being carried off the stage. The museum preserves the Gumms' little white house with its cast-iron stove and furnishings from the mid-1920s. There's also a straightforward presentation of Garland's career, tracing her life with photographs and mementos such as her Tony Award (though the original ruby slippers were stolen).

Sharing the building is the **Children's Discovery Museum** (2727 Hwy. 169 S., 218/326-1900 or 866/236-5437, www.cdmkids.org, 10 A.M.–5 P.M. daily summer, Fri.–Sat. only rest of year, $7), full of hands-on educational exhibits and an incredible doll exhibit.

There is more Judy Garland memorabilia at the **Itasca Heritage Center** (10 5th St. NW, 218/326-6431, www.itascahistorical.com, 9:30 A.M.–5 P.M. Mon.–Fri., 10 A.M.–4 P.M. Sat., closed Sun., $4 adults, $12 family), housed in the Old Central School, an imposing 1895 Romanesque stone structure with a yellow brick road leading to the front door. Other exhibits found at the top of the beautiful wooden central staircase cover logging, mining, papermaking, and the history of the famous photograph *Grace,* which was taken in town.

Entertainment and Events

Grand Rapids is more than a little proud to be the birthplace of Judy Garland. The **Judy Garland Festival** takes over town on the fourth weekend in June and usually attracts several of the original Munchkins. The festival also includes a candlelight vigil celebrating Judy's birthday, *Wizard of Oz* screenings, and a collector's exchange with Judy and Oz memorabilia.

The city's biggest summer bash is the **Tall Timber Days Festival,** the first weekend in August, featuring lumberjacking events, chainsaw carving, turtle and bed races, and a craft show.

The **Mississippi Melodie Showboat** (866/336-3426, 9 P.M. Thurs.–Sat., $10) is a summer re-creation of the days when entertainment traveled up the Mississippi River by steamboat. During the last three weekends in July a small paddlewheel steamboat arrives and docks at an outdoor stage on the riverbank, then disgorges costumed performers who sing and dance with a live band.

The **Myles Reif Performing Arts Center** (720 Conifer Dr., 218/327-5780, www.reifcenter.org) is a large space in a beautiful modern building on the forested edge of Grand Rapids. Offerings include everything from jazz combos to comedians to children's theater.

Shopping

The **MacRostie Art Center** (405 1st Ave. NW, 218/326-2697, www.macrostieartcenter.org, 10 A.M.–5 P.M. Mon.–Sat., closed Sun.) is a nonprofit art gallery with an eclectic mix of artworks by local artists. The Old Central School houses several craft shops, including **Stained Glass with Class** (218/327-7964, 9:30 A.M.–5 P.M. Mon.–Sat., closed Sun.) and **ABC's of Quilting** (218/326-9661, 9:30 A.M.–5 P.M. Mon.–Sat., 11 A.M.–4 P.M. Sun.). The gift shops at both museums sell a plethora of Judy Garland items.

Recreation

The **Mesabi Trail** is still a work in progress, but when finished this ribbon will run 132 miles to Ely, making it one of the longest paved recreational trails in the country. At the time of publication, the trail is completed between Grand Rapids and Aurora, running across the Iron Range through Hibbing, Virginia, and Eveleth, along with shorter sections between Tower and Soudan and in Ely. The early reports are enormously positive: Cyclists rave about the beauty of the scenery and the quality of the trail. A $5 two-day or $15 annual Wheel Pass is required; you can buy one at the trailhead (at the fairgrounds on the northeast side of town) or Itasca Trail Sports (316 4th St. NE, 218/326-1716).

The **Taconite State Trail** is another long-distance trail stretching to Ely, though it is not surfaced and is used primarily by snowmobilers.

Mount Itasca (218/245-3487), a few miles north of town near the village of Coleraine, is a year-round recreational park, though it is busiest in the winter for downhill skiing and snowboarding. There are also some challenging cross-country ski trails, a biathlon course, and a year-round ski jump. The CVB can direct you to many other skinny-ski trails in the area.

Accommodations

With 124 rooms, the **Sawmill Inn** (2301 Hwy. 169 S., 218/326-8501 or 800/235-6455, $89) is not only the city's largest hotel, but also arguably the best. It has a rustic logging-themed decor, and the pool, whirlpool, and sauna are in a skylit courtyard.

The **Itascan Motel** (610 Hwy. 169 S., 218/326-3489 or 800/842-7733, www.itascan.com, $48), a very good value, has one-, two-, and three-bedroom units, including some kitchenettes.

South of town on the north shore of Sugar Lake is the upscale **Ruttger's Sugar Lake Lodge** (218/327-1462 or 800/450-4555, www.sugarlakelodge.com, $195), a well-known golf resort. For nongolfers, or those who need a diversion between tee times, there are also bikes, boats, Mississippi River kayak trips, and more. Lodging options range from studio lodge rooms to three-bedroom town homes, and there is a two-night minimum stay on summer weekends.

Food

The often-recommended **Forest Lake Restaurant** (1201 4th St. NW, 218/326-3423, breakfast and lunch 7–11:30 A.M. Mon.–Fri., 7 A.M.–1 P.M. Sat.–Sun., dinner 4–9 P.M. Mon.–Fri., 4–10 P.M. Sat.–Sun., $10–22) features a pair of dining rooms. The expensive steakhouse has entrees like roasted prime rib au jus and seafood manicotti, while the more casual upstairs has some of the same plus plenty of sandwiches.

Pastie's Plus (1405 4th St. NW, 218/326-2234, 10 A.M.–7 P.M. Mon.–Fri., 10 A.M.–5 P.M. Sat. summer, reduced hours rest of year, $4.50) makes several varieties, including rutabaga, of the beloved Iron Range hand pie.

Rivers Italian (208 3rd St. NE, 218/327-3471, www.riversitalian.com, lunch 11 A.M.–3 P.M., dinner 5–9 P.M. Mon.–Sat., closed Su n., $13–32) has a relaxed wine-bar atmosphere and a reassuringly short menu: Rather than being everything to everyone, they focus on great small plates to go with a glass of wine, a handful of thin-crust pizzas, and classic Italian pastas and entrees.

Brewed Awakenings (24 4th St. NE, 218/327-1088, 6:30 A.M.–8 P.M. Mon.–Fri., 7 A.M.–9 P.M. Sat., 7 A.M.–6 P.M. Sun., $5–10) is known far and wide not just for its coffee but for its homemade soups—an ever-changing array of 55 original recipes—and panini.

Other Practicalities

Visit Grand Rapids (1 3rd St. NW, 218/326-9607 or 800/335-9740, www.visitgrandrapids.com, 8:30 A.M.–5 P.M. Mon.–Fri., closed Sat.–Sun.) tracks lodging vacancies, which can be useful during the summer.

HILL ANNEX MINE STATE PARK

One mile long, three quarters of a mile wide, and 500 feet deep, the Hill Annex open pit mine gave up 63 million tons of iron ore during its 65 years of operation. The massive cavity, now partly filled with water, was turned into a tourist attraction shortly after the mine shut down in 1978. The 90-minute tours—one by land and one by boat—lead past many original mining facilities and detail mine operations, which began with horsepower before this became the Iron Range's first all-electric mine. Guides also lead fossil hunts, and the snails, clams, and shark's teeth you'll dig up prove this area was under water during the Cretaceous period (some 144 to 66 million years ago).

The old Clubhouse (218/247-7215, 9:30 A.M.–5 P.M. Wed.–Sat., closed Sun.–Tues., free admission) has been converted into the park office and a museum with exhibits about the mine and fossil displays (including a crocodile jaw found here). You can also view the mine from the overlook. Each tour is available daily on Friday, Saturday, and Sunday (fossil at 10 A.M., boat at 10:30 A.M. and 3 P.M.) during the summer and costs $9.

SAVANNA PORTAGE STATE PARK

Remote and peaceful Savanna Portage State Park (55626 Lake Pl., 218/426-3271) is a lovely tract of near-wilderness centered on a historic portage between the Mississippi River watershed and Lake Superior–bound St. Louis River. The six-mile Savanna Portage connecting the

East Savanna River with the West Savanna River was used for centuries by Dakota and Ojibwe and then by fur traders who arrived in the region in 1763. After poling or dragging their canoes down miles of narrow, sharp turns the voyageurs had to trudge through at least 1.5 miles of knee-deep muck while shouldering 150-pound packs. Even with a canal dug to shorten the walk this was one of the most dreaded portages in the entire Northwest. The entire transit used to take the men as long as five days. The savanna of the name doesn't refer to an actual grassland, but rather the marsh along the eastern portion of the trail.

In total there are 17 miles of hiking trail crossing the park's 15,818 acres, with 10 miles open to mountain bikes and groomed for cross-country skiers of all abilities. You can retrace part of the voyageurs' route along the remote **Savanna Portage Trail,** an often wet and somewhat challenging 11-mile round-trip—the early-summer mosquito hordes add a bit of historical authenticity. Another popular path is the hilly, two-mile **Continental Divide Trail,** suitable for hikers as well as bikers, which follows the divide and offers a great vista of the forest along the way. It connects to the flatter **Wolf Lake Trail** with an observation deck overlooking Wolf Lake and the surrounding tamarack lowlands at the end. As the easy **Lake Shumway Trail** encircles its namesake lake it traverses a beaver dam and provides a good opportunity to see other wildlife along its 1.5-mile path—a short **bog boardwalk,** lined by orchids and carnivorous pitcher plants, branches off the north end. The 1.6-mile **Esker Trail** attests to the park's glacial past and takes you past a spruce-tamarack bog. Explore more spruce forest and spot the myriad warblers that inhabit it along the mile-long **Black Spruce Trail.** There's a historic homestead and excellent wildflower-viewing along the one-mile **Anderson Road Trail.** The **Remote Lake Trail** on the west side of the park connects to the trail system in the **Remote Lake Solitude Area** of the adjacent Savanna State Forest.

Besides hiking, people come to Savanna Portage to swim in Loon Lake and to fish for panfish, trout, and bass on this and other waterways—only electric trolling motors are allowed on the four main lakes. Canoeists may prefer the island-studded and aptly named Remote Lake. Canoes and fishing boats are available for rent. In the south end of the park, at the confluence of the Prairie and West Savanna Rivers, there's a wild rice field and more fishing.

Those spending the night have many options. The park has 61 campsites, some on the lakefront. Both loops are woodsy and pleasant, but the northern one is quieter since the 18 electric sites are all in the southern loop. The best places to pitch a tent are the seven backpacking sites scattered around the park; two can be reached by canoe. Noncampers can enjoy the surroundings in either the rustic camper cabin or the modern Garni Cottage, with all the comforts of home.

Waters of the Dancing Sky

Although it's just a puddle compared to Lake Superior, **Lake of the Woods** is a pretty remarkable body of water. The nation's largest lake after the five Great Lakes and Great Salt Lake sprawls over 1,486 square miles and has 65,000 miles of shoreline and an ocean-like feel, especially when strong winds toss up six-foot waves. A remnant of Glacial Lake Agassiz, Lake of the Woods is relatively shallow, averaging just 26 feet in depth. It encompasses 14,582 islands, and despite the area's brief summers and frigid winters (40-below-zero nights are not rare), some of them harbor prickly pear cactus.

Needless to say, if you are here to fish you will find everything you need; area towns seemingly have as many bait shops and fishing guides as the lake has fish. The lake competes with Lake Mille Lacs as the state's top walleye factory (some proud locals call this the "Walleye Capital of the World"), though muskie, northern pike, and smallmouth bass are also abundant, and lake sturgeon are recovering. The recreational fishing scene here churns on year-round, with ice fishing becoming more popular each year. Heated-fish-house rental is big business, and you can even spend the night out on the lake in a sleeper fish house stocked with full kitchens and beds. Dozens of resorts ring the lake, and unlike elsewhere in Minnesota, most rent by the day rather than the week. Just about all are geared exclusively for hunters and anglers, but that doesn't mean those who don't fish (or just don't want to spend all their time doing it) won't enjoy themselves up here. There are some beautiful state parks, and each of the small communities around the lake has something worth seeing.

Several designated scenic touring routes through Lake of the Woods County highlight natural and historical points of interest. The **Waters of the Dancing Sky Scenic Byway** (so named because the chance of seeing the Northern Lights is good up here) stretches 191 miles across the top of Minnesota, following Highway 11 from Karlstad to International Falls. The 75 miles of this route between Baudette and Greenbush, known as the **Wildflower Route,** once sported upward of two million orchids (over 20 varieties) every summer, principally Minnesota's state flower, the showy lady's slipper. The widening of the highway has reduced their numbers, but it is still an impressive show in some places, especially if you take a look on the side roads. The peak blooming season is usually late June. Scenic auto routes through the wildlife-rich **Beltrami Island State Forest** (218/425-7504) include a Bog Drive, Blueberry Pickers' Drive (the berries ripen in mid-summer), Homestead Drive (passing pioneer cemeteries and remnants of early houses), and Fall Color Drive.

BAUDETTE

The border town of Baudette (pop. 1,000) is 12 miles up the Rainy River from Lake of the Woods; nevertheless, with most of the resorts nearby, it is the primary hub for those fishing the lake. The **Lake of the Woods County Museum** (119 8th Ave. SE, 218/634-1200, 10 A.M.–4 P.M. Tues.–Fri., 10 A.M.–2 P.M. Sat., closed Sun.–Mon. summer, free admission) covers local history, both human and natural. There are exhibits on early settlers and the industries that have driven the area's economy over the years: logging, commercial fishing, agriculture, and pharmaceuticals. One highlight is the 1924 Model T.

Jenny Moorman, who runs **Lake of the Woods Nature Tours** (218/634-1059, $100/half day for up to 6 people, by reservation only), offers three types of customized, guided trips: bird-watching, wildflowers, and Native American culture. She knows where to find many rare orchids and birds, most notably golden-winged warblers, and the cultural outings can include stops at the Native American burial mounds along the Rainy River or a visit to Fort St. Charles.

Any doubts about the locals' love of fishing will be put to rest when you see **Willie Walleye.** The region's 2.5-ton, 40-foot-long mascot "leaps" out of the Rainy River along Highway 11.

Accommodations

The **AmericInn** (1179 Main St. E. near Hwy. 11, 218/634-3200 or 866/370-8008, $77) has a pleasant fireplace in the lobby, plus a pool, hot tub, sauna, and heated fish-cleaning house.

The **Wildwood Inn** (3361 Cottonwood Rd. NW, 218/634-1356 or 888/212-7031, www.wildwoodinnbb.com, $90) is in a choice spot on wooded Wheeler's Point at the mouth of the Rainy River. This large bed-and-breakfast has five guestrooms, each with a private bath and unique decoration; some have fireplaces.

Typical of the many fishing resorts in the area is the friendly **Schuster's** (3140 Hwy. 172 NW, 218/634-2412 or 800/243-2412, $50) with 15 simple one- to three-bedroom cabins. There are boats and sleeper fish houses for rent, plus a launch service, and anglers appreciate the calm waters here.

Food

The aging **Ranch House** (203 Main St. W., 218/634-2420, 5:30 A.M.–10 P.M. Mon.–Sat., 6 A.M.–10 P.M. Sun., $2–16) offers some massive cholesterol vessels like the two-steak-and-three-eggs breakfast and the sodbuster burger. The atmosphere is homey, and locals gather here to catch up on town gossip.

You can get a good cup of coffee or tea at **The Smiling Moon** (121 Main Ave. N., 218/634-2976, 7 A.M.–4 P.M. Mon.–Fri., 7 A.M.–7 P.M. Tues., 8 A.M.–2 P.M. Sat., closed Sun.).

Information

Lake of the Woods Tourism (930 Main St. W., 218/634-1174 or 800/382-3474, www.lakeofthewoodsmn.com, 9 A.M.–6 P.M. Mon.–Fri., 10 A.M.–4 P.M. Sat., closed Sun.) offers information for the entire region.

ZIPPEL BAY STATE PARK

Zippel Bay State Park (3684 54th Ave. NW, 218/783-6252, $16 non-electric) protects nearly 3,000 acres of forest, though it is defined by water. Not surprisingly, swimming, fishing, boating, and beachcombing bring in most visitors. The nine miles of hiking trail through the forest—the system is expanded to eleven miles for cross-country skiing—afford a chance to spot wildlife and wildflowers. Though you would be lucky to see one, the adorable piping plover, one of the nation's most endangered birds, nests on the miles of sandy beach here. In Zippel Bay itself, a fishing pier, boat ramp, and marina serve anglers in search of walleye, sauger, and northern pike. Four campgrounds with 57 rustic sites are nestled in the woods.

BIG BOG STATE RECREATION AREA

Aptly named Big Bog (218/647-8592, $18 non-electric, $50 camper cabin) protects part of a 500-square-mile peat bog, one of the largest in the country. An accessible mile-long boardwalk lined by interpretive panels cuts through the spruce-tamarack forest and ends in an open muskeg where a binocular-viewer helps you spy bear, bobcat, bog lemmings, and some of the over 300 species of bird, including great gray owl, that inhabit the park. The three other easy, level trails that circle Ludlow Island, where the boardwalk begins, are also good wildlife-watching destinations, and your odds of seeing a moose aren't that bad. The bog also harbors many insectivorous plants like bladderworts, pitcher plants, and sundews, and many orchids bloom in June.

The South Unit, 8.5 miles south of the boardwalk, has an accessible fishing area at the mouth of the Tamarack River and a petite beach on Upper Red Lake. Interpretive panels here discuss the lake environment, including the collapse of the walleye population in the early 1990s caused by overfishing. The half-mile Old Marina Trail, a level, wooded path with many wildflowers, leads along the shore to an observation platform on the Tamarack. The somewhat shady campground has 31 sites (26 electric) and six camper cabins along the Tamarack River.

WARROAD

Warroad, the only American port on Lake of the Woods, lies along what was once a well-traveled route, a figurative war road followed by the Dakota and Ojibwe who frequently attacked each other in an effort to control this fertile area. Today Warroad is a busy, sprawling town with thousands of petunias lining the main route in the summertime.

The town's biggest employer is **Marvin Windows and Doors** (802 State Ave. N., 218/386-4222), and the largest made-to-order window and door manufacturer in the world offers factory tours by reservation. The **William S. Marvin Training and Visitor Center** (802 State Ave. N., 218/386-4334, http://visitor.marvin.com, 8 A.M.–6 P.M. Mon.–Fri., 1–4 P.M. Sat.–Sun., free admission), on the east side of town at the junction of Highways 11 and 313, both tells the company's history and promotes its products. The professionally assembled displays tell an interesting tale—from George Griffin Marvin's start in the lumber business in 1906; to how buying a $300 saw in 1939 changed the family, company, and city forever; to selling windows out of a station wagon in the 1950s; to the innovations of today that make them an industry leader.

Most of Warroad's 1,700 residents eat, sleep, and breathe hockey (they've dubbed themselves "Hockeytown USA," and four locals are in the United States Hockey Hall of Fame), so it's only appropriate that **Christian Brothers Hockey Sticks,** one of the most respected names in the sport, was founded here by native sons and 1960 Olympic gold medalists Bill and Roger Christian. Bill's son David got a second-generation gold during 1980's Miracle on Ice run. Ask at the **Warroad Area Chamber of Commerce** (311 State Ave. N., 218/386-3543 or 800/328-4455, www.warroad.org, 9 A.M.–4 P.M. Mon.–Fri., closed Sat.–Sun.) about factory tours.

Regional history is laid out at the little **Warroad Heritage Center** (201 Main Ave. NE, 218/386-2500, 1–4 P.M. Mon.–Sat., free admission) next to the library. On display are historical artifacts relating to Native Americans, the fur trade, European settlement, commercial fishing, plus current industries of hockey sticks and windows.

The **Ka-Beck-A-Nung Trail** is a 2.5-mile walk through town highlighting various historical sites; pick up a brochure with directions at the Heritage Center. Highlights are the burial mounds by the lake and the 1904 **Father Aulneau Memorial Church** (202 Roberts Ave. NE), said to be the largest all-weather log church in the world. Bird-watchers shouldn't be in too much of a rush to get out of town since the marshes and sandbars on The Point near Warroad Marina are very productive for waterbirds, and two observation towers offer wide views.

Though only a small patch of their reservation lands lie here, the Red Lake Band Ojibwe operate the **Seven Clans Casino** (1012 E. Lake St., 218/386-3381 or 800/815-8293, www.sevenclanscasino.com) and host the **Warroad Traditional Powwow** in August.

Practicalities

The city's three hotels are simple but modern. With 80 rooms the **Patch Motel** (801 State Ave. N., 218/386-2723 or 800/288-2753, www.patchmotel.com, $50) is the city's largest. It has a game room, as does the **Can-Am Motel** (406 Main Ave. NE, 218/386-3807 or 800/280-2626, $50).

Four miles northeast of town, on a wooded cove on Lake of the Woods, **Springsteel Resort and Marina** (38002 Beach Rd., 218/386-1000, www.springsteelresort.net, $85–150 nightly, $395–675 weekly cabins, $22 campsite, $25 with hookup) is a rustic angler's haven. The cabins are converted mobile homes, and the RV sites are tightly packed. But the lush, remote location makes it worth it.

The **Warroad City Campground** (218/386-1004, $25 full hookup) is huge—165 sites including 68 electric—and crowded, but it has plenty of shade and a good location near the marina.

The menu at the **Patch Restaurant** (701 State Ave. NE, 218/386-2082, 6 A.M.–8 P.M. daily, $4–13) spans buffalo burgers to pizza to burritos to walleye, and breakfast is available all day. Its popularity is primarily due to the all-you-can-eat buffets.

Daisy Gardens (115 Wabasha Ave., 218/386-1763, 10 A.M.–9 P.M. Mon.–Fri., 11 A.M.–9 P.M. Sun., $5–10), the city's only Chinese restaurant, offers some variety.

ROSEAU

Roseau (pop. 2,800) is the largest and fastest-growing city in this part of the state. It was established as a fur trade post on Roseau Lake by the Hudson's Bay Company way back in 1822. The lake, really more of a wetland area, was later drained for agriculture. Like Warroad, its principal on-ice rival, this town is hockey-mad—even more so than most other Minnesota towns. The Rams have made more appearances at the state high school hockey tournament than any other team in Minnesota and have sent nine alumni to the NHL, including the Broten brothers, Neal, Aaron, and Paul.

Roseau bills itself as the "Snowmobile Capital of the World," and though many people and publications call it the birthplace of the snowmobile, that just isn't true. It was, however, a player in snowmobiling's infancy. **Polaris Industries** (301 5th Ave. SW, 218/463-4999) opened here in 1944 as a manufacturer of farm equipment, but 11 years later they became the first company to mass-produce a snowmobile for individual use. Today Polaris is a billion-dollar corporation and one of the world's leading manufacturers of recreational vehicles. You can see snowmobiles and ATVs being assembled during a free tour (4 P.M. Mon.–Fri.) of their 500,000-square-foot facility. Just north of the plant is the **Polaris Experience Center** (205 5th Ave. SW, 218/463-3218, 11 A.M.–7 P.M. Mon.–Fri., 11 A.M.–5 P.M. Sat., closed Sun., free admission) museum and gift shop. It is packed with old sleds, plus some of the company's other products.

Two miles west of town on Highway 11, the **Pioneer Farm and Village** (218/463-3052, www.roseaupioneerfarm.com, noon–5 P.M. Mon.–Fri., May–Sept., free admission) tells the story of the early settlers in reconstructed buildings, including a cabin, general store, church, and cigar factory. Several special events, such Scandinavian Days (second weekend in June) are held on the grounds.

The **Roseau County Historical Museum** (121 Center St. E., 218/463-1918, www.roseaucohistoricalsociety.org, 9:30 A.M.–5 P.M. Mon.–Fri., closed Sat.–Sun., museum free, $5 research center) focuses on industry, agriculture, transport, and natural history, with features on Polaris and hockey. There are also taxidermied animals native to the region.

Practicalities

Travelers here on business with Polaris stay at either the **North Country Inn** (902 3rd St. NW, 218/463-9444 or 888/300-2196, www.northcountryinnandsuites.com, $77) or the **AmericInn** (1110 3rd St. NW, 218/463-1045 or 800/634-3444, www.americinn.com, $66). Both have modern rooms plus swimming pools and whirlpools; the latter also has a sauna.

Brickhouse Bar & Grille (205 5th Ave. SW, 218/463-0993, 11 A.M.–11 P.M. Mon.–Thurs., 11 A.M.–1 A.M. Fri.–Sat., 11 A.M.–9 P.M. Sun., $6–22) is an attractive space in a renovated creamery (the same building as the Polaris Experience Center) and is the best restaurant for many miles. It has a broad menu featuring steaks, seafood, pastas, salads, and the like.

Carhops deliver floats, burgers, chili, ribs, fried chicken, and gizzards at **Earl's Drive-In** (1001 3rd St. NE, 218/463-1912, 10:30 A.M.–10 P.M. daily May–Sept., $1–10).

HAYES LAKE STATE PARK

Swimming and fishing in the 200-acre man-made lake are the top draws to Hayes Lake State Park (218/425-7504), but thanks to its remote location this 2,950-acre park is also an excellent destination for nature lovers, and there is a lot to see along the 13 miles of level hiking trail hugging the lake and river. Rare wetland plants, like orchids and gentians, grow in the large bogs, and you can see them along the short **Bog Walk** near the campground. The half-mile **Pine Ridge Nature Trail** is an easy, interpretive trail at the end of the lake offering the chance to see a beaver lodge and maybe some of its residents. On the **Homestead Interpretive Trail** you'll pass the remains of an early 1900s homestead and gravesite, as well as get scenic views of the Roseau River. For longer hikes the **Moose Ridge Trail** on the lake's south shore is the least used and thus the preferred option for spotting wildlife, perhaps even moose, bobcat, lynx, or wolf. Seven miles of path are open to horseback riders, five for mountain bike riders, and six are groomed for cross-country skiing. The 35 sites (18 electric) in the modern campground and two nearby walk-in sites overlooking the lake are all very private. For those less inclined to rough it, there are two camper cabins, one with electricity.

NORTHWEST ANGLE

One of the strangest quirks of geography in the United States, the Northwest Angle is a large, wooded peninsula completely cut off from the rest of the nation by a corner of Manitoba. Due to crude maps and a surveyor's error, early government officials believed the Mississippi River headwaters lay west of Lake of the Woods.

This caused a long period of confusion, starting with the 1783 treaty that gave the United States independence from Great Britain. The treaty mandated that the international boundary should follow the Rainy River to Lake of the Woods, cut through the lake, then head due west from the northwest corner of the lake to the Mississippi River. When the British realized that the Mississippi is actually 140 miles to the south, the question of the boundary was reopened—the issue wasn't completely resolved until 1925. Astronomer I. L. Tiarks located the northwesternmost point of the lake and dropped a line south from there to the 49th parallel, creating the "chimney" shape that rises from the top of Minnesota today. It is the northernmost point in the continental United States, making little Angle Inlet the Lower 48's northernmost town.

Today, the Angle is still defined by its separateness. The vast majority of the land is uninhabited and officially a part of the Red Lake Ojibwe Reservation, and telephone service didn't reach the Angle until the 1990s. Angle Inlet residents—there are around 100—are a tight-knit group. Children, from kindergarten through sixth grade, attend the only state-funded one-room schoolhouse in Minnesota before being bused to Warroad to continue their education. Though tourism is the main industry, dirt roads and a harsh climate ensure that visitors don't overwhelm the place. When visitors do come, they usually do so to fish, though bird-watching is growing in popularity. The "town" of Angle Inlet isn't much more than a large fishing camp, and everything is quite basic and laid-back. Life seems to happen out on the lake, fishing and exploring islands, more than it does on land. The Northwest Angle also encompasses a few inhabited islands, including Oak and Flag.

Sights and Recreation

The only actual tourist attraction on the Angle is **Fort St. Charles,** a reconstruction of the longest-occupied French fort on Minnesota soil. St. Charles was established in 1732 by Pierre Gaultier de Varennes, Sieur de La Verendrye, and a band of French-Canadian voyageurs. The fort served as a center of exploration and fur trading, and La Verendrye spent his years venturing west desperately searching for the Northwest Passage. The fort was abandoned in 1763 when Great Britain gained control of the territory. When built it sat on the mainland, but now, due to a rise in the lake level, the re-created log cabins and stockade (on the exact locations of the original structures) sit a short ways off it on Magnuson's Island. The free site is maintained by Angle Outpost Resort (218/223-8101 or 800/441-5014).

On Harrison Creek, west of Angle Inlet, are the ruins of **North West Angle,** a 19th-century Canadian village that had 800 inhabitants at its peak. It's in an advanced state of decay but still worth poking around, especially the cemetery. You can also paddle out to **"The Wagon Wheel,"** an old steel tractor tire that marks the very northernmost point in the Lower 48—unless the lake level is very high you won't reach it in a fishing boat, though a guide from **Jake's Northwest Angle Resort** (9270 Golf Course Dr. NW, 218/223-8181 or 800/729-0864, www.jakesnorthwestangle.com) can get you out here as well as show you some petroglyphs on the Ontario side. You'll see a lot of waterfowl and warblers on the journey to these places, but you probably won't find the actual sites without a guide or some luck.

Out in the center of the lake, 19 miles from Angle Inlet, is the 762-acre **Garden Island State Recreation Area** (218/783-6252). Named after the corn, squash, pumpkin, and potato gardens tended here by Native Americans as early as the 18th century, Garden Island is today primarily used by anglers wanting to stretch their legs or fry up the day's catch at the picnic area. There are sandy beaches for swimming or strolling, and during the annual migrations the island is a productive bird-watching locale. In the winter, wolves cross the frozen lake to hunt, and snowmobilers stop for a rest in the park shelter. Camping is prohibited.

DRIVING TO THE ANGLE

The drive from Warroad or Roseau to Angle Inlet is about 60 miles, with the first 40 miles paved. You will first pass through a manned Canadian Customs station. Have your vehicle registration and passport with you. The Warroad station never closes in either direction; the Roseau station is open 8 A.M.-midnight daily.

After a remote drive through Manitoba (remember that posted speed limits are in kilometers/hour) you'll reenter the United States and travel eight more miles to Jim's Corner, a four-way intersection. Stop at the videophone and press the American flag button to report to U.S. Customs. Stop here again when leaving to call Canadian Customs. They will give you a number to prove that you cleared customs, just in case you're stopped. If the videophone isn't working, use the regular payphone to call either country's customs office (800/505-8381 for the United States, 888/226-7277 for Canada).

Practicalities

There are about a dozen resorts up here—half on the mainland and half out on Oak and Flag Islands—and most offer all-inclusive fishing packages. **Jake's Northwest Angle Resort** (9270 Golf Course Dr. NW, 218/223-8181 or 800/729-0864, www.jakesnorthwestangle.com, $49/person with a $120 minimum/cabin) is a mainland mainstay. They've got six cabins with full kitchens and decks that sleep up to eight people and a 32-site campground ($20 electric). In winter, Jake's provides fish houses for ice fishing and transportation to the best fishing spots via bombardier.

Sportsman's Oak Island Lodge (Oak Island, 218/223-8411 or 800/772-8411, www.oakislandlodge.com, $120) offers more upscale lodging in two- and three-bedroom condos, each with kitchens, lake views, and access to a shared hot tub. A restaurant and rental boats are available. They can arrange a boat from the Angle or from Baudette.

Jerry's Restaurant & Bar (7609 Young's Bay Dr. NW, 218/223-8381, 7 A.M.–9 P.M., $3–15) on the mainland is more bar than grill. Some resorts also serve meals.

Basic supplies are available at Jake's and **J&M Company** (9385 Golf Course Dr., 218/223-4381), but it's worth stocking up on most of what you'll need in Warroad or Roseau before making the trip. Also, don't plan on buying gas up here. The fuel available is primarily meant for boats and is quite expensive.

Island Passenger Service (218/223-8261) offers water-taxi service out to Oak and Flag Islands, or anywhere else you need to get to. They will also customize tours, whether you want to do some bird-watching on Garden Island or you just want a lift to Fort St. Charles.

Getting There

The only way to get to the Angle overland is to go through Canada, which means you need to have your passport with you. It also means you need to be aware of Canadian immigration and customs law. Canada excludes anyone with a DWI on their record in the past 10 years and limits the amount of alcohol and cigarettes you can bring.

You can clear customs at the border 10 miles north of either Warroad or Roseau, about 60 miles away (the last third of your drive will be on gravel). When you get to Angle Inlet, you need to check back in with U.S. customs via one of the three videophone booths (you'll see them at the main intersection in town, the church, and at Young's Bay).

To get here by water (a 40-mile trip) or seaplane, arrange this with the resort where you plan to stay.

RED RIVER VALLEY

Few would rank the stretch of Minnesota tucked up against North Dakota as the state's most beautiful or exciting region. Nevertheless, it is anything but boring. While endless farm fields checker the improbably flat terrain that covers most of the area, sandwiched between the farms are the lakes and hills around Fergus Falls and Detroit Lakes, some excellent parks and wildlife refuges, and a touch of big-city energy in Fargo-Moorhead.

There is no denying that agriculture is the heart and soul of the region. This is, in fact, the east end of the Great Plains, where the West begins. The Red River Valley (more properly the Valley of the Red River of the North to distinguish it from the Red River Valley in Texas and Oklahoma), a remnant from the last Ice Age, spreads an average of 50 miles wide along the Red River of the North. This mucky, meandering groove flows north to Canada and forms the upper half of Minnesota's western border along the way. A sea of tallgrass and wet prairie, broken only by the occasional riverbottom forest, once covered this land. Today all but a few scattered fragments of the prairie have been plowed under and most of the wetlands drained to access some of the most fertile farmland in the world. Though the growing season is short, the rich soil, coupled with abundant rain and snow, makes this excellent farming territory. Wheat, sugar beets, potatoes, corn, and sunflowers are some of the top crops. The latter are a beautiful sight in the fall when fields of the golden giants stretch to the horizon.

HIGHLIGHTS

Historical and Cultural Society of Clay County: Also known as the Hjemkomst Center, named after the Viking-style ship it was built around, Moorhead's top attraction offers a unique and entertaining look at Norse and local history (page 285).

Buffalo River State Park: One of Minnesota's largest and healthiest prairies covers part of this park and stretches well beyond. If you are here in April, reserve a viewing blind and watch prairie chickens strut their stuff during their colorful courtship dance (page 289).

Otter Trail Scenic Byway: A Minnesota microcosm, this lovely 150-mile scenic drive zigs and zags past a variety of small towns, historic sites, oversized statuary, and natural areas. A particularly lovely sight along the way is Phelps Mill, an iconic flour mill near Fergus Falls (page 292).

Tamarac and Agassiz National Wildlife Refuges: Lying at the ecological transition zone between forest and prairie, these two large, natural oases are excellent wildlife-watching destinations (pages 299 and 301).

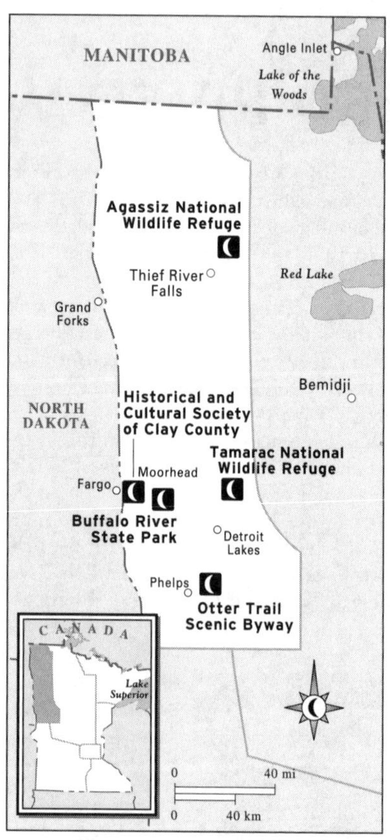

LOOK FOR ☾ TO FIND RECOMMENDED SIGHTS, ACTIVITIES, DINING, AND LODGING.

PLANNING YOUR TIME

The Red River Valley can be covered adequately in three days. Spend one touring the **Otter Trail Scenic Byway,** the second getting to know Moorhead, and the third driving north through the eerily endless checkerboard farms to surprisingly wild natural oases like **Tamarac and Agassiz National Wildlife Refuges.**

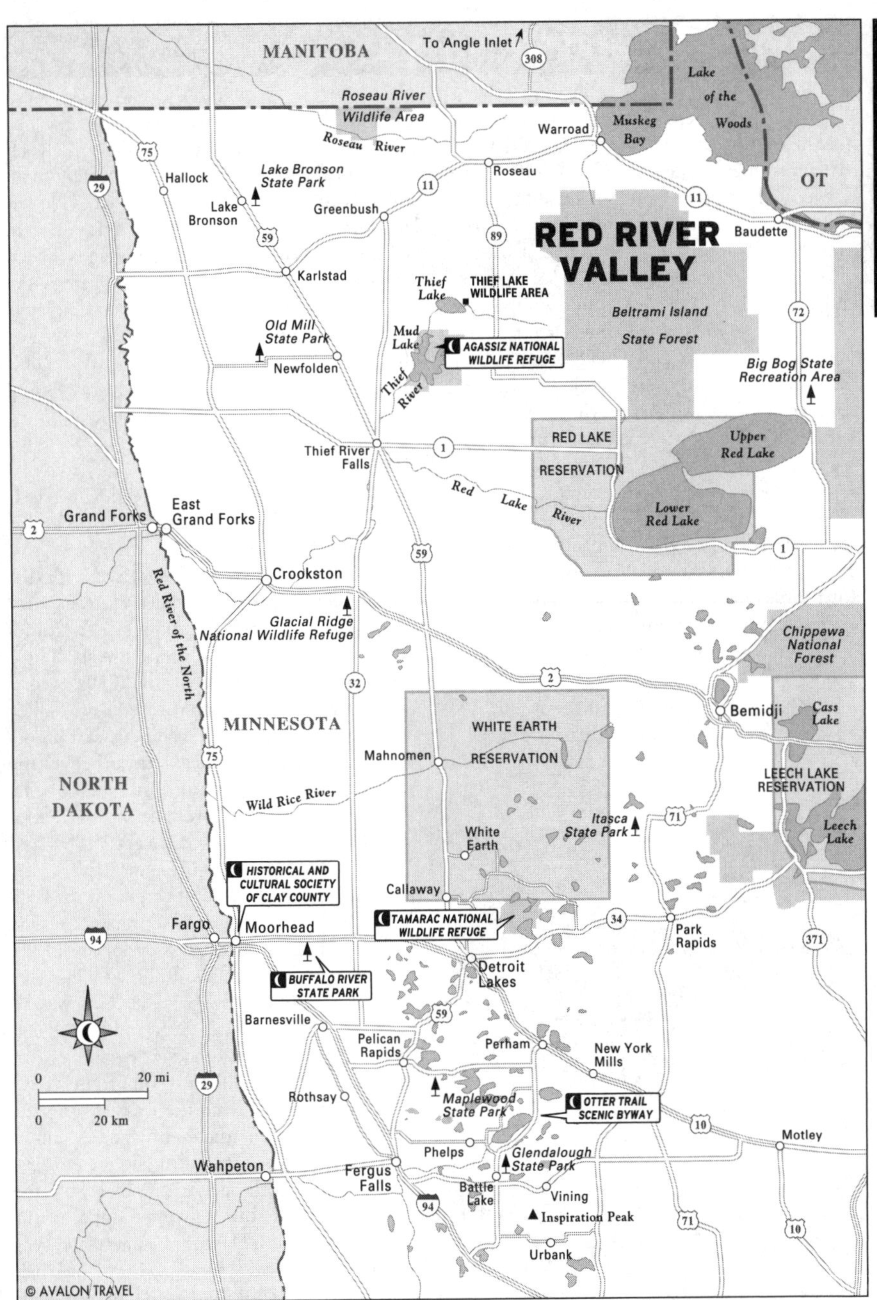

RED RIVER VALLEY
MANITOBA
To Angle Inlet
Roseau River Wildlife Area
Roseau River
Lake of the Woods
Muskeg Bay
Warroad
Roseau
OT
Hallock
Lake Bronson State Park
Lake Bronson
Greenbush
Baudette
Karlstad
Thief Lake
THIEF LAKE WILDLIFE AREA
Beltrami Island State Forest
Old Mill State Park
Mud Lake
AGASSIZ NATIONAL WILDLIFE REFUGE
Newfolden
Thief River
Big Bog State Recreation Area
Thief River Falls
RED LAKE RESERVATION
Upper Red Lake
Lower Red Lake
Red Lake River
Grand Forks
East Grand Forks
Crookston
Glacial Ridge National Wildlife Refuge
Red River of the North
Chippewa National Forest
Bemidji
Cass Lake
MINNESOTA
WHITE EARTH RESERVATION
Mahnomen
LEECH LAKE RESERVATION
NORTH DAKOTA
Wild Rice River
Itasca State Park
White Earth
Leech Lake
HISTORICAL AND CULTURAL SOCIETY OF CLAY COUNTY
Callaway
TAMARAC NATIONAL WILDLIFE REFUGE
Fargo
Moorhead
Park Rapids
Detroit Lakes
BUFFALO RIVER STATE PARK
Barnesville
Pelican Rapids
Perham
New York Mills
0 20 mi
0 20 km
Rothsay
Maplewood State Park
OTTER TRAIL SCENIC BYWAY
Motley
Phelps
Glendalough State Park
Wahpeton
Fergus Falls
Battle Lake
Vining
Inspiration Peak
Urbank
© AVALON TRAVEL

Moorhead and Vicinity

Minnesota's western outpost, along with its bosom buddy Fargo, North Dakota, forms the largest metropolitan area (175,000 people) between Minneapolis and Spokane. Still, it remains off the beaten path for tourists. Fargo-Moorhead is rightly considered one place, and, unlike the bickering siblings of Minneapolis and St. Paul, it is a cordial and cooperative partnership—most of the time.

In most regards Moorhead plays second fiddle to Fargo, but even with just a third the population of its western neighbor, Moorhead (pop. 32,177) has a wide range of attractions for visitors, many thanks to the city's 10,000 students enrolled at Minnesota State University–Moorhead and Concordia College. Fargo may have earned considerable national attention when the Coen brothers named their movie after it, but don't come looking for movie locations—almost none of the story or filming took place here.

The area also occasionally attracts national attention for a reason that's a lot less fun: The combination of the north-flowing Red River (water upstream thaws sooner than water downstream, causing ice dams) and the flat, wide valley surrounding it makes the area prone to floods. In 2009, the river was above flood stage (18 feet) for 61 days and crested at a record-setting 40.8 feet, covering many low-lying areas completely in water. As a visitor, you are unlikely to see any aftereffects beyond a remarkable sense of community engagement that comes from helping one's neighbors through tough times.

© TRICIA CORNELL

Moorhead retains its small-town feel.

History

Transportation made Moorhead what it is today. By the 1820s caravans of huge-wheeled oxcarts, made entirely of wood, screeched across the prairie (grease would have mixed with dirt and quickly worn away the axles; as it was, they still had to be changed up to four or five times per trip) to service the pioneer outposts. These trains, up to 200 carts long by the 1840s, carried tons of pelts south through the Red River Valley along the Pembina Trail, then cut east across the Minnesota River Valley to the offices of the American Fur Company at Fort Snelling. The first steamboat, hauled overland in pieces from Little Falls, ran up the Red River in 1859, and soon the oxcart caravans came here to transfer their loads on the boats and barges for the five-day journey north toward Winnipeg. Settlers poured in, and a proper town developed in 1871 when the Northern Pacific Railroad chose this site to cross the Red River. The "Gateway to the West" opened a year later, and by the end of the decade Moorhead had grown into one of Minnesota's largest and most important cities.

As settlers moved into the western frontier, Fargo would become the dominant city, but at the end of the 19th century Fargo seemed to exist largely to fuel Moorhead's growth. By 1885 Fargo became known as the "Divorce Capital of the World," since North Dakota residents could get a "10-minute divorce." Those seeking to end their nuptials came to Fargo and lived it up across the

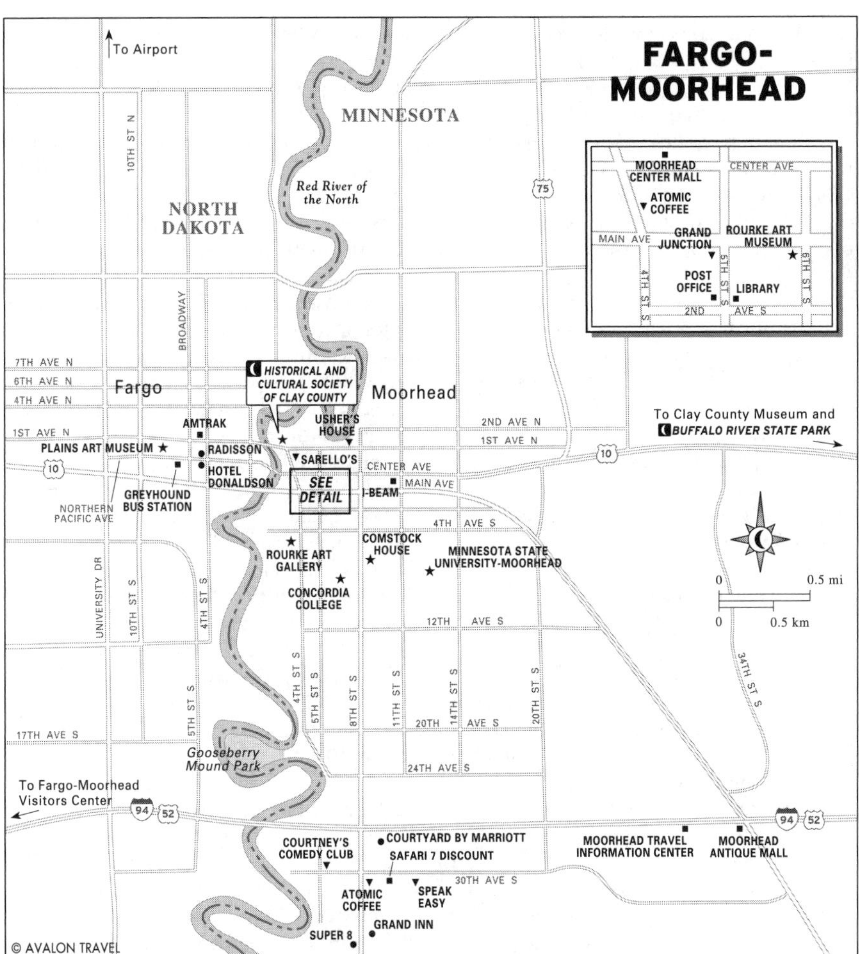

river in Moorhead at the city's symphony, opera, and bars for 90 days until they could get their business over with and go home. In 1889 North Dakota went dry and Moorhead's bars thrived, at least until Clay County followed suit.

SIGHTS

Historical and Cultural Society of Clay County

The focal point of the Historical and Cultural Society of Clay County (202 1st Ave. N., 218/299-5511, www.hjemkomst-center.com, 9 A.M.–5 P.M. Mon. and Wed.–Sat., 9 A.M.–8 P.M. Tues., noon–5 P.M. Sun., $7 adults) is the 76-foot Viking ship built in a potato warehouse by local guidance counselor Robert Asp, who had long dreamt of sailing to Norway. Although Asp died shortly after finishing construction, the *Hjemkomst* (YEM-komst, "homecoming" in Norwegian) completed the 6,000-mile voyage from Duluth, Minnesota, to Bergen, Norway, in 1982. The museum, literally built around the ship, also houses a handful of displays about the construction, the voyage, and Vikings.

Just as interesting and historically accurate is the **Hopperstad Stave Church,** another labor of love by a local resident. The rocket-like chapel, topped by carved dragons, is a full-sized replica of a 12th-century church in Vik, Norway. Built entirely of wood, except where modern building codes demanded otherwise, it is an impressive sight. A guide takes visitors inside on the hour from April to October.

Downstairs inside the main building of the Historical and Cultural Society of Clay County are the often-overlooked free historical displays of the **Clay County Museum** (14 Main St. N., 816/792-1849, www.claycountymuseum.org, 1–4 P.M. Mon.–Sat., closed Sun. and all of Jan., call ahead to confirm hours) including their Scandinavian cultural exhibit in the hallway, and the **Red River Valley Exhibit.**

Comstock House

Moorhead wouldn't be what it is today if it weren't for the Comstock family. Solomon, the patriarch, earned a fortune in banking and railroads and used his wealth and influence to create the college that would grow to become Minnesota State University–Moorhead (MSUM). He also served as a state senator and along with his wife, Sarah, helped establish Moorhead's first public library. Their daughter Ada continued the family's interest in promoting education; she was named the first dean of women at the University of Minnesota and later rose to president of Radcliffe College. Their 1882 11-room Victorian mansion (506 8th St. S., 218/291-4211, 5–8 P.M. Thurs., 1–4:30 P.M. Sat.–Sun. summer, $6 adults) was the largest and fanciest house in Moorhead.

Art Museums

The small but grand 1913 Federal Post Office Building makes a lovely home for the **Rourke Art Museum** (521 Main Ave., 218/236-8861, 1–5 P.M. Fri.–Sun., $5 adults). The permanent collection spans ancient to modern and includes a large selection of African and Native American works, plus temporary exhibits are always coming in. A few blocks away, in an 1875 mansion, is the smaller **Rourke Art Gallery** (523 4th St. S., 1–5 P.M. Fri.–Sun.), their satellite space.

Although it's in Fargo, the **Plains Art Museum** (704 1st Ave. N., Fargo, 701/232-3821, www.plainsart.org, 11 A.M.–5 P.M. Tues.–Wed. and Fri., 11 A.M.–8 P.M. Thurs., 10 A.M.–5 P.M. Sat., 1–5 P.M. Sun., $5 adults, free 1st and 4th Thurs. of each month) got its start in Moorhead and spent over three decades there before moving to this wonderfully adapted 1904 warehouse. Only a fraction of the 2,600-piece permanent collection, which includes such artists as Warhol and glassblower Dale Chihuly, is on display at any one time, but the three floors host a continuous stream of exhibitions.

Both MSUM and Concordia College have small school-year-only art galleries with varying hours on campus. Concordia's **Cyrus M. Running Gallery** (218/299-4623, free admission) is on the second floor of the Frances Frazier Comstock Theatre, and MSUM's art gallery is in the **Rolland Dille Center for the Arts** (218/236-2151, free admission).

SS *Ruby*

For the full scoop on the Red River's history and ecology, take a ride on the SS *Ruby* (701/793-7829, www.riverkeepers.org, 5–8 P.M. Tues. and Fri., 1–7 P.M. Sat.–Sun. summer, $8). The 45-minute cruises on the 20-passenger pontoon boat depart from under the First Avenue Bridge in Moorhead and offer a surprisingly scenic experience.

ENTERTAINMENT AND EVENTS

Moorhead isn't devoid of entertainment options, but you'll find much more happening across the river.

The best cultural calendar is in the free weekly ***High Plains Reader*** (www.hpr1.com).

Nightlife

Courtney's Comedy Club (600 30th Ave. S., 218/287-7100, www.courtneyscomedyclub.biz)

at the AmericInn laughs it up Thursday through Saturday, though they take the summer off. Best for dancing is the **I-Beam** (1021 Center Ave., 218/233-7700, www.thei-beam.com, 9 P.M.–2 A.M. Fri.–Sat.), the only gay bar around.

On Campus

MSUM (1104 7th Ave. S., 218/477-4000, www.mnstate.edu) offers everything from musicians to mentalists, and the public is usually invited. Find their arts calendar online at www.mnstate.edu/cah/calendar.html. **Concordia College** (901 8th St. S., 218/299-4000, www.cord.edu) also hosts concerts and lectures. Both the **MSUM Theatre** (218/477-2126, mnstate.edu/theatre) and the **Concordia College Theatre** (218/299-3314) produce plays year-round. The MSUM Planetarium (218/477-2920, $3) presents six shows throughout the year in Bridges Hall.

Classical Music

The **Fargo-Moorhead Symphony Orchestra** (218/233-8397, www.fmsymphony.org) performs in various locations on both sides of the river. Their most popular performances are theme nights (such as science fiction–related songs), which try to bring symphonic music to new audiences. They often perform with the **Fargo-Moorhead Civic Opera** (701/239-4558, www.fmopera.org).

The **Jazz Arts Group of Fargo-Moorhead** (218/359-4529, www.jazzartsfm.com) hosts concerts and workshops in locations throughout the area.

Cinema

Moorhead's only movie theater is the **Safari 7 Discount** (925 S. 30th Ave., 701/461-8902), which shows second-run movies. MSUM's **Summer Cinema** presents silver screen classics in June and July at Weld Hall's Glasrud Auditorium. Pipe organ music is played during silent films and before every show.

Events

The **Scandinavian Hjemkomst Festival** (www.scandinavianhjemkomstfestical.org) is one of the nation's largest celebrations of Nordic heritage. You can discover the ethnic music, dance, crafts, food, and more over three days around the fourth weekend in June.

Barnesville, 20 miles southeast of Moorhead, hosts **Potato Days** (www.potatodays.com), one of Minnesota's finest festivals. Events include potato sculpture, a potato-sack fashion show, mashed-potato wrestling, and a hotly contested potato-picking competition. The excessive silliness draws upward of 15,000 people (over seven times the population) to this quiet town every year on the weekend before Labor Day.

SHOPPING

Moorhead lacks the classic small-town boutique shopping district. If that's what you're looking for, head across the river to Broadway and 1st Avenue in Fargo.

The **Moorhead Antique Mall** (2811 Main Ave. SE, 218/287-1313, www.moorheadantiquemall.com, 10 A.M.–6 P.M. daily) out along I-94 has 70-odd dealers in twin buildings.

For basic needs, hit **Moorhead Center Mall** (510 Center Ave., 218/233-6117, www.moorheadcentermall.com, 10 A.M.–9 P.M. Mon.–Fri., 10 A.M.–5:30 P.M. Sat., noon–5 P.M. Sun.), anchored by Herberger's department store.

RECREATION

The Red River is an almost forgotten asset amongst locals, but it makes for a great day of lazy canoeing. Even right in the city you get a near-wilderness experience along its wooded banks, while extended journeys north pass a mix of farms, forest, and prairie. On land, paved bike trails run up and down both sides of the Red River, and the two towns are connected by several bridges.

River Keepers (325 7th St. S., Fargo, 701/793-7829, www.riverkeepers.org) rents canoes, kayaks, and bikes ($7/hour) from the SS *Ruby* dock, but only when the boat is running.

MSUM's Recreation and Outing Center (615 14th St. S., 218/477-2265, 10 A.M.–5 P.M. Mon.–Fri.), in the Comstock Memorial Union, also rents canoes and camping equipment.

Usher's House restaurant and bar is housed in a WPA building.

© TRICIA CORNELL

ACCOMMODATIONS

Most of the city's hotels are out at the junction of I-94 and U.S. Highway 75. The **Grand Inn** (810 Belsly Blvd., 218/233-7501 or 800/628-4171, www.grandinnmotels.com, $45) and **Super 8** (3621 8th St. S., 218/233-8880 or 800/800-8000, $59) are two quality cheapies.

The **Courtyard by Marriott** (1080 28th Ave. S., 218/284-1000, www.mhdcourtyard.com, $119) is spiffy and clean, with a large-ish indoor pool. Some rooms have whirlpools and all have refrigerators.

The hotels nearest to downtown Moorhead are actually in downtown Fargo. Completely, and refreshingly, out of place on the prairie, **Hotel Donaldson** (101 Broadway, Fargo, 701/478-1000 or 888/478-8768, www.hoteldonaldson.com, $179) is a thoroughly modern boutique hotel in a renovated 1893 brick building. Each of the 17 oversized suites was decorated by a local artist and has lots of little extras. There is a rooftop patio with a hot tub and bar and a swank restaurant and bar down below.

At 18 stories the **Radisson** (201 N. 5th St., Fargo, 701/232-7363 or 800/333-3333, www.radisson.com, $84) is the second-tallest building in North Dakota. It's quite a bargain if you can get their lowest rate. Amenities include a lap pool, sauna, whirlpool, and exercise room.

FOOD

One of Fargo-Moorhead's best restaurants, **Sarello's** (28 4th St. N., 218/287-0238, www.sarellos.com, lunch 11 A.M.–1 P.M. Fri., dinner 5–10 P.M. Tues.–Sat., $15–32) is superb from start to finish. The food, wine list, and service are excellent, but the best thing is how affordable dishes like roasted rack of lamb and lobster ravioli are.

A popular Moorhead original is **Speak Easy** (1001 30th Ave. S., 218/233-1326, 11 A.M.–11 P.M. Mon.–Sat., 10 A.M.–11 P.M. Sun., $5–26), where the menu is Italian and the decor is 1930s gangster chic.

Usher's House (700 1st Ave. N., 218/287-0080, www.ushershouse.com, 11 A.M.–2 A.M., Mon.–Sat., closed Sun., $10–24) serves upscale steaks and sandwiches (vegetarians are pretty nearly out of luck) in an incongruous but beautiful WPA building with a big, glassed-in dining room overlooking the river.

Better than the chains, **Grand Junction** (435 Main Ave., 218/287-5651, 11 A.M.–9 P.M. Mon.–Sat., noon–8 P.M. Sun., $3–7) serves grilled (and cold) subs, and their french fries are quite good too.

Tops for Java is **Atomic Coffee** (16 4th St. S., 218/299-6161, 6:30 A.M.–10 P.M. Mon.–Fri., 7 A.M.–10 P.M. Sat., 8 A.M.–10 P.M. Sun.), with art on the walls, board games on the shelves, and free Wi-Fi. A second outlet (805 30th Ave. S., 218/477-6161, 5:30 A.M.–7 P.M. Mon.–Fri., 6:30 A.M.–5 P.M. Sat., 8 A.M.–3 P.M. Sun.) near the hotels has a drive-through.

INFORMATION AND SERVICES

The **Fargo-Moorhead Visitors Center** (2001 44th St. SW, Fargo, 701/282-3653 or 800/235-7654, www.fargomoorhead.org, 7:30 A.M.–6 P.M. Mon.–Fri., 9 A.M.–4 P.M. Sat., 10 A.M.–4 P.M. Sun.) is located in a mock grain elevator along I-94 in Fargo. While there, check out the **Celebrity Walk of Fame,** where more than 100 notables have left handprints, from Richard Simmons to Gene Simmons. The **Moorhead Travel Information Center** on I-94 has information on the rest of Minnesota.

The best source for local information is ***The Forum,*** Fargo-Moorhead's daily newspaper. **KMSC** (1500 AM), MSUM's student radio station, plays everything from Mana to Marilyn Manson.

GETTING THERE

Hector International Airport (www.fargoairport.com) in Fargo is served by **Delta** (800/221-1212) with up to eight flights a day to Minneapolis and two to Salt Lake City, by **Allegiant** (702/505-8888) once daily to Las Vegas, **United** (800/241-6522) with four a day to Chicago O'Hare, and **Frontier** (800/432-1359) to Denver.

The **Amtrak** (420 4th St. N., Fargo, 701/232-2197 or 800/872-7245, www.amtrak.com) Empire Builder stops in Fargo at 2:13 A.M. on its way to Chicago and 3:35 A.M. on its way to Seattle/Portland. Bear in mind that hours-long delays often nab the train in the Rockies.

The **bus station** (402 Northern Pacific Ave., Fargo, 701/293-1222) is also in Fargo. **Greyhound** (800/231-2222, www.greyhound.com) goes to Minneapolis ($40 one-way) twice a day. **Jefferson Lines** (888/864-2832, www.jeffersonlines.com) has a daily run in each direction to Sioux Falls, South Dakota ($55 one-way), and Winnipeg, Manitoba ($55 one-way). **Rimrock Stages** (800/255-7655, www.rimrocktrailways.com) goes west to Billings ($99 one-way) once a day.

GETTING AROUND

Metropolitan Area Transit (701/232-7500, www.matbus.com) covers both Moorhead and Fargo, though service after 7 P.M. is very limited and there are no buses on Sundays. The regular adult fare is $1. Call **Doyle's Yellow Checker Cab** (218/233-1354) for taxi service.

The only national car rental agency in Moorhead is **U-Save** (1036 1st Ave. N., 218/271-8994, www.usave.com, 7 A.M.–6 P.M. Mon.–Fri., 8 A.M.–5 P.M. Sat., closed Sun.), though many of the big name agencies have branches at Fargo's airport.

BUFFALO RIVER STATE PARK

One of Minnesota's largest and healthiest prairies, Buffalo River State Park (565 155th St. S., 218/498-2124, www.dnr.state.mn.us) straddles the Buffalo River 13 miles west of Moorhead. Restoration of this vanishing ecosystem began back in 1979 with the cooperation of The Nature Conservancy, who owns the adjoining 2,855-acre Bluestem Prairie Scientific and Natural Area. If you want to see prairie chickens strut their courtship dance in April, reserve a viewing blind (218/498-2679) as early as possible. The mile-long **Wide Sky Trail** north of the river offers the easiest views of the park's annual floral explosion plus good bird-watching opportunities, while other stretches of the 12-mile trail system (six miles groomed for cross-country skiing) wind through the native hardwood forest along the riverbottom. The best way to learn about the 1,322-acre park's four distinct habitats (river, forest, oak savanna, and prairie) is to follow the half-mile **Savanna Cutoff Trail,** which passes through each of them. A picnic area, swimming pond, and 44 campsites (35 electric) sit in the woods near the river and it is these, not the prairie, that draw most visitors—even on a busy summer weekend, the trails are likely to offer a peaceful escape once you get beyond earshot of the beach. Call 218/498-2124 with any park questions.

The adjacent **Minnesota State University-Moorhead's Regional Science Center** (1104 7th Ave. S., 218/477-2904, www.mnstate.edu/regsci, 6 A.M.–11 P.M. daily, free admission) is a great place for a quiet stroll—or ski—through tallgrass prairie and hardwood forests. The interpretive center houses a small natural history exhibit, and the 16-inch telescope at its Paul Feder Observatory is often open to the public.

Lakeland

Although its waters drain to the Red River, the area southeast of Moorhead has little else in common with the rest of the region. Glaciers carved out 1,277 lakes in what are now Otter Tail and Becker Counties, making this the surprising site of one of Minnesota's greatest concentration of lakes. The 20-mile-wide swath of hills and valleys is known as the Leaf Hills, and it extends all the way south to Willmar. The Otter Tail River, which crosses the county, is the principal source of the Red River of the North.

FERGUS FALLS

Unlike its neighbors Detroit Lakes and Alexandria, the seat of Otter Tail County doesn't rely on tourism for its economic health. This makes it a less exciting, but more pleasant, place to visit. Fergus Falls straddles the Otter Tail River, and it grew up as a milling town; when the railroad arrived its future was guaranteed. Today Fergus Falls is a rapidly growing town of nearly 13,500 people with a lovely main street—Lincoln Avenue in this case—where cobblestone sidewalks and trees front the 19th-century brick facades. Joseph Whitford, who in 1857 staked out the town site, named it after James Fergus, the man who financed his expedition. Neither witnessed the town's growth: Fergus never set foot in the area, and Whitford died soon after he came, years before the first settlers arrived.

Sights and Recreation

Locals are rightly proud of the excellent **Otter Tail County Historical Museum** (1110 Lincoln Ave. W., 218/736-6038, www.otchs.org, 9 A.M.–5 P.M. Mon.–Fri., 1–4 P.M. Sat., $4 adults). The lifelike displays on a wide variety of topics make this one of the state's best local history museums. Most impressive are the 1916 Main Street and the agricultural displays.

The **Prairie Wetlands Learning Center** (602 Hwy. 210 E., 218/736-0938, 8 A.M.–4 P.M. Mon.–Fri. year-round, plus 9 A.M.–4 P.M. Sat. summer, free admission) is a 330-acre environmental education center run by the U.S. Fish & Wildlife Service. Inside, hands-on exhibits cover ecology, land management, and history, but the main reason to visit is to admire the prairie and wetlands along the 3.5 miles of trails, which are open dawn to dusk daily year-round.

The **RiverWalk** following the Otter Trail River downtown is a pleasant half-mile stroll with a steady stream of historical markers commemorating the city's early days. Call the Otter Tail County Historical Museum to ask about summer guided tours.

Fergus Falls is the western terminus of the **Central Lakes Trail** (www.centrallakestrail.com), which stretches 55 paved miles along an abandoned rail line to Osakis, where it connects with the Lake Wobegon Trail.

Birders can also start a unique journey in

© TRICIA CORNELL

Flowers bloom at the Prairie Wetlands Learning Center.

Fergus Falls: The **Pine to Prairie Birding Trail** (800/433-1888, www.mnbirdtrail.com) winds north 200 miles to Warroad, with 45 stops on public land or private reserves. Free guidebooks with checklists are available on the website or from the tourist information office in Fergus Falls.

Don't leave town without taking a look at the **world's largest otter** in Adams Park just southeast of downtown along County Highway 82. Rothsay, 16 miles up the freeway, has its own entry in the Minnesota big-statue contest: a 13-foot-tall, 18-foot-long **prairie chicken** in full mating display—it, too, is the world's largest.

Entertainment

A Center for the Arts (124 Lincoln Ave. W., 218/998-2787, www.fergusarts.org), a restored 1921 vaudeville theater, is the pride and joy of Fergus Falls. It hosts movies, music, plays, and more throughout the year. If you get a chance, attend one of the silent movies to hear the accompaniment of the Mighty Wurlitzer pipe organ.

Kaddatz Art Gallery (111 Lincoln W., 218/998-4405, www.kaddatzgalleries.org, 10 A.M.–5 P.M. Tues.–Wed. and Fri., 10 A.M.–8 P.M. Thurs., 10 A.M.–3 P.M. Sat.) hosts an anything-goes open mic the first Thursday of the month.

Shopping

Regional artists (several of them live in the loft apartments upstairs) sell their works at the downstairs **Kaddatz Art Gallery** (111 Lincoln Ave. W., 218/998-2787, www.kaddatzgalleries.org, 10 A.M.–5 P.M. Tues.–Wed. and Fri., 10 A.M.–8 P.M. Thurs., 10 A.M.–3 P.M. Sat.).

Collector's Corner (221 Lincoln Ave. W., 218/736-2210, 10 A.M.–5 P.M. Mon.–Fri., 9:30 A.M.–4 P.M. Sat., closed Sun.), the city's only antiques store, shares a building with the Scandinavian gift shop **Nordic Galleri** (218/739-9665, 9 A.M.–5:30 P.M. daily, except 9 A.M.–7 P.M. Thurs.).

Accommodations

Most of Fergus Falls' hotels are clumped together around I-94 and Highway 210. The barn-like **Motel 7** (616 Frontier Dr., 218/736-2554, www.motel7fergusfallsmn.com, $44) surrounds decent, larger-than-average rooms.

One of the best hotels in town is the **Best Western The Falls Inn** (925 Western Ave., 218/739-2211 or 800/293-2216, $99), which is connected to the city's convention center. It has a pool, whirlpool, and fitness center.

Outside of town, the luxurious, full-service **Thumper Pond** (300 Thumper Lodge Rd., Ottertail, 877/294-7981, www.thumperpond.com, $279) is great for a family getaway, with a golf course, Northwoods-themed indoor waterpark, restaurants, and spa. More than a summer destination, the resort also attracts skiers and vacationers in the winter months.

Food

Ask anyone in town which of Fergus Falls' restaurants is the best and they'll probably tell you **Mabel Murphy's** (3401 Hwy. 210 W., 218/739-4406, www.mabelmurphysmn.com, lounge 11 A.M.–1 P.M. daily, dining room 11 A.M.–2 P.M. and 7–9 P.M. Mon.–Fri.,

7–10 P.M. Sat.–Sun., $10–27). The menu has steaks, salads, seafood, and pastas, and the Old World atmosphere is warm and inviting, if a bit on the kitschy side.

The **Viking Cafe** (203 Lincoln Ave. W., 218/736-6660, 5:30 A.M.–7 P.M. Mon.–Fri., 5:30 A.M.–6 P.M. Sat., 7 A.M.–2 P.M. Sun., $2–8) opened in 1946, and about the only thing that has changed since then are the prices—one of many reasons why locals love it so much.

Barringer's Coffee House (127 Lincoln Ave. E., 218/736-2090, 8 A.M.–5 P.M. Mon.–Fri., closed Sat.–Sun.) has soup, sandwiches, and snacks.

Information and Transportation

The **Fergus Falls Area Chamber of Commerce** (202 Court St. S., 218/739-0125 or 800/726-8959, www.visitfergusfalls.com, 8 A.M.–4:30 P.M. Mon.–Fri.) is downtown along the RiverWalk.

Greyhound (800/231-2222, www.greyhound.com) buses stop at the Olson Oil Company (1425 Lincoln Ave. W., 218/736-3292).

OTTER TRAIL SCENIC BYWAY

Although the land right around Fergus Falls is pretty dry, Otter Tail County has 784 lakes. Besides the great fishing, there are plenty of small towns, historic sites, and natural areas worth a visit and some excellent places to spend the night, whether you want to pitch a tent or be pampered. Even more appealing than the sights themselves is driving between them. This is rural Americana at its best. All of the following, except artsy New York Mills, lie along the **Otter Trail Scenic Byway,** a circular 150-mile marked route along country roads. Get an early start and you can cover it all in a day, but that would be seriously rushing things. Better to take your time and enjoy the ride.

Phelps Mill

There's no point in saving the best for last. The first stop along the byway, if traveling clockwise from Fergus Falls, is the impressive Phelps Mill (29024 County Hwy. 45, Underwood, 218/826-6159, 8 A.M.–8 P.M. daily May, 8 A.M.–9 P.M. daily summer, 8 A.M.–5 P.M. daily Sept.–Oct., free admission). Not only is it a beautiful sight from the outside, but the original equipment is still in place, and you can walk through all four levels to learn how the process, advanced for its day, worked. The Maine Roller Mills, as it was known, began producing flour in 1889. It continued grinding wheat and rye until 1939, when it was abandoned and the town that grew up alongside it slowly vanished. The **Phelps Mill Festival** (www.phelpsmillfestival.org), an arts and crafts fair with music and a children's activity area, takes over the grounds the second weekend in July.

Pelican Rapids

Surprisingly, little Pelican Rapids (pop. 2,374) is one of the most ethnically diverse cities in the state. Mexicans and Vietnamese came some time ago for jobs, and more recently hundreds of Bosnian, Kurdish, Sudanese, and Somali refugees have left their war-torn lands and found a safe haven here; many work at the West Central Turkey plant. This cultural diversity is celebrated, primarily in its edible form, in June during the **International Friendship Festival** (iff12.blogspot.com). The main reason to stop the rest of the year is for a look at the **world's largest pelican.** The 18-foot-tall steel bird sits below Mill Pond Dam.

About 11 miles east of town on Spirit Lake, **The Log House & Homestead** (44854 Fredholm Dr., 218/342-2318 or 800/342-2318, www.loghousebb.com, $165) sits on 115 wild acres with a mile of lakefront. Five rooms, full of all the little extras, and each with a private bath, are split between the 1889 log house, built by the innkeeper's great-great-grandfather and later moved here, and the 1902 homestead. Breakfast includes as many locally grown ingredients as possible.

Several small, family-owned resorts in the area offer lakeside cabins by the week. **Cross Point Resort** (39870 Cross Point Ln., 218/863-8593, www.crosspointresort.com, $555/week for a four-person cabin) is a typical one, with nine tidy cabins in a quiet, woodsy spot on Lake Lida. The beach is good for swimming, and there are boats available for fishing and exploring. You might find your neighbors a bit close for comfort.

Just north of town, the **Pelican Motel** (900 N. Broadway, 218/863-3281, $57) has 16 basic rooms.

At **Riverside Coffee** (18 Broadway N., 218/863-2326, 8 A.M.–4 P.M., Tues.–Sat., $5–9) you can enjoy panini sandwiches, mango smoothies, and fair-trade Guatemalan coffee on the outdoor deck.

Jimmy's Pizza (41 Broadway N., 218/863-7777, 11 A.M.–8 P.M. Tues.–Thurs., 11 A.M.–9 P.M. Fri.–Sat., 4–8 P.M. Sun., closed Mon.) is a popular spot for passable pizza, along with a few pasta and Tex-Mex dishes.

Maplewood State Park

Soaring tree-covered hills and deep lake-filled valleys define Minnesota's seventh-largest state park (39721 Park Entrance Rd.). The basswood, maple, and oak that dominate the forest put on a fantastic display of fall color, while the park's prairie has its own brilliant show during the summer. Hikers have 25 miles of trail, ranging from gentle to wild, leading across the 9,250 acres, and come winter 13 miles of these are groomed for cross-country skiing. The easiest walking routes are the **Grass Lake Interpretive Trail** and the **Woodland Nature Trail,** both of which have signs discussing park ecology. Boats and canoes can be rented to explore the various lakes. Seventy-one campsites (32 electric) and a camper cabin are spread over four campgrounds; the shaded and secluded Knoll and Hollow Camps are the best. For even more privacy get one of the three backpacking sites in the south end of the park. Horseback riders touring the 20 miles of trails open to them have their own camp. Call 218/863-8383 for more information or visit www.stayatmnparks.com for reservations.

Perham

Perham's claim to fame are the faster-than-you'd-expect **International Turtle Races.** The 10-foot sprints take place downtown in City Hall Park every Wednesday at 10:30 A.M. throughout the summer. Between heats kids can take a ride on the **Perham Express,** a mock train that runs up and down the city's streets. Next to the reptilian speedway is the **Tourist Information Center** (135 E. Main St., 218/346-7710 or 800/634-6112).

In Their Own Words (805 W. Main St., 218/346-7678, www.itowmuseum.org, 10 A.M.–5 P.M. Mon.–Sat., 1–4 P.M. Sun., $4, free Veterans Day and Fourth of July., free for veterans) has interactive displays where veterans tell war stories from World War I to the present, both about the battlefield and the home front.

The **History Museum of East Otter Tail County** (230 1st Ave. N., 218/346-7676, www.historymuseumeot.org, 10 A.M.–5 P.M. Mon.–Sat., 1–4 P.M. Sun., free admission) is housed in a former Episcopal church built in 1887. The collection is modest, but well presented. Their archives are all searchable online, a boon for genealogists.

Just outside of town on Big Pine Lake, **Whispering Pines Resort** (46362 County Hwy. 8, 218/346-3188, www.whisperingpinesmn.com, $400–1,075/week) is a homey collection of eight fully-stocked cottages with one to four bedrooms, each of which comes with its own boat. Nightly rates ($100–180) are available after Labor Day and before June 1.

The **Station House** (103 E. Main St., 218/346-7181, 6 A.M.–9 P.M. daily, $5–16) has a broad menu ranging from spaghetti to taco salads to vegetarian garden burgers to steaks.

Out on the highway, the spacious **Mrs. B's** (junction of 78 and 10, 218/346-6772, 5:30 A.M.–4 P.M. daily) is known for homemade pies and pastries.

For a hit of coffee and a dose of community, stop at **Gathering Grounds Coffee Shop** (134 1st Ave. S., 218/346-7069, 7:30 A.M.–5 P.M. Mon.–Fri., 9 A.M.–5 P.M. Sat., closed Sun.), with frilly decorations, antiques for sale, free wireless, and a great small-town attitude.

New York Mills

Though the Otter Trail Scenic Byway turns south at Perham, a detour on U.S. Highway

10 to this unique community is definitely in order. The **New York Mills Regional Cultural Center** (24 Main Ave. N., 218/385-3339, www.kulcher.org, 10 A.M.–5 P.M. Tues.–Fri., 10 A.M.–3 P.M. Sat., free admission to gallery) is a true anomaly—a town this small (pop. 1,158) shouldn't have an arts center this good. Housed in a lovingly restored 1885 redbrick mercantile, the center hosts an impressive calendar of exhibits, music, theater, storytelling, and more. Their low-priced workshops are even more diverse and have included painting, bookbinding, mime, and playing the jaw harp.

Arguably the center's greatest contribution is the **Great American Think-Off** (www.think-off.org), an annual philosophy competition held each June since 1993. Entries are received from around the globe and the final debate is usually broadcast live on C-SPAN.

Five miles outside of town is the **Finn Creek Museum** (55442 340th St., 218/385-2233, 1–5 P.M. daily summer, free admission), a Finnish farm site with the original 1900 house and sauna, as well as many other relocated buildings from that era. To get there head east on Centennial 84 Drive and follow the signs. The best time to visit is the last weekend of August during the **Finn Creek Festival.**

At the **Whistle Stop B&B** (107 Nowell St. E., 218/385-2223 or 800/328-6315, www.whistlestopbedandbreakfast.com, $80) guests choose between three turn-of-the-20th-century railroad cars (including an 1893 caboose), a southwestern-themed cottage, and two plush rooms in the lovely 1903 Victorian home.

For a relaxed morning pastry, casual lunch, or afternoon snack, you can't beat **Mills Creamery** (100 Centennial Dr., 218/385-5282, www.millscreamery.com, 7:30 A.M.–4 P.M. Mon., 7:30 A.M.–5 P.M. Tues.–Fri., 7:30 A.M.–3 P.M. Sat., 7–11 A.M. Sun.).

The **Bake Shoppe** (32 Main Ave. N., 218/385-2665, 7 A.M.–5:30 P.M. Mon.–Fri., 7 A.M.–4 P.M. Sat., closed Sun.) has coffee and bakery items, including lefse.

Glendalough State Park

Though Glendalough (25287 Whitetail Ln., 218/864-0110) is one of Minnesota's newest state parks, it is also one of its oldest protected natural areas. The various owners had limited impact on their land, and much of the park's 1,931 acres of marsh, hardwood forest, and remnant prairie, and more than nine miles of undeveloped shoreline on six lakes, is remarkably pristine. The most unusual feature of the park is Annie Battle Lake, a designated **Heritage Fishery.** Because fishing was limited on the 335-acre lake over the last century, largemouth bass, panfish, and walleye are large and plentiful. To preserve the status quo for future generations, strict regulations, including no motors (even electric), no fish-finding devices, and catch-and-release only for some species, are in effect.

Fish aren't the only species found in abundance. Waterfowl, including loons, are common on Glendalough's lakes, bald eagles nest on the shores, and you are almost certain to spot deer in the prairie along the entrance road in the early evening. Lake Emma, which has a floating observation blind, is the park's premier wildlife-viewing spot. The 1.4-mile **Beaver Pond Interpretive Trail** is another good spot, and Sunset Lake is excellent for bird-watching. In total there are 10 miles of trails, with 8 miles groomed for cross-country skiing. The park office rents canoes, kayaks, rowboats, cross-country skis, and snowshoes. When you are not communing with nature there is a picnic area and sandy beach. Glendalough's campground is one of the state's best. All 22 cart-in sites are wooded and well spaced. There are also four camper cabins (two with heat and electric), and five sites on the far side of Annie Battle Lake are reached by boat, bike, or foot.

Battle Lake

Battle Lake is home to **Chief Wenonga,** a towering fiberglass sculpture overlooking the lake on the north end of town. In 1795 the real chief, leading a band of Ojibwe warriors, suffered a massive defeat by the Dakota on this spot in a battle for control of these productive hunting and fishing grounds. Tucked in amongst the many gift shops along Lake

Avenue is the nonprofit **Art of the Lakes Gallery** (108 Lake Ave. S., 218/864-8606, 10 A.M.–5 P.M. daily), with works for sale in all media by some 50 member artists. They also sponsor various workshops throughout the year and the **Art & Craft Affair** the second weekend in August.

If shopping isn't your thing—though that is really what Battle Lake is all about—two area stables, **Silver Sage Guest Ranch** (15381 410th Ave., 218/864-8007, www.silversagemn.com) and **Shady Oaks Riding Stable** (40927 County Hwy. 128, 218/367-2699), offer horseback riding.

One of the region's best places to spend the night is **Xanadu Island** (35484 235th St., 218/864-8096 or 800/396-9043, www.xanadu.cc, $105), five miles out of town. In the 1920s and '30s this five-acre island on the north end of Elbow Lake was a luxurious summer retreat for the rich and famous. A one-lane road, enshrouded by a lovely tunnel of trees, now connects the island to the mainland. The rustic main lodge, with an enclosed porch and open deck, has five bed-and-breakfast rooms, some with fireplaces and hot tubs. Behind the main house the old servants' quarters have been converted into spacious and fully equipped cottages, though they lack the charm of the rooms in the house.

The recently renovated **Battle Lake Motel** (102 Glenhaven Dr., 218/864-5208, www.battlelakemotel.com, $55) is just a stone's throw north of Chief Wenonga on Highway 78. It's a good value.

Stub's (211 Lake Ave. S., 218/864-9929, 5–10 P.M. Mon.–Sat. summer, Thurs.–Sat. May and Sept., Fri.–Sat. Apr. and Oct.–Nov., $12–26) specializes in steak and seafood and has a whole section of the menu dedicated to combinations of the two, such as "steak and walleye" and "ribs and lobster chunks."

Many locals swear by the hamburgers at **Shoreline Lanes** (505 Lake Ave. N., 218/864-5265, 6 A.M.–9 P.M. Sun.–Thurs., 6 A.M.–10 P.M. Fri.–Sat., $3–15). In fact, one area nurse tells me that she has had patients on their deathbeds whose last wish was to have just one more. They also serve pizza and host a Friday-night fish fry.

Vining

If it weren't for local construction worker Ken Nyberg, the only reason to stop in Vining would be to fill up your gas tank. Nyberg makes larger-than-life steel sculptures and uses Highway 210 as his gallery. Spread out along the length of the tiny village you'll find a square knot, pliers about to squash a roach, and many more amusing items.

Inspiration Peak

The views from the second-highest point in Minnesota make this hill worthy of its name, though when autumn color arrives you might think its original name, Leaf Hill, is most appropriate. A steep quarter-mile walk on a paved path from the picnic area takes you to an overlook at the summit of the 1,750-foot hill for panoramic views. It is 4.5 miles west of Urbank on County Highway 38.

DETROIT LAKES

The village of Detroit was founded in 1871 as a service center along the newly built Northern Pacific rail line. "Lakes" was added in 1926 because of continued postal mix-ups between it and some other city way off in Michigan. The town of about 7,000 people sits at the north end of the glacially formed lakes and hills (known as the Leaf Hills), and it is these bodies of water that serve as its livelihood today. The economy is heavily dependent on the thousands of families who flock here each summer to pass a week at one of the over 50 resorts in the vicinity.

Sights and Recreation

Almost everyone will find something of interest at the **Becker County Museum** (714 Summit Ave., 218/847-2938, 10 A.M.–4 P.M. Tues.–Sat., until 6 P.M. on Thurs., free admission), whether it be something from Native American or military collections (the latter dating back to the Civil War), the 1890s settler's cabin, the horse-drawn hearse, or the two-headed cow.

The narrow, mile-long **City Beach** is a

© TRICIA CORNELL

Detroit Lakes is a popular beach destination.

huge summertime draw. Boat launches and boat rentals are available. There is a miniature golf course and boat rental at the end of Washington Avenue. South of town is the larger **Go Putt N Bump** (15802 U.S. 59, 218/847-7083, 10 A.M.–9 P.M. daily weather permitting), with go karts, bumper boats, mini golf, and batting cages.

McLaughlin's RV and Marine (12211 Hwy. 59 S., 218/846-9950 or 866/262-8332, www.fundealer.com, 8 A.M.–7 P.M. Mon.–Thurs., 8 A.M.–6 P.M. Fri., 9 A.M.–3 P.M. Sat., closed Sun.) rents boats, as well as RVs, ATVs, and snowmobiles.

Two companies sitting side by side on Highway 34 seven miles west of town, **KK Tubing** (33551 Hwy. 34, 218/847-5734) and **Charlie's Ottertail Tubing** (33505 Hwy. 34, 218/847-3258), run two-hour trips on the Otter Tail River for $6 and $7 respectively.

If Detroit Lakes itself starts to feel a little too hectic and resort-y, peace and quiet are only a short drive away. **Hamden Slough National Wildlife Refuge** (218/847-4431) is just six miles northwest of Detroit Lakes at the intersection of County Road 104 and 210th Street. The 3,000-acre refuge is home to 225 species of birds, including prairie chickens, and has been named an Important Bird Area by the Audubon Society. There's little in the way of facilities out on the rolling grassland and wetlands, beyond quiet hiking trails where you are unlikely to meet another soul.

Shopping

There's a handful of small shops along Washington Avenue, including **Washington Square Mall** (808 Washington Ave., 218/847-1679, 10 A.M.–8 P.M. Mon.–Fri., 9:30 A.M.–5:30 P.M. Sat., noon–5 P.M. Sun.) hidden stealthily behind the classic downtown storefronts.

Across the street, **Book World** (815 Washington Ave., 218/847-0133, www.bookworldstores.com, 9 A.M.–7 P.M. Mon.–Sat., 10 A.M.–5 P.M. Sun.) has a fantastic regional section with a ton of local cookbooks.

Entertainment and Events

The **Historic Holmes Theatre** (806 Summit Ave. 218/844-7469, www.dlccc.org) hosts local arts groups and touring acts, from comedy

© TRICIA CORNELL

Hamden Slough National Wildlife Refuge is home to 225 species of birds.

revues to plays for preschoolers to classical and pop music.

The **Northwest Water Carnival** has grown from humble beginnings in 1935 to eight days of family events. Highlights are a chili cook-off, water fights, and a massive parade. It begins the week after the Fourth of July.

Each August, 50,000 people pack the Soo Pass Ranch south of town for **WE Fest** (www.wefest.com), one of the largest country music festivals in the world.

Thirty-five miles north of Detroit Lakes is the White Earth Ojibwe's **Shooting Star Casino** (777 Casino Rd., Mahnomen, 218/935-2711 or 800/453-7827, www.starcasino.com). A 390-room hotel is attached and they bring in big-name entertainment. The band also sponsors the **White Earth Powwow** in the village of White Earth on the weekend closest to June 14th.

Accommodations

Holiday Haven Motel (220 Lake Dr. W., 218/847-5605, $85) is one of a dying breed of simple lodging in town on the lake.

Heading east out of town you'll find the **Best Western Holland House** (615 Hwy. 10 E., 218/847-4483 or 800/338-8547, $99), whose primary attraction is a 133-foot indoor waterslide. Other amenities include a pool, whirlpool, and sauna.

Modern and welcoming, **The Lodge** (1200 East Shore Dr., 218/847-8439 or 800/761-8439, www.thelodgeonlakedetroit.com, $169) is an upscale lakeside property where all 55 rooms have lake views. Amenities include a beach, pool, business center, and fitness center.

The **Acorn Lake B&B** (30680 Acorn Lake Rd., 218/334-5545 or 888/571-9904, $55–99), five miles southeast of town along U.S. Highway 10, has five guest rooms ranging from shared bath to a two-room whirlpool suite with private entrance.

Maplelag (30501 Maplelag Rd., Callaway, 218/375-4466 or 800/654-7711, www.maplelag.com), 20 miles north of Detroit Lakes on Little Sugarbush Lake, attracts guests from around the world who want to experience one of Minnesota's best winter resorts. Cross-country skiing is the main focus, and 36 miles of groomed trails for all abilities cross their 660 acres. Lessons are available and

WHITE EARTH RESERVATION

- Total Area: 1,167 sq. miles
- Tribally Owned: 10 percent
- Total Population: 9,192
- Native Population: 3,378
- Tribal Enrollment: 19,366

The White Earth Reservation was never the historic homeland of any Ojibwe people. The U.S. Government created it with the intent of relocating all the Ojibwe people from Minnesota, Wisconsin, and Michigan. Due to pressure and payoffs from the government, many did settle in scattered communities across the reservation, but most refused or returned home after arriving. The village of White Earth, named for the white clay found in abundance here, is the largest native community on the reservation and home to the tribal headquarters. The other notable native communities are Naytahwaush, Pine Point, Rice Lake, and Elbow Lake. Fifty-three wild rice beds are spread out across the reservation, and hundreds of thousands of pounds of the sacred grain are harvested each year by the tribal-owned Manitok Wild Rice Company. The tribe also owns a garment manufacturing plant and the Shooting Star Casino in Mahnomen, the area's largest employer.

The White Earth band's most famous member is the environmentalist Winona LaDuke, who was Ralph Nader's vice presidential running mate for the Green Party in 1996 and 2000. LaDuke's White Earth Land Recovery Project is part of a larger effort by the tribe to regain land that it has lost over the years, much of it due to unscrupulous land sales authorized by the 1889 Nelson Allotment Act and other similar laws, as well as tax delinquency.

top-quality equipment is available for rent. Guests can also try snowshoeing, kicksledding, and ice-skating. After a long day on the trails, unwind in the hot tub and sauna, get a massage, or dip into the bottomless cookie jars before heading back to relax in your TV- and telephone-less rooms. A three-day winter weekend package including excellent meals runs $225–338. They are closed most of the summer.

If you just need a basic room for the night, **Morningside Motel** (31348 County Hwy. 10, 218/334-5021, $55), seven miles out of town, in Frazee, offers clean, no-frills, inexpensive rooms with unexpectedly homey decorative touches. There's a small fridge and microwave in every room.

Food

The casual and ever-popular **Lakeside Tavern** (200 Lake Dr. W., 218/847-1891, 11 A.M.–1 A.M. daily, kitchen closes at 10 P.M., $6–11), set in a historic hotel, has pizzas and sandwiches. There's a big patio with a lake view and lots of bar games.

Speak Easy (1100 Shore Dr. N., 218/844-1326, 10 A.M.–11 P.M. daily, lounge open until 2 A.M., $5–25) serves a 1930s theme—waitresses wear period dresses and a 1931 Model A Ford is parked in the bar—along with its Italian and American menu.

Another blast from the past is **The Fireside** (1462 Shore Dr. E., 218/847-8192, 5–11 P.M. daily, brunch 9 A.M.–1 P.M. Sun., $19–41), which retains much of the elegance of its 1940s heyday. It's known for its supper club classics (shrimp cocktail, iceberg lettuce wedges, and ribs) and great view.

Young people and a surprising number of families with kids have been enjoying the party at **Zorbaz** (402 Lake Dr. W., 218/847-5305, www.zorbaz.com, 10 A.M.–2 A.M. daily, $7–15) since 1969. It's part of a small chain of conspicuously fun restaurant/bars in Minnesota's resort towns. There's a warren of indoor seating and outdoor patios vaguely reminiscent of Key West, serving pizza, tacos, and other crowd-pleasers.

For ice cream and snacks, and high-quality sandwiches with your coffee, stop at **Brewed Awakenings** (910 Washington Ave.,

218/847-5104, www.lakesbrewedawakening, 6 A.M.–7 P.M. Mon.–Thurs., 6 A.M.–6 P.M. Fri., 6 A.M.–4 P.M. Sat., closed Sun.), which also has free Wi-Fi.

Information and Transportation

The **Detroit Lakes Regional Chamber of Commerce** (700 Summit Ave., 218/847-9202 or 800/542-3992, www.visitdetroitlakes.com, 8 A.M.–5 P.M. Mon.–Fri.) has information about the city and surrounding lakes area.

Amtrak (800/872-7245, www.amtrak.com) trains stop at the downtown depot (116 Pioneer St.) around 3 A.M. on their east- and westbound runs.

TAMARAC NATIONAL WILDLIFE REFUGE

The beautiful Tamarac National Wildlife Refuge (35704 County Hwy. 26, 218/847-2641, www.fws.gov/midwest/tamarac) is spread across 43,000 acres at the convergence of Minnesota's three primary ecosystems—prairie, northern hardwood forest, and northern pine forest—creating an impressive variety of flora and fauna. Nearly half the area is wetlands, which increases the biological diversity even more. Tamarac is one of the best bird-watching destinations in the state, and you've got a shot at seeing over 250 species, including common loon, bald eagle, ruffed grouse, great gray owl, mourning warbler, and trumpeter swan. The more than 50 mammalian species include black bear, beaver, otter, fisher, moose, and wolf. Visitors are welcome to pick the berries and chokecherries that grow in the refuge for personal use.

Just about everything of interest to visitors is in the southern third of the refuge (below County Highway 26), which is open year-round; the northern section is generally off-limits March–September. The best place to begin a visit is the centrally located **visitors center** (7:30 A.M.–4 P.M. Mon.–Fri. year-round, plus noon–5 P.M. Sat.–Sun. summer), which has a short, informative video, interpretive displays, a gift shop, and knowledgeable staff on hand to answer your queries. They lead free guided tours at 10 A.M. on Thursdays during the summer and offer special films and programs nearly every summer weekend. The five-mile **Blackbird Auto Tour,** starting near the visitors center, is both scenic and excellent for wildlife observation. It is open to cars when the weather permits, which is generally May through October. The best bet for hiking is the **Old Indian Trail,** which leads two miles through a maple forest. Winter visitors can ski, snowshoe, and ice fish.

The Far Northwest

Few tourists to Minnesota make it out this far, and with all there is to see and do in the rest of the state that's understandable. That doesn't mean, however, that there is no reason to visit this forgotten corner. For someone who has never been to the Great Plains, just driving through here will be a worthy new experience. As you approach the widely scattered towns, grain elevators loom in the distance, looking larger than the Sears Tower. Up close though, you can almost see the small towns dying right before your eyes. On the other hand, a few mid-sized cities have diversified their economies and are thriving. But towns are the exception—here farms are the rule. Being surrounded for so long by so little you can quickly come to feel lonely—sometimes it even seems a little eerie—and when a rumbling thunderstorm is rolling toward you it can be downright scary. Just imagine how the pioneers felt as they stared out across the endless sea of prairie, unlike anything they had ever seen before, that was to become their new homes. Their legacy is to be found in both the rusting farm equipment and crumbling shells of old houses sprinkled along the roads and in the shiny new silos and tractors in the fields.

THIEF RIVER FALLS

Thief River Falls is the largest and fastest-growing city in northwest Minnesota. It sits where the Thief River joins the larger Red Lake River, and this waterpower was first exploited for sawmills in the 1880s. Norwegians were amongst the earliest settlers, and today half of the city's 8,410 residents claim at least some Norse ancestry, making this the most Norwegian city in the nation. Before this, the Dakota and later the Ojibwe made it their home, and an Ojibwe village remained at the river junction until 1904—a statue of Chief Red-Robe overlooks the site. The city really began to grow when the Great Northern and Soo Line railroads made this a center for shipping wheat.

Sights and Recreation

The city's most interesting attraction is the area's second-largest employer, the **Arctic Cat factory** (601 Brooks Ave. S., 218/681-8558), where you can watch snowmobiles and ATVs being born. Your tour guide will lead you right through the factory floor along the assembly lines and under conveyor belts to show you the whole operation from start to finish. Many things have changed since 1962 when the plant opened, but, while you'll see robotic welding and computerized diagnostics, most of the work is still done by hand. The free, hour-long tours depart weekdays at 1 P.M. throughout the year, but call ahead to make sure the lines aren't down.

Seventeen historic buildings have been moved from across the county to **Peder Engelstad Pioneer Village** (825 Oakland Park Rd., 218/681-5767, 1–5 P.M. daily summer, $5 adults), which is just off Highway 32. All of them, including the one-room schoolhouse, barbershop, general store, and candy shop, are stocked with appropriate furnishings and provisions. The museum also has interesting Native American and Norwegian exhibits.

The city's 7.3-mile **Riverwalk** trail system roughly follows the Red Lake River through town and has 15 historical markers along its path. The parts that get away from city streets are quite pleasant. For a more active outing you could canoe the **Red Lake River** all the way to East Grand Forks, a 127-mile trip. The Red Lake River is one of the few canoeable rivers in the region and is generally a quiet paddle, though there are some easily navigable boulder fields between St. Hilare and Crookston, which can create up to Class II rapids. The wooded banks are steep until around Red Lake Falls before giving way to low farmland.

The Red Lake Band of Chippewa operate the **Seven Clans Casino** (20595 Center St. E., 218/681-4062, www.sevenclanscasino.com), along with sister establishments in Red Lake and Warroad. It's far from the biggest or the flashiest casino in Minnesota, but there are large banks of slot machines, many tables, a 1950s "malt shop," and even a large water park and hotel.

Thirteen miles outside of Thief River Falls, in tiny Plummer, is Minnesota's northernmost vineyard, the appropriately named **Two Fools Vineyard** (12501 240th Ave. SE, 218/465-4655, www.twofoolsvineyard.com, noon–5 P.M. Sat.–Sun. June–Oct.). They grow primarily cold-hardy varieties developed by the University of Minnesota and operate a small tasting room with a modest and relaxing patio.

Practicalities

The **T-59 Motel** (1510 Hwy. 59 SE, 218/681-2720, www.t59moteltrf.com, $50) has basic rooms, but the price is right.

The newer **C'Mon Inn** (1586 Hwy. 29 SE, 218/681-3000 or 800/950-8111, www.cmon-inn.com, $85) has a pool and whirlpool.

There are 64 campsites crammed between the river and Highway 32 in the city-owned **Thief River Falls Tourist Park** (218/681-2519, $19 full hookup).

Evergreen Eating Emporium (700 Hwy. 32 S., 218/681-3138, 11 A.M.–2 P.M. Mon.–Fri. and 5–9 P.M. Mon.–Thurs., 5–10 P.M. Fri.–Sat., $8–27) has an English Tudor decor, but serves up a solid American menu, including build-your-own pastas.

The **Thief River Falls Visitors and Convention Bureau** (2017 Hwy. 59 SE,

218/681-3720 or 800/827-1629, www.visitthiefriverfalls.com, 8:30 A.M.–5 P.M. Mon.–Fri.) is at the southeast entrance to town. **Thief River Falls Regional Airport** (13722 Airport Dr., 218/681-7680, www.citytrf.net/transportation.htm) is two miles south of town on Highway 17. **Delta Airlines** (800/225-2525) flies to the Twin Cities twice a day.

CROOKSTON

While Crookston is home to the **Polk County Historical Museum** (719 E. Robert St., 218/281-1038, noon–5 P.M. Tues.–Sun. May–Sept., free admission), with its assortment of relocated historic buildings, the lovely downtown's living history is more interesting.

Widman's Candy Shop (116 Broadway S., 218/281-1487, 7 A.M.–5 P.M. Mon.–Fri., 7:30 A.M.–2 P.M. Sat., 7 A.M.–12:30 P.M. Sun.) opened in 1911 and hasn't changed much since then. Now run by a fourth-generation Widman, the store still sells homemade candy, their famous hand-dipped potato chips, and old-fashioned fountain drinks. Even the prices hark back to the bygone days.

A few blocks over, the **Grand Theatre** (124 2nd St. E., 218/281-1820, www.crookstontheatre.com) opened in 1910 as a vaudeville stage and is now one of the oldest continually running movie theaters in the country.

The **Pembina Trail Memorial**—explorer Joe Rolette and his oxcart—on the north side of town along U.S. Highway 2 is dedicated to the father of the Pembina Trail and certainly worthy of a road-trip photo.

The **Red Lake River,** one of the few canoeing rivers in northwest Minnesota, offers 50 miles of gentle paddling to East Grand Forks, where it joins the Red River.

Nine miles east of town is **Glacial Ridge National Wildlife Refuge** (17788 349th St. SE, 218/687-2229), the country's newest national wildlife refuge and also the largest tallgrass prairie restoration project in the nation. There are currently 5,000 acres of native prairie, much of it acquired with the help of The Nature Conservancy, and more than three times that of old cropland is ready to be returned to prairie and wetlands, though it is a long-term project. For the time being, there are few visitor facilities, but roadside bird-watching is productive for sandhill cranes, marbled godwit, and prairie falcon, and viewing blinds are available for watching greater prairie chickens do their mating dance in April and May. Reserve a blind through the **Crookston Convention & Visitors Bureau** (107 2nd St. W., 218/281-4320 or 800/809-5997, www.visitcrookston.com, 8 A.M.–4:30 P.M. Mon.–Fri.).

Crookston's annual festival is **Oxcart Days,** held the third weekend in August. Revelers enjoy parades, a corn feed, foot races, canoe races, kayak races, bed races, and a torchlight parade to wrap it all up.

Practicalities

The **Golf Terrace Motel** (1731 University Ave., 218/281-2626, $39) has decent enough rooms. A big step up in quality is the **Northland Inn** (2200 University Ave., 218/281-5210, www.northlandprairieinn.com, $69) with a pool and hot tub.

Among Crookston's most popular restaurants is **University Station** (2200 University Ave., 218/281-5210, 6:30 A.M.–2 P.M. Sun.–Sat. and 5–9:30 P.M. Sun.–Thurs., 5–10 P.M. Fri.–Sat., $7–30) at the Northland Inn, which spans steaks, salads, pastas, and stir fries.

For a drink or a snack try **Novel Cup** (101 W. Robert St., 218/281-4830, 7:30 A.M.–5:30 P.M. Mon.–Fri., 10 A.M.–2 P.M. Sat.–Sun.), a tiny coffee shop and bookstore.

The small **University of Minnesota-Crookston** (2900 University Ave., 218/281-8520, www.crk.umn.edu) campus is the town's cultural anchor, and the public is welcome at most events.

Jefferson Lines (888/864-2832, www.jeffersonlines.com) buses stop at the Tri–Valley Heartland Express (1345 Fairfax Ave.) near the university.

AGASSIZ NATIONAL WILDLIFE REFUGE

Twenty-three miles northeast of Thief River Falls is Minnesota's largest National Wildlife

Refuge and one of its oldest. Named for Glacial Lake Agassiz, which shaped this land some 10,000 years ago, Agassiz (22996 290th St. NE, 218/449-4115, www.fws.gov/midwest/agassiz) has 61,500 acres, most of it wetlands, in the ecological transition zone between the pine forests of the east and tallgrass prairies to the west. Wetlands like these once covered a much larger area of the Red River Valley, but a massive network of drainage ditches opened up the land to farming. They also increased the severity of spring floods along the Red River.

Two wolf packs roam the refuge, and bear, fisher, otter, and bobcat are among the other 49 species of mammal found here. Moose numbers have dropped dramatically in recent years, but they are still seen sometimes, and elk even wander in on occasion. One hundred thirty-one bird species nest here, and more than twice that can be observed over the course of a year. Rare species, such as great gray owl and marbled godwit, have earned Agassiz recognition as one of the best bird-watching sites in the United States.

Despite its size, public access is limited. Other than County Highway 7, which crosses the southern half of the refuge, casual visitors are restricted to the four-mile **Lost Bay Habitat Drive,** which leads you right through some prime wildlife-viewing territory and three concise, wooded hiking trails. All of these routes are open May–October. Bird-watching is also good on roads along the edge of the refuge. For an impressive panorama, climb the 100-foot-tall **observation tower** on County Highway 7 next to the headquarters (7:30 A.M.–4 P.M. Mon.–Fri.). Several free, primitive campsites are available on the adjacent state-managed wildlife lands.

OLD MILL STATE PARK

This peaceful 287-acre wooded preserve (218/437-8174) circles a small collection of historic structures. The namesake Old Mill is a steam-powered flour mill that was built along the Middle River in the 1890s. A furnished log cabin next door adds to the experience. The mill is powered up each year on the last Sunday in August during **Grinding Days.** The park hosts a decent sampling of wildlife, including moose, beaver, and long-eared owls, which might be spotted on the seven-mile web of hiking trails crossing the mostly forested park. In winter the trails are groomed for cross-country skiing, and skis and snowshoes can be rented from the park office. There is also a sledding hill. Twenty-six campsites (10 electric) and a swimming pond round out the facilities. The park office is located at 33489 240th Avenue NW.

LAKE BRONSON STATE PARK

You know that if such an off-the-beaten-path park (218/754-2200) attracts nearly 120,000 visitors a year it must be pretty good. Following a major drought in the 1930s that dried up wells in Bronson and Hallock, the South Branch Two River was dammed as a hedge against future disasters. As one of the few lakes in the area, 330-acre Lake Bronson became a magnet for locals looking to swim, fish, and canoe. While the lake draws the vast majority of visitors, this is a well-rounded park with 14 miles of trails, abundant wildlife, and several minor historic sites. The 3,598-acre park encompasses a mix of prairie and aspen-oak forests, and if you'd like to see a moose in the wild, this is an excellent place to look. The easy 1.5-mile **Aspen Parklands Interpretive Trail** is a good place to learn about the park's ecology, but if you really want to get away from it all head through the forest and oak savanna in the far east end of the park. The eastern half of the five-mile trail around the lake is also scenic, while the western portion is paved for biking. The seven miles of groomed cross-country ski trails are some of the best in the region. Campers are well covered with 157 sites (35 electric) in three campgrounds. The mostly wooded **Two Rivers Campground** is quieter and has more-secluded sites, but if you can get a site on the water in the **Lakeside Campground,** take it for the views. Additionally, four backpacking sites are set along the river, and there are a couple of canoe-in sites (canoes can be rented) on Moose Island: These sites can't be reserved, but they are almost always available.

In Hallock, 15 miles northwest, even, of the very northerly Lake Bronson State Park is an unlikely dining destination. In fact, once you're this far north anyway, you really shouldn't miss it. Locally farmed elk steaks and burgers are the specialty at **Caribou Grill** (225 Broadway E., 218/843-3748, www.wiktel.com/menus/caribougrill, 11 A.M.–10 P.M. Mon.–Sat., 11 A.M.–8 P.M. Sun., $10–18). The rest of the menu includes shrimp, jumbo salmon, pork chops, and pastas, and as much locally grown produce as is feasible up here.

PRAIRIELAND

Minnesota's southwest corner is relentless farm country speckled with historic sites, most related to the region's original cultures. Though it is still romantically linked with its prairie, all but tiny fragments of the original landscape have been plowed under. In its place are some of the nation's highest-yielding corn and soybean fields, and most of the harvest is sold by some of the most innovative and profitable farmer-owned cooperatives in the world. Prairie restorations, some quite extensive, are under way in many places, and at Blue Mounds State Park bison roam free once again, albeit behind 4.5 miles of fence.

The region has several unusual attractions. One-of-a-kind must-sees include the world's largest ball of twine rolled by just one man and an actual two-story outhouse, and Pipestone National Monument and Jeffers Petroglyphs are two of the most important Native American spiritual sites in the state. For some, a pilgrimage to Walnut Grove, former home of Laura Ingalls Wilder, is just as spiritual. This may not be what you came to Minnesota for, but to ignore this part of the state is to miss the variety that makes it so special.

PLANNING YOUR TIME

Pretty much everything of interest in southwest Minnesota lies on a convenient, if somewhat convoluted, crisscross route beginning and ending in the Twin Cities. Head west on U.S. Highway 12 where you pass **Darwin** and its famous twine ball. Eventually you'll hit the Minnesota River and some beautiful scenery near the **Big Stone National Wildlife Refuge.**

HIGHLIGHTS

New Ulm: On a per capita basis, New Ulm is the United States' most German city, and there is plenty of Old World history, hospitality, and cuisine to enjoy (page 316).

Harkin Store: The village of West Newton died in the late 19th century, but this stuck-in-time general store was left behind (page 319).

Lac Qui Parle State Park: This lovely little stretch of bottomland forest and prairie hillsides along the Minnesota River is one of the best wildlife-watching destinations in the state. There's plenty of peace and solitude, except in late fall when hundreds of thousands of geese crash the party (page 325).

Sod House on the Prairie: This pair of authentic sod houses sits amidst a healthy tallgrass prairie and can be visited during the day or rented for the night (page 328).

Jeffers Petroglyphs: Not only are these islands of etched bedrock among the nation's most important Native American spiritual sites, Jeffers is also one of the most beautiful patches of prairie still standing (page 328).

Walnut Grove: The former home of Laura Ingalls Wilder, author of *Little House on the Prairie*, celebrates her extraordinary family with a multifaceted museum; several original buildings from Laura's life still stand (page 329).

Pipestone: With a sacred quarry and some active organizations, Native American culture in this crimson town is as much a part of the present as it was the past (page 332).

Blue Mounds State Park: Buffalo graze once again atop this dramatic prairie-covered ridge. The hiking is some of the best in southern Minnesota, and the rock climbing is even better (page 337).

Darwin: This sleepy little village wouldn't even warrant a pit stop if it weren't for one of Francis Johnson's peculiar hobbies: From 1950 until 1979 he rolled miles of baler twine into a nine-ton orb, the largest ball of twine ever rolled by one man. A museum displays some of Johnson's other odd obsessions (page 344).

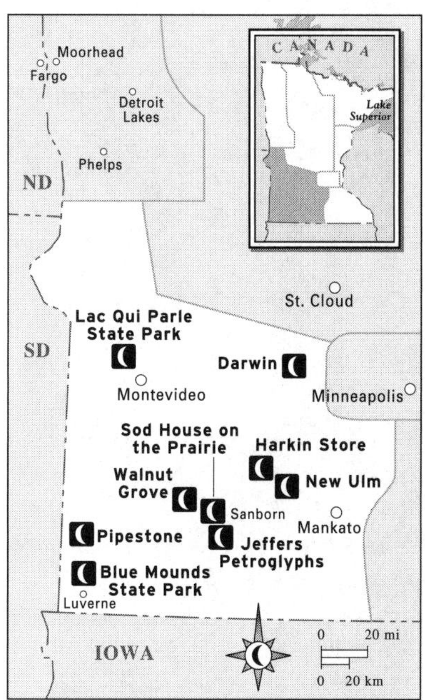

LOOK FOR TO FIND RECOMMENDED SIGHTS, ACTIVITIES, DINING, AND LODGING.

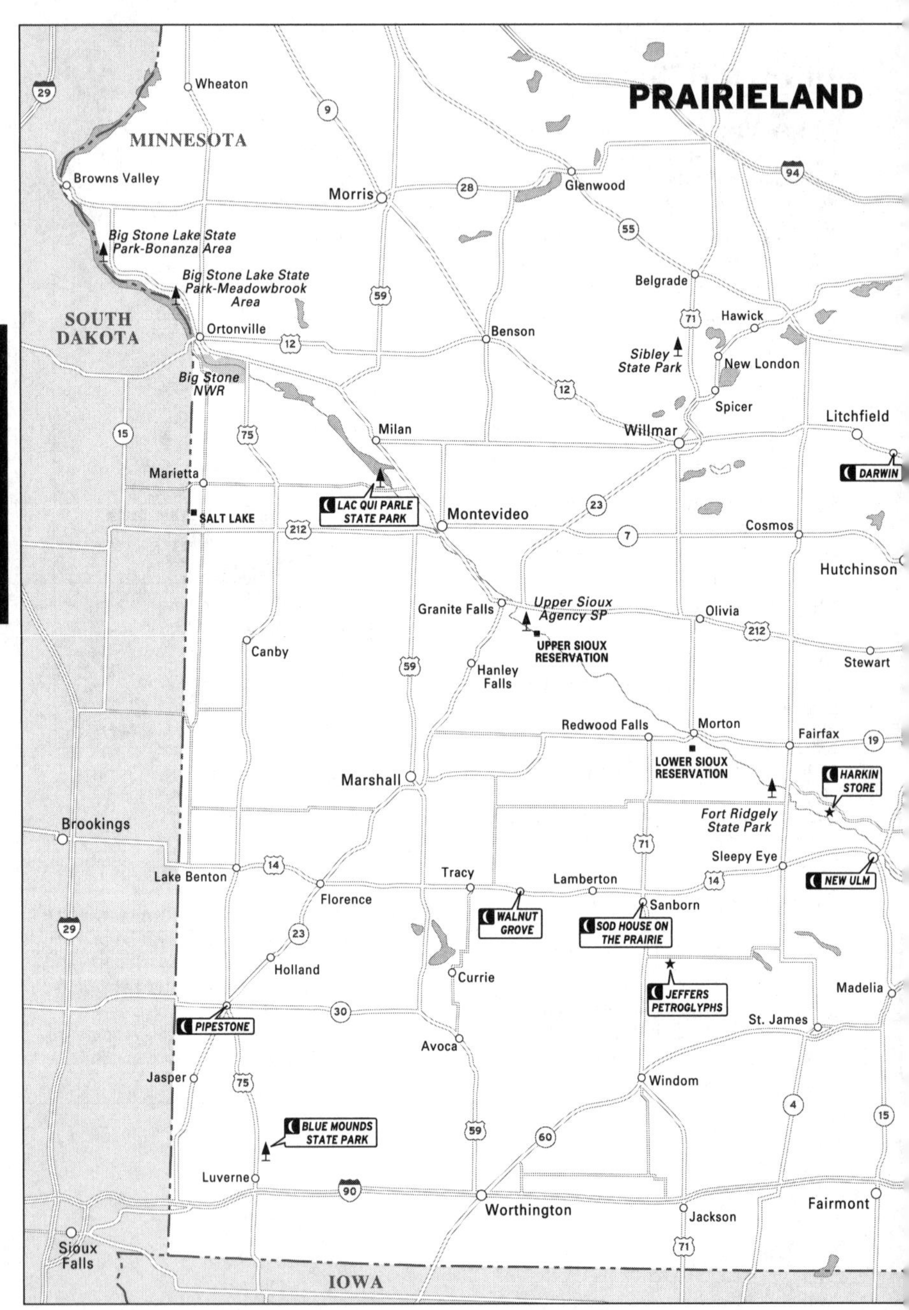
PRAIRIELAND
MINNESOTA
SOUTH DAKOTA
IOWA
Wheaton
Browns Valley
Big Stone Lake State Park-Bonanza Area
Big Stone Lake State Park-Meadowbrook Area
Ortonville
Big Stone NWR
Morris
Glenwood
Belgrade
Hawick
Benson
Sibley State Park
New London
Spicer
Willmar
Litchfield
DARWIN
Milan
Marietta
SALT LAKE
LAC QUI PARLE STATE PARK
Montevideo
Cosmos
Hutchinson
Granite Falls
Upper Sioux Agency SP
UPPER SIOUX RESERVATION
Olivia
Stewart
Canby
Hanley Falls
Redwood Falls
Morton
Fairfax
LOWER SIOUX RESERVATION
HARKIN STORE
Marshall
Fort Ridgely State Park
Brookings
Sleepy Eye
NEW ULM
Lake Benton
Tracy
Lamberton
Florence
Sanborn
WALNUT GROVE
SOD HOUSE ON THE PRAIRIE
Holland
Currie
JEFFERS PETROGLYPHS
Madelia
PIPESTONE
St. James
Avoca
Jasper
Windom
BLUE MOUNDS STATE PARK
Luverne
Worthington
Jackson
Fairmont
Sioux Falls
29
9
28
94
55
59
71
12
15
75
23
212
7
19
14
30
4
60
90

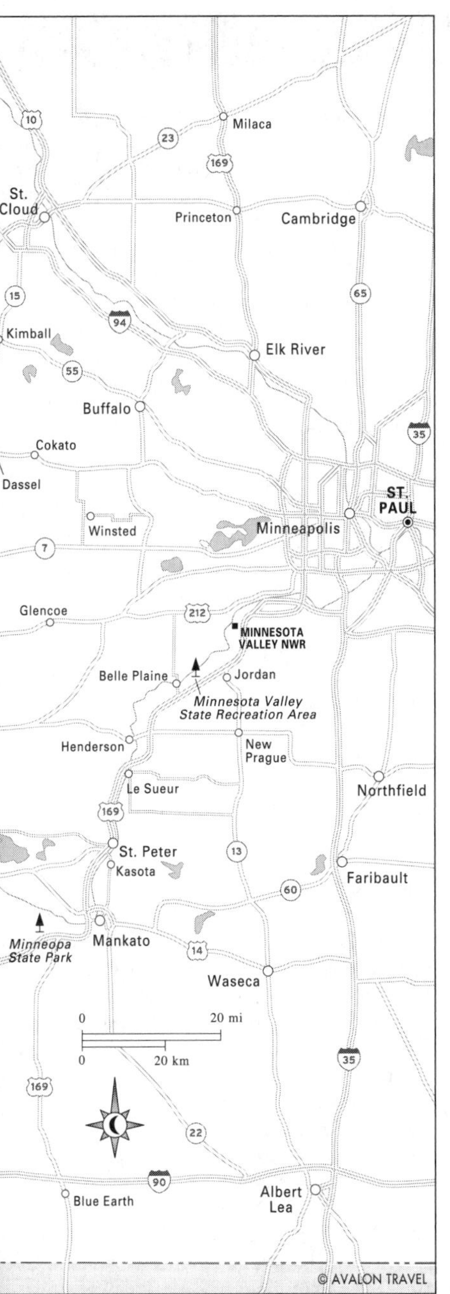

Head downstream, making sure not to miss **Lac Qui Parle State Park, Birch Coulee Battlefield,** and the **Harkin Store** before soaking up some German heritage in **New Ulm.** Turn back along U.S. Highway 14, the Laura Ingalls Wilder Historic Highway, taking in not only the sights related to the famous author in **Walnut Grove,** but also **Jeffers Petroglyphs** and the **Sod House on the Prairie.** Turn south again when you hit the wind farms lining the Buffalo Ridge, and spend some quality time in **Pipestone** and **Blue Mounds State Park** before zipping back along I-90 and U.S. Highway 169, making a last stop at **Belle Plaine** to see the double-decker skycrapper. Plan on five days to do it right.

If you've only got a couple of days, that's still enough time to hit most of the highlights. Base yourself in New Ulm and make two day trips, one down U.S. Highway 14 and the other up the Minnesota River, or make a loop from New Ulm combining the two.

Minnesota River Valley

The Minnesota River cuts 330 miles across the bottom of the state before joining the Mississippi River at the Twin Cities. The first major tributary of the Mississippi flows through a deep, miles-wide valley cut during the last Ice Age by the draining of Glacial Lake Agassiz. The state took its name from the river, adapting the Dakotas' Minnay Sotar (Sky-tinted Water). The best way to visit the towns and parks along it is to follow the various highways and back roads of the **Minnesota River Valley Scenic Byway,** a 300-mile route from Belle Plaine to Browns Valley. Unlike the monotonous driving elsewhere in southwest Minnesota, the journey is very beautiful. Distinctive pink signs with a bald eagle in flight mark the route, but with so many twists and turns it can be difficult to keep your bearings, so a map (available for free from any tourist office along the way) is highly recommended.

EASTERN MINNESOTA RIVER VALLEY

Minnesota Valley State Recreation Area

Most of the low-lying valley between Belle Plaine and the Mississippi River is protected by a series of parklands, including this 5,490-acre multi-unit state park that covers most of the ground upstream of Shakopee. The landscape is principally wet meadow and floodplain forest, though the valley walls and bluff tops are lined by oak forest and oak savanna remnants. The **Minnesota Valley Trail,** a 45-mile riverside route open to hikers, mountain bikers, horseback riders, and snowmobilers, is a pretty easy ride overall, though there are some sandy areas and heavy rains that can make mud pits out of long stretches. If you want to follow the river by canoe or kayak, you can put in along Highway 25 north of Belle Plaine. It's an easy rapids-free route with numerous canoe-in campsites. Boat ramps are found at every road crossing downstream to Shakopee and most of the rest on toward the Mississippi River.

The trail center (952/492-6400, 8 A.M.–10 P.M. daily), campground, and the restored 1857 **Samuel B. Strait House** (952/492-6400, 9 A.M.–3 P.M. Sat.–Sun. summer)—go inside to read historical panels about how the former settlement here grew up with the steamboat and died with the railroad—are found along County Road 57 just north of Belle Plaine. The rustic Quarry Campground has 33 shady and well-spaced campsites, including eight walk-ins, and there is also a horse-rider campground.

Belle Plaine

The "Beautiful Prairie" is home to one of the most unusual tourist attractions in the nation—a real **two-story outhouse.** The five-holer is connected by a skywalk to the **Hooper-Bowler-Hillstrom House** (410 N. Cedar St., 952/873-6109, 1–4 P.M. Sun. summer, $5 adults), as the Belle Plaine Historical Society calls it. Samuel Bowler, the home's second owner, added the "skycrapper" to accommodate his many children. It's actually not as ominous as it seems, the upper chamber is set back a few feet so everything drops behind a wall. The rest of the rooms in the 1871 home are furnished from three periods: the 1850s, the 1890s, and the early 1900s.

Le Sueur

This former steamboat stop, founded as a city in 1853, was named after Pierre Le Sueur, a French explorer credited as the first European to travel up the Minnesota River. He was sent here in the late 17th century by the King of France to keep the peace between the Dakota and the Ojibwe.

One small house in the center of this unassuming town gave birth to two of America's most well-known and successful enterprises: the Mayo Clinic and Green Giant. English-born Dr. William Mayo built this boxy home himself in 1859 and set up his first medical practice on the second floor. Five years later, after an appointment to the Civil War draft-

© TIM BEWER

Le Sueur is the humble birthplace of the Mayo Clinic and Green Giant.

enrollment board, he relocated to Rochester, where his practice grew into the Mayo Clinic. A decade later the Cosgrove family moved into the house, and in 1903 Carson Nesbit Cosgrove founded the Minnesota Valley Canning Company, later renamed Green Giant because of the overwhelming popularity of its mascot. Hour-long tours of the **W. W. Mayo House** (112 N. Main St., 507/665-3250, www.mayohouse.org, 10 A.M.–4:30 P.M. Tues.–Sat., $4 adults), offer a glimpse of life in the 1860s, the time period reflected in the house's furnishings, a few of which were used by the Mayo family. Costumed guides recount the family's histories (Louise Mayo's story is as interesting as her husband's) and daily lives. In early December the house is decorated for 1860s- and 1920s-style Christmases. Tours start next door in the **Mayoview History Center,** which has a short video introduction and a gift shop.

ST. PETER

St. Peter is just your average small city (pop. 11,000), but things could have been much different. In February 1857, shortly before Minnesota would become a state, a bill moving the capital from St. Paul to this young city passed the Territorial Legislature. But, before the bill could reach the desk of Governor Willis A. Gorman, who happened to be from St. Peter, Representative Joe Rolette of Pembina, the committee chair, took the bill and hid out in a St. Paul hotel room playing poker until the session adjourned. The governor did sign a copy of the bill, but the courts overturned the law because it was not the actual bill passed by the legislature. As a reminder of the shenanigans, Highway 169 runs down an especially wide main street (Minnesota Avenue, lined with classic brick storefronts) laid out in anticipation of the move.

Sights

A mile north of town is a natural ford in the Minnesota River (then named the St. Peter River, hence the city's name) known as Traverse des Sioux (Sioux Crossing). Over several weeks in the summer of 1851 the Sisseton and Wahpeton bands of Dakota met with American negotiators at a busy trading post here and eventually signed the Traverse des Sioux Treaty giving up over 24 million acres of land in southern Minnesota, as well as Iowa and South Dakota. The unkept promises made in this treaty (and the Mendota Treaty signed by the Mdewakanton and Wahpekute Dakota two weeks later) played a large part in the Dakota Conflict a decade later.

The **Treaty Site History Center** (1851 Minnesota Ave. N., 507/934-2160, www.nchsmn.org, 10 A.M.–4 P.M. Tues.–Sat., 1–4 P.M. Sun., $4 adults) details the events leading up to the signing and the tragedies following it. The museum also covers other events in Nicollet County history. The restored prairie surrounding the museum is a state historic site, and a mile-long trail with interpretive signs leads down to the river. The best guess at where the actual signing ceremony took place is just up and across the highway, but there is nothing to see there except a boulder with a plaque embedded in it.

The historical society also runs the **E. St. Julien Cox House** (500 Washington Ave. N., 507/934-4309, 10 P.M.–4 P.M. Thurs.–Sat. summer, $4 adults), an excellent example of Gothic/Italianate architecture. The striking red-and-gold house is fully restored and furnished with 1880s Victorian period pieces. A costumed guide will tell you about upper-class life from this time during an hour-long tour. The popular Christmas at Cox House is held the first two weekends in December.

Up on the hill is **Gustavus Adolphus College** (800 College Ave. W., 507/933-8000, www.gustavus.edu), which opened here in 1876. Over 30 bronze **sculptures** by noted artist Paul Granlund, the college's longtime sculptor-in-residence, are spread about campus. A tour brochure, available at the tent-like **Christ Chapel,** points out all of them. Other artists get display time in the little **Hillstrom Museum of Art** (Jackson Campus Center, 507/933-7200, 9 A.M.–4 P.M. Mon.–Fri., 1–5 P.M. Sat.–Sun., free admission). The **Olin Observatory** (507/933-7306, 9–11 P.M. Sun.–Thurs. Sept.–May) has regular public viewing. **Linnaeus Arboretum** (507/933-6181, grounds open daylight hours daily) on the edge of campus features 55 acres of formal gardens and examples of the Minnesota's primary ecosystems; follow signs from the campus entrance on College Avenue.

The small **Arts Center of St. Peter** (315 Minnesota Ave. S., 507/931-3630, www.artscentersp.org, 1–8 P.M. Thurs., 1–5 P.M. Tues.–Sun.) has art from local and regional artists on display.

There's a **Pharmacy Museum** (201 3rd St. S., 507/931-4410, 8:30 A.M.–7 P.M. Mon.–Fri., 8:30 A.M.–2 P.M. Sat., free admission) featuring an ornamental soda fountain (free root beer, but no food) and a whole wall of antique medicine bottles inside Soderlund Village Drug.

Accommodations

Luxury arrived in St. Peter in 2008 with the opening of the **Konsbruck Hotel** (408 3rd St. S., 507/934-3154, www.konsbruckhotel.com, $174–194). The boutique hotel has five unique rooms that all mix a little of the historic building's charm with modern hospitality (flat screen TVs and fully stocked complimentary minibars). Book well in advance, as Twin Citians looking for a luxury escape have discovered the Konsbruck.

Your other options in town are more modest, including the **AmericInn** (700 N. Minnesota Ave., 507/931-6554 or 800/634-3444, www.americinn.com, $81), with a pool, whirlpool, and sauna.

Riverside Park ($20 electric hookup), near downtown, off Front Street north of the river, has 11 first-come, first-served campsites along the water. Campers must register with the police department (207 Front St. S., 507/931-1550).

Food

St. Peter's finest dining is at **Richard's Restaurant and Pub** (408 S. 3rd St., 507/934-4988, www.richardsrestaurantandpub.com, lunch 11 A.M.–2 P.M. Tues.–Sun., dinner 5–9 P.M. Tues., Wed., and Sun., 5–10 P.M. Thurs.–Sat., $18–25), located inside the historic Konsbruck Hotel. The brief, refined menu shows its European flair in truffle sauces and gastrique under fine cuts of meat.

The deli section of the long-lived and much-loved **St. Peter Food Co-op** (119 Broadway W., 507/934-4880, 8 A.M.–8 P.M. daily, $5–6) has a large variety of sandwiches, salads, and even entrees, with a heavy emphasis on the local and seasonal.

Locals gather at the **Riverrock Coffee** (301 Minnesota Ave. S., 507/931-1540, 6:30 A.M.–9 P.M. Mon.–Sat., 8 A.M.–9 P.M. Sun.) for fair-trade organic coffees and an outdoor patio.

Information and Transportation

The St. Peter Chamber of Commerce maintains a small **Tourist Information Office** (101 Front St. S., 507/934-3400, http://tourism.st-peter.mn.us) near the heart of town.

Jefferson Lines (888/864-2832, www.jeffersonlines.com) buses stop at the Freedom Valu Center (625 S. Minnesota Ave.), and **Land to Air Express** (507/625-3977 or 888/736-9190, www.landtoairexpress.com) vans, which run between Mankato and the Twin Cities, stop at Hometown Travel (400 3rd St. S.).

MANKATO

Settled in February of 1852, before the terms of the Traverse des Sioux Treaty were even formalized, Mankato sits right where the Minnesota River takes a sharp left turn toward the Mississippi. The origin of the city's name is something of a mystery. Mahkato means Blue Earth in Dakota and refers to the clay found along the Blue Earth River, which empties into the Minnesota on the west side of town. Legend has it that this was the name chosen by the founders, and a later printing error was never corrected. The story has been repeated so often and for so long that it is now accepted as fact by many people, but more likely than not that actual origin lies with a survey map published in 1843 by Joseph Nicollet. The name Mahkato reminded the famous explorer and cartographer of a German folktale about a "water-spirit" named Mankato (he was in fact mistaken, according to the Blue Earth County Historical Society there is no such character), so he used that name on his map.

There is absolutely nothing special about this Mahkato clay, but in the late 17th century Pierre Charles Le Sueur, a French lieutenant who explored the area, sent a sample back to France, where it was declared copper-bearing. Le Sueur returned several years later and reportedly shipped two tons of the blue earth down the Mississippi River toward France in 1701, though somehow it never made it. The clay, in fact, did not contain copper. Le Sueur was almost certainly aware of this and simply used the sample as a ruse to procure a license to trade furs in the area, an endeavor that proved very lucrative.

The city grew rapidly as a transportation and supply center for the prairie frontier. Steamboats led the way, but were unreliable due to the shallow river, and stagecoaches soon came from St. Paul along a military road. The railroad arrived in 1868, and Mankato became a hub for four different lines. By 1880 it was the fourth-largest city in the state, and the success of surrounding farms made it very prosperous. Today Mankato is the largest city in the southwest and a considerable arts hub, though farming remains important to the economy.

The most infamous chapter in the city's history came very early. The 303 prisoners convicted and sentenced to death following the Dakota Conflict in 1862 were brought to Mankato. President Lincoln, after hearing an urgent plea from Bishop Henry Whipple, spared the lives of all but the convicted murderers and rapists, and 38 men were hung simultaneously from a single gallows on December 26, 1862. A crowd of 3,000 (watched over by 2,000 soldiers there to keep the peace) waited hours in the bitter cold to witness what remains the largest mass execution in U.S. history. A nine-foot buffalo sculpted from local Kasota limestone stands in Reconciliation Park, near the site of the execution, as a memorial to that time.

Sights

Mankato's principal attraction is the **R. D. Hubbard House** (606 Broad St. S., 507/345-5566, 10 A.M.–4 P.M. Fri.–Sat., 1–4 P.M. Sun., $3 adults), a three-story white-brick French

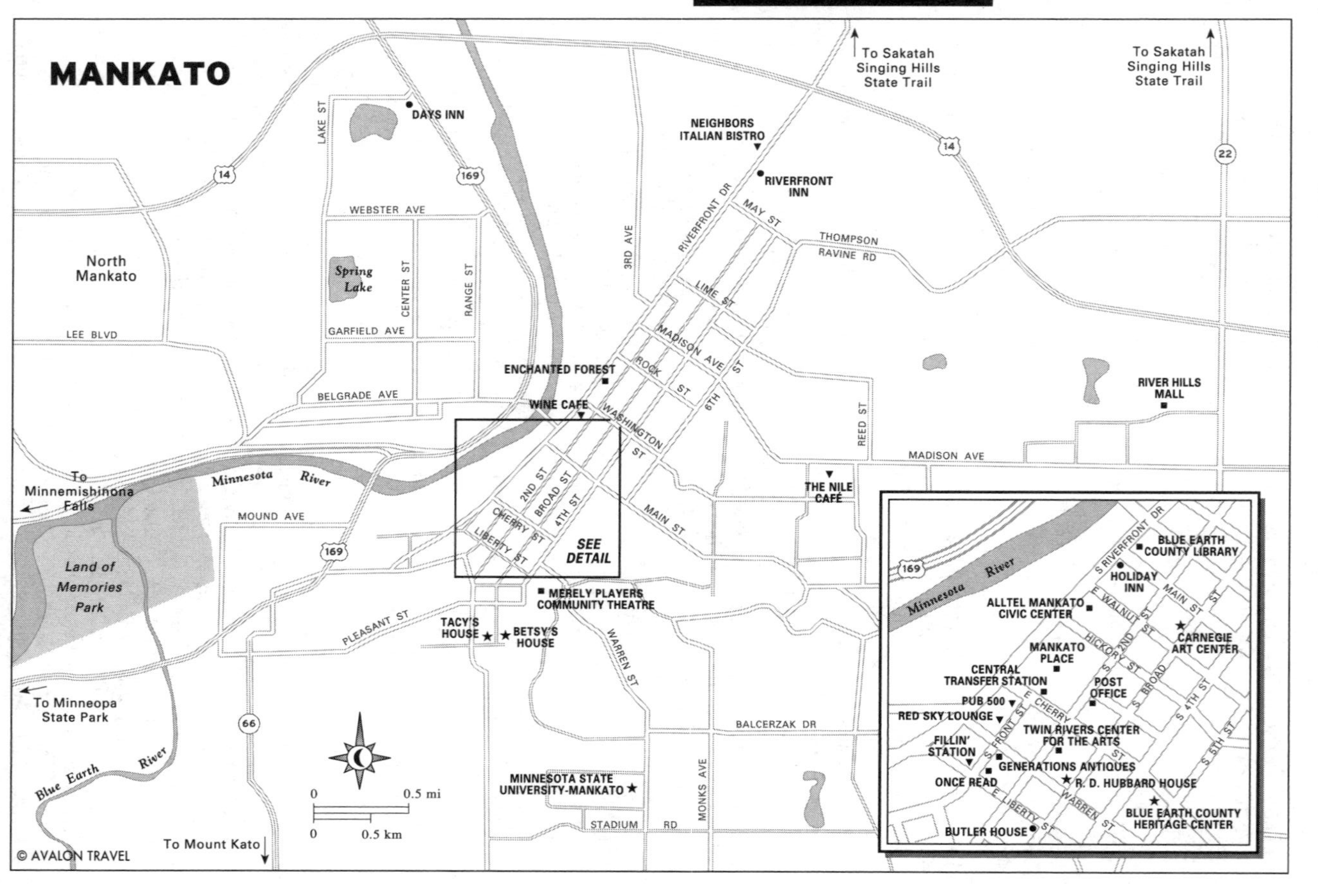
MANKATO
DAYS INN
LAKE ST
WEBSTER AVE
North Mankato
Spring Lake
CENTER ST
RANGE ST
LEE BLVD
GARFIELD AVE
BELGRADE AVE
To Sakatah Singing Hills State Trail
To Sakatah Singing Hills State Trail
NEIGHBORS ITALIAN BISTRO
RIVERFRONT INN
RIVERFRONT DR
MAY ST
THOMPSON
RAVINE RD
3RD AVE
LIME ST
MADISON AVE
ROCK ST
6TH ST
ENCHANTED FOREST
WINE CAFE
WASHINGTON ST
REED ST
MADISON AVE
RIVER HILLS MALL
To Minnemishinona Falls
Minnesota River
THE NILE CAFÉ
2ND ST
BROAD ST
4TH ST
CHERRY ST
LIBERTY ST
MAIN ST
SEE DETAIL
MOUND AVE
Land of Memories Park
MERELY PLAYERS COMMUNITY THEATRE
PLEASANT ST
TACY'S HOUSE
BETSY'S HOUSE
WARREN ST
To Minneopa State Park
BALCERZAK DR
MINNESOTA STATE UNIVERSITY-MANKATO
MONKS AVE
STADIUM RD
Blue Earth River
0 0.5 mi
0 0.5 km
To Mount Kato
© AVALON TRAVEL
Minnesota River
S RIVERFRONT DR
BLUE EARTH COUNTY LIBRARY
HOLIDAY INN
ALLTEL MANKATO CIVIC CENTER
E WALNUT ST
MAIN ST
CARNEGIE ART CENTER
MANKATO PLACE
HICKORY ST
S 2ND ST
CENTRAL TRANSFER STATION
POST OFFICE
S BROAD
S 4TH ST
PUB 500
E CHERRY
RED SKY LOUNGE
S FRONT ST
TWIN RIVERS CENTER FOR THE ARTS
FILLIN' STATION
GENERATIONS ANTIQUES
S 5TH ST
ONCE READ
R. D. HUBBARD HOUSE
WARREN ST
E LIBERTY ST
BLUE EARTH COUNTY HERITAGE CENTER
BUTLER HOUSE

THE DAKOTA CONFLICT

Taoyateduta is not a coward and he is not a fool. Kill one-two-10, and 10 times that many will come to kill you. Braves, you are little children – you are fools. You will die like the rabbits when the hungry wolves hunt them in the Hard Moon. Taoyateduta is not a coward. He will die with you.

– Chief Little Crow

Prompted by a decade of broken promises and underhanded dealings by the U.S. government, the Dakota in Minnesota, led by Chief Little Crow (Taoyateduta), began attacking white towns and farmsteads in August 1862 in order to take back the land they had ceded a decade earlier. With the army occupied by the Civil War, many Dakota believed that they could defeat the Americans, and initially it looked like they were right. The attacks resulted in widespread panic and abandonment of just about every settlement in southwestern Minnesota. Before the army, led by former governor Sibley, rounded up hundreds of combatants and chased most of the other warriors west, nearly 500 civilians and soldiers had been killed. An estimated 71 Dakota, including 38 hung in unison in Mankato – the largest mass execution in the country's history – died in the uprising. Almost all remaining Dakota, including many who had risked their own lives to protect settlers, were evicted from the state, though this action served both as punishment and protection since vigilantes would have almost certainly killed anyone who remained. The tragic episode essentially spelled the end of Native American resistance in Minnesota, though subsequent battles between the Dakota and the United States, such as Little Big Horn and Wounded Knee, flared out west through the rest of the century.

Second Empire mansion full of fancy woodwork, marble fireplaces, stained-glass windows, and Tiffany lamps. Built in 1871, the house has been restored and refurnished to its 1905 appearance by the Blue Earth County Historical Society.

The historical society also runs the nearby **Blue Earth County Heritage Center** (415 Cherry St. E., 507/345-5566, 10 A.M.–8 P.M. Tues., 10 A.M.–4 P.M. Wed.–Sat., $3 adults), a small local history museum with various historical artifacts, including some really nice Dakota pieces.

The museum also has a display about hometown hero Maud Hart Lovelace, author of the classic Betsy-Tacy books. The Deep Valley setting for her stories was really Mankato, and if you are a fan of the series you'll want to get a copy of the ***Betsy-Tacy Places in Mankato*** self-guided tour brochure; it's available at the Heritage Center and the Blue Earth County Library (100 Main St. E., 507/304-4001). The tour, created in part by Lovelace herself, leads you past 55 sites featured in the 13 books, including Betsy's and Tacy's houses (333 Center St. and 332 Center St., respectively), both owned by **The Betsy-Tacy Society** (507/345-9777, www.betsy-tacysociety.org). Betsy's fictional home was also Lovelace's real-life home; Tacy's is now a little museum (1–3 P.M. Sat., free admission).

The Carnegie Library, mentioned frequently in Lovelace's books, is now the **Carnegie Art Center** (120 Broad St. S., 507/625-2730, 1–4 P.M. Wed.–Sat., 1–7 P.M. Thurs., free admission). The building itself is on the National Registry of Historic Places, but the inside has been thoroughly modernized and is now among the best visual arts museums in southern Minnesota. The Broad Street Gift Shop, located inside, is a great place for a unique souvenir.

Students, faculty, and visiting artists show their work at the small **Conkling Gallery** (Nelson Hall, 507/389-6412, 9 A.M.–4 P.M. Mon.–Fri., free admission) at **Minnesota State University-Mankato** (228 Wiecking Center, 507/389-1866 or 800/722-0544, www.mnsu.edu).

Minneopa State Park

Southern Minnesota's largest waterfall sits about three miles west of Mankato on Highway 169 in Minneopa State Park (54497 Gadwall Rd., 507/389-5464). The 45-foot twin falls dropping into a rocky gorge on Minneopa Creek (Minneopa is a poor transcription of a Dakota word meaning "water falling twice") is the favorite feature of the park and has been attracting sightseers since the mid-19th century. A short-lived summer resort was built here in 1858, and a village grew up around the nearby train station. Both went bust following the grasshopper plagues of the 1870s, though the train continued to bring thousands of tourists each summer. Recognizing the beauty and popularity of the area, the legislature made this Minnesota's third state park. The arms of the German-style Seppman windmill, completed in 1864, were blown off by a tornado and never replaced, but the medieval-looking tower is still a beautiful sight. From this perch you get the best views of the boulder-strewn prairies of the river valley below—or take an up-close look along the 4.5 miles of hiking trail (groomed for cross-country skiing in winter) that loop through it. Birdwatchers will be rewarded with both grassland and woodland species like bluebirds, bobolinks, shrikes, belted kingfishers, and both eastern and western meadowlarks. Take one of the spurs that lead down to the river and you might see beaver, bald eagle, or northern green heron.

Nightlife

MSU's 14,000 students keep the nightlife active. The best bet for barhopping is the Entertainment District along South Front Street and in the **Mankato Place** mall (12 Civic Center Plz., 507/625-1400, www.mankatoplace.mn)—a motley mix of government offices, a church, second-run movie theater, and a couple of bars.

Down the block, and a little more refined, is the spacious **Pub 500** (500 Front St. S., 507/625-6500, www.pub500.com, 11 A.M.–2:15 A.M. daily). You'll find something going on most nights, from live music to trivia to free poker.

Also downtown, the **Red Sky Lounge** (520 Front St. S., 507/625-8131, www.myredskylounge.com, 4 P.M.–midnight daily) offers some truly tasty bites (like vegetable tempura and sweet potato fries) to go with their long list of cocktails.

Wine Cafe (301 Riverfront Dr. N., 507/345-1516, 11 A.M.–2 A.M. daily) has light rock and jazz on Friday and Saturday nights.

Entertainment and Events

To find out about just about any cultural event taking place in Mankato or the immediate area, stop by the **Twin Rivers Center for the Arts** (Emy Frentz Arts Guild, 523 2nd St. S., 507/387-1008, www.twinriversarts.org, noon–4 P.M. Mon.–Wed. and Fri., noon–8 P.M. Thurs., closed Sat.–Sun.), which operates a centralized box office. Local artists also have studio space here and show and sell their work.

The biggest events in town, from professional wrestling to Broadway musicals, take place at the **Alltel Mankato Civic Center** (1 Civic Center Plz, 507/389-3000, www.alltelcenter.com).

Overall the best source of entertainment in town—from plays to lectures—is **Minnesota State University-Mankato** (228 Wiecking Ctr., 507/389-1866 or 800/722-0544, www.mnsu.edu), and most events are open to the public.

The **Mankato Symphony Orchestra** (523 S. 2nd St., 507/625-8880, www.mankatosymphony.com) mixes classical music and pops in fun and well-attended concerts at the Mankato West High School auditorium and other venues.

The **Merely Players Community Theatre** (Lincoln Center, 110 Fulton St., 507/388-5483, www.merelyplayers.com) has been putting on popular contemporary plays for both adults and children since 1981.

Some of the hottest sports tickets in town are for the **MSU Mavericks** (www.msumavericks.com) men's hockey team, who take on their WCHA (a premier Division I conference, all other MSU sports are Division II) rivals at the Verizon Wireless Center (1 Civic Center Plaza, 507/389-3000, www.verizonwirelesscentermn.com).

Fans of the purple and gold flock to MSU from late July to mid-August for **Minnesota Vikings training camp.** Practices (autograph sessions usually follow morning workouts) are free and open to the public, though tickets (612/338-4537) are required for intra-squad scrimmages and games against other NFL teams.

The annual **Mankato Pow-wow** is held in Land of Memories Park the third weekend of September.

Shopping

Most day-to-day shopping is east of town along Madison Avenue and around the large **River Hills Mall** (1850 Adams St., 507/388-1100, www.riverhillsmall.com, 10 A.M.–9 P.M. Mon.–Sat., 11 A.M.–6 P.M. Sun.), an area known as Hilltop.

For more interesting shopping, stroll along North Riverfront Drive in **Old Town,** where you'll find a handful of antiques and gift shops, including **Enchanted Forest** (529 N. Riverfront Dr., 507/385-1448, 10 A.M.–5 P.M. Tues.–Fri., 10 A.M.–3:30 P.M. Sat.), which has many Minnesota-related books.

Shoppers will also have some luck downtown along South Front Street. **Generations Antiques** (615 S. Front St., 507/345-7551, 11 A.M.–5 P.M. Wed.–Fri., 10 A.M.–4 P.M. Sat.) is dusty and musty and delightful.

Once Read (629 S. Front St., 507/388-8144, 10 A.M.–5 P.M. daily) is the quintessential college-town used book store, with an inviting sign on the window saying, "Coffee welcome."

Recreation

The paved **Sakatah Singing Hills State Trail** follows 39 miles of former railroad bed through farms, forest, and small towns between Mankato and Faribault, while other paved trails hug the Minnesota River.

In its peak season, **Mount Kato** (20461 Hwy. 66, 507/625-3363 or 800/668-5286, www.mountkato.com) has 19 downhill ski and snowboard runs, the largest dropping 240 feet, and a tubing park. From May through October mountain bikers ride the seven miles of trail, most of it wooded single-track.

Accommodations

The cheapest motel in town is the small **Riverfront Inn** (1727 Riverfront Dr. N., 507/388-1638, $45), with very basic but clean rooms, stocked with refrigerators and microwaves. Don't expect to watch the sunset over the river—it's named for the street, not the scenery.

A few dollars more gets you a small pool and whirlpool at the **Days Inn** (1285 Range St., 507/387-3332 or 800/329-7466, www.daysinn.com, $50) on the north side of town along Highway 169.

The city's biggest and best hotel is the **Holiday Inn** (101 Main St. E., 507/345-1234 or 888/890-0242, www.holidayinn.com, $95). Besides the good location you get a pool, whirlpool, sauna, fitness center, and game room.

The **Butler House** (704 Broad St. S., 507/387-5055, www.butlerhouse.com, $99), the city's first and only bed-and-breakfast, is a lovely and cozy 1905 English-style home. Two of the five guestrooms have double whirlpools, and one has a fireplace. They all have private baths.

Minneopa State Park (507/389-5464, $18 campsites, $20 with electricity, $50 cabin) has 61 decent campsites (six electric) and one camper cabin.

Food

The vine-entwined **Wine Cafe** (301 Riverfront Dr. N., 507/345-1516, www.winecafebar.com, 11 A.M.–2 A.M. daily, $4–9) serves over 80 wines by the glass, and although the menu is limited to soup, sandwiches, pizza, and cheese plates, it is still one of the most recommended restaurants in town.

Another local favorite, **Neighbors Italian Bistro** (1812 Riverfront Dr. S., 507/625-6776, www.neighborsitalianbistro.com, 11 A.M.–10 P.M. Mon.–Sat., 10 A.M.–9 P.M. Sun., $10–18) serves fresh and flavorful Italian (not Italian-American) food, from a basic penne alla vodka to a rich osso bucco.

For something entirely different, try **The Nile Café** (1021 Madison Ave. E., 507/344-0878, 11 A.M.–9 P.M.), which serves a mix of Ethiopian stews and brighter Mediterranean fare, including lamb and chicken gyros, in a casual, friendly space.

As this is a college town, there are plenty of casual choices for top-quality java. Downtown, the **Fillin' Station** (634 Front St. S., 507/344-0345, 7 A.M.–7 P.M. Mon.–Fri., 8 A.M.–5 P.M. Sat., 9 A.M.–2 P.M. Sun.) is like a home away from home for some patrons, and serves house-made sandwiches and soups.

Information

The **Greater Mankato Convention & Visitors Bureau** (507/345-4519 or 800/657-4733, www.greatermankato.com, 8 A.M.–5 P.M. Mon.–Fri., closed Sat.–Sun.) is inside the Civic Center, and it also staffs a booth in the River Hills Mall.

Getting There and Around

Jefferson Lines (888/864-2832, www.jeffersonlines.com) buses stop at Express Way Mankato (51674 Hwy. 169) on their way to and from Minneapolis. It can be more convenient to travel to the Twin Cities with **Land to Air Express** (434 Patterson Ave., 507/625-3977 or 888/736-9190, www.landtoairexpress.com), which does the trip to the airport five times a day during the week and thrice on weekends for $30.

Heartland Express (507/625-7433) buses provide a limited city service, but not at night or on Sunday. Most routes stop at the Central Transfer Station on Cherry Street in front of Mankato Place. The fare is $1.25. For a taxi call **Kato Cab** (507/388-7433).

NEW ULM

New Ulm revels in its Teutonic heritage. Sixty-six percent of the city's 13,500 residents claimed German ancestry in the last census, which gives New Ulm the nation's largest percentage of any single ethnicity among cities with 5,000 or more residents. The Brown County seat was settled in 1854 by two groups of German colonists who established a "planned socialist utopian German community on the American prairie." Germans continued to immigrate to the growing city, and within 15 years the town had five breweries. The mother tongue could still be heard on city streets well into the 1960s, and even today a large percentage of locals can get by in German. A completely unrelated claim to fame is that most of the world's Velveeta is made here.

Sights

The better-than-average **Brown County Historical Museum** (2 Broadway N., 507/233-2616, 10 A.M.–4 P.M. Mon.–Fri., 10–3 P.M. Sat., closed Sun., $3 adults) is most noteworthy for its layered German Renaissance design; the 1910 building originally served as the post office. The principal exhibits are the Dakota room, with a wonderful collection of exquisite artwork and displays about the Dakota Conflict, and Made in Brown County (aka the "beer, brats, and bricks exhibit"), about the industries that the town grew up on.

The **Minnesota Music Hall of Fame** (27 Broadway N., 507/354-7305, www.mnmusichalloffame.org, 10 A.M.–2 P.M. Wed.–Sat., $3) began as a way to preserve the work of "Whoopee John" Wilfahrt, the local king of old-time music, but now 100 state notables have been inducted. The displays are pretty static, mostly just photos and concertinas.

The **Wanda Gág House** (226 Washington St. N., 507/359-2632, 10 A.M.–4 P.M. Sat., 11 A.M.–2 P.M. Sun. summer and Dec., $2) is the childhood home of the famous children's book author and illustrator (*Millions of Cats, ABC Bunny, Tales From Grimm,* and more), whose prints now hang in galleries around the world. The rooms of the restored house have family photos and some of her art hanging on the walls.

If you've ever traveled across central Europe, you'll recognize many of the design elements in the 1893 Baroque twin-spired **Cathedral of the Holy Trinity** (605 N. State St., 7 A.M.–5 P.M. daily). And even if you are not Catholic, the **Way of the Cross** is worth a (respectful) visit. Completed in 1904, the series of large statues arranged on a steep path off Loretto Street depict 14 scenes in the life of Jesus Christ. Halfway up is a grotto dedicated

© TIM BEWER

New Ulm takes pride in its German heritage.

to Our Lady of Lourdes, and at the top of the hill is the small Lady of Sorrows Chapel, as well as a beautiful view of the river.

American-, German-, and French-style wines are made at **Morgan Creek Vineyards** (23707 478th Ave., 507/947-3547, www.morgancreekvineyards.com, 11 A.M.–9 P.M. Fri.–Sat., noon–5 P.M. Sun. May–Oct., 11 A.M.–6 P.M. Fri.–Sat., noon–5 P.M. Sun. Nov–Dec., closed Jan.–Apr.), eight miles south of town. Among Minnesota's earliest wineries, it was founded in 1993. Tours (1–4 P.M. Sat.–Sun. May–Oct., $3) are available.

NEW ULM'S GERMAN HERITAGE

New Ulm's 45-foot-tall **Glockenspiel,** one of the few freestanding carillon clock towers in the world, stands at the north end of downtown at Minnesota Street and 4th Street North. The bells—all two tons of them—chime and the three-foot-tall polka figures spin around daily at noon, 3 P.M., and 5 P.M., plus 10:30 A.M. and 1 P.M. during festivals.

The towering **Hermann Monument** (9 A.M.–7:30 P.M. daily summer and Oktoberfest weekends, $1), officially the National German-American Monument, was erected in 1897 to honor Hermann of Cherusci, who united the German tribes and drove out the Romans in the year A.D. 9. The 32-foot statue of the sword-bearing warrior stands at the top of a 102-foot tower, itself perched atop one of the city's highest points. The views across the town and the Minnesota River Valley from the top are fantastic. To get there follow Center Street west out of downtown to Hermann Heights Park.

Continuing a proud German tradition, the **New Ulm Turner Hall** (1st South & State St., 507/354-4916, www.newulmturnerhall.org, 10 A.M.–10 P.M. daily) has been a private gymnastics and social club since 1857. In recent years, it has opened its *ratskellar* to nonmembers. While you can certainly have an inexpensive, meat-heavy German lunch or dinner here, the real attraction is the murals, which cover 70 feet of the walls in the basement. Painted over in 1917 to forestall anti-German sentiment, they were restored in the late 1990s.

The most noteworthy bit of German heritage in the city is the **August Schell Brewing**

Company (1860 Schell Rd., 507/354-5528 or 800/770-5020, www.schellsbrewery.com, 8 A.M.–dusk daily). The popular local brewery has remained at the same lovely riverside setting and under the same family of owners since its founding in 1860. Though you only see a dash of the brewery's operations, the one-hour tours (1, 2:30 and 4 P.M. Mon.–Fri. and on the hour between 1 and 4 P.M. Sat.–Sun. summer, on the hour between 1 and 4 P.M. Sat. and 1 and 2:30 P.M. Sun. rest of year, $3) are entertaining nonetheless. Your ticket includes a post-tour tasting session. Tours start in the **Museum of Brewing** (11 A.M.–5 P.M. daily summer, noon–4 P.M. Sat. and noon–3 P.M. Sun. rest of year, free admission), which features old brewery and family items. After the tour, roam the lush grounds among butterflies and peacocks.

Flandrau State Park

Tucked into the Cottonwood River Valley on the west edge of the city is 1,006-acre Flandrau State Park (1300 Summit Ave., 507/233-9800). The most popular features are the campground and the large sand-bottomed swimming pool, but the eight miles of hiking trails aren't bad. The least used, though arguably the best, trails in the park are the forested **Old Island Loop** and **River Loop** in the south end. A steep set of steps climbs up the oak-covered bluff and then gradually drops down into the valley again, where the rest of the two-mile figure-eight is generally level. Probably the most popular trail is the half-mile round-trip up to the overlooks at the end of the **Indian Point Trail.** The **Bluebird Trail** is an easy half-mile loop through the grasslands at the north end of the park. The trails are groomed for cross-country skiing in the winter, and both skis and snowshoes are available for rent.

Events

The city's biggest shindig is **Bavarian Blast** (www.bavarianblast.com), which celebrates all things German the third weekend in July. There's entertainment on four stages (including bands from the homeland), a parade, a craft fair, and the hundreds-strong "tuba mania" concert. Photogenic masked Narren stroll the festival grounds and the **New Ulm Battery,** a most unusual relic, perform. The horse-drawn artillery unit was formed following the Dakota Conflict and is the only Civil War outfit of its kind still in existence.

Of course, the city celebrates **Oktoberfest** (www.newulmoktoberfest.com) with dancing, music, food, and free-flowing Schell's beer the first two weekends in October. **Fasching,** the "German Mardi Gras," designed to chase winter away, is held on the Saturday before Ash Wednesday, while Schell's Brewery hosts a **Bock Fest** on the same afternoon.

Shopping

Downtown remains a vibrant shopping district, though many more stores are stretched out along Broadway to the south. Shop to a serenade of polka music and cuckoo clocks at **Domeiers** (1020 Minnesota St. S., 507/354-4231, 9 A.M.–4 P.M. Sat.), an Old World store bursting with imported German goods.

Just as the name suggests, it's always the holiday season at **Christmas Haus** (203 Minnesota St. N., 507/233-4350, 9 A.M.–5 P.M. Tues.–Wed. and Fri.–Sat., 9 A.M.–8 P.M. Mon. and Thurs., noon–4 P.M. Sun.).

Old World heritage of a different sort is available at **The Sausage Shop** (301 Broadway N., 507/354-3300 or 886/656-8910, www.thesausageshopllc.com, 8 A.M.–5:30 P.M. Mon.–Fri., 8 A.M.–5 P.M. Sat., 10 A.M.–2 P.M. Sun.), where dozens of varieties, like wild rice brats and blood sausage, are made in-house.

Antiques Plus (117 Broadway N., 507/359-1090, www.antiquesplusnewulm.com, 10 A.M.–5 P.M. Mon.–Sat., noon–4 P.M. Sun.) is the city's largest antiques shop.

Sven and Ole's Books (2 N. Minnesota St., 507/354-6421, www.svenandolesbooks.com, noon–3 P.M. Mon.–Fri., 10 A.M.–5 P.M. Sat.) stocks a good selection of Minnesota-focused books and about equal numbers of new and used books—with a heavy emphasis on genre fiction. Make yourself at home at the chessboard.

Accommodations

The **Holiday Inn** (2101 S. Broadway, 507/359-2941 or 800/359-2941, www.holidayinn.com, $86) is the city's top hotel. Facilities include a pool, whirlpool, exercise room, and arcade.

A little less expensive, the **Super 8** (1901 S. Broadway, 507/359-2400 or 800/800-8000, www.super8.com, $59) has clean and modern rooms.

Several of New Ulm's large, lovely homes are now bed-and-breakfasts. **The Bohemian** (304 S. German St., 507/354-2268 or 866/499-6870, www.the-bohemian.com, $89) is in a flashy 1899 East Lake Victorian bedecked with stained glass and even has an Asian-inspired parlor. Each of the seven main house and carriage house guestrooms has a private bath, and four have their own whirlpool tubs.

The homey **Bingham Hall** (500 S. German St., 507/354-6766 or 800/486-3514, www.bingham-hall.com, $99–199) has four guestrooms with private baths and large beds (two have fireplaces and three have whirlpool tubs) in a completely renovated 1893 Queen Anne.

Flandrau State Park (1300 Summit Ave., 507/233-9800, $20) has a pair of campgrounds with 92 (34 electric) rather crowded and moderately shaded sites. The three walk-in sites offer a semblance of solitude.

Food

German food is easy to come by in New Ulm. The rather formal **Veigel's Kaiserhoff** (221 Minnesota St. N., 507/359-2071, 11 A.M.–8:30 P.M. daily, often open later, $7–22) opened its doors in 1938 and is the city's oldest and most beloved restaurant. The meat-laden menu (a ⅓-pound hamburger is the weight-watchers special, vegetarians are completely out of luck) has both German and American favorites.

The **Ulmer Café** (115 Minnesota St. N., 507/354-8122, 7 A.M.–2 P.M. daily, $3–7) is a classic small-town café, the sort of place where the mid-day meal is still called "dinner" and you can't spend $10 even if you try. Get a gravy-slathered open-face sandwich or the Oktoberfest, a grilled sausage patty sandwich with sauerkraut.

For something a little more up-to-date, **Lola's** (16 Minnesota St. N., 507/359-2500, 7 A.M.–5:30 P.M. Mon.–Wed., 7 A.M.–9 P.M. Thurs.–Sat., closed Sun., $7–16) serves salmon en papillote, pesto chicken, and hanger steak with blue cheese. The long, dim room with brick walls and intimate nooks is also a great place for just a cup of coffee.

Information and Services

The staff of the city's **Visitor Information Center** (1 Minnesota St. N., 507/233-4300 or 888/463-9856, www.newulm.com, 8 A.M.–5 P.M. Mon.–Fri., 10 A.M.–3 P.M. Sat., closed Sun.) are very friendly and knowledgeable.

WESTERN MINNESOTA RIVER VALLEY

Harkin Store

The wonderful little Harkin Store (507/354-8666, 10 A.M.–5 P.M. Tues.–Sun. summer, 10 A.M.–5 P.M. Sat.–Sun. May, Sept., and first half of Oct., $3 adults), eight miles northwest of New Ulm on County Road 21, really transports you back to a bygone era. The village of West Newton, a steamboat stop halfway between New Ulm and Fort Ridgely, was a bustling place in 1870 with mills, hotels, saloons, a school, and, of course, a general store. When the railroad came through in 1873 it bypassed West Newton, and the town, which was also suffering from a grasshopper plague, quickly faded away. The store, however, didn't close until 1901, but it did little business in the ensuing years, serving almost exclusively as the local post office. When it finally shut its doors, much of the original stock—cigars, fabric, boxes of soap, nails, and patent medicines—were still on the shelves. Today costumed staff, reliving the heydays of the 1870s, can give you prices and explain what some of the unusual gadgets are for.

Fort Ridgely State Park

Fort Ridgely (72158 County Rd. 30, 507/426-7840) was built in 1853 at the edge of the newly created Dakota reservation lands to keep the peace as settlers poured into southwest

Minnesota. Nine years later the fort was attacked twice during the Dakota Conflict, but neither offensive was successful. The fort had no stockade, just six cannons. With ravines on three sides, it was in a poor defensive position, so had the 1,000 or so Dakota been better organized or more aggressive they surely could have overtaken the 180 soldiers bunkered down here. The fort became obsolete after the war since the Dakota had been exiled, and it was abandoned just a decade later. The **commissary** (10 A.M.–5 P.M. Sat. and noon–5 P.M. Sun. June–Oct., 10 A.M.–5 P.M. Fri. summer, free admission), the only remaining building, has been restored by the Minnesota Historical Society and now houses displays about life in the fort.

Eleven miles of hiking trail cross the 477-acre park, and those on the east side are hilly and forested, while those through the prairie to the west are generally level. All but a mile are open to horses, and five miles are groomed for cross-country skiing, though the sledding hill (inner tubes can be rented for $2) is the more popular winter destination. There's also a nine-hole golf course and a paved bike trail connecting the park to Fairfax. The campground has two sections. The Creekside camp has 22 sites (15 electric) with some along Fort Ridgely Creek. The quieter Rustic camp has 17 shady and widely spaced sites; three walk-in sites offer extra seclusion. Horseback riders have their own camp.

Morton

Historic sites and a large casino lure tourists to this small town. It developed alongside the granite quarries first dug here in 1886, and the Cold Spring Granite Company still works several of them on a limited basis.

Just north of town, at the junction of County Highways 2 and 18, is the **Birch Coulee Battlefield** (507/697-6321, free admission), scene of one of the bloodiest battles of the Dakota Conflict. Though the site amounts to little more than an empty field with a few sticks in the ground, this is by far the most interesting site relating to war because the design lets you imagine yourself as an observer at the real event. Captain Joseph Anderson and his men from Fort Ridgely were out on a mission to bury the civilians killed over the previous two weeks. Wrongly assuming that the Dakota had left the area, they set up camp on a hill near Birch Coulee Creek on the evening of September 1, 1862. During the night, 200 Dakota warriors, led by Wamditanka (Big Eagle), surrounded them and, just before dawn, attacked. The Dakota kept the U.S. soldiers under siege for 36 hours, killing 20 men and 90 horses in the process. They only fled when reinforcements arrived the next afternoon. Quotes from Captain Anderson and Chief Wamditanka, along with sketches done by one of the soldiers, provide a full accounting of the battle, as well as perspectives on its cause. The **Gathering of Kinship Powwow** is held at Birch Coulee in early September. The field is three miles north of Morton; take Highway 71 and follow the signs.

To learn more about the causes of the war and the history of the Dakota, cross the river to the **Lower Sioux Agency** (32469 Hwy. 2, 507/697-6321, 10 A.M.–5 P.M. Sat., noon–5 P.M. Sun. summer, $6 adults). The post, established in 1853, served as the distribution center for food and funds called for by the Traverse des Sioux Treaty. It was also an educational center for the few Dakota who wanted to learn the European way of life. In their first organized attack of the war, the Dakota looted and then destroyed the post on August 18, 1862. Just one building, a restored 1861 warehouse built of stone, remains standing, though interpretive signs along the trails point out the locations and functions of others. Life at the agency and other aspects of Dakota culture and resistance are discussed in the visitors center.

The Lower Sioux Community's **Jackpot Junction** (39375 County Hwy. 24, 507/697-8000 or 800/946-2274, www.jackpotjunction.com) was Minnesota's first casino. Besides gaming, this complex has the fancy **Lower Sioux Lodge** hotel ($62), three restaurants, big-name entertainment, and **Dacotah Ridge Golf Course** (507/644-5050, 18 holes starting

LOWER AND UPPER SIOUX RESERVATIONS

LOWER SIOUX

- Total Area: 2.7 sq. miles
- Tribally Owned: 100 percent
- Total Population: 335
- Native Population: 294
- Tribal Enrollment: 1,113

UPPER SIOUX

- Total Area: 2 sq. miles
- Tribally Owned: 100 percent
- Total Population: 57
- Native Population: 47
- Tribal Enrollment: 438

The original Dakota (aka Sioux) reservations in Minnesota, as established by the Traverse des Sioux and Mendota Treaties, stretched along the Minnesota River, ten miles wide on each side. The Lower Sioux Reservation extended from Little Rock Creek (just west of the Harkin Store) to the Yellow Medicine River; the Upper Sioux lands continued from Yellow Medicine up to Big Stone Lake. After the Dakota were expelled from Minnesota following the 1862 Dakota Conflict, some 7,000 people fled to South Dakota or were resettled in Nebraska. In the 1880s a few Dakota families defied the government and returned to their homeland in the Minnesota River Valley. By the end of the decade the federal government recognized these settlements, though the reservations weren't formalized until the 1930s, at which time they were granted additional lands.

The Lower Sioux Community, across the river from Morton, got its start in 1884 when Chief Good Thunder returned from South Dakota and purchased 80 acres near where Bishop Henry Whipple had run his mission, a spot traditionally known to the Dakota as Cansa'yapi ("where they marked the trees red"). Whipple was a faithful friend of the Dakota and the man who had convinced President Lincoln to spare the lives of most of those condemned for their roles in the uprising. Good Thunder and other returning Dakota were soon joined by a few families who had managed to remain in the state under the protection of influential fur trader Alexander Faribault. The tribe's major industry, besides their Jackpot Junction casino, is traditional hand-thrown, hand-painted pottery.

The families of the Upper Sioux community returned to Pejuhutazizi Kapi ("the place where they dig for yellow medicine") near the far southeast end of their former reservation lands, just south of Granite Falls. Though not as profitable as most others in the state, their Prairie's Edge Casino has been a vital economic stimulant for the band.

at $49), one of the state's best. The **Lower Sioux Community Wacipi** (powwow) is held the second weekend in June.

In town you'll find some gift and antiques shops and the **Renville County Museum** (441 Park Dr. N., 507/697-6147, www.renvillecountyhistory.com, 10 A.M.–4 P.M. Tues.–Sat. and 1–4 P.M. Sun. June–Sept., 1–4 P.M. Tues.–Fri. rest of year, $2 adults), with the usual assortment of historic artifacts.

Redwood Falls

The waterfalls from which this city took its name run through **Alexander Ramsey Park.** Larger than the city itself, "The Park" has six miles of trail winding past Ramsey Falls, a beautiful dual waterfall, and smaller Redwood Falls. Also in the park are some quiet picnic areas, an 18-hole golf course (Redwood Falls Golf Club, 101 Oak St., 507/627-8901, www.redwoodfallsgolf.com, $24–47 for 18 holes), and a little zoo with buffalo (333 Washington St. S., 507/637-5755, free admission). Ramsey Creek is stocked with brown trout each spring.

A half-mile west of town on Highway 19 is the **Redwood County Museum** (507/641-3329, 1–4 P.M. Sat.–Sun. May–Sept., $2 adults) with 27 rooms of the former Redwood County Poor Farm now filled with historical artifacts and displays. Highlights of the diverse collection, quite large for such a small town, include a foot-and-a-half-long meteorite, frightening old medical instruments, and dozens of mounted birds. There is also a small display about Richard W. Sears. The founder of the Sears, Roebuck Co. was the depot agent for the Minneapolis and St. Louis Railroad in North Redwood when he sold his first shipment of watches in 1886 and realized there was money to be made in the mail-order business.

Downtown, at East 2nd Street and South Jefferson, is the restored 1860s **Redwood County Jail,** still used as a jail. The **Gilfillan Estate** (507/249-3451, 9 A.M.–4 P.M. Tues.–Fri., $3 adults) is eight miles southeast of town on Highway 67. In 1882 St. Paul lawyer and businessman Charles Duncan Gilfillan left the big city and purchased 13,000 acres here to raise cattle. Remarkably, the home he built in 1882 was turned over to the historical society with all of its possessions, much of it dating back to the 1920s. The grounds also host **FarmFest,** an annual farmers' convention, in early August.

Mad-scientist types arrive in town the second weekend in June to show off their latest creations at the **Minnesota Inventors Congress** (www.invent1.org), the nation's oldest invention convention. While none of the products displayed here have changed the world, some might end up on store shelves after being examined by manufacturers who arrive incognito.

Your best bet for lodging is the **Redwood Valley Lodge** (1382 Bridge St. E., 507/644-5700, www.redwoodvalleylodge.com, $70). Although the rooms look an awful lot like a chain hotel's, the lobby is spacious and charming and, best of all, there is a truly hot sauna for guests' use.

The cheapest rooms in town are at the simple but spotless **Motel 71** (1020 Bridge St. E., 507/637-2981 or 800/437-4789, $40).

With three rooms on the Minnesota River, **Tatanka Bluffs** (103 2nd St. E., 507/627-1875, www.tatankabluffsbandb.com, $110) is a bed-and-breakfast for those who love the personal service, but not the usual overstuffed Victoriana.

Alexander Ramsey Park (333 Washington St. S., 507/637-5755, $20) has a 28-site (15 electric) first-come, first-served campground.

With made-from-scratch soups and breads, the **Calf Fiend Cafe** (220 2nd St. E., 507/637-3728, 6 A.M.–2 P.M. Mon.–Wed., 6 A.M.–11 P.M. Thurs., 6 A.M.–midnight Fri.–Sat., $4–7), a bright-yellow coffeehouse, is a popular place for breakfast, lunch, and late-night weekend eats. Besides the usual long list of drinks, they serve soups, sandwiches, and salads.

Upper Sioux Agency State Park

Perched on the riverside bluffs where the Yellow Medicine River joins the Minnesota, 1,280-acre Upper Sioux Agency State Park (5908 Hwy. 67, 320/564-4777) affords some quality views of the Minnesota River Valley, but was actually established for its historical significance. This was the site of the Yellow Medicine (aka Upper Sioux) Agency, established in 1853 to administer the terms of the Traverse des Sioux Treaty. Food and cash, as provided by the treaty, were doled out here, and, though most rejected attempts to "civilize" them, some Dakota families came to learn modern farming methods. By 1862 the site had grown into a small village, but the warring Dakota destroyed it during their failed uprising that summer. The local Dakota opposed the conflict and helped lead residents to safety. While the story is interesting, the remains are not. Only one brick employee duplex still stands; signs mark the foundations of others. To see an actually interesting bit of history, come the first full weekend in August for the **Upper Sioux Wacipi** (powwow).

Though small, the park has a lot of natural diversity, ranging from restored prairies to forest to wetlands, and 18 miles of hiking and horseback riding trail lead through it all. In winter, most of the trails are claimed by snowmobilers, though cross-country skiers have two miles of groomed track, and the office has snowshoes available. The long, steep sledding hill is one of the park's most popular features.

The **Yellow Medicine River Campground,** on the edge of the prairie, has 34 (14 electric) widely spaced sites ($20 a night), including three walk-ins, in a mix of shade and sun. Two authentic tepees are available from Memorial Day through October for $30—they are very popular, so reserve well in advance. The **Riverside Campground** is an open grassy area along the Minnesota River with all sites available first-come, first-served. There is also a horse-rider campground.

Granite Falls

The founders of this city of 3,000 came to run mills along the fast-dropping Minnesota River, and even today a hydroelectric plant still generates the town's power. Andrew J. Volstead, former mayor of Granite Falls and long-serving Minnesota congressman, is best remembered as the author of the Volstead Act that established enforcement provisions for Prohibition. He wrote the bill not as a crusader, but only because as chair of the House Judiciary Committee the job fell in his lap. Volstead was most proud of his work to establish farmer cooperatives in the United States.

The **Volstead House** (163 9th Ave., 320/564-2255, open by chance or appt., $3), now a National Historic Landmark, has a few informational panels about Volstead and the history of cooperatives.

The rest of the county's history, from its ancient geology to pioneer life, is laid out at the **Yellow Medicine County Museum** (98 Hwy. 67 E., 320/564-4479, 11 A.M.–5 P.M. Fri.–Sun., $1). There are many Native American displays inside, and an old log cabin and log church sit behind the main building.

Nine miles south of town, just off Highway 23 in Hanley Falls, the **Minnesota Machinery Museum** (5th St. S., 507/768-3522, www.mnmachinerymuseum.com, 10 A.M.–4 P.M. daily May–Sept.) is a massive shrine to the past and present of Minnesota agriculture. Five buildings of a former school—26,000 square feet in all—are filled with artifacts from tractors to butter churns to farm toys. Each fall, the museum hosts a threshing show.

Three miles southeast of town on Highway 67 is the small **Prairie's Edge Casino** (5616 Prairies Edge Ln., 320/564-2121 or 866/293-2121, www.prairiesedgecasino.com) operated by the Upper Sioux Dakota. Their hotel is among the best in town (from $59 a night), and there's a 55-spot RV park ($24 full hookup).

The **Super 8** (845 Hwy. 212 W., 320/564-4075 or 800/800-8000, www.super8.com, $59) isn't fancy, but it is a pretty good deal.

For a huge plate of steak or fish or a one-third-pound burger, visit **Bootlegger's Supper Club** (1940 11th Ave., 320/564-4003, www.bootleggerssupperclub.com, 5–9 P.M. Wed.–Thurs., 5–10 P.M. Fri.–Sat., 10:30 A.M.–1:30 P.M. Sun., $10–15).

For something lighter, the **Granite Grinder & Café** (176 Hwy. 212 E., 320/564-4244, 7 A.M.–5 P.M. Mon.–Fri., 8 A.M.–3 P.M. Sat., closed Sun.) is ideal. With mismatched chairs and tables inside a rustic cabin and drinks served in glass jars, it's got charm galore, as well as tasty sandwiches and wraps.

Jefferson Lines (888/864-2832, www.jeffersonlines.com) buses stop at the Tri-County Co-op (1297 Granite St.).

Swensson Farm Museum

Olof Swensson, a Norwegian immigrant, settled here in 1873. His family lived in the 22-room brick home (115 Co. Rd. 15 SE, 320/269-7636, 1–5 P.M. Sun. summer, $4 adults), built in 1901, until the 1960s, and many of the original furnishings remain. During your visit you will also learn a little about Olof's dabbling as a writer, preacher, and political activist. The museum is located halfway between Granite Falls and Montevideo on County Road 15, three miles southeast of the hamlet of Wegdahl. The building and grounds were the used as the set of the 2008 movie *Sweet Land* about the experiences of immigrant farmers in Minnesota.

Montevideo

Montevideo's founders were so impressed by the views of the Minnesota and Chippewa River Valleys that they borrowed the name of the Uruguayan capital, which in Latin means

From the Mount I See. They now maintain a sister-city relationship with their southern counterpart, and the downtown plaza is named in honor of Jose Artigas, the father of Uruguayan independence. The 11-foot bronze statue of Artigas was a gift from Uruguay in 1949.

The city's primary attraction is **Historic Chippewa City** (320/269-7636, 9 A.M.–5 P.M. Mon.–Fri. and 1–5 P.M. Sat.–Sun. summer, Mon.–Fri. only in the month of September, $4 adults), an interesting collection of relocated and restored historic buildings at the junction of Highways 59 and 7. The two dozen structures include a general store, blacksmith shop, one-room schoolhouse, firehouse, newspaper office, and bank. Each is filled with tools of the trade creating what approximates a late-19th-century village. Just south of downtown is the **Milwaukee Road Heritage Center** (Park Ave. and 1st St. S., 320/226-0384, 8 A.M.–5 P.M. Mon.–Fri., free admission). The restored 1901 Chicago, Milwaukee & St. Paul Railroad Depot houses a small collection of railroad-related artifacts, and across the street are a few old railroad cars around a functional turntable. Also in the depot are the offices of the Land Stewardship Project (320/269-2105, www.landstewardshipproject.org), and they can direct you to local farms that sell direct to the public and offer tours. A mile to the east on Highway 212 is a 51-foot granite obelisk and historical marker commemorating the release of 269 Dakota-held captives and the surrender of some 1,200 warriors at the end of the Dakota Conflict. The small park, now known as **Camp Release,** was the site of Col. Henry Sibley's military camp.

© TRICIA CORNELL

A statue of Jose Artigas stands in downtown Montevideo.

If you will be staying here you've got several good options. Four miles northwest of town, the **Broodio at Moonstone Farm** (9060 40th St. SW, 320/269-8971, $60) attracts many writers and artists looking for peace and quiet. Richard and Audrey Arner run an antibiotic- and hormone-free beef farm and have converted their old henhouse into a simple cottage heated by a wood-burning stove. Guests can use the bathroom facilities in the main house or the outhouse and eat a simple continental breakfast.

The **Crossings Inn and Suites** (1805 Hwy. 7 E., 320/269-8000 or 800/936-7829, www.crossingsinn.com, $75) is the best hotel for many miles around. Besides comfy rooms, there is a pool and whirlpool.

The 10-site **Lagoon Park Campground** (103 Canton Ave., 320/269-6575, $20 full hookup), along the Chippewa River just northwest of downtown, is a shady, better-than-average municipal campground.

The locals' runaway favorite for dining out is the fantastic **Valentino's** (110 1st St. S., 320/269-5106, 8 A.M.–4:30 P.M. Mon.–Wed. and Fri., 8 A.M.–8 P.M. Thurs., 7 A.M.–2 P.M. Sat., open Sun. for lunch Oct.–May, $4–8), probably the classiest, not to mention tastiest, small-town café you'll ever find.

An even bigger surprise is **Java River** (210 1st St. S., 320/269-7106, 6:30 A.M.–5:30 P.M. Mon.–Fri., 7 A.M.–2 P.M. Sat., $2–5) coffeehouse. In addition to the roster of fair-trade coffees, they serve low-priced soups and sandwiches using as many locally grown ingredients as possible—right down to locally milled flour for the house-made bread. They also offer computers for Internet access and sometimes host live music, in which case they stay open late.

For something entirely different, fill up at the authentic buffet at **El Paraiso** (102 1st St. N., 320/269-9801, 9 A.M.–7 P.M. Mon.–Sat., 9 A.M.–4 P.M. Sun., $4–8), a grocery store catering to the area's large and growing Mexican population.

Lac Qui Parle State Park

Lac Qui Parle State Park (14047 20th St. NW, 320/734-4450), sits at the foot of the Lake That Speaks, as the Dakota called it, though just what it was they were listening to is lost to history. Some people wrongly assume it was migrating geese because flocks of up to 150,000 gather on this natural widening of the Minnesota River during the early November peak (back then there were many other places for geese to stop, and so the numbers here were much smaller), more than at any other spot in the state, and their collective honking is an astonishingly loud experience. Though the park is only 1,057 acres in size, the adjacent **Lac Qui Parle Wildlife Management Area** manages another 34,000 acres along a 25-mile-long stretch of the river. This well-managed area accounts for the remarkable abundance of not just geese but many other species of birds and other wildlife. Notable species nesting here include white pelican, prairie chicken, and bald eagle. The latter congregate each winter and can be seen feeding on the Minnesota River below the Lac Qui Parle (aka Churchill) dam. They also sometimes feast on geese that overwinter on the lake.

The park has five miles of trails for hiking, horseback riding, and cross-country skiing; all are flat and easy, though sometimes a bit wet. The 2.5 miles of loops through the bottomland forest behind the campground are some of the best wildlife-watching trails anywhere in Minnesota. Canoeing down the Lac Qui Parle and Minnesota Rivers or along the shore of the lake itself is another good way to see animals. **Mitlyng's Bait & Tackle** (320/269-5593, hours vary) down by the dam has rentals. If you are just looking to relax, there is a small sandy beach. The **Lower Campground** has 24 (12 electric) widely spaced sites, some with shade, while the westernmost of the 46 (37 electric) wide-open sites in **Upper Campground,** including the three walk-ins, have lake views. Sites are $18, $22 with electric.

Just outside the park is **Lac Qui Parle Mission** (Hwy. 13 north of Hwy. 59, 320/269-7636, 8 A.M.–8 P.M. daily May–Aug., free admission), a Minnesota Historical Society historic site. Joseph Renville, an independent fur trader with a French father and Dakota mother, established his trading post here in 1826. A decade later he invited missionaries to educate and Christianize the Dakota, though few accepted the overtures. The Lac Qui Parle Mission was shut down in 1854, but during their time here Renville and the missionaries wrote the first translation of the Bible into the Dakota language and completed the first Dakota dictionary. Inside the small wooden church, a reconstruction of the 1841 original, are a few displays about the Dakota, their language, and the missionaries' work. The first church bell to ring in Minnesota hung in the steeple of this church and what is believed to be that bell is on display. A mile up County Road 32 is an overlook of the site of **Fort Renville,** his original fur-trading post, which operated until the 1830s. It's most interesting for the lake view, especially when migrating geese congregate here in the fall.

Milan

Exactly why this tiny village, founded by Norwegians, was named after the Italian city is unknown. Some of its Scandinavian past is on display at the **Arv Hus Museum** (236 Main St., 320/734-4868 or 320/734-4829, 10 A.M.–4 P.M. Tues.–Sat. or by appt., free admission), an eclectic little collection of local history and Norwegian art in an old harness shop. Ask at the gift shop if it looks like no one's around.

There's a fantastic mural next to the museum, and around the corner is Karen Jenson's **Trestuen Gallery & Studio** (104 Lincoln, 320/734-4715, open by appt. or chance). She sells her own rosemaling, as well as wood carvings and other Scandinavian crafts from several local artists.

Chippewa Prairie

If you look south across this 1,143-acre tallgrass prairie preserve, you can begin to imagine what most of western Minnesota looked like before it was turned into farms. This land, too rocky to plow, was used largely for grazing and mowing hay and has over the past few decades grown into one of the Minnesota chapter of The Nature Conservancy's largest preserves. Bird-watchers can look for upland sandpipers, short-eared owls, and prairie chickens, which have been successfully reintroduced here by the DNR. To get here, head four miles northwest of Milan on Highway 59 and then turn west on Chip-Swift Street, which forms the county line. Continue two miles to the large sign marking the preserve.

Big Stone National Wildlife Refuge

Named by the Dakota for the tall granite outcroppings rising along the river, Big Stone National Wildlife Refuge (44843 County Rd. 19, 320/273-2191) is a vital haven for migrating birds and a magnet for bird-watchers. The 11,586 acres of bottomland forest and grassland (including 1,700 acres of native prairie) fronting 11.5 miles of the Minnesota River host 240 bird species over the course of a year, most notably waterfowl and warblers. The easiest way to see the refuge and its inhabitants is along the six-mile **Prairie Drive Auto Tour.** The easy 0.75-mile **Rock Outcrop Hiking Trail** is also worthwhile. Along both you'll learn about local history and ecology, see the prairie, and get a chance to walk among the beautiful, lichen-encrusted granite mounds. For the best views of the huge autumnal waterfowl concentrations, drive along the **East Pool Wildlife Observation Drive** off Highway 75 at the refuge's eastern border. All other refuge roads not posted as restricted are also open to hiking. A canoe is a great way to explore the refuge, though paddling is only allowed on the Minnesota River from mid-April through the end of September. A fantastic river trip begins at the main entrance (along Highway 75, two miles south of Ortonville) and continues down to the Highway 75 bridge. The NWR abuts the Lac Qui Parle Wildlife Management Area, so you can continue the scenic paddle much further down river.

Ortonville

Ortonville, which grew up on granite quarrying and corn canning, sits at the foot of Big Stone Lake. The narrow 30-mile lake is the source of the Minnesota River and also forms the Minnesota–South Dakota border. The main building of the **Big Stone County Museum** (985 U.S. 12, 320/839-3359, 10 A.M.–4 P.M. Mon.–Sat., 1–4 P.M. Sun., free admission) houses a hodge-podge collection of antique items for home and work, plus a few locally discovered fossils and Native American artifacts.

Right on Big Stone Lake, **Rustling Elms Resort** (74637 Rustling Elms Rd., 800/839-3845, www.rustlingelmsresort.com, $179 cabin for four people, $32 campsite) has three very home-like cabins available, as well as full-hookup RV sites available nightly, weekly, and seasonally.

The **Econo Lodge** (650 U.S. 75, 320/839-2414 or 800/553-2666, $70) atop the hill is Ortonville's best hotel, and there are a few no-frills cafés for meals.

The enormous **Lakeshore RV Park** (39445 Lakeshore RV Park Dr., 800/266-7883, $29.95 full hookup, $24 tent site) on Big Stone Lake has about 150 sites to choose from, as well as a pool, mini golf, and canoe and fishing boat rentals.

Big Stone Lake State Park

Big Stone Lake State Park (35889 Meadowbrook State Park Rd., 320/839-3663), created in 1961 to preserve some land on the lakeshore before it was all developed, is a three-for-one deal. The first unit you come to, the **Meadowbrook Area,** contains most of the park's 986 acres and has the most facilities, including the basic 37-site (10 electric) campground. Right next to the campground is a beach, and you can also rent canoes. The half-mile Bluebird Trail, noted for its spring and summer wildflowers, has two easy loops through a prairie restoration. Eleven miles up the road is the smaller **Bonanza Area,** much of which is covered by a rare undisturbed glacial till hill prairie and oak savanna and has been designated a Scientific and Natural Area. The mostly wooded **Hiking Club Trail** hugs the shore and then loops past tiny Benkowski Falls. The little **Overlook Area** between the other two is perched high above Big Stone Lake. Both the Meadowbrook and Bonanza units have lakeside picnic areas and boat launches. The majority of visitors are here to fish—Big Stone Lake is noted for walleye, but also yields bluegill, perch, northern, and channel catfish.

Browns Valley

Continue to the end of Big Stone Lake, and you'll pass several apple orchards before ending up in this small village stuck out at the end of Minnesota's hump. Browns Valley was founded in 1866 by Joseph R. Brown, a leader in the formation of the Minnesota Territory, cowriter of its constitution, and prominent lobbyist of the federal government on behalf of the local Dakota. His son Sam made a famous "Paul Revere Ride" that year to warn settlers of threatened attacks by the Dakota. **Sam Brown Memorial Park** (2nd Ave. N., west of Hwy. 7) contains a restored log cabin that served as Sam's home, a trading post, stagecoach stop, tavern, and inn. It now houses a **local history museum** (320/695-2110, 1–6 P.M. Fri.–Sun. summer, free admission). The park also has a furnished one-room schoolhouse. Famous among archaeologists, **Browns Valley Man** was discovered in 1933 by local farmer William H. Jensen in the gravel ridge just south of town. The skeleton has been dated to 8,000 B.C., making it one of the oldest found in the Americas.

South of the River

LAURA INGALLS WILDER HISTORIC HIGHWAY

Walnut Grove, twice the home of the famous children's author Laura Ingalls Wilder and the setting of the TV show *Little House on the Prairie,* is one of the most popular destinations in southwest Minnesota. A few other towns along U.S. Highway 14 also have Laura connections. No matter what brings you here, don't miss Jeffers Petroglyphs.

Sleepy Eye

Although the real Ingalls family likely passed through here on their way to Walnut Grove, they had next to no connection to the town. The TV family, however, visited often, and Laura even married Almanzo Wilder there—in real life the marriage took place in De Smet, South Dakota. The village took its name from Sleepy Eye Lake on the northwest edge of town, which honors the Sisseton Dakota chief Ish-Tak-Ha-Ba (Sleepy Eyes), who lived here near the end of his life. Remembered fondly by explorers and settlers as "a friend of the Whites," he died in South Dakota in 1860, but in 1902 his remains were returned to his homeland, and he now rests below a 50-foot-tall granite obelisk in front of the **Sleepy Eye Depot Museum** (100 Oak St. NW, 507/794-5053, 10 A.M.–4 P.M. Tues.–Sat. May–Dec., free admission). The museum itself has a small collection of random artifacts from the town's past and present, including plenty of Sleepy Eye Milling Co. memorabilia, now hot collector's items. A larger-than-life bronze statue of the chief stands across the street. **Del Monte Foods** (22977 9th Ave. SW, 507/794-2151) have been in Sleepy Eye since 1930, and they offer tours (by reservation, free admission) of their pea- and corn-canning facility during the production season, generally June through October.

The best hotel in town is the **Inn of Seven**

© TRICIA CORNELL

Sheep graze on the southern Minnesota prairie.

Gables (1100 Main St. E., 507/794-5390 or 800/852-9451, www.innof7gables.net, $79), with large rooms plus a pool and whirlpool.

The **W. W. Smith Inn** (101 Linden St. SW, 507/794-5661 or 800/799-5661, www.wwsmithinn.com, $90) is a friendly bed-and-breakfast with four guestrooms (some private bath, some shared) and a carriage house with hot tub. The 1901 Queen Anne Victorian is filled with stained glass, carved woodwork, and period furnishings.

The **Orchid Inn** (500 Burnside St. SE, 507/794-3211, dinner 5–9 P.M. Thurs.–Sat., $4–16) is an old-fashioned supper club with a prime-rib smorgasbord on weekends.

Sod House on the Prairie

Two authentically constructed soddies sit in the middle of a restored tallgrass prairie, and this is the closest you'll come to seeing how the pioneer families of Laura Ingalls's day lived. The main house is furnished with period pieces, and interpretive signs on the grounds explain what Laura Ingalls's real life was like. To get the full pioneer experience, don't just visit, spend the night. You cook on a wood-burning stove, read by oil-burning lamps, carry in your own water and, yes, use a sod outhouse. If you want, there is even period clothing to wear. Though obviously not for everyone, the house is much nicer than you would expect and has a wood floor (the Ingallses' was earthen) and plaster walls. The Sod House (12598 Magnolia Ave., 507/723-5138, www.sodhouse.org, open until dusk daily summer, $4 adults) is half a mile east of Sanborn and spending the night costs $125 for a couple, more for families.

Jeffers Petroglyphs

The 80-acre Jeffers Petroglyphs Historic Site (507/628-5591, www.jefferspetroglyphs.com, 10 A.M.–5 P.M. Fri.–Sat. and noon–5 P.M. Sun. May, 10 A.M.–5 P.M. Mon.–Fri., 10 A.M.–8 P.M. Sat., and noon–5 P.M. Sun. June, 10 A.M.–5 P.M. Thurs.–Sat. and noon–5 P.M. Sun. July–Aug., various days throughout Sept., $6) protects over 2,000 ancient petroglyphs. Many of the buffalo, deer, elk, turtles, thunderbirds, humans, weapons, and other similar subjects were cut by Native Americans in the exposed shelf of

© TRICIA CORNELL

A guide shows off the Jeffers Petroglyphs.

bedrock as far back as 3,000 B.C. Others, it appears, are as recent as the 1750s. The glyphs likely served a ceremonial purpose, and this remains sacred ground for many tribes—religious ceremonies are still held here on occasion. The shapes are most dramatic during the long shadows of early morning and late evening. Even if there weren't a single carving this would be a worthwhile trip, the small islands of pink quartzite surrounded by the sea of prairie make this one of the most beautiful spots in Minnesota. It is also a great place to see the subtleties of prairie ecology since each of the three main prairie types—wet, mesic, and dry—are represented, and together they contain well over 100 species of flower and forb. Amongst the many plants are prickly pear cactus and the federally threatened prairie bush clover. The 33 acres surrounding the rocks are native prairie, while the rest is a very healthy restoration.

After appreciating the glyphs most people just return to the parking lot, but if you continue around the site on the mile-long trail you'll pass a shiny and smooth "buffalo rub" (bison would rub themselves up against rocks to help shed their thick winter coats). Interpretive programs begin at 2 P.M. daily.

Jeffers is located 12 miles south of Sanborn. Take Highway 71 to County Road 10 and follow the signs. On your way, take a short detour north on 460th Avenue to see the 30-foot waterfall at **Red Rock Falls County Park.** If you arrive outside of normal opening hours, leave a donation in the box, take a brochure, and walk around to the back of the park building to the petroglyphs.

Walnut Grove

Walnut Grove was settled and grew like just about every other small prairie town in southwestern Minnesota and would be as unremarkable as the rest of them if it weren't for one former resident. Laura Ingalls Wilder, author of the "Little House" series of books that inspired the TV show *Little House on the Prairie,* arrived as a seven-year-old girl and lived here for about five years (1874–1876 and 1877–1879). The Ingalls family and other homesteaders who made their way west to this spot along the banks of Plum Creek found rich soil

LITTLE HOUSE *OF* THE PRAIRIE

Early settlers on the prairie built sod houses for one logical reason – there weren't very many trees. But out on the frontier, dirt dwellings had many other practical advantages. They were strong, dirt-cheap (pardon the pun), and could be quickly taken down and reassembled elsewhere should the need arise. The sod bricks, cut three to four inches thick, were held together by the dense network of prairie roots and formed remarkably durable walls and ceilings. The two-foot thick walls not only made a sturdy home, but a climate-controlled one: warm in the winter and cool in the summer. Soddies did have a downside, of course. They could suffer smoke drafts (especially irritating considering that buffalo chips were the primary fuel source), and they would get damp if the roof wasn't up to snuff. Practical matters aside, living in a well-built soddy was not the unpleasant experience one would expect. Interior walls would be smoothed down with an ax and covered with lime whitewash, clay, canvas, or newspaper. Most pioneers also built a window or two into their homes. Although most settlers were very poor, over time they could enhance their soddy with all the comforts of a city home.

Eventually, railroads brought cheap lumber to the prairie and sod walls were slowly replaced, though some farming families didn't give up their soddies until the middle of the 20th century. The art of sod construction hasn't died out completely: The **Sod House on the Prairie** (12598 Magnolia Ave., 507/723-5138, www.sodhouse.org), half a mile east of Sanborn, lets you live like the resourceful pioneers for a night.

Sod House on the Prairie

and plentiful game, which made the difficulty of living in the prairie frontier worthwhile. The family lived alternately out on the farm and in town where Charles Ingalls worked various jobs. The settlement quickly grew into a proper village, and Walnut Grove was incorporated in 1879. Charles was elected the first justice of the peace, but later that year his insatiable wanderlust and lack of farming success prompted a move to De Smet in the Dakota Territory. Laura described life here in her book *On the Banks of Plum Creek.* Although her books, written while she was in her 60s and 70s, are fictional and were never meant to be historical records, many of the episodes she describes really did happen or are based loosely on real events. The TV show, however, just borrowed a few names and general events and is nearly 100 percent fiction.

The real story of Laura and her family, both in Walnut Grove and elsewhere, is told at the **Laura Ingalls Wilder Museum** (330 8th St., 507/859-2358 or 888/528-7298, www.walnutgrove.org, 10 A.M.–6 P.M. daily summer, 10 A.M.–5 P.M. Mon.–Sat. and noon–5 P.M. Sun. May and Sept., 10 A.M.–4 P.M. Mon.–Sat. and noon–4 P.M. Sun. Apr. and Oct., gift shop only Nov.–Mar., $5 adults). The collection includes many family photos and mementos, such as Laura's sewing basket and quilt, plus displays about several of the real people she mentioned in the Plum Creek book, such as Johnny Johnson and the Olesons, who in real life were the Owens. You can also roam the original **Ingalls Dugout** (daily until dusk May–Oct., $4), now a spic-and-span farm that Charles would be proud of. The sod home alongside Plum Creek, which Laura described as "small, but clean and pleasant," that they lived in before building a proper cabin is long gone, but you can still make out the outline of where it stood. It is located 1.5 miles north of town on County Road 5. Fanatical Little Housers will not want to miss **"Pa's Bell,"** which hangs in the steeple of the English Lutheran Church at the corner of 5th and Wiggins Streets. Charles donated his last $3 toward its purchase, and Laura tells the story in her Plum Creek book. People at the museum can direct you to other Wilder sites, such as where Laura worked and went to school. To get an idea of what the land looked like when the Ingallses lived here, take a look at The Nature Conservancy's 80-acre **Wahpeton Prairie** tucked up against the Cottonwood River. It is located six miles north of town on County Road 5, a mile east on 170th Street, and then half a mile north on Duncan Avenue. The best time for "Little House" fans to visit town are any of the first three weekends in July for the **Wilder Pageant** (888/859-3120, $10), a theatrical reenactment of Laura's life. The pageant is a mighty big production and is held in an outdoor amphitheater on the banks of Plum Creek. Besides the play, a craft show, Laura and Nellie look-alike contest, and historical reenactments take place during some or all of these weekends.

Surprisingly, considering all the tourists who come here, Walnut Grove has no lodging, just a 70-site campground at **Plum Creek Park** (507/859-2005, $20 with electric). The nearest place with a bed is seven miles down the road in Tracy. There is also the **Lamberton Motel** (601 1st Ave. W., 507/752-7242, $45), ten miles east on U.S. Highway 14, with basic but clean rooms. Also in Lamberton is the **Hanzlik Blacksmith Shop** (Douglas St. and 2nd Ave., 507/752-7086, open by appt.), built in 1895 and now a museum full of original tools. The no-frills **Nellie's Cafe** (550 Hwy. 14, 507/859-2384, 6 A.M.–6 P.M. Mon.–Fri., 6 A.M.–4 P.M. Sat., 6 A.M.–1 P.M. Sun., $2–8) has sandwiches, but no cinnamon chicken.

Tracy

Laura Ingalls's first train ride was the eight-mile hop from Walnut Grove to Tracy, fancifully described in her book *By the Shores of Silver Lake,* so it's fitting that the highlight of the **Wheels Across the Prairie Museum** (3297 Hwy. 14, 507/629-3661, 1–5 P.M. daily summer, $5 adults) is the railroad display. The original depot no longer exists, however, the bench inside the one here now is one of the six that was in the original, and some people come just to sit in it hoping that they are sitting where Laura once did. (You can raise your odds of sitting in history by visiting the **End-O-Line Railroad Park and Museum** (440 Mill St. N., 507/763-3708, www.endoline.com, 10 A.M.–5 P.M. Mon.–Sat., 1–5 P.M. Sun., $4 adults), 13 miles south in Currie, which has a pair of the original benches.) The rest of the museum's collection includes just about anything old they can get their hands on and, as the name suggests, a large number of old vehicles.

The **Valentine Inn** (385 Emory St., 507/629-3827, $95), a 1902 Victorian home that once served as a hospital, was saved from the wrecking ball and lovingly restored. The four guestrooms each have a private bath and some have private porches.

The family-owned **Wilder Inn** (1000 Craig Ave., 507/629-3350 or 866/211-7877, $42), along U.S. Highway 14, is a good value, but they only accept cash.

Quiet **Swift Lake Park** (County Rd. 11, 507/629-5528, $15 with electric) just north of town has a dozen lakeside campsites.

Right in the historic downtown area, the **Tracy Bakery** (136 3rd St., 507/629-3130, 6 A.M.–4 P.M. Mon.–Fri., 6 A.M.–2 P.M. Sat., closed Sun.) serves breakfast and deli sandwiches, in addition to breads and pastries. It's a popular local gathering spot.

PIPESTONE

Pipestone's first settler didn't put down roots until 1873, and the village wasn't incorporated until almost a decade later. The city developed later than many other towns in southwest Minnesota because people feared living so close to the sacred quarries being worked by the Dakota. Once the settlers did finally come, though, it grew fast. By the end of the 19th century, four railroads passed through town, and promoters took to calling it Little Chicago. It never grew into a metropolis, but the city's former prosperity is evident in the ornate buildings gracing the downtown. Constructed with distinctive red Sioux Quartzite (the dark red was quarried in Pipestone and the pink comes from nearby Jasper), the downtown looks like no other. It is a much older history, though, that brings most visitors to Pipestone. Native American culture remains strong here, and the quarries that once kept people away now make Pipestone one of the most visited cities in western Minnesota.

Pipestone National Monument

For many Native Americans the Pipestone National Monument (36 Reservation Ave., 507/825-5464, www.nps.gov/pipe, 8 A.M.–5 P.M. daily year-round, 8 A.M.–6 P.M. Fri.–Sun. summer, $3) is one of the most sacred places in North America. Quarrying of pipestone, so named because it is carved primarily into ceremonial pipe bowls (peace pipe is a common misnomer), is believed to have begun here in the late 16th century. Though there are other sources of pipestone, the Catlinite found here exists nowhere else in the world. The finished pipes from these quarries were so highly revered that tribes across most of North America traded for them, and this land was neutral ground at various points in history. It became a unit of the National Park Service in 1937 after the Yankton Dakota, who had been guaranteed unrestricted access through an 1858 treaty, sold their rights to the federal government; however, Native Americans are still the only ones allowed to quarry here. The process nearly died out in the first half of the 20th century, but today interest has been revived and quarriers from across the United States and Canada still dig through some 10 feet of solid quartzite by hand to reach the 1- to 3-inch-thick layer of pipestone. During late summer and fall you will probably see people working one of the many pits. The visitors center not only explains the entire process of making a pipe, but from April to October you can watch local Dakota artists carving them. The finished products, along with other Native crafts, are for sale in the gift shop.

Although the stone is the main focus, there is much more to see in this 282-acre park. The 0.75-mile **Circle Trail** leads along a beautiful ridge of quartzite with a waterfall and many interesting rock formations. Much of the site

© TRICIA CORNELL

The Three Maidens is a grouping of six rocks in Pipestone.

is covered by virgin tallgrass prairie and signs along the trail point out many of the plants as well as some of the uses the Dakota had for them. On your way in or out of the park take a look at the **Three Maidens,** six large granite boulders, originally part of one enormous rock, named in honor of two (who said names have to be logical?) legendary women who live inside them. The Dakota leave offerings of food and tobacco here for the guardian spirits of the quarry.

Other Sights

For more information on the history and art of pipe-making or Dakota culture visit the **Little Feather Center** (317 4th St. NE, www.littlefeathercenter.com, 10 A.M.–5 P.M. daily, free admission), which has a good museum of Dakota cultural art and artifacts in back, and **Keepers of the Sacred Tradition of Pipemakers** (400 Hiawatha Ave. N., 507/825-3734, 10 A.M.–4:30 P.M. Tues.–Sun.), a cultural center in the restored 1880 Rock Island Railroad Depot—look for the 28-foot pipe sculpture. The latter has pipe-making workshops and summer cultural events and a small coffee shop, both sell pipes and other crafts.

The **Pipestone County Museum** (113 Hiawatha Ave. S., 507/825-2563 or 866/747-3687, 10 A.M.–5 P.M. daily summer, closed Sun. rest of year, $3 adults) has an interesting collection of items related to the city's history and a good Native American collection. While there pick up the ***Pipestone: Past and Present*** walking-tour booklet, which details three dozen buildings in one of Minnesota's largest historic districts. One must-see is the **Moore Block** next to the museum, which is adorned with whimsical gargoyle-like sculptures.

Fort Pipestone (104 9th St. NE, 507/825-4474, 9 A.M.–6 P.M. daily summer, 10 A.M.–6 P.M. daily May, Sept., and Oct., free admission) is really just a gift shop with a selection of generic bric-a-brac to go along with its high-quality Native American goods, but you should visit to see the replica 19th-century fort surrounding it.

Entertainment and Events

The American Indian Movement hosts the **Sacred Pipes Sundance** in mid-July. This deeply spiritual gathering draws Native Americans from across the United States and Canada, and while non-Native visitors are allowed at this event, it is not meant for them. If you have a deep interest in Native American issues and culture and are interested in attending, contact the Pipestone Convention & Visitor Bureau (117 8th Ave. SE, 507/825-3316 or 800/336-6125, www.pipestoneminnesota.com) for more information.

Civil War Days, held the second weekend of August in even-numbered years, attracts around 400 living history reenactors and over ten times as many onlookers. Admission is $5.

The **Pipestone Center for Performing Arts** (104 Main St. E., 507/825-2020 or 877/722-2787, www.pipestoneminnesota.com/artscenter) offers a year-round schedule of music, theater, dance, and other special events.

Shopping

Ceremonial pipes and other Native American crafts are for sale all over town. Stores selling antiques include **The Meadowlark Shop** (110 Main St. W., 507/825-5424, 10 A.M.–5 P.M. Mon.–Sat.), and **Monk's Secondhand** (213 Main St. W., 507/562-4001, 9 A.M.–5 P.M. Mon.–Sat., 1–5 P.M. Sun.).

Accommodations

The **Calumet Inn** (104 Main St. W., 507/825-5871 or 800/535-7610, www.calumet-inn.com, $82) is so good that spending a night here is reason enough to visit Pipestone. The 1888 hotel has been completely modernized, but the historic character is omnipresent, from the grand staircase to the claw-foot tubs.

The large, basic rooms at the **Arrow Motel** (600 8th Ave. NE, 507/825-3331, $37) are among the cheapest in town. Even better is the **Super 8** (605 8th Ave. SE, 507/825-4217 or 800/800-8000, $68).

The **Pipestone RV Campground** (919 Hiawatha Ave., 507/825-2455, www.pipestonervcampground.com, Apr.–Oct., $30 full hookup) is a standard RV park, except that they rent a pair of tepees. These cost $30 per night and can fit six people.

PRAIRIELAND

Food

Lange's Cafe (110 8th Ave. SE, 507/825-4488, open 24/7, $4–20) is a casual Pipestone institution with brilliant home cooking. Try the chicken with almond-raisin sauce or a hotdish daily special, and leave room for their homemade ice cream and pies for dessert. Jane and Michael Stern of *Gourmet* magazine declared that Lange's has "the best sour cream raisin pie ever made."

The **Calumet Inn** (104 Main St. W., 507/825-5871, 11 A.M.–2 P.M. daily, 5–9 P.M. Sat.–Sun., $5–17) also has excellent dining. Filet mignon, apple-smoked pork chop, and Cajun chicken fettuccine are typical of the meat-heavy menu, though they are most proud of their wild rice soup.

For excellent baked goods follow your nose to **Brummel's Bread Basket** (214 Main St. E., 507/825-5911, 7 A.M.–4 P.M. Mon.–Fri., 7 A.M.–noon Sat., closed Sun.).

Information and Transportation

Tourism information is available at the **Pipestone Convention & Visitor Bureau** (117 8th Ave. SE, 507/825-3316 or 800/336-6125, www.pipestoneminnesota.com, 8:30 A.M.–5 P.M. Mon.–Fri., closed Sat.–Sun.) and the **Pipestone County Museum** (113 Hiawatha Ave. S., 507/825-2563 or 866/747-3687, 10 A.M.–5 P.M. daily summer, closed Sun. rest of year).

Jefferson Lines (888/864-2832, www.jeffersonlines.com) buses stop at Lange's Café (110 8th Ave. SE).

NORTH OF PIPESTONE

Lake Benton

This quiet town of 700 hugs the southern end of its 2,875-acre namesake lake, a popular boating destination. The city is best known for sitting right at the center of the world's largest wind-power project: a nearly 10-mile chain of over 600 modern **wind turbines** stretching along the Buffalo Ridge. This new generation of generators can soar 400 feet high and are so efficient that on a windy day just one creates more than enough energy for all 250 of the town's homes. The towers, which continue to be erected on area farms, are Minnesota's newest cash crop, bringing much-needed money into one of the poorest parts of the state. Studies show that this area could conceivably produce enough electricity for the entire state. Local officials are so enamored with the future of wind energy that they have declared themselves the "Original Wind Power Capital of the American Midwest" and even worked a three-blade design into the downtown streets. Not only are the turbines producing cheap, clean energy for tens of thousands of people and providing new jobs, they have become a tourist attraction. For an up-close view, head two miles west on U.S. Highway 14 and then take the unnamed road north to the towers. You can learn more about wind energy, as well as local history, at the **Heritage and Wind Power Learning Center**

© TRICIA CORNELL

Wind turbines are manufactured and put to good use in southern Minnesota.

(110 Center St., 507/368-9577, 10 A.M.–5 P.M. Mon.–Fri., 10 A.M.–3 P.M. Sat., closed Sun., free admission).

On the way to the aforementioned wind-turbine-viewing spot is **Hole-in-the-Mountain County Park** (507/368-9350), 1.5 miles south of Lake Benton on Highway 75, with an 1860 pioneer cabin, hiking trails, a small tubing hill with towrope, and cross-country and small downhill ski trails, as well as a lift. The **Te Tonka Ha Rendezvous** fur trade reenactment takes place in the park the second weekend of August. Two miles south of town along Highway 75, the 1,157-acre **Hole-in-the-Mountain Prairie** preserve crosses a line of steep hills and valleys. The best views of the wildflowers and other flora are available along the dirt road just south of the sign. The preserve is managed by the Nature Conservancy (800/628-6860, www.nature.org).

The lovely **Lake Benton Opera House** (120 Benton St., 507/368-4620, www.lakebentonoperahouse.org), an 1896 downtown edifice that looks like the offspring of a church and a fire station, hosts several dramatic and musical productions each year. Finally, if you love to shop you are in luck—Lake Benton has an unexpected proliferation of gift and antiques shops.

The Burk family restored an 1888 Italianate home following a destructive fire, filled it with lovely decorations, and opened the **Benton House** (211 W. Benton St., 507/368-9484, www.itctel.com/bentonhs, $75) bed-and-breakfast. The three guestrooms all have a private bath, and one has a heart-shaped tub.

If price is the only consideration, head for the **Highway 75 Motel** (605 Hwy 75 N., 507/368-9354, $25), which has tiny, old rooms.

Hole-in-the-Mountain County Park (507/368-9577, $18 with electric) has 51 campsites.

The **Country House Supper Club** (405 Benton St. E., 507/368-4223, 5–9 P.M. Wed.–Sun., $8–18), just east of town on U.S. Highway 14, is the city's top restaurant. Their specialty, prime rib, is served on Friday and Saturday nights in the main dining room, and there is also a more casual lower dining room.

Prairie Coteau Scientific and Natural Area

Ten miles northeast of Pipestone on Highway 23, just past the village of Holland, is one of the region's few large remnants of original prairie. The healthy 421-acre grassland blankets a steep hill, allowing for a progression from dry prairie species along the ridge to wet prairie vegetation at the bottom. Over 40 species of butterfly flutter amidst the more than 200 species of wildflower. There are no trails, but you are welcome to explore on your own. The field is most colorful along the ridge top, so don't be put off by the steep climb.

Salt Lake

Serious bird-watchers will want to detour south to this shallow 312-acre lake straddling the South Dakota border. Bird-watching is particularly productive on the state's only salinated lake during the spring, when many migratory species, particularly shorebirds, make an appearance. American avocet, eared grebe, piping plover, and snow geese might be spied from the accessible observation deck, and 100-species days are not unheard of. The lake is three miles south of Marietta on Country Road 7, and one mile west on the township road to the parking area.

I-90 Corridor

LUVERNE

The Rock County seat was founded as a mail stop along the military road between Blue Earth, Minnesota, and Yankton in the Dakota Territory. The original plan called for the city to sit below the cliffs of Blue Mounds State Park, but town founder Philo Hawes, who upon first seeing the hills called this area a Garden of Eden, found a better supply of lumber a short ways south. Luverne had a short day in the sun when it hosted the world premiere of Ken Burns's documentary *The War* in 2007. The mini-series highlighted the columns Al McIntosh, editor of the *Rock County Star Herald,* wrote about life on the homefront during World War II.

Sights and Entertainment

In 2009 the city of Luverne completed an ambitious cultural project. The **Galleries at Rock County Courthouse** (213 Luverne St. E., 507/283-4061, 8 A.M.–5 P.M. Mon.–Fri., 10 A.M.–5 P.M. Sat., closed Sun., free admission) opened in the old Rock County jailhouse. The building is now the home of three museums. The **Brandenburg Gallery,** showcases the work of internationally renowned photographer Jim Brandenburg (sales benefit Touch the Sky Prairie), who was born in Luverne. On the second floor, the **Herreid Military Museum** honors Rock County veterans of all branches of the armed forces. On the third floor, the **Heritage Museum** honors the contributions of civilians during World War II. The **Veteran's War Memorial** stands in front of the building, and the **Kahler Terrace** hosts community events.

The city's other worthy attraction is the **Hinkly House Museum** (217 Freeman Ave. N., 507/449-2115, 2–4 P.M. Tues., Thurs., and Sat. summer, free admission), a 12-room Victorian mansion filled with many of original furnishings.

A block over is the **Rock County Historical Museum** (123 Freeman Ave. N., 507/283-2122, 2–4 P.M. Tues., Thurs., and Sat. summer, free admission), though its collection is primarily of interest to local residents.

Between the two museums is the **Carnegie Cultural Center** (205 Freeman Ave. N., 507/283-8294, 1–5 P.M. Tues.–Fri., noon–4 P.M. Sat., free admission). The former library now hosts monthly art and historical exhibitions and special events such as music and storytelling. Work from local artists is sold in the gift shop.

For a blast from the past watch a flick at the **Verne Drive-In Theatre** (1607 Kniss Ave.

S., 507/283-0007, www.vernedrivein.com) or the 1915 **Palace Theatre** (104 E. Main St., 507/283-8294, www.palacetheatre.us), a former vaudeville house.

Although there is a lot going on during **Buffalo Days,** held the first weekend in June, the most notable event is the **buffalo chip-throwing contest.** For those who don't know what a buffalo chip is, here's a clue—contestants take aim at a toilet.

Accommodations

Nothing fancy, but still tops in town, the **Comfort Inn** (801 Kniss Ave. S., 507/283-9488 or 877/424-6423, $70) has a small pool and whirlpool.

The **Sunrise Motel** (114 Sunshine Ave. S., 507/283-2347 or 877/641-2345, www.sunrisem.com, $29) is off the main drag on a quiet side street. The 14 units are basic, but all have Wi-Fi, HBO, refrigerators, and microwaves.

Food

For a simple but delicious meal head to **J J's Tasty Drive-In** (804 Kniss Ave. S., 507/283-8317, 11 A.M.–9 P.M. daily Mar.–Nov.), where $5 will get you a burger, fries, and a malt. Motorcycle fans can admire the 1949 Harley Davidson displayed inside.

Magnolia Steak House (1202 Kniss Ave. S., 507/283-9161, www.magnoliasteakhouse.com, 5–10 P.M. Tues.–Thurs., 5–11 P.M. Fri.–Sat., $5–26) is famous for their steaks (they have their own meat market attached so you know the beef is top quality), but it has a pretty broad menu.

The Coffey Haus (111 Main St. E., 507/283-8676, www.thecoffeyhaus.com, 7 A.M.–4:30 P.M., Mon.–Fri., 8 A.M.–3 P.M. Sat., closed Sun., $3–7) has the perfect casual coffeehouse atmosphere and serves filling sandwiches, like barbecue brisket, as well as ice cream and coffee.

Getting Here

Jefferson Lines (888/864-2832, www.jeffersonlines.com) buses stop at the Phillips 66 gas station along I-90.

BLUE MOUNDS STATE PARK

Although it receives far fewer visitors than most of Minnesota's state parks and can't offer the deep wilderness of the state's largest, in many ways Blue Mounds State Park (1410 161st St., 507/283-1307) is one of the best. The namesake mound at the heart of the park, which appeared blue to the earliest settlers passing by in the distance, is a massive outcrop of Sioux quartzite bedrock rising gradually from the west and ending in a spectacular 1.5-mile-long cliff. This ridge, nearly 100 feet tall in many places, is one of the best rock-climbing sites in the state, all climbers must get a free permit from the park office. The mound and most of the 1,826-acre park is topped by original tallgrass prairie that, although degraded by livestock grazing, was never plowed, thanks to the shallow, rocky soil. Bison graze on the prairie once again as they did through the early 19th century: The only difference is that this herd of over 100 remains inside a 500-acre enclosure. Though the bison are behind a fence, they do remain wild, so never walk right up to them since they can break through the mesh as if it were a paper bag—and they sometimes do.

The hiking here is arguably the best in southwest Minnesota, and all 13 miles of trail crossing the prairie are beautiful. The easiest is the **Mound Creek Trail,** leading around the lakes and campgrounds. The distant vistas from the **Upper Cliffline Trail** are spectacular, and when combined with the scenic views of the cliff itself from the **Lower Cliffline Trail,** makes an ideal though somewhat difficult hike, several cutoffs let you take in the best of both without hiking the full five-mile loop. The fairly easy **Western Loop Trail** in the south end of the park leads right through the heart of Blue Mounds' prairie. Bird-watchers seeking western species could have a field day along these trails. It's about a mile round-trip from the parking lot along County Road 8 to the park's highest point near Eagle Rock via the **Mound Trail.** Along the way up to the peak, stop to investigate the 1,250-foot line of rocks perfectly aligned to east and west. No one knows who built them or why. A six-mile paved bike trail connects the park to Luverne. The large campground overlooking Upper Mound Lake has 73 sites (40 electric), though the separate 14-site cart-in campground offers a more peaceful and secluded night.

WORTHINGTON

Some of the first settlers to arrive on the shore of Lake Okabena were members of the National Colony Company, a temperance group whose influence on local law lasted well into the 20th century. Those seeking out the 785-acre lake today include a large number of windsurfers who love the steady and strong winds—many contests have been held here, including the 2003 U.S. Nationals.

Sights and Events

Its sheer size makes **Pioneer Village** (501 Stower Dr., 507/376-3125, 10 A.M.–5 P.M. Mon.–Sat., 1–5 P.M. Sun. summer, $6 adults) out at the fairgrounds one of the best local history museums in the state. Over three dozen historic buildings, including a print shop, one-room schoolhouse, farm house, and general store, have been moved from around the county. Most are filled with appropriate furnishings and fixtures. Other interesting displays are a sod house, a large assortment of old vehicles, and the barbed-wire collection.

The **Nobles County Historical Society Museum** (407 12th St., 507/376-4431, noon–4 P.M. Mon.–Fri., free admission) has a small collection of artifacts in the basement of the library. Also at the library is the small **Nobles County Art Center** (507/372-8245, 2–4:30 P.M. Mon.–Fri., free admission), with exhibits by regional artists.

If something cultural is happening in town it's probably at the large art deco **Memorial Auditorium Performing Arts Center** (714 13th St., 507/376-9101, www.friendsofthe-auditorium.com).

The town's biggest claim to fame is the **Great Gobbler Gallop.** Worthington annually pits a turkey in a main-street race against a contender from Cuero, Texas, which also claims to be the Turkey Capital of the World. They've been squaring off since 1973 and Worthington's bird, always named Paycheck ("Nothing goes faster than a paycheck"), leads the overall series. Other events during **King Turkey Day** (www.kingturkeyday.com), the second Saturday after Labor Day, include a parade and pancake feed.

The two-day **International Festival** held in mid-July usually includes African, Asian, Latin American, and Scandinavian performers and foods, celebrating Worthington's increasingly diverse population.

Accommodations

You can spend the night in the **Historic Dayton House** (1311 4th Ave., 507/727-1311, www.daytonhouse.org, $130), an 1890 Georgian/Colonial Revival built by George Draper Dayton, who founded what is now Target Company. It is filled with period antiques, though the twin two-room suites on the second floor have a few modern touches, such as flat-screen TVs.

The best of the ordinary hotels is the **Holiday Inn** (1250 Ryan's Rd., 877/863-4780, $89), with updated rooms, a welcoming lobby area, and an indoor pool and fitness area.

The **Sunset Inn** (1923 Dover St., 507/376-9494, $41), at the junction of Highways 59 and 60 is one of Worthington's better cheapies.

Food

Super-friendly **Queen of Sheeba** (304 10th St., 507/376-5102, 11 A.M.–9 P.M. Mon.–Fri., 10 A.M.–2 P.M. Sat., noon–8 P.M. Sun., $4–8) serves Ethiopian food and coffee, including a buffet lunch on Saturdays.

You can't beat the urbane, welcoming atmosphere at **Benlee's** (212 10th St., 507/343-3400, 8 A.M.–5 P.M. Mon.–Fri., 8 A.M.–4 P.M. Sat., closed Sun.), a coffee shop with a full menu of sandwiches, soups, salads, and desserts. Local musicians often play here.

Panaderia Mi Tierra (424 10th St., 507/343-0324, 7 A.M.–8 P.M. Mon.–Fri., 8 A.M.–8 P.M. Sat.–Sun.) is a Mexican grocery store with a great selection of Mexican pastries.

Getting There

Jefferson Lines (888/864-2832, www.jeffersonlines.com) buses stop at the Cenex gas station (1710 N. Humiston) at I-90 and Highway 59.

JACKSON

Jackson was born in 1856 when the Wood brothers built their trading post on the Des Moines River. Six years later 11 Norwegian immigrant families rode out the Dakota Conflict in a small log cabin circled by a rough hexagonal stockade. **Fort Belmont** (507/847-3867, 10 A.M.–4 P.M. Mon.–Fri., 9 A.M.–3 P.M. Sat., noon–4 P.M. Sun. summer, $3 adults), at the junction of I-90 and U.S. Highway 71, is a re-creation of their simple shelter. Elsewhere on the grounds are a sod house, blacksmith shop, and other old buildings. The **Fort Belmont Rendezvous** has historical reenactments the weekend after Labor Day.

There are over a dozen more period buildings at **Historic Fair Village** (only open during fair week, but you can look at them from the outside any time) on the fairgrounds east of downtown.

The 1922 **Historic State Theater** (600 2nd St., 507/847-4360, www.histstatetheatre.com), an art deco gem that seats 500 people and still shows movies, is one of many lovely buildings along the sleepy Main Street.

The **Earth Inn** (1051 Hwy. 71, 507/847-5603, $43) is a spotless hotel built largely underground.

The **Old Railroad Inn** (219 Moore St., 507/847-5348 or 888/844-5348, $65) bed-and-breakfast has four guestrooms (which share two baths) in an 1888 home built for railroad workers. The antiques-filled house has loads of character.

Jackson doesn't have many restaurants, but you can fill up at **New China** (300 Ashley St. W., 507/847-2800, 9:30 A.M.–9:30 P.M. daily, $6–17).

Get your caffeine fix at **Reggie's Cinema Barista** (600 2nd St., 507/847-4360, 7:30 A.M.–9:30 P.M. daily).

FAIRMONT

Fairmont, the Martin County seat, hugs a long chain of lakes. It was founded in 1857 by E. Banks Hall and William Budd, whose names still grace the waters on which they built their cabins. A decade and a half later a group of Oxford- and Cambridge-educated English settlers arrived, and the new methods of growing beans they developed helped save the town during the grasshopper plague of the 1870s. The English, riding in full crimson regalia, also introduced fox hunting to Minnesota and soon became known statewide as the Fairmont Sportsmen.

Sights

Some of the more unusual artifacts in the large Martin County Historical Society's **Pioneer Museum** (304 Blue Earth Ave. E., 507/235-5178, 8:30 A.M.–noon and 1–4:30 P.M. Mon.–Fri., free admission) are a motorcycle from 1912, a radio from 1924, and a pair of wooden roller skates.

Next door, the **Red Rock Center for the Arts** (222 Blue Earth Ave. E., 507/235-9262) is a striking building with occasional art displays. Ask here if you'd like to tour the 1867 **Chubb House** (209 Lake Ave.), the oldest brick building in the city.

Heritage Acres (827 Lake Ave., 507/235-5547, open by appt.) is a private agricultural history museum overlooking Sisseton Lake. The 40-acre site holds several historic structures including a church, train depot, and one-room schoolhouse. You can walk the grounds anytime, though the buildings can only be visited during festivals or by appointment. There's an enclosed **prairie dog colony** at the entrance.

Another animal attraction, a herd of **Texas Longhorns,** grazes behind the McDonalds on Highway 15 just south of the freeway.

If you are staying in town be sure to see what's on stage at the **Fairmont Opera House** (45 Downtown Plz., 507/238-4900, www.fairmontoperahouse.com), built in 1901 and added to the National Register of Historic Places 80 years later after almost being demolished for a parking lot.

Accommodations

The **Holiday Inn** (1201 Torgeson Rd., 507/238-4771 or 800/785-4066, www.hifairmont.com,

$95), right off the freeway on Highway 15, has a pool, hot tub, sauna, exercise room, game room, putting green, and other diversions.

Across the road, the **Super 8** (1200 Torgeson Rd., 507/238-9444, www.super8fairmont.com, $79) is another good choice, though without the pool, fitness center, or other amenities.

Food

The Ranch (1330 State St. N., 507/235-3044, 6 A.M.–9 P.M. Sun.–Thurs., 6 A.M.–10 P.M. Fri.–Sat., $5–15) serves standard family fare and is one of Fairmont's most popular restaurants.

El Mariachi (62 Downtown Plz., 507/235-8835, 11 A.M.–9 P.M. Sun.–Thurs., 11 A.M.–10 P.M. Fri.–Sat., $4–13) serves excellent Mexican meals.

For something just a little fancier, try **Kak's Lounge and Steakhouse** (1500 Albion Ave., 507/235-8210, 11:30 A.M.–1 A.M. Tues.–Sun., closed Mon., $8–15) with a meat-heavy menu.

Getting There

Jefferson Lines (888/864-2832, www.jeffersonlines.com) buses stop at the Freedom Valu Center (407 Blue Earth Ave. E.).

BLUE EARTH

Who's green, stands 47 feet tall, weighs 8,000 pounds, and greets visitors with a hearty "Ho, Ho, Ho?" No, not Godzilla doing his Santa Claus impression—it's the **Jolly Green Giant,** of course. Arms akimbo and a smile on his face, he surveys the pea and corn fields around town that are harvested by General Mills, the latest owner of this merry mascot. He wears a leather vest and bandana at times in July and August (as a gesture to motorcycle riders heading to rallies in South Dakota and Iowa) and a red scarf in the winter. The jolly one isn't Blue Earth's only claim to fame. In 1917, Walter Schwen devised a process for coating ice cream in chocolate and the Eskimo Pie was born, though back then it was called a Chocolate Dream.

Although the giant is the primary reason to stop in Blue Earth, if you are here you might as well visit the city's twin museums. The **James B. Wakefield House** (405 6th St. E., 507/526-5421, 10 A.M.–4 P.M. Tues.–Fri., free admission), built in 1868 by one of the city's founders, is laid out as though a family from around the turn of the 20th century was still living here and happened to label all their possessions with index cards.

Kitty corner, in the old library, the **Etta C. Ross Museum** (324 6th St. E., 507/526-5421, 10 A.M.–4 P.M. Tues.–Fri., free admission) has a hodge-podge collection of anything old they can get their hands on.

The Faribault County Historical Society also maintains a one-room schoolhouse, log cabin, blacksmith shop, and post office (all appropriately equipped) at the fairgrounds and opens them up during the County Fair at the end of July.

As you drive west out of Blue Earth on I-90, keep your eyes peeled for a strip of red concrete that marks the exact middle of the highway as it stretches from coast to coast.

Both of the town's hotels are along I-90. The **Super 8** (1420 Giant Dr., 507/526-7376 or 800/800-8000, $62) is a good choice, but you get a pool and hot tub at the **AmericInn** (1495 Domes Dr., 507/526-4215 or 800/396-5007, $69).

Camping is free for two nights along the Blue Earth River at the fairgrounds north of downtown.

Carhops still take your order at the **Cedar Inn** (326 Grove St. N., 507/526-5612, 11 A.M.–8:30 P.M. daily Apr.–Sept., $2–5), and the prices are equally old-fashioned. The Cedar Inn is the home of the Pink Elvis—a strawberry shake with black licorice.

Another local favorite is the **Double Play Bar & Grill** (115 6th St., 507/526-3032, 11 A.M.–10 P.M. daily, $6–12). Lively in the evenings when bands often play, it's a great place for a burger or a pizza.

Little Crow Lakes

Though Kandiyohi and Meeker Counties have a high concentration of lakes, this is still, like the rest of southwest Minnesota, thoroughly farm country. Except for drivers racing along Highway 12 from the Twin Cities to South Dakota and anglers shacking up for a week at a resort for some fishing in the summer, this part of Minnesota sees few visitors. Darwin, however, is worth going out of your way for.

WILLMAR

The Kandiyohi County seat is a growing, though not very exciting, city of over 19,000 that serves as the regional commercial center. Though the first settlers built log cabins around Foot Lake over a decade earlier, the city of Willmar was founded as a railroad town in 1869. It soon became a hub of James J. Hill's Great Northern empire, and it remains an important rail center, with the Burlington Northern & Santa Fe Railway's busy switching yard one of Willmar's major employers.

Sights

Area history is on display at the **Kandiyohi County Historical Museum** (610 Hwy. 71 NE, 320/235-1881, www.kandimuseum.com, 9 A.M.–5 P.M. Mon.–Fri. year-round and 1–5 P.M. Sat.–Sun. summer, $2 adults). The Native American display is small but interesting, and the horseless carriage, circa 1900, is another highlight.

A pair of privately owned museums will appeal to fans of internal combustion. The **Mikkelson Collection** (418 Benson Ave. SE, 320/231-0384, www.fallsflyer.com, open by chance or appt., $6 adults) is packed with vintage boats (including over a dozen rare Falls Flyers, "The Jaguar of Boats") and outboard motors, various other boating artifacts, and hundreds of toys.

Across town is the **Schwanke Museum** (3310 U.S. 71 S., 320/231-0564, www.schwanketractor.com, 1–4 P.M. Mon.–Sat. May–Nov., $5 adults), which covers most of the rest of the motorized spectrum. The private collection has over 400 classic cars, trucks, tractors, and related items.

Entertainment and Events

Touring music and theatrical acts, plus the **Willmar Area Symphonic Orchestra,** take the stage at the **Willmar Education and Arts Center** (611 5th St. SW, 320/231-8560, www.willmararts.org), while locals produce seven shows a year at the **Barn Theatre** (321 4th St. SW, 320/235-9500, www.thebarntheatre.com).

Willmar's biggest bash is late June's **Willmar Fests** (www.willmarfests.com). A sand sculpture contest, bed races, international banquet, and performance by the award-winning Little Crow Water Ski Team (which performs to big crowds every Friday night during the summer in nearby New London) are highlights.

Recreation

The **Glacial Lakes State Trail** is an 18-mile path connecting Willmar with Spicer, New London, and Hawick. The 12 miles from Willmar to New London is paved, while the last section is crushed granite. The trail continues to Richmond, but it is still being developed, and some bridges are out. **Robbins Island Park,** covering the peninsula dividing Foot Lake from Willmar Lake, has a beach, short nature trail, and plenty of shady space for picnics.

Accommodations

The large **Holiday Inn** (2100 Hwy. 12 E., 320/235-6060 or 877/405-4466, www.hiwillmar.com, $82) is attached to the Willmar Conference Center and has a pool, whirlpool, sauna, game room, and exercise equipment.

Lakeview Inn (1212 N. Business 71, 320/235-3424 or 800/718-3424, www.lakeviewinnmn.com, $50) doesn't quite have a lake view, but it's friendly and homey.

Two sister properties right next door to each

other, the **Corner Cottage** and **A'Venue** (615 Becker Ave. SW, www.grandcottages.com, $65–150) together have five rooms available. A'Venue has an outdoor in-ground pool and has a fully stocked kitchen for guests to use, while the Corner Cottage operates as a bed-and-breakfast and offers a more luxurious suite. Both are invitingly furnished, with some country touches. The same folks also rent out **The Lodge** (22483 5th St. NW, $350), a whole-house rental that sleeps up to ten next to Sibley State Park.

Food

Willmar's historic downtown is in transition, as immigrant populations find their footing here. Nearly every chain restaurant imaginable has an outpost on the highway (1st Street).

One of a few authentic Mexican restaurants in town, **Antonio's** (304 4th St. SW, 320/235-1072, 11 A.M.–9 P.M. daily, $5–12) serves good food in a historic space with a big skylight.

Rosita's (308 4th St. SW, 320/235-1072, 11 A.M.–9 P.M. daily) is usually packed with families and young people who come for the authentic Mexican barbecue known as *carnitas*.

Northern Grounds (333 Litchfield, 320/235-9775, www.northerngroundswillmar.com, 6:30 A.M.–9 P.M. Mon.–Thurs., 6:30 A.M.–9 P.M. Fri., 7:30 A.M.–9 P.M. Sat., closed Sun.) is an excellent coffee shop, but it is so much more. They have a wine license and serve small plates (like blue cheese potatoes, roasted asparagus, and smoked salmon) to go with a nice glass in the evening. For lunch they have a nice list of panini on offer and a couple of soups.

Information and Transportation

The **Willmar Lakes Area Convention and Visitors Bureau** (2104 Hwy. 12 E., 320/235-3552 or 800/845-8747, www.seeyouinwillmar.com, 9 A.M.–4:30 P.M. Mon.–Fri., closed Sat.–Sun.) has a rack of brochures for all of Kandiyohi County.

Jefferson Lines (888/864-2832, www.jeffersonlines.com) buses stop at the Kum and Go gas station (2550 Hwy. 12 E., 320/214-7813). **Executive Express** (320/253-2226 or 888/522-9899, www.executiveexpress.biz) runs an airport shuttle to the Twin Cities from the Holiday Inn (2100 Hwy. 12 E., 320/235-6060 or 877/405-4466) several times a day.

SPICER

Spicer is a mini resort town on Green Lake, the largest body of water in the area. While it hops during the summer it is very quiet the rest of the year.

Sights and Recreation

Besides swimming, fishing, boating, or sailing on the lake, you can get your kicks on go-karts and the like at **Big Kahuna** (190 Progress Way, 320/796-2445, 11 A.M.–9 P.M.) along Highway 23.

Spicer Bike and Sports (178 Progress Way, 320/796-6334, 9 A.M.–6 P.M. Mon.–Fri., 9 A.M.–3 P.M. Sat.) along the **Glacial Lakes State Trail** rents bikes and in-line skates.

The **Prairie Woods Environmental Learning Center** (12718 10th St. NE, 320/354-5894, www.prairiewoodselc.org,) has seven miles of trails in varied terrain. They are open for hiking and skiing during daylight hours and rent cross-country skis.

The two-week-long **Spicer WinterFest** in late January and early February includes sports tournaments and races (yes, WinterFest), as well as warmer, indoor events. Some years they build an ice castle with blocks taken from the lake.

Accommodations

A dozen small, summer-only resorts dot the many lakes surrounding the town, but by far the best lodging is the charming **Spicer Castle** (11600 Indian Beach Rd., 320/796-5870 or 800/821-6675, www.spicercastle.com, $110) on Green Lake. This English country-style mansion, built in 1895 by town founder John Spicer, is now an exquisite eight-room inn with other rooms in cottages on the grounds. Rooms all have private baths, and a few have fireplaces and whirlpools. You don't need to spend the night to join one of their five-course **Murder Mystery dinners** or **Dinner Cruises.**

If you just want a regular hotel, the

Northern Inn (154 Lake Ave. S., 320/796-2091 or 800/941-0423, www.northern-inn.com, $80), right in town across from big and busy Saulsbury Beach, has modern rooms plus a pool, whirlpool, and sauna.

Food

Melvin's (159 Lake Ave. S., 320/796-2195, www.melvinsonthelake.com, 11 A.M.–11 P.M. Sun.–Wed. summer, 11 A.M.–1 A.M. Thurs.–Sat. year-round, closed Sun.–Wed. in off-season, $7–17) has a mostly American menu and a lakeside deck. The adjacent nightclub has live music on weekends.

The best place for breakfast is **Westwood Café** (142 Lake St., 320/796-5355, www.westwoodcafe.com, 6 A.M.–1:30 P.M. Sun., 6 A.M.–2 P.M. Mon., 6 A.M.–8 P.M. Tues.–Sat., $5–12). The malted Belgian waffle topped with blueberries is especially a treat. Lunch is soup and sandwiches, but the dinner menu brings the kinds of hearty home-cooked meals you need after a day out on the lake: meatloaf, fried chicken, and battered walleye.

Getting There

Executive Express (320/253-2226 or 888/522-9899, www.executiveexpress.biz) runs a shuttle to the Minneapolis–St. Paul airport from Melvin's Restaurant (159 Lake Ave. S.).

SIBLEY STATE PARK

Sibley State Park (800 Sibley Park Rd. NE, 320/354-2055) sits near the southern end of the Alexandria Moraine, a band of glacially formed hills and lakes stretching north to the city of Detroit Lakes. **Mount Tom,** the tallest hill, was once a lookout for the local Dakota and, like most high places, it held spiritual significance for them too. From the observation tower you can take in a broad vista of the surrounding lakes, forest, and farms. Historically, oak savanna and prairie were the main landscapes, but today forest covers most of the 2,510-acre park. Shortgrass prairie remnants remain on some of the hills, and many old farm fields are being restored to the native prairie and oak savanna. With a mix of grasslands, woodlands, and lakes, bird-watching can be pretty good here.

Eighteen miles of hilly hiking trails, half open to horseback riders, wind through the park. The **Mt. Tom Trail,** a four-mile loop climbing from Lake Andrew to Mt. Tom, is the most popular. Several shorter loops branch off the south end, and the **Oak Hills Trail** lets you cut off the not-so-scenic southern tip. Arguably more scenic, and definitely more peaceful, is the horse path along the north end of the park. For a short, easy hike try the **Pondview Interpretive Trail,** a granite-surfaced loop around a pond with signs discussing park ecology. More interpretive signs are found on the **Woodland Wildlife Trail,** which follows the beginning of the five-mile paved bike trail. Both are a mile long and start by the interpretive center. **Lake Andrew** bustles with swimmers, boaters, and anglers all summer long, while smaller **Henschien and Swan Lakes,** connected by a portage and a small stream, offer some scenic canoeing. Canoes and rowboats can be rented during the summer. In winter, a ten-mile web of challenging groomed cross-country ski trails covers the main part of the park. The western half of the park has no trails, but would be a good place to explore by snowshoe.

Campers have 132 sites (53 electric) in two campgrounds. A little over half of them, including all the electric, are crammed together next to the beach and main picnic area. They are shady and convenient if you have kids, but the **Oak Ridge Campground** ($20), a mix of open and wooded sites, all widely spaced, is much more peaceful and scenic. Horseback riders have their own camp.

HIGHWAY 12 EAST OF WILLMAR

Litchfield

The Meeker County seat is a quiet city of 6,542 whose main claim to fame is the 1885 **Grand Army of the Republic Hall** (308 Marshall Ave. N., 320/693-8911, noon–4 P.M. Tues.–Sun., $2 adults), one of the few remaining in the nation and the last in Minnesota. The

Ladies of the G. A. R., descendents of Union veterans, still hold their annual meeting here. It houses a small but interesting collection of Civil War artifacts, but the building itself is the most interesting feature. It was designed to resemble a military fort, giving the diminutive structure a degree of stature. An addition in back houses the **Meeker County Historical Society Museum,** two floors of the usual historical artifacts highlighted by an 1868 log cabin. A Civil War living-history encampment takes place across the street in Central Park on Labor Day weekend (most of the action is on Saturday) in even-numbered years.

Another historical relic, the **Starlite Drive-In Theatre** (Hwy. 22 & Hwy. 12, 320/693-6990, www.starlitemovies.com), still screens double and triple features.

On the other side of town is **Lake Ripley,** very popular for boating and fishing. Surrounding its shore you'll find a small floral garden, beach, **municipal campground** (320/693-7201, $17 with full hookup), and the 18-hole **Litchfield Golf Club** (405 Pleasure Dr. W., 320/693-6059, www.litchfieldgolfclub.com, $32 18 holes).

The modern **Scotwood Motel** (1017 Frontage Rd. E., 320/693-2496 or 800/225-5489, $80) has a pool and whirlpool.

The very friendly **Marshall Estate** (611 Marshall Ave. N., 320/593-8170, www.themarshallestate.com, $80) bed-and-breakfast has four guest rooms sharing a bath in a quaint 1920 Tudor Revival home.

Six miles southwest of town, on 300 acres fronting Star Lake, is the luxurious **Birdwing Spa** (21398 575th Ave., 320/693-6064, www.birdwingspa.com, $250 day spa, $315 overnight). A few of the many rejuvenation options include mud massages, pedicures, yoga, herbal wraps, gourmet meals, and canoe trips.

The best bets for a bite to eat are the solid home-cooked meals at the **Main Street Cafe** (226 N. Sibley Ave., 320/693-9067, 6 A.M.–4 P.M. Mon.–Fri., 6 A.M.–2 P.M. Sat., 7 A.M.–2 P.M. Sun., $4–8).

Executive Express (320/253-2226 or 888/522-9899, www.executiveexpress.biz) airport shuttle picks up next door at Swan's Cafe (1015 Frontage Rd. E.).

Darwin

Everyone should make the trip to tiny Darwin (pop. 296), just over an hour from Minneapolis, to experience the extraordinary, one-of-a-kind genius of Francis A. Johnson. Johnson, son of U.S. Senator Magnus Johnson, gave the tiny village its one claim to fame: the **world's largest ball of twine made by just one man.** This "magnificent sphere" is 11 feet tall, 12 feet, nine inches wide, and weighs nearly nine tons—it used to weigh 11 tons, but all the water has finally evaporated out. He rolled his first strand of baler twine in March of 1950 and didn't stop until 1979. There are other giant twine balls out there, some even a bit bigger, but they are just imitations—all were collective efforts inspired by Johnson's creation. When Johnson died in 1989 the city spurned a generous offer from the *Ripley's Believe It or Not!* folks and moved it into a Plexiglas-enclosed shelter downtown. The ball has since been made vaguely famous by the epic Weird Al Yankovic song *The Biggest Ball of Twine in Minnesota.* Weird Al had befriended Johnson and, according to the folks in Darwin, still visits town when he gets a chance.

Though he will always be known as the man who rolled the twine ball, Johnson was also an obsessive whittler and collector—he died with nearly 500 hammers and 7,000 pencils. A few of the tens of thousands of functional wooden pliers he carved—one cut from a matchstick and another stretching 6.5 feet, with 19 progressively smaller pliers cascading from the handles—are now on display in the adjacent **Darwin Twine Ball Museum** (320/693-7544, www.darwintwineball.com, 9:30 A.M.–4:30 P.M. daily Apr.–Sept., by appt. rest of year, free admission) along with a handful of historical Darwin photos and artifacts. The whole town celebrates **Twine Ball Days** on the second Saturday in August.

Dassel

Any railroad enthusiasts passing by will want

© TIM BEWER

Darwin is home to the world's largest ball of twine rolled by just one man.

to stop at **The Old Depot Museum** (651 Hwy. 12 W., 320/275-3876, www.theolddepot.com, 10 A.M.–4:30 P.M. daily June–Sept., $2.50 adults), a 1913 Great Northern Depot filled with one of the state's top collections of railroad art and artifacts.

The **Universal Laboratories Building Museum** (901 1st St. N., 320/275-3077, 10 A.M.–4 P.M. Tues.–Fri. year-round and 9 A.M.–1 P.M. Sat. summer, free admission) has local history displays, but its focus is on ergot, a fungus that grows on wheat and is used in blood-clotting medicines. The medicines once produced here were particularly important during World War II.

Cokato

The city's name, roughly derived from the Dakota for "in the midst of," is an appropriate enough title today since it lies halfway between Minneapolis and Willmar. The well-presented **Cokato Museum** (175 W. 4th St., 320/286-2427, 9 A.M.–4:30 P.M. Tues.–Fri., 9 A.M.–3 P.M. Sat., noon–4 P.M. Sun., free admission) focuses on the town's Swedish and Finnish roots. Displays include a reconstructed log home, a Finnish sauna, and an early dentist's office that will make you cringe, but the real gem is the **Akerlund Photo Studio** up the street. It was opened in 1902 and looks just as it did when operations ceased in the 1950s; the owner's apartment has been left nearly exactly as it was when furnished in 1927.

A classic among small-town festivals, the **Cokato Corn Carnival** has been celebrated every year since 1950 with roasted corn, kiddie rides, and music in mid-August.

BLUFF COUNTRY

When the last five to ten glaciers bulldozed their way across North America, they spared most of southeast Minnesota. Though their icy lobes slid around this area, the torrential meltwaters rushed right through it, carving away hundreds of feet of sandstone and limestone. The gorgeous result is a rugged region of steep valleys capped by limestone bluffs and lined by wildly meandering streams. This unique region is often errantly called the Driftless Area. The true Driftless Area is a 10,000-square-mile wedge across parts of Wisconsin, Illinois, and Minnesota that wasn't gouged by any glaciers over the last million years—in Minnesota it only encompasses a thin strip along the Mississippi River in Winona and Houston Counties. The rest of the region beyond this, which some geologists call the Pseudo Driftless Area, was buried by earlier glaciations, though it is visually identical to the real thing, hence the confusion. Even geologists can only differentiate it by locating the scattered pockets of thin, highly eroded glacial till that remain.

There is a lot of variety in this little corner of the state. Moving inland from the spectacular 500-foot bluffs and historic river towns hugging the Mississippi you'll find blue-ribbon trout streams, the state's most popular bike trails, Minnesota's largest Amish settlements, and cosmopolitan Rochester. The land levels out as it moves west, slowly fading into the Great Plains.

PLANNING YOUR TIME

Geographically speaking, Rochester is the heart of the region, so you can use it as a hub for

© TRICIA CORNELL

HIGHLIGHTS

Eagle Watching: Thanks to the rapid current that keeps the river from freezing near Wabasha, this area has some of the best eagle-spotting opportunities in the country, especially in the winter (page 359).

LARK Toys: With everything from hand-carved puzzles to chemistry sets, not to mention a whimsical carousel, Lost Arts Revival by Kreofsky in little Kellogg is one of the world's greatest toy stores (page 362).

Great River Bluffs State Park: This park offers some of the best Mississippi River views anywhere, and a good campground to boot (page 372).

Lanesboro: This little town in the heart of the Driftless Area's scenery, near the middle of the Blufflands State Trail and on the edge of Amish country, is just too lovely to miss (page 385).

Forestville and Mystery Cave State Park: In this lovely and diverse park, you can explore Minnesota's longest cave, step back to the 19th century in the village of Forestville, and hike wooded hills and valleys (page 392).

Harmony: From the goat farm to the wood-carving museum to the Amish tours, Harmony surprises as much as it delights (page 393).

SPAM Museum: This humorous and high-tech celebration of the mystery meat is one of the state's best museums (page 406).

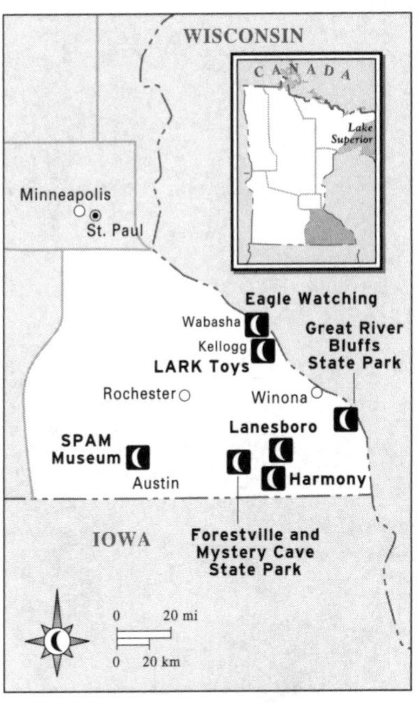

LOOK FOR ☾ TO FIND RECOMMENDED SIGHTS, ACTIVITIES, DINING, AND LODGING.

making multiple day trips. On the other hand, just about everything detailed in the chapter except Rochester lies along a conveniently circular route, so you can also loop through it all and detour to Med City for a look at the Mayo family legacy when it's most convenient. Either way, count on four days for a quick look at the best of the best.

Along the Mississippi-hugging Great River Road, which is the one place to go if you have just one day to spend (though it can't be done justice without spending two), do some sightseeing and shopping in Red Wing, Wabasha, and Winona, soak up the scenic vistas from John A. Latsch and **Great River Bluffs State Park,** and take a spin on the **LARK Carousel.** Turning inland to Amish Country, weave through the contorted hills and valleys to little **Lanesboro,** which is just too lovely to miss. After visiting some Amish farms around **Harmony,** head over to the **SPAM Museum** in Austin. Owatonna, for a look at Louis Sullivan's breathtaking National Farmer's Bank, and Northfield, for a riverside stroll, are the two mandatory stops on your way up I-35 back to the Twin Cities.

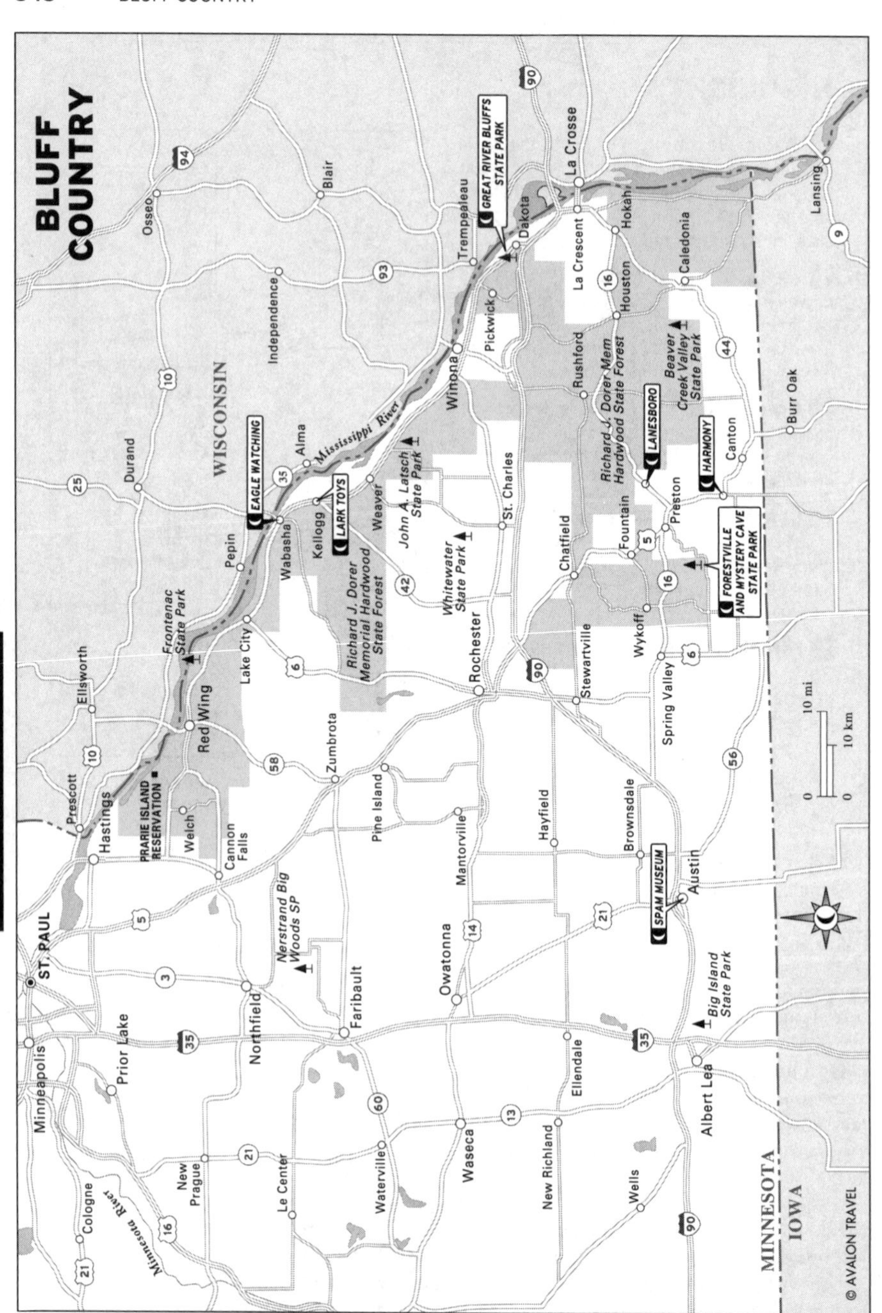

BLUFF COUNTRY
WISCONSIN
MINNESOTA
IOWA
Mississippi River
Minnesota River
GREAT RIVER BLUFFS STATE PARK
EAGLE WATCHING
LARK TOYS
LANESBORO
HARMONY
FORESTVILLE AND MYSTERY CAVE STATE PARK
SPAM MUSEUM
PRAIRIE ISLAND RESERVATION
Frontenac State Park
Richard J. Dorer Memorial Hardwood State Forest
Richard J. Dorer Mem Hardwood State Forest
John A. Latsch State Park
Whitewater State Park
Beaver Creek Valley State Park
Nerstrand Big Woods SP
Big Island State Park
ST. PAUL
Minneapolis
Prior Lake
Cologne
New Prague
Le Center
Waterville
Waseca
New Richland
Wells
Albert Lea
Ellendale
Northfield
Faribault
Owatonna
Austin
Brownsdale
Hayfield
Mantorville
Pine Island
Zumbrota
Cannon Falls
Welch
Hastings
Prescott
Ellsworth
Red Wing
Lake City
Frontenac
Pepin
Wabasha
Kellogg
Weaver
Alma
Durand
Osseo
Blair
Independence
Trempealeau
Winona
Pickwick
Dakota
La Crescent
La Crosse
Hokah
Houston
Caledonia
Rushford
Rochester
St. Charles
Chatfield
Stewartville
Spring Valley
Wykoff
Fountain
Preston
Canton
Burr Oak
Lansing
0 10 mi
0 10 km
© AVALON TRAVEL

Great River Road

We move up the river – always through enchanting scenery, there being no other kind on the Upper Mississippi.

– Mark Twain, *Life on the Mississippi*, 1883

Life on the Mississippi has changed considerably since Twain penned these words, but the statement remains as true as ever. Below its confluence with the St. Croix River, the "Father of Waters" quickly expands, spanning up to five miles across, while towering half-dome bluffs hedge it in along the rest of its Minnesota journey. Highway 61 hits the bluffs as it approaches Red Wing and meets the river at Lake City, and from this point on you'll have unrivaled scenery. There is ample opportunity to turn inland and climb the mountain-like terrain for glorious valley views. Though you are never far from one of the historic river towns, the floodplain and impossibly steep hills thwart development, allowing moments where you can imagine yourself deep in a lost wilderness. Wildlife, best enjoyed from a canoe in the river's backwaters, but quite often seen from behind the wheel, abounds all year long. Each fall waterfowl, shorebirds, and raptors follow the valley south to warmer wintering grounds. For bald eagles the river *is* their winter residence—well over a thousand of them fish in the open waters along Minnesota.

© TRICIA CORNELL

Pleasure boats speed up and down the wide Mississippi River south of Red Wing.

Though the age of paddlewheel steamboats peaked even before Mark Twain did, for many they remain synonymous with the Mississippi. A few paddlewheelers still ply these waters, though today you are much more likely to view one of the river's many massive barges.

HASTINGS AND VICINITY

Hastings's first European settler, Henry Bailly, came to this strategic spot, where the St. Croix River meets the Mississippi, in 1850 under the guise of running a trading post, but he really was in wait to claim the site for development the moment the ink dried on the Dakota treaties. That, as anticipated, happened the next year, and a city was soon plotted and named for Henry Hastings Sibley, the future first governor of Minnesota. It was a city poised for greatness. Steamboat travel was difficult upriver of this point, so many warehouses, mills, banks, and other businesses associated with river trade rose here, and the city prospered. Navigational improvements later organized by shippers allowed the commercial emergence of Minneapolis and St. Paul and spelled the end of Hastings's prominence.

Just 20 minutes from St. Paul, this city of 18,000 is a popular day trip from the Twin Cities. Most come to shop the galleries, gift shops, and antiques stores along historic Second Street, whose two busiest blocks remain largely intact from the beginning of the 20th century.

Sights

The **Hastings Area Chamber of Commerce & Tourism Bureau** (111 3rd St. E., 651/437-6775 or 888/612-6122, www.hastingsmn.org, 8:30 A.M.–5 P.M. Mon.–Fri., closed Sat.–Sun.) gives out a free map with a detailed walking tour that highlights most of the 64 buildings listed on the National Register of Historic Places, including the modest **Fasbender Clinic** (now Edward Jones Investments), a Frank Lloyd Wright design at the corner of Highway 55 and Pine Street, and the imposing **LeDuc Historic Estate** (1629 Vermillion St., 651/437-7055, 10 A.M.–5 P.M. Wed.–Sat., 1–5 P.M. Sun. May–Oct., $6 adults), an 1865 Gothic Revival home in the process of being filled with period furnishings.

An elevated observation platform at **Lock and Dam #2,** just northwest of town, lets you watch boats and barges get a 12-foot lift. Another worthy diversion is **Vermillion Falls,** located on the west side of town just off U.S. Highway 61. The small falls lies behind the Gardner Flour Mill (now known as ConAgra), the oldest continuously operating flour mill in the state, and drops into a narrow gorge that runs around the city. Downstream is the almost haunting **Ramsey Mill** ruins, built by the state's first territorial governor in 1857.

Outside of town, the **Alexis Bailly Vineyard** (18200 Kirby Ave., 651/437-1413, www.abvwines.com, 11 A.M.–5:30 P.M. Fri.–Sun. June–Nov.), the state's first winemaker using all locally grown grapes, opens their doors for tastings ($2–5) and sales. To get there head south on U.S. Highway 61 to 170th Street East, and then west for two miles.

Although it is only open to the public the last weekend in July during the **Antique Power Show,** you should drive past the **Little Log House Pioneer Village** (13746 220th St. E., 651/437-2693, www.littleloghouseshow.com, $12 adults), a large and impressive collection of old buildings and vehicles spread across 40 acres. It's six miles south of town.

Recreation and Events

Across the Mississippi River from downtown Hastings, the **Carpenter St. Croix Valley Nature Center** (12805 St. Croix Trl., 651/437-4359, www.carpenternaturecenter.org, 8 A.M.–4:30 P.M. daily) is a private 725-acre facility. The small interpretive center has a few nature displays, plus animals caged and mounted. Outside are a flower and herb garden and environmentally friendly apple orchard. Ten miles of scenic trail cross the forest, savanna, and restored prairie; some trails overlook the St. Croix River, others lead down the bluffs to its shore. Unfortunately you can't escape the Highway 10 traffic hum.

This is a great area to explore on a bike. **The Route** (200 2nd St. E., 651/437-4010, www.theroute.net, 10 A.M.–7 P.M. Mon.–Fri., 10 A.M.–5 P.M. Sat., noon–5 P.M. Sun.) will rent you one for $25 a day.

No matter the season, **Afton Alps** (6600 Peller Ave. S., 651/436-5245 or 800/328-1328, www.aftonalps.com) is a one-stop recreational hub, with downhill skiing, golf, and mountain-bike trails.

During the summer, classic cars (built in 1976 or earlier) converge in downtown Hastings for **Cruise-ins** every other Saturday night. There are food and merchandise vendors and a general atmosphere of old-fashioned summertime fun.

Accommodations

All of Hastings's hotels are on the south side of town on or near U.S. Highway 61. The cheapest is the locally owned **Hastings Inn** (1520 Vermillion St., 651/437-3155, $50–60), with large, basic rooms.

Much newer and nicer is the **Country Inn & Suites** (300 33rd St., 651/437-8870 or 800/456-4000, www.countryinns.com, $83), also with a pool and whirlpool.

For something special try the 1880 **Classic Rosewood Inn** (620 Ramsey St., 651/437-3297, www.classicrosewoodinn.com, $117), one of the city's most beautiful historic homes, which has been renovated for all-out luxury. Your hosts have plenty of experience: They opened Minnesota's first bed-and-breakfast in 1982, the now-closed Thorwood Inn. Ask

PRAIRIE ISLAND RESERVATION

- Total Area: 1.9 sq. miles
- Tribally Owned: 100 percent
- Total Population: 199
- Native Population: 166
- Tribal Enrollment: 700

The small island home of the Prairie Island Mdewakanton Dakota sits on the Mississippi River 30 miles downriver from St. Paul. Like the rest of the state's Dakota, the Prairie Island band was expelled from Minnesota following the bloody Dakota Conflict. The Secretary of the Interior established the present reservation in 1889 for the Dakota who returned to their homes instead of staying in exile in South Dakota, and they continued to purchase land for the tribe through 1934, expanding their home to its present size. The reservation was officially recognized in 1936. Soon after this, the U.S. Army Corp of Engineers built Lock and Dam #3, burying about half of the tribe's low-laying island under the river and adding about half of the rest to the floodplain.

Their Treasure Island Casino, opened in 1984, is one of the state's most profitable, but the biggest issue for the tribe today is "The Nuke." In 1973 Northern States Power (NSP, now Xcel Energy) built the Prairie Island Nuclear Generating Plant less than half a mile from the community, an act the tribe calls the second invasion. Despite not having an adequate evacuation plan for this busy island (with casino guests there can be as many as 11,000 people on the island at a time, and the only road out is both vulnerable to floods and crossed by 20 to 25 trains a day), NSP was granted permission to store spent nuclear fuel on the island. Though the tribe has resisted the plant and its expansion from the start, they have had only minor victories in the courts and the legislature.

about packages including massages and tours of nearby wineries, as well as arranging a private dinner at the inn.

Food

Casual, but still white-tablecloth, the popular **Levee Café** (100 Sibley St., 651/437-7577, www.leveecafe.com, 11 A.M.–9 P.M. Mon.–Thurs., 11 A.M.–10 P.M. Fri., 8:30 A.M.–10 P.M. Sat., 8:30 A.M.–8 P.M. Sun., $6–27) has a wide-ranging menu of sandwiches, pasta, steak, and seafood. This is a popular place for weekend brunch.

The **Red Rock Café** (119 2nd St. E., 651/437-5002, 6 A.M.–2 P.M. Mon.–Fri., 7 A.M.–2 P.M. Sat., 8 A.M.–1 P.M. Sun., plus dinner 5–9 P.M. Wed.–Sat.) is a classic diner with a to-go espresso counter in the front. Breakfasts are fresh and filling—the eggs Benedict are lovely—and lunches and dinners are hearty meat-and-potatoes stuff.

Getting There

Visiting boaters can dock up and stock up at **Hastings Marina** (1111 1st St. E, 651/437-9621).

Go Carefree Shuttle (651/437-8877, www.gocarefreeshuttle.com, $35 one-way, reservations required) vans go to the Twin Cities from the AmericInn (2400 Vermillion St., 651/437-8877) twice a day.

Prairie Island

The Prairie Island Dakota's massive **Treasure Island Resort and Casino** (5734 Sturgeon Lake Rd., 800/222-7077, www.treasureislandcasino.com) has a Caribbean decor and one of the largest nonsmoking gaming spaces in the Midwest. If you are here in July you can join the **Prairie Island Dakota Wacipi** (powwow). The 125-passenger ***Spirit of the Water*** (Wed.–Sun. June–Oct., $29–37) cruise boat runs on the Mississippi River, and lunch, brunch, and dinner cruises are available. The casino's 250-room hotel features a swimming pool with a waterfall, a pair of hot tubs, fitness center, and rooms from $109. If you are driving your bedroom it can be parked in the large RV park. You can also come by boat since they have a large full-service marina. There are several restaurants on-site including the Las Vegas–worthy **Tradewinds Buffet** ($8 lunch, $13 dinner).

Turn down the road just before the casino, and you'll pass the Prairie Island Nuclear Generating Plant before coming to **Lock and Dam #3,** the busiest lock on the Upper Mississippi River. Over 11,000 recreational boats get an eight-foot lift each year, and you can watch them from the elevated viewing platform.

Welch

Well away from the Mississippi River, but just 2.5 miles south of Highway 61, quaint and quiet Welch is worth a detour even if you just drive down into the valley for a quick peek. The tiny bluff-ringed town on the Cannon River so resembles a New England village that it stood in as one in the film *Here on Earth.* Welch is at the midpoint of the **Cannon Valley Trail** (www.cannonvalleytrail.com), a 19.7-mile paved bike and cross-country ski path between Red Wing and Cannon Falls.

Just as beautiful as a ride on the trail is a trip on the river. **Welch Mill Canoeing & Tubing** (26389 County Road 7 Blvd., 651/388-9857 or 800/657-6760, www.welchmillcanoeandtube.com) will set you up for easy 5- or 12-mile canoe trips down the Cannon for $25 and $30 respectively. Tubing trips are just $10. Added to the recreation mix in winter is **Welch Village** (26685 County Road 7 Blvd., 651/258-4567, www.welchvillage.com) with 50 downhill ski and snowboard runs, the largest dropping 360 feet, plus a half-pipe and terrain park.

If you want to stay overnight, you can choose between the six slope-side bunkhouses (a two-day lift ticket plus one night lodging cost $66) or **Hidden Valley Campground** (27173 144th Ave. Way, 651/258-4550, www.hvcamping.com, $35 full hookup) just outside town along the Cannon Valley Trail.

The **Trout Scream Café** (14689 Welch Trl., 651/388-7494, 7:30 A.M.–2 P.M. Mon.–Sat., dinner 5–8 P.M. Fri.–Sat., $3–16) downtown is an unexpected place for an out-of-the ordinary meal (Reuben soup? Wonder why no one ever thought of that before), as well as inexpensive omelets, sandwiches, and ice cream by day, and pasta and steak by night.

RED WING

The answers are yes. Both Red Wing Pottery and Red Wing Shoes hail from this flower-filled river town, one of the prettiest on the whole of the Mississippi. Just an hour from St. Paul and Rochester, this vibrant city of 16,000 has a largely intact 19th-century downtown, a gift to all from previous city leaders who were ahead of their time in historic preservation. You can enjoy the results by just strolling through downtown and the residential neighborhood next to it.

History

A Dakota summer village stood at the base of Barn Bluff since at least 1805, the year Lieutenant Zebulon Pike came through to explore the new lands acquired by the United

The city of Red Wing clings tightly to the Mississippi River.

States in the Louisiana Purchase. Half a century later the city was named for the chief that Pike met, Whoo-pa-doo-to (Wing of Scarlet), whose descendents resided in town through the middle of the 20th century. The first European settlers were Swiss Protestant missionaries who established an outpost here in 1837. Though they left eight years later, Rev. John Aiton revived the mission in 1848, and an official post office was opened two years later. The town didn't really take off, however, until the U.S. Land Office opened here in 1855. Waves of settlers claiming property on the western prairies filtered through, and a busy trade center emerged to serve them. By the end of the decade the population exceeded 1,250.

Even with the Civil War raging to the south, the city thrived through the 1860s (the population more than tripled) with wheat leading the way, and soon Red Wing was the world's largest wheat port. As farmers shifted to other crops and the steamboats lost most of their business to the railroads its importance as a wheat market soon declined, but Red Wing never experienced the predictable economic bust because so many other industries had sprung up here. By the end of the century Red Wing had swapped superiorities by becoming one of the nation's largest flour-milling centers. The innovative La Grange Mill, one of dozens in and around Red Wing, ground its first wheat in 1877, and their Gilt Edge and Old Glory brands earned such acclaim that the company exported half of their output to Europe.

Pottery also rose to prominence in the 1870s. The area's first potter was German immigrant Joseph Pohl, who sold some of his creations to neighbors in 1861, though he only remained in the area for a couple of years. A few potters followed in his footsteps, but with very limited success. In 1878 the Red Wing Stoneware Company finally got the business model right, and five years later they were joined in the clay trade by the Minnesota Stoneware Company. Eventually the companies merged and operated under the Red Wing United Stoneware and Red Wing Potteries names until the company folded in 1967. Their early crocks, water coolers, and butter jars are the most famous and desirable products with collectors, but as populations shifted to the cities the company diversified into flower pots, dinnerware, and even sewer pipe—if you live in the Midwest there's a good chance that some still runs under your town. Today two small companies keep the Red Wing Pottery tradition alive.

The city's first shoe factory opened in 1861. Red Wing Shoes, just "The Shoe" to locals, sewed its first pair of boots in 1905, and within a decade production reached 200,000 pairs a year. Though they now annually manufacture millions of shoes in over 150 styles at three plants (one here plus one each in Missouri and Kentucky), it remains a family-owned enterprise.

Sights

The **Goodhue County History Center** (1166 Oak St., 651/388-6024, www.goodhuehistory.mus.mn.us, 10 A.M.–5 P.M. Tues.–Fri., 1–5 P.M. Sat.–Sun., $5 adults), perched high above the town, has a better-than-average local history collection on display. Highlights are the fossils and agates in the geology room, the ancient pottery and modern crafts in the Native American exhibit, and Red Wing Pottery.

There's an even larger pottery display at the **Red Wing Pottery Museum** (2000 Old West Main St., 651/388-4004, www.redwingpottery.com, 9 A.M.–5 P.M. Mon.–Fri., free admission) at historic **Pottery Place,** a former pottery factory that has been transformed into a beautiful shopping mall. The extensive collection, organized by the Red Wing Collectors Society, spans the earliest salt-glazed crocks to the expensive dinnerware made at the end of the company's history.

The story of the city's other famous industry is told at the **Red Wing Shoe Museum** (315 Main St., 800/733-9464, free admission), relocated and expanded in 2009. Displays show the history of the company and the whole shoemaking process, from cutting the hide to final inspection. Red Wing's pride and joy, a 16-foot-tall work boot, is finally home here, as well, after years in storage.

© TRICIA CORNELL

Boat trips on the Mississippi River depart from Levee Park in Red Wing.

Barn Bluff, looming nearly 350 feet over downtown, has always been a dominant landmark on the river, and its magnetic appeal has lured countless visitors to the top. Most famous was Henry David Thoreau, who climbed it during his 1861 journey to Minnesota. A set of steps leading up the backside makes the climb easier these days, though the steep route means you still have to earn the wonderful city and river views. (To find the stairs, follow 5th Street East as it passes under Highway 61, toward the river.) The extensively bolted bluff faces are a popular rock-climbing destination. You can follow Scenic Skyline Drive to the top of **Sorin's Bluff** for another scenic overlook of the city. The view isn't quite as good, but it comes with a lot less effort.

Each winter over 100 bald eagles winter in the Red Wing area, and they can be seen up close and personal at **Colvill Park,** where dozens perch in the cottonwood trees when not fishing in the Mississippi. Spotting scopes are set up during Eagle Watch Weekends in February and March. To get to Colvill Park, follow 7th Street East as it passes under Highway 61, toward the river.

Red Wing River Boat Rides (Levee Park, 651/388-3047, 2 P.M. and 4 P.M. daily May–Oct., $15, call ahead) offers an hour-long Mississippi River trip, poking into the backwaters when possible.

Botanist Alexander Anderson, inventor of the process behind "puffed" wheat and rice, built his country estate and laboratory five miles west of downtown. After he died his family donated the land and home to promote the arts, and today the **Anderson Center** (163 Tower View Dr., 651/388-2009, www.andersoncenter.org, 9 A.M.–4 P.M. Mon.–Thurs., 9 A.M.–noon Fri., free admission) offers classes and hosts artist retreats. You can stop by to see the art—the collection includes minor works by Calder, Matisse, Chagall, Dali, and more—climb the water tower, or stroll the 15-acre grounds and sculpture garden.

Narrated tours on the **Red Wing Trolley** (420 Levee St., 11 A.M.–4 P.M. May–Oct., www.redwingtrolley.com, $10) leave from Red Wing Depot and wind through town for 45 minutes.

Entertainment and Events

The immaculately restored 1904 **Sheldon Theatre** (443 3rd St. W., 651/388-8700 or 800/899-5759, www.sheldontheatre.org) has a busy year-round schedule of theatrical and musical performances.

Weekend acoustic acts play at **Blue Moon** (427 3rd St. W., 651/385-5799, 7:30 A.M.–8 P.M. Mon.–Fri., 8 A.M.–10 P.M. Sat., 8 A.M.–8 P.M. Sun.).

The city's biggest blowout is **River City Days,** the first weekend in August, with a parade, talent show, ice cream social, arts and crafts fair, and dragon boat races. There are several autumn arts events, including the **Studio Ramble** in late September.

Shopping

Shopping is a key component of the Red Wing experience, and many people make special trips for the pottery and antiques. Most shops are found in two main areas: Up along Old West Main Street in what's known as the Historic Pottery District, you'll find several outlet stores, and specialty shops downtown lean toward the refined.

Two companies continue the city's pottery heritage, and you can watch the products being made by hand at both of them. The revival began in 1987 at the **Red Wing Stoneware Company** (4909 Moundview Dr., 651/388-4610 or 800/352-4877, www.redwingstoneware.com, 9 A.M.–5 P.M. Mon.–Sat., 11 A.M.–4 P.M. Sun.), 4.5 miles west of town along U.S. Highway 61, which throws the classic crocks and jugs plus other customary and contemporary products. You can also take a **factory tour** (10:30 A.M., 1 P.M. and 3:30 P.M. Mon.–Fri., $3 adults).

Red Wing Pottery (1995 Old West Main St., 651/388-3562 or 800/228-0174, 9 A.M.–6 P.M. Mon.–Fri., 8 A.M.–6 P.M. Sat., 10 A.M.–5 P.M. Sun.) has produced salt-glazed wares since 1996.

Antiques lovers could easily browse for a day. The best place to start is at **Pottery Place** (2000 Old West Main St.) mall. Here you'll find **Pottery Place Antiques** (651/388-7765, 10 A.M.–6 P.M. Mon.–Sat., 11 A.M.–5 P.M. Sun.) and **Old Main Street Antiques** (651/388-1371, 10 A.M.–6 P.M. Mon.–Sat., 11 A.M.–5 P.M. Sun.), two superb multi-dealer showrooms with plenty of Red Wing Pottery merchandise.

© TRICIA CORNELL

Hobgoblin Music ships harps all over the world.

You can buy footwear direct from the source at the **Red Wing Shoe Store** (314 Main St., 651/388-6233, 9 A.M.–8 P.M. Mon.–Fri., 9 A.M.–6 P.M. Sat., 11 A.M.–5 P.M. Sun.).

Falconer Vineyards (3572 Old Tyler Rd., 651/388-8849, noon–5 P.M. Fri. and Sun., 10 A.M.–6 P.M. Sat. May–Thanksgiving, www.falconervineyards.com), in the hills just west of town (turn south on Tyler Road by the Econo Foods and follow the signs), is open weekends for sales and tastings.

Further west, **Hobgoblin Music** (920 Hwy. 19, 877/866-3936, 9 A.M.–5 P.M. daily) sells dulcimers, guitars, bagpipes, drums, flutes, and similar folk instruments from their restored barn, and you can watch harps being made.

Recreation

The paved **Cannon Valley Trail** follows the bluffs above the Cannon River for 20 miles from

Red Wing to Cannon Falls along a former railroad bed. A $3 Wheel Pass ($20 for the season), available from local merchants or at trailhead pay stations, is required for adult bike riders. **Wheelhouse Cycles** (1932 Old West Main St., 651/388-1082, www.wheelhousecycles.com, 10 A.M.–7 P.M. Mon.–Fri., 10 A.M.–5 P.M. Sat.–Sun.) rents bikes for $25/day, and they also have tandems and recumbents.

Hikers should head inland to the Hay Creek unit of the **Richard J. Dorer Memorial Hardwood State Forest** (651/345-3401), where 17 miles of rugged trail climb the steep valleys and follow the ridge tops. In winter about a third are groomed for cross-country skiing. The principal trailhead, which also has a quiet picnic area and good trout fishing nearby, is four miles south of town on Highway 58, and then 1.5 miles north on the gravel road by Dressen's.

Paddlers can run the lovely 25 miles of the Cannon River from the city of Cannon Falls back to Red Wing. With just a few Class I rapids, it's an easy run suitable for families. There are no rentals available in Red Wing, though you can arrange this and shuttle service from **Cannon Falls Canoe & Bike** (615 5th St. N., Cannon Falls, 507/263-4657 or 877/882-2663, www.cannonfallscanoeandbike.com) at the start of the run or in the village of Welch. Exploring the labyrinth of Mississippi River backwaters surrounding town can also be great fun.

Accommodations

Red Wing has several top-notch bed-and-breakfasts, each in antiques-filled, historic homes. A few miles outside of downtown Red Wing, you'll find the intimate **Round Barn Farm** (28650 Wildwood Ln., 651/385-9250, www.roundbarnfarm.com, $159–249), which calls itself a B&B&B—or bed & breakfast & bread—after the sourdough bread the proprietors bake in the wood-fired stone oven. Five double rooms with feather beds, massage tubs, and fireplaces make this a welcoming retreat, and with extensive hiking trails on the farm itself, you may never feel the need to explore much further.

The colorful **Moondance Inn** (1105 W. 4th St., 651/388-8145 or 866/388-8145, www.moondanceinn.com, $185) is an 1874 Italianate with a large front porch and museum-quality living room. Two of the five large guestrooms have views of Barn Bluff, where the stone for the house was quarried, and each has its own double whirlpool.

The **Pratt-Taber Inn** (706 4th St. W., 651/388-7392, www.pratttaber.com, $99–150) was quite a stunner in its day. The 1876 red-brick Italianate home with a wrap-around porch has intricate wood carvings and other details just not seen today. After years of neglect, the current owners have lushly restored the home and created four guest rooms—decorated with seasonal themes—with private baths.

The only hotel right downtown is the venerable **St. James Hotel** (406 Main St., 651/388-2846 or 800/252-1875, www.st-james-hotel.com, $129), which opened in 1875. It now oozes with European elegance and charm; there's even a pipe organ in the lobby. All 61 rooms are decorated with Amish quilts and antiques, and most have river or bluff views.

There are a number of chain hotels out on the highway. The nicest is the **Best Western Rivertown Inn and Suites** (Hwy. 61 & Withers Harbor Dr., 651/388-1577, $139), with indoor and outdoor pools, whirlpool suites, and specialized decor. Ask about ski packages at Welch Village.

For something a little different on longer trips, rent a houseboat from **Great River Houseboats** (1009 Main St. E., Wabasha, 651/565-3376, www.greatriverhouseboats.com). The family-owned company rents boats sleeping two to four people for a minimum of two nights ($600), or 10 people for the long weekend ($1,100–1,600) or the week ($1,700–2,400). The boats are fully equipped and—provided you're ready to pilot a 48-foot boat—can move up and down the river within a 70-mile range.

Food

The Port (651/388-2846, 5–9 P.M. Tues.–Sat., $16–40) at the St. James Hotel is the cream of the crop of Red Wing restaurants.

The seasonal menu features such choices as almond-encrusted walleye, gnocchi, and roasted duck with apple raisin wild rice stuffing. The decor is suitably elegant for the prices and reservations are recommended.

Also in the St. James, **The Veranda** (6:30 A.M.–9 P.M. Mon.–Sat., 7:30 A.M.–9 P.M. Sun., $8–13) overlooks the river and has an outdoor patio. Much more casual than The Port, it's still the second most formal restaurant in town.

The only Red Wing restaurant that gets mentioned in the same breath as the Port and Veranda is the **Staghead** (219 Bush St., 651/388-6581, 11 A.M.–9 P.M. Mon.–Sat. year-round, plus 11 A.M.–7 P.M. Sun. summer, $11–30). The steak, seafood, and pasta menu is served in an unpretentious, but beautifully restored, 1884 setting. They also have an excellent beer and wine list.

A relative newcomer on the scene, **The Norton's Restaurant** (307 Main St., 651/388-2711, www.thenortonsrestaurant.com, $12–26) is likely to give the old stand-bys a real run for their money, with a more modern take on fine dining. There's chicken, salmon, and steaks, of course, but with them you'll get Indian, Southern, and other daring flavors. (A bit of trivia: Greg Norton, co-owner with his wife, Sarah, played bass in the 1980s band Hüsker Dü.)

A more casual—and thoroughly modern—meal is available at **Lily's Coffee House** (419 W. 3rd St., 651/388-8797, www.lilyscoffeehouse.com, 7 A.M.–5:30 P.M. Mon.–Fri., 7 A.M.–4:30 P.M. Sat., closed Sun.). Generous, classic sandwiches and updated wraps can be had for under $7.

Near Pottery Place, **Smokey Row Café and Jenny Lind Bakery** (1926 Old West Main St., 651/388-6025, www.jennylindbakery.com, $5–8) makes all their breads in house, from baguettes to cracked wheat carrot bread, and then uses them to make sophisticated sandwiches, served alongside homemade soups.

Information

The helpful **Red Wing Visitor Center** (420 Levee St., 651/385-5934 or 800/498-3444, www.redwing.org, 8 A.M.–5 P.M. Mon.–Wed., 8 A.M.–7 P.M. Thurs.–Fri., 10 A.M.–4 P.M. Sat., 11 A.M.–4 P.M. Sun. June–Oct., 8 A.M.–5 P.M. Mon.–Fri. rest of year) is in the city's historic train depot.

Getting There and Around

The train is a great way to visit Red Wing from the Twin Cities. **Amtrak** (800/872-7245, www.amtrak.com) arrives at the city's historic depot from St. Paul at 7:50 A.M., while the westbound service comes through at 8:52 P.M. A walk-up single ticket costs $10–14.

Go Carefree Shuttle (608/781-5181, www.gocarefreeshuttle.com, $35 one-way, reservations required) vans go to the Twin Cities from the AmericInn (1819 Old West Main St.) twice a day.

If you are arriving by boat there is short-term dockage downtown at Levee Park. For additional boating services, **Bill's Bay Marina** (651/388-0481, www.billsbaymarina.com), **Ole Miss Marina** (651/388-5839, www.olemissmarina.com), and **Red Wing Marina** (651/388-8995, www.redwingmarina.com) can meet your needs.

FRONTENAC STATE PARK

The 2,803 acres of Frontenac State Park (29223 County 28 Blvd., 651/345-3401) stretch along four miles of Lake Pepin, a gorgeous 28-mile-long widening of the Mississippi River. Most facilities, including a picnic ground with great Mississippi views on Point-No-Point, are perched atop a forested 430-foot bluff. Moving inland down the back of the bluff you'll find a diverse ecosystem of prairie, oak savanna, floodplain forest, and a small lake. The varied habitats make for great bird-watching, and some 261 species reside here. Most noteworthy are the many species of migrating warbler that pass through in early May, while the prothonotary and Cerulean warblers, rare in Minnesota, nest in the bottomland forests.

Frontenac has nearly 13 miles of hiking trails. The most popular is the short and easy **Bluffview Trail,** an interpretive path that offers both forest and grassland scenery. Heading for 1.5 miles atop the 430-foot ridge in the opposite direction and returning down along the river is the more rewarding **Bluffside Trail.** At the far end of the trail, behind the campground, is **In-Yan-Teopa,** a giant rock with a hole carved through its heart by glacial meltwaters. There is an overlook with a historical marker above the stone, but to see the hole you must walk down the trail. Beginning at the parking area along U.S. Highway 61, the 0.75-mile **Sand Point Trail** cuts through wetlands on a long boardwalk and leads out to Lake Pepin, where you can stroll the beach. This is the most noteworthy spot in the park for bird-watchers, and interpretive signs along the way discuss the history and ecology of the area. The other trail starting here is a short and easy unnamed walk that loops past some small Native American burial mounds. In the winter the park maintains a steep sledding hill and grooms 5.7 miles of cross-country ski trails, which, unfortunately, intersect with snowmobile trails at several points.

The 58 shady sites in the **campground** (www.stayatmnparks.com for reservations) are spaced close together, but all have trees between them. The 19 electric sites are in the first two loops, so if you are tenting, reserve a site in the back two. Better yet, take one of the six cart-in campsites, which are less than half a mile down a trail.

LAKE CITY

Stretched out along the length of Lake Pepin, Lake City gives itself over to water-loving tourists all summer long and then retreats into a quiet winter.

Sights and Recreation

On June 28, 1922, 18-year-old Ralph Samuelson strapped two eight-foot pine boards to his feet, grabbed hold of an old clothesline, and let an airplane pull him across the Mississippi River just offshore of Lake City: On that day, water-skiing was born. Replicas of his skis (he broke the originals while skiing) are on display at the **Lake City Area Chamber of Commerce** (101 Center St. W., 651/345-4123 or 877/525-3248, www.lakecitymn.org, 9 A.M.–5 P.M. Mon.–Fri., closed Sat.–Sun.).

Lake Pepin, as this 28-mile widening of the Mississippi River is known, is the Upper Mississippi's top spot for sailing, water-skiing, and boating, and with 625 slips, the city-owned **Lake City Marina** (201 S. Franklin St., 651/345-4211) is the largest marina on the Upper Mississippi.

If you don't have your own boat you can rent one from **Hansen's Harbor** (35853 Hwy. 61 Blvd., 651/345-3022, boats start around $300 a day plus tax and fuel) or take a ride on the replica paddlewheeler ***Pearl of the Lake*** (651/345-5188, www.pearlofthelake.com, 1 P.M. Wed.–Sun. public excursions, $15).

The Hale Irwin–designed **Jewel Golf Club** (1900 Clubhouse Dr., 800/738-7714, $40 off-season 18 holes, $70 in season 18 holes) is the tops of the city's golf course trio and also brings in many tourists.

Great River Vineyard (35680 Hwy. 61, 877/345-3531, www.greatrivervineyard.com, open Aug.–Oct., call before coming), three miles north of town, has seven acres of trellises, but instead of fermenting their grapes they produce juice, jelly, and jam. You can also pick your own grapes. There are also a couple of apple orchards selling directly to the public (Aug.–Nov.) along the highway near town.

Accommodations

The family-friendly **Sunset Motel** (1515 Lakeshore Dr. N., 651/345-5331 or 800/945-0192, $55) has an outdoor heated pool, game room, and fish-cleaning house, and they'll even pick you up at the marina.

The guest rooms at the **Red Gables Inn** (403 High St. N., 651/345-2605 or 888/345-2605, www.redgablesinn.com, $99–150) are all named for old Mississippi paddlewheelers. Now a bed and breakfast, the Victorian home was built in 1865 just off the main highway. The comfortable porch is unbeatable.

From the road, it looks like a rundown fishing village—because that's what it once was—but now **Camp Lacupolis** (71000 Hwy. 61, 651/565-

4318 summer, 507/324-5216 winter, www.camplacupolis.com, $109–120), at the southern end of Lake City, is a vacation spot with unexpected charm. The dozen cabins are all mismatched and lined up along the water. They come fully equipped, and some are even air conditioned. There is limited space for RV parking, as well. It is particularly popular with anglers.

Hok-Si-La Municipal Park and Campground (2500 Hwy. 61 N., 651/345-3855, www.ci.lake-city.mn.us, $15) has 41 tent camping sites, a few of them secluded enough to feel private. It's a short walk to the beach and hiking trails.

Food

The relaxing **Rhythm & Brew Coffeehouse** (220 Chestnut St. E., 651/345-5335, 7 A.M.–2 P.M. Mon.–Sat., 8 A.M.–2 P.M. Sun., $2–7) has a small menu of soups and sandwiches. Musicians sometimes take the stage on Sunday; otherwise, you can take a seat at the piano.

The local choice for home-cooking away from home is **The Galley** (100 Lyon Ave. E., 651/345-9991, 6 A.M.–8 P.M. daily, $3–11), a no-frills joint with a typical all-American roster of steak, seafood, and sandwiches. They also serve a Friday fish fry and a Sunday breakfast buffet.

For something a little fancier, there's **Nosh** (310 Washington St. S., 651/345-2425, www.noshrestaurant.com, 5–9 P.M. daily except closed Tues., $16–25), with upscale treats like handmade pasta, local lamb chops, and paella.

Getting There

Go Carefree Shuttle (608/781-5181, www.gocarefreeshuttle.com, $35 one-way, reservations required) vans go to the Twin Cities from the AmericInn (1615 N. Lakeshore Dr.) twice a day.

WABASHA

Wabasha is Minnesota's most timeless river town; replace the cars on Main Street with horses and buggies, and you'd have a scene almost straight out of the last act of the 19th century. Only about 15 buildings in the seven-block historic district were erected after 1900, and the Wabasha Bridge hanging behind it adds a scenic flourish.

In 1826 fur trader Augustine Rocque, whose father was French and mother Dakota, built a trading post here, and since the site has been continuously occupied since that day, Wabasha claims to be Minnesota's oldest city. It acquired the name Cratte's Landing in 1838 after Oliver Cratte built a home and blacksmith shop here, but five years later the growing settlement was renamed in honor of the respected Dakota chief Wa-pa-shaw, who held sway over the area at that time. The town thrived as a lumbering, milling, and boatbuilding center between 1850 and 1880 and at that time was one of the largest wheat markets along the river. As the railroads usurped its importance as a shipping center the town stagnated, and for most of the 20th century the beautiful downtown was pretty much left alone.

The town's current claim to fame comes as the home of Jack Lemmon and Walter Matthau in the *Grumpy Old Men* movies, though they were filmed almost entirely elsewhere in the state: Faribault for the downtown and St. Paul for the neighborhood. The only Wabasha location is the St. Felix Church shown for a few seconds during the opening credits in the original. Screenwriter Mark Steven Johnson grew up nearby in Hastings, and his grandfather—Old Man Gilbert—lived in Wabasha. Though the movies are fictional, many of the characters and incidents are based on real people and events.

Eagle Watching

Each winter the Mississippi River around Wabasha is home to one of the largest concentrations of bald eagles in the Lower 48. They come south to Wabasha because the rapid current keeps the river open year-round, allowing them to fish. The early birds show up around the beginning of November, though the best viewing, when over 200 can be seen on most days, doesn't begin until December. Most stick around through March. Just before they leave, a sharp peak occurs (the record daily count is over 700) as other eagles that went further

© TRICIA CORNELL

Eagles and other raptors congregate under this bridge in Wabasha, south of Red Wing.

south stop here on their trip back home. While sightings are all but guaranteed in the winter, they aren't exactly rare the rest of the year, since 40 pair nest in the area. You can learn about the national bird at the **National Eagle Center** (50 Pembroke Ave., 651/565-4989 or 877/332-4537, www.nationaleaglecenter.org, 10 A.M.–5 P.M. daily, open 1 hour later weekends Mar.–Nov., $6), which has educational displays, knowledgeable staff, and four resident eagles that cannot be released back into the wild because of injury. Spotting scopes are set up on the deck overlooking the river.

You can also get some up-close looks from several pullouts along the highway just to the north of Wabasha between Reads Landing and Camp Lacupolis. The best viewing times are morning and early evening when they dive into the river for fish; during the middle of the day they can be seen perched in trees.

Other Sights and Recreation

Two museums sit about two miles outside of town. To the north, in the hamlet of Reads Landing, is the **Wabasha County Historical Museum** (70537 206th Ave., 651/565-0357, www.wabashacountyhistory.org, 1–4 P.M. Sat.–Sun., mid-May–mid-Oct., free admission), which occupies a musty 1870 schoolhouse, the second brick school built in Minnesota. The most interesting parts of the historical hodgepodge are the pearl-button display (this was once a very lucrative industry all along the river) and the copies of letters sent by Pa and Laura Ingalls to family across the river in Pepin, Wisconsin, the town where Laura was born. There is farm machinery in the back annex.

To the south along Highway 60 is the far more interesting **Arrowhead Bluffs Museum** (17505 667th St., 651/565-3829, 10 A.M.–5 P.M. daily May–Nov., $5 adults), an eclectic private collection of old farming and logging tools, arrowheads, bottles, and one of every Winchester gun model (including commemoratives) from 1866 to 1982. Mounted wildlife from across North America includes moose, polar bear, javelinas, and scorpions.

Believe it or not, the world's largest collection of wedding kimonos—more than 4,000—are for sale in Wabasha at **Wind Whisper West**

UPPER MISSISSIPPI RIVER NATIONAL WILDLIFE AND FISH REFUGE

Established in 1924 to protect smallmouth bass spawning grounds, the Upper Mississippi River National Wildlife and Fish Refuge follows the river for 261 miles from just above Wabasha, Minnesota, south to Rock Island, Illinois. Along the way it encompasses nearly 240,000 acres of river, islands, forest, marshes, sloughs, backwater lakes, sandbars, and scattered prairie remnants – almost all of it in the floodplain. It is the longest wildlife refuge in the Lower 48. The refuge headquarters in Winona (51 E. 4th St., 507/452-4232 or 888/291-5719) has maps and brochures and can answer just about any question you might have.

WILDLIFE

The refuge is home to 57 species of mammals including white-tailed deer, coyote, fox, otter, and beaver; the endangered Blanding's and wood turtles and 51 other reptile and amphibian species; and 118 kinds of fish ranging from minnows to sturgeon.

Birds have been the biggest winners in the U.S. Fish and Wildlife Service's conservation efforts. Over 300 species have been recorded here and the river is one of the continent's principal migration corridors. Geese and ducks are especially abundant. Each fall up to 75 percent of the North American population of canvasback ducks may be seen on Mississippi River Pools 7 and 8 around La Crosse, Wisconsin. Up to 12,000 tundra swans can be seen in late October and early November around Weaver Bottoms. Bald eagles are year-round residents – nearly 100 pair nest in the refuge – though they are most impressive in winter when they congregate below dams and at the mouths of tributaries, where the water doesn't freeze over. The Wabasha and Red Wing areas are the top winter viewing spot on the Minnesota side. Heron and egret rookeries, often hundreds of nests strong, are found in the more remote areas. Other birds commonly found in the refuge are sandhill crane, turkey vulture, pheasant, wild turkey, Eastern bluebird, yellow warbler, and an increasing number of American white pelicans. Endangered and threatened species residing here include osprey, peregrine falcon, red-shouldered hawk, great egret, and yellow-crowned night heron.

PADDLING

Lazy canoeing is fantastic in the quiet backwaters where countless side channels and sloughs wind through hundreds of wooded islands. In the summer, acres of water lilies and other flowering water plants are in bloom. In addition to the up close and personal look at the river's rich flora and fauna, the backwaters offer adventure and solitude; you can explore at will, enjoy getting lost, and for the most part motorboats can't make it back here. The braided backwater labyrinths are most abundant in the upper sections of each pool where the construction of the locks and dams has had less effect on the river. Because of heavy boat and barge traffic, the main river channel is not a good place to canoe; even just crossing it can be difficult. The largest barges need a mile to stop and they cannot steer out of your way!

Boaters of all kinds can camp on refuge islands for up to 14 days at a single site. During waterfowl hunting season (generally late September to mid-November in Minnesota), camping is only allowed outside closed areas and on sites visible from the main channel. Downed wood may be used for campfires, though cutting of any tree is, of course, prohibited.

(128 Main St., 651/565-2002, www.windwhisperwest.com, 10 A.M.–4 P.M. Mon.–Fri., noon–4 P.M. Sat.–Sun.). Now that most Japanese women wear western-style dresses, these *uchikake* are collected as art. Richard Fuller, who opened the store when his hobby got out of hand, can tell you everything you want to know about these vibrant gowns.

Coffee Mill Bluff (99 Coulee Way, 651/565-2777, www.coffeemillski.com) ski area has 11 runs, the longest dropping 425 feet, making it the tallest in southern Minnesota.

Entertainment and Events

Wabasha's biggest bash is the **Riverboat Days Festival** held the last weekend in July. Highlights include a classic car show, dog Frisbee, and a craft and antiques fair. Come February it's time for the **Grumpy Old Men Festival,** with motorcycle racing on ice, softball in the snow, and a look-alike contest. Friday-night **Meet Me Under the Bridge Concerts** take place all summer long.

Accommodations

The rooms at **Coffee Mill Motel and Suites** (50 Coulee Way, 651/565-4561, www.coffeemillmotelandsuites.com, $59–149) are an excellent value for the money, with more charm than a basic chain hotel. "Chalet rooms" have vaulted ceilings under the eaves, and some have whirlpools.

The **Bridgewaters Bed and Breakfast** (136 Bridge Ave., 651/565-4208, www.bridgewatersbandb.com, $130–185) has six guest rooms—some share a bath—in a lovely 1903 Queen Anne Victorian. The location couldn't be better: right off the main street, near the river and the Eagle Center.

The cheapest rooms in town are at the small **Wabasha Motel** (1110 Hiawatha Dr. E., 651/565-9932 or 866/565-9932, $59). There are also seven RV campsites here ($32 full hookup).

The **Kruger Campground** (Richard J. Dorer Memorial Hardwood State Forest, 651/345-3401, $12), five miles west of town along Highway 60, is a peaceful primitive campground with 19 shady and widely spaced sites. Nine miles of hiking trails, including a 0.75-mile wheelchair-accessible path, lead through the forested bluffs.

Food

Your fanciest choice in Wabasha is **Vinifera** (260 Main St. W., 651/565-4171, www.viniferarestaurant.com, $10–18), a wine store, wine bar, and fine restaurant. The menu is brief, but varied, and changes seasonally. You might find a hearty Argentine-inspired beef plate or lighter seared scallops. Definitely get a seat on the patio to watch the river float by.

Though not the actual bar from the *Grumpy Old Men* movies, **Slippery's** (10 Church Ave., 651/565-4748, 10 A.M.–10 P.M. Mon.–Sat., 8 A.M.–10 P.M. Sun., $6–16) did lend them its name. The casual boat-in restaurant has an outside deck, while interior decoration includes several set pieces from the movies. The menu has Putz burgers, Catfish Hunter sandwiches, Italian dishes, and they also do a popular Friday-night fish fry.

Information

The **Wabasha-Kellogg Convention and Visitors Bureau** (160 Main St. W., 651/565-4158 or 800/565-4158, www.wabashamn.org, 8 A.M.–5 P.M. Mon.–Fri., 9 A.M.–3 P.M. Sat.) has tons of area information.

Getting There

Go Carefree Shuttle (608/781-5181, www.allwayscharter.com, $39 one-way, reservations required) vans go to the Twin Cities from the AmericInn (150 Commerce Dr.) daily. If you are arriving via the Mississippi, there is a courtesy dock right behind downtown, while the full-service **Wabasha Marina Boatyard** (1009 Main St. E., 651/565-4747, www.wabashamarinamn.com) and **Parkside Marina** (829 3rd St. W., 651/565-3809, www.parksidemarina.com) can take care of any other boating needs.

KELLOGG

LARK Toys

The last thing you would expect to find in little Kellogg, population 439, is one of the world's greatest toy stores, but there it is. LARK (63604 170th Ave., 507/767-3387, www.larktoys.com, 9:30 A.M.–5:30 P.M. Mon.–Fri., 10 A.M.–5 P.M. Sat.–Sun. Mar.–Dec., 9 A.M.–5 P.M. Fri., 10 A.M.–5 P.M. Sat.–Sun. Jan.–Feb.) stands for Lost Arts Revival by Kreofsky, and the family-run enterprise, which now attracts hundreds of thousands of visitors annually, began in 1983 when Donn and Sarah Kreofsky began making wooden toys in their garage. Word spread and soon they were stocking FAO Schwarz and 2,500 other retailers. Burned out by the big-business side of things, they decided to open their own toy store. Now the largest independent toy store in North America sells everything from board games to chemistry sets to Russian nesting dolls to wind-up toys, plus, of course, the handmade wooden toys that started it all. The whimsical **LARK Carousel** ($1) takes riders for a spin on 18 hand-carved creatures, like a goldfish and an otter. The thousands of antique toys on display throughout the store will no doubt bring back memories. Also on-site is a restaurant and miniature golf course.

WEAVER BOTTOMS

One of Minnesota's most impressive migrations begins in mid-October when tundra swans swoop down from above the Arctic Circle and take a month-long break on the Mississippi before continuing to their East Coast wintering grounds. In good years this shallow backwater area, stretching four miles between the hamlets of Weaver and Minneiska, has seen as many as 12,000 swans in a single day: The peak always comes within a few days of November 10. The best viewing spot is at the top of the hill next to St. Mary's Cemetery, 1.75 miles south of Weaver—look for the bald eagle nest here. Another good spot is the observation deck at Weaver Landing. Occasionally you might also spot them from downtown Minneiska. Because of the heavy traffic, stopping along U.S. Highway 61 to take a look is a bad idea. The best swan-watching is actually across the river in Alma, Wisconsin (www.almaswanwatch.org), where volunteers are available daily to answer questions.

Drive along County Highway 84 (which joins U.S. 61 about 1.5 miles north of Weaver), and you'll pass 1,000 acres of rolling sand dunes, some as high as 30 feet. Most are protected as the **Kellogg-Weaver Dunes Scientific and Natural Area** on land owned and managed by The Nature Conservancy (800/628-6860, www.nature.org).

JOHN A. LATSCH STATE PARK

Twelve miles before Winona a trio of 500-foot-tall bluffs—Faith, Hope, and Charity—are perched high above the Mississippi in this seldom-visited state park. The aptly named **Riverview Trail,** a lung-chugging half-mile set of steps, climbs 450 feet through the forest and past a prairie remnant to the top of Charity Bluff, the tallest of the three. The views, of course, are superb. The only camping is at seven walk-in sites. Call 507/643-6849 with any questions or go to www.stayatmnparks.com for reservations.

The park is named in honor of a Winona businessman and avid Mississippi River angler who, around the turn of the 20th century, was chased off a farmer's land when he attempted to take shelter from a storm. In order to prevent similar affronts from occurring to anyone else ever again, he spent two million dollars to purchase over 18,000 riverside acres and then gave it away for use as parks and wildlife habitat. His campaign later inspired the creation of the Izaak Walton League, whose first act was to promote the creation of the Upper Mississippi River Wildlife and Fish Refuge.

Directly across from the park is **Lock and Dam #5,** where you can watch boats get a nine-foot lift.

WHITEWATER STATE PARK

The large Whitewater River Valley, filled with spring-fed streams and tall limestone bluffs, cuts through the heart of southeast Minnesota before merging with the Mississippi near Weaver. The name, bestowed by the Dakota, speaks not of frothy rapids but rather its milky springtime color, caused by clay deposits accumulating during high water. When European settlers moved into the valley to farm, they cleared the steep hills, and, by the turn of the 20th century, as a direct result of their actions, severe flooding began. By the 1930s the floods had become epidemic—the village of Beaver flooded 28 times in 1938 alone—and frustrated people abandoned their homes. The DNR purchased the most erosion-prone lands and taught remaining farmers to change their land-use practices. Today, the 28,000-acre Whitewater Wildlife Management Area covers nearly half the valley, and the restoration efforts have made this something of a natural paradise. The popular 2,700-acre park lies adjacent to the WMA, but was established for its beauty decades before the state stepped in to stop the floods.

The valley is a great bird-watching destination, and the 237 recorded species include Cerulean warbler, Louisiana waterthrush, Acadian flycatcher, and other species at the far northwest extent of their ranges. Whitewater is also one of the best places in the state to enjoy spring wildflowers. For more information about the natural and human history of the valley, stop by the park's **Whitewater Valley Visitor Center** (507/932-3007, 9 A.M.–9 P.M. summer, 9 A.M.–4 P.M. rest of year), at the north end of the park near the entrance off Highway 74. The most popular of the many naturalist programs held here discusses rattlesnakes and includes a chance to see a live one.

Recreation

There are two kinds of hiking trails at Whitewater: steep and flat. The best representative of the latter is the mile-long **Trout Run Creek Trail,** a self-guided interpretive path that cuts back and forth across its namesake creek. The 2.7-mile **Coyote Point Trail** and 4.2-mile **Dakota Trail** climb the 250-foot bluffs on the west side of the park, leading to some wonderful vistas, particularly Eagle Point and Signal Point along the latter trail. The 0.75-mile **Chimney Rock Trail** is the easiest and, thus, most popular, bluff-top climb. Steps on the steepest parts of all three trails ease the climbs considerably. In the winter the level trails are groomed for cross-country skiing, while snowshoe rentals let you explore the rest of the park. The most popular spot in the park on hot summer days is the wide, sandy beach.

The Whitewater River and some of its tributaries are some of the state's top trout runs, with ample browns, brooks, and rainbows, and there's a winter catch-and-release season on a portion of the river. The river can be canoed down to the Mississippi River, though low water levels and frequent snags make it a tough journey. If you want to go anyway, start the 17-mile trip in the village of Elba, the last town in the valley. Despite the name the river has no natural rapids, though there are some riffles around bridges.

Camping

Whitewater has a pair of campgrounds and, in an exception to the general rule, the larger one is the better of the two (make reservations at www.stayatmnparks.com). The 75 sites (47 electric) in the **Cedar Hill Campground** are mostly shady and widely spaced, while most of the 31 sites across the river at **Gooseberry Glen** are crowded closely together. The park also has four walk-in sites and a camper cabin with electricity is available April–October.

Elsewhere in the Valley

Several unique natural and historic attractions are found near the park. A map, available at the park office, details these and many others, and park naturalists often lead tours to these satellite sites. The **Elba Fire Tower** is perched atop a bluff three miles northeast of the park. Some 600 steps lead up to the tower, which you can climb (during daylight hours between Apr. and Oct.) for spectacular views of the valley's farms and forests. You can hunt for (and almost certainly find) **fossils** to the west of the park along County Highway 9, about seven miles from Highway 74; the site is between the river and the church. Scan the sedimentary rock that was cut away for the road, and you'll find the calcified remains of ancient plants and animals that lived here hundreds of millions of years ago, back when this land was buried under the ocean. Most common are clam-like brachiopods, snails, moss animals (bryozoans), and sea lilies. The **Crystal Springs Hatchery** (14674 County Rd. 112, Altura, 507/796-6691, 7 A.M.–3:30 P.M. Mon.–Fri., free admission) rears about 400,000 brook, rainbow, lake, and splake trout annually.

WINONA

The largest of Minnesota's river towns below St. Paul was founded as Montezuma in 1851 by Orrin Smith, captain of the steamboat *Nominee,* who needed a location between Galena and St. Paul to load fuel wood. Within two years it had grown into a town of 300 and was renamed Winona ("firstborn daughter" in the Dakota language). Not only did steamboats resupply themselves here, but when the local land office opened, settlers heading west poured in to secure farms and purchase provisions for a new life on the prairie. By the end of the decade nearly a dozen sawmills were turning, and the town thrived. Flour mills also went up in the 1850s, and the settlers who had previously passed through town continued to enrich it by shipping their harvest back from as far west as South Dakota, first by oxcart and then, in 1862, along the Winona and St. Peter Railroad. Ironically, by the 1880s this treeless, barren plain had become one of Minnesota's greatest lumber towns and the fourth-largest grain market in the country, reportedly producing more millionaires than any other similarly sized city in the nation.

By the late 19th century, cities to the west had appropriated much of the flour business, and around the turn of the 20th century the surrounding forests had largely been cleared. As the old industries died out new ones, such as brick-making, dairying, meatpacking, sauerkraut-making (at one time Winona produced more than any place west of Chicago), and quarrying, arose to keep the city prosperous. **Sugar Loaf Mountain,** visible from across the city and well beyond, is a 500-foot-tall monument to the latter industry. The 85-foot pinnacle at the top appears natural, but is, in fact, the remains of an 1880s quarry. If you want to climb it, a well-worn trail leads up the south side of the peak from the redbrick building (West Burns Valley Rd.) serving the city's water reservoirs. Today, despite a population of over 27,000, it is a fairly sleepy town most of the time.

Sights

HISTORY

The **Winona County Historical Museum** (160 Johnson St., 507/454-2723, www.winonahistory.org, 9 A.M.–5 P.M. Mon.–Fri., noon–4 P.M. Sat.–Sun., weekdays only Jan.–Feb., $5 adults) is one of the state's most interesting local history museums. Most impressive are the lumber mill diorama and the balcony-level timeline beginning during the Ice Age and ending in the 1960s. Children can explore replicas of a cave, tepee, and steamboat pilothouse. In 2009 the museum broke ground on an addition that nearly doubled their space for exhibits and educational programs.

The historical society also maintains two sites outside of downtown. The **Bunnell House** (10 A.M.–5 P.M. Wed.–Sat., 1–5 P.M. Sun. summer, $5 adults) is five miles south of town, just off Highway 61 in the hamlet of Homer. Willard Bunnell, a trader who supplied lumber to passing steamboats, was Winona County's first permanent white settler. He built this Rural Gothic wood-frame house in the early 1850s, making it one of the oldest surviving houses in the state. From the outside it looks like a movie-set haunted house, and inside it is furnished as it might have been in the mid-1800s.

Nine miles west on Hwy. 14, between Stockton and Lewiston, is the **Arches Museum of Pioneer Life** (507/523-2111, www.winonahistory.org, 1–5 P.M. Wed.–Sun. June–Aug., free admission). Folk artist Walter Rahn created working models of farm machinery and displayed them here for years in his private roadside museum. You'll also find a one-room schoolhouse, log home, and a few pieces of farm equipment, as well as a lovely picnic spot.

During the last half of the 19th century, several thousand Polish immigrants settled in Winona's east end, and today the city has the

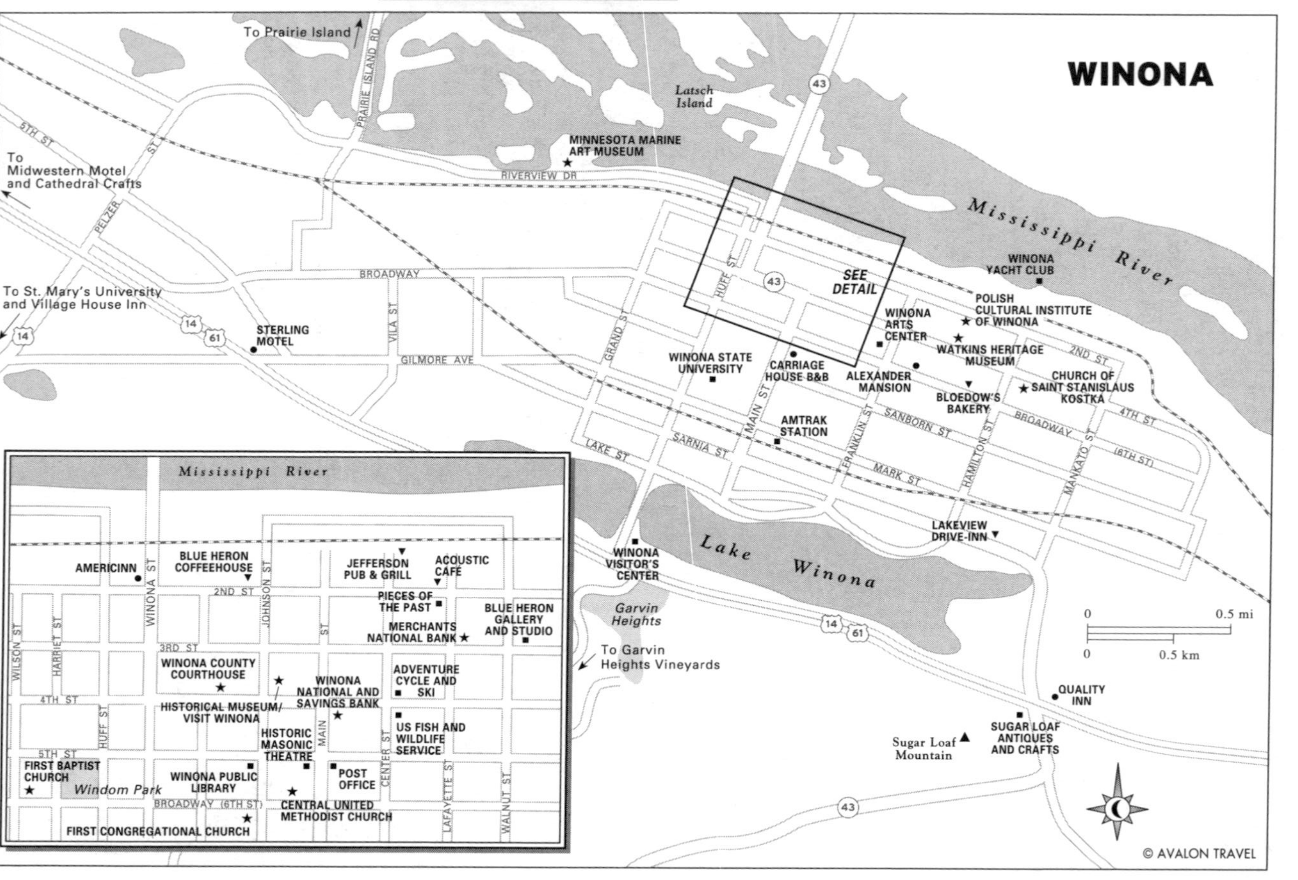

BLUFF COUNTRY

THE MODERN MISSISSIPPI

Before the 1840s steamboats had a hard time navigating the Upper Mississippi River because of the abundance of sandbars, low water, and snags. In 1845 wheat interests formed the Mississippi River Improvement Company to aid navigation by removing wrecks and snags. The U.S. Army Corps of Engineers dredged a four-and-a-half-foot-deep shipping channel in 1878 and over time it was expanded, but despite these efforts, cargo continued to shift to the more reliable railroads. By 1918 river transport was virtually dead. Business leaders, concerned about a lack of competition, pushed Congress for action to restore commerce on the river, and they authorized a nine-foot channel maintained by a series of locks and dams. Construction on what was then one of the world's largest public works projects began in 1931. Today 29 locks and dams, the last completed in 1964, move 90 million tons of cargo, principally wheat, logs, oil, and fertilizer, up the river between St. Louis and Minneapolis. A typical 15-barge tow stretches a quarter mile and carries the equivalent of 990 semi-trucks or 225 train cars.

The 670-mile aquatic stairway brought commerce back, but it also changed the river forever. Originally the Mississippi had several winding channels with many rapids and shifting sand bars, but the series of pools created by the dams made it more like a lake habitat than that of a river. The current was slowed by both the main dams and the smaller wing dams (underwater rock piles) that help maintain the channel. The excessive sedimentation that has resulted has become a serious threat to the river, and many fish populations are in serious decline. Critics also claim that the barges' wakes erode the shoreline.

Although it's unlikely to happen in our lifetimes, many would like to remove the dams and let the real river return. This would spell the end of commercial river transport, but shipping by rail is cheaper anyway since maintaining commerce on the river costs hundreds of millions of federal dollars annually. The Corps, which is addicted to enormous projects and hates to take no for an answer, has other plans: For many years they have pushed a one-billion-dollar lock expansion plan. When their own lead economist determined that the benefits couldn't even come close to justifying the costs, Corps leaders removed him from the study. A resulting investigation showed that top brass at the Corps – who had met behind closed doors with barge interests, including ConAgra, Cargill, and American Commercial Barge Lines – cooked the books to justify the program. Some of the evidence uncovered in a resulting investigation included internal emails and memos with phrases such as "He directs that we develop evidence or data to support a defensible set of capacity enhancement projects" and "The push to grow the program is coming from the top down." Independent analysis has backed up the original conclusions, but the Corps continues to study the project. This is just one of many controversial projects that make the Corps one of the most reviled federal agencies by both environmentalists and taxpayer advocates.

nation's largest concentration of Poles from the Kashubian region. The little **Polish Cultural Institute of Winona** (102 Liberty St., 507/454-3431, 10 A.M.–3 P.M. Mon.–Sat. May–Oct., limited hours rest of year, $2 adults) makes an effort to both tell and preserve their history.

One block over on East 3rd Street is the **Watkins Heritage Museum** (150 Liberty St., entrance on 3rd St., 507/457-6095, 10 A.M.–4 P.M. Mon.–Fri., 10 A.M.–2 P.M. Sat., free admission). Displays cover the entire history of the company, from the days of peddling Dr. Ward's Vegetable Anodyne Liniment, "good for man or beast," via horse-drawn wagon in 1868 to its current line of nearly 400 products sold by 80,000 North American salespeople. Though primarily just a collection of old bottles, boxes, and tins, it is far more interesting than you would expect.

Though many historic buildings have been lost over the years, downtown Winona is still the most architecturally interesting city

© TRICIA CORNELL

Watkins was the first company to sell door to door, with salesmen peddling liniments and spices in wagons like this one at the company headquarters, adjacent to the Watkins Heritage Museum.

between St. Paul and Galena, and over 100 structures are listed on the National Register of Historic Places. The ***Explore Historic Downtown Winona*** map, available at the visitors center and Historical Museum, details about two dozen of them, most dating from the last half of the 19th century. They also offer a driving tour ($4) on cassette.

The banks designed by prominent Prairie School architects are the most noteworthy edifices. The 1912 **Merchants National Bank** (102 3rd St. E., 507/457-1100, 9 A.M.–4 P.M. Mon.–Thurs., 9 A.M.–5 P.M. Fri.), designed by William Purcell and George Elmslie, has an intricate terra-cotta arch over the front door and amazing stained-glass windows that are even beautiful from the outside.

The 1914 George Maher–designed **Winona National and Savings Bank** (204 Main St., 507/454-8800, 8:30 A.M.–5 P.M. Mon.–Fri., 8 A.M.–noon Sat.) creatively combines Egyptian Revival with the classic Prairie School style. An odd little museum on the second floor has a couple of placards on the bank's history, a wall full of antique guns, and dozens of trophies from African safaris, including various hippo, baboon, wildebeest, and elephant body parts.

Many of the city's fanciest Victorian homes surround **Windom Park,** which is bounded by Harriet Street and West Broadway. The bronze statue in the center of the fountain is of the city's namesake, a Sioux maiden who, according to legend, threw herself off a Mississippi bluff rather than marry a man she did not love.

Also, don't miss the impressive **Church of Saint Stanislaus Kostka** (625 E. 4th St., 507/452-5430). Topped by a towering, silver dome, the 1894 church combines a Greek cross plan with Romanesque and Baroque elements.

ART

It all started with a single painting. Businessman Bob Kierlin and his wife Mary Burrichter needed a very large painting to hang on a particularly hard-to-decorate spot in their home. The painting of sailing ships at sea pleased them so much that they started to collect other pieces of marine art and eventually had

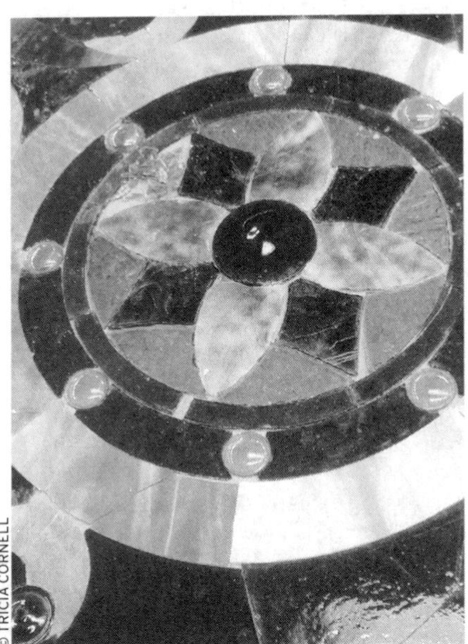
© TRICIA CORNELL

Winona is known as the Stained Glass Capital. This piece was restored by Cathedral Crafts.

so many they decided to share them with the world. Their collection became the **Minnesota Marine Art Museum** (800 Riverview Dr., 507/474-6626, www.minnesotamarineart.org, 10 A.M.–5 P.M. Tues.–Sat., 11–5 P.M. Sun., $9 adults). The permanent collection in this remarkable building on the river—newly built, but reminiscent of dockside warehouses—is a surprising gem. An entire hall is dedicated to Impressionist and Hudson River School paintings, with Monets, Renoirs, Homers, and others in the mix.

The greatest reminders of Winona's past wealth are its stained-glass windows, many made by Tiffany and other famous studios. These fabulous works of art adorn churches and other buildings all over town. The aforementioned banks and Church of Saint Stanislaus Kostka are three of the most spectacular examples. The **Watkins Company headquarters** (150 Liberty St., 507/457-3300) and **Winona County Courthouse** (171 3rd St. W., 8 A.M.–4:30 P.M. Mon.–Fri.) are also worth a look. Though less easy to visit, the **First Baptist Church** (368 Broadway St. W., 507/452-9133), **Central United Methodist Church** (114 Broadway St. W., 507/452-6783), and **First Congregational Church** (161 Broadway St. W., 507/452-4829) are also impressive. The **Winona County Historical Museum** (160 Johnson St., 507/454-2723, www.winonahistory.org, 9 A.M.–5 P.M. Mon.–Fri., noon–4 P.M. Sat.–Sun., weekdays only Jan.–Feb., $5 adults) has displays about stained glass, as well as a large window of its own. It's not just the number of stained-glass windows that lead some to call Winona the "Stained Glass Capital" of the United States. Winona is also home to seven studios that make, restore, and repair windows worldwide. A couple of them give tours to large groups. **Cathedral Crafts** (730 54th Ave., 507/454-4079, www.cathedralcrafts.org) welcomes visitors in its showroom and might allow you to watch the artists in action if they're not too busy.

Entertainment and Events

Both **Winona State University** (264 Mark St. W., 507/457-2456, www.winona.edu) and the smaller **St. Mary's University** (400 Terrace Heights, 507/457-1600, www.smumn.edu) have varied schedules of music, theater, speakers, films, and similar cultural events. The general public is welcome at most of them. St. Mary's **Page Theatre** (700 Terrace Heights, 507/457-1715, www.pagetheatre.org) and **Valencia Arts Center** (1164 West Howard St.) have particularly rich schedules.

Theatre du Mississippi (Historic Masonic Theatre, 255 Main St., 507/459-8090, www.tdmwinona.org) hosts national productions, stages its own plays, and puts on the surprisingly good **Frozen River Film Festival** in January, among many other things.

The **Winona Arts Center** (228 E. 5th St., 507/453-9959, www.winonaarts.org, no regular hours, call ahead) is a small volunteer-run venue hosting music, art displays, and many films.

Having played their first gig in 1915, the **Winona Municipal Concert Band** (Lake Park Band Shell, 8 P.M. Wed. summer) is reportedly the oldest continuously performing municipally sponsored musical group west of the Mississippi.

Winona's diverse calendar of festivals is highlighted by a month of the Bard in July during the **Great River Shakespeare Festival** (www.grsf.org) and, almost concurrently, the **Minnesota Beethoven Festival** (www.mnbeethovenfestival.org). Both festivals attract visitors from across the state and the region, a great boon for the local tourism industry.

Winona also celebrates its Polish past with **Polish Heritage Days** in early May and **Polish Apple Day** in mid-October.

Shopping

As you'd expect, most of the city's shopping is out along Highway 61, though a number of shops have claimed homes in historic buildings downtown. One of the largest is **Pieces of the Past** (79 2nd St. E., 507/452-3722, 9:30 A.M.–6:30 P.M. Tues.–Fri.), which sells things that look old, including handcrafted furniture.

Sugar Loaf Antiques and Crafts (1023 Sugar Loaf Rd., 507/452-9593, www.sugarloafantiquesandcrafts.com, 10 A.M.–5 P.M. Mon.–Fri., 10 A.M.–4 P.M. Sat., 11 A.M.–4 P.M. Sun.) fills the massive old brewery on the hillside, including the storage caves.

The **Blue Heron Gallery and Studio** (168 3rd St. E., 507/474-6879, www.blueheronstudio.net, 10 A.M.–5 P.M. Thurs.–Sat. May–Sept., 11 A.M.–4 P.M. Fri.–Sat. Oct.–Apr.) shows works by a handful of local painters, potters, and furniture makers.

Visitors are welcome to taste and shop at **Garvin Heights Vineyards** (2255 Garvin Heights Rd., 507/454-71719, www.ghvwine.com, 1–5 P.M. Fri.–Sun., hours vary by season) on the bluff above town.

Recreation

There are a lot of options in and around Winona to keep the active set busy—what follows just scratches the surface. If you'll be spending any amount of time here, get copies of the excellent maps and brochures published by the CVB for detailed biking, hiking, paddling, cross-country skiing, and bird-watching advice.

The most challenging, but also the most remote and rewarding, off-road biking is the six-mile Plowline Trail west of Winona in the Bronk Unit of the **Richard J. Dorer Memorial Hardwood State Forest** (651/345-3401). To reach the trailhead go northwest of town on U.S. Highway 61 to County Highway 23 and follow it south for three miles. For a leisurely family ride, follow the 5.5-mile path that circles Lake Winona. Road riders will find the country roads through the narrow valleys surrounding Winona to be peaceful, beautiful, and quite challenging territory. The most popular cross-country skiing right in the city is on the nine miles of groomed trail through the forested hills behind **St. Mary's University** (400 Terrace Heights, 507/457-1600, www.smumn.edu).

St. Mary's is also home to the popular 18-hole disc golf course **The Woods** (www.smumn.edu/thewoods), which visitors are welcome to use free of charge.

Adventure Cycle and Ski (178 Center St., 507/452-4228, 9:30 A.M.–7 P.M. Mon.–Fri., 9:30 A.M.–5 P.M. Sat., 11 A.M.–3 P.M. Sun.) rents bikes and cross-country skis. Winona, home of We-no-nah Canoes, one of the world's leading canoe and kayak manufacturers, is a great spot to begin an exploration of the maze of Mississippi River backwater channels. There are canoe rentals at Prairie Island Park. The Winona District office of the **Upper Mississippi River National Wildlife and Fish Refuge** (51 4th St. E., 507/452-4232 or 888/291-5719, 7 A.M.–4:30 P.M. Mon.–Fri.) has maps and information.

Accommodations

Rooms in Winona can be very hard to come by on summer weekends, so plan as far ahead as possible.

Best of the budget lodging is the **Midwestern Motel** (7115 Martina Rd., Minnesota City, 507/452-9136 or 800/213-9136, www.midwesternmotel.com, $49), a few miles north of town on U.S. Highway 61. Little has changed at the **Sterling Motel** (1450 Gilmore Ave., 507/454-1120 or 800/452-1235, $45) since it opened in the 1950s.

The best-located hotel is the **AmericInn** (60 Riverview Dr., 507/457-0249 or 877/946-6622, $90), which sits by the river and has a two-story lighthouse room with Mississippi views. Facilities include a pool, whirlpool, and sauna.

The **Carriage House Bed & Breakfast** (420 Main St., 507/452-8256, www.chbb.com, $99–159), one of the longest-operating bed-and-breakfasts in the state, has its four guestrooms in a renovated 1870 carriage house that still maintains some original features. Each of the rooms has a private bath, and two have whirlpool tubs and fireplaces. After eating the continental breakfast, guests can borrow bikes, including a tandem, to explore the city, or they can take a ride in the owners' Model A Ford.

Perhaps the most sumptuously, meticulously decorated bed-and-breakfast in Winona—or in the state—is the **Alexander Mansion** (274 Broadway E., 507/474-4224, www.alexandermansionbb.com, $149–179). The four guest rooms in this 1886 mansion show an over-the-top dedication to Victorian detail. Your hosts have reimagined the rooms as they might have been used by the family at the time—right down to Maude Alexander's dressing gown hanging in the closet. Evening wine and hors d'oeuvres may be the highlight of your visit.

The rooms are plainer, but the views are unbeatable at the **Village House Inn** (Hwy. 14 & Knopp Valley R., 507/454-4322, www.villagehouseinn.com, $90), a brick house built in the 1870s at the base of the bluffs. The four rooms each have a private bath. The continental breakfast is self-serve and guests have access to a kitchen.

The 195-site **Prairie Island Campground** (1120 Prairie Island Rd., 507/452-4501, www.prairieislandcamp.com, $21 with electric hookup) north of town is your typical large municipal campground, though the riverside location, complete with a beach, is a bonus. Campers looking to enjoy natural surroundings should consider the nearby state parks or, better yet, take a boat or canoe out to one of the myriad islands around the city.

Food

Ask anyone in town where to eat, and after telling you about the great restaurants across the river in Wisconsin, they will probably suggest the casual **Jefferson Pub & Grill** (58 Center St., 507/452-2718, www.jeffersonpub.com, 11 A.M.–10 P.M. daily, $6–18). The menu spans spicy black-bean burgers, walleye-fillet sandwiches, fajitas, and steaks, and the attached Sidetrack Tap bar has an impressive roster of beers.

There is also really good food—much of it organic, vegetarian, and made with locally grown ingredients—at the **Blue Heron Coffeehouse** (162 2nd St. W., 507/452-7020, 7 A.M.–6 P.M. Mon.–Sat., 8 A.M.–4 P.M. Sun., $4–10).

The **Acoustic Café** (77 Lafayette St., 507/453-0394, 7 A.M.–10 P.M. daily, $3–7) is a busy, but still cozy, coffeehouse that roasts its own beans, some of which are fair trade and organic. They also serve pita and hoagie sandwiches.

Carhops still take your order at the **Lakeview Drive-Inn** (610 Sarnia St. E., 507/454-3723, 10:30 A.M.–8:30 P.M. Mar.–Sept., $1–7). They serve sandwiches (including elk and buffalo burgers), ice cream, and homemade root beer. Classic car collectors gather here to show off their wheels.

You'll no longer find Krispy Kreme doughnuts in Winona since **Bloedow's Bakery** (451 Broadway St. E., 507/452-3682, 6 A.M.–5:30 P.M. Mon.–Fri., 7:30 A.M.–3 P.M.) beat them at their own game.

Information

The **Winona Visitor's Center** (924 Huff St., 507/452-2278, 9 A.M.–5 P.M. Mon.–Sat., 11 A.M.–4 P.M. Sun. May–Oct., Sat.–Sun. only May and Nov.–Dec.) is just off the highway on Lake Winona. You can also get information from **Visit Winona** (160 Johnson St., 507/452-0735 or 800/657-4972, www.visitwinona.com, 9 A.M.–5 P.M. Mon.–Fri., noon–4 P.M. Sat.–Sun., Mon.–Fri. only Jan.–Feb.) in the Winona County Historical Museum.

KQAL (FM 89.5), Winona State University's student radio station, is a welcome break from the usual vanilla of commercial music stations.

Getting There and Around

The **Amtrak** (65 Mark St. E., 507/452-8612 or 800/872-7245, www.amtrak.com) Empire Builder service arrives from St. Paul about 10 A.M., and the western service comes through at 7:50 P.M. A walk-up return ticket from St. Paul costs $20.

Jefferson Lines (888/864-2832, www.jeffersonlines.com) buses, which connect to Minneapolis via Rochester, stop at the Quality Inn (956 Mankato Ave.).

Go Carefree Shuttle (608/781-5181, www.gocarefreeshuttle.com, $45 one-way, reservations required) vans go to the Twin Cities from the Quality Inn (956 Mankato Ave.), St. Mary's University (400 Terrace Heights), Winona State University (264 Mark St. W.), and the Amtrak Station (65 Mark St. E.) five times a day.

Locally, **Winona Transit** (507/454-6666) has a limited bus service available weekdays until around 6 P.M. The city also has two cab companies: **Economy Cab** (507/454-7433) and **Yellow Cab** (507/452-3331). **Hertz** (275 W. 2nd St., 507/454-2888, www.hertz.com, 7 A.M.–5 P.M. daily) and **Enterprise** (1111 Service Rd. W., 507/454-4462, www.enterprise.com, 7:30 A.M.–5 P.M. Mon.–Sat., 9 A.M.–noon Sun.) are the national car rental agencies in town.

There is public dockage for short-term visitors on Front Street downtown. For overnighters there is the **Winona Yacht Club** (24 Laird St., 507/454-5590) near downtown and **Dick's Marine** (507/452-3809) over on Latsch Island—both are full-service facilities.

SOUTH OF WINONA

Pickwick Mill

Two miles off Highway 61 is the restored **Pickwick Mill** (26421 County Rd. 7, 507/452-9658, www.pickwickmill.org, 10 A.M.–5 P.M. Tues.–Sat., 1–5 P.M. Sun. summer, Sat.–Sun. only May, Sept., and Oct., $3 adults), which operated from 1856 to 1980. Today the building has been extensively fixed up inside, but most of the original machinery and some assorted supplies remain, much of it just lying around where the last owners left it. The mill no longer grinds grains, but the 20-foot waterwheel still turns the complex series of wooden gears. While the inside is interesting, the solid, six-story limestone building is just as impressive from the outside. You can dine with a mill view across Big Trout Creek at the popular **Pickwick Inn** (24731 County Rd. 7, 507/454-7750, 11 A.M.–9 P.M. Tues.–Fri., 11 A.M.–10 P.M. Sat., 11 A.M.–9 P.M. Sun., closed Mon., $7–25).

Great River Bluffs State Park

This 3,026-acre bluff-top park (43605 Kipp Dr., 507/643-6849) is managed as a "natural" park, so development is limited to a small picnic area, campground, and 6.5 miles of wide, level hiking trails linking eight scenic overlooks. The north-facing vistas offer some of the best Mississippi River views anywhere, but don't miss the valley views to the south, which are also impressive. If you don't want to walk to the overlooks, there is a good one of the river along the road to the campground. As you walk the trails you'll also see several small goat prairies (on slopes so steep that only goats could graze them) riding some of the bluff tops. Ironically, they get more sunlight than any other natural community in Minnesota, but because they freeze easily woody plants that would otherwise establish themselves are killed off. The **King's Bluff Nature Trail,** a 2.5-mile round-trip, has interpretive signs along it discussing these and other ecological topics. In winter these trails, plus a few miles of additional loops, are groomed for cross-country skiing. Snowshoes can be rented at the park office, and there is a steep sledding hill. The primitive campground has 31 shady and widely spaced sites and is one of the best campgrounds along the river. Additionally, a five-site bicycle campground down along U.S. Highway 61 is available for those pedaling the Great River Road.

La Crescent

Little La Crescent is all about apples. The first orchard in the state was planted here in 1857 and today, with growers working over 500

BLUFF COUNTRY

acres, La Crescent has justifiably declared itself the "Apple Capital of Minnesota." Nine orchards, most selling direct to the public, ring the town, with some located along the **Apple Blossom Scenic Drive.** The 17-mile marked route climbs the bluffs above La Crescent and then returns along the river, many people just follow the most scenic first half of the route, which turns back at Dakota. The trees are in their glorious white bloom in early May, and apples are available from late July until mid-November, though the valley views are superb all year long. La Crescent is also the east end of the 88-mile **Historic Bluff Country Scenic Byway.** Three miles upriver from town is **Lock and Dam #7,** where an elevated platform and visitors center lets you watch boats get an eight-foot lift. In the winter you'll likely see bald eagles fishing here. Next door is a **Minnesota Travel Information Center** full of brochures. The city's **Applefest** (www.applefestusa.com), held over four days around the third weekend in September, has orchard and packing-plant tours, big-wheel races, an arts and crafts fair, and the King Apple Grand Parade. It's a mighty big event for such a small town.

All of your lodging and most of your dining choices are across the river in La Crosse, Wisconsin.

Beaver Creek Valley State Park

Beaver Creek Valley State Park (159454 County 1, 507/724-2107), 22 miles southwest of La Crescent, is a fine example of Minnesota's driftless topography. Spring-fed Beaver Creek cuts a deep, narrow valley through the bluffs, and this cool and quiet 1,187-acre park straddles nearly six miles of it. Because the park protects the majority of land in the upper part of the watershed, the little creek and surrounding landscape are remarkably pristine. The valley is filled with virgin hardwood forests, and native patches of prairie cling to some south and west facing slopes. Fly fishers will appreciate the challenge of the naturally reproducing trophy-sized brown and brook trout—there is a special winter catch-and-release season. The park is a top bird-watching spot, and several species, like Cerulean warbler, Louisiana waterthrush, and the rare Acadian flycatcher, that are at the far northwestern ends of their range nest in the park.

Eight miles of hiking trail follow the valley. For a complete Beaver Creek experience, climb 250 feet up the bluffs to the first overlook along the **Switchback Trail** for a long view down the valley, and then walk through what you've just been admiring along the **Beaver Creek Valley Trail,** a level and easy two-mile round-trip leading along the creek and out to a prairie. If you're lucky, you might spy a five-lined skink with its bright blue tail along the adjoining **Plateau Rock Trail** and **Quarry Trail.** The campground has 42 sites (16 electric) and a camper cabin with electricity right along the road—the valley is just too narrow for any setback—and the farther in you go the more peaceful and secluded the sites become. Half a dozen cart-in sites sit way at the end.

Just north of the park, off County Highway 10, is **Schech's Mill** (507/896-3481 or 651/245-5566, 1–6 P.M. Fri., 8 A.M.–6 P.M. Sat.–Sun. summer, $5), a working water-powered flour mill built in 1876. If you call ahead someone will crank it up for you. They also sell burlap sacks and flour bags, and other rustic handicrafts.

Rochester

The average Minnesotan knows just two things about Rochester: It is home to the Mayo Clinic, and it is an exceedingly dull city. "I don't need to go to Rochester, I'm not sick" is a common attitude. The "boring" label is so strongly ingrained, in fact, that the CVB gives locals familiarization tours just so that if someone asks them what there is to do in town they don't answer, "Nothing." While the prevailing wisdom is not completely wrong—frankly Rochester does rank fairly low on the excitement scale—the odd combination of big city and small town surprises most first-time visitors, of whom, between "The Clinic" and conventions, there are hundreds of thousands annually. It really is worth a visit.

Though the city is synonymous with modern technology (besides the Mayo Clinic, Rochester has IBM's largest single building), the giant corncob water tower on the south side of town is a reminder of Rochester's agricultural roots. Olmsted County's first settlers were New England farmers. In 1854 one of them, George Head from Rochester, New York, built a log cabin home–hotel–saloon at a waterfall on the South Branch Zumbro River. A proper town, fueled by flour mills, soon sprang up here, and when a name was needed Head suggested Rochester because the rapids here reminded him of the Genesee River in his former hometown.

After an 1883 tornado devastated the city, Dr. William Mayo opened a hospital that would later grow into the world-renowned Mayo Clinic. Today the Mayo name and legacy permeate the city. The clinic has brought gleaming skyscrapers and some cosmopolitan flair to this city of 86,000. This sophistication, along with a deep civic pride, makes Rochester a regular chart-topper on "Most Livable" city rankings. Rochester was doing all right before the hospital opened and might have even become southern Minnesota's leading city without it, but Dr. Mayo single-handedly put Rochester on the map, and it certainly would not be the economic axis that it is today without him.

Orientation

Though many of the city's top attractions sit on the southeast end of the city, you can find just about anything you want or need downtown. Beyond the center most businesses stretch out along Highways 52 and 63. There is very little of interest in the eastern half of the city. Rochester is divided into quadrants and all addresses have a NE, NW, SE, or SW suffix. The dividing intersection is Center Street and Broadway (U.S. 63). A downtown pedestrian subway and skyway system connects the main Mayo Clinic buildings, Civic Center, Centerplace Galleria mall, parking ramps, and most of the large hotels.

SIGHTS

Olmsted County History Center

The county historical museum (1195 W. Circle Dr. SW, 507/282-9447, www.olmstedhistory.com, 9 A.M.–5 P.M. Tues.–Sat., $5 adults) has a classic soda fountain, an early IBM display, and, of course, quite a bit on the Mayo Clinic. Kids can get up close and personal with the hands-on log cabin, tepee, and rag-rug loom. The most fascinating display is the chunk of wood impaled by blades of grass during the 1883 tornado. The furnished 1862 log cabin and 1885 one-room schoolhouse in back are open during the summer only.

Mayowood Mansion

Mayowood (3720 Mayowood Rd. SW, 507/282-9447, 11 A.M., noon, 1 P.M., and 2 P.M. Tues. and Sat. May–Oct., plus Wed.–Thurs. summer, $12), the country estate of clinic cofounder Dr. Charles Mayo, once covered 3,000 acres and included eight farms, a man-made lake with landscaped islands, a greenhouse made of old X-ray plates, and extensive Japanese, English, and Italian gardens.

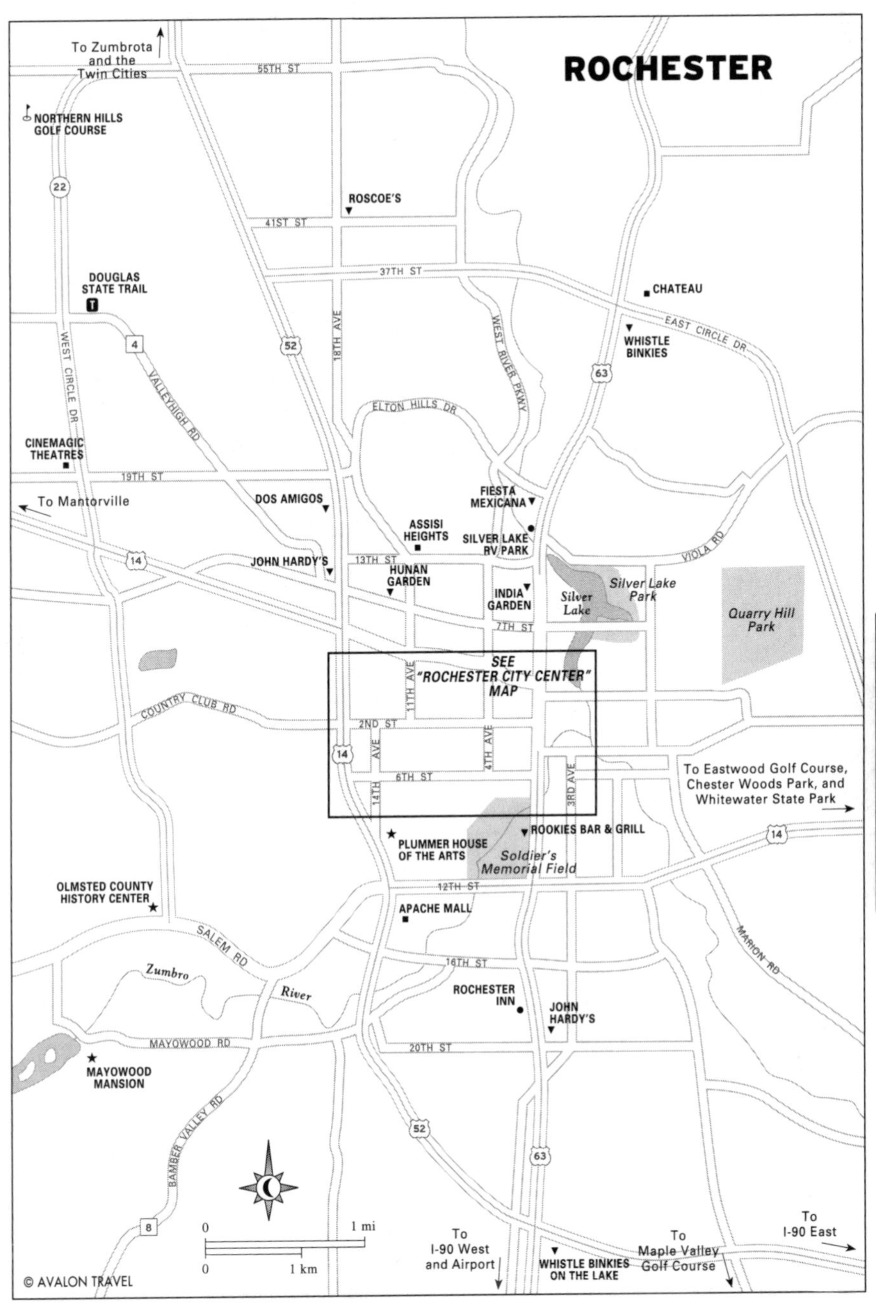
ROCHESTER
To Zumbrota and the Twin Cities
55TH ST
NORTHERN HILLS GOLF COURSE
22
ROSCOE'S
41ST ST
37TH ST
DOUGLAS STATE TRAIL
CHATEAU
EAST CIRCLE DR
WHISTLE BINKIES
4
52
18TH AVE
WEST RIVER PKWY
63
WEST CIRCLE DR
VALLEYHIGH RD
ELTON HILLS DR
CINEMAGIC THEATRES
19TH ST
To Mantorville
DOS AMIGOS
FIESTA MEXICANA
ASSISI HEIGHTS
SILVER LAKE RV PARK
VIOLA RD
14
JOHN HARDY'S
13TH ST
HUNAN GARDEN
INDIA GARDEN
Silver Lake
Silver Lake Park
Quarry Hill Park
7TH ST
SEE "ROCHESTER CITY CENTER" MAP
11TH AVE
COUNTRY CLUB RD
2ND ST
14
AVE
4TH AVE
6TH ST
14TH
3RD AVE
To Eastwood Golf Course, Chester Woods Park, and Whitewater State Park
PLUMMER HOUSE OF THE ARTS
ROOKIES BAR & GRILL
14
Soldier's Memorial Field
OLMSTED COUNTY HISTORY CENTER
12TH ST
APACHE MALL
SALEM RD
MARION RD
16TH ST
Zumbro
River
ROCHESTER INN
JOHN HARDY'S
MAYOWOOD RD
20TH ST
MAYOWOOD MANSION
BAMBER VALLEY RD
52
63
8
0
1 mi
0
1 km
To I-90 West and Airport
WHISTLE BINKIES ON THE LAKE
To Maple Valley Golf Course
To I-90 East
© AVALON TRAVEL

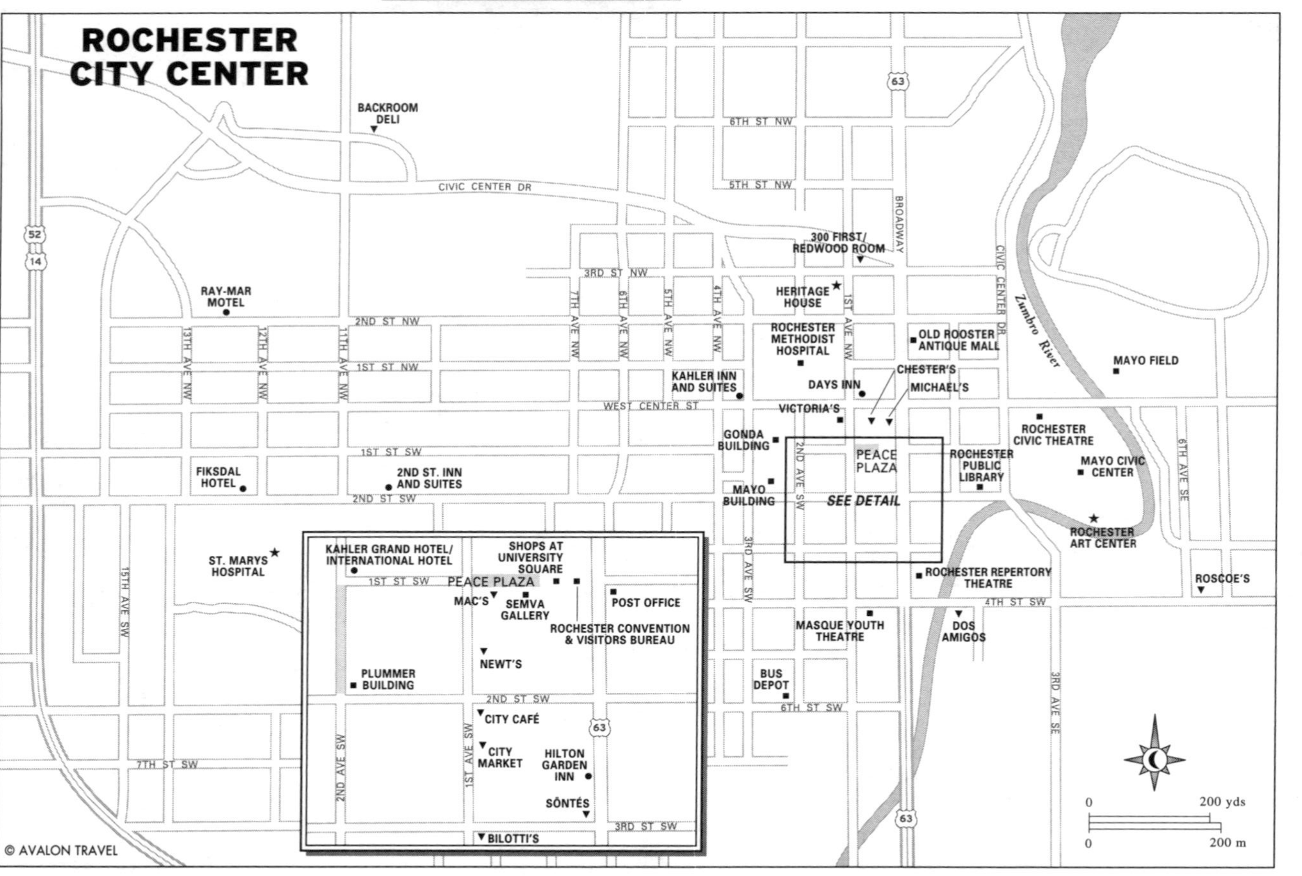
ROCHESTER CITY CENTER
BACKROOM DELI
CIVIC CENTER DR
52
14
RAY-MAR MOTEL
63
6TH ST NW
5TH ST NW
BROADWAY
300 FIRST/ REDWOOD ROOM
3RD ST NW
7TH AVE NW
6TH AVE NW
5TH AVE NW
4TH AVE NW
HERITAGE HOUSE
1ST AVE NW
CIVIC CENTER DR
Zumbro River
ROCHESTER METHODIST HOSPITAL
OLD ROOSTER ANTIQUE MALL
MAYO FIELD
2ND ST NW
13TH AVE NW
12TH AVE NW
11TH AVE NW
1ST ST NW
KAHLER INN AND SUITES
DAYS INN
CHESTER'S
MICHAEL'S
WEST CENTER ST
VICTORIA'S
ROCHESTER CIVIC THEATRE
GONDA BUILDING
PEACE PLAZA
ROCHESTER PUBLIC LIBRARY
MAYO CIVIC CENTER
1ST ST SW
FIKSDAL HOTEL
2ND ST. INN AND SUITES
2ND AVE SW
6TH AVE SE
MAYO BUILDING
SEE DETAIL
2ND ST SW
ROCHESTER ART CENTER
ST. MARYS HOSPITAL
KAHLER GRAND HOTEL/ INTERNATIONAL HOTEL
SHOPS AT UNIVERSITY SQUARE
1ST ST SW
PEACE PLAZA
3RD AVE SW
ROCHESTER REPERTORY THEATRE
ROSCOE'S
MAC'S
SEMVA GALLERY
POST OFFICE
4TH ST SW
15TH AVE SW
ROCHESTER CONVENTION & VISITORS BUREAU
MASQUE YOUTH THEATRE
DOS AMIGOS
NEWT'S
PLUMMER BUILDING
BUS DEPOT
2ND ST SW
6TH ST SW
3RD AVE SE
CITY CAFÉ
63
7TH ST SW
2ND AVE SW
1ST AVE SW
CITY MARKET
HILTON GARDEN INN
SÖNTÉS
3RD ST SW
BILOTTI'S
63
0
200 yds
0
200 m
© AVALON TRAVEL

The elegant 38-room mansion at the center of it all was built as a summer home in 1911, and sometime in the 1920s he added a hydroelectric dam and moved out here permanently. Another two generations of Mayos resided here until 1965, when the family left the "Big House," as Dr. Charlie called it, and most of its furnishings to the Olmsted County Historical Society. Special Christmas tours are held in November, and the grounds are one stop on a citywide gardens tour held each June.

Plummer House of the Arts

Henry Plummer, another doctor made obscenely wealthy during his time at the Mayo Clinic, built this 49-room English Tudor mansion (1091 Plummer Ln. SW, 507/328-2525, noon–6 P.M. Wed. June–Aug., $3 adults) in 1917. Plummer (designer of the clinic's Plummer Building) was also a noted engineer, and he worked such innovative features as a central vacuum system, power garage-door opener, intercom, and gas furnace into his Quarry Hill home. All of the furniture was left behind with the house, though it still feels somewhat empty. Despite the name, there are no art displays. The arts label stems from his wife Daisy, a tireless cultural promoter. Today the home is used primarily for weddings and other special events, though you can take a look around it, and the 11-acre grounds with forested trails and a small floral garden are free and open to the public year-round from sunrise to sunset. Private tours for groups of ten or more can be arranged.

© TIM BEWER

The Mayo Clinic's Plummer Building houses a 56-bell carillon.

The Rochester Carillon

Inside the pinnacle atop the Mayo Clinic's grand Plummer Building is one of the most complete carillons in North America. The 56 bronze bells cover four-and-a-half octaves; the largest stands six feet tall and weighs in at four tons, while the smallest is just 19 pounds. **Live concerts** (7 P.M. Mon., noon Wed. and Fri., plus various holidays) encompass everything from show tunes to hymns. The best place to hear them is about 500 feet downwind, but since that is unpredictable it is probably best to take a seat around the *Boy With a Dolphin* statue in front of the Mayo Building. Call 507/284-8294 to arrange a tour.

BLUFF COUNTRY

Heritage House

For a look at a more modest, though still upper-class, home, visit Heritage House (225 1st Ave. NW, 507/282-2682, 1–3:30 P.M. Tues., Thurs., and Sun. summer, $4). When the wrecking ball threatened it in 1972, citizens raised some money, moved it to Central Park (the city's original town square), and restored it. The 1875 home was one of the few downtown buildings to survive the 1883 tornado, and many of the original features and furnishings remain. The guides know the story behind just about every chair, lamp, and doorknob and will tell you as little or as much as you want to know about family life in the late 19th century.

Rochester Art Center

The riverside Rochester Art Center (40 Civic Center Dr. SE, 507/282-8629,

THE CLINIC IN THE CORNFIELD

The Mayo Clinic began with a tragedy. In August 1883 a tornado leveled half of Rochester, killing 31 and injuring hundreds more. Rochester had no medical facility, so hotels, offices, and dance halls transformed into emergency rooms. Desperate doctors, including William Worrall Mayo and his sons, enlisted nuns from the Sisters of St. Francis as nurses. The crisis inspired Mother Alfred Moes to propose building a hospital, and she enlisted the support of Dr. Mayo. The order raised $40,000 and opened St. Marys Hospital in 1889. The "Clinic in the Cornfield," as it was known, was southern Minnesota's first hospital, and it served the needs of rural residents for hundreds of miles.

While W. W. Mayo created the clinic, his sons, William J. and Charles H., both expert surgeons, were the pioneers who made it the world-renowned center it is today. Back then doctors washed their hands after surgery, but not before. Dr. Charlie and Dr. Will were among first doctors in the nation to sterilize equipment before surgery, and they made the new aseptic techniques standard procedure in their hospital. They also pioneered the concept of medicine as a cooperative science with specialists consulting amongst themselves in a teamwork approach to patient care. This revolutionary concept made the Mayo Clinic the world's first integrated group practice; today it is the largest. By the 20th century the Mayo name was known far and wide and the actual clinic was growing as fast as its reputation. Patients weren't the only ones flocking to Rochester to take advantage of the Mayo doctors' skill and ingenuity; other physicians came to learn from the best, and in 1915 the clinic organized the world's first formal graduate-training program for physicians.

In 1919 the Mayo brothers transferred all of the clinic's assets and the bulk of their life savings to a charitable nonprofit group now called the Mayo Foundation. From that point on, all profits have gone toward medical education and research. Many breakthroughs have come out of Rochester, including the first test of surgical samples that was quick enough to allow diagnosis and repair in a single operation, the cure for tuberculosis, the first hip-replacement surgery, and, most recently, a rapid anthrax test. Dr. Charlie, noticing that milk was the source of illness in a large percentage of his patients, even went as far as establishing his own dairy herd at his Mayowood estate to prove to area farmers that pasteurizing milk was cost effective.

Today the Mayo Clinic continues to rank among the best health care facilities in the world. The country hospital that began with 27 beds now has its own zip code and has treated over six million people from over 100 countries, including presidents and royalty. Branches have since opened in Florida and Arizona, and the Rochester facility alone occupies 13 million square feet, has more than 1,500 doctors, and treats well over 300,000 patients a year.

www.rochesterartcenter.org, 10 A.M.–5 P.M. Tues.–Wed. and Fri.–Sat., 10 A.M.–9 P.M. Thurs., noon–5 P.M. Sun., $5 adults, free on Thurs.) hosts a variety of exhibitions and events featuring Midwest artists.

Silver Lake Park

If you've been wondering why the goose theme is so prevalent in Rochester, visit this large park just north of downtown, where upward of 35,000 Canadian honkers congregate over the winter, a result of the local power plant keeping the lake ice-free. They are here the rest of the year too, though in much smaller numbers. If you don't have your own bread you can buy goose food at the parking lot north of 7th Street on the west side of the lake. Paddleboats and canoes are available for rent.

ENTERTAINMENT AND EVENTS

The noticeably slim Entertainment section in the Thursday edition of the ***Rochester Post-Bulletin*** (www.postbulletin.com) is the best source of what's going on in town.

BLUFF COUNTRY

CLINIC VISITS

Guided tours (507/284-2511) begin at 10 A.M., though come early because it is preceded by an interesting 15-minute film on the history of the Mayo family and the early years of the clinic. You don't see anything beyond the main public areas during the 90-minute tours – they can't exactly walk you into the operating rooms – but you'll get the full scoop on the history and daily operations, plus some of the artistic highlights will be pointed out. A more detailed hour-long art and architecture tour begins in the afternoon at 1:30. The collection, mostly donated by patients and benefactors, includes such heavyweights of the art world as Warhol, Rodin, and Chihuly, as well as work by renowned local sculptor Charles Gagnon. Both tours are free, offered weekdays only, and start in the Judd Auditorium on the subway level of the Mayo Building.

If you don't mind missing the stories or having someone around to answer questions, you can see everything and more on your own – maps are available at the information desks. Currently there is no self-guided-art-tour brochure, but supposedly one is in the works.

The **Gonda Building,** referred to as the "Front Door" of the Mayo Clinic, is the newest of the clinic's 70 buildings. It holds some of the largest works of art (including a much talked about Dave Chihuly blown-glass chandelier) and an interesting modern design; a self-guided-tour brochure is available.

In contrast to the sleek, modern Gonda Building is the gargoyled **Plummer Building.** The city's showpiece edifice cost three million dollars to build in 1928, and even Bill Gates probably couldn't finance it today. Henry Plummer joined the Mayo brothers in 1901 and became the clinic's jack-of-all-trades. Not only was he an accomplished physician, but he introduced the now-ubiquitous dossier medical records system where a single file is kept for a patient, designed the first large-scale intercom system, and was even such a skillful architect that he designed the building named after him. The **Mayo Historical Suite** (8 A.M.-5 P.M. Mon.-Fri., free admission), a mini-museum on the third floor, has lots of old photos, the Mayo brothers' original office furniture, and some frightening surgical instruments from the past. Also worth a look are the lobby, the massive front doors, and the Medical Library Reading Room on the 14th floor.

Unique X-rays, such as a snake that swallowed a pair of light bulbs, are displayed in the Patient Education Center on the subway level of the **Siebens Building,** and more historical displays are found in the adjacent hallway.

St. Mary's Hospital also has a self-guided-tour brochure, though pretty much the only thing worth seeing is the small historical display near the Francis Building's main entrance. It has some of W. W. Mayo's original surgical tools and the hospital's first operating table.

Nightlife

With two locations, **Whistle Binkies** packs in crowds at both. Their Old World Pub (3120 Wellner Dr. NE, 507/289-9200, www.whistlebinkiespub.com, 11 A.M.–midnight Sun.–Wed., 11 A.M.–1 A.M. Thurs.–Sat.) hosts live music ranging from polka to classic rock. Whistle Binkies on the Lake (247 Woodlake Dr. SE, 507/424-1227, 10 A.M.–midnight Sun., 11 A.M.–midnight Mon.–Wed., 11 A.M.–1 A.M. Thurs.–Sat.) has a great patio on the water.

The dance floor at **Rookies Bar & Grill** (1201 Broadway S., 507/252-5161, www.rookiesbar.com) is among the most popular in town, whether there's a live band or a DJ. It's a something-for-everyone sort of place, with sports on the TV sets and pool tables in back.

For something a little more grown-up, have a glass of wine at **Söntés** (4 3rd St. SW, 507/292-1628, www.sontes.com, 4–10 P.M. Mon.–Thurs., 4–11 P.M. Fri.–Sat., closed Sun.). Whether you take a table or a lounge chair by the fire, you're welcome to stick around a while. There's a long menu of creative small plates, more filling than your usual tapas options.

Classical Music

The **Rochester Orchestra and Chorale** (507/286-8742, www.rochestersymphony.org), founded in 1919, serves up seven shows a season at the Mayo Civic Center. Tickets start at $21. Also popular is the **Choral Arts Ensemble** (507/252-8427, www.choralartsensemble.org), a 40-voice choir performing classical and jazz pieces several times a year at the beautiful Assisi Heights convent (1001 14th St. NW). Ticket prices begin at $15.

Theater

Both the **Rochester Civic Theatre** (20 E. Civic Center Dr. SE, 507/282-8481, www.rochestercivictheatre.org) and the **Rochester Repertory Theatre** (103 7th St. NE, 507/289-1737, www.rochesterrep.org) offer comedies, dramas, and musicals at their respective homes. Tickets are around $15 at each. Children take the stage between October and June at the **Masque Youth Theatre** (14 4th St. SW, 507/287-0704, http://themasque.bravehost.com), performing anything from fairy tales to Shakespeare, and tickets are as low as $3.

Cinema

Rochester has two large movie theaters: **CineMagic** (507/280-0333, www.cinemagictheatres.com) on the west side and **Chateau** (507/536-7469, www.chateautheatres.com) not too far north of downtown.

Spectator Sports

The **Rochester Honkers** (www.rochesterhonkers.com) play in the Northwoods Baseball League, made up of top Division I college players who get minor league experience while keeping their college eligibility. Home games are played at **Mayo Field** (403 Center St. E., 507/289-1170, $6–28).

The **Rochester Giants** (www.rochestergiants.com) are a semi-pro team in the Great Plains Football League; they won the first three league championships. Home games for the summer season are played at **Soldiers Field** (244 Soldiers Field Dr. SW, 507/358-7075, $6) south of downtown.

Events

The city's biggest blowout is **Rochesterfest** (www.rochesterfest.com), a nine-day affair with a sandcastle contest, kite festival, hot air balloon races, and an 1860s baseball game—not to mention the usual food, parade, music, and carnival rides. It begins the third weekend in June. The ever-popular **Midwestern Lumberjack Championships** are always held concurrently with Rochesterfest.

SHOPPING

Rochester is the regional shopping center for a large chunk of southeast Minnesota, so there is little you can't find here. The **Apache Mall** (507/288-8056, www.apachemall.com, 10 A.M.–9 P.M. Mon.–Sat., 11 A.M.–7 P.M. Sun.), at the junction of Highways 52 South and 14 East, with around 80 stores, is the largest outlet, though the smaller **Shops at University Square** (111 Broadway S., 507/281-1364, 9:30 A.M.–8:30 P.M. Mon.–Fri., 9:30 A.M.–5:30 P.M. Sat., noon–5 P.M. Sun.) right in the heart of downtown has a more interesting selection of shops.

Rochester is a good place to shop for antiques. The largest store, with about 20 dealers, is the **Old Rooster Antique Mall** (106 Broadway N., 507/287-6228, 9 A.M.–7 P.M. Mon.–Fri., 9 A.M.–5:30 P.M. Sat.–Sun.).

The large **SE Minnesota Visual Artists (SEMVA) Gallery** (16 1st St. SW, 507/281-4920, www.semva.com, 10 A.M.–6 P.M. Mon.–Wed. and Sat., 10 A.M.–9 P.M. Thurs.–Fri., noon–4 P.M. Sun.) fronting Peace Plaza has work for sale in just about all possible media.

RECREATION

Two-hundred-seventy-acre **Quarry Hill Park** (507/281-6114) is no lost wilderness, but for an urban park it's not too shabby. Five miles of hiking trail wind through the woods and grassland, though wherever you decide to hike includes a pass though the 20-acre hilltop savanna at the center of the park. In the winter cross-country skis and snowshoes can be rented. The kid-focused **Nature Center** (9 A.M.–5 P.M. Mon.–Sat., noon–5 P.M. Sun., free admission) has interactive displays, touch tables, an indoor bee hive, a 1,700-gallon Minnesota fish aquarium, a life-size T-Rex skull model, and over 100 animal mounts. The main entrance is located off County Highway 22.

The paved **Douglas State Trail** follows a former railroad bed through 13 miles of farmland between the northwest edge of Rochester and Pine Island. Bikers have many more miles of paved trail crisscrossing the city along the Zumbro River and the smaller creeks that empty into it.

The best of the city's public golf courses are **Northern Hills Golf Course** (4721 W. Circle Dr. NW, 507/281-6170, $27 for 18 holes) and **Eastwood Golf Course** (3505 Eastwood Rd. SE, 507/281-6173, $27 for 18 holes). Though it's not very challenging, the limestone bluffs at the **Maple Valley Golf Course** (8600 Maple Valley Rd. SE, 507/285-9100, www.maplevalleygolf.com, $19 for 18 holes) make it the area's most scenic by far.

ACCOMMODATIONS

Hotels in Rochester offer very good value. Most have shuttle service available to the hospitals, and most have kitchenettes available.

Under $50

The **2nd St. Inn and Suites** (1013 2nd St. SW, 507/289-3363 or 800/533-2226, www.rgilodging.com, $40) opened its doors in 1906, and today a night in the very small and simple rooms is kind of like stepping back to that time.

A row of older no-frills hotels catering almost exclusively to patients and their families, fronts St. Marys Hospital. The **Ray-Mar Motel** (1416 2nd St. NW, 507/282-7468 or 800/625-7468, www.raymarmotel.com, $49) tries to make visitors feel at home with free breakfast and afternoon snacks. Weekly and monthly rates are also available.

There's no shortage of cheap, basic hotels along Broadway on the south side of town either. The **Rochester Inn** (1837 Broadway S., 507/288-2031 or 800/890-3871, $38) is typical.

$50–150

The historic **Kahler Grand Hotel** (20 2nd Ave. SW, 507/280-6200 or 800/533-1655, www.kahler.com, $79) opened its doors in 1921. It has a grand lobby, 668 rooms, 15 suites, and a domed, skylit recreation area with pool, whirlpool, sauna, and exercise room. The standard rooms are small, though larger rooms are available. Its sister hotel, the **Kahler Inn and Suites** (9 3rd Ave. NW, 507/285-9200, www.kahler.com, $99) is more modern, but less interesting and opulent. It also has top-notch facilities, including a pool, fitness center, and on-site shopping and restaurants. Both are connected directly to the Mayo Clinic by indoor walkways.

Less fancy, but also full of character, is the **Days Inn** (6 1st Ave. NW, 507/282-3801 or 800/329-7466, www.daysinn.com, $62), a renovation of a 1917 building with smallish rooms. The larger kitchenettes don't cost all that much more.

The **Hilton Garden Inn** (225 Broadway S., 507/285-1234 or 877/782-9444, $139), one of the most recently constructed downtown hotels, has well-appointed rooms plus a pool, whirlpool, and exercise room.

The **Fiksdal Hotel** (1215 2nd St. SW, 507/288-2671 or 800/366-3451, www.fiksdalhotel.com, $75) is a bit nicer than most of the other hotels by St. Mary's and has microwaves and refrigerators in all the rooms, plus a 2nd-floor patio.

Over $150

A hotel within a hotel, the **International Hotel** (20 2nd Ave. SW, 507/328-8000 or 800/940-6811, www.internationalhotelmn.com, $450) is a 26-room boutique facility on the top floors of the historic Kahler Grand. It's a brand-new facility shooting for five-diamond service.

Campgrounds

The miserably crowded **Silver Lake RV Park** (1409 Broadway N., 507/289-6412 or 888/284-6412, $34 for full hookup including cable TV) is the closest camping to downtown and the Mayo Clinic. **Chester Woods Park** (507/285-7050, May–Oct., $18 with electricity), seven miles east of the city on U.S. Highway 14, has a far better campground.

FOOD

Rochester goes to sleep early, and during the week many restaurants have the chairs on the tables by 9 P.M.

American Upscale

300 First (300 1st Ave. NW, 507/281-2451, www.300first.com, 4–11 P.M. Mon.–Thurs., 4 P.M.–midnight Fri.–Sat., 4–10 P.M. Sun., $15–30) makes excellent use of the old warehouse building it calls home, with copper-topped tables playing off the exposed brick. The atmosphere is relaxed in the way that only people who can afford $29 steaks can pull off. Downstairs, the **Redwood Room** (507/281-2978, www.redwoodroom.com) is a romantic candle-lit, jazz-infused basement space with thin-crust pizzas and homemade pastas.

Before you walk through the wall of wine into the candle-lit dining room, check out the photos of celebrities who have dined at the venerable **Michael's** (15 Broadway S., 507/288-2020, www.michaelsfinedining.com, 11 A.M.–10 P.M. Mon.–Sat., $10–40). Greek dishes are the specialty of the house, but make up only a small part of the meat and seafood menu. The filet mignon with wild mushrooms has been called the best steak in Rochester.

Everything changes once you step inside **Chester's** (111 Broadway S., 507/424-1211, www.chesterskb.com, 11 A.M.–10 P.M. Mon.–Thurs., 11 A.M.–11 P.M. Fri.–Sat., 10 A.M.–9 P.M. Sun., $8–18): You were in a strip mall; now you're in one of Rochester's top fine-dining restaurants. Locals rave about the rotisserie chicken dinner, thin pizza, and pork chops.

American Casual

The more casual, but no less class, sibling of 300 First and the Redwood Room, **City Café** (216 1st Ave. SW, 507/289-1949, www.cccrmg.com/city_cafe.htm, 11 A.M.–11 P.M. Mon.–Fri., 5–11 P.M. Sat., 5–10 P.M. Sun., $12–18) specializes in seafood, from tuna sliders to mussels in curry sauce. The parmesan-crusted grouper in basil cream sauce was voted Rochester's best seafood dish.

Ask any local, and they'll tell you the best place to get burgers and fries is at **Newt's** (216 First Ave. SW, 507/289-0577, www.ccrmg.com, 11 A.M.–11 P.M. Mon.–Thurs., 11 A.M.–midnight Fri.–Sat., 11 A.M.–10 P.M. Sun., $7–10). Half-pound patties sit next to tall piles of crispy, hand-cut fries.

Mac's (20 1st St. SW, 507/289-4219, 6 A.M.–9 P.M. Mon.–Fri., 7 A.M.–9 P.M. Sat.–Sun., $4–13) is a simple café on Peace Plaza where they will serve you a heaping platter in no time flat, though you are welcome to linger like many of the coffee-sipping regulars do. The menu includes some Greek standards and breakfast is served all day.

City Market (212 1st Ave. SW, 507/536-4748, 7 A.M.–6 P.M. Mon.–Fri., $5–6) is a small gourmet grocer with deli sandwiches and salads. The lunch-hour lines may look long, but they zip right along. The roast beef and gouda sandwich on a Portuguese bun is more than worth the short wait.

In the back of the Good Food Store Co-op hides a little vegetarian restaurant, the **Backroom Deli** (1001 6th St. NW, 507/289-9061, www.rochestergoodfood.com, 9 A.M.–7 P.M. Mon.–Sat., closed Sun., $5–8), a favorite with locals in the know who love the house-made hummus and hearty vegetable stews.

There are several very cheap (and healthy, of course) cafeterias in the main **Mayo Clinic** buildings.

Asian

India Garden (1107 Broadway N., 507/288-6280, lunch 11 A.M.–2:30 P.M. Mon.–Fri. and 11 A.M.–3 P.M. Sat.–Sun., dinner 5–10 P.M. daily, $9–17) has an extensive menu covering the whole of the subcontinent, though their tandoori dishes are the specialty of the house.

Rochester's best Chinese restaurant is **Hunan Garden** (Northgate Shopping Center, 1120 7th St. NW, 507/285-1438, 11 A.M.–9:30 P.M. Sun.–Thurs., 11 A.M.–10 P.M. Fri.–Sat., $8–13). Its huge menu covers nearly the whole of China and it is noted for its use of fresh ingredients.

Barbecue

This isn't Memphis, but Rochester takes its barbecue seriously. Though the competition is stiff, **John Hardy's** (929 W. Frontage Rd. N., 507/288-3936, and 1940 S. Broadway, 507/281-1727, www.johnhardysbbq.com, 10:30 A.M.–9 P.M. Mon.–Thurs., 10:30 A.M.–10 P.M. Fri., 11 A.M.–10 P.M. Sat., 11 A.M.–9 P.M. Sun., $4–30) is many locals' top pick. Its wildly popular sauce—available in seven levels of heat, three of them hotter than just plain "hot"—is also available to go.

The other strong contender for the title is **Roscoe's** (3456 E. Circle Dr. NE, 507/281-4622, and 603 4th St. SE, 507/285-0501, www.roscoesbbq.com, 11 A.M.–9 P.M. Tues.–Sun., $5–21), locally owned roadhouses.

Italian

With an astonishingly large menu, ordering a meal at **Victoria's** (7 1st Ave. SW, 507/280-6232, www.victoriasmn.com, 10:30 A.M.–10 P.M. daily, $6–29) can be tough. The choices run from mix-and-match pastas to pork tenderloin Sorrento, and there's even walleye with Alfredo sauce.

The red-vinyl **Bilotti's** (304 1st Ave. SW, 507/282-8668, 11 A.M.–10 P.M. Mon.–Thurs., 11 A.M.–11 P.M. Fri.–Sat., 4:30–9 P.M. Sun., $4–12) has a full Italian and American menu, but it is their piled-high, thin-crust pizzas that keep them so popular.

Mexican

Once the only Mexican restaurant in Rochester, **Fiesta Mexicana** (1645 Broadway N., 507/288-1116, 11 A.M.–10 P.M. Sun.–Thurs., 11 A.M.–11 P.M. Fri.–Sat., $5–20) is still the best. This friendly, family-run place has a large menu with all the usual fare, plus some less-common additions like potato chimichangas.

Also popular is **Dos Amigos** (20 4th St. SE, 507/282-3300, 11 A.M.–10 P.M. daily, $5–14), which serves an interesting *salsa blanca* with the complimentary chips. They have another location (1611 Hwy. 52 N., 507/536-4527, same hours) north of downtown.

INFORMATION AND SERVICES

Tourist Information

The **Rochester Convention & Visitors Bureau** (111 Broadway S., Ste. 301, 507/288-4331 or 800/634-8277, www.rochestercvb.org, 8 A.M.–5 P.M. Mon.–Fri.) in the Shops at University Square has a very knowledgeable and friendly staff.

The weekly ***Rochester Area Visitor*** brochure (www.rochestervisiter.com) and the monthly ***Rochester Magazine*** (www.rochesermagazine.com) are available along the skyway and in most hotels.

Media

The city's daily newspaper is the ***Rochester Post-Bulletin*** (www.postbulletin.com), though the Twin Cities papers are also widely available.

Post Office

The main post office (1445 Valley High Dr. W., 507/287-1240, 8:30 A.M.–5 P.M. Mon.–Fri., closed Sat.–Sun.) is right downtown.

GETTING THERE

By Air

Rochester International Airport (7701 Helgerson Dr. SW, 507/282-2328, www.rochesterintlairport.com) is eight miles south of the city along Highway 63. **Delta Airlines** (800/225-2525) makes the short hop to the Twin Cities several times a day and also flies direct to Detroit. **American Airlines** (800/433-7300) flies nonstop to Chicago O'Hare Airport.

Yellow Cab Rochester Airport Shuttle (507/282-2222) runs between the airport and major hotels for $11.50 per person up till the last flight of the evening. A taxi will cost about $25 to downtown.

By Bus

Jefferson Lines (888/864-2832, www.jeffersonlines.com) buses stop at the Sinclair gas station (205 6th St. SW) downtown. **Go Rochester Direct** (507/280-9270 or 800/280-9270, www.gorochesterdirect.com, $29 one-way) runs vans to the Minneapolis–St. Paul

International Airport, Mall of America, and Winona (coinciding with Amtrak trains), with drop off and pick up at most of the city's major hotels. Reservations are required for the outbound trips and recommended for the return.

GETTING AROUND

By Bus

Rochester City Lines (507/288-4353, www.rochestercitylines.com, $2) is a comprehensive bus system, though there is no Sunday service. All routes begin and end downtown at the transit information center on 2nd Street SW.

By Taxi

Taxis aren't rare in Rochester, but waving one down isn't routine. If you need one, call **Yellow Cab** (507/282-2222).

Car Rentals

Most national car rental companies have airport branches. **Avis** (507/288-5222, 8 A.M.–11 P.M. Mon.–Fri., 9 A.M.–5 P.M. Sat., 11 A.M.–11 P.M. Sun.) is also downtown at the Kahler Grand Hotel (20 2nd Ave. SW, 507/280-6200).

AROUND ROCHESTER

Mantorville

This petite community (it's actually home to over 1,000 people, but you'd never know by looking at it) survives on tourism—half of all shops in town are antiques and gift stores—but it grew up on limestone. The Mantor Brothers, Peter, Riley, and Frank, came here from out east in 1853 and built a sawmill and gristmill on the Zumbro River, though they chose this particular spot with eyes on opening a quarry. Mantorville limestone has built buildings across the state and beyond. Naturally it was the material of choice for local architects, a factor that led to the entire downtown's inclusion on the National Register of Historic Places.

Up the hill and across from the 1871 Dodge County Courthouse (the oldest working courthouse in the state, unfortunately ruined aesthetically by the incompatible modern annex) is the **Dodge County Historical Society Museum** (615 Main St., 507/635-5508, 10 A.M.–4 P.M. Tues.–Sat. May–Oct., 10 A.M.–4 P.M. Thurs.–Sat. rest of year, closed one month starting mid-December, $2 adults). The main building, the former St. John's Episcopal Church, built in 1869, now contains a small but eclectic collection of historical curios, plus there's an 1856 house and 1883 one-room schoolhouse on the grounds.

Just down the street is the **Restoration House** (540 Main St. N., 507/635-5140, noon–5 P.M. Tues.–Sun. May–Oct., $2 adults), a fully restored and furnished 1856 home. It once served as a county office building, and what was then the county's only prison cell is still in the basement. In back is the even more interesting **Old Log Cabin,** built at roughly the same time. It was home to the cooper for the nearby Mantorville Brewery (now in ruins, though a new microbrewery, Mantorville Brewing, keeps the tradition alive) and many barrel-making tools are on display in the basement. The ***Mantorville Walking Tour*** brochure will lead you to dozens of other historic buildings. The **covered bridge** in Riverside Park is a modern addition, though it makes a nice photo.

The city's top historic site is a restaurant, not a museum. The **Hubbell House** (502 Main St. N., 507/635-2331, 11:30 A.M.–2 P.M. and 4–9 P.M. Mon.–Thurs., 11:30 A.M.–2 P.M. and 4–10:30 P.M. Fri., 11:30 A.M.–3 P.M. and 4–10:30 P.M. Sat., 11:30 A.M.–9 P.M. Sun., $7–28) has been in continuous operation since 1854, when it opened as a stagecoach stop. The current building, filled with antiques and Civil War memorabilia, went up in 1856, replacing the original log hotel. The varied menu includes such choices as walleye almondine, vegetable lasagna, raspberry chicken, and filet mignon.

The **Mantorville Theatre Company** (507/635-5420, www.mantorvillain.com) is best known for their boo-able summer melodramas ($8), though they do other productions during the rest of the year too. Their home base is the **Mantorville Opera House** (5 5th St. NE), a 1918 vaudeville theater.

The purely functional **Stussy Memorial RV**

Park (507/635-5170, $22 full hookup) has ten sites along the river.

Zumbrota

On your way to or from Rochester, be sure to stop for a look at Minnesota's only remaining original covered bridge. The 116-foot **Zumbrota Covered Bridge** was built in 1869 to serve the stagecoach route between St. Paul and Dubuque, Iowa. When a modern steel span replaced the barn-like structure in 1932, sensible locals insisted on preservation not demolition, though it didn't actually make it back over the riffling Zumbro River again until 1997. It now sits a block from where it originally stood.

Amish Country

Take some of the best scenery southeast Minnesota can throw at you, add bucolic bike trails, trophy trout streams, and the old order way of life, mix with a dash of luxurious indulgence, and you get Fillmore County, southern Minnesota's most popular destination. The state's largest Amish communities ring Harmony, and a chance to brush up against their way of life is a big draw, but the bike trails snaking through the deep valleys bring in most of the masses and have given Lanesboro hegemony in the county's tourist trade. While this is primarily a summer and fall destination—the Root River Valley is a remarkable fall-color canvas—more and more people are heading here in the winter to ski.

Most of what is detailed in this section lies along or near Highway 16, the federally designated **Historic Bluff Country Scenic Byway,** a winding 88-mile ribbon coming up the bluff-lined Root River Valley from La Crescent on the Mississippi River. West of Lanesboro the road leaves the valley to wind through the rolling farm fields trimmed with patches of forest and streams.

If you are here to cast a fly, the South Branch Root River above Preston and the streams that feed it are considered by many to be the best trout waters in the state, while Duschee Creek outside Lanesboro and Trout Run Creek east of Chatfield also come highly recommended.

LANESBORO

Little Lanesboro is one of Minnesota's loveliest towns. The entire downtown business district is listed on the National Register of Historic Places, and the plumb limestone bluff rising 320 feet behind it couldn't be any more perfect a backdrop.

The Southeastern Minnesota Railroad reached the valley in 1868, and Lanesboro was founded as a summer resort by and for East Coast bigwigs that year. The financiers dammed the Root River to create a lake for sailing and summer homes and built the three-story Phoenix Hotel, a luxurious dwelling filled with hand-carved oak woodwork, imported crystal chandeliers, and marble-topped dressers. The Phoenix did decent business until it burned down in 1885. (Despite the name, it was not rebuilt.) Though Lanesboro never became the great resort area its promoters had hoped, it turns out they were just ahead of their time. The city did thrive during the 19th century and well into the 20th, though it was milling, not tourism, that created the initial boom. Lanesboro hit the skids in the 1960s and, during two decades of decline, saw most businesses go belly up, leaving a downtown filled with vacant storefronts.

The rail line that created the town almost single-handedly re-created it in 1985 when the first five miles were converted into the Root River State Trail. Lanesboro is now one of the most popular travel destinations in the state, and, though fewer than 800 people reside here, many times that number pass through the city every weekend during the summer and fall—you'll probably tour half the town while searching out a parking space. Dozens of businesses

© TIM BEWER

Amish country scenery

now cater to the mostly affluent visitors who pedal the trails and shop by day, and pamper themselves with the fine dining and historic lodging at night.

Sights

The **Lanesboro Historical Museum** (105 Parkway Ave. S., 507/467-2177, 10 A.M.–3 P.M. Tues.–Fri., 11 A.M.–4 P.M. Sat.–Sun., free admission) began with the donation of wood carvings of local barber Hans Olson, and, though these are still the highlight of the collection, it has now expanded to include various other historical artifacts from the town's early days.

The **Eagle Bluff Environmental Learning Center** (28097 Goodview Dr., 507/467-2437 or 888/800-9558, www.eagle-bluff.org, free admission) is primarily a residential group conference center with educational and team-building programs, though the small **nature center** (8 A.M.–4:30 P.M. Mon.–Fri., 10 A.M.–4 P.M. Sat.–Sun.) with displays on karst geology and some of the hiking trails, which continue into the surrounding Richard J. Dorer Memorial Hardwood State Forest, are also open to the public. The monumental overlook of the Root River Valley, an easy quarter-mile stroll from the nature center, is alone worth the trip up here. Take County Highway 8 two miles west of town, turn right on County Highway 21, and follow the signs.

The DNR's **Lanesboro Fish Hatchery** (23789 Grosbeak Rd., 507/467-3771, 7 A.M.–3:30 P.M. Mon.–Thurs., 7 A.M.–4:30 P.M. Fri., free admission) produces around 750,000 brown and 300,000 rainbow trout annually. A video shown in the office presents the beginnings of the rearing process, and then you can see the rest of it in person. You'll see the biggest fish in the ponds and raceways during April and May. The fish farm is located along Duschee Creek (one of the state's best trout streams) a mile south of town on Highway 16.

To see something you just don't see every day, drop by the **Lanesboro Sales Barn** (402 Coffee St., 507/467-2192) on the east end of town. This is one of the largest livestock markets in the Upper Midwest, and an average of 1,000 head of cattle, often twice that, are auctioned off during the slaughter auction

BLUFFLANDS STATE TRAIL

A pair of immensely popular trails, collectively known as the Blufflands State Trail, are the ideal way to experience the beauty of southeast Minnesota. The 60 miles of paved path lead through the wooded valleys and past the towering limestone bluffs and rolling farm fields that define this corner of the state. As a bonus, deer, pheasant, and wild turkey encounters are quite common. The bikers and in-line skaters who flock here to use these trails are largely responsible for the area's economic resurrection. Heaviest use comes during the summer, but cross-country skiers make the trails year-round attractions.

The shade-covered **Root River State Trail** winds along its eponymous waterway for most of the 42 miles between Fountain and Houston, crossing 47 bridges along the way. The trail largely follows an abandoned railroad grade and is almost completely level except for a steep half-mile climb about five miles from the Houston end. Riders doing one-way trips should note that there is an appreciable downhill from west to east.

The just as beautiful **Harmony-Preston Valley State Trail,** an offshoot of the Root River Trail, leads 18 miles south to Harmony and has two distinct segments. The northern half crisscrosses Camp Creek, Watson Creek, and the South Branch Root River – like the Root River Trail, it is generally flat and pleasantly shady. Beginning at County Highway 16, about five miles south of Preston, the trail leaves the old railroad grade and climbs out of the valley over leg-burning hills. For many, it is a welcome break from the usual flat and straight miles of rail-to-trail conversions. Eventually you are rewarded for the effort with a sweeping view of the path you just traced. Beyond this there are just rolling hills on into Harmony.

Lanesboro, located along the western half of the Root River Trail and just five miles from the Harmony-Preston Valley Trail, is the main base for most riders, though most of the quaint rural communities along the trail have lodging and/or camping.

(8:30 A.M. Wed.). The regular livestock auction (10:30 A.M. Fri.) is mostly cattle, but also pigs, sheep, and goats.

R & M Amish Tours (507/467-2128, www.rmamish.com, 10 A.M., 1 P.M., 4 P.M. Mon.–Sat. year-round, $25 per person) will take you out to Amish farms in their vans. Tours depart from the Amish Experience gift shop (105 North Pkwy.). **Cheryl's Apparel** (102 Beacon St. E., 507/467-4466, www.cherylsapparel.com) arranges narrated city tours on **Molly the Trolley** (1 P.M. Sat. May–Oct., plus by demand, $10 adults).

Entertainment and Events

The respected **Commonweal Theatre Company** (208 Parkway Ave. N., 507/467-2525 or 800/657-7025, www.commonwealtheatre.org, $25) produces six shows throughout the year. During the summer the theater hosts the live radio broadcast of the *Over the Back Fence* musical variety show (7 P.M. Sun., $5); you can also listen in on KFIL (103.1 FM/1060 AM).

Also during the summer, live bands, blues and rock more often than not, play the patio at the **Riverside on the Root** (109 Parkway S., 507/467-3663, 11 A.M.–8 P.M. Sun.–Thurs., 11 A.M.–9 P.M. Fri.–Sat.) restaurant on Wednesday and Sunday nights. The public is always welcome at the monthly summer **barn dances** in the Sons of Norway Hall (200 Parkway S., 507/498-5452).

The artistic home of many local artists is the **Cornucopia Art Center** (103 Parkway Ave. N., 507/467-2446, www.lanesboroarts.org, 10 A.M.–5 P.M. Mon.–Thurs., 10 A.M.–7 P.M. Fri.–Sat., 11 A.M.–3 P.M. Sun.), where you will find single and group exhibitions, as well as a juried sales gallery filled with paintings, ceramics, textiles, and more.

Buffalo Bill Cody, a friend of David Powell, a famous Dakota doctor who lived in town, spent

© TIM BEWER
downtown Lanesboro

a great deal of time in Lanesboro in the years before and after forming his Wild West Show, and the town celebrates the connection by naming its biggest festival **Buffalo Bill Days.** The community blast has music, theater, canoe races, a parade, and lots of food the first weekend in August. **Art in the Park,** every third Sunday in June, attracts nearly 100 vendors and thousands of buyers. Two weeks earlier is the wacky **Rhubarb Festival** (www.rhubarbfestival.org). There's a **standstill parade** (www.standstillparade.org) the third Saturday in May in Whalen, four miles east of Lanesboro.

Shopping

Many businesses downtown sell antiques or Amish goods. You can buy the latter, plus produce and baked goods, directly from the source on Saturday mornings when a small **farmers market** convenes in Sylvan Park. There is a smaller market on Wednesday afternoons. The **Cornucopia Art Center** (103 Parkway Ave., 507/467-2446, 10 A.M.–5 P.M. Mon.–Thurs., 10 A.M.–7 P.M. Fri.–Sat., 11 A.M.–3 P.M. Sun.) carries top-quality and often reasonably priced work by dozens of regional artists.

Frank Wright (106 Coffee St. E., 507/467-3376, 10 A.M.–6 P.M. Thurs.–Sat., 10 A.M.–4 P.M. Sun., by appt. or by chance on other days), woodworker extraordinaire, primarily carves spoons, and you can pick up artistic utensils at his workshop.

The **Scenic Valley Winery** (101 Coffee St., 507/467-2958 or 888/965-0250, www.scenicvalleywinery.com, 10 A.M.–5 P.M. Mon.–Sat., 1 P.M.–5 P.M. Sun.) mainly produces fruit vintages such as cranberry, rhubarb, and apple, plus green pepper and garlic cooking wines. Free samples are always available.

Recreation

The **Root River State Trail** cuts straight through the heart of town, while the **Harmony-Preston Valley State Trail** begins about five miles away. Canoeists, kayakers, and inner tubers run the **Root River.** Both the north and south branches cut past towering bluffs and sheer limestone cliffs and are easy routes with generally nothing more than the occasional Class I rapid. The North Branch is widely considered the most scenic trip and is thus the most popular. The 30 miles between Chatfield and the confluence of the two branches near Whalen can be done in about 12 hours, though several campsites make it a great overnight trip, and a landing at Moen's Bridge right in the middle allows for more manageable day trips too. Below Whalen the valley widens and continues to expand for all of the 55 miles to the Mississippi River. Highway 16 hugs the river most of the way down, and though this makes for an incredible drive, it diminishes the quality of the paddling. For just a short jaunt consider the winding five-mile, 90-minute trip between Lanesboro and Whalen. A pair of outfitters in town can set you up with everything you need for some time on the trail or the river.

The **Little River General Store** (105 Coffee St., 507/467-2943 or 800/994-2943, 9 A.M.–6 P.M. daily, open until 8 P.M. Sat.–Sun. summer) rents canoes and kayaks and has a most impressive array of bikes, including

© TIM BEWER

riding side by side on the Root River State Trail

tandems, recumbents, tandem recumbents, and even side-by-side four-seater surreys. Shuttle service for bikers is available along the entire trail system with advanced notice.

The smaller, though generally cheaper, **Root River Outfitters** (109 Parkway Ave. S., 507/467-3400, www.rootriveroutfitters.com, by appt. Mon.–Fri., 8 A.M.–4 P.M. Sat.–Sun.) has bikes, canoes, and inner tubes. Both companies provide shuttle service with watercraft rentals.

Accommodations

With well over a dozen in and around town, little Lanesboro is the bed-and-breakfast capital of Minnesota. Yet, even with many other hotels, historic inns, and cottages, it is often difficult to find a room on summer weekends without booking months in advance. The Lanesboro Visitor Center keeps a list of vacancies in and around town for last-minute visitors, and when the city is full up don't fret; there are plenty of quality options in the nearby towns. Two-night minimum stays are the norm on summer weekends.

Proudly gay-owned ("Expect all the positive stereotypes!" they boast) **Belle Rive** (302 Ashburn St. E., 507/467-2407, www.bellerivebandblanesboro.com, $125–150) has just one guest room, so guests get plenty of privacy, including their own deck and ample living space. Arriving here feels just like coming home to your own comfortable, friendly, well-kept house.

Newly built on 50 acres, **The Inn at Sacred Clay Farm** (23234 Grosbeak Rd., 507/467-9600 or 866/326-8618, www.sacredclayfarmbandb.com, $140–235) offers a true escape—you won't even find TVs, telephones, or computer hookups in the rooms). There are five rooms, from a simple ground-floor double flooded in light to a private loft retreat with a whirlpool, arranged around a vaulted sitting room.

The colorful ☾ **Scandinavian Inn** (701 Kenilworth Ave. S., 507/467-4500, www.scandinavianinn.com, $99), a bright and lovely 1893 home with original woodwork, period furnishings, assorted items gathered during extensive foreign travel, and four cozy guestrooms (two with private bath), prides itself on environmentally friendly policies: Cleaning products are all natural while breakfast is organic and locally grown. Ask about their Ukrainian egg painting lessons.

If you really want to be pampered, book a room at the **Berwood Hill Inn** (22139 Hickory Rd., 507/765-2391 or 800/803-6748, www.berwood.com, $95), a museum-quality Victorian mansion surrounded by an incredible garden four miles west of town. Each of the four eclectic and luxurious guestrooms has a private bath, while a simple cottage (the bathroom is inside the main house) is also available. A gourmet breakfast is included in the price, plus afternoon tea and dinner options—not to mention their renowned chocolate tastings—are available with advance notice.

The venerable **Mrs. B's** (101 Parkway Ave. N., 507/467-2154 or 800/657-4710, www.mrsbsinn.com, $125) is right along the river and trail—this is one of the few businesses that predates it—in the heart of town. Each of the nine cozy rooms in the impressive 1870 limestone inn have a unique character, including some rosemaled and hand-carved Norwegian beds and fireplaces.

Another classic 19th-century limestone structure on the north end of town has been converted into the **Stone Mill Suites** (100 Beacon St. E., 507/467-8663 or 866/897-8663, www.stonemillsuites.com, $100). Many original features, such as the thick interior walls and wooden beams, have been left exposed, and some of the larger of the 10 themed rooms have lofts and fireplaces.

The friendly and attractive **Brewster's Red Hotel** (106 Parkway Ave. S., 507/467-2999, www.brewstersredhotel.com, $70) is in an 1870 home that climbs church hill. The nine individually decorated rooms are a good value, and the patio and deck are great places to unwind.

What the **Coffee Street Inn** (305 Coffee St. E., 507/467-2674, www.coffeestreetinn.com, $60–245) lacks in style, it makes up for with its friendly staff and excellent location: just off Main Street and within walking distance of much of what you came to Lanesboro to see, including theater, shopping, and restaurants.

The city runs a pair of first-come, first-served **campgrounds** (202 Parkway Ave. S., 507/467-3722, $25 RVs, $10 tents): 27 RV sites with water and electric hookups are jammed together at **Sylvan Park,** though the pond-side tent sites are decent enough. The 16 RV sites between the river and the high school football field at the nearby **Riverview Campground** are a bit more spread out, but you need to head over to the park for showers.

Food

The most talked-about restaurant in town is the casual and creative **Old Village Hall** (111 Coffee St., 507/467-2962, www.oldvillagehall.com, 5–8 P.M. Mon. and Wed., 5–9:30 P.M. Fri., 4:30–9:30 P.M. Sat., 4:30–8:30 P.M. Sun., hours change seasonally, $14–25). The trailside deck is a popular place to dine on salmon with Thai curry or lamb chops with mint pesto sauce and drink from the award-winning wine list.

Naturally, most of the tables at the laid-back, blues-infused **Riverside on the Root** (109 Parkway Ave. S., 507/467-3663, 11 A.M.–8 P.M. Sun.–Thurs., 11 A.M.–9 P.M. Fri.–Sat., limited schedule Nov.–Mar., $6–25), overlook the river. They serve burgers and pizzas throughout the week and step it up a notch on weekends with seafood, steak, and chops on the outdoor grill.

For more small-time charm, have an elk burger or a hearty omelet at the **Chat-n-Chew** (701 Parkway Ave. S., 507/467-3444, 6 A.M.–2 P.M. Mon.–Fri., 7 A.M.–1:30 P.M. Sat.–Sun.). The wooden booths are usually filled with regulars.

Last, but certainly not least, is **Das Wurst Haus** (117 Parkway Ave. N., 507/467-2902, 11 A.M.–5 P.M. daily Apr.–Nov., $3–6). The meat, bread, sauerkraut, and mustard for their brats, Reubens, and other German-style sandwiches are all made in-house. They also brew their own root beer and serve an extraordinary number of ice cream cones, and at any time you might hear a random act of polka.

Information and Services

The **Lanesboro Visitor Center** (100 Milwaukee Rd., 507/467-2696 or 800/944-

2670, www.lanesboro.com, 10 A.M.–5 P.M. Mon.–Sat., noon–4 P.M. Sun. June–Oct., noon–5 P.M. Fri.–Sat. Nov.–Feb., plus Mon. in Mar. and Tues. and Thurs. Apr.–May) is located one block east of Parkway Avenue along the Root River Trail.

WEST OF LANESBORO

Preston

The Fillmore County seat is quite a bit larger than Lanesboro, but a whole lot quieter due to the scarcity of tourists. "America's Trout Capital," as Preston has declared itself, is tucked into a deep bend of the **South Branch Root River,** and the fishing is superb from here all the way up to Forestville/Mystery Cave State Park. For most, the main reason to come to Preston is to leave it, either along the river or via the **Harmony-Preston Valley State Trail.** The 14-mile trip by water to Lanesboro has just a few small riffles and is a much less traveled route than that below Lanesboro, though this is in part because it is a difficult run when water levels are low. If you call ahead you can tour the **Pro-Corn Ethanol Plant** (701 Industrial Dr. N., 507/765-4548, 8 A.M.–4 P.M. Mon.–Fri., free admission).

The simple **Trailhead Inn** (112 Center St., 507/765-2460, www.trailhead-inn.com, $55), sitting right where it says it does, has 11 fairly large rooms.

The fanciest rooms in town are at the **JailHouse Inn** (109 Houston St. NW, 507/765-2181, www.jailhouseinn.com, $82). The 1869 brick building did serve as the courthouse and jail, but it has been completely gutted and gussied up, and now the only evidence of its former use are the room names and the original bars left behind in the "Cell Block." Each of the 12 cozy rooms has a unique touch, whether that's Amish furnishings, antique decorations, or claw-foot tubs, and there are some whirlpool suites. A full breakfast is included.

One mile south of town, off County Highway 17 right between the river and the trail, is **The Old Barn Resort** (507/467-2512 or 800/552-2512, www.barnresort.com, $34 with full hook-up, $25 hostel bed). The massive campground (130 RV and 40 tent sites) is as crowded as you'd expect it to be, but the location makes it a good choice anyway. The barn itself houses the offices, a busy restaurant, a game room, and a four-room, 44-bed hostel in the basement, while a swimming pool and 18-hole golf course surround it.

Another vast campground is the grassy **Maple Springs Campground** (21606 County Road 118, 507/352-2056, www.maplespringscampground.com, $18 tent, $25 full hookup), as groomed as a city park. There are 69 sites and a well-stocked store on-site.

Locals looking for a nice night out come from across the county to dine at the **Branding Iron** (1100 Circle Heights Dr., 507/765-3388, 11:30 A.M.–9 P.M. Tues.–Thurs. and Sun., 11:30 A.M.–9:30 P.M. Fri.–Sat., $7–22), a casual supper club perched above town along U.S. 52.

Get sandwiches to go or eat in the simple bakery at the **Sweet Stop & Sandwich Shop** (110 St. Anthony St. S., 507/765-9956, www.sweetstop.net, 7:30 A.M.–7 P.M. Mon.–Fri., 7:30 A.M.–4 P.M. Sat., closed Sun.).

The Trailhead Inn and Old Barn rent bikes, and the Old Barn also has inner tubes and canoes.

Fountain

Other than to access the **Root River State Trail,** which has its western terminus here, the main reason to stop in Fountain is to visit the **Fillmore County History Center** (202 County Hwy. 8, 507/268-4449, 9 A.M.–4 P.M. Mon.–Fri., free admission), the largest museum in the area by far. The historical medley contains thousands of objects from the distant and not-so-distant past, such as fossils, old toys, housewares, clothes, classic cars, and farm equipment. Their 36 restored Oliver tractors date back to the 1920s. Outside are a furnished one-room schoolhouse and a spruced-up log cabin from the late 1860s.

Fountain is named for the abundant natural springs in the area, and the results of those springs has lent the town its motto: "Sink Hole Capital of the U.S.A." There are about 100 of these small, usually shallow pits right around town; look for clumps of trees. One is fenced off directly across from the museum. You can see many more along County Highway 8 west of town and from a viewing platform just down the Root River Trail.

Wykoff

Until 1989, when Ed Krueger died, there was little reason for visitors to come to this sleepy village. Unlike anything you've ever seen, **Ed's Museum** (100 Gold St. S., 1–4 P.M. Sat.–Sun. summer, free admission) is a meticulously organized monument to messiness. The town's most colorful character ran this Jack Sprat grocery store and resided upstairs. When his wife died in 1940, Ed pretty much stopped throwing things away, and he left the store, and everything in it, to the town on the condition that it be turned into a museum. The local historical society fixed up the building, tossed out tons—literally—of what they decided was rubbish, and organized the rest of his hoard to a degree of orderliness that would pass boot camp muster—and probably make Ed turn in his grave. Still, the collection is amazing, and careful scanning of the boxes and shelves will reveal some surprising finds, like his mummified cat Sammy and a jar with 25 gallstones. Other things laying about the store include junk mail, every magazine he ever subscribed to, and unsold store merchandise. Thankfully some things, such as his desk, were left in their original state, and there are photos of the store before its unfortunate rearranging. If the museum is closed, inquire across the street at **The Bank Gift Haus** (105 Gold St. N., 507/352-4205, call for hours).

The Historic Wykoff Jail Haus (219 Main St. S., 507/352-4205, $75) is an original 1913 jailhouse that the town has renovated into a little bed-and-breakfast. You can sleep on bunks in the two original cell blocks or use the fold-out bed in the sitting room. It's not fancy, but hey...you're in jail!

The best place in town to grab a light meal is **Margaret's Tea Room** (105 Gold St. N., 507/352-4205, 11 A.M.–3 P.M. Mon.–Sat.) in the back of the Bank Gift Haus.

Spring Valley

Spring Valley has just over 2,500 inhabitants, enough to make it the largest town in the county. Laura Ingalls Wilder and her husband, Almanzo, whose parents moved here from New York when he was 13, attended the Methodist-Episcopal Church in Spring Valley during 1890 and 1891. Today the simple church with its lovely stained-glass windows houses part of the **Spring Valley Historical Museum** (221 Courtland St. W., 507/346-7659, www.springvalleymnmuseum.org, 10 A.M.–4 P.M. daily summer, Sat.–Sun. Sept.–Oct., $4 adults). Naturally, the handful of Wilder photos and memorabilia are the primary draw. The rest of the historical hodgepodge includes an antique camera collection, 1874 horse-drawn fire wagon, funeral wreaths woven from human hair, and an exhibit on Richard Sears, founder of Sears, Roebuck & Co., who was born in nearby Stewartville. Across the street is the 1865 Washburn-Zittleman House, furnished as it would have been at the turn of the 20th century. Another building has school, military, and agricultural displays. The Wilder's home is gone, but if you want to see their barn ask the staff for directions.

Spring Valley Inn & Suites (745 Broadway N., 507/346-7788 or 888/254-6835, www.springvalleyinnsuites.com, $72) has modern rooms.

Elaine's Café (125 Broadway S., 507/346-7492, 6 A.M.–6 P.M. Tues.–Thurs., 6 A.M.–1 P.M. Mon. and Sat.–Sun., 6 A.M.–7 P.M. Fri., $2–10) is a no-nonsense joint where locals linger over coffee and catch up on town news. If you're lucky the daily special will be the Tater Tot hot dish.

FORESTVILLE AND MYSTERY CAVE STATE PARK

You can do more in one afternoon at this diverse park (507/352-5111) than most vacationers do all weekend. You can explore Minnesota's longest cave, step back to the 19th century in the village of Forestville, hike the wooded hills and valleys, dip a line in three of Minnesota's best trout streams, and much more.

Historic Forestville

Founded in 1853, Forestville, like many other fledgling communities in the south of the state, became a rural trade center for area farmers. One hundred and ten people lived here at its peak, but when the newly formed Southern Minnesota Railroad bypassed it in 1868 it faltered, and by 1890 Thomas Meighen had acquired the entire town and much of the surrounding land. Each of the fifty remaining residents worked for Meighen on his farm, in his general store, or at his saw and feed mills. Today part of the village is brought to life, as it would have been in the summer of 1899, by costumed interpreters portraying actual town residents. During the hour-long **living-history tours** (21899 County Rd. 118, 507/765-2785, 10 A.M.–5 P.M. Tues.–Fri., 11 A.M.–6 P.M. Sat., noon–5 P.M. Sun. summer, 10 A.M.–5 P.M. Sat., noon–5 P.M. Sun. Sept.–Oct., $6 adults), you'll get to compare prices in the General Store (much of the original stock was left on the shelves when it closed in 1910), sample something fresh from the oven in the Meighen's kitchen, and help the farm laborers in the garden.

Mystery Cave

The entrance to Minnesota's longest-known cavern is five miles west of the main park. Thirteen miles of winding passage were carved into the limestone bedrock over many thousands of years, and the South Branch Root River still feeds this living cave before flowing through the park proper. The standard one-hour **tour** (507/937-3251, 10 A.M.–5 P.M. daily summer, 10 A.M.–4 P.M. Sat.–Sun. Apr.–May and Sept.–Oct., $10 adults) follows a lighted wheelchair-accessible concrete path past the stalactites, stalagmites, and underground pools. At least twice a day during summer weekends a two-hour tour using handheld lanterns leads along a gravel path through a different level of the cave. There are fewer formations along the way, but you will see larger passages. Bring something warm to wear since the cave remains a constant 48 degrees.

Trails

Most of the 17 or so miles of trail in the 3,296-acre park have some climbs, though they are generally very scenic, so your effort is rewarded. One of the more popular routes is the mile-long climb up the **Sandbank Trail** to the overlook. Follow the **Ravine** and **Maple Ridge** trails to enjoy the profusion of spring wildflowers. The only level hike is the **Big Spring Trail,** though it can be very wet, and there is no bridge over Canfield Creek near the end. If you hike the whole two miles to the Big Spring at the head of the valley, you'll experience a microclimate 10 degrees cooler than the rest of the park. Look carefully in the winter and spring when there is no vegetation in the way, and you'll find hidden caves and springs near many of the trails. Most of the trails are open to and popular with horseback riders, and over half are groomed for cross-country skiing in the winter.

Camping

The quiet campground has 73 sites in three loops. Those in Loop A are the best, all shaded and widely spaced, while B and C are mostly shady. All 23 electric sites are in Loop C. Horse riders have a 60-unit (23 electric) camp of their own.

HARMONY

This friendly town lies right between the area's two largest Amish communities. The Amish drop into town quite frequently and you are much more likely to pass their horse-drawn buggies around here than anywhere else. The region's biggest tourist draw after Lanesboro got its name rather spontaneously. When a discussion of what to call the newly formed town became overly heated, one exasperated member of the group stood up and exclaimed: "Let's have harmony here!" The opposing sides pondered the statement briefly, and they've had Harmony ever since.

A PEOPLE APART, A PEOPLE TOGETHER

And be not conformed to this world: but be ye transformed by the renewing of your mind, that ye may prove what is that good, and acceptable, and perfect, will of God.

– Romans 12:2

The country roads around Harmony are lined with Amish farmsteads. Spend even a little time here and you'll pass bearded men (sans mustaches since they associate these with the military) and bonneted women in their plain, home-sewn clothes clopping along in horse-drawn buggies or out working the fields.

Scattered pockets of Amish dot Minnesota farm country, about 1,000 in total, but Fillmore County's community is the largest. Driven west by rising land prices, the first Amish relocated here from Ohio in 1974. Southeast Minnesota appealed to the transplants because of the abundance of wood, natural springs, and creameries. From just an initial few, the tight-knit community has grown to about 114 families (800 people) in five church districts. A second and entirely separate group of about 40 families came up from Iowa in the mid-1990s and now resides to the southwest of Harmony. Both are strict Old Order sects. A less austere community, also relocated from Iowa, resides not too far away to the north near St. Charles.

THE ORDNUNG

Though the Amish were born of the Radical Reformation, today they constitute the most conservative faction of American society. While some Amish sects are less strict, the Old Order of Fillmore County have retained much of their 17th-century culture. They travel by horse and buggy, light their homes with kerosene lamps, and cook on wood-burning stoves. Children study English in school, though their mother tongue remains the German dialect known as Pennsylvania Dutch (Deutsch), and Sunday worship is conducted in High German. Among the modern developments that they reject are indoor plumbing, musical instruments (emotions might be stirred), daylight savings time, zippers, rubber tires, and insurance.

Amish doctrines, while varying slightly from community to community (there is no central Amish organization), all stem from the core belief that the Bible is the literal word of God and are maintained in the *Ordnung* (Order), a strict, unwritten moral code. The twin tenets remain separation and obedience; the latter referred to as *Gelassenheit* (literally "submission to authority," though often translated as humility), which promotes exclusive and tightly knit communities. The simplicity and self-denial that defines the Amish lifestyle wards off temptation and promotes self-sufficiency.

Church elders are willing to strike a balance between change and tradition, and though they always aim toward the latter, the Amish are not quite as stuck in the past as they appear. While they do not use electricity in their homes (if you see an Amish household with power lines it is because most deeds require the electrical system to remain in working order until the property is paid off), diesel engines are one technology that the Amish have widely embraced. Motors are used in woodworking shops, to pump water, and in many aspects of farming. Commercial dairying in particular requires adherence to strict storage and sanitation laws that simply cannot be met without a touch of technology. Automobiles too are an accepted part of Amish life, though owning and driving them are not, since this would result in inequality and make travel too easy. Just about every Amish family in Fillmore County has a close relationship with someone who owns a car whom they can pay for rides. They also ride Greyhound and Amtrak when visiting relatives back east.

MODERN CONFLICTS

From the start the Amish have been at conflict with the society around them, or more accurately society has been in conflict with the Amish around them. Today's Amish are almost completely free to practice their beliefs as they desire, though problems occur when their strict biblical interpretations run counter to the law. One of the most important examples is in education. Amish children attend private one-room schools through the 8th grade – the Old Order prohibits formal education beyond this – a belief that by the 1950s had created quite an uproar in many places. The issue was, for the most part, settled in 1972 by a unanimous Supreme Court decision (Wisconsin v. Yoder) exempting the Amish and similar groups from compulsory school attendance laws.

A more recent and enduring example is the use of slow-moving vehicle signs. In the interest of public safety many Amish affix the familiar orange triangles to the rear of their buggies, but others, mostly elders, refuse because doing so means putting their faith in "worldly symbols" rather than God. An outline of silver reflective tape was a solution accepted reluctantly by most states, but not Minnesota. Back in the 1980s the Highway Patrol argued that this method was insufficient because it only let drivers know that something is ahead but does not communicate that it is moving at a slow speed. A 1986 compromise permitting black triangles with a white outline pleased neither side completely and lasted just a year. The state and other proponents of mandatory signage, including most Harmony area residents, argued that safety concerns outweighed a religious view that was not even held by all church members. Additionally they pointed out that the Amish opposition to the orange safety signs was inconsistent with their use of orange hunting attire. As many Fillmore County Amish ended up in jail over repeat violations, the Minnesota Supreme Court, citing Wisconsin v. Yoder amongst other things, overturned the convictions. Today very few use the orange triangles.

MEET THE AMISH

Signs like "Quilts" or "Eggs and Honey" fronting Amish farms don't just advertise what the farm produces, they invite you to stop and buy. In some cases you will meet the family, though many rely on the honor system. On Saturdays during the summer and fall many drive their buggies into Harmony and Lanesboro or park along U.S. Highway 52 to sell their wares: Bread, produce, jellies and jams, honey, candy, baskets, furniture, and one-of-a-kind quilts are all common.

Though you are welcome to ask, they tend not to like discussing their culture or religion with the English, as all outsiders are called. Fact is, they don't let you onto their property to be sociable, they just want your money. To learn about their lives and customs or just get an explanation of what you are seeing, join a tour or hire a ride-along guide in Harmony or Lanesboro. A typical tour lasts about 2.5 hours and visits a woodworking shop and around five farms with different items for sale. While the van tours are becoming the method of choice, the ride-along guides have the advantage of letting you set the route: Decide what sorts of things you wish to see or buy and they will lead you to a farm that has it.

Whether touring with a guide or on your own, do not take photos of people, a practice they believe is forbidden by the Second Commandment. Also, never stop at an Amish house on a Sunday or a religious holiday.

Sights and Recreation

Amish Tours of Harmony (94 2nd St. NW, 507/886-2303 or 800/752-6474, www.amish-tours.com, $40 in your car, $20 per person in their van) next to the visitors center offers guided tours year-round.

In 1924 a farmer followed the squeals of his missing pigs and found they had fallen into a deep cavern, and **Niagara Cave** (507/886-6606 or 800/837-6606, www.niagaracave.com, 9:30 A.M.–5:30 P.M. daily summer, 10 A.M.–4:30 P.M. daily May and Sept., 10 A.M.–4:30 P.M. Sat.–Sun. Apr. and Oct., $10.50 adults) opened to the paying public ten years later. Stalactites, stalagmites, flowstone, and fossils are found in many of the large caverns, though the highlight of this living, growing cave is the 60-foot underground waterfall. The cave is four miles outside Harmony: Take Highway 139 south, and follow the signs. Amish Tours will drive you out and back for a few bucks.

Slim's Woodshed (160 1st St. NW, 507/886-3114, www.slimswoodshed.com, 9 A.M.–5 P.M. Mon.–Sat. year-round, noon–4 P.M. Sun. May–Dec., $4) is a combination classroom, store, and museum, and the collection of carvings from around the globe is most enjoyable. Slim figures that the more than 4,000 pieces makes this the largest collection in the world.

Harmony is the southern terminus of the **Harmony-Preston Valley State Trail.** A sinkhole located along the trail has been developed as a **Karst Interpretive Site,** with signs describing the geology of the area. **Kingsley Mercantile** (2 Main Ave. N., 507/886-2323, 7:30 A.M.–6:30 P.M. Mon.–Fri., 8 A.M.–5 P.M. Sat., 11 A.M.–2 P.M. Sun.) rents bikes, and though there is no regular shuttle service here, if you are staying in town the proprietors of your hotel or bed-and-breakfast might be able to make arrangements. Whether you are riding the trail or not, check out the **Historic Hobo Camp** woodcarvings at Trailhead Park.

The **Jem Theatre** (14 Main Ave. N., 507/886-7469, $4) is a small renovated 1940s movie house showing first-run films on weekends. The popcorn is topped with real butter.

Shopping

Many shops downtown sell Amish goods and/or antiques, and an informal **Amish farmers and craft market** sets up by the grain elevator on Saturday mornings during the summer and fall.

Arranged around **The Village Green** (90–92 2nd St. NW, 507/886-2409, www.village-depot.com, 10 A.M.–5 P.M. Mon.–Sat., noon–4 P.M. Sun. mid-Apr.–Dec., Sat. only rest of year) are a handful of old buildings stocked to the rafters with authentic Amish quilts, baskets, furniture, and more.

Accommodations and Food

The **Country Lodge** (525 Main Ave. N., 507/886-2515 or 800/870-1710, $71) is a very friendly and homey hotel in a renovated creamery.

Harmony Guest House (115 2nd Ave. SW, 507/886-4331, $90) offers a pair of cozy little one-bedroom houses; one has a deck with a hot tub and barbecue pit.

Austin's Mohair (11484 331st Ave., 507/886-6731, $10) has four primitive campsites along a road traveled frequently by their Amish neighbors, and children from neighboring farms will come by to sell you firewood.

Locals catch up on gossip at **Harmony House** (57 Main Ave. N., 507/886-4612, 5:30 A.M.–1:30 P.M. daily) over burgers, pork chops, beer-battered fish dinners, and good pie.

Get pizza, sandwiches, and homemade pies at the **Village Square** (51 Main Ave. N., 507/886-4406, 11 A.M.–9 P.M. Tues.–Sat., 4–8 P.M. Sun.).

Information

Get all the local information you need at the **Harmony Visitor Center** (15 2nd St. NW, 507/886-2469 or 800/288-7153, www.harmony.mn.us, 9 A.M.–5 P.M. daily June–Sept., 10 A.M.–4 P.M. daily May and Oct.).

Historic Bluff Country (507/886-2230 or 800/428-2030, www.bluffcountry.com, 9 A.M.–5 P.M. Mon.–Fri. year-round), across the hall, covers the whole region and keeps a list of lodging vacancies.

I-35 Corridor

The west side of southeast Minnesota lies just beyond the hills and valleys that define this corner of the state. This is the start of the flat farm country of the Great Plains, and agriculture is the principal industry. Excepting Northfield, a vibrant college town, these interstate-hugging cities, all county seats with populations roughly around 20,000, are exceptionally ordinary, but herein lies their charm. Blocks of unblemished 19th-century storefronts line the streets as a testament to their former prosperity; architecture and history fans can get walking tour brochures for each town at the local history museums or chambers of commerce. Yet, unlike some other cities chock-full of classic architecture—Stillwater for instance—with businesses aimed primarily at the throngs of tourists, Faribault, Owatonna, Albert Lea, and Austin remain genuine Main Street shopping districts, with family-owned shoe stores, pharmacies, lunch counters, and the like still thriving. So stop, have a look around, and take the pulse of Middle America.

NORTHFIELD

This charming city straddling the Cannon River exudes a European charm. John North, a progressive-thinking lawyer from New York, founded The City of Cows, Colleges and Contentment in 1855. He constructed the Ames Mill (today the home of Malt-O-Meal) the next year, and the flour it produced, using a new and improved milling process, won an award at the 1876 Centennial Exposition World's Fair in Philadelphia. Milling declined toward the end of the 19th century, and many locals turned to dairy cows—area farmers were amongst the first in the nation to raise Holsteins for their livelihood—and by the early 1900s Northfield was one of America's leading dairy centers. Agriculture remains the area's top industry, though Northfield's fortunes rest squarely on its two high-ranking colleges. Tops is Carleton College, known as the "Harvard of the Midwest" for attracting more National Merit Scholars than any other liberal arts college in the country. St. Olaf College, well known for its music program, holds tightly to its Norwegian roots and is the home of the national archives of the Norwegian-American Historical Society. Together the pair, founded in 1866 and 1874 respectively, have nearly 5,000 students, and while it's impossible to know what would have come of Northfield had the schools not thrived, it certainly wouldn't be the vibrant place it is today.

Northfield is most famous for a violent bank robbery. On September 7, 1876, the James-Younger gang, led by the infamous Jesse and Frank James, rode into town and raided the First National Bank, but the robbery was foiled by the courageous townsfolk. Joseph Heywood, the acting cashier, refused to assist, even though the safe was unlocked (none of the outlaws tried to open it on their own and they only got away with $26.60, all in coins), a brave act of resistance for which he was fatally shot. Alerted men took up the fight on the streets, killing two of the eight outlaws. The remaining six, including the James brothers, were pursued across the state by a posse that grew as large as 1,000, and eventually each gang member was captured or killed. Hollywood has rehashed the affair many times, but never once bothered to do so accurately. Though the robbers later told conflicting stories about the heist, Cole Younger asserted that they ventured all the way up to Minnesota from Missouri because the bank held funds of two carpetbaggers they despised (Adelbert Ames, who ran the mill, had been a Northern general and was later appointed governor of Mississippi by President Grant, and General Benjamin Butler of Massachusetts), thus some observers consider it the last battle of the Civil War.

Sights

The First National Bank is now part of the **Northfield Historical Society Museum**

© TRICIA CORNELL

Northfield's Bridge Square is a popular gathering place.

(408 Division St., 507/645-9268, www.northfieldhistory.org, 10 A.M.–4 P.M. Tues.–Sat., 1–4 P.M. Sun. year-round, plus 10 A.M.–4 P.M. Mon. summer, $4 adults). Though the counter is a replica, the safe, clock (permanently set to 1:50), and other items are original, and it looks exactly as it did on that fateful day. One room has displays about the robbery, including some of the outlaws' guns and a saddle, plus a small back room hosts rotating exhibits on other aspects of city history. If you can't be in town for the annual reenactment of the shoot-out, you can watch it on video. The ***Outlaw Trail*** brochure available at the museum and chamber details sites in Northfield and beyond where they ate, slept, rendezvoused, and hid out. The ***Northfield Historic Points of Interest*** brochure leads you on an architectural tour of the town; one of the stops is the modest home of Norwegian-born author O. E. Rolvaag. For many visitors, a wander through downtown and a stroll along the riverwalk, followed by a rest in lovely **Bridge Square,** is the highlight of a visit to Northfield. The downtown park hosts special events such as concerts every Thursday night during the summer, plus special events at other times.

The scenic St. Olaf and Carleton campuses possess several minor attractions. The **Carleton College Art Gallery** (507/646-4469, 11 A.M.–4 P.M. Mon.–Wed., noon–10 P.M. Thurs.–Fri., noon–4 P.M. Sat.–Sun., free admission) is in the lower level of the school's Concert Hall. The **Goodsell Observatory** (507/646-4000) is a beautiful 1887 Richardsonian Romanesque building. If the skies are clear on the first Friday of the month, you can gaze at the planets through its original 16.2-inch refractor during the first two hours after dark. Both buildings are centered on the Bald Spot (where you'll probably have to dodge flying disks—this school is mad about ultimate Frisbee) in the center of campus. Nearby, behind the Cowling Recreation Center, is a petite **Japanese Garden.** St. Olaf's **Flaten Art Museum** (507/646-3248, 10 A.M.–5 P.M. Mon.–Wed. and Fri., 10 A.M.–8 P.M. Thurs., 2–5 P.M. Sat.–Sun., free admission) features work by regional, national, and international artists.

Entertainment

The very active **Northfield Arts Guild** (304 Division St., 507/645-8877, www.northfield-artsguild.org) produces six musical, comedic, and dramatic plays a year, including some for children, at the **NAG Theater** (411 W. 3rd St.) and hosts concerts, readings, and more.

There is usually something interesting going on at **Carleton College** (1 College St. N., 507/646-4000) and **St. Olaf** (1520 St. Olaf Ave., 507/646-3002), and the public is welcome.

Two wonderful basement pubs face each other across the river. While both the **Contented Cow** (302 Division St., 507/663-1351, 3 P.M.–midnight Mon.–Thurs. and Sat.–Sun., 3 P.M.–1 A.M. Fri.) and **Froggy Bottoms** (305 Water St. S., 507/664-0260, 10 A.M.–10 P.M. daily) have their own personal faunal theme, they have much in common, including riverside patios, live music, and smoke-free air. **Hogan Brothers' Acoustic Café** (415 Division St. S., 507/645-6653, 9 A.M.–9 P.M. daily) also has live music on weekends.

Events

The **Defeat of Jesse James Days,** one of Minnesota's biggest festivals, spans five days, but the highlight takes just seven minutes. The infamous raid and shoot-out is reenacted in front of the First National Bank six times on Saturday and Sunday. The festival begins on Wednesday with a graveside service for Joseph Lee Heywood and Nicolaus Gustavson, the two innocent men killed during the robbery attempt, and is followed by an antique tractor pull, rodeo, arts and crafts show, and parade, among other things. It all takes place the weekend after Labor Day. The city of Madelia, 65 miles to the east, reenacts the capture of the Younger Brothers the following weekend.

The **St. Olaf Christmas Festival,** begun in 1912, draws thousands to Northfield in early December and reaches a much larger audience with a national broadcast on PBS. Hymns, carols, and other choral works are performed by the acclaimed St. Olaf Choir and other vocal groups, with accompaniment from the St. Olaf Orchestra: over 500 student musicians in total. Another musical event is the **Bridge Chamber Music Festival** the first weekend in June.

Shopping

Downtown Northfield has many specialty shops along Division Street. The little **Northfield Arts Guild Gallery** (304 Division St., 507/645-8877, 10 A.M.–5 P.M. Tues.–Fri., 11 A.M.–3 P.M. Sat.) displays and sells the work of artists from across southeast Minnesota.

The gift shop at the **Northfield Historical Society Museum** (408 Division St., 507/645-9268, www.northfieldhistory.org, 10 A.M.–4 P.M. Tues.–Sat., 1–4 P.M. Sun. year-round, plus 10 A.M.–4 P.M. Mon. summer, $4 adults) has seemingly every Jesse James book in print, plus other Minnesota-related titles.

Recreation

The gem of the Carleton campus is the **Cowling Arboretum,** 880 acres of natural beauty originally dubbed "Cowling's Folly" by those who disagreed with then-President Donald Fowling's investment. But, like so many so-called "follies" in history, the Arb, as it is known, has been vindicated and is now central to campus life. The Upper Arb, the area closest to the main campus, includes playing fields and is crisscrossed by paved and unpaved paths for running and biking. The much larger portion, the Lower Arb, is less developed and a lovely place for more solitary hiking and running (but no biking is allowed). The easiest place to access the Lower Arb is behind the West Gymnasium (321 Division St. N.). Cross Division Street and walk north a few hundred yards to access the Upper Arb. (Note that the Lower Arb, so named because it lies low in the Cannon River valley, actually lies to the north of the Upper Arb.)

If you'd rather paddle down the Cannon, a state-designated Wild and Scenic River, it's 11 easy miles through a mix of forest and farm to **Lake Byllesby Regional Park,** just before the city of Cannon Falls. The river's best scenery lies along the final 25 miles between Cannon Falls and the Mississippi River. Above Northfield it's a generally peaceful 16-mile, six- to eight-hour paddle down the mostly wooded

© TRICIA CORNELL

Division Street in downtown Northfield is a lively shopping district full of independent boutiques.

valley from Faribault, and there are several campsites along the way.

Accommodations

Rooms in and around Northfield fill up fast—as in four years in advance—for St. Olaf and Carleton graduation and homecoming weekends. During the Defeat of Jesse James Days festival (the weekend after Labor Day) and the St. Olaf Christmas Festival, rooms are also hard to come by.

The undisputed top lodging option is the **Archer House** (212 Division St., 507/645-5661 or 800/247-2235, www.archerhouse.com, $75–160), a grand French Second Empire inn right downtown. Erected in 1877, the hotel has been completely modernized without sacrificing its historic character. The 36 individually decorated rooms have various little extras, such as claw-foot tubs and four-poster beds.

If the Archer House is full, consider the completely modern **Country Inn** (300 Hwy. 3 S., 507/645-2286 or 800/456-4000, $95) across the river.

For longer stays, or for more convenience during a single overnight, the **Froggy Bottoms Suites** (309 Water St. S., 507/650-0039, www.froggybottoms.com), next door to the pub of the same name, are a unique option. The one- and two-bedroom suites sleep four or six people and come with fully equipped kitchens and on-site laundry facilities. The price is the same no matter how many in your party: $100–150 for a weekday overnight, more on weekends and during special events, $600–900 weekly, and $1,800–2,700 monthly. The suites are homily decorated, like spare, comfortable student apartments, with a goofy frog theme throughout. Several have decks directly overlooking the river.

Food

In a college town like Northfield, academic types need a place to gather over a pint or a meal. **The Contented Cow** (302 Division St., 507/663-1351, www.contentedcow.com) offers just that, informally and formally, with its Politics and a Pint gab fests on Sunday nights, starting at 6 P.M. The pub also hosts live music, poetry readings, and outdoor barbecues. The menu is lighter in the summer (salads and sandwiches) and heavier in the winter, with the addition of dishes like shepherd's pie and pork stew, and there are 13 beers on tap.

Another pub with a great riverside view is **Froggy Bottoms** (302 Water St. S., 507/664-0260, www.froggybottoms.com, 11 A.M.–11 P.M. Mon.–Sat., $8–12), a cozy, stone-walled main dining room and a small, flower-filled patio right on the river. The menu includes filling sandwiches, pizzas, and pasta dishes. There's also karaoke on Thursdays and Saturdays starting at 9 P.M., for those who want to watch professorial types at the mike.

The cozy **Tavern of Northfield** (212 Division St., 507/663-0342, www.tavernofnorthfield.com, 6:30 A.M.–10 P.M. Sun.–Thurs., 6:30 A.M.–11 P.M. Fri.–Sat., $5–18), below the Archer House Inn, has something for everyone. The menu spans lamb pitas, steak sandwiches, jambalaya, roast duck, lasagna, and bean burritos.

You can get soup, a hoagie, and a beer for around $7 at **Hogan Brothers' Acoustic Café** (415 Division St. S., 507/645-6653, 9 A.M.–9 P.M. Sun.–Thurs., 9 A.M.–10 P.M. Fri.–Sat.).

Chapati (214 Division St. S., 507/645-2462, lunch and dinner Tues.–Sun., $8–18) serves some wonderful tandooris, biryanis, and curries. Mild is the standard, but if you request it spicy, they will deliver. The menu is large, though you are limited to the about $11 buffet during weekday lunches.

With everything delicious and cheap, the **Quality Bakery** (410 Division St., 507/645-8392, 6 A.M.–5:30 P.M. Tues.–Sat.) lives up to its name.

Information and Transportation

You can pick up tourism brochures at the **Northfield Area Chamber of Commerce** (205 3rd St. W., 507/645-5604 or 800/658-2548, www.northfieldchamber.com, 8 A.M.–5 P.M. Mon.–Fri.) and the museum.

If you aren't driving, the easiest way to get here from the Twin Cities is with **Care Tenders** (507/664-3859 or 888/492-7433), who will pick you up at the airport and deliver you right to your destination in town. **Jefferson Lines** (888/864-2832, www.jeffersonlines.com) buses stop at the Big Steer Travel Center (8051 Bagley Ave.) west of town at the junction of I-35 and Highway 19. With 24 hours' notice **Northfield Transit** (507/645-7250, $4) will pick you up or drop you off at Big Steer.

NERSTRAND BIG WOODS STATE PARK

Midway between Northfield and Faribault is Nerstrand Big Woods State Park (507/333-4840), a nearly 3,000-acre remnant of the Big Woods, once a vast island of forest in the surrounding prairie and oak savanna, that stretched from Mankato almost to St. Cloud. Although there are 13 miles of trails crossing the peaceful rolling hills and valleys, most visitors are here to see petite Hidden Falls, which is very impressive in high water, almost looking man-made. The best time to visit is in the spring when not only is the waterfall at its peak, but over 50 varieties of wildflower bloom in the park. Look for sharp-lobed hepatica, nodding trillium, March marigold, bloodroot, and the endemic Minnesota trout lily, the only federally endangered plant in Minnesota. You'll pass one of the greatest blossom concentrations on the way down the steep hill to the falls. The vivid bloom begins in mid-April and lasts about a month. The seven miles of trail in the north half of the park are groomed for cross-country skiing, and snowshoes for rent from the park office let you explore the rest of the forest. The campground has 51 sites, plus four walk-in sites sit nearby. For the most part the 24 sites without electricity are fully shaded, while the others are not.

FARIBAULT

While you may have never heard of Faribault (FAIR-ih-bo) you likely are familiar with its products: Tilt-A-Whirl carnival rides, Faribault Woolens, and Butter Kernel canned vegetables. You might also have seen the city before since its historic downtown stood in as

Wabasha in the *Grumpy Old Men* movies. Fur trader Alexander Faribault established his first post in the area in 1826 before moving to the present town site, where the Straight River joins the Cannon, a decade later. He established the town in 1852, immediately following ratification of the Traverse des Sioux Treaty, and within a few years it was a prosperous city. Today this quiet town has more buildings on the National Register of Historic Places than any other community of its size in Minnesota. The many schools established during the 1860s, including the Minnesota State Academy for the Blind and the Minnesota State Academy for the Deaf, both still in operation (the Faribault Regional Center—variously known as the School for Idiots and Imbeciles, the Minnesota Institute for Defectives, and the School for Feeble-Minded and Colony for Epileptics—closed in 1998), led to the moniker "Athens of the West."

A good time to visit town is the third weekend in September for the **Faribault Area Airfest** (www.faribaultairfest.com), which features a variety of airplanes and hot air balloons. The **Tree Frog Music Festival** (www.treefrogmusic.org) runs concurrently.

Sights

The oldest building in the city, the **Alexander Faribault House** (12 1st Ave. NE, 507/332-2121, call to schedule a tour, $2) was built in 1853 by the city's founding father. It was one of the first (possibly *the* first) wood-frame homes constructed in southern Minnesota and is one of the state's oldest surviving buildings.

More history is on display at the **Rice County Historical Museum** (1814 2nd Ave. NW, 507/332-2121, 9 A.M.–4 P.M. Mon.–Fri., plus 1–4 P.M. Sat.–Sun. summer, $3 adults), where much of the space is taken up by a well-executed mock Main Street display. The Native American artifacts are also interesting. A log cabin, church, one-room schoolhouse, and shed filled with farm machinery sit out back. The adjacent **Faribault Woolen Mills** (www.faribaultmills.com), the last sheep-to-blanket mill left in the nation, diverts the largest number of visitors off the freeway (just follow the signs). They have been weaving top-quality wool fabrics, most famously Faribo blankets, since 1865, and free tours (10 A.M. and 2 P.M. Mon.–Fri.) of the entire operation are available; tours begin at their large outlet store (1819 2nd Ave. NW, 507/334-1644 or 800/448-9665).

Recreation

Faribault is the eastern terminus of the **Sakatah Singing Hills State Trail,** a 39-mile paved path leading to Mankato along an old railroad bed. The trailhead is along Highway 21, just north of the **Faribault Area Chamber of Commerce** (530 Wilson Ave., 507/334-4381 or 800/658-2354, 8 A.M.–5 P.M. Mon.–Fri., www.visitfaribault.com). You can also depart town along the **Cannon River,** a state-designated Wild and Scenic River. It's a generally peaceful 16-mile, six- to eight-hour paddle down the mostly wooded valley to Northfield, and there are several campsites along the way. For a quiet hike, follow the 10 miles of trails at the **River Bend Nature Center** (1000 Rustad Rd., 507/332-7151, www.rbnc.org), particularly those along the Straight River. The 743 acres of forest and prairie is a good bird-watching area, and the Interpretive Center is filled with animal mounts. It is located on the southeast edge of town: Take Highway 60 and follow the signs.

Practicalities

If you are going to stay in town it should be at the family-run **Lyndale Motel** (904 Lyndale Ave. N., 507/334-4386 or 800/559-4386, $49), which sits on the Cannon River—you can watch herons wade in the river right from your room.

Outside of town, guests at **Dancing Winds Farmstay** (6863 Country 12 Blvd., 507/789-6606, www.dancingwinds.com, $85–119) can spend time with the resident goats, help with chores, cook for themselves, go on long hikes—or not, according to their own schedules.

Faribaultians love **The Depot Bar & Grill** (311 Heritage Pl., 507/332-2825, 11 A.M.–10 P.M. Sun.–Thurs., 11 A.M.–11 P.M. Fri.–Sat., bar open until 1 P.M. Sun.–Thurs. and until 2 P.M. Fri.–Sat., $6–23), in a renovated train depot downtown by the river. The menu covers sandwiches, salads, steak, seafood, and Southwestern.

South of town near the junction of Lyndale and I-35 is the wonderful **El Tequila** (951 Faribault Rd., 507/332-7490, 11 A.M.–9:30 P.M. daily, $3–15), with real-deal Mexican.

You can sample some Somali at **Banadir** (211 Central Ave. N., 507/209-1624, 6 A.M.–9 P.M. daily, $6–8).

Jefferson Lines (888/864-2832, www.jeffersonlines.com) buses stop at Nelson's Market Place (430 2nd Ave. NW).

OWATONNA

Legend has it that Chief Wadena once relocated his entire village south to this spot so that his daughter Owatonna, deathly ill following the famine of the harshest winter they had ever seen, could drink the healing waters of the area's mineral springs. Though there is likely no truth to the tale, generations of Native Americans did travel here to quaff the curing waters of the springs feeding the "Ouitunya" River. Mapmakers ironically translated this crooked river's name to Straight, though a better translation would be "morally strong" or "honest." The city's founding fathers, the earliest of whom built their cabins here in 1854, kept the original name for the town. Like most cities around here it prospered early, first with milling and soon after with the railroad.

Sights

Though the claim seems dubious, according to Explore Minnesota Tourism, hunting and fishing superstore **Cabela's** (3900 Cabela Dr., 507/451-4545, 8 A.M.–9 P.M. Mon.–Sat., 10 A.M.–6 P.M. Sun.) is the second most-visited tourist attraction in the state. Regardless of where it ranks, this 150,000-square-foot center is a big deal. Literally hundreds of animal mounts—at least 100 white-tailed deer alone—are on display throughout the store. A 35-foot-tall mountain features North American species such as polar bear and elk, while creatures from the African plains such as elephant, rhino, hartebeest, and baboon are spread out along the north wall and Minnesota fish swim in the 60,000-gallon aquarium. It's not exactly the American Museum of Natural History, but it's an impressive collection. It is located just off of I-35 approximately 60 miles south of Minneapolis, just off the Clinton Falls exit.

Even if you are in a hurry to get elsewhere, exit the freeway and take a moment to admire the Louis Sullivan–designed **National Farmer's Bank** (101 Cedar Ave. N., 507/451-5670, 8:30 A.M.–6 P.M. Mon.–Sat.), a Prairie School masterpiece inside and out. Now Wells Fargo, the world-renowned 1908 building is a National Historic Landmark and was even featured on a postage stamp. Inside you can admire the stained-glass arches (even beautiful from the outside), murals, and 2.25-ton chandeliers. It sits across from Central Park, one of the few town squares in the state.

The Steele County Historical Society's **Village of Yesteryear** (1448 Austin Rd., 507/451-1420, guided tours 1:30 P.M. Tues.–Sun. May–Sept., $5 adults), on the south side of town at the fairgrounds, has 15 19th-century structures such as log cabins, a blacksmith shop, general store, one-room schoolhouse, and print shop. Each is appropriately equipped, and the furnishings of the 1876 St. Wenceslaus of Moravia Church are largely original. The Please Touch stickers on many items are a nice feature.

The Minnesota State Public School for Dependent and Neglected Children opened in 1886 and served nearly 13,000 children during its 60 years of operation. At its peak in the 1920s it housed 500 children, making it the largest in the nation. Owatonna was chosen, in part, because it was believed that area farmers in need of workers would adopt kids. The **State School Orphanage Museum** (540 West Hills Cir., www.orphanagemuseum.com, 8 A.M.–5 P.M. Mon.–Fri., 1–5 P.M. Sat.–Sun., free admission) is really just a small collection of photos, plus a few artifacts in a City Hall hallway, but the accompanying stories are both frightening and heartwarming. It's hard to believe that in its day this was a very progressive institution. The **Owatonna Arts Center** (507/451-0533, 1–5 P.M. Tues.–Sun., free admission) in the same building has monthly exhibits by area artists and a tiny sculpture garden.

About 15 miles west of Owatonna, just outside Waseca, is a site nearly everyone who went to school in Minnesota will recognize. **FarmAmerica** (7367 360th Ave., Waseca, 507/835-2052, www.farmamerica.org, 9 A.M.–2 P.M. Tues.–Fri. June–Aug., $5 adults), also known as the Minnesota Agricultural Interpretive Center, welcomes school groups in May and the general public throughout the summer to experience life on the farm in the 1850s and the 1930s. There are plenty of ways to get your hands dirty—even milking a (pretend) cow.

Practicalities

The **Holiday Inn** (2365 43rd St. NW, 507/446-8900 or 800/920-4402, www.greatserengeti.com, $125) next to Cabela's features an indoor water park with waterslides, lazy river, waterfall whirlpool, and more. There is also a game room and fitness center.

The aging but clean **Oakdale Motel** (1418 Oak Ave. S., 507/451-5480, www.owatonnalodging.com, $40) is on the south side of town. **Jefferson Lines** (888/864-2832, www.jeffersonlines.com) buses stop here.

Ideally situated in the heart of town, the **Northrop-Oftedahl House B&B** (358 Main St. E., 507/451-4040, www.northrophouse.com, $80–90) has seven guest rooms filled with family heirlooms.

The most unusual menu in the region is at the **Northwoods Restaurant** (3900 Cabela Dr., 507/451-4545, 8 A.M.–9 P.M. Mon.–Sat., 10 A.M.–6 P.M. Sun., $5–7) at Cabela's. Wild-game ingredients include ostrich and elk sandwiches and bison and venison bratwurst.

Costas' (112 Cedar Ave. N., 507/451-9050, 8 A.M.–3 P.M. daily, open until 6 P.M. for candy sales, $5–8) has Greek and American favorites on the menu, and the homemade sweets in the candy counter are awfully tough to resist.

The **Owatonna Area Chamber of Commerce and Tourism** (320 Hoffman Dr., 507/451-7970 or 800/423-6466, www.owatonna.org, 8 A.M.–5 P.M. weekdays) is very helpful.

ALBERT LEA

The Freeborn County seat is centered on a low hill between Fountain and Albert Lea Lakes. Lieutenant Albert Lea, who led a surveying expedition across the region in 1835, initially named the larger of the two Fox Lake after spying a white fox run by it. Several years later, the famous French explorer Joseph Nicollet came through the area and renamed it in Lea's honor. Even though I-35 and I-90 intersect here, making it "The Crossroads of the Upper Midwest," the town sees few tourists. The city's museums, however, are worth a stop.

Sights

The **Freeborn County Museum** (1031 Bridge Ave., 507/373-8003, 10 A.M.–5 P.M. Tues.–Fri. year-round, $5 adults) is the area's best local history collection. The main hall houses the usual artifacts, plus gold records and quite a bit of memorabilia from native son Eddie Cochran. The old toys are interesting too. During the summer you can visit the one-room schoolhouse, cobbler shop, 1853 log cabin, and other historic structures out back. Ask at the museum to see the **Itasca Rock Garden,** a unique outdoor folk sculpture; it is on private property, but visits are allowed.

Just about everyone will find something of interest at the **Story Lady Doll & Toy Museum** (131 Broadway Ave. N., 507/377-1820, noon–4 P.M. Tues.–Fri., 11 A.M.–3 P.M. Sat., $2 adults), whether it be the Raggedy Ann, Princess Diana, Cat in the Hat, or handmade Navajo dolls. There are over 1,500 dolls (and despite the name, hardly any toys) in total.

It's easy to dismiss small-town art centers, but you'll probably be surprised by the creative offerings at the **Albert Lea Art Center** (224 Broadway Ave. S., 507/373-5665, noon–2 P.M. Tues.–Sat., free admission). New displays by serious Midwest artists are hung monthly, and work by local artists is sold in the shop.

During the summer you can float around

Albert Lea Lake on the **Pelican Breeze Cruise Boat** (507/383-2630, www.pelicanbreeze.org, 4 P.M. Sat., 1:30 P.M. Sun. June–Sept., $15), a double-decker pontoon that departs from Frank Hall Park for 90-minute narrated tours. There's also a Friday-evening pizza cruise (6 P.M., $20, reservations required).

October's **Big Island Rendezvous** (www.bigislandfestivalandbbq.com, $10 adults) is Minnesota's largest fur-trade-era reenactment. Over 1,000 costumed traders camp out and demonstrate the crafts, games, and music of the early 1800s.

Big Island State Park

Across Albert Lea Lake from the city is Big Island State Park (19499 780th Ave., 507/379-3403). Oak savanna and prairie, including expansive prairie wetlands, dominate most of the park, though the 116-acre island itself, protected from the fires that perpetuated the prairies, is covered by a dense northern hardwood forest. The 2,028-acre park protects 8 of the lake's 20 miles of shoreline, and hundreds of migrating waterfowl converge on the wetlands. Some 16 miles of hiking trail loop through the park. The best destination for bird-watchers is the 1.5-mile **Great Marsh Trail,** which follows the rolling hills around a large pond. The freeway hum is pretty loud, but the birds don't mind.

The **Bur Oak Esker Trail** crosses four miles of similar terrain, plus adds some lakeshore. The glacial moraine of the last Ice Age not only formed the lake, but also an esker, and the north end of this trail follows it. Four lakeside backpack sites, reached by foot, mountain bike, or canoe, are stretched out along this trail.

The easiest path, the mile-long **Big Island Trail,** is also the most popular. Five miles of trail, including those on Big Island, are groomed for cross-country skiing. The 34 campsites (half of them electric) and camper cabin in the Big Island Campground are in the woods, while most of the 59 sites (15 electric) in the White Fox Campground are out in the open. The lake is too shallow for a beach, but there is a picnic area and boat launch, and rental canoes are available.

The paved **Blazing Star Bike Trail** leads from the park to near downtown, a six-mile trip.

Practicalities

Not far off I-35, the **Country Inn** (2214 Main St. E., 507/373-5513 or 800/456-4000, $105) has a pool, whirlpool, and fitness center, plus rooms have the chain's usual cozy touches.

Just down the street is the simpler **Countryside Inn Motel** (2102 Main St. E., 507/373-2446 or 888/373-1188, www.countrysidemotel.com, $45).

Ten miles south of town the **1858 Log Cabin B&B** (11859 755th Ave., 507/448-0089, www.1858logcabin.com, $110, $85 for lodging only) is just what the name claims. Antique furnishings are mixed with modern amenities such as electricity, refrigerator, and bathroom, but it still has a pioneer feel. They welcome families with young children.

One of the biggest surprises in all of Minnesota is **Crescendo** (118 Broadway Ave. S., 507/377-2425, www.crescendodining.com, 5–9 P.M. Thurs.–Sat., $13–25), a gourmet bistro with a Mediterranean-inspired menu. The choices change with the seasons, but sweet-potato ravioli and sautéed Atlantic salmon fillet with rhubarb marmalade are typical. Locally grown and organic ingredients feature prominently, and the wine list is impressive.

At the other end of the spectrum are **Taco King** (104 Broadway Ave. S., 507/377-2485, 10:30 A.M.–8 P.M. Mon.–Fri., 10:30 A.M.–5 P.M. Sat.–Sun., $3–7), a counter-service place with excellent Mexican, and **The Trumble's** (1811 Main St. E., 507/373-2638, 6 A.M.–9 P.M. Mon.–Thurs., $5–20), a local favorite for family fare.

The friendly staff of the **Albert Lea Convention and Visitors Bureau** (2566 Bridge Ave., 507/373-2316 or 800/345-8414, www.albertleatourism.org, 8:30 A.M.–5 P.M. Mon.–Fri.) at the Northbridge Mall will be happy to help you with any questions you have.

Jefferson Lines (888/864-2832, www.jeffersonlines.com) buses stop at the Shell gas station (2222 Main St. E.).

AUSTIN

The area's first European settler, a trapper named Austin Nichols, built his cabin along the Cedar River in what would become the city of Austin in 1853. The city became an important regional rail center in 1867, though it could be said that the modern town was born in 1887 when George Hormel opened his butcher shop. This trivial operation grew into the Hormel Foods Corporation, maker of SPAM and much more. Hormel, now a Fortune 500 company (the only one in Minnesota outside the Twin Cities metro area), is still headquartered here and also keeps its research and development arm in town. Spend even a moment here and it will become evident just how proud the 23,000 residents of the Mower County seat are to live in the land of SPAM: The Hormel name pops up all over town, the high school athletes are Packers, **SPAMtown USA** banners line the streets, and you'll even find the mystery meat on many restaurant menus.

© TIM BEWER

SPAM Museum

SPAM Museum

Learn everything you always wanted to know about SPAM (but were afraid to ask) at Hormel Foods' humorous SPAM Museum (1101 Main St. N., 507/437-5100 or 800/588-7726, 10 A.M.–5 P.M. Mon.–Sat., noon–5 P.M. Sun., free admission), just north of downtown along Main Street. Believe it or not, this celebration of America's luncheon meat is one of the best-executed museums in the state. Following the 15-minute film *SPAM, A Love Story,* the endless conveyor belt of navy and yellow cans will lead you past interactive multimedia displays on George Hormel's first butcher shop, SPAM at war, historic ads, including those by George Burns and Gracie Allen, and much more. One of Monty Python's greatest achievements airs continuously, and you can also show off your SPAM knowledge by playing the SPAM Exam game show. At the end you can purchase a SPAM-emblazoned doll, necktie, basketball, or wine glass in the gift shop.

Other Sights

The rest of the town's history—plus more about George Hormel—is told at the **Mower County Historical Center** (700 12th St. SW, 507/437-6082, 10 A.M.–4 P.M. Tues.–Fri., $5 adults), a collection of historic buildings, including a log cabin, blacksmith shop, and one-room schoolhouse, plus an M-4 Sherman tank and steam locomotive. None of the buildings are left open, so if you want to visit them you'll need to be led around by a volunteer.

The ***SPAMtown Belle*** (507/433-1881, 5:30–8:30 P.M. Fri., 1–4 P.M. Sat. and Sun., $2 adults), a toy-like miniature paddlewheeler built in 1956, chugs around East Side Lake during the summer.

Although it's now an events center, not a museum, if you stop by the **Hormel Historic Home** (208 4th Ave. NW, 507/433-4243, 10 A.M.–4:30 P.M. Mon.–Fri., closes 4 P.M. summer, $2 donation recommended) you can look around the luxurious former residence of the meat plant's founder. It was built in 1871 and has been restored to the glory of the 1920s, when the family moved out.

Cycling fans will enjoy a look at the nearly 90 bicycles dating back to 1868 on display at

Rydjor Bike Shop (219 Main St. N., 507/433-7571, 9 A.M.–6 P.M. daily.).

Although it doesn't happen every year, Hormel hosts **SPAM Museum Jam,** the town's biggest bash, in mid-June. There is music (including the harmonies of the SPAMettes female quartet), celebrity appearances, a classic car show, SPAM cooking contests, and much more. Another noteworthy event is the **Minnesota Storytelling Festival** the first weekend in March. Storytellers from across the United States come to spin yarns and lead workshops, and there are opportunities for audience participation. Many events take place at the historic **Paramount Theatre** (125 4th Ave. NE, 507/434-0934, www.paramounttheatre.org), a 1929 Spanish Colonial gem.

Practicalities

Most of the city's hotels line I-90 on the north side of town, including the **Holiday Inn** (1701 4th St. NW, 507/433-1000 or 800/985-8850, $105), easily the city's best. There's a pool, whirlpool, sauna, fitness center, game room, and putting green under the dome.

The **Countryside Inn** (3303 Oakland Ave. W., 507/437-7774 or 800/277-7579, www.countrysideinnaustin.com, $45) further west is a good value. It has a whirlpool.

Austin has a good variety of restaurants. **Jerry's Other Place** (1207 Main St. N., 507/433-2331, www.jerrysotherplacemn.com, 6:30 A.M.–9 P.M. Mon.–Sat., 6:30 A.M.–3 P.M. Sun., $3–25), a family-style restaurant near the SPAM Museum, seems to always be busy.

For a table with a view there is **The Old Mill** (54446 244th St., 507/437-2076, 11:30 A.M.–2 P.M. and 5:30–9 P.M. Mon.–Fri., 5:30–10 P.M. Sat., $9–30) north of town. Known far and wide as much for being in an 1873 flour mill—the dining room overlooks the waterfall cascading down Ramsey Dam—as the food, the Old Mill has been a restaurant since 1950. The supper-club menu is mostly steak and seafood at night and sandwiches at lunch.

Piggy Blue's Bar-B-Que (323 Main St. N., 507/434-8485, www.piggybluesbbq.com, 11 A.M.–8 P.M. Mon.–Thurs., 11 A.M.–9 P.M. Fri.–Sat., $7–22) sauces up hardwood-smoked meats.

White's Tendermaid (217 4th Ave. NE, 507/437-7907, 11 A.M.–7 P.M. Mon.–Fri., 11 A.M.–3 P.M. Sat., $2–4) is a classic closet-sized lunch counter. The Tendermaid burger is not so much a burger as a pile of seasoned ground meat on a bun. Once you get used to the concept, you'll love it.

You can relax with deli sandwiches and caffeine at **Coffee House on Main** (329 Main St. N., 507/433-1200, 7 A.M.–5 P.M. Mon.–Fri., 7 A.M.–midnight Sat., $4–6).

The friendly **Austin Convention and Visitors Bureau** (104 11th Ave. NW, 507/437-4563 or 800/444-5713, www.austincvb.com, 8 A.M.–5 P.M. Mon.–Fri.) is across the street from the SPAM Museum.

BACKGROUND

The Land

Minnesota covers 84,068 square miles, making it the 12th-largest state in the nation and just a wee bit smaller than Great Britain. The Twin Cities, a little south of the state's waistline, sit right on the 45th parallel, halfway between the equator and the North Pole. Angle Inlet (49.22° North), up at the top of the Northwest Angle, a chunk of land completely cut off from the rest of the United States due to a surveyor's error, is the northernmost town in the Lower 48. Minnesota's highest point, Eagle Mountain (2,301 feet above sea level), is just 13 miles from its lowest point, Lake Superior (602 feet). The rest of the state works out to an average elevation of 1,200 feet.

Officially, the Land of 10,000 Lakes has 11,842. Red Lake, at 288,800 acres, is the largest entirely within the state's borders, with Lake Mille Lacs coming in second at 132,520 acres. Due to the myriad lakes, Minnesota has more shoreline than California and Florida combined, or so they say. Some 92,000 miles of rivers and streams cross the state, with the Mississippi River, the granddaddy of them all, accounting for 681 of those miles. Including wetlands, over 6 percent of Minnesota's surface area is water.

© TRICIA CORNELL

JUST HOW MANY LAKES ARE THERE IN THE LAND OF 10,000 LAKES?

The simple answer is...a lot. It seems that the only thing people can agree on is that there are far more than the titular 10,000. I've seen official publications from various state and municipal agencies and other respectable sources claim 11,842, 12,034, and 15,291. Before you decide that Minnesotans can't count, let's back up a minute. In order to determine how many lakes there are, we have to define exactly what a lake is. According to the *Merriam-Webster's Collegiate Dictionary*, a lake is "a considerable inland body of standing water." So what's considerable? Proud Minnesotans, who are most likely to cite totals over 15,000, are counting even the smallest ponds. For their own purposes the Department of Natural Resources classifies a lake as a body of water 10 acres or larger, and it has officially tallied 11,842 of these. While this is as close to a final word as there is, even this answer is not set in stone because many factors such as rainfall, shoreline erosion, and sedimentation can alter a lake's surface area. So, when the DNR resurveys Minnesota's bodies of water, ponds that missed the cut last time might be added to the tally while some lakes might drop off the list.

GEOLOGY

Beginning some 2.7 billion years ago and lasting for over a billion and a half years, the shifting of tectonic plates and volcanic activity created immense mountain ranges in Minnesota. During this time, the Canadian Shield, a layer of bedrock underlying most of Greenland, half of Canada, and extending into the northeast United States, was formed. In Minnesota this massive slab extends down to the upper reaches of the Minnesota River Valley, where some of the planet's oldest rock, Morton Gneiss (estimated at 3.6 billion years), is exposed in several places. The Canadian Shield is also often revealed along Lake Superior and the Boundary Waters, lending a special beauty to the northeast. Also during this time, iron particles settled at the bottom of the great sea that covered the state forming the Vermilion, Mesabi, and Cuyuna Iron Ranges. Over the rest of the Precambrian era, seas continued to sweep in and out and, along with the wind and ice of early glaciers, wore away the once-mighty mountains. During the Paleozoic era (540–245 million years ago), when animals evolved, and the Mesozoic era (245–66 million years ago), the age of dinosaurs, Minnesota was floating down around the equator and had a tropical climate. As the North American continent broke away from the supercontinent Pangaea, it drifted north to cooler climes.

Two million years ago the Quaternary period, commonly referred to as the Ice Age, began. During this time the Laurentide Ice Sheet, centered near Hudson Bay, advanced and retreated four times. The first three glaciations, separated by long ice-free periods, reached well into the middle of the United States, covering all of Minnesota. Despite such a long, active, and violent past, Minnesota as we now know it didn't begin to really take shape until about 75,000 years ago when the last advance of ice, the Wisconsin Glaciation, swept south. The ice sheet wiped away just about everything in its path, though it spared the southeast and southwest corners. The glaciers began their latest retreat about 12,000 years ago. As they melted away, the various glacial lobes deposited the countless tons of rock and other earthly debris they had picked up on the trip south. This moraine formed most of Minnesota's hills and, when massive chunks of ice got buried in it, the lakes and wetlands. The meltwater cut most of Minnesota's riverbeds, including those of its four largest rivers: the Mississippi; its first major tributary, the Minnesota; the St. Croix; and the Red River of the North.

While gently rolling hills cover most of the state, its four corners are each a unique

© TRICIA CORNELL

Lake Superior is Minnesota's lowest point.

exception. The northeast has many steep, rugged hills, the final remnants of Minnesota's former mountains, while the Red River Valley in the northwest is improbably flat. The southeast corner has many deep, highly eroded valleys with much exposed bedrock and many caves. The southwest corner is more or less flat except for some deep river valleys and the long, tall Buffalo Ridge, a plateau that stretches well into South Dakota. Perhaps Minnesota's most unusual geological quirk is that its waters empty in three different directions: south to the Gulf of Mexico via the Mississippi River, east to the Atlantic Ocean via Lake Superior, and north to Hudson Bay via the Red River of the North.

CLIMATE

Minnesotans love to talk (and, in the company of outsiders, boast) about their weather, and they have plenty of fodder for the discourse. Minnesota lies at the same latitude as France, but lacks an ocean to moderate the climate, leading to a true theater of seasons and occasional extremes like tornadic thunderstorms and blizzards, as well as drastic temperatures. Meteorologists here really earn their pay—there are no "weather girls" or comedic Willard Scott–like "weather reporters" on the local TV news. Still, despite the occasional flare-up, Minnesota's weather is usually very pleasant.

Temperatures and Precipitation

Statewide summer (June–Aug.) and winter (Dec.–Feb.) mean temperatures are 67 and 11 degrees respectively, though the north and south differ by as much as 15 degrees. You never know exactly what you will get during the autumn. Duluth, for instance, has seen 37 inches of snow during a Halloween storm, but also a Thanksgiving high of 66 degrees. Minnesota's record high temperature is 115°F (July 29, 1917, Beardsley), beating out such notorious hot spots as Atlanta (105°), Los Angeles (112°), and El Paso (114°). The all-time low is 60 below zero (Feb. 2, 1996, near Tower).

While temperatures are warmest in the southwest corner and coolest in the northeast, precipitation runs contrary, increasing from about 18 inches in the northwest to 32 inches in the southeast. Most falls during the May

to September growing season. Total annual snowfall is around 40 inches in the south and over 60 inches in the north. There is at least one inch of snow on the ground an average of 160 days in the northeast and 85 days in the southwest. In an average year, Minnesota sees about 16 snowstorms with an inch or more of accumulation, though usually only one of those is a full-on blizzard. While an inch or two of snow will slow down travel a bit, a winter storm doesn't become a real nuisance to Minnesotans until about six inches have fallen.

Lake Effect

Lake Superior is so big that it creates its own weather. With an average annual temperature of just 39 degrees, Superior cools the surrounding air in the summer and warms it in the winter, moderating the climate by as much as 15 degrees over inland temperatures. The effect does not extend very far because it is blocked by the Sawtooth Range and pushed back by winds that normally blow out of the west. Some of Minnesota's larger inland lakes have a similar but smaller effect in the summer. Lake Superior also creates its own snowstorms. When moist air blows inland from the east and up the hills lining the North Shore, it condenses and falls as snow, making the North Shore the snowiest part of the state by far.

Flora and Fauna

FLORA

Three of North America's eight major biomes converge in Minnesota: Coniferous Forest, Deciduous Forest, and Prairie Grassland. Minnesota is the only place where these three communities come together, and one of the few nonmountainous regions on earth to contain any three biomes in such a small space. This convergence results in a tremendous statewide biodiversity. On a macro scale the change from one to the next is quite sudden, though on the ground the zones co-mingle, creating biologically rich areas many miles wide that contain species from both.

The largest biome in Minnesota, **Coniferous Forest,** covers 40 percent of the state. While it only dips into a few northern reaches of the eastern United States, this region extends north across most of Canada and Alaska before petering out into arctic tundra. Vegetation must contend with shallow soils and a short growing season, so most species have evolved to economize energy use. The dominant trees are pines (red, white, and jack), spruce, fir, aspen, and birch. The tallest tree is the **eastern white pine,** which often tops out above 100 feet, and Minnesota's state tree, the **red (Norway) pine,** is not far behind. Vast open peatlands, some of the largest in the world, are spread throughout the central and western parts of the region and contain **tamarack,** a conifer that sheds its needles in the winter, turning a beautiful orange in the process.

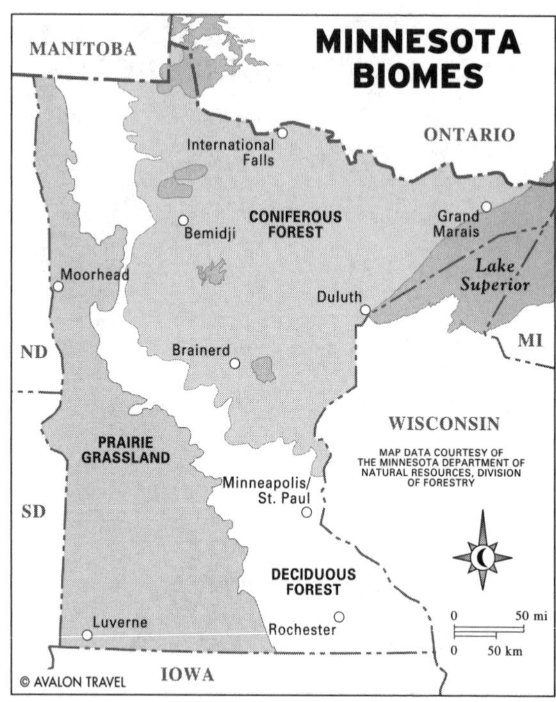

The **Prairie Grasslands** of the Great Plains follow the entire western border of Minnesota and sweep across most of the south. This is the state's most fractured landscape, but the prairie that hasn't been lost to the plow is some of North America's most diverse. Nearly 1,000 species of grass and forb thrive in the nutrient-rich soils of the Minnesota prairie, and small individual plots can contain over 200 species. Despite this incredible richness, five grasses—**big and little bluestem, Indian grass, prairie dropseed,** and **porcupine grass**—account for as much as three-quarters of the vegetative cover in dry prairies. It's the flowers that really capture the imagination, though: Favorites include **wood lily, purple coneflower, gray-headed coneflower, pasqueflower, purple and white prairie clovers, goldenrods,** and **asters.** Prairie wetlands, home to **small white lady's slippers** and **golden alexander,** are scattered through the region, mostly in the north. **Bur oaks,** their thick bark resistant to fire, sometimes manage to invade a prairie, creating an **oak savanna.**

Though it covers most of the eastern United States, **Deciduous Forest** exists in Minnesota as just a narrow band separating the prairie and the coniferous forest. The most common trees are oak, maple, elm, basswood, hickory, butternut, birch, and aspen. The **sugar maple,** turning bright yellow to deep reddish-orange, is the most spectacular fall-color tree. Spring sees a profusion of ephemeral wildflowers such as **trillium, hepaticas, anemones, bellworts,** and **Dutchman's britches** that bloom before the canopy of leaves returns. Other shade-tolerant species, such as **asters, elm-leaved goldenrod,** and **woodland sunflower,** wait until the summer to flower. North of Polk County onward into Canada, the forest consists mostly of scattered stands of aspen interspersed with the prairie—known as **brush prairie** or aspen parkland, it is sometimes considered a separate biome.

FAUNA

Mammals

Eighty species of mammal inhabit Minnesota. Those you are most likely to encounter are **raccoon, eastern cottontail,** various

© TRICIA CORNELL

Wildflowers blanket northern Minnesota in the late spring and early summer.

squirrels and **chipmunks,** and **white-tailed deer,** all of which are common throughout the state—even in the Twin Cities.

About seven thousand **moose** lumber across the northern tier of the state, the majority of them in the northeast corner. While spotting a moose is a distinct possibility, you'll be far luckier to see any of the few dozen **elk** that call Minnesota home. Once common in the state, the only remaining herd—about 40 strong—lives near Agassiz National Wildlife Refuge, though others wander down from Canada into the far northeast counties and some have begun to spend much of the year south of the border. The occasional **caribou,** also once common in northern Minnesota, still slips across the border from Canada, but there are no more breeding populations.

Black bear are common in the northern half of the state, with the population having risen to nearly 30,000 in recent years. Some of Minnesota's black bears are actually colored a light brown, but this is just a minor variation; they are still the same species. Visit the Vince Shute Wildlife Sanctuary near Orr for a guaranteed close encounter with a wild *Ursus americanus.*

Three big cats—**lynx, bobcat,** and **mountain lion**—roam the state's northern forests, but are rarely seen. Also count yourself lucky if you spy a **badger, river otter, pine marten, fisher** or **gray wolf.**

Birds

As a result of habitat diversity, well over 400 species of bird have been recorded in Minnesota, with 312 of them residents or regular visitors. No species typifies Minnesota more than its official state bird, the **common loon,** which is prevalent in the northern two-thirds of the state. Other common Minnesota waterbirds include **mallards, Canada geese, great blue heron, great egret, black-crowned night-herons,** and **double-crested cormorant.**

Red-tailed hawks and 30 species of **warbler** (24 in the northeast) are some of the defining forest species, and the state's northern forests are home to many **great gray owl** and **boreal owl.** The Lake Superior shore attracts **herring gulls** and many species of migrating **hawks.** Arctic species like **gyrfalcon** and **snowy owl** migrate to northern Minnesota each winter. The most common birds on the prairie are **savannah sparrow, western meadowlark,** and **bobolink.**

Sandhill crane, bald eagle, osprey, and **greater prairie chicken** all came very close to disappearing from Minnesota, but thanks to ongoing habitat restoration, reintroduction, and other environmental projects, they have been saved. The first three are thriving again (over two dozen pair of bald eagle even nest in the Twin Cities metro area) and sightings are actually quite common in much of the state these days. The prairie chicken is still very rare, only hanging on naturally in the northwest and a couple of spots along the Minnesota River where it was recently reintroduced. **Sharp-tailed grouse** is another species whose numbers have been dramatically reduced, but they still converge to mate on over 200 dancing grounds in the north of the state each spring.

Reptiles and Amphibians

Most of Minnesota's reptiles and amphibians are found in the southeast corner, which has the warmest climate, but many species, such as the northern leopard frog, snapping turtle, and common garter snake, range across the entire state. Most survive the winter freeze by burrowing below the frost line or hibernating at the bottom of lakes and streams.

Seventeen of the state's 29 species of reptiles are snakes. Largest is the brown-and-yellow **gopher snake,** which can grow in excess of six feet and is most common in grasslands along the St. Croix, Mississippi, and Minnesota Rivers. Gopher snakes, as well as the slightly smaller **fox snake,** which has a similar range, are non-venomous, but resemble timber rattlers and, because they sometimes vibrate their tails along the ground when frightened, are often confused with them. Actual rattlesnakes elevate their tails to rattle. The **western painted turtle** is by far the state's most visible reptile, inhabiting just about every body of water with a log or rock to bask on.

Frogs account for half of Minnesota's 21 amphibian species. One of the most interesting is the **bullfrog,** the United State's largest frog species, reaching eight inches in body length. Adult bullfrogs eat almost anything they can swallow, including fish, snakes, turtles, rodents, birds, and other frogs. Though they naturally inhabit just the far southeast corner of Minnesota along the Mississippi River, there are now many healthy, introduced populations elsewhere in the state. Just as exceptional are the **eastern gray treefrog** and **Cope's gray treefrog,** nearly identical-looking species distinguished primarily by their calls. They can change their skin color to match their surroundings and are excellent climbers. Their range extends throughout most of the state, and on summer evenings they are commonly found clinging to cabins and other rural buildings waiting to snare insects that fly by. The most common and widespread of Minnesota's seven salamander species is the **tiger salamander,** which thrives in all kinds of habitats in all parts of the state. Black with yellow spots, they can reach lengths of over 13 inches, though eight to ten is more common. It is not the state's largest salamander though; that honor falls to the wholly aquatic **mudpuppy,** which measures 13 to 16 inches.

Fish

While the state abounds in the usual game fish such as **walleye, muskellunge, northern pike, bass, perch, bluegill, crappie, salmon,** and **trout,** Minnesota's waters have several other unique residents.

The largest of Minnesota's 158 fish species is the **lake sturgeon,** a relic from the age of dinosaurs with no teeth or scales and, like sharks, cartilage instead of bone. Back in the 19th century, before they were nearly fished to extinction for the caviar market, anglers caught eight-foot, 300-pound sturgeon in Minnesota. They are making a slow comeback today, thanks to the Clean Water Act and strict fishing regulations, though few top out over 100 pounds. They are found in many lakes and rivers (to the surprise of everyone a six-foot, 105-pounder washed up on the shore of Lake Harriet in Minneapolis in 1998), though the healthiest population is in Lake of the Woods. Not too far behind in the monstrous category are **flathead catfish,** which also sometimes exceed 100 pounds, though the Minnesota record catch is 70 pounds.

Some other fish that haven't changed in millions of years are **paddlefish** and the **longnose gar** and **shortnose gar,** all with massive snouts. Paddlefish proboscises have sensors that detect the electrical impulses emitted by the microscopic plankton it eats. Though they can grow up to 140 pounds, in Minnesota, where they are rare, the largest are just over 50 pounds. The much smaller gar have long cylindrical snouts filled with razor-sharp teeth and skin so tough that it can't be cut with a fillet knife.

THREATENED AND ENDANGERED SPECIES

Like most other places in North America, the first European settlers to arrive on the scene either plowed, drained, or logged much of the state's original habitat, creating permanent

MINNESOTA'S SIGNATURE SPECIES

Minnesota's state bird, the **common loon,** is easily its most beloved wild resident. About 12,000 of these ancient birds, one of the earth's oldest living bird species, reside on lakes in the northern two-thirds of the state – only Alaska has more. With speckled black and white bodies and dark iridescent heads, loons are beautiful creatures, but it's their haunting calls – a long, sad wail and a maniacal tremolo – that so enchant people. Helped by the extra weight of their dense bones, these large birds can dive down 250 feet and remain underwater for up to 10 minutes in search of a meal. Their distinct red eyes help them see underwater. They're not bad in the air either and have been clocked at 75 mph. While they are masters of seas and sky, they are horribly clumsy on land. The only time they go to shore is to nest, and this they will only do on the cleanest and quietest of lakes. Come early June, when the eggs hatch, you'll catch the solid-black fledglings sailing on their parents' backs to stay warm and out of the mouths of hungry fish and turtles.

Upward of 8,000 **moose** reside in the northern corners of Minnesota. The giants of the north have long spindly legs, shoulder humps, and thick flaps of skin (called a bell) hanging from their throats, and the male's flat antlers spread six feet wide. A full-grown adult can stand six-and-a-half-feet high at the shoulder and weigh 1,300 pounds. Despite their size moose can sprint at 35 mph and outswim two people paddling a canoe. The name, coming from the Algonquin language, means twig eater, and these do get them through the winter, but the rest of the year they prefer leaves and aquatic vegetation – they can close their nostrils when foraging below the surface. Moose have a keen sense of hearing and smell, but their eyesight is so poor that they have been known to mistake cars for potential mates.

While the **gray wolf** (sometimes called a timber wolf) was wiped out from all the rest of the Lower 48 by the early 1960s, a small population held on in Minnesota. Since bounties were eliminated at that time and the Endangered Species Act was passed in 1973, they have staged a remarkable comeback. Today about 3,000 wolves roam the northern third of the state, and they are expanding their territory south. A typical pack averages around seven wolves and defends an 80-mile territory. Adults stand three feet tall, often exceed 100 pounds, and are seemingly all muscle. With their "steel-strong jaws," they are efficient killing machines, but, despite the widespread belief to the contrary, they are no threat to humans. Wolf advocates are quick to point out that there has never been a documented case of a healthy, wild wolf killing a human in North America. They don't howl at the moon either.

changes—the effects of which most plants and animals are still feeling today. The loss of habitat is the primary reason for the disappearance or decline of most species. Pollution, hunting, and dam construction are a few other causes. Minnesota currently lists 27 animal species as endangered and 32 as threatened. Nearly 80 others are species of special concern. The plant kingdom has 69 threatened and 69 endangered species and 145 on the special concern list.

The only mammal on Minnesota's list of threatened species is the **eastern spotted skunk** (noted for spraying its opponents while doing a "handstand" on its front feet).

The two most notable birds at risk are the **trumpeter swan** and **peregrine falcon,** both state-threatened species once completely extirpated from Minnesota. The Department of Natural Resources (DNR), Minnesota Zoo, University of Minnesota's Raptor Center, and private organizations have worked together to successfully reintroduce them to the state, and both continue to increase in number: Biologists recently counted over 1,500 trumpeter swans and 30 breeding pairs of the high-diving falcons. Thankfully the long-term outlook for both is excellent. On the other hand, the state-endangered **piping plover,** hanging on by a feather on Lake of the Woods, and the prairie-dwelling **burrowing owl,** which is gone as a nesting species and only arrives every few years as a vagrant, are in a very precarious position. The **paddlefish,** mentioned above, is Minnesota's only threatened fish.

The animal group in the gravest danger in Minnesota, and around the country, is **mussels.** Over half of the 48 species of mussel found in Minnesota are threatened, endangered, or of special concern, and at least two species have recently disappeared. Like frogs, mussels are valuable biological indicators, so the current trend doesn't speak well for the state's waterways. Many disparate factors—all of human origin—including reduced water quality, dam construction, stream channelization, and, in the past, overharvesting for buttonmaking and the cultured-pearl industry, affect their declining numbers. The invasion of zebra mussels has also severely harmed many species of native mussels. Thousands of zebra mussels can attach themselves to a larger native mussel, eventually killing it. This rapidly reproducing species with few predators arrived in the United States on a freighter from the Black Sea in the mid-1980s and has spread rapidly through the Great Lakes and up the Mississippi River. It appears that these exotics may also be a threat to fish populations.

The endemic **Minnesota dwarf trout lily** is the state's only federally endangered plant species. It survives in about a dozen locations just south of the Twin Cities in the forests of Rice, Goodhue, and Steele Counties, and, because each of the few remaining colonies is a genetic clone, they are especially vulnerable to disturbances. It usually blooms in late April. Once wildly abundant in the state's deciduous forests, **American ginseng** was almost brought to extinction in the mid-20th century when the root became a valuable export to China (the Chinese believe that, as a folk medicine, our ginseng is more powerful than theirs), and it has never fully recovered. It is now listed as a species of special concern. Of Minnesota's three biomes, the prairie has the most plant species at risk. While once abundant and widespread, both **western prairie fringed orchid** and **prairie bush clover** are now federally threatened species, and the latter is one of the rarest plants in the Midwest. Farming caused most of the destruction of the prairie, and while new technologies have allowed expansion into areas once unworkable, a new and growing threat to this vanishing ecosystem is the alternative medicine fad. People sneak into nature preserves under cover of darkness and dig up whatever plant is the hot new trend, as well as everything else around it, destroying large swatches of prairie.

History

FIRST ARRIVALS

The Beringia land-bridge theory—that the first humans in the Americas migrated from Asia to North America over the Bering Strait 12,000 years ago—has been seriously challenged. The discovery of important new archaeological sites, such as Serra Da Capivara in northeast Brazil, Monte Verde in southern Chile, and Meadowcroft in Pennsylvania, appear to show that humans had arrived in the Americas in several waves as much as 20,000–30,000 years ago, though these later figures are somewhat speculative and remain in dispute amongst experts. It appears the first peoples of the Americas came by boat from the South Pacific and only later by foot from Siberia. Despite these exciting new finds, there is still no reason to think that humans came to what would become Minnesota any time before about 9,000–10,000 B.C., since most of the land was covered by ice before this.

Little is known about the first Minnesotans, the nomadic **Paleo-Indians,** who followed the melting glaciers north, hunting large game such as mastodon, musk ox, and giant beaver along the way. It is assumed they did not make pottery or fabrics since none from this time have been found. What have been uncovered in large numbers are their weapons. The finely made projectile points were attached to spears and thrown by atlatls, a powerful and accurate weapon. After these megafauna became extinct (debate continues about whether over-hunting or climate change was the primary factor) around 6,000 years ago, so did the Paleo-Indian way of life.

With less game to sustain them, the hunter-gatherers of the **Archaic** period began to settle into longer-term campsites near bodies of water and rely more on what they could find locally. They still hunted, but also learned to fish and relied more on harvesting edible plants like acorns, cherries, blueberries, and plums. Technology advanced and people made knives, scrapers, axes, and drills. Toward the end of this period people began to construct burial mounds, and those living along the northwestern Great Lakes, including Minnesota, pounded tools out of copper nuggets.

After 1000 B.C. the **Woodland** culture began to rise in the Ohio River Valley, climaxing in the area's Hopewell societies. There were many large societal advances during this time, but most came slowly to Minnesota. Most notable was the manufacture and use of pottery. Tools became more specialized and eventually these people learned to use bows and arrows. People soon settled in permanent villages, and their sedentary lifestyle led to the cultivation of plants like sunflower, ragweed, and wild rice. People made simple jewelry, decorated their pottery, and became increasingly ceremonial. Burial mounds became larger, more complex, and more common as the importance of individual leaders grew. For unknown reasons the Woodland culture began to decline around A.D. 500–600, but it lingered on in Minnesota until about A.D. 1700 in the northern part of the state.

Beginning about A.D. 1000, a new series of cultures known as **Mississippian** either moved in and replaced some of the Woodland peoples or the Woodland peoples evolved into them. Mississippian culture was heavily influenced by ideas from Mexico, and it flourished across the eastern half of the continent. Cahokia, its spiritual and cultural heart, was a city of over 30,000 people across the Mississippi River from present-day St. Louis. In Minnesota, which was again far from the center of power, the influence was tempered somewhat. Villages grew large, possibly upward of 800 people, and were often fortified. Corn (a Mexican import) was the era's most important crop, but since it did not grow well in the north, wild rice became the staple in Minnesota. Pipes carved from stone quarried at what is now the Pipestone National Monument in southwest Minnesota spread across North America due to their deep spiritual import. Though several cultures related to the Cahokians, such as the **Great Oasis** and **Cambria,** lived amongst each other in Minnesota, the **Oneota** were the most advanced and widespread.

By the time Europeans first arrived in the state, the Mississippian cultures had largely faded away, though their modern descendents, the **Dakota** (aka Sioux), were spread across the center of Minnesota and occupied the majority of the state. Other Mississippian progeny, the **Iowa** and **Oto** tribes, remained in the far south. The **Cree** controlled the far north, and the **Assiniboine,** descendents of but enemies with the Dakota, inhabited the northwest corner. Some **Omaha** and **Cheyenne** might have been in the southwest corner and far west-central regions respectively, though we may never know for sure.

The **Ojibwe** (aka Chippewa or Anishinaabe), Minnesota's other major historic Indian culture, were centered around Sault Ste. Marie in Upper Michigan when the French came up the Great Lakes. Beginning in the 1640s the League of the Iroquois, in an effort to monopolize the fur trade, attacked other tribes in the area, and most Ojibwe fled west, eventually settling in northern Wisconsin and forcing some Dakota villages to pick up and move west in the process. As they became more enamored with the goods they received from the French in return for the furs they trapped, the Ojibwe moved into northern Minnesota to occupy the most fertile lands. The resulting animosity between the two tribes would eventually lead to over a century of on-again, off-again war; the Ojibwe usually came out on top.

EUROPEAN CONTACT

The Spanish (and Portuguese), in the latter part of the 15th century, blazed the trail west looking for the East. Their goal was to circumvent the Arabs, reach the courts of the Great Khan, and establish methods to appropriate the riches of the new lands. Along the way, the natives, if any, were to be "pacified" under papal hegemony. After England came to naval power under the Tudor monarchies and began taking swipes at the French, the New World became the proving ground for European powers.

New France: Black Robes and the Fur Trade

The French were relative latecomers to maritime, and thus expansionist, endeavors and, thanks to the Reformation, conveniently freed of papal dicta for divvying up the new continent and its inherent wealth. With the Spanish controlling most of the Caribbean and Gulf Coast and the up-and-coming English dominating what would become the mid-Atlantic colonies, France was effectively forced to penetrate the new land via the northern frontier.

Jacques Cartier first opened the door to the Great Lakes region with his exploration of the St. Lawrence River in 1535 during his second expedition to find the Northwest Passage to the Orient. He sailed as far as what would become Montreal and spent that winter at the future site of Quebec City with the Iroquois. They told him stories of vast seas and wealthy kingdoms to the west. Cartier, figuring these waters must be the coveted maritime route to Asia he had been seeking, claimed the entire river valley for France. His tales, however, lacking mention of lustrous gold and silver, failed to woo France's insular King Francis I, who was busy fighting Spain and invading Italy. As a result, the French, content to fish the shoals of Newfoundland, left the scattered outposts to simmer for another 40 years—except for several fur traders, who, it turns out, were on to something.

When, with an eye to creating a permanent "New France," the French did establish settlements, they were dismayed by the lack of ready riches, the roughness of the land, and the bitter weather. The original traders, however, possessed one superlative talent: forging relationships with the natives, who became enamored of French metal implements—firearms in particular—and eventually, the French found their coveted mother lode: beavers. Paris hatmakers saw that beaver pelts made a superior grade of felt for hats, and these soon became the rage in Paris and other parts of Europe. As beaver was readily available and easily transportable to France from the wilds, it became the lifeblood of the colonies.

Facilitating both the fur trade and French control over the colonies were the missionaries of the Society of Jesus—the Jesuits. These "Black Robes" (so-called by the Huron and Ottawa because of their long dark frocks) first arrived during a time of atavistic religious fervor in France. The Jesuits became the foundation upon which New France operated, serving crucial secular and religious needs. The traders needed them to foster harmony with Native Americans. More important, the often complicated French system of operation required that all day-to-day affairs be carried out at the local level. By 1632, all missionary work in French Canada was under the auspices of the Jesuits. The Jesuits also accompanied *voyageurs* (literally "travelers," but specifically it refers to the men who paddled the canoes for the New World fur traders) as New France attempted to widen its sphere of influence westward. Eventually the Black Robes themselves, along with renegade fur traders, were responsible for the initial exploration and settlement of present-day Minnesota.

Samuel de Champlain, who first arrived in Quebec in 1603 as part of a fur-trading party and later was given charge of New France, was obsessed with finding the Northwest Passage. Convinced that the Great Lakes were the way to the riches of the East, he personally explored Lakes Ontario and Huron, where, in 1615, he made first contact with the Ojibwe, who would become the French's most important partners in Minnesota. Men such as Étienne Brûlé and Jean Nicolet were dispatched west to trade and foster good relations with the natives and explore sea routes along the way.

THE VOYAGEURS REACH MINNESOTA

Brûlé explored Lake Superior as early as 1618, two years before the Mayflower landed at Plymouth Rock, but he never reached the western shore. Following Champlain's death in 1635 the official desire to push west withered, and it wasn't until 1660 that the first Europeans set foot in what would become Minnesota. On their second illicit trading journey along the south shore of Lake Superior, Pierre Esprit Radisson and his brother-in-law Médard Chouart, Sieur des Groseilliers, an enterprising duo of unlicensed traders, spent the winter of 1659 with the Ottawa in northern Wisconsin, during which time they became the first Europeans to meet the Dakota. The following spring they reached the "Head of the Lake" at present-day Duluth and paddled up along the lake's western shore before returning to Montreal, where they expected to be welcomed as heroes. Instead French officials confiscated their colossal haul of illegally obtained fur. Radisson and Groseilliers soon allied with the British and headed for Hudson Bay, where their explorations led to the formation of the Hudson's Bay Company, which, ironically, later played a large role in the downfall of the French empire in North America.

Following Radisson and Groseilliers, a few others poked around Lake Superior's western shore, including Father Claude Allouez, who contributed greatly to a 1670 Jesuit map of the lake. No one, however, headed inland until 1679 when Daniel Greysolon, Sieur du Lhut (Duluth's namesake), paddled up the St. Louis River and crossed overland to Lake Mille Lacs, where he forged an alliance with the Dakota at the village of Izatys and claimed all this land for King Louis XIV. A year later the Dakota, who apparently weren't too impressed by du Lhut's overtures, seized a group of explorers traveling north from Illinois to explore the upper Mississippi River and held them captive near Mille Lacs before du Lhut returned to secure their release. Upon his return to Europe, one member of that fateful party, Father Louis Hennepin, published *Description of Louisiana*, an account of their ordeal. Though full of inaccuracies, the first book written about Minnesota became a best-seller.

Fur traders soon followed du Lhut and Hennepin and were operating along the Mississippi and Minnesota Rivers. In 1686 Nicholas Perrot built Fort St. Antoine on the Wisconsin side of the Mississippi River at Lake Pepin, and soon after he erected Fort Bon Secours, the first white settlement in Minnesota, just below Lake Pepin. A few more small posts were later constructed in Minnesota, including the short-lived Fort l'Huillier near Mankato in 1700, but most New World positions were abandoned at the start of the 18th century as France fought a vast and expensive war against the British across the European continent.

The War of the Spanish Succession ended in 1714, and a few years later the French revived their quest for beaver pelts and the legendary Northwest Passage. The last French explorer of any significance in North America was the Canadian-born Pierre Gaultier de Varennes, Sieur de La Vérendrye, who built Fort St. Charles on Lake of the Woods in 1732. This Jesuit mission and fur-trading post thrived despite its remote location. La Vérendrye passed on the opportunity to enrich himself in the fur trade and spent most of the rest of his life venturing west desperately searching for the Pacific, eventually expanding the French influence all the way to the Canadian Rockies. By the 1750s the fur trade was thriving and several other large forts had sprung up in Minnesota, including La Jonquiére near Brainerd.

NEW REGIMES

The Dakota initially tolerated the French partnership with the Ojibwe because their longtime enemies served as an intermediary, bringing valuable French goods to the Dakota. After the increasingly expansionist French moved into Minnesota permanently and fostered alliances with (and supplied weapons to) the Cree and Assiniboine to the north, also both enemies of the Dakota, the Dakota attacked Fort St. Charles in 1736. The Ojibwe decided to cement their relationship with the French, increase their territory, and settle old scores by attacking the Dakota. Allied with the Cree and Assiniboine and supplied with firearms and military advice by the French, the highly motivated Ojibwe slowly swept across Dakota territory in Minnesota, Wisconsin, and Canada. At the bloody, three-day Battle of Kathio (about 1750), the Ojibwe routed the Dakota in their spiritual and political heart on the western shore of Mille Lacs. Though this was the decisive clash (that is, assuming it really happened; some historians doubt it), the war continued, and so did the Dakota exodus to the south and west. By 1780 the Dakota had been pushed completely south of the Minnesota River, where these forest-dwellers had to adapt their lifestyle to the prairies.

The French and British were at each other's throats again by 1754. The French and Indian War, the North American campaign that led to the Seven Years' War in Europe (1756–1763), began with the British, led by a 23-year-old George Washington, trying to evict the French from western Pennsylvania. The British trounced the French on both continents in this, the last of four major conflicts between the colonial powers during the previous 75 years, and took Canada and all French territories east of the Mississippi. Spain had received all French land west of the Mississippi a year earlier in a scheme to keep it out of British hands.

Under the British and Spanish Flags

Spain did nothing with its lands in Minnesota, but the British continued searching for a water route to the Pacific and trading for furs with the Ojibwe and Dakota. To appease the Ojibwe the British continued to employ French voyageurs to trade and transport furs. Jonathan Carver spent two years exploring in and around Minnesota as part of a larger expedition to find the Northwest Passage and published a wildly exaggerated and frequently inaccurate (except for those passages he plagiarized from earlier French explorers) account of his journey. *Travels Through the Interior Parts of North America, in the Years 1766, 1767, and 1768,* the first English-language book about Minnesota, was an immediate and enduring success, going through 32 printings. British fur traders opened dozens of trading posts in Minnesota's interior and also made Spanish Louisiana their domain since no one was there to keep them out.

THE AMERICAN REVOLUTION

Twenty years after Great Britain acquired the land east of the Mississippi River, the 1783 Treaty of Paris, which recognized the independence of the United States, took it away. No fighting took place in or even near Minnesota during the Revolutionary War, and fur traders continued their work with scant regard to the battles in the East since a British defeat was unimaginable. Their defeat sent shock waves around the world, but life for the British in Minnesota, a western outpost far too remote for the Americans to worry about, continued just as before.

The year after the treaty was signed, Simon McTavish's newly organized North West Company, the primary competitor of the Hudson's Bay Company, based its inland operations at Grand Portage. All pelts coming out of northern Minnesota and western Canada passed through this gateway, which was conveniently located as far west as the voyageurs could travel in a year and still make it back to Montreal. This isolated site had been a busy trading center for many decades, but McTavish transformed it into one of the most important fur-trading posts in the New World.

In 1800 the French briefly returned to Minnesota after they reacquired the Louisiana Territory from Spain, but the land west of the Mississippi joined the United States just three years later when Thomas Jefferson and Napoleon completed the Louisiana Purchase. That same year the North West Company's Grand Portage settlement was abandoned. Inland operations were moved up the shore to Fort William in Canada under the assumption that the Americans would soon try to tax them.

The Americans Take Control

Though the North West Company packed up their main base, trade at most of their other outposts continued unabated. In order to secure their hold on the new land and its inhabitants, both British and Indian, 20 soldiers led by Lieutenant Zebulon Pike set out on the first U.S. expedition through Minnesota in 1805. His orders were to find the source of the Mississippi River, choose sites for army posts, reel in the British, and foster peace between the Dakota and Ojibwe. Land along the Mississippi at the mouths of the St. Croix and Minnesota Rivers was purchased from the Dakota for future military posts, but this was the only goal of the expedition that was truly met. Pike misidentified the mighty river's source as Leech Lake, and the North West Company never kept their promise to begin paying duties on their furs.

Although many factors contributed to the War of 1812, it was the quest for land that ultimately led the Americans to declare war against the British. The Dakota, Ojibwe, and most other northeastern tribes fought alongside the British, who almost immediately retook most of the Great Lakes region before the Americans put up a strong, and often successful, fight there. Though the British had also sacked Washington, D.C., torching the Capitol and White House in the process, two years of fighting had resulted in a near stalemate; thus, the Treaty of Ghent, which required each side to return conquered territory and join a commission to formalize the Canadian border, was a logical move.

The Convention of 1818 set the U.S.-Canadian border between Lake Superior and Lake of the Woods as the Pigeon River and then the forty-ninth parallel west of Lake of the Woods, but because the 1783 Treaty of Paris was based on errant maps, nit-picking over the exact boundary along Minnesota continued until 1931. Following the (theoretical) drawing of the border, British traders finally faced reality and left Minnesota or accepted the American offer to remain and become citizens. John Jacob Astor's American Fur Company filled the void in Minnesota and elsewhere in the western United States until the fur trade crashed in the 1840s.

The United States officially staked its claim in Minnesota in 1819 with the construction of Fort St. Anthony (renamed Fort Snelling upon its completion in 1825) high atop a bluff at the confluence of the Mississippi and Minnesota Rivers. For a decade and a half this was Minnesota's main white settlement, and its founding marked the beginning of modern Minnesota history.

Even up to this point little was known of Minnesota beyond its major rivers. A bevy of explorers, some on government business, set out for the thrill and glory of the adventure, all seeking the fame sure to befall the discoverer of the source of the Mississippi River. In 1832 Henry Rowe Schoolcraft, who had been poking around the state for over a decade, set out on an official mission to quell disturbances between the Ojibwe and Dakota and vaccinate as many of them against smallpox as possible. Though diligent in his orders (Douglass Houghton, the party's doctor, vaccinated over 2,000 people), he also decided to solve once and for all the great mystery of the Mississippi. So confident was he this time that he derived the grand name Itasca (in Latin "true head" is *veritas caput;* Schoolcraft just trimmed the outer syllables) before even setting out. Schoolcraft's Ojibwe guide Ozawindib led him upstream to what the Ojibwe knew as Elk Lake, and though he wasn't the first white man to visit it, none before had recognized its importance. Schoolcraft gained eternal fame for his explorations, but his most important work came as an ethnologist, and he is regarded as the foremost pioneer of Native American studies.

Land Rush

By 1837 four states—Ohio, Indiana, Illinois, and Michigan—had been carved out of the Old Northwest and tens of thousands of immigrants had flowed into what would become Wisconsin, but most of the land in Minnesota remained with the Dakota and Ojibwe nations. That year the inevitable began, and they signed treaties relinquishing their lands (5,000 sq. miles) between the Mississippi and St. Croix Rivers. Congress ratified the treaties the next year and on July 15, the very day word of the final agreement reached Fort Snelling, settlers branched out to make claims. Pierre "Pig's Eye" Parrant, an aging voyageur with a nasty disposition, settled at the future site of St. Paul and built a shanty tavern. The eventual state capital soon became a steamboat port and trading center, replacing Fort Snelling as the most important settlement on the Upper Mississippi River.

While some settlers came here to claim land for farms, most, including a large number of New Englanders, had their sights set on the vast and valuable stands of timber. Orange Walker and L. S. Judd came to the St. Croix River from Illinois and had a sawmill, the state's first (besides the small one used for the construction of Fort Snelling), running at their new town, Marine on St. Croix, by August of 1839. Franklin Steele also had lumbering in mind when he made his claim at the Falls of St. Anthony on the Mississippi River, an obvious place to build a sawmill, but it would take him a decade to get things up and running. His settlement later evolved into Minneapolis.

MINNESOTA TERRITORY

When Wisconsin was admitted to the union in 1848, the land between the Mississippi and St. Croix Rivers, which had been part of the Wisconsin Territory, was not included in its borders, leaving thousands of people in political limbo. A group of influential civic leaders hastily schemed amongst themselves and, at an August summit in Stillwater, elected Henry Sibley, a director of the American Fur Company, to represent them in Washington. Though technically Sibley had no right to a seat in Congress, a point that both he and his opponents were well aware of, the country was in all-out Manifest Destiny fever, which prompted legislators to accept him as a delegate. Despite partisan bickering and a white population well below the 5,000 legally required for territorial status, the Minnesota Territorial Act was passed in March of the next year. The new territory had the same borders as the current state on all sides except the west, where it stretched out to the Missouri and White Earth Rivers, making it twice the size of the present state. The only part of the Stillwater Convention plan that went awry was the timing. Minnesota was a thoroughly Democratic state, but the law was signed too late for Democratic president James K. Polk to appoint Sibley as territorial governor. The choice instead fell to his successor Zachary Taylor, a Whig, who chose Pennsylvanian Alexander Ramsey. Sibley, who would later be elected the state's first governor, was unanimously chosen as Minnesota's first official delegate to Congress.

Before word of the new territorial status reached this far west (the first boat of the season arrived up the Mississippi with the good news in April of 1849), Minnesota had but a handful of towns, and no more than two dozen buildings stood in St. Paul, but by the time Ramsey stepped off the boat in May his new home had already doubled in size. When the legislature convened in September, 1,000 people had arrived and stores, hotels, bowling alleys, a school, and the state's first newspaper (the *Minnesota Pioneer,* now the *Pioneer Press*) had all sprung up in the capital. Growth in the rest of the state remained modest, however, and the 1850 census tallied just 6,077 residents.

The first order of business for the new government was land. Ramsey and Sibley almost immediately set to work securing funds from Washington with which to negotiate treaties. In 1851 the Dakota relinquished most of southern Minnesota, some 20 million acres, in exchange for $1,665,000—about seven cents an acre. Not only did the United States fail to honor all terms of the treaties in the coming years, but at the official ceremony the chiefs were tricked into signing another document agreeing to use $275,000 of the just-appropriated funds to repay debts owed to fur traders. While the issue of traders' debts was legitimate, the total claimed for them was grossly exaggerated. This whole underhanded affair was partly to blame for the Dakota Conflict a decade later.

Ramsey and his agents continued to buy land from the Ojibwe, and by 1857, when all but a small stretch of land along the northern border had been ceded, the territory's population had swelled to a previously unfathomable total of 150,092. Most of these eager pioneers were American-born farmers who took horse and plow to the southern prairies to raise wheat, while others swept through the great forests of the north with ax and saw. Speculators penciled in hundreds of new villages with enough homesites for over eight times the population. The financial Panic of 1857 dampened many grand plans and created a fair share of ghost towns, but it didn't suppress overall enthusiasm for Minnesota's future, and a constitutional convention was held that year.

OFFICIAL MINNESOTA STATE SYMBOLS

Bird: Common Loon
Butterfly: Monarch
Drink: Milk
Fish: Walleye
Flower: Pink-and-White Showy Lady's Slipper
Gemstone: Lake Superior Agate
Grain: Wild Rice
Muffin: Blueberry
Mushroom: Morel
Photograph: *Grace*, by Eric Enstrom
Song: "Hail! Minnesota"
Tree: Norway Pine

STATEHOOD

Minnesota officially joined the union as the 32nd state on May 11, 1858, but like the rest of the nation it was in for a tough haul over the next seven years—the depression resulting from the Panic of 1857 struck Minnesota particularly hard because of the excessive land speculation, a severe drought in 1862 and 1863 created food shortages, and in April 1861 Confederate troops fired on Fort Sumter, sending the young nation into Civil War. Governor Ramsey, who had been elected in 1859 in part because his Republican Party echoed the anti-slavery convictions of the majority of Minnesotans, was the first governor to offer troops to the Union cause, doing so a day before President Lincoln even requested volunteers. While the battles of the Civil War raged far away, war struck home in 1862 when Chief Little Crow led the Dakota in a devastating, though ultimately unsuccessful, rebellion.

Since wheat and timber supplied Northern armies, the Civil War had the unexpected effect of reviving Minnesota's economy. By 1867 railroads connected the Twin Cities to Chicago, an important event since frozen rivers prevented steamboat traffic for much of the year. The Homestead Act of 1862, which allowed Americans and immigrants who had started the naturalization process 160 acres of free land if they built a dwelling on it and lived there for five years, eventually brought hundreds of thousands of new farmers to the state. Most newcomers were New Englanders, while immigrants came primarily from Britain, Ireland, and Germany. To promote foreign settlement, the State Board of Immigration was established in 1867, and, because of similar climates, it focused its efforts on luring Scandinavians. With the ringing endorsement of earlier immigrants from Norway and Sweden, hundreds of thousands arrived by the end of the 19th century, and today Scandinavians collectively constitute, by far, the largest ethnic group in the state. German is the largest single nationality.

Progressive Politics

Three industries dominated Minnesota's economy in the second half of the 19th century: logging, agriculture, and iron mining. Logging yields doubled in each decade between 1860 and 1900, with two billion board feet felled at the turn of the 20th century. During this time Minnesota was amongst the leaders nationally in the amount of lumber supplied to the growing nation, but throughout it all agriculture was the state's lifeblood, and the vast majority of Minnesotans were farmers. By 1860 wheat was king, and it continued to increase in importance so that by 1878 the golden grain accounted for nearly three-quarters of the state's agricultural production. The total might have risen higher, but the blizzard of 1873, followed immediately by a four-year grasshopper plague, forced a reluctant move toward crop diversification.

During the 1880s and 1890s the percentage of land cultivated with wheat dropped by more than half, but overall production still increased substantially, and Minnesota led the nation in wheat production during these decades. With the boom in wheat around the state and the active development of new technologies, men like Cadwallader Washburn and John Pillsbury made Minneapolis a world-famous flour-milling center. Mill City, as it was known, thrived as the nation's leading flour producer for half a century. Minneapolis's supremacy in this one industry attracted tangential businesses such as banks, railroads, and food manufacturers, turning it into Minnesota's metropolis. Had it not been for wheat, St. Paul would almost surely be the state's leading city instead.

Despite growth in agriculture, farmers' discontent was almost universal. At the mercy of the railroads, which charged extortionate shipping rates and habitually cheated them at the scales, they were routinely forced into debt. The 1870s was a particularly challenging decade since the natural disasters came side by side with a severe downturn in the national economy (the Panic of 1873), cutting prices for their products. Their first champion was Oliver Kelley, a farmer from Elk River, who believed cooperatives and scientific agriculture were the answers farmers needed. Kelley had founded The Grange in 1867 to promote these ideals and lobby against the monopolistic pricing of the railroads. The Grange also opposed many of the practices of millers, farm-equipment dealers, and bankers. Surprisingly they had little trouble convincing the governor and legislature to take on the railroads; a railroad commissioner was appointed and rates were fixed in 1871. The railroads, however, simply ignored the new directives. Two years later the Grangers moved directly into politics when former Congressman and Lieutenant Governor Ignatious Donnelly, a brilliant public speaker, formed the Anti-Monopoly Party. Several Anti-Monopolist legislators, including Donnelly, were sent to St. Paul the next year but had no success reeling in the railroads, and the party quickly faded away. While they affected little legislatively, they did herald the progressive era in Minnesota and the tradition of third-party movements that continues to this day. The Anti-Monopoly Party was followed by the Greenback Party, Farmers' Alliance, and Populist Party, all of which continued to campaign for rural issues, largely by promoting currency expansion that would have assisted indebted farmers. Donnelly, who became famous nationally for his crackpot books on Atlantis and other bizarre topics, was involved in all of them, but never again won elected office.

The first iron was shipped out of Two Harbors from the Soudan Mine up on the newly discovered Vermilion Range in 1884. Six years later iron was found on the even richer Mesabi Range, and Minnesota soon became the nation's leading iron-producing state, an honor Minnesota has maintained ever since. The mines also helped make Duluth the Great Lakes' largest port. Tax revenues endowed the Iron Range boomtowns with some of the best schools and public services in the nation, but the difficult and dangerous conditions that the miners labored in bred anger and protest. In later years the Finns, many of whom were Socialists who had fled the Russian Czar's crackdown on the political left, were well known as effective organizers and agitators.

When organized labor joined the reform cause in the 1890s, they brought great success to the Populist Party in both Minnesota and the nation. Though the Populists were Minnesota's second party, by the 1894 elections they faded when the Democrats, led nationally by firebrand populist William Jennings Bryan and locally by former Republican and political moderate John Lind, co-opted many of their positions. In the 1898 elections Lind became the state's first Democratic governor since Henry Sibley won the initial election in 1857, but it didn't exactly break the Republicans' hold on the executive; Lind was defeated two years later, and the GOP took 10 of the next 15 governorships.

EARLY 20TH CENTURY

Despite the death of the Populist Party, the first decade of the 20th century saw progressive ideals like trust-busting and government reform expand beyond partisan politics. In 1901 Governor Van Sant spearheaded the national effort to bring the hammer down on the Northern Securities Company railroad monopoly, a crusade President Theodore Roosevelt enthusiastically supported; however, the reform movement really came to a head with the 1904 election of the humble Democrat John Johnson. Over the course of his three terms the moderate Johnson promoted tax reforms, appointed nonpartisan judges, expanded powers for the Bureau of Labor, reformed the insurance and banking industries, and further regulated the railroads. Johnson took repeated verbal shots from both the Right and Left but remained exceedingly popular with the public and gained national prominence. His legitimate presidential potential was dashed by his untimely death in 1909. Johnson's successor, Republican Albert Eberhart, another Swede, continued to take on corporate industrialism, signed the state's first workers' compensation laws, and pushed through a sweeping program of government reforms, though he did so out of political necessity rather than personal conviction.

As World War I raged across Europe and dominated the political debate in this country, renewed agrarian discontent swept the Nonpartisan League into Minnesota. This political-pressure group supported some socialistic programs like state ownership of grain elevators and flour mills. Though Nonpartisans had taken control of the governorship and legislature in North Dakota, where the movement had been born, they had less success in the more industrial Minnesota. The labor movement had strengthened during this time too, and by 1914 over 400 labor organizations were operating across the state, pushing for reforms like the minimum wage and the eight-hour workday. Arthur C. Townley, the league's founder and a Minnesota native who had moved the headquarters to St. Paul in 1917, realized that to succeed in the state he would need to forge an alliance with labor.

Almost overnight in 1918 the new Farmer-Labor Party, capitalizing on the post-war depression, became the state's second-largest political party. By 1923 it held both of the state's U.S. Senate seats, and, on the heels of the Great Depression, the flamboyant Floyd B. Olson took the governorship in 1930. The party lost support by the end of the decade for supporting increasingly radical ideas like the public ownership of banks, transportation, utilities, and other essential services. By 1938 a more moderate Republican Party was back on top in the state when Harold Stassen, the Boy Governor, took office at age 31 and Republicans won both houses of the legislature. Both Stassen and the revitalized party accepted most of the major New Deal programs like Social Security and promoted "enlightened capitalism" as an alternative to the socialistic aims of the Farmer-Laborers. The moderate stance kept the Republicans on top of the political scene in Minnesota until the mid-1950s.

The state's tradition of championing reform continued in 1933 when the first sit-down strike took place at Austin's Hormel meatpacking plant. After three days Hormel agreed to submit their wage dispute to binding arbitration. The next year the Minneapolis Teamster Strike, one of the most important events in American labor history, resulted in over 200 strikers injured and 4 killed, and a declaration of Martial Law. Not only did the truck drivers and warehouse workers win the right to organize, but the tragedy resulted in the National Labor Relations (Wagner) Act of 1935, which guaranteed all workers the right to organize and bargain collectively. It also prohibited interference in union action by employers and established national standards for resolving labor disputes.

Though the state was rapidly industrializing,

farming and mining remained vital to the economy. The lumber industry in Minnesota had peaked in 1899 and the last of the virgin forests were felled by the 1930s, but iron had taken up the slack and by then over half of the ferric ore mined on earth came from Minnesota. The increasing prevalence of automobiles brought visitors to Minnesota's many lakes, allowing tourism to replace logging as one of the state's leading three enterprises.

WORLD WAR II TO THE PRESENT

It was only natural that the Farmer-Labor Party and the Democrats would merge. Though politicians had promoted the union for many years, the Democratic-Farmer-Labor (DFL) Party was officially forged in 1944. Soon DFLers like Hubert H. Humphrey, Eugene McCarthy, and Walter Mondale took to the national stage. While DFL politicians have spent more time in the spotlight and the party has been in control more often than not from the 1950s on, power in both St. Paul and Washington has seesawed between the Democrats and Republicans.

World War II led to record iron production in Minnesota's mines, but at the same time it became clear that the high-grade iron ore was running out. In response, the state invested heavily with research funding and tax breaks to encourage mining companies to begin extracting iron from abundant low-grade taconite (a low-grade iron-bearing rock). Engineers had been trying for decades to develop a cost-effective process to extract the iron from the solid rock, and, thanks to generous state funding, Dr. E. W. Davis at the University of Minnesota School of Mines perfected one. The world's first taconite plant opened at Silver Bay in 1956, and a decade later taconite production exceeded regular ore—the last direct ore shipment left the Mesabi Range in 1984.

The war not only stimulated the iron industry, but it also spurred Minnesota's industrial sector (led by companies like 3M, Honeywell, and Medtronic), and by 1948 manufactured goods exceeded the value of farm products for the first time. Though agriculture remains vital, the resulting diversification distinguishes the state's economy today. In 1973 *Time* magazine put Governor Wendell Anderson on the cover and proclaimed "Minnesota: A State That Works," lauding Minnesota for doing just about everything right. The overall solid economy of the past half-century has made Minnesota the fastest-growing state in the Midwest and Northeast regions of the country.

Two of the most remarkable events of Minnesota's 20th century came right at the end. The Mall of America opened in 1992 and proved doubters wrong by thriving. And, in a scenario so unlikely that the writers for the WWE wouldn't have dreamed it up, former professional wrestler Jesse "The Body" Ventura was elected governor in 1998.

Government and Economy

GOVERNMENT

Minnesota's parties are the most unusual feature of the state's political scene. The primary party of the left is the DFL (Democratic-Farmer-Labor), which resulted from a merger of Farmer-Labor Party and the much smaller Democratic Party after World War II. The right got into the autonomy act in the 1970s. Following the Watergate scandal, Minnesota's Republicans distanced themselves from the national disgrace by changing their name to the Independent Republican Party, but the Independent was dropped during the party's wave of national success in the mid-1990s. The leftist and progressive Green Party of Minnesota has won a handful of local races, though as of yet it is taken no more seriously statewide than the Greens are at the national level. White Earth Reservation activist Winona LaDuke helped raise the party's profile when she ran as the Greens' vice presidential candidate for the 1996 and 2000 elections.

The newest player in Minnesota politics is the Independence Party of Minnesota, which sits squarely in the middle of the road. They began as part of the Reform Party, Ross Perot's anti-deficit crusade of the late 1990s, but split in 2000. Since its founding, only five party members have won a seat at the polls, including former professional wrestler Jesse "The Body" Ventura. Ventura's tenure as governor was, as the *Star Tribune* called it, "a riotous four years of controversy, publicity-seeking, outside moneymaking, tri-partisan gridlock and, yes, governance." DFL and Republican critics were outspoken from the start (an inevitable aspect of political life that the thin-skinned Ventura did not handle very maturely), though his candor and his independence from special interests kept his approval ratings high throughout most of his term. The sudden downturn in the polls—a March 2002 *Star Tribune* poll showed only 31 percent of Minnesotans felt that he "deserves to be reelected"—and his fervent hatred of the media were no doubt significant factors in his decision to not run for reelection. It is still too early to tell if the Independence Party will have much success beyond its most visible spokesman, though it seems unlikely.

As its parties demonstrate, politically Minnesota has a strong independent streak, though historically it is one of the nation's more liberal states. Democrats have won every presidential election in the state since 1960 with the exception of Richard Nixon's victory in 1972—most by wide margins—yet Minnesotans have consistently seesawed between the left and right in Congressional, gubernatorial, and state legislative elections over the same period. The DFL took control of the state Senate in 1972 (the first year legislators again began running with party labels) and hasn't let go since. They also currently hold a solid majority in the House. Governor Tim Pawlenty, elected in 2002, announced that he would not seek reelection in 2010, under speculation that he was leaving to national political aspirations.

ECONOMY

The industries most closely associated with Minnesota—agriculture, forestry, and mining—amount to just two percent of the state's Gross State Product (GSP). With over 90 percent of the country's primary industries represented, Minnesota has one of the nation's most diverse economies. Generating one-quarter of the state's $262 billion GSP, service industries are the state's leading—and fastest-growing—sector. Following services are finance, insurance, and real estate services; trade; and manufacturing.

The economy is consistently one of the strongest in the nation. Throughout the 1990s and on into the 21st century, job and GSP growth in Minnesota soundly outpaced the national average; unemployment in all major industries and for all major occupations has consistently been several points lower than the national rate, exports outpace imports by over 50 percent, and per capita income has risen to ninth-highest in the nation. Additionally, with 17 of them headquartered here, Minnesota ranks first in the number of Fortune 500 companies per capita. Target, U.S. Bancorp, 3M, Best Buy, General Mills, and Hormel Foods are some of the best known.

Agriculture

Even though farming accounts for just a tiny fraction of the state's economy and, for the most part, only occurs in the southern and western tiers, Minnesota ranks sixth nationally in total farm income, with annual receipts topping $15.8 billion. One significant factor behind the agricultural success is that Minnesota farmers have always been national leaders in supporting cooperative business organizations.

The top five agricultural products are, in order, corn, soybeans, hogs, dairy products, and cattle: Together they account for more than 75 percent of all agricultural cash receipts. Also, Minnesota raises more sugar beets, sweet corn, green peas, and turkeys than any other state and is second for wild rice and canola. Other crops ranking in the top five include corn, soybeans, oats, sunflowers, dairy products, honey, and hogs.

Mining

The first iron mine opened in northeastern Minnesota in the 1880s, and the state has been the nation's leader in ore production ever since. Virtually all of it was dug out of the Vermilion, Cuyuna, and Mesabi Iron Ranges in northern Minnesota. Only the Mesabi Range, by far the largest of the three, is still worked these days, but it manages to provide two-thirds of the United States' supply of iron ore. The industry—notoriously volatile—suffered setbacks and shutdowns in the economic turmoil of 2008 and 2009, but has at times contributed more than $750 million to the state's economy. While that is just half a percent of the state's GSP, it's the lifeblood of many Iron Range communities. The Mesabi still has enough ore to keep the mines operating at current rates for over 200 years. There is relatively little mining besides iron, though Minnesota also leads the nation in granite production, most of it quarried around St. Cloud, and is near the top in sand, gravel, and peat.

Forestry

Minnesota was the leading lumber-producing state for most of the last half of the 19th century, but the Paul Bunyan cut-and-run era of logging died out in the early 20th century. Today logging is just a shadow of its former self, but associated paper- and wood-manufacturing companies are much bigger players in the economy and employ nearly 60,000 people.

Manufacturing

While manufacturing employment has fallen nationally, it has been on the increase in Minnesota, and high-tech industries are leading the sector's rise. It began in the 1980s with computing pioneers Control Data and Cray Research, and today the state is a leader in e-commerce technology and medical instruments. Medtronic, inventors of the cardiac pacemaker, is one of hundreds of members of Medical Alley, the state's influential trade association. In 2007, Minnesota ranked third nationally in the number of U.S. patents issued per capita, a strong indicator of available talent and commitment to research. Minnesota's high-tech success comes from several factors, not the least of which is the highly educated workforce. Another advantage Minnesota has is that unlike other high-tech hotspots, such as the Silicon Valley, there is a very low employee turnover because people who come to Minnesota generally want to stay. The state has recently begun a push to make Minnesota a leader in biotechnology.

Food processing remains an important part of the manufacturing sector with meatpacking, dairy products, and sugar-refining all major contributors. Relatively little milling takes place in Minnesota today, though many of the leading companies such as Cargill and General Mills remain headquartered in the Twin Cities. On the marketing end, the Pillsbury Doughboy, Jolly Green Giant, and Betty Crocker all hail from Minnesota.

The People

Minnesota's population of 5,220,393 (2008 estimate) ranks 21st in the nation, though its population density of 61.8 people per square mile ranks 31st. Fifty-five percent of Minnesotans live in the seven-county Twin Cities metro area, which is the fastest-growing part of the state. Another 20 percent live in the triangle formed by the Twin Cities, Duluth, and Moorhead. Since the 1990s, Minnesota has been by far the fastest-growing state in the Midwest. Its five most populous cities are Minneapolis, 390,131; St. Paul, 288,055; Rochester, 102,437; Duluth, 85,220; and Bloomington, 85,238.

The state's ethnic breakdown is 89 percent white, 4.6 percent black, 3.5 percent Asian, 1.2 percent Native American, and 1.3 percent biracial. Latinos totaled 4.1 percent of the population. Although per capita immigration totals are average compared to the rest of the nation, and the foreign-born population is just six percent of the population (compared to 12 percent nationally), more refugees choose Minnesota than just about any other state.

Although immigration peaked at the beginning of the 20th century, few Minnesotans have completely let go of their heritage. Just about every town still celebrates at least some of the traditions of its founders in annual festivals, and local historical museums usually feature cultural displays from the motherland. Scandinavian traditions are the most widespread and still so ingrained that the Swedish and Norwegian royal families visit Minnesota occasionally. Lutefisk and lefse remain vital to many family celebrations; a multitude of cities have Scandinavian import stores; and most Minnesotans still love a good Ole and Lena joke. The newest immigrants, like Somali and Hmong, have brought their own food, crafts, and traditions to the state, and Native American pride is as strong as ever.

NATIVE AMERICANS

Since the time the first Europeans came in search of furs, the Native Americans residing in Minnesota have been almost exclusively the **Dakota** and **Ojibwe.** Historically bitter enemies, the Ojibwe, with the help of the French, slowly pushed the Dakota south and west. The current distribution of reservations, Dakota south of the Minnesota River and Ojibwe to the north, generally reflects the balance of power that was achieved between them by the time Europeans began to appropriate their lands. The Dakota have four reservations, all under two thousand acres, while the Ojibwe, by far the larger of the two, have seven reservations, none smaller than 48,000 acres. The Dakota lands are so small because following the Dakota Conflict they were expelled from the state and only a few later returned, at which time the government gave them new land.

Minnesota, with about 53,000 Native American residents, has the 14th-largest Native population in the United States. Only about a third actually live on the reservations, while nearly 40 percent live in the Twin Cities metro area.

EUROPEANS

While many Europeans came to the New World hoping to strike it rich, most were fleeing poverty or religious and political persecution. Minnesota's land rush began at the end of the 1830s and most people were drawn here by cheap land, though some sought logging and iron mining jobs. Initially most settlers came from the eastern United States and Canada, though some northern European immigrants arrived during the early years too.

The first arrivals in Minnesota were the **French,** who spread the fur trade across the Northwest. Most who came to Minnesota did so not directly from Europe, but through Canada. The most notable of the French-Canadians were the **Métis,** an ancestral mix of French and Native American, who ran oxcart trains of furs and supplies between St. Paul and Winnipeg.

Despite the widespread reputation of its Scandinavian heritage, **German** is actually the most common ancestry of today's Minnesotans, and it has been that way almost from the start. Germans settled across the whole of the state but with the densest concentrations in the southern and central counties, as towns such as Cologne, Hamburg, Heidelberg, New Germany, New Munich, and New Ulm attest. Minnesota remains one of the country's most ethnically German states, and New Ulm is not only the nation's most German city, but has the greatest percentage (66 percent) of any single ethnicity in cities with 5,000 or more residents.

Collectively the state's **Scandinavian** descendants outnumber the Germans, and they have left the most indelible mark on Minnesota. The rush of **Norwegians** and **Swedes,** who share not only similar backgrounds in Europe but also similar experiences in early Minnesota, began in the 1850s. More Norwegians and Swedes came to Minnesota than went to anywhere else in the world, and more than the next two states, Wisconsin and North Dakota, combined. Scandinavian ethnic supremacy in the state was achieved by the end of the 19th century, and immigration en masse didn't tail off until around 1930. Even today, Thief River

ST. URHO'S DAY

There is no St. Urho (pronounced OOR-hoe, with a heavy trilling of the R), but that doesn't stop Minnesotans from celebrating his heroic deeds. Legend has it that thousands of years ago wild grapes once grew in Finland. (This fact has been proven by studying the archaeological remains of bears.) When a plague of grasshoppers descended on Finland, Urho drove the locusts into the sea by loudly exclaiming *Heinäsirkka, heinäsirkka, mene täältä hiiten* (Grasshopper, Grasshopper, get the hell out of here!) and waving his pitchfork. Having conquered the locusts and saved the grapes, he thus became the patron saint of the Finnish vineyard workers. To honor this great linguistic feat, Finnish women and children, dressed in royal purple, line up along lakeshores at sunrise on March 16th and recite the magnificent Urho's mighty words. The men, wearing green costumes, gather atop the hills and upon hearing the chant change into purple garb. When the ritual is over the celebrants dance the polka, drink wine and grape juice, and eat the traditional *mojakka* (fish soup) that gave Urho the strength to succeed. Although it has yet to be proven by scholars, some Finns contend that the Irish stole the idea of celebrating St. Patrick, the Emerald Isle's patron saint, from them. The strongest evidence of this claim comes from the fact that St. Patrick's Day lands on the day immediately following St. Urho's Day. Apparently the Irish felt a celebration of their own would be a good reason to party for two days instead of just one.

None of the above tale is true, of course, though the real story behind St. Urho is just as entertaining. Urho was born to Richard Mattson in the spring of 1953 at Ketola's Department Store in Virginia, Minnesota. Mattson's tall tales of the Finnish saint who drove the poisonous frogs out of Finland, initially created as a counterpart to the Irish's beloved St. Patrick, eventually led to actual celebrations in his hometown. The frogs were changed to grasshoppers by Dr. Sulo Havumäki, a psychology professor at Bemidji State University who helped spread the legend.

St. Urho's Day is now celebrated in towns with Finnish heritage across the United States and Canada – there are even St. Urho's pubs in Finland – though it is still primarily a Minne-

Falls and Cambridge are respectively the nation's most Norwegian and Swedish cities of 5,000 or more residents. While the climate was a factor in their choice, the primary reason so many chose Minnesota was timing: Lands were opening up for settlement in Minnesota just as food shortages, overpopulation, and economic strife hit the homeland. They settled throughout the state (statistically Swedes are a little more common in the north, and denser Norwegian distribution is found in the south and west) and dominated state politics even before surpassing Germans in number. The **Danish** population, a much later arrival than other Scandinavians, is only about a fifth the size of either that of the Swedish or Norwegians, but it is still one of the largest Danish communities in the United States. Tyler, in the far southwest, is Minnesota's main hotbed of Danish culture. For the most part the **Finns** came even later than the Danes did, though in equal numbers, and Minnesota's Finnish descendants also constitute one of the largest such populations in the United States. Though some farmed, most notably around New York Mills and Embarrass, the vast majority dug the mines of the Iron Range. The "Red Finns," as they were known across the north, were persistent and effective union organizers and fought hard for improved working conditions—they were often severely persecuted for their efforts. Finnish saunas are still prevalent across the northeast. The number of **Icelandic** immigrants was minimal, but because the population of the island was so small, the percentage of Icelanders who left their homeland and came to Minnesota during the end of the 19th century was higher than for most other

sota thing. Menahga, home to a giant St. Urho statue, has the best-known celebration. Some of the festivities include a costume-changing of the guard, Finnish music, and plenty of *moj-akka*. The highlight of the celebrations in the town of Finland, Minnesota, is the crowning of Miss Helmi – all contestants are male. Other Minnesota towns that celebrate this holiday include New York Mills, Silver Bay, and Finlayson. It's now a big enough deal in some towns that celebrations begin on March 15th, while others, for some reason, ignore tradition and hold the festivities on the 23rd. There is more about the heroic saint and the celebrations in his honor at www.sainturho.com.

ODE TO ST. URHO

by Gene McCavic and Richard Mattson, Virginia, Minnesota

Original Finglish version

Ooksi kooksi coolama vee
Santia Urho is ta poy for me
He sase out ta hoppers as pig as pirds
Neffer peefor haff I hurd tose words
He reely tolt tose pugs of kreen
Braffest Finn I effer seen
Some celebrate for St. Pat unt hiss nakes
Putt Urho poyka kot what it takes
He kot tall and trong from feelia sour
Unt ate kala moyakka effery hour
Tat's why tat kuy could sase toes peetles
What krew as thick as chack bine neetles
So let's give a cheer in hower pest vay
On Sixteenth of March, St. Urho's Tay

English translation

One two three five
St. Urho is the boy for me
He chase out the hoppers as big as birds
Never before have I heard those words
He really told those bugs of green
Bravest Finn I ever seen
Some celebrate for St. Pat and his snakes
But Urho boy got what it takes
He got tall and strong from sour milk
And ate fish soup every hour
That's why that guy could chase those
beetles
What grew as thick as jack pine needles
So let's give a cheer in our best way
On Sixteenth of March, St. Urho's Day

countries. Most took up sheep farming on the prairies of Lyon, Lincoln, and Yellow Medicine Counties in the far southwest.

Minnesota's fourth-largest immigrant group, the **Irish,** made their new homes primarily in the southeast corner of the state, and, unlike most other Irish immigrants to the United States, farming was their principal livelihood. One of the first ethnic groups to arrive in large numbers in Minnesota, the roughly 12,000 exiles from the Emerald Isle living here in 1860 constituted one-fifth of the state's foreign-born population. The Irish continued to arrive in large numbers through the early 20th century and because, unlike other foreigners, they arrived with a mastery of the English language, a large number became political leaders of the state's new towns. While always outnumbered by Germans, St. Paul is still considered an Irish town.

British immigrants were also early arrivals and included enough **Welsh** that when the push for statehood began, the proposed constitution was translated into their ancient tongue. Though best known as miners, most Welsh in Minnesota came to farm. A few **Cornish** miners relocated from Michigan with the discovery of iron ore in the northeast. Though most eventually relocated elsewhere in the United States, their practical meat-and-potato-filled pasties remain an Iron Range staple. **Scots** were noted fur traders, and Simon McTavish's North West Company set up its inland operations at Grand Portage, but few settled here permanently. Many **English** professionals relocated here in the 1870s to start new lives as gentleman farmers, and though they gained fame across the state from newspaper accounts of their crimson foxhunts and horse races, they weren't cut out for rural living, and the grand settlements failed.

While **Russian** and Eastern Slavic (**Ukrainian, Belarusian,** etc.) immigration dates back to the 19th century, the main surge began in the 1990s following the collapse of the Soviet Union. Many Russians chose Minnesota because they liked the climate, and they were one of the largest immigrant groups of that decade. Today's Russo-Minnesotans tend to be highly educated professionals, and they include many Jewish and Pentecostal Christian refugees. Most settled in the Twin Cities.

While **Poles,** most of whom arrived in Minnesota between 1900 and 1915, settled across the state, the most distinct community has always been in Winona, where the Church of Saint Stanislaus Kostka and the Polish Cultural Institute memorialize the city's Polish past and present. **Czechs** and **Slovaks** came during the same time, but in smaller numbers. The former are pretty widespread around the state (though most notably in New Prague, where much effort is made to maintain the culture), while the latter took residence almost exclusively in Minneapolis.

Almost all of the **Serbian, Croatian, Macedonian, Slovene,** and **Montenegrin** (the peoples of the former Yugoslavia) arrivals worked the mines of the Iron Range. The Iron Range was, in fact, Minnesota's great melting pot. Three dozen ethnicities came to dig, and, at the turn of the 20th century, half the population was foreign born. This accounts for the tremendous number of taverns in Iron Range towns—the multitude of ethnicities worked together during the day, but drank separately at night. In the 1990s a group of **Bosnians** fled the civil war and ended up in Pelican Rapids.

Other nationalities who migrated here in small but significant numbers include **Italians,** who came to the cities (principally St. Paul and Duluth) and the Iron Range, and **Dutch,** who are predominantly rural. The small number of **Swiss,** who were at Fort Snelling as early as 1821, settled throughout the state.

AFRICANS AND AFRICAN AMERICANS

African Americans are the largest minority group in Minnesota. Although black migration to Minnesota began in earnest after World War I—as Southerners came north looking for factory work—Africans have been in Minnesota from the start. They first came as fur traders back in the late 18th century, most famously the Bonga (sometimes spelled Bungo) family. Pierre Bonga had settled in north-central Minnesota after gaining his freedom and opened a series of trading posts across the region. His son George, educated in Montreal, garnered such respect and fame as a trader, explorer, interpreter, and negotiator that his death in 1885 was reported in newspapers around the country. Bungo Township and Bungo Brook in Cass County are named for the family.

In the early 19th century many slaves accompanied their owners to Fort Snelling, none more famously than Dred Scott, who unsuccessfully sued for his freedom based upon his two years of residence in free territory. The case, which reached the Supreme Court, and its far-reaching legal ramifications fanned the already strong antislavery fires of Minnesota and the rest of the North. The census of 1850, the year after Minnesota officially became a territory, tallied 39 "free colored," and they earned the right to vote in Minnesota in 1868. Minnesota was one of the few states to grant this right prior to passage of the 15th Amendment. Following the Civil War, new arrivals came slowly but steadily up the Mississippi River. Many settled in rural areas to farm, but most eventually made their way to the Twin Cities. Today 91 percent of Minnesota's 172,000 blacks live in the Twin Cities metro area, though an increasing number have relocated to other parts of the state in recent years.

East Africans, principally **Somalis,** but also **Ethiopians, Eritreans,** and **Sudanese,** are the newest group of immigrants in Minnesota, arriving as refugees in large numbers since the mid-1990s. For some of those years Somalis were the largest immigrant group coming to Minnesota, and today there are an estimated 25,000 in the state (unofficial estimates range as high as 60,000)—the largest Somali population in the United States. Most live in Minneapolis, but other significant populations are found in St. Paul, St. Cloud, Rochester, Marshall, Owatonna, and Mankato.

LATINOS

Latinos are the most widely distributed minority group in the state. Two-thirds of Minnesota's Latinos are of **Mexican** descent, though over 20 countries from Central and South America and the Caribbean are represented. Latinos have been arriving since the mid-19th century, but only in large numbers since the last half of the 1990s. Minnesota had a grand total of two residents of Mexican descent at statehood, but a population explosion of sorts led to the tripling of that total by 1880 and a further quadrupling by the turn of the 20th century. One of those 24 was an oboe player named Luis Garzon who, while on tour with the Mexico City Orchestra in 1886, fell ill and was left behind—he remained in Minneapolis for over 50 years.

Labor shortages north of the border during World War I drew many Mexicans to the United States looking for work, and, in Minnesota, a few migrant workers found employment in the sugar beet fields. By the 1920s, as the sugar industry expanded, thousands of migrants came for a few months each summer, and some, finding work with the railroads or in meatpacking plants, "settled out." By 1990 the state's Latino population was 53,884 and during the next decade, thanks in part to the state's low unemployment rate, it climbed to 143,382, and Minneapolis surpassed St. Paul as the city with the largest Latino population. The population is primarily urban, with over 100,000 in the Twin Cities metro area, but thriving populations exist in many southern and western agricultural towns like Willmar, Worthington, Pelican Rapids, St. James, and Albert Lea. Despite a decreased need for field workers due to new technologies the state's farm fields still see thousands of migrant workers each summer.

ASIANS

Like all the state's other minority groups, Minnesota's Asian residents are centered in the Twin Cities, with 85 percent of the nearly 142,000 calling the metro area home. More reside in St. Paul, most notably in Frog Town, than any other city. While significant immigrant populations have come from **India, China, Nepal, Tibet, the Philippines,** and **Vietnam,** the 60,000 or so Laotian **Hmong** (about one-quarter of all those in the United States; only California has more) are most noteworthy. The first Hmong arrived in Minnesota in the late 1970s following the Vietnam War. Hoping that they could carve out an independent homeland, many Hmong joined the United States in the fight against the North Vietnamese. When the war was lost, tens of thousands of Hmong, facing reprisals by the government that they had fought against (most, in fact, had nothing to do with the war, but the often-violent revenge was indiscriminate), fled to refugee camps in Thailand and, over the next two decades, slowly picked up their lives and filtered into other countries, primarily the United States. Since the Hmong are traditionally an agrarian people residing in small mountain villages, the Twin Cities now has the world's largest urban Hmong population. Many continue to farm, and Hmong vendors are regulars at local farmers markets. Mee Moua of St. Paul, whose family fled Laos when she was five, was elected to the State Senate in 2002, becoming the first Hmong legislator in the United States. With about 1,500 living here, mostly in Minneapolis, Minnesota has the nation's second-largest **Tibetan** community.

Culture

Minnesotans are a fiercely independent, resilient, and self-reliant people. Harrison Salisbury, the *New York Times'* Pulitzer Prize–winning journalist, once attributed much of his success to "the Minnesota spirit, skeptical, contrarian, often out-of-step, hostile to the Bigs." This deeply ingrained temperament explains why many of the small, struggling towns you pass through in western farm country haven't died out yet, why Minnesota leads the nation in sales by business cooperatives, and why large chains have a harder time pushing out Mom-and-Pop restaurants and retail stores than most places in the country.

As pervasive as the state's independent streak is, the defining quality of the native Minnesotan is what has come to be called "Minnesota Nice." Minnesotans are friendly, easy-going, eager to please, humble (often to the point of self-deprecation), and do not want to stand out too much. Apologies are offered for simple acts like returning something to a store, and sincere pleases and thank yous are the norm. Some people joke that it should really be called Minnesota "Ice" because people can be so reserved; but don't be fooled—being quiet and restrained is considered polite here. No matter how frequently Minnesota Nice is joked about, it remains a point of pride.

Language

The language played up in movies such as *Fargo* is real but rare. The Minnesota tongue spoken by most natives has a more typically neutral Midwestern diction, but it does share some of those now-famous characteristics and vocabulary. Space does not permit more than a cursory scan of the many delicate subtleties of formal Minnesotan, but Howard Mohr, in his definitive text *How To Talk Minnesotan,* lays them out in hilarious detail. "Minnesotan is not a musical language," Mohr explains. "Some people with an ax to grind have said it is the musical equivalent of a one-string guitar. What I say is, what's wrong with a monotone—at least you don't startle anybody." Minnesotans are not an excitable bunch and, unless discussing a Viking Super Bowl victory (which would be exciting because the purple and gold have choked in the big game all four times they've made it) or bagging a thirty-point buck, their conversations reflect this. Again, Mohr says it best: "Get that excited about something in Minnesota and you might as well paste a bumper sticker on your forehead that says I'M NOT FROM AROUND HERE."

All joking aside, there are several uniquely Minnesotan words and phrases you are likely to hear. The state's true workhorse phrase is **you bet.** It can be a positive response to just about any question—"Were the fish biting today?"—or even most statements—"It's gonna be a hot one." As Mohr explains, "You bet is meant to be pleasantly agreeable and doesn't obligate you to a strong position." You bet also replaces "You're welcome" as the most common reply to a thank you. **You betcha** serves as an enthusiastic "you bet."

Yah, which is drawn out when spoken (*yaahh*), is an equally versatile word. It usually means "yes" or "sure," but it can also mean "Really?" when pronounced with a rising tone. Yah also serves as a verbal filler like "um-hmm." A **Yah, for sure** construction offers added emphasis.

Uff da is the only Norwegian expression that has survived assimilation. It is a general exclamation similar to "Oops" or "Damn it," though uff da is never impolite. Charlie Brown's "Good grief" could be expressed as uff da.

A uniquely Minnesotan word, one you are likely to encounter either in menus, newspapers, tourist brochures, or on Garrison Keillor's *A Prairie Home Companion,* is **hot dish**—this is just Minnesota vernacular for casserole. It should also be pointed out that during the winter most Minnesotans go **sliding** rather than sledding.

Less common than the others, and used

primarily by women, the **Oh, for?** construction ("Oh, for fun!," "Oh, for cute!," "Oh, for gross!," and so on) is an exclamation that can describe things good or bad.

Minnesota Cuisine

While any blue-blooded Minnesotan regards the hot dish (local vernacular for a casserole) as a gourmet meal, Midwestern cuisine should not be dismissed out of hand. Featured prominently are locally grown ingredients such as cranberries, raspberries, morel mushrooms, pumpkin, wild rice, fresh fish, and wild game such as venison and elk—sounds pretty good, right? Many of the poshest restaurants specialize in imaginative uses of these ingredients, using them in various ethnic recipes and creating new takes on American classics, but even some small-town greasy spoons feature them.

Walleye, the most prevalent Minnesota specialty (though it almost always come from Canada), is usually served batter-fried, and menus will often have multiple variations of it. Increasingly common is **wild rice,** which was historically so important to the Ojibwe (it once constituted as much as a quarter of their diet) that it remains a sacred food, and its harvest from the shallow lakes of northern and central Minnesota a sacred event. Wild rice, or *manomin* (good berry) to the Ojibwe, has a slightly nutty flavor and is a remarkably versatile ingredient. While most common as a side dish or soup ingredient (a good wild rice soup is a truly glorious thing!), it can also be used to make tortilla chips, bread, beer, pancake flour, and much more. Its increased popularity has led to the creation of commercial paddies where water levels can be controlled. Gourmets claim that naturally grown rice is a superior product, though there is absolutely nothing wrong with the cultivated variety. However, if your only experience with wild rice is from Uncle Ben, then you haven't really tasted it.

Pasties (PASS-tees), stuffed pastry pockets with the look of mini-calzones, are a great snack, though they can easily make a meal. The basic filling is potato, onion, carrot, and beef, though chicken, ham and cheese, pizza, veggies, and breakfast (ham and eggs) are some common variations. They were brought to Minnesota by Cornish miners (who took them into the tunnels with them for lunch), and they remain an Iron Range fixture but are sometimes found in bakeries and restaurants elsewhere in the state. **Potica** (po-TEET-sah), a walnut-filled sweet bread brought by south Slavic immigrants, and **porketta,** a highly seasoned pork roast, are other Iron Range specialties.

Though you won't find it on too many menus, the state's most distinctive cuisine is Scandinavian. Swedish meatballs are well known throughout the country, but it's the three Ls, **lutefisk, lefse,** and **lingonberries,** that most intrigue visitors. These and other Scandinavian staples are largely reserved for church and lodge suppers and family get-togethers, but you'll find them on the occasional restaurant menu. Lefse comes in many varieties, but the most common combines potato (occasionally rice), flour, butter, and salt. The mix is rolled flat and baked on a griddle producing a bread that resembles a thick tortilla. Traditionally lefse was wrapped around meat or fish—today it is mostly eaten on the side with butter and a sprinkling of sugar, brown sugar, or cinnamon, or with a spread of jam. Lingonberries are similar to cranberries, and are sometimes called mountain cranberries. A much greater culinary adventure is lutefisk—dried North Atlantic cod reconstituted in water for three days, soaked in lye for another three, and then put back into water for up to a week. Yes, really. If not prepared properly it becomes a gelatinous, foul-smelling mess. When done right it is a flaky, foul-smelling mess. Traditionally Norwegians top it with butter and Swedes with a cream sauce, while a mustard sauce helps many non-fans get it down year after year. Minnesotans consume several tons of it annually, mostly between October and December. A few churches also host communal **Lapskaus** (a traditional Norwegian beef stew) dinners, which might include a side course of sing-along. If you want to sample some of this ethnic cuisine, you can always pick some up at Scandinavian gift shops and many grocery stores. Microwaveable lutefisk dinners are a new option.

You might also stumble upon the German immigrant-bred tradition of the **Friday-night fish fry** (Catholics were once prohibited from eating meat on Fridays), where fillets of perch, cod, walleye, or whitefish are deep-fried, usually in a beer batter, and served as all-you-can-eat feasts along with french fries and coleslaw. If you're not from Minnesota you'll be surprised to find how popular they are—unless you're from Wisconsin, in which case you'll be shocked by their scarcity. **Fish boils,** where chunks of fish, potatoes, and onions are cooked up outdoors in a large communal cauldron, are sometimes found along the North Shore, usually during town festivals, but some restaurants also prepare them on weekends. A boilmaster, equal parts chef and showman, finishes the preparation by dumping fuel onto the flames, creating a short-lived inferno. This boil-over not only garners a collective cheer from the crowd, but also sends the fat and other undesirables up and out of the cauldron.

Maple syrup from Minnesota often beats out that from New England in competitions, so be sure to pick some up when you see it for sale. If you like the idea of picking up farm-fresh produce while out on the road, get a free copy of the **Minnesota Grown Directory** (651/296-5029, www.mda.state.mn.us/mngrown). It lists hundreds of homegrown vendors selling everything from blueberries to bison brats.

Visitors are often surprised to learn that some 20 commercial wineries operate in frosty Minnesota, and even more surprised at how good some of the finished products are. Traditional grape vines must be buried each winter, but several new cold-hardy hybrids, such as Frontenac and La Crescent, have been developed in recent years, allowing the **Minnesota Grape Growers Association** (www.mngrapes.org) to become one of the largest viticulture groups in the nation. Several vintners deal with winter by using other fruits like raspberry, strawberry, plum, and apple exclusively. There are also some beloved local breweries. The most widely tapped are **Summit** and **Schell's.** The **Minnesota Craft Brewer's Guild** (www.mncraftbrew.org) and **MNBeer.com** are good resources.

Crafts

Minnesota's diverse cultures afford some interesting shopping opportunities. Native American arts are found throughout the state. Beadwork and silver jewelry are most common, though the least Minnesotan. Baskets made of birch bark can be true works of art, while other birch-bark items, such as toy canoes, make cheap mementos. Though sold across the nation, pipestone carvings come from Minnesota.

Also common at craft fairs and in gift shops are Scandinavian folk arts, like rosemaling—a decorative painting characterized by flowers and flowing scrolls—and chip carving. Most large and mid-sized cities have Scandinavian gift shops. Hmong handiwork is less common. The principal craft is *paj ntaub* (pronounced pahn dow), which combines reverse applique with intricate embroidery to create colorful geometric designs containing hidden symbolism. While the "flower cloths" are traditionally part of the elaborate costumes worn at weddings, New Year's celebrations, and other important events, you can buy wall hangings, bedspreads, Christmas-tree skirts, wallets, and much more with the artistic patterns. A new take on the ancient art that developed in the refugee camps of Thailand, and has proven very popular in Minnesota, are storycloths that tell family histories or stories of the Hmong's exodus from their tribal homelands. Prices are high, but a quick look at the intricacy shows why; large quilts or wall hangings can take months to complete. The best place to look is the Hmong Arts, Books, & Crafts Store in St. Paul. You will also find artists selling their creations at craft fairs and farmers markets.

Many people go to Lanesboro and Harmony

just to buy Amish crafts, principally basketry, quilts, and furniture. The selection and quality in the shops is excellent, but many signs in front of farms invite shoppers to stop by homes (never go to a home on a Sunday) and purchase direct from the source. Others park their horses and buggies along busy highways to sell to passing motorists.

ESSENTIALS

Getting There and Around

BY AIR

Minneapolis-St. Paul International Airport (MSP), conveniently located right on the edge of the Twin Cities, is one of the Midwest's largest hubs. Airports in Rochester and Duluth also have a handful of flights to other states and Hector International Airport in Fargo, North Dakota, can also be convenient.

To find a good fare to Minnesota, it's important to know that Delta—which merged with the once Minnesota-based Northwest Airlines—accounts for around 80 percent of all flights, and thus holds a monopoly on many routes. Price pressure from discount airlines has alleviated this somewhat in recent years.

Small airports in Bemidji, Brainerd, Hibbing, International Falls, St. Cloud, and Thief River Falls have regular propjet service to and from Minneapolis with Northwest. Fares from Minneapolis to elsewhere in the state aren't cheap, unless bought as part of a connecting flight.

BY TRAIN

The **Amtrak** (800/872-7245, www.amtrak.com) Empire Builder service between Chicago and Seattle/Portland passes through Minnesota

The Empire Builder crosses Minnesota on its way from Chicago to Seattle and Portland.

once a day in each direction with stops in Winona, Red Wing, St. Paul, St. Cloud, Staples, Detroit Lakes, and Fargo, North Dakota (for Moorhead). Though no trains go there, Amtrak provides connecting bus service to Duluth. The train can be a good way to reach Minnesota, but, because of limited service and inconvenient hours, it's not too practical for getting around. It is, however, possible to make day trips from the Twin Cities to Winona and Red Wing.

Amtrak rail passes, such as **Explore America Fares,** which allow three stops during a 45-day period, are some of the best travel bargains around. Amtrak also offers an **Air Rail** option, allowing you to travel in one direction by train and the opposite with Continental Airlines. Students, seniors, veterans, and children are all eligible for various discounts.

BY BUS

Getting to Minnesota by bus is easy, but using buses to get around is impractical due to limited service. **Greyhound** (800/231-2222, www.greyhound.com), the nation's largest carrier, has routes from Minneapolis north through Duluth ($31 one-way), east through Chicago ($31 one-way), and west to Fargo ($40 one-way), but the most extensive service in Minnesota is with **Jefferson Lines** (888/864-2832, www.jeffersonlines.com), which connects Minneapolis to far more outstate towns. **Megabus** (877/462-6342, www.megabus.com), a low-cost express carrier, connects Minneapolis to many Midwestern cities through Chicago. **Lorenz Bus Service** (800/784-3611, www.lorenzbus.com) runs daily from Minneapolis to the town of Virginia, taking a roundabout route past Lake Mille Lacs, and **Happy Time Tours and Travel** (807/473-5515, www.httours.com) vans make round-trip runs between Duluth and Thunder Bay, Ontario, three days a week.

Several small companies run van service between the Twin Cities airport and towns across the state. Some of the cities served include Red Wing, Winona, Northfield, Rochester, Mankato, Willmar, and Brainerd. Ticket counters for all of them are in the Lindbergh Terminal, just below the baggage claim area. Reservations are highly recommended and often required.

HOUSEBOATS

You really are the captain of your own ship when you travel by houseboat, a popular option on large northern lakes and the lower Mississippi River. Take in the scenery and soak up the sun by day, and moor up in a secluded cove at night; or if you want to spend a night on the town, dock up at a marina. The RVs of the aquatic world have everything a hotel room would, plus fully equipped kitchens and outdoor lounge space. Many models also include grills, hot tubs, and waterslides. No experience (or license) is needed to drive a houseboat. A quick course on piloting and navigation will make you an expert before you even leave the dock.

BY CAR

Though major cities, and a few small towns in between, are connected by public transportation, to really see Minnesota you need your own vehicle. The Minnesota Department of Transportation maintains a 24-hour statewide road-condition hotline (dial 511) that points out congestion and construction information.

Minnesota has designated 22 official **Scenic Byways,** but the system is something of a joke. The problem is that these signed routes primarily stick to the busier trunk lines, instead of leading off the beaten track. Don't get me wrong, you won't be disappointed if you follow any of these official tours, it's just that overall you'll find much more natural beauty and rural Americana (and a lot fewer Pizza Huts) along the back roads. A few major exceptions to this rule are the Otter Trail Scenic Byway, Rushing Rapids Parkway, North Shore Scenic Drive, Historic Bluff Country Scenic Byway, and Great River Road below Lake City, which truly deserve special designation.

Rules of the Road

All drivers and passengers must wear seat belts; failure to do so is a primary violation and the police can pull you over for it. Children age seven and under must be in a federally approved car seat or booster. Motorcycle helmets are required for any drivers or passengers under 18 or anyone driving with a learner's permit. The maximum speed limit on the interstates is 70 mph, though it is reduced in all urban areas. All drivers must have insurance.

Winter Driving

The first rule of winter driving is to be prepared. Take a few minutes to winterize your vehicle: Top off the antifreeze (it should test to at least 35 degrees below zero) and wiper fluid and inflate your tires to the manufacturer's suggested psi—despite the myth, underinflated tires do not provide more traction. Also, do as locals do and keep an emergency kit—warm blanket, nonperishable munchies like candy bars, a container of sand or kitty litter, and a small snow shovel—in the trunk. A flashlight, flare or reflectors, and a first aid kit are good additions. Of course you shouldn't drive without an ice scraper and jumper cables.

Winter driving is second nature for Northerners (few things are more entertaining for us than watching news footage of a Southern city crippled by a one-inch snowstorm), but if it's new to you there are a few techniques to remember. Above all, just SLOW DOWN! Posted speed limits are only meant for dry and clear conditions. Allow at least twice as much distance between your car and the one in front of you than you normally would, and try to anticipate lane changes, turns, and stops so you can brake sooner and more gently. If you are driving a manual transmission, downshift to reduce your speed instead of using the brakes. Use extra caution on bridges and overpasses because these are the first spots to freeze. At temperatures below zero, intersections are another problem spot because car exhaust no longer evaporates, but instead forms black ice. If you do skid, immediately remove your foot from the brake (fight that instinct!) or accelerator and steer in the direction you want the car to go; be prepared to countersteer if you overcorrected the first time. Extra weight in the trunk of a rear-wheel-drive car can aid traction.

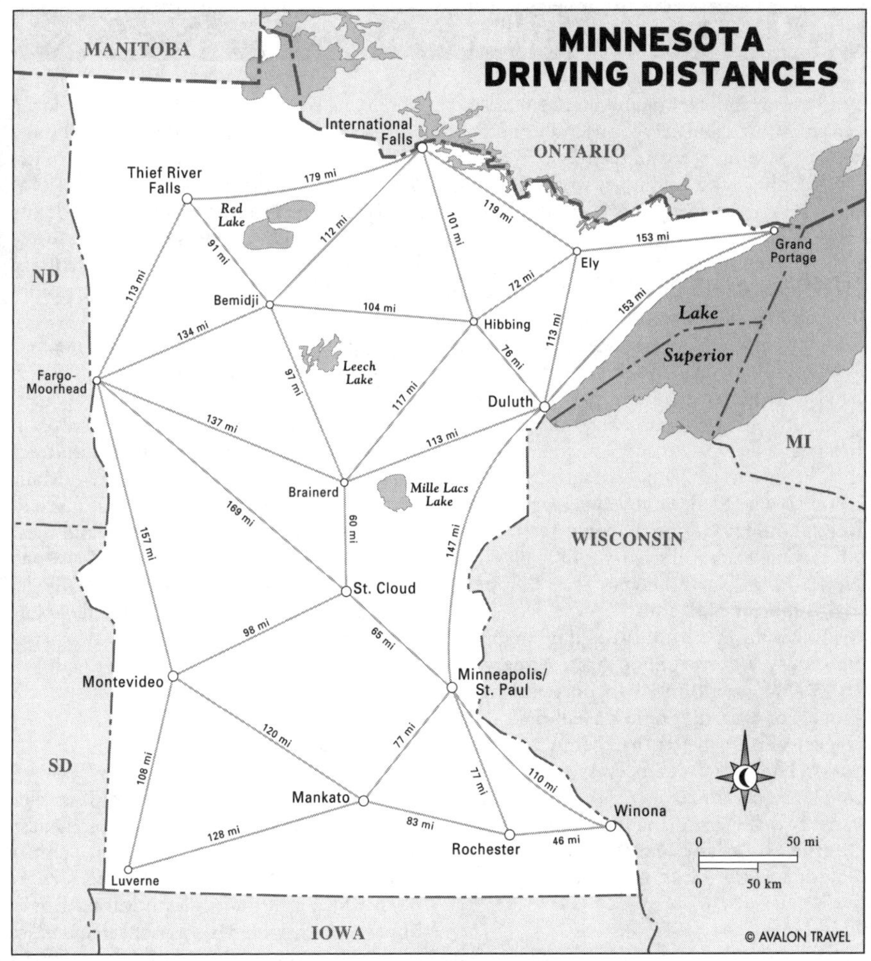

No matter how cold the temperature is outside, take the time to scape the ice off *all* your windows, as well as your lights, before you drive.

If you get stranded in your car during a blizzard, tie something colorful to the antenna and stay with the vehicle—help will find you. Make sure the exhaust pipe is not blocked by snow and crack the window slightly when running the heater to prevent carbon monoxide poisoning. Finally, don't leave your car running (either to warm it up or keep it warm) when it is unattended. Every year there are many cases of thieves driving off with a target they found too easy to resist. (The police won't prosecute and in Minneapolis and some other municipalities, you, the owner, will get ticketed.)

Outdoor Recreation

With the exception of mountain climbing, you can enjoy just about every conceivable outdoor activity in Minnesota and then some. The hiking, paddling, and fishing are world class, and Lake Superior even attracts a handful of surfers year-round.

HIKING AND BACKPACKING

The undisputed champion of long-distance foot trails in Minnesota is the **Superior Hiking Trail** (SHT), which runs 205 miles along the length of the North Shore passing through some of the loveliest scenery in the state. Readers of *Backpacker* magazine have ranked this the second-best long-distance trail in the country. The SHT is now a segment of the **North Country National Scenic Trail,** which, when completed, will stretch 4,400 miles from New York to North Dakota. The **Chippewa** and **Superior National Forests** have hundreds of miles of other trails, and hiking in the **Boundary Waters Canoe Area Wilderness (BWCAW)** isn't limited to portaging your canoe. For a day hike or just a half-hour stroll, you can't do any better than Minnesota's state parks. The system covers every possible environment and fitness level, and trails are invariably well marked and maintained. **Itasca, George H. Crosby Manitou,** and **Savanna Portage State Parks** are among the wildest.

BIKING

With rarely anything more challenging than gently rolling hills between all its amazing scenery, Minnesota can be great for bike travel. Despite Minnesota's southeast corner's many long climbs, most saddle jockeys consider it the top place to tour on two wheels. Besides mixing rural farm scenery, including the state's largest Amish community, with unique glacial topography, the back roads are well maintained. West-central Minnesota between St. Cloud and Fergus Falls, the center of Minnesota's dairy industry, has many paved back roads and little traffic on the trunk routes. Minnesota is a leader in converting abandoned railroad beds into trails, and nearly 600 miles of these are paved (as are many other routes that are not rails-to-trails). The **Root River** and **Harmony-Preston Valley State Trails** in the southeast, the **Paul Bunyan State Trail** through the heartland, and the **Willard Munger State Trail** outside Duluth are probably the most scenic.

Off-road riders will find a lot to like here too, from extreme single-track to quiet forest touring trails. The national forests have hundreds of miles of seldom-followed paths to ride, and the state forests have hundreds of miles more of even less used trails. Many of the state's downhill ski areas open up trails to mountain bikers in the summer, and these are justifiably popular. **Minnesota Off Road Cyclists** (www.morcmtb.org) have many detailed trail reviews on their website and Explore Minnesota Tourism's handy *Explore Minnesota Biking* brochure has a comprehensive listing of paved and mountain bike trails.

ROCK CLIMBING

It's been said that Minnesota has the best rock climbing between Seneca and Boulder. The four main climbing areas are perpetually busy **Interstate State Park,** sometimes-empty **Blue Mounds State Park,** extensively bolted **Barn Bluff,** and the endlessly varied **North Shore,** which includes some spectacular sea cliffs at Tettegouche State Park (please respect the decades-old no-chalk/no-bolts tradition). Climbers in state parks must get a free permit from the office before going up. The only current statewide climbing guidebook out there is the invaluable *Rock Climbing Minnesota and Wisconsin* by Mike Farris.

CANOEING, KAYAKING, AND RAFTING

With over 11,000 lakes, 92,000 miles of rivers and streams, and the wild Lake Superior coast, you bet the canoeing and kayaking

GET IT BEFORE YOU GO

You can order state park permits, obtain free maps and brochures about all varieties of state-owned lands, and get answers to almost any outdoors- or nature-related questions from the **DNR Information Center** (500 Lafayette Rd., 651/296-6157 or 888/646-6367, 8 A.M.-4:30 P.M. Mon.-Fri.) in St. Paul, and most of these can be downloaded from www.dnr.state.mn.us. The **Recreation Compass** (www.dnr.state.mn.us/maps/compass.html) is an interactive map with links to information about Minnesota's parks, forests, wildlife areas, lakes, and more – including federally owned lands. It is an extremely handy resource.

For a $3.50 fee you can buy hunting and fishing licenses or a ski pass by phone at 888/665-4236 or online at www.wildlifelicense.com/mn. There is no need to wait for them to arrive in the mail, as they are valid instantly.

are good here. The pinnacle of paddling in Minnesota is the **Boundary Waters Canoe Area Wilderness** (BWCAW), a million acres of portage-linked lakes and streams. The remoter parts of **Voyageurs National Park,** the largest water-based park in the nation, offer a similar experience. The **Superior National Forest** (SNF) beyond the BWCAW has other wonderful but often overlooked rivers and lakes.

Most of the state's rivers offer quiet canoeing with a mix of natural scenery and rural life. Although experienced paddlers can find some challenges, beginners generally have little to worry about since most rapids, if there are any, are tame. Overall, the **Kettle, Cloquet,** and especially the **St. Croix,** along Minnesota's border with Wisconsin, come most highly recommended for a wilderness experience. While the number of streamside towns and farms increases as you move south, that doesn't necessarily mean that heading north is always the best option. The scenic rivers cutting the deep valleys of Minnesota's southwest, such as the **Cannon** and **Root,** are rightly popular, and poking around the **Mississippi River** backwaters in the far south can be a lot of fun too.

Although most of the state is pretty flat, the northeast has no shortage of white water, with many rivers along the North Shore dropping over 200 feet per mile. Kayakers experienced or foolish enough to run some of these monsters should note that for the most part there is only enough water in the spring or after very heavy rains. The **St. Louis River** below Cloquet, with rapids up to Class V and a steady flow through the entire season, is the state's premier whitewater route, while the **Kettle River** through Banning State Park is also popular. **Superior Whitewater** in Carlton leads commercial whitewater rafting trips down the St. Louis.

The **Lake Superior Water Trail** (www.lswta.org) is drawing an increasing number of sea kayakers each year. The goal is to have a campsite or rest area every three or so miles, and though there are still a few gaps due to private land (the longest is eight miles, though you can get on shore in an emergency), most of the work is done between Two Harbors and Grand Marais. Someday the trail will circle the entire lake. Because of the lake's perpetually cold water and fickle temperament, beginning paddlers should take a guide or at least stay very close to shore. Contact the **Lake Superior Water Trail Association** (www.lswta.org) for further information. Voyageurs National Park's larger lakes are also good sea kayaking territory.

The best single source of information is Greg Breining's *Paddling Minnesota,* published in cooperation with the Department of Natural Resources (DNR). The **Minnesota Canoe Association** (www.canoe-kayak.org) is also a good resource. The DNR's Canoeing webpage (www.dnr.state.mn.us/canoeing) has detailed descriptions of two dozen rivers (pocket-sized maps are free), a list of outfitters, and water-level reports. Explore Minnesota

Tourism publishes the handy *Explore Minnesota Canoeing* brochure, with general information on the major paddling areas and the businesses that serve them.

BIRD-WATCHING

Minnesota's remarkable variety of habitats leads to excellent bird-watching, and many people come here with binoculars and field guides in hand. In total, over 312 regular visitors, plus another 115 casuals and accidentals, have been recorded in Minnesota. While bird-watching opportunities are excellent year-round, winter bird-watching in Minnesota stands out. Arctic species like the common and hoary redpoll, gyrfalcon, Ross's gull, and snowy owl head south to Minnesota when the snow flies. There are also exciting resident species, such as the spruce grouse, three-toed woodpecker, and boreal chickadee, who reach the southernmost ends of their nesting range in Minnesota.

Where to go depends on what you want to see and when you visit, but many people consider the **Sax-Zim Bog** north of Duluth to be the single best bird-watching site in the state because of the ease of spotting northern species that are tough to find elsewhere. On the other hand, some of these species can be seen in Duluth where there is a greater overall variety of birdlife. The endlessly varied **Agassiz National Wildlife Refuge** north of Thief River Falls has gained a good reputation among bird-watchers nationwide, and the **Minnesota Valley National Wildlife Refuge,** just a stone's throw from the Mall of America, is one of the best urban bird-watching sites in the nation.

Minnesota lies right at the heart of the Mississippi Flyway, one of North America's four main migration corridors, and this brings some tremendous congregations to the state each fall. Anywhere from 40,000 to over 200,000 (the record count for a single day is over 100,000) raptors soar past Duluth's **Hawk Ridge** between August and November. Other fall migration hotspots include **Lac Qui Parle Wildlife Management Area** along the upper reaches of the Minnesota River, where as many as 150,000 Canada geese flock; and **Weaver Bottoms** along the Mississippi River north of Winona, which has seen upward of 12,000 tundra swans in a single day.

The **Minnesota Ornithologists' Union** website (www.moumn.org) offers a wealth of information including bird-watching hot spots, trip announcements, and the definitive Minnesota species checklist. The MOU's **Rare Bird Alerts** are available online or by phone. There are separate numbers for the Duluth area (218/834-2858), northwest Minnesota (800/433-1888), and the rest of the state (763/780-8890). No book is more invaluable than Kim Eckert's *A Birder's Guide To Minnesota.*

Anyone heading to the Red River Valley should get a copy of the ***Pine to Prairie Birding Trail*** booklet (available free from all area tourism agencies or at www.mnbirdtrail.com), which details 43 top sites between Fergus Falls and Warroad. The Audubon Society has also developed the **Great River Birding Trail** (608/784-2992) along the Mississippi River and the **Minnesota River Valley Birding Trail** (651/739-9332, www.birdingtrail.org).

FISHING

Many a professional angler will insist, with good reason, that the best inland fishing in the United States is in Minnesota. With all those lakes, not to mention 15,000 miles of fishable streams, how could the fishing not be great? The love of fishing explains why Minnesota has more recreational boats and sells more fishing licenses per capita than any other state.

Of the two dozen game species in Minnesota waters, none excite anglers like the state fish, the **walleye.** Though found across the state, generally the action is hottest in the large cool lakes of north-central and northeast Minnesota. And though more than four million are taken each year, 75–90 percent are naturally produced. People talk so much about walleye that some forget Minnesota has the most varied **bass** fishing in the nation. Largemouth are most plentiful in central Minnesota, while the largest smallmouth swim in the northeast. Minnesota's northern and central lakes also produce copious trophy

© TIM BEWER

In Minnesota, there are nearly as many bait shops as lakes.

muskie and **northern pike.** The largest rivers are well known for their **catfish.** Flatheads topping 60 pounds swim in the Mississippi, St. Croix, and Minnesota Rivers, while the more widespread channel cats can exceed 20 pounds in and around the Red River of the North. Other popular Minnesota catches include **tiger muskie, sauger, bullhead, crappie** (black and white), and **sunfish.** The latter even out-bite walleye, making it the most-caught fish in the state.

Fly fishers focus on the 2,600 miles of **trout** streams carving the valleys of the southeast and climbing the hills along the North Shore. The brown trout is the top catch, while rainbow (steelhead) and the native "brookie" round out the state's inland trout species. Several southern streams have a winter (Jan.–Mar.) catch-and-release season.

Lake Superior, deep and always cold, adds another dimension to the Minnesota angling experience. Lake trout are the most frequent catch, while walleye, rainbow trout, and **salmon** (Chinook, pink, and coho) are all frequently landed. Duluth is charter-boat central, but you will find licensed captains in most North Shore towns.

Regulations, Maps, and Information

In order to ensure the future of fishing in Minnesota, the DNR has enacted an extensive and somewhat complicated set of fishing regulations, and there are a variety of new rules created every year. Generally the fishing season is May through February, but there are many exceptions, so always inquire locally before casting a line. All anglers should pick up the annual *Minnesota Fishing Regulations* booklet, available free wherever licenses are sold.

Anyone age 16 and older must posses a Minnesota fishing license, and penalties for fishing without one can be pretty severe, potentially including jail time and confiscation of your boat. A standard adult license for the season is $17 for Minnesota residents and $39.50 for nonresidents; one-, three-, and seven-day passes are also available. Trout and salmon stamps are generally required for designated lakes, streams, and Lake Superior. Licenses

STATE PARK AND NATIONAL FOREST CAMPGROUNDS

Depending on what facilities are available, state park campsite prices range $12-24, plus $4 each for electricity and water/sewer. Camper cabins cost $50 with electricity and $45 without. You can make reservations or check availability online at www.stayatmnparks.com or call 866/857-2757 (TDD 866/290-2267) from the United States or Canada or 605/718-3030 from anywhere else in the world. Phone lines are open 7 A.M.-10 P.M. daily. Campsites can be reserved 2-90 days in advance when paying by credit card, and 10-90 days in advance when paying by check. The $8.50 reservation fee is nonrefundable.

Campgrounds in Minnesota's national forests are generally smaller and quieter than those in the state parks. An added bonus is that most campgrounds generally only fill up on Memorial Day and Labor Day weekends, so reservations are rarely necessary, though always still a good idea. Only two of the 23 "developed" campgrounds in the Superior National Forest have electricity: Fall Lake near Ely and Whiteface Reservoir near Aurora. Prices range $10-20. An additional 17 rustic campgrounds with pit toilets, none with more than six sites, are free. Most of the developed campgrounds in the Chippewa National Forest are also small, quiet, and rustic. Only three, Stony Point near Walker, O-Ne-Gum-E near Deer River, and the Norway Beach Recreation Area near Cass Lake, have showers and electrical hookups. Rates range $14-20. Reservations for all national forest campgrounds can be made online at www.reserveusa.com or by calling 518/855-3639 or 877/444-6777 (TDD 877/833-6777). If you don't know exactly where you want to camp, it is easiest to book by phone. The lines are open 7 A.M.-11 P.M. weekdays and 7 A.M.-8 P.M. weekends April 1 through Labor Day and 9 A.M.-6 P.M. weekdays and 9 A.M.-4 P.M. weekends the rest of the year. Reservations are accepted up to eight months in advance, and there is a $9 fee. It costs $10 to change or cancel a reservation.

and stamps can be bought at bait shops, sporting goods stores, marinas, resorts, hardware stores, gas stations, and DNR offices; by phone at 888/665-4236; or online at www.wildlifelicense.com/mn.

It won't replace the advice from down at the bait shop, but the *Minnesota Fishing Guide* published by Explore Minnesota Tourism offers a good overview. The DNR's Lake Finder (www.dnr.state.mn.us/lakefind) has lake surveys, depth maps, stocking reports, and other information for over 4,500 lakes statewide.

Ice Fishing

As author Thomas Huhti so perfectly explains in *Moon Wisconsin,* "Driving the truck out on a frozen lake to a village of shanties erected over drilled holes, sitting on an overturned five-gallon pail, stamping your feet quite a bit, and drinking a lot of schnapps is a time-honored tradition in the Great White North." Despite what one would assume, the ice-fishing scenes from the movie *Grumpy Old Men* were not exaggerated for comic effect; if anything they were understated to make them believable to the rest of the country. Shantytowns connected by plowed and signed roads spring up on lakes across the state between December and March. Frostbite Flats, a temporary city of 6,000 homes on Mille Lacs, is the most famous. Many of these fish houses, ranging from simple wooden shacks to "sleepers" decked out with furnaces, electrical generators, and even satellite TVs, are available for overnight rental by the day or week.

Ice fishing isn't difficult, but there are a few things first-timers need to know. If there is a big crowd out on the ice you can probably assume it is safe, but never take ice safety lightly. Every year several knuckleheads foolishly push the limits and lose their vehicles or even their lives. If there is any doubt, ask. Resort owners, bait shops, sheriff's departments, and the DNR will usually have the most current ice conditions. A depth finder keeps you from making Swiss cheese out of the ice while looking for the perfect spot. And bring a cooler so the beer doesn't freeze.

HUNTING

Love it or hate it, hunting is an indelible part of Minnesota life. Nearly 600,000 people take up a gun or bow each year, and the first deer hunt is an important rite of passage for many kids. The littered six-packs and Stop-sign targets found all too often around wildlife areas and public forestlands show that many trigger-happy idiots still roam the woods, but most hunters are, in fact, far more conservation-minded than the average citizen. The revenue raised by hunting licenses and stamps, as well as funds donated by conservation organizations like Ducks Unlimited, Pheasants Forest, and the Izaak Walton League, have paid for over half of the one million acres of wildlife management land found around the state. Thanks largely to hunters, Minnesota has more public wildlife lands than any other state in the Midwest. And in many cases hunting is an essential management tool—I know a vegetarian ecology professor who takes up a rifle during the deer season.

Minnesota has over 100 legal game species. Deer, goose, duck, ruffed grouse, and pheasant are some of the most popular. Any questions you have about seasons (most are between September and December), locations, or licenses can be answered by the DNR Information Center. Licenses can be obtained in person at sporting goods stores, bait shops, resorts, hardware stores, gas stations, and DNR offices; by phone at 888/665-4236; or online at www.wildlifelicense.com/mn.

GOLF

Minnesota ranks number one in the nation in golfers per capita, and some 480 courses have been carved into the Minnesota countryside to meet demand. Greens fees are a veritable bargain, and the season usually runs from April through October, though over the past several years warmer-than-average autumns have extended playing time into November and even a few Decembers. The season may run year-round in Arizona, Florida, and other hotspots, but who wants to walk nine holes under the sun of a Southern summer?

Minnesota's two best courses are **Interlachen** in Edina and **Hazeltine National** in Chaska, which both *Golf Digest* and *Golf* magazines rank in their top 100 for the United States—but you'll have to befriend a member to get a whack at them. A few of the best public courses are **The Classic at Madden's** (Brainerd), **Dacotah Ridge** (Morton), **Giants Ridge** (Biwabik), **Legends** (Prior Lake), **The Pines at Grand View Lodge** (Nisswa), **Rush Creek** (Maple Grove), **Superior National** (Lutsen), and **Wilds** (Prior Lake).

Explore Minnesota Tourism's *Explore Minnesota Golf* brochure lists 300 courses and their website (www.golf.exploreminnesota.com) has a searchable database with detailed information about all of the state's courses.

WINTER PURSUITS

Downhill Skiing and Snowboarding

Though Minnesota is no French Alps or Colorado Rockies, ski bums could do a lot worse—and pay a lot more. Over a dozen downhill ski areas dot the state, and most are open by early November. Minnesota's big three, **Lutsen Mountains** (the Midwest's largest and highest), **Giants Ridge,** and **Spirit Mountain,** sit just a few hours from each other in Minnesota's northeast corner. The www.mnsno.net website has a nearly complete list of ski areas, plus information on slope conditions and ski schools.

Cross-Country Skiing

Skinny skiing is excellent right across the whole of Minnesota, and large parks that don't have groomed trails are the exception rather than the rule. The **Gunflint Trail** area, with over 200 kilometers of signed and well-maintained trails

LEAVE NO TRACE

Leave No Trace is a wilderness ethic designed to minimize your impact when visiting the outdoors. It has been officially adopted by federal agencies including the U.S. Forest Service, U.S. Fish and Wildlife Service, and National Park Service, and should be followed every time you venture into the wild.

The core principles are:

- Plan ahead and prepare
- Travel and camp on durable surfaces
- Dispose of waste properly
- Leave what you find
- Minimize campfire impacts
- Respect wildlife
- Be considerate of other visitors

For more specific information about these guidelines check out www.lnt.org or call 800/332-4100.

along it, is arguably the top spot to stride and glide, but even Twin Cities parks like **Battle Creek** in St. Paul and **Lebanon Hills** in Eagan will challenge experienced skiers. The Three Rivers Park District trail system (in and around Minneapolis) has 22 kilometers of lighted ski trail. Special candlelight skiing nights are held in most state parks and along other popular trails. Skiers should also know about the winter-focused **Maplelag Resort** near Detroit Lakes and **Giants Ridge** on the Iron Range.

Skiers 16 and older must carry a **Minnesota Ski Pass** on most public trails—including all in the state parks and national forests. A daily pass costs $5 and a season pass is $15. Passes can be purchased by phone (888/665-4236); online (www.wildlifelicense.com/mn); and at sporting goods stores, resorts, hardware stores, gas stations, and DNR offices.

A great source for trail reports is **Adelsman's Cross-Country Ski Page** (www.skinnyski.com). They also feature race information, weather forecasts, and more. Another good resource, the *Explore Minnesota Skiing* brochure published by Explore Minnesota Tourism, has a fairly comprehensive list of trails.

Snowshoeing

The classic wood-and-rawhide tennis racket–style snowshoes are more likely to be found decorating a resort wall than strapped to someone's feet. High technology has made this ancient art one of the fastest-growing sports in the nation. Today's modern shoes are constructed with aircraft-quality aluminum frames and high-grade polymer decks, allowing these smaller, lighter models to carry just as much weight and be far more maneuverable than the classic styles. And, unlike cross-country skiers, shoers with an adventurous spirit and a good sense of direction can go almost anywhere. Small streams, thick woods, and steep hills can all be crossed without a hitch.

The learning curve for mastering the higher, wider step required for walking with webbed feet is about as flat as for chewing gum, and, other than the shoes themselves, no special equipment is needed. Some people use poles for balance, but they really aren't necessary unless you are venturing off into steep or rocky terrain. Minnesota's state parks are a great place to give snowshoeing a try. With the obvious exception of groomed ski trails, snowshoeing is allowed anywhere, and shoes can be rented from many park offices. Shoes can also be found at most of the same places that rent cross-country skis. The "anywhere but groomed trails" rule applies to most public lands, from county parks to the national forests.

Dogsledding and Skijoring

Dogsledding's popularity is increasing in Minnesota and so are the opportunities for rookies to give it a try. Most large resorts in the north can arrange it for you, and many mushers have their own operations in northern towns. Either just go for a ride or, after about 45 minutes of instruction, drive your own team. Several sled dog races are held across the north, most notably the

John Beargrease Sled Dog Marathon, running 400 miles along the North Shore from Duluth to Grand Marais and back. It is considered the toughest race in the Lower 48.

Skijoring is a pared-down version of dogsledding; just strap on your cross-country skis and harness your dog (or dogs) to your waist. There are fewer opportunities to try this simple, fast-growing Scandinavian import, but many of the outfitters and resorts that arrange dogsledding can hook you up. If you want to try it on your own, check out **Skijor Now** (651/486-6824 or 888/486-6824, www.skijornow.com), which sells equipment and offers information about getting started in the sport.

Snowmobiling

Snowmobiling is more than just a popular pastime in Minnesota—for many it's nearly a religion. Minnesota is second in the nation with over 270,000 registered sleds, or roughly nine percent of all snowmobiles in the United States and Canada. Beginning with the first substantial snowfall, a 17,000-mile winter highway system with road signs, billboards, and bridges is laid out across the state, making it possible to travel straight through from Luverne to Grand Marais by snowmobile. Restaurants, hotels, and other businesses advertise what trail they are located on and set up parking lots for riders. Even schools have lots for students' sleds. Snowmobile rentals are fairly common in the north, though not exactly cheap—expect to pay $125 a day at the very least. All riders on state-funded trails must display a State Trails Sticker, available for $16 from sporting goods stores, resorts, hardware stores, gas stations, and DNR offices; by phone at 888/665-4236; or online at www.wildlifelicense.com/mn. All riders born after 1976 must take a snowmobile safety course (unless already certified in another state), available in person or on a self-study CD. Call 800/366-8917 for details. The best source of information for riders is the **Minnesota United Snowmobilers Association** (763/577-0185, www.snowmobile-mnusa.org). Explore Minnesota Tourism publishes the handy *Explore Minnesota Snowmobiling* booklet.

Information and Services

TOURIST INFORMATION

Explore Minnesota Tourism (651/296-5029, 888/868-7476, or 800/627-3529 TTY, www.exploreminnesota.com) can answer just about any Minnesota questions you have. Counselors are available from 8 A.M. to 4:30 P.M. Mon.–Fri., while a host of recorded information on topics such as snow depths and fishing reports is available 24 hours.

If you are driving to Minnesota, chances are you will pass one of the ten **Travel Information Centers** that have been set up along the major highways near the borders. You can also visit the **Explore Minnesota USA** store in Mall of America.

Maps

The foldout road map available free from Explore Minnesota Tourism is more than adequate to get you around the state. If you want to explore any back roads during your trip, you can't do any better than the *Minnesota Atlas and Gazetteer* published by DeLorme.

If you'll be spending a lot of time in the outdoors, one of the DNR's 51 Public Recreation Information Maps (PRIMs) could prove handy. PRIMs show all county, state, and federal public lands and plot campgrounds, fishing piers, boat launches, parking lots, long distance trails, and the like. They cost $5.95 and are available at DNR offices, state parks, sporting goods shops, and online (www.dnr.state.mn.us/maps/prim.html).

MONEY

If you can, either come to Minnesota with American dollars or don't leave the airport without changing most of the foreign currency you

RESORT LIFE, MINNESOTA STYLE

A week "Up North" at the lake is a summer ritual for many Minnesota families, and those who don't have their own cabins usually take up residence at their favorite resort. Resort, it should be pointed out, has a different definition in Minnesota than it does in Colorado or Cancùn. Sure, there are plenty of fancy lodges with golf courses, marinas, and other four-star facilities, but the classic Minnesota resort is a dozen or so rustic cabins with faux wood paneling, linoleum floors, furniture the owners bought back in the 1950s, and fully equipped kitchens for frying up the day's catch. Most people raised in the Upper Midwest, myself included, have fond memories of a week at the lake in a cabin just like this and are happy to relive them again and again and again. Clearly these aren't for everyone, but many get so much repeat business that they don't advertise. Not all of the small, family-run resorts are stuck in a time warp, so if you're looking for something a little fancier and more modern, but with the same olden-days character, you'll have no problem finding it.

There are some things that all resorts have in common, no matter what the era. First, all are on a lake or a river, and it's common for each cabin to come with its own boat. Few resorts rent for less than a week during the summer and most close up shop for the winter. Pricing terms you may encounter are *American plan,* which includes three meals a day; *modified American plan,* which signifies only certain meals are provided; and *European plan,* meaning no meals are included. A *housekeeping* cabin comes fully equipped and you do the cleaning. Always ask whether linens, dishes, and towels are provided; often they aren't or they cost extra.

While there are plenty of resorts listed in this book, I would still recommend calling the local tourism office if you're interested in this type of lodging. Tell them what sort of vacation you are looking for, and they can recommend places that best fit your needs.

think you will need. It's not that you can't do foreign exchange elsewhere, but only a handful of banks and high-end hotels in the largest cities offer this service, and even then usually only for the most common currencies. The exception to the rule is Canadian dollars, which are not only easy to exchange at banks across the north, but, depending on the exchange rate, can get you some serious savings since many businesses in the north accept Canadian dollars (from Canadian citizens) at par.

The scarcity of exchange facilities doesn't matter very much anymore, since Automatic Teller Machines (ATMs) are found just about everywhere these days. Both credit cards (primarily Visa, MasterCard, and American Express) and travelers checks (in U.S.-dollar denominations) are widely accepted, though it would be best to ask first in small-town hotels and restaurants.

Taxes are high in Minnesota, but visitors won't likely notice since prices, compared with the rest of the country, are generally low. The statewide sales tax is 6.5 percent, and a handful of cities and counties tack on an additional half or one percent. There is no sales tax on most clothing and groceries.

Lodging Prices

Unless otherwise stated, prices in this guide are the lowest available for double-occupancy rooms on weekends during the summer high season and do not include taxes, which will add about ten percent. Some large resorts also tack on their own service charges, a shamefully deceptive practice. Off-season prices can be over 50 percent less, though 20 percent is more typical. AAA and AARP members get significant discounts at just about all hotels, though many will automatically give the same reduced rate to anyone who simply asks if there are any specials.

WEIGHTS AND MEASURES

Minnesota, like the entire country, shuns the metric system, and, except for cross-country ski trail distances, which are usually given in kilometers, you will rarely encounter it.

Minnesota is in Central Standard Time (CST). Daylight Saving Time (clocks are turned forward one hour, moving one hour of sunshine from the morning to the evening) begins on the first Sunday of April and ends on the last Sunday of October. If you will be crossing into Canada, note that the portion of Ontario along Lake Superior is Eastern Standard Time, one hour ahead of CST. The rest of Canada that borders Minnesota is CST.

TRAVEL TO AND FROM CANADA

Minnesota has seven road border crossings with Canada, one by Grand Portage, another at International Falls, and the rest to the west from Baudette on. (Some maps show one at Noyes, but this was recently closed.) The four easternmost ones are open 24 hours a day year-round, while the others close at either 10 P.M. or midnight. Everyone needs a passport to cross the border, and children under 18 traveling with just one parent need a notarized letter of consent from the absent parent or proof that the traveling parent has sole custody. Crossings are generally quick and smooth, even at the Fort Frances/International Falls port of entry, the state's busiest.

Officially U.S. Customs allows 200 cigarettes or 50 cigars and one liter of alcohol to be brought into the country duty free. Returning to Canada you can bring $50 (Canadian) worth of goods duty free, excluding alcoholic beverages and tobacco products, if your stay exceeded 24 hours. If you stay in the United States for 48 hours or more, the duty exemption is $200; the limit rises to $750 if you stay for seven or more days. For stays of two days or more, the exemption can include 200 cigarettes, 50 cigars, 40 ounces (1.14 L) of liquor, 1.6 quarts (1.5 L) of wine, or 24 12 oz. bottles of beer. Canada excludes all foreign citizens with a criminal record—even a DUI—from entering its territory (recent exceptions have been made for older driving infractions; check before you travel).

United States and Canadian citizens and permanent residents who wish to cross the

ANNUAL EVENTS

This brief list highlights some of the state's most popular and peculiar events. A nearly complete roster of statewide happenings is available at www.exploreminnesota.com/events.

JANUARY

Third weekend – Brainerd Jaycees Ice Fishing Extravaganza, Brainerd. Thousands of anglers make Swiss cheese out of Gull Lake during the world's largest ice-fishing tournament.

Third weekend – Icebox Days, International Falls. The Icebox of the Nation celebrates the snowy season.

Last Friday – St. Paul Winter Carnival, St. Paul. A 10-day celebration of all things winter, sometimes highlighted by an ice castle.

FEBRUARY

Second weekend – Eelpout Festival, Walker. A fish-house parade, polar plunge, and other events close out the ice-fishing season.

MARCH

Mid-March – St. Urho's Day, several towns. What began as a fictional festival for a fictional Finnish saint is now celebrated far and wide.

APRIL

Late April – Minnesota's rarest plant, the Minnesota dwarf trout lily, blooms.

MAY

Week of May 24 – Dylan Days, Hibbing. Native son Bob Dylan is feted with song and poetry.

JUNE

First weekend – Buffalo Days, Luverne. The principal event is a buffalo chip-throwing contest.

Third weekend – Rochesterfest, Rochester. The highlight of this nine-day affair is the Midwestern Lumberjack Championships.

Fourth weekend – Scandinavian Hjemkomst Festival, Moorhead. Three days of music, dance, crafts, and food make for one of the nation's largest celebrations of Nordic heritage.

Fourth weekend – Judy Garland Festival, Grand Rapids. Garland's hometown celebrates all things Oz, and several of the original munchkins usually attend.

JULY

First three weekends – Wilder Pageant, Walnut Grove. A large, theatrical reenactment of Laura Ingalls Wilder's life.

First Tuesday after Fourth of July – Bean Hole Day, Pequot Lakes. One hundred fifty gallons of baked beans are buried in a rock-lined pit and then dug up the next day at noon to feed thousands.

Mid-July – Two Harbors Folk Festival, Two

border by boat along the North Shore of Lake Superior, Lake of the Woods, or through the wilderness of the BWCAW/Quetico Provincial Park area can apply for a **CANPASS-Remote Area Border Crossing Permit.** BWCAW outfitters can take care of the paperwork or you can get it at www.queticopark.com/rabc. You can also apply in person at the Pigeon River, Fort Frances, and Rainy River ports of entry, but a decision can take 48 hours.

TIPS FOR TRAVELERS

Crime is not something visitors to Minnesota need to worry about very much, though don't be lulled into forgetting common sense. Women traveling alone need to take the usual big-city precautions in Minneapolis and St. Paul, but have little to worry about elsewhere. You can dial 911 statewide for emergencies. Minnesota's reputation for tolerance and kindness is justified, and gay and lesbian travelers or those whose ethnic background isn't Caucasian are unlikely to encounter any problems; although outside the Twin Cities and busy resort destinations you will be a rarity. Discretion is still the best approach for same-sex couples throughout most of the state, but pretty much anything goes in Minneapolis and St. Paul, which have active gay scenes. The best overall gay resource is **OutFront Minnesota** (612/822-0127

Harbors. Three days of music and dance beloved by both spectators and performers.

Late July – Minneapolis Aquatennial, Minneapolis. Milk carton-boat races and the largest fireworks display west of the Mississippi are just a few of the dozens of events during this 10-day celebration of summer.

Last two weekends in July and first weekend in August – Song of Hiawatha Pageant, Pipestone. A high-tech outdoor performance based on the famous Longfellow poem.

AUGUST

Early August – Minnesota Fringe Festival, Minneapolis. Ten days of avant-garde theater, dance, and spoken word during the largest nonjuried theater festival in the United States.

Second weekend – Grand Portage Rendezvous Days and Powwow, Grand Portage. A recreation of the annual summer gathering held here during the 18th century.

Twelve days ending on Labor Day – Minnesota State Fair, St. Paul. The Great Minnesota Get-Together, famous for food on a stick, is one of the largest fairs in the nation.

Weekend before Labor Day – Potato Days, Barnesville. Minnesota's most spud-tacular celebration has mashed-potato wrestling, potato sculpture, a potato-sack fashion show, and much more.

SEPTEMBER

Second weekend – Defeat of Jesse James Days, Northfield. The primary attraction is the reenactment of the famously foiled bank raid by the James-Younger gang.

Third weekend – King Turkey Days, Worthington. Worthington squares off against Cuero, Texas, in the Great Gobbler Gallop turkey race down Main Street.

OCTOBER

Mid-October – Tundra Swan migration to Weaver Bottoms begins.

NOVEMBER

Day after Thanksgiving – Fish House Parade, Aitkin. Dolled up ice-fishing shanties and other humorous floats herald the arrival of winter.

DECEMBER

First weekend – St. Olaf Christmas Festival, Northfield. Over 500 musicians sing hymns and other choral works for a national broadcast on PBS.

or 800/800-0350, www.outfront.org), and you can pick up the free biweekly *Lavender* magazine (www.lavendermagazine.com) at coffeehouses, theaters, bookstores, and other spots across the Twin Cities. Travelers with disabilities will find access pretty limited outside cities, though the national forests and parks, state parks, and state historic sites are welcome exceptions. **Access for All** (www.accessminnesota.org) is a handy resource.

Health and Safety

A visit to Minnesota is not completely devoid of risk, but none of the potential concerns are extreme, and simple common sense is pretty much all you need to stay safe and healthy. **911** is the statewide emergency number.

WINTER WEATHER

The first thing a winter visitor to Minnesota has to understand is that **wind chill** is not just something northerners talk about. It is real and it can be very dangerous. The wind-chill factor is an estimated measure of the rate at which exposed skin will lose body heat due to the combination of wind speed and temperature. So, for example, if the temperature outside is 5°F and the winds are blowing at 30 mph, your body will feel as if the temperature is 19°F below zero and the winds were calm.

A low wind chill (or just a low temperature) can quickly lead to **frostbite,** the freezing of skin. The initial symptoms of redness and pain are followed by a loss of feeling and color. Fingers, toes, ears, and the tip of the nose are most susceptible. If your skin does freeze, rewarm it slowly by immersing the affected area in warm (not hot) water. If that is not possible, use body heat, an armpit for example. Do not use a heat source, such as a fire or radiator, because the affected areas can burn easily. As it thaws, the skin turns red and painful with a severe tingling or burning sensation. If damage was limited to the skin, there will probably be no long-term effects, but if blood vessels were damaged there can be serious complications. Severe cases need immediate medical assistance.

Another cold-weather concern is **hypothermia,** a life-threatening condition where core body temperature falls below 95°F, the point at which the body can no longer produce enough heat to warm itself. Symptoms come on slowly and include uncontrolled shivering, slurred speech, confusion, drowsiness, loss of coordination, pale and cold skin, and bluish lips. Because the cold affects brain function, the victim may not even be aware of his or her own condition and must rely on companions, even when insisting he or she feels fine. Hypothermia can occur even in the summer if you spend too much time in cold lakes. Anyone suffering from hypothermia needs immediate medical attention. If that is not an option, get the victim out of the cold as best as possible. People with hypothermia are at high risk for cardiac arrest, so be as gentle as possible if moving them. Remove any wet or constrictive clothing and cover them with warm blankets or a sleeping bag. A metallic emergency blanket that conserves body heat should be in every backpack and canoe; they weigh just a couple of ounces and cost just a couple of dollars. Warm the body SLOWLY, starting with the chest, neck, head, and groin. In the wilderness, sharing body heat, skin-to-skin, is the best method of recovering victims. If they are conscious, give them warm (nonalcoholic) beverages and food. Even someone found out in the cold, unconscious and with no apparent pulse, should be treated. Many people who appeared dead on initial examination have been revived.

Prevention is the best medicine for cold-weather ailments. The key to staying warm in the winter is to wear loose-fitting layers. Not only is this the most effective for warmth, but you can shed layers as your exertion level rises, avoiding sweating, which leads to later chills or worse. A thin layer of wool, silk, or synthetics that can wick away sweat should be worn against the skin with a wind- and waterproof breathable outer shell as the top layer. Insulating layers of wool and lighter-weight polyester fleeces will keep you warm even if wet. Cotton should be avoided as much as possible because it retains moisture. Over half of body heat lost escapes through the head, so a good hat, one that covers the ears, is a must. Mittens are warmer than gloves and large ones can be worn over gloves. Your feet, which are exposed to the most moisture, need warm socks, preferably a thin inner sock, a wool outer sock, and warm waterproof boots.

OUTDOORS

The biggest concern for those venturing into Minnesota's outdoors is **Lyme disease,** but like most things, with just a bit of simple protection there's no need to worry. This bacterial disease is transmitted by the bite of the tiny deer tick. Deer ticks are smaller, and thankfully much less common, than wood ticks, which don't carry the disease. It is important to note that bites rarely lead to infection, and the incidence of the disease is much lower in Minnesota than New England. Lyme disease is almost always caught from May through July when nymphal-stage ticks are feeding. Adult ticks can also spread Lyme, but since they are much larger (an unfed nymph is no bigger than a poppy seed, while the adult grows to sesame seed size), people are much more likely to spot them and thus remove them quickly. A tick must be attached for at least 24 hours, usually 48 or more, before the bacteria can spread. If you have become infected, a distinctive "bull's-eye" rash may occur at the site of the bite in 7 to 14 days, and it might be accompanied by fever, fatigue, headache, muscle and joint pains, and other flu-like symptoms. See a doctor if any of these symptoms occur following a bite. In almost all cases, if diagnosed in the early stages, Lyme disease can be cleared up with standard antibiotics. While not life threatening, if left untreated it can lead to arthritis or complications of the nervous system or heart. Prevention is easy: Wear light-colored clothing so you can easily spot any ticks crawling on you, tuck long pants into socks to reduce access to the skin, and use a good insect repellent. Do a daily tick check on yourself and your pets after spending time outdoors. Remove embedded ticks with tweezers by grasping as close to the mouth as possible—do not grab the body as this might squeeze the infected contents into the wound—and slowly pull. Cleanse the bite with an antiseptic.

Minnesota has a few bloodthirsty flying insects that can be serious annoyances. Only a few species of **black flies** (sometimes called buffalo gnats) can bite through the skin with their razor-like mouths, but when they swarm around your head they can be pretty irritating. Thankfully black flies produce just one generation a year and they only feed over a three-week period, generally from mid-May through June. They are only active during the day. **Mosquitoes** are the most likely to put a damper on summer fun. Jokingly referred to as Minnesota's state bird on many postcards and coffee mugs, mosquitoes feed from May until the first frost but are most abundant in the early summer and are rare in the fall. Southeast Minnesota, away from the Mississippi River, is relatively mosquito free due to the lack of lakes. Repellents containing the chemical DEET last the longest and are the most effective (though they do little to discourage black flies), but there can be side effects if too much is absorbed through the skin; this is primarily a concern for long-term use and most people use it with absolutely no problems. Still, to be on the safe side, use a brand containing no more than 35 percent DEET (those with higher percentages aren't much more effective anyway), do not put it directly on children's skin, and do not use it at all on children under two. Effective non-DEET repellents using oil of lemon eucalyptus and picaridin are available too, though they have to be applied more frequently. Long-sleeved shirts and pants are also helpful, and a hat makes a world of difference with black flies.

No matter how clean and pure the water looks in Minnesota, you should never drink it straight from the source or you might just win weeks of diarrhea, abdominal cramps, bloating, flatulence, fatigue, and nausea. The culprit is *Giardia lamblia,* a hardy single-celled parasite found in lakes and streams worldwide. Symptoms begin one to two weeks after ingestion and continue for one to four weeks in most people, though chronic infections can last months or years and lead to weight loss and nutritional deficiencies. Giardiasis, as the illness is called, usually resolves itself, though a doctor should be consulted if there is dehydration, blood in the stool, or symptoms that persist beyond two weeks. Children and pregnant women should see a doctor immediately.

Water can be purified by boiling (one minute is enough for Giardia and most other biological hazards, but five is often recommended to kill them all), filtering (choose one with an absolute pore size of at least one micron, 0.2 is best, or one NSF rated for "cyst removal"), or treating (iodine kills almost everything, though it doesn't taste so good).

Coming into contact with **poison ivy** might cause a red rash, blistering, and extreme itching that can last up to two weeks. Poison ivy is found in wooded areas throughout the state and prefers moist, shaded spots; it is common along riverbanks, paths, and fencerows. It grows primarily as a woody vine; however, if it is growing in full sunlight it will become a shrub. The primary method of identification is by its leaves, which grow in groups of three—always remember "Leaves of Three, Let Them Be." The size and shape of the leaflets can vary considerably, but are usually 2–4 inches in length with pointed tips, smooth or toothed edges, and shiny faces; the middle leaflet has a longer stalk than the two on the side. Small yellowish-green, five-petaled flowers bloom in May–July, and clusters of small white berries emerge from August–November. In the fall the leaves turn red.

If you are unlucky enough to brush up against poison ivy, wash the area thoroughly with cold water (hot water will open your pores and make the reaction worse) as quickly as possible. You generally have at least an hour to wash away the poisonous urushiol oil before it is absorbed into the skin. Washing with rubbing alcohol during the first six hours can also help remove the oil and prevent or diminish symptoms. Ask a pharmacist about lotions to relieve the itching, though if it is severe you should see a doctor. A pre-exposure, over-the-counter lotion called Ivy Block reacts with the urushiol, blocking the allergic reaction. It must be applied 15 minutes before contact and lasts up to four hours.

Thin ice claims several lives each year in Minnesota. Generally speaking, ice four inches deep is considered safe for walking or skating, five inches for snowmobiles, and eight to twelve inches for cars and small trucks. The main problem is that ice is never uniform. Ice formed over currents will be weaker, so be especially cautious around bridges, outside river bends, and near the lakeshore. Also, don't assume that just because you see tracks that the ice is safe. Many Minnesotans, ever impatient to begin their winter rituals, rush out too early. Local bait shops, resorts, and sheriff's departments are your best source of advice. If you plan on going out on a lake or river, carry something sharp, such as picks or screwdrivers, to pull yourself out with if you fall through. If you are driving on a lake, keep your windows down to facilitate a quick escape.

ANIMALS

Despite their reputation, **bears** are more of a nuisance than a danger. Bears are common throughout northern Minnesota, but while attacks on humans are not unheard of, they are *extremely* rare. If you do run across a bear, stay calm and back away slowly; it will likely leave the moment it senses you. Occasionally bears will woof, snap their jaws, slap the ground, stand upright, or make a bluff charge. While frightening, these actions are not a prelude to an attack. If you are in your campsite, or for some other reason it needs to be the bear that leaves instead of you, shout, bang pots, or throw rocks and wood at the bear. Do not be gentle, though make sure it has an escape route before you begin. Capsaicin (hot pepper) sprays are another effective, and harmless, bear repellent. Food raids are the real concern with bears, since they will seek out and eat anything that even smells or looks like food. Keep your campsite clean: Never eat or store food in your tent, do not burn or bury food scraps at your site, and store all food and anything else with a strong odor, such as toothpaste, in your car. If you are camping in the wilderness, hang your food in a tree 10 feet off the ground and 4 feet from the trunk and any branches. There are many campsites in the BWCAW without large standing trees, so it would be wise to take a bear-proof storage container—local outfitters sell and rent them. These precautions must be followed even on islands, since bears are excellent swimmers.

Just two Minnesota **snakes**—the timber rattlesnake and the massasauga rattlesnake—are venomous, and both are rare and found only in limited areas in southeast Minnesota, primarily right along the Mississippi River. Both are timid and slow to rattle or strike. Bites are rare and rarely fatal; in fact, it has been over a century since anyone has died from a snakebite in Minnesota, but snakebites should still be treated as a medical emergency. First, keep the victim calm and limit physical exertion as much as possible. Squeeze and suck venom from the wound. Remove jewelry since swelling can occur rapidly. Keep the stricken limb below the heart. Attempt to identify the snake, killing it if possible, but do not waste time or put yourself at risk; observing symptoms gives a doctor enough information to choose the proper anti-venom. Get the victim to a hospital as soon as possible. Note the times that symptoms first occur. DO NOT cut the wound, use a tourniquet, or apply ice. These treatments do more harm than good.

Of all the animals in Minnesota, Bambi is the one most likely to do you harm. Annually there are some 20,000 **deer-vehicle collisions** reported in the state, and the Minnesota Department of Transportation estimates that twice as many go unreported. These crashes, or crashes as a result of attempts to avoid deer, cause an average of $2,000 in damage per car and even result in two or three deaths annually. Always keep an eye out for deer, especially in wooded areas and where deer warning signs are posted. Deer will cross roads throughout the year and at any time of the day, but they are most active at dawn and dusk and during October and November (while in rut and thus moving around much more than usual) and March and April (when some of the year's first greenery sprouts on roadsides). If you spot one anywhere near a road, decelerate as safely as possible—panicked deer will sprint off unexpectedly in any direction, and if you see one deer there are likely to be more nearby. And, though instincts say otherwise, hitting a deer is often safer than swerving out of its way, which might result in losing control of your vehicle. According to the DNR, studies have shown that whistles and other warning gadgets attached to vehicles do not frighten deer.

RESOURCES

Suggested Reading

For Minnesota books, no store can compete with the exhaustive inventory at the Minnesota History Center in St. Paul.

REQUIRED READING

Martin, Janet and Suzann Nelson. *Growing Up Lutheran: What Does This Mean?* Minnesota: Martin House Publications, 1997. The book that spawned a trio (so far) of *Church Basement Ladies* plays will have you rolling in the aisles and nodding in recognition, no matter how much time you've spent in Minnesota.

Mohr, Howard. *How To Talk Minnesotan.* New York: Penguin, 1987. A thoroughly hilarious primer on not only how to talk like, but how to be, a Minnesotan. Although Mohr claims that his book is only "a good deal," it is absolutely a heckuva deal.

HISTORY

Carley, Kenneth. *The Dakota War of 1862.* St. Paul, MN: Minnesota Historical Society Press, 2001. A balanced and accessible account of Minnesota's own civil war.

Folwell, William Watts. *A History of Minnesota.* St. Paul, MN: Minnesota Historical Society Press, 1969. This encyclopedic four-volume set is unquestionably the best historical resource available—at least up to the 1920s, when its account terminates.

Meier, Peg. *Bring Warm Clothes.* Minneapolis, MN: Minnesota Historical Society Press, 2009. Meier's compilation of letters and diary entries offers a fascinating look at Minnesota's past—from the early explorers through World War II.

Risjord, Norman K. *A Popular History of Minnesota.* St. Paul, MN: Minnesota Historical Society Press, 2005. The most recent recitation of Gopher State history available ties in the events of the past with places you can visit today.

PEOPLE

Cary, Bob. *Root Beer Lady: The Story of Dorothy Molter.* Minneapolis, MN: University of Minnesota Press, 2002. One of the most remarkable legends of Minnesota's Northwoods, city girl Dorothy Molter left Chicago to live off the land on remote Isle of the Pines in what is now the Boundary Waters Canoe Area Wilderness.

Holmquist, June D. (editor). *They Chose Minnesota: A Survey of the State's Ethnic Groups.* St. Paul, MN: Minnesota Historical Society Press, 1988. An in-depth but not too scholarly look at the people who made Minnesota. Many updated and expanded individual chapters of *They Chose Minnesota* are also available as part of *The People of Minnesota* series of books.

Yang, Kao Kalia. *The Latehomecomer: A Hmong Family Memoir.* Minneapolis, MN: Coffee House Press, 2008. A young Hmong woman tells the story of her family's—and her people's—journey from the refugee camps in Thailand to a new life in St. Paul.

Zochert, Donald. *Laura: The Life of Laura Ingalls Wilder.* New York: Avon, 1977. The true story of the author whose books inspired the *Little House on the Prairie* TV series.

LITERATURE

Enger, Leif. *Peace Like a River.* New York: Atlantic Monthly Press, 2002. This beautifully told tale, which begins and ends in small-town Minnesota in 1962, tends toward fable and fantasy yet still captures the character of Minnesota and Minnesotans.

Ervin, Jean (editor). *The North Country Reader.* St. Paul, MN: Minnesota Historical Society Press, 2000. This diverse anthology of Minnesota writers spans the state from the prairie to the North Shore and from the pioneer days of the mid-19th century to the turn of the 21st. The 37 authors include F. Scott Fitzgerald, Sinclair Lewis, Garrison Keillor, and Carol Bly.

Keillor, Garrison. *Lake Wobegon Days.* New York: Viking Penguin, 1985. Keillor's classic novel shares the complete story of the fictional small Minnesota town he made famous on his *A Prairie Home Companion* radio show. A truly delightful read whether you've ever heard the show or not.

Kling, Kevin. *The Dog Says How.* St. Paul, MN: Borealis Books, 2007. A beloved playwright and storyteller, Kling spins tales of his Minnesota childhood and his recovery from a terrible motorcycle accident. His voice—on the page and on the stage—is pure Minnesota.

Lewis, Sinclair. *Main Street.* New York: Signet Classics, 1998. This full frontal attack on the small-mindedness of small-town America is one of Lewis's most acclaimed works. Though he named the town Gopher Prairie, it was a very thinly veiled portrayal of Sauk Centre, his hometown.

Wilder, Laura Ingalls. *On the Banks of Plum Creek.* New York: Harper & Row, 1973. The only one of the nine Little House books set primarily in Minnesota, it gives a good account of the hardships of pioneer life in the 1870s.

NATURE

Eckert, Kim. *A Birder's Guide to Minnesota.* Plymouth, MN: Williams Publications, 2002. Minnesota's bible of bird-watching covers over 1,000 sites with detailed maps. It also provides superb background information on Minnesota species and seasons.

Henderson, Carrol, Andrea Lambrecht, et al. *Traveler's Guide to Wildlife in Minnesota.* St. Paul, MN: Minnesota's Bookstore, 1997. A bulky but excellent guide to 120 of the top wildlife-viewing spots, with maps and information about what to look for where and when.

Madson, John. *Where the Sky Began: Land of the Tallgrass Prairie.* Ames, IA: Iowa State Press, 1996. A beautifully written yet intricately detailed look at the complex ecology and long history of the tallgrass prairie.

Moyle, John B., and Evelyn W. Moyle. *Northland Wildflowers: The Comprehensive Guide to the Minnesota Region.* Minneapolis, MN: University of Minnesota Press, 2001. The standard reference to Minnesota's wildflowers. It details over 300 species and is filled with photos for easy identification.

Ojakangas, Richard W., and Charles L. Matsch. *Minnesota's Geology.* Minneapolis, MN: University of Minnesota Press, 1982. As close to the complete story of the state's formation as one could hope for. It is filled with maps, charts, and photos, which make following the detailed descriptions fairly easy, even for those without a geology background.

Olson, Sigurd. *Songs of the North.* New York: Penguin, 1995. Olson was such a powerful force for conservation in the Boundary Waters that reading his essays is the next best thing to being there.

Seeley, Mark. *Minnesota Weather Almanac.* St. Paul, MN: Minnesota Historical Society Press, 2006. Beyond the when and what of Minnesota's favorite topic of conversation—the weather—meteorologist and lifelong Minnesotan Seeley shares the why and the how.

Tester, John R. *Minnesota's Natural Heritage: An Ecological Perspective.* Minneapolis, MN: University of Minnesota Press, 1995. This excellent book, beautifully illustrated and filled with helpful charts and graphs, offers a detailed and comprehensive overview of Minnesota ecology. It's required reading in many college courses, but so well written that those without a science background can easily take it all in.

OUTDOOR RECREATION

Breining, Greg. *Paddling Minnesota.* Helena, MT: Falcon Publishing, 1999. The bible of Minnesota paddling describes and maps over 100 lake and river trips.

Farris, Mike. *Rock Climbing Minnesota and Wisconsin.* Helena, MT: Falcon Publishing, 2000. A very useful guide covering 10 locales in Minnesota. Photos and maps help you identify the hundreds of routes.

Johnson, Mickey. *Flyfisher's Guide to Minnesota.* Belgrade, MT: Wilderness Adventures Press, 2001. A very comprehensive listing of where, when, and how.

Johnson, Steve. *Mountain Biking Minnesota.* Guilford, CT: The Globe Pequot Press, 2002. Sixty-three off-road rides for all abilities.

Pauly, Daniel. *Exploring the Boundary Waters.* Minneapolis, MN: University of Minnesota Press, 2005. With recommended routes from every entry point, this is an invaluable resource for planning a trip in the Boundary Waters Canoe Area Wilderness.

Pukite, John. *Hiking Minnesota.* Helena, MT: Falcon Publishing, 1998. The 87 featured hikes, each of them mapped, offer a good selection of what the whole state has to offer.

Weinberger, Mark. *Short Bike Rides in Minnesota.* Guilford, CT: The Globe Pequot Press, 1998. A handy little guide that describes and maps 40 scenic rides across the state, most of them loops.

DESCRIPTION AND TRAVEL

Ayen, Norm, and Shane Weibel. *Wineries & Breweries of Minnesota.* Cambridge, MN: Adventure Publications, 2005. The full skinny on 39 wineries, breweries, and brewpubs.

Dregni, Eric. *Minnesota Marvels: Roadside Attractions in the Land of Lakes.* Minneapolis, MN: University of Minnesota Press, 2001. Minnesota loves its giant fiberglass whatevers, from walleye to the Jolly Green Giant. Dregni finds the high points and tells you the stories behind them.

Federal Writers' Project of the Works Progress Administration. *The WPA Guide to Minnesota.* St. Paul, MN: Minnesota Historical Society Press, 2002. Originally published in 1938 as *Minnesota: A State Guide,* this wonderful document is far too outdated to be of any help as a travel guide, but it offers a fascinating look at the state's folklore and remains an invaluable historical resource.

Gebhard, David, and Tom Martinson. *A Guide to the Architecture of Minnesota.* Minneapolis, MN: University of Minnesota Press, 1991. This book will be a welcome resident in your glove box. It contains quick profiles of thousands of buildings in nearly 300 towns across the state.

Thornley, Stew. *Six Feet Under.* St. Paul, MN: Minnesota Historical Society Press, 2004. A graveyard guide to the final resting places of nearly 400 notable Minnesotans.

Wurzer, Cathy. *Tales of the Road: Highway 61.* St. Paul, MN: Minnesota Historical Society Press, 2008. Minnesotans love the highway that stretches from the Mississippi bluff country and up along Superior's North Shore so much that they named it among the "Minnesota 150"—people, places, and things honored on the state's sesquicentennial. Wurzer, a Minnesota Public Radio journalist, travels the length of it and digs up unique stories along the way.

PHOTOGRAPHY

Minnesota is so singularly beautiful that I've seen very few photo collections that aren't spectacular. These are a few personal favorites.

Brandenburg, Jim. *Chased By the Light.* Chanhassen, MN: Creative Publishing International, 2001. These Boundary Waters and North Shore photos would be special no matter what circumstances they were taken under, but for this collection Brandenburg limited himself to just one photo a day for 90 autumn and winter days. Truly amazing.

Keillor, Garrison, and Richard Olsenius. *In Search of Lake Wobegon.* New York: Viking Studio, 2001. A look, through the words of Keillor and black-and-white photos of National Geographic photographer Olsenius, at the small towns of Stearns County that the fictional Lake Wobegon is based on.

Ryan, Greg, and Sally Beyer. *Minnesota: Simply Beautiful.* Helena, MT: Farcountry Press, 2001. Stunning photos of city and country (mostly the latter).

Ryan, Greg, and Douglas Wood. *Minnesota: The Spirit of the Land.* Stillwater, MN: Voyageur Press, 1995. A celebration of Minnesota wilderness, from the tallgrass prairie to the boreal forest.

CUISINE

Hauser, Susan Carol. *Wild Rice Cooking.* New York: The Lyons Press, 2004. Wild rice is more than just a food to Native Americans, and this beautiful little book tells the complete story of the official state grain. It also has 80 recipes.

Legwold, Gary. *The Last Word on Lutefisk.* Minneapolis, MN: Conrad Henry Press, 1996. Everything you always wanted to know about reconstituted cod soaked in lye (but were afraid to ask). Includes a lutefisk dinner directory.

McKey, Gwen, and Barbara Moseley (editors). *Best of the Best from Minnesota.* Brandon, MS: Quail Ridge Press, 1997. Over 400 of just what the name says, from Minnesotan dishes such as Norwegian flat bread and wild rice soup to the just plain delicious, like meatless lasagna and frozen mint dream dessert.

Ojakangas, Beatrice. *The Best Casserole Cookbook Ever.* San Francisco: Chronicle Books, 2008. Casserole—or hot dish, as the locals call it—is practically the state food. And Duluth-based Beatrice Ojakangas has written 20 cookbooks on baking, Scandinavian specialties, and more. Put them together and you have a quintessentially Minnesotan cookbook.

Renewing the Countryside. *The Minnesota Homegrown Cookbook: Local Food, Local Restaurants, Local Recipes.* Stillwater, MN: Voyageur Press, 2008. Through well-told stories of local chefs—from renowned Twin Cities restaurants and tiny outstate B&Bs—this richly illustrated book celebrates the food and places we love.

CHILDREN

Bowen, Betsy. *Antler, Bear, Canoe: A Northwoods Alphabet Year.* Boston: Houghton Mifflin Co., 2002. An alphabet book that takes children through typical sights and activities during a year in the Northwoods. Even adults will love Bowen's woodblock prints in this or any of her other children's books.

Butler, Dori Hillestrand. *M is for Minnesota.* Minneapolis, MN: University of Minnesota Press, 1998. A fun, fact-filled picture book.

Button, Sara. *Black Bear, Loon, and Walleye: A Fable From the Northwoods.* Minneapolis, MN: Beaver's Pond Press, 2007. Three familiar Minnesota friends want to trade places with each other—and learn a little bit about walking in someone else's shoes. The illustrations have a classic look, and the book comes with an audio CD.

McCarthy, Ann E. *Critters of Minnesota Pocket Guide.* Cambridge, MN: Adventure Publications, 2000. This little book has facts and photos of 50 Minnesota mammals and birds.

Shaw, Janet. *Kirsten's Story Collection.* Middleton, WI: American Girl, 2005. Kirsten, of the popular American Girl series, is a nine-year-old Swedish girl whose family immigrates to Minnesota in 1854. During the six-story series, combined into one book, she encounters a bear, goes to school, and has her house burn down.

Stong, Phil. *Honk: The Moose.* Duluth, MN: Trellis Publishing, 2001. A classic Newbery Medal–winning tale from 1935 of a moose who comes to live in town. Based on a true story from Biwabik.

MAGAZINES

From deep political reporting to shopping tips, ***Minnesota Monthly*** (www.minnesotamonthly.com) has some of the state's best magazine writers. Watch for well-researched travel roundups, but otherwise the focus is heavily on the Twin Cities metro.

Mpls.St.Paul (www.mspmag.com) is *Minnesota Monthly's* opposite number, with a little more emphasis on lifestyle features for the wealthier set. Their forte is making recommendations, from the driest martini to the best doctors, and their opinions carry a lot of weight around town.

Because no metro area can have too many glossy general-interest magazines, we've got three. ***Twin Cities Metro*** (www.metromag.com) aims for a younger audience, perhaps with more aspirations and attitude than cash.

The Boundary Waters Journal (www.boundarywatersjournal.com), a thick quarterly published out of Ely, covers travel and natural history for the Boundary Waters Canoe Area Wilderness and around.

Lake Superior Magazine (www.lakesuperior.com) is a quality bimonthly covering the entire Lake Superior region, but as it is published in Duluth, the Minnesota portion gets a great deal of coverage. The photography is invariably excellent.

The hard-to-find ***Big River*** (www.bigrivermagazine.com) is an enthusiastic bimonthly focusing on the past, present, and future of the Mississippi River between St. Cloud, Minnesota, and Davenport, Iowa.

Lake Country Journal (www.lakecountryjournal.com) is a bimonthly lifestyle magazine for north-central Minnesota.

Internet Resources

TRAVEL PLANNING

Access for All
www.accessminnesota.org

Travel information about Minnesota for people with disabilities.

Explore Minnesota Tourism
www.exploreminnesota.com

The official web home of Explore Minnesota Tourism has loads of statewide information.

Minnesota Bed and Breakfast Association
www.minnesotabedandbreakfasts.org

All member bed-and-breakfasts undergo quality inspections.

HISTORY AND NATURE

Minnesota Department of Natural Resources
www.dnr.state.mn.us

Besides plenty of practical information on state parks, outdoor recreation, licenses, and the like, there is a lot of information on Minnesota's natural history.

Minnesota Ornithologists' Union
http://moumn.org

A wealth of information for bird-watchers.

Visual Resources Database
http://collections.mnhs.org/visualresources

The Minnesota Historical Society's online archive is a fascinating collection of nearly 120,000 photos and drawings.

SPORTS AND ENTERTAINMENT

Adelsman's Cross-Country Ski Page
www.skinnyski.com

The state's best cross-country-skiing resource.

Explore Minnesota Golf
www.golf.exploreminnesota.com

Detailed information about all of the state's courses.

Fishing Minnesota
www.fishingminnesota.com

More than anyone could ever want to know about landing a lunker in Minnesota, including regularly updated fishing reports from across the state.

Minnesota Gaming Directory
www.minnesotagaming.com

A listing of all Minnesota casinos.

MnSNO
www.mnsno.net

Information on downhill skiing and snowboarding in Minnesota.

OTHER USEFUL SITES

Minnesota Grown
www.minnesotagrown.com

The Minnesota Grown Directory is a searchable database of agricultural products, from blueberries to buffalo, available for purchase straight from the producer.

Minnesota Newspaper Directory
www.mnnews.com

Get the latest news and gossip from Minnesota towns. If a paper has a website, you'll find the link here.

Index

C

D

E

F

G

H

I

J

K

L

M

N

O

P

V

WXYZ

List of Maps

MAP SYMBOLS

Expressway	Highlight	Airfield	Golf Course
Primary Road	City/Town	Airport	Parking Area
Secondary Road	State Capital	Mountain	Archaeological Site
Unpaved Road	National Capital	Unique Natural Feature	Church
Trail	Point of Interest	Waterfall	Gas Station
Ferry	Accommodation	Park	Glacier
Railroad	Restaurant/Bar	Trailhead	Mangrove
Pedestrian Walkway	Other Location	Skiing Area	Reef
Stairs	Campground		Swamp

CONVERSION TABLES

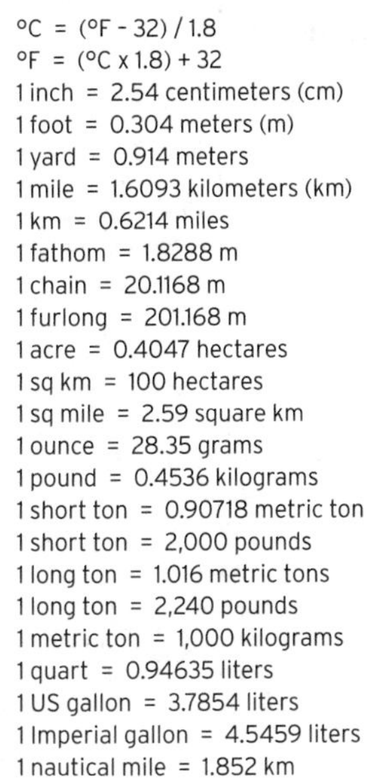
°C = (°F - 32) / 1.8
°F = (°C x 1.8) + 32
1 inch = 2.54 centimeters (cm)
1 foot = 0.304 meters (m)
1 yard = 0.914 meters
1 mile = 1.6093 kilometers (km)
1 km = 0.6214 miles
1 fathom = 1.8288 m
1 chain = 20.1168 m
1 furlong = 201.168 m
1 acre = 0.4047 hectares
1 sq km = 100 hectares
1 sq mile = 2.59 square km
1 ounce = 28.35 grams
1 pound = 0.4536 kilograms
1 short ton = 0.90718 metric ton
1 short ton = 2,000 pounds
1 long ton = 1.016 metric tons
1 long ton = 2,240 pounds
1 metric ton = 1,000 kilograms
1 quart = 0.94635 liters
1 US gallon = 3.7854 liters
1 Imperial gallon = 4.5459 liters
1 nautical mile = 1.852 km

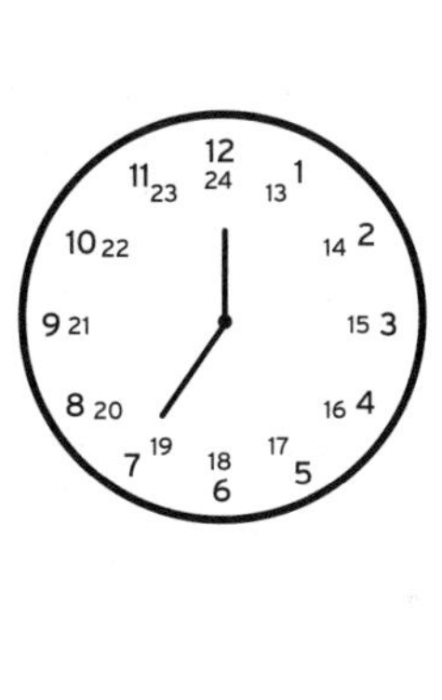

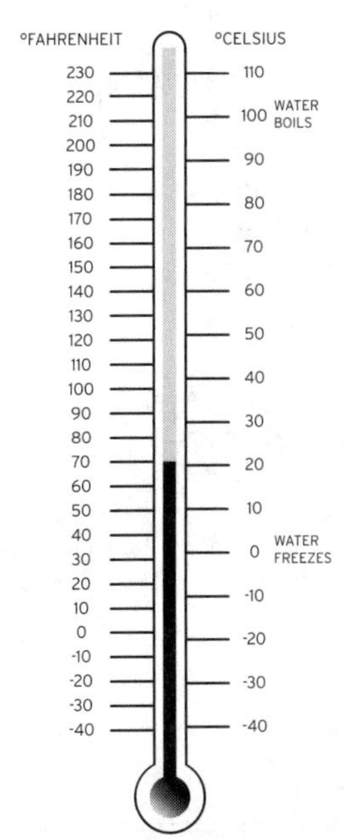

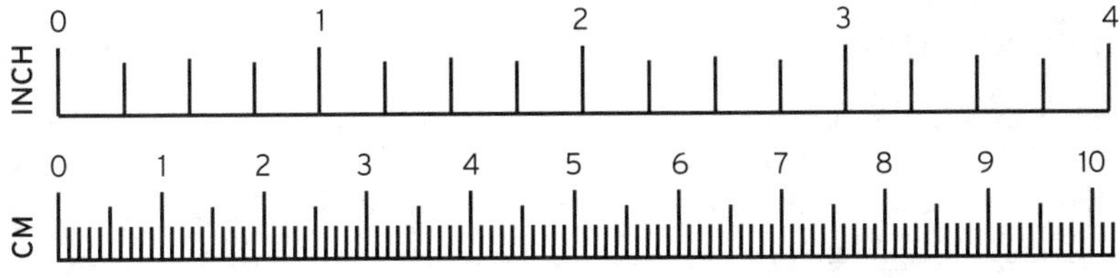

MOON MINNESOTA
Avalon Travel
a member of the Perseus Books Group
1700 Fourth Street
Berkeley, CA 94710, USA
www.moon.com

Editor and Series Manager: Kathryn Ettinger
Copy Editor: Annie M. Blakley
Graphics Coordinator: Lucie Ericksen
Production Coordinators: Lucie Ericksen, Amber Pirker
Cover Designer: Lucie Ericksen
Map Editor: Brice Ticen
Cartographers: Kat Bennett, Mike Morgenfeld
Indexer: Greg Jewett

ISBN: 978-1-59880-369-3
ISSN: 1545-2158

Printing History
1st Edition – 2004
3rd Edition – May 2010

5 4 3 2 1

Front cover photo: colorful leaves on a wet road, Father Hennepin State Park © Richard Hamilton Smith/CORBIS
Title page photo: Tettegouche State Park on the North Shore of Lake Superior © John McLaird/123RF
Other front matter photos: pages 4, 6, 7 bottom & top-left, 11-12, 14 bottom, 16 bottom, 17: © Tricia Cornell; pages 5, 7 top-right, 8, 13, 16 top, 18: © Bruce Manning; page 10: © George Burba/123RF; page 14 top: © Brynn/Wikimedia Commons; page 15: © Michael Hicks/Wikimedia Commons; page 19: © Rigadoun/Wikimedia Commons; page 21: © Wikimedia Commons; page 22: © Mark Evans/Wikimedia Commons; page 23: © Bobak Ha'Eri/Wikimedia Commons

Printed in Canada by Friesens

KEEPING CURRENT

If you have a favorite gem you'd like to see included in the next edition, or see anything that needs updating, clarification, or correction, please drop us a line. Send your comments via email to feedback@moon.com, or use the address above.